THE MEANING OF DIFFERENCE

THE MEANING OF DIFFERENCE

American Constructions of Race, Sex and Gender, Social Class, and Sexual Orientation

A Text/Reader

THIRD EDITION

Karen E. Rosenblum

George Mason University

Toni-Michelle C. Travis

George Mason University

Boston Burr Ridge, IL Dubuque, IA Madison, WI New York San Francisco St. Louis
Bangkok Bogotá Caracas Kuala Lumpur Lisbon London Madrid Mexico City
Milan Montreal New Delhi Santiago Seoul Singapore Sydney Taipei Toronto

McGraw-Hill Higher Education

A Division of The ***McGraw-Hill*** *Companies*

THE MEANING OF DIFFERENCE
American Constructions of Race, Sex and Gender, Social Class, and Sexual Orientation

Published by McGraw-Hill, a business unit of The McGraw-Hill Companies, Inc., 1221 Avenue of the Americas, New York, NY 10020.

This book is printed on acid-free paper.

2 3 4 5 6 7 8 9 0 FGR/FGR 0 9 8 7 6 5 4 3 2

ISBN 0-07-248782-8

Publisher: *Phillip A. Butcher*
Sponsoring editors: *Sally Constable/Sherith Pankratz*
Developmental editor: *Katherine Blake*
Senior marketing manager: *Daniel M. Loch*
Producer, media technology: *Jessica Bodie*
Project manager: *Christina Thornton-Villagomez*
Production supervisor: *Susanne Riedell*
Coordinator of freelance design: *Mary L. Kazak*
Supplement associate: *Kate Boylan*
Photo research coordinator: *Alexandra Ambrose*
Illustrator interior: *James O'Brien*
Cover design: *Sarah Studnicki*
Cover illustrator: *©SuperStock/Diana Ong*
Typeface: *10.5/12 Times Roman*
Compositor: *GAC Indianapolis*
Printer: *Quebecor World Fairfield, Inc.*

Library of Congress Cataloging-in-Publication Data

The meaning of difference : American constructions of race, sex and gender, social class, and sexual orientation / [editors] Karen E. Rosenblum, Toni-Michelle C. Travis. — 3rd ed.
p. cm.
ISBN 0-07-248782-8 (softcover : alk. paper)
1. United States—Social conditions—1980- 2. Pluralism (Social sciences)—United States. I. Rosenblum, Karen Elaine. II. Travis, Toni-Michelle, 1947-
HN59.2.M44 2003
306′.0973—dc21 2002069597

www.mhhe.com

ABOUT THE AUTHORS

KAREN E. ROSENBLUM is vice president for University Life and a faculty member in sociology at George Mason University in Fairfax, Virginia. She is a former director of Women's Studies and the Women's Studies Research and Resource Center. Professor Rosenblum received her Ph.D. in sociology from the University of Colorado, Boulder. Her areas of research and teaching include sex and gender, language, and deviance. With David W. Haines, she is coeditor of *Illegal Immigration in America: A Reference Handbook.* (Greenwood Press, 1999).

TONI-MICHELLE C. TRAVIS is associate professor of government and politics at George Mason University in Fairfax, Virginia. She is also a faculty member in the Women's Studies and African American Studies programs. Professor Travis received her Ph.D. in political science from the University of Chicago. Her areas of research and teaching include race and gender in political participation and urban politics. She has served as the president of the National Capital Area Political Science Association and the Women's Caucus of the American Political Science Association. She hosts "Capital Region Roundtable," a cable television show, and is a frequent political commentator on Virginia politics.

CONTENTS

PREFACE

In teaching in our respective fields, we regularly face classrooms filled with students who are questioning their identity in American society. With a population over one-third students of color, George Mason University has experienced in microcosm the traditional and the new American divide. As we shared our classroom experiences, we began to consider the similarities in the operation of race, sex and gender, social class, sexual orientation, and—later—disability. Our conversations led us to conclude that there was an overarching conceptual structure that could be applied to this material, and applied in a way that would provide students with a positive, rather than divisive, classroom experience. Thus, the genesis of the first edition of *The Meaning of Difference* in 1996.

The Meaning of Difference (or *MOD*) is, first and foremost, an effort to understand how *difference* is constructed in contemporary American culture: How do categories of people come to be seen as "different"? How does being "different" affect people's lived experience? What meaning does difference have for social interaction, social institutions, or cultures? What difference does difference make?

MOD focuses on the most significant categories of difference on the American landscape—race, sex and gender, sexual orientation, social class, and disability—and asks: What is *shared* across these categories? What can be learned from their commonalities? That the *Meaning of Difference* is now in its third edition makes us hopeful that such an approach is useful in understanding American conceptions and constructions of difference.

ORGANIZATION AND CONCEPTUAL FRAMEWORK

MOD is divided into three sections. Each section opens with a Framework Essay that provides the conceptual architecture by which to understand the readings. The readings have been carefully selected to illustrate the Essay's concepts and structure. Thus, the Essays are not merely introductions to the readings; they are the "text" portion of this *text/reader.*

The first Framework Essay describes how categories of difference are created; the second considers the experience of difference; and the third examines the meanings assigned to difference by law, politics, public policy, the economy, science, popular culture, and language. The readings that illustrate and extend each essay were specifically selected because of their applicability to multiple categories of people. For example, M. Annette Jaimes's article on the "blood quantum" required to classify a person as Native American can be applied to a discussion about the criteria people use to classify one another as gay or straight. Similarly, Eric Liu's discussion of finding himself "Asian American" parallels many people's "discovery" of their membership in race, sexual orientation, or disability groups.

DISTINGUISHING FEATURES

Several features make *The Meaning of Difference* distinctive:

- First, it offers a conceptual framework by which to understand the commonalities among categories of difference. We believe this encompassing approach makes *MOD* unique.
- Second, *MOD* provides an accessible and historically grounded discussion of the Supreme Court decisions critical to the creation of these categories of differences.
- Third, *MOD* has been designed with an eye toward the pedagogic difficulties that often accompany this subject matter. Our experience has been that when the topic is *simultaneously* race, sex and gender, social class, and sexual orientation, no one group can be easily cast as victim or victimizer.

CHANGES IN THE THIRD EDITION

The third edition includes 25 *new* readings and nine *more* readings than the previous edition. Specific changes and additions include the following:

- More readings focusing on whiteness as an identity.
- More readings examining the intersections of race, social class, sex and gender, and sexual orientation.

- Coverage of the 2000 Census in its process and results.
- An entirely new section on social class.
- Increased attention to the topic of disability, including discussion of a recent Supreme Court case on disability rights, *PGA Tour, Inc., v. Casey Martin.*
- An Index to provide easier access to the topics.

The third edition also includes several new readings that we think will become classics. "At the Slaughterhouse," by Charlie LeDuff, was part of the 2001 *New York Times* Pulitzer-Prize-winning series, "How Race Is Lived in America." LeDuff paints an unforgettable image of race and ethnic conflict at a North Carolina slaughterhouse. In "All Souls' Night," Michael Patrick MacDonald provides a personal account of the lives of poor and working-class whites in South Boston—"the best place on earth to live." Michael Zweig's, "Why Is Class Important?" and Sherry B. Ortner's, "Preliminary Notes on Class and Culture," draw our attention to social class as a hidden aspect of American social relations.

Several readings from the previous editions have been retained here because of their wide popularity among students and faculty. Certainly, John Larew's, "Why Are Droves of Unqualified, Unprepared Kids Getting into our Top Colleges," has been a revelation for students trying to understand affirmative action policies. Robert Moore's, "Racism in the English Language," paints a vivid, and still relevant, picture of the values embedded in the language of color. Finally, in the two articles by Anne Fausto-Sterling—one from the previous edition of *MOD*—we can observe changing notions about people who are intersexed.

SUPPLEMENTS

Instructor's Manual/Test Bank

Jamey Piland, a colleague at Trinity College in Washington, DC, has used *MOD* in several interdisciplinary courses and, from that experience, has produced a thoughtful Instructor's Manual that focuses especially on how to teach this material. Melissa Milne, a graduate student at George Mason, developed the discussion questions for our new readings.

New for the third edition is a Test Bank combined with the Instructor's Manual. The Test Bank, developed by Susan Weldon of Eastern Michigan University, includes multiple-choice and true-false questions for the Framework Essays and each of the readings.

Companion Website

This website provides an overview of the book, summaries of key features, what's new in the third edition, information about the authors, and Practice Test Questions.

Other content on this site include an annotated list of weblinks to useful sites, a list of professional resources (e.g., professional journals), links to websites offering Census 2000 information, a glossary, flashcards, and a comprehensive film and video guide.

Visit the companion website by going to

www.mhhe.com/raceclassgender

ACKNOWLEDGMENTS

Many colleagues and friends have helped us clarify the ideas we present here. David W. Haines has been unfailingly available to help Karen think through conceptual and technical dilemmas. She could not imagine a colleague more supportive or wise. Theodore W. Travis provided insight on Supreme Court decisions, their relationship to social values, and their impact on American society. The third edition also benefited from the comments of colleagues who have used the volume: Victoria Rader, Rose Pascarell, and Jamey Piland—master teachers all.

We owe special thanks to our students at George Mason and Simmons College for sharing their experiences, and to Melissa Milne for her research assistance and commitment to keeping us on track. We are particularly grateful to Beth Omansky Gordon for convincing us to broaden our scope to include disability. Thanks go to John Ameer of Clark University for his compilation of video and film titles included on the companion website. Thanks also go to Nancy Murphy for again keeping the administrative side of Karen's life in order during the completion of this revision.

We continue to be grateful to Joan Lester and the Equity Institute in Emeryville, California, for their understanding of the progress that can be made through a holistic analysis.

Proving itself as committed to a thorough review of the third edition as it had for previous editions, McGraw-Hill put together a panel of accomplished scholars with broad expertise. All offered detailed, insightful, and invaluable critiques, and we are much in their debt:

Kelly Dagan, Illinois College
Jennifer Eichstedt, Humboldt State University
Jill Fuller, The University of North Carolina at Greensboro
Tom Gerschick, Illinois State University
Carol Holdt, Portland State University
Joon Kim, Colorado State University
Steven Kogan, Valdosta State University
Melissa Latimer, West Virginia University

Rubén Martinez, University of Southern Colorado
Magalene Harris Taylor, University of Arkansas
Susan Weldon, Eastern Michigan University

Karen Rosenblum

Toni-Michelle Travis
George Mason University

THE MEANING OF DIFFERENCE

SECTION I

CONSTRUCTING CATEGORIES OF DIFFERENCE

FRAMEWORK ESSAY

The Meaning of Difference (MOD) addresses the social construction of difference as it operates in American conceptions of race, sex and gender, social class, and sexual orientation. These categories, so often taken for granted, will be systematically questioned throughout this text.

Race, sex, class, and sexual orientation may be described as *master statuses.* In everyday speech, the term *status* conveys prestige. In most social science literature and in this text, however, a status is understood as a position or slot in a social structure. For example, office manager is an occupational status, college graduate is an educational status, and cousin is a kinship status. At any point in time, each of us occupies multiple statuses; that is, one may be an office manager, a college graduate, and a cousin simultaneously. Among these statuses, master statuses are those that "in most or all social situations will overpower or dominate all other statuses. . . . Master status influences every other aspect of life, including personal identity" (Marshall, 1994:315).

We will examine the similarities in the master statuses of race, sex, social class, and sexual orientation. The circumstances of African Americans, Latinos, and Asian Americans differ in many ways, just as the experiences of racial minorities differ from those of sexual orientation minorities. Nonetheless, similar processes are at work when we "see" differences of color, gender, class, and sexual orientation. There are also commonalities in the consequences of these statuses for people's lives. Indeed, we suggest that many of the same processes occur in the operation of other master statuses, such as disability.

In preparing this volume, we noticed that talk about racism, sexism, homophobia,[1] and class status seemed to be everywhere—film, music, news reports, talk shows, sermons, and scholarly publications—and that the topics carried considerable intensity. These are controversial subjects; thus, readers may have strong reactions to these issues. Two perspectives—essentialism and constructionism—are core to this book and should help you understand your own reaction to the material.

The Essentialist and Constructionist Orientations

The difference between the *constructionist* and *essentialist* orientations is illustrated in the tale of the three umpires, first apparently told by social psychologist Hadley Cantril:

> Hadley Cantril relates the story of three baseball umpires discussing their profession. The first umpire said, "Some are balls and some are strikes, and I call them as they are." The second replied, "Some's balls and some's strikes, and I call 'em as I sees 'em." The third

[1]The term *homophobia* was coined in 1973 by psychologist George Weinberg to describe an irrational fear of, or anger toward, homosexuals. While the psychological application has been abandoned, the word remains in common use to describe a strong opposition to or rejection of same-sex relationships. The term leaves much to be desired, but the alternative that has emerged, *heterosexism,* is not yet in conventional usage. *Heterosexism* is the presumption that all people are heterosexual and that heterosexuality is the only acceptable form of sexual expression.

> thought about it and said, "Some's balls and some's strikes, but they ain't nothing 'till I calls 'em." (Henshel and Silverman, 1975:26)

The first umpire in the story takes an essentialist position. In arguing that "I call them as they are," he indicates his assumption that balls and strikes are entities that exist in the world independently of his perception of them. For this umpire, "balls" and "strikes" are easily identified, and he is merely a neutral observer of them. This umpire "regards knowledge as objective and independent of mind, and himself as the impartial reporter of things 'as they are'" (Pfuhl, 1986:5). For this essentialist umpire, balls and strikes exist in the world; he simply observes their presence.

Thus, the essentialist orientation presumes that items in a category all share some "essential" quality, their "ball-ness" or "strike-ness." For essentialists, the categories of race, sex, sexual orientation, and social class identify significant, empirically verifiable differences among people. From the essentialist perspective, racial categories exist apart from any social processes; they are objective categories of real difference among people.

The second umpire is somewhat removed from pure essentialism. His statement, "I call 'em as I sees 'em," conveys the belief that while an independent, objective reality exists, it is subject to interpretation. For him the world contains balls and strikes, but individuals may have different perceptions about which is which.

The third umpire, who says "they ain't nothing 'till I calls 'em," is a constructionist. He operates from the belief that "conceptions such as 'strikes' and 'balls' have no meaning except that given them by the observer" (Pfuhl, 1986:5). For this constructionist umpire, reality cannot be separated from the way a culture makes sense of it; strikes and balls do not exist until they are constructed through social processes. From this perspective, difference is created rather than intrinsic to a phenomenon. Social processes, such as those in political, legal, economic, scientific, and religious institutions, create differences, determine that some differences are more important than others, and assign particular meanings to those differences. From this perspective, the way a society defines difference among its members tells us more about that society than the people so classified. *MOD* operates from the constructionist perspective, since it examines how we have arrived at our race, sex, sexual orientation, and social class categories.

Few of us have grown up as constructionists. More likely, we are essentialists who believe that master statuses such as race or sex entail clear-cut, unchanging, and in some way meaningful differences. Still, not everyone is an essentialist. Those from mixed racial or religious backgrounds are familiar with the ways in which identity is not clear-cut. They grow up understanding how definitions of self vary with the context; how others try to define one as belonging in a particular category; and how in many ways, one's very presence calls prevailing classification systems into question. For example, the experience Jordan Lite describes in Reading 23 of being asked "What are you?" is a common experience among mixed-race people. Such experiences make evident the social constructedness of racial identity.

Most of us are unlikely to be exclusively essentialist or constructionist. As authors we take the constructionist perspective, but we have still relied on essentialist terms we find problematic. The irony of questioning the idea of race but still talking about "blacks," "whites," and "Asians," or of rejecting a dualistic approach to sexual identity while still using the terms "gay" and "straight," has not escaped us. Indeed, throughout our discussion we have used the currently favored essentialist phrase "sexual orientation" over the more constructionist "sexual preference."[2]

Further, there is a serious risk that a text such as this falsely identifies people on the basis of *either* their sex, race, sexual orientation, or social class, despite the fact that master statuses are not parts of a person that can be broken off from one another like the segments of a Tootsie Roll (Spelman, 1988). All of us are always *simultaneously* all of our master statuses, and it is that complex package that exists in the world. While Section I of the readings may make it seem as if these were separable statuses, they are not. Indeed, even the concept of master status suggests that there can be only one dominating status in one's life. However, we would reject that position.

Both constructionism and essentialism can be found in the social sciences. We present constructionism as a useful approach to contemporary master status formulations, but essentialism has nonetheless been a critical element in the development of modern science. It has been the basis of probability theory and statistics (Hilts, 1973), and it forms the bedrock for most social scientific research.

Both perspectives also are evident in social movements, and those movements sometimes shift from one perspective to the other over time. For example, some feminists and most of those opposed to feminism have held the essentialist belief that women and men are inherently different. The constructionist view that sexual identity is chosen dominated the gay rights movement of the 1970s (Faderman, 1991), but today most members of that movement take the essentialist approach that sexual identity is something one is born with, whereas those opposed to gay relationships take the constructionist view that it is chosen. In this case, language often signals which perspective is being used. For example, sexual *preference* conveys active, human decision making with the possibility of change (constructionism), while sexual *orientation* implies something fixed and inherent to a person (essentialism). Gallup polls show an increasing percentage of Americans believe homosexuality is a genetic trait. In 1977, 13 percent indicated they believed that to be the case; in 2001, 40 percent agreed with that statement. Indeed, now as many people believe homosexuality is genetic as say it is attributable to upbringing (Newport, 2001).

In telling the life story of a friend, journalist Darryl Rist explained the shift to a more essentialist approach on the part of gay rights activists as a response to heightened prejudice against same-sex relationships:

> [Chris Yates's parents were] . . . Pentecostal ministers who had tortured his adolescence with Christian cures for sexual perversity. Shock and aversion therapies under born-again doctors and gruesome exorcisms of sexual demons by spirit-filled preachers had culminated in a plan to have him castrated by a Mexican surgeon who touted the procedure as

---

[2]The term "sexual identity" may now be replacing "sexual orientation." It could be used in either an essentialist or a constructionist way.

> a way to make the boy, if not straight, at least sexless. Only then had the terrified son rebelled.
>
> Then, in the summer of 1991, the journal *Science* reported anatomical differences between the brains of homosexual and heterosexual men. . . . The euphoric media—those great purveyors of cultural myths—drove the story wildly. Every major paper in the country headlined the discovery smack on the front page. . . . Like many others, I suspect, Chris Yates's family saw in this newly reported sexual science a way out of its wrenching impasse. After years of virtual silence between them and their son, Chris's parents drove several hundred miles to visit him and ask for reconciliation. Whatever faded guilt they might have felt for the family's faulty genes was nothing next to the reassurance that neither by a perverse upbringing nor by his own iniquity was Chris or the family culpable for his urges and actions. "We could never have condoned this if you could do something to change it. But when we finally understood that you were *born* that way, we knew we'd been wrong. We had to ask your forgiveness." (Rist, 1992:425–26)

Understandably, those under attack would find essentialist orientations appealing, just as the expansiveness of constructionist approaches would be appealing in more tolerant eras. Still, both perspectives can be used to justify discrimination, since people can be persecuted for the choices they make as well as for the genes they were born with.

Why have we spent so much time describing the essentialist and constructionist perspectives? Discussions about race, sex, sexual orientation, and social class generate such great intensity partly because they involve the clash of essentialist and constructionist assumptions. Essentialists are likely to view categories of people as "essentially" different in some important way; constructionists are likely to see these differences as socially created and arbitrary. An essentialist asks what causes people to be different; a constructionist asks about the origin and consequence of the categorization system itself. While arguments about the nature and cause of racism, sexism, homophobia, and poverty are disputes about power and justice, from the perspective of essentialism and constructionism they are also disputes about what differences in color, sexuality, and social class *mean.*

The constructionist approach has one clear advantage, however. It is from that perspective that one understands that all the talk about race, sex, sexual orientation, and social class has a profound significance. Such talk is not simply *about* difference and similarity; it is itself the *creation* of difference and similarity. In the sections that follow, we examine how categories of people are named, dichotomized, and stigmatized—all toward the construction of difference.

Naming

Difference is constructed first by naming categories of people. Therefore, constructionists pay special attention to the names people use to refer to themselves and others—the times at which new names are asserted, the negotiations that surround the use of particular names, and those occasions when people are grouped together or separated out.

Asserting a Name Both individuals and categories of people face similar issues in the assertion of a name. A change of name involves, to some extent, the claim of a new identity. For example, one of our colleagues wanted to be called by her first name rather than by its abbreviated version because the diminutive had come to seem childish to her. It took a few times to remind people that this was her new name, and with most that was adequate. One colleague, however, argued that he could not adapt to the new name; she would just have to tolerate his continued use of the nickname. This was a small but public battle about who had the power to name whom. Did she have the power to enforce her own naming, or did he have the power to name her despite her wishes? Eventually, she prevailed.

A more disturbing example was a young woman who wanted to keep her "maiden" name after she married. Her fiancé agreed with her decision, recognizing that he would be reluctant to give up his name were the tables turned. When his mother heard of this possibility, however, she was outraged. In her mind, a rejection of her family's name was a rejection of her family. She urged her son to reconsider getting married. We do not know how this story ended.

Thus, asserting a name can create social conflict. On both a personal and societal level, naming can involve the claim of a particular identity and the rejection of others' power to impose a name. For example, is one Native American, American Indian, or Sioux; African American or black; girl or woman; Asian American, Korean, or Korean American; gay or homosexual; Chicano, Mexican American, Mexican, Latino or Hispanic?

> Geographically, *Hispanic* is preferred in the Southeast and much of Texas. New Yorkers use both *Hispanic* and *Latino.* Chicago, where no nationality has attained a majority, prefers *Latino.* In California, the word *Hispanic* has been barred from the Los Angeles *Times,* in keeping with the strong feelings of people in the community. Some people in New Mexico prefer *Hispano.* Politically, *Hispanic* belongs to the right and some of the center, while *Latino* belongs to the left and the center. Historically, the choice went from *Spanish* or *Spanish-speaking* to *Latin American, Latino,* and *Hispanic.* (Shorris, 1992:xvi–xvii)

Deciding what name to use for a category of people is not easy. It is unlikely that all members of the category use the same name; the name members use for one another may not be acceptable for outsiders to use; nor is it always advisable to ask what name a person prefers. We once saw an old friend become quite angry when asked whether he preferred the term *black* or *African American.* "Either one is fine with me," he replied, "*I* know what *I* am." To him, the question meant that he was being seen as a member of a category, not as an individual.

Because naming may involve a redefinition of self, an assertion of power, and a rejection of others' ability to impose an identity, social change movements often lay claim to a new name, and opponents may express opposition by continuing to use the old name. For example, *black* emerged in opposition to Negro as the Black Power movement sought to distinguish itself from the Martin Luther King–led moderate wing of the civil rights movement. The term *Negro* had itself been put forward by influential leaders W. E. B. Du Bois and Booker T. Washington as a rejection of the term "colored" that had dominated the mid- to late 19th century. "[D]espite its association with racial epithets, 'Negro' was defined to stand for a new way of thinking about Blacks" (Smith, 1992:497–98). Similarly, in 1988 Ramona H. Edelin, president of the National Urban Coalition, proposed that *African American* be substituted for *black,* and now both terms are in use (Smith, 1992).[3] Ironically, *people of color* is now a common reference to all nonwhite Americans, while *colored people* refers exclusively to African Americans, who may take offense.

Each of these changes—from *Negro* to *black* to *African American*—was first promoted by activists as a way to demonstrate their commitment to change and militance. A similar theme is reflected in the history of the terms *Chicano* and *Chicanismo.* Although the origin of the terms is unclear, the principle was the same. As reporter Ruben Salazar wrote in the 1960s, "a chicano is a Mexican-American with a non-Anglo image of himself" (Shorris, 1992:101).

Similarly, the term *homosexual* was first coined in 1869 by a Hungarian physician who sought to have same sex relationships recognized as a medical rather than a criminal issue. The term was then adopted by the medical and psychological literature of the time, which, as Jonathan Katz explains in Reading 16, depicted all nonprocreative sex as pathological. When activists of the 1960s rejected the pathological characterization, they rejected the name associated with it as well, substituting *gay* for *homosexual.* Presently *gay* is used both as a generic term encompassing men and women and as a specific reference to men.[4]

The 1990 founding of Queer Nation may have signaled the demise of *gay,* however. This use of *queer*—as in the slogan "We're here. We're queer. Get used to it."—attempts to transform an epithet into a label of pride and militance. Nonetheless, use of the word is also debated within the gay community. Some argue that it reflects the internalization of homophobic attitudes, while others argue that it signals defiance of straight culture.

Just as each of these social movements has involved a public renaming that proclaims pride, the women's movement has asserted *woman* as a replacement for *girl.* A student who described a running feud with her roommate illustrates the significance of these two terms. The student preferred the word *woman,* arguing that the word *girl* when applied to females past adolescence was insulting. Her female roommate just as strongly preferred the term *girl* and regularly applied it to the females she knew. Each of them had such strong feelings on the matter that is was apparent they would not last as roommates.

How could these two words destroy their relationship? It appears that English speakers use the terms *girl* and *woman* to refer to quite different qualities. *Woman*

---

[3]Thus, one can find Black Studies, Afro-American Studies, and African American Studies programs in universities across the country.

[4]In the 17th century, *gay* became associated with an addiction to social pleasure, dissipation, and loose morality, and was used to refer to female prostitutes (e.g., "gay girl"). The term was apparently first used in reference to a male homosexual in 1925 in Australia. "It may have been both the connotations of femininity and those of immorality that led American homosexuals to adopt the title 'gay' with some self-irony in the 1920s. The slogan 'Glad to Be Gay,' adopted by both female and male homosexuals, and the naming of the Gay Liberation Front, which was born from the Stonewall resistance riots following police raids on homosexual bars in New York in 1969, bear witness to a greater self-confidence" (Mills, 1989:102).

(like *man*) is understood to convey adulthood, power, and sexuality; *girl* (like *boy*) connotes youth, powerlessness, and irresponsibility (Richardson, 1988). Thus, the two roommates were asserting quite different places for themselves in the world. One claimed adulthood; the other saw herself as not having achieved that yet. This is the explanation offered by many females: It is not so much that they like being *girls,* as that they value youth and/or do not yet feel justified in calling themselves *women.* Yet this is precisely the identity the women's movement has asserted: "We cannot be girls anymore, we must be women."

Creating Categories of People While individuals and groups may assert names for themselves, governments also have the power to create categories of people. The history of the race and ethnicity questions asked in the U.S. Census illustrates this process.

Every census since the first one in 1790 has included a question about race. By 1970, the options for race were white, Negro or black, American Indian (with a request to print the name of the enrolled or principal tribe), Japanese, Chinese, Filipino, Hawaiian, Korean, and Other (with the option of specifying). (Reading 3 charts the evolution of the census's race categories.) The 1970 census began the practice of allowing the head of the household to identify the race of household members: before that, the census taker had made that identification. Thus, the bureau began treating race as primarily a matter of *self*-identification. Still, it was assumed that a person could only be a member of *one* racial group, so respondents were allowed only one option for each household member.

The 1970 "long form" also posed the first ethnicity question, asking whether the individual was of Hispanic or non-Hispanic ancestry, and providing four checkoff categories with space to fill in other possibilities. (Ethnicity, which generally refers to ancestry, is a subject we will return to shortly.) The Hispanic/non-Hispanic question was added at the recommendation of the Census Bureau's Hispanic Advisory Committee as a way to correct for the *differential undercount* of the Hispanic population. A differential undercount means that more people are undercounted in one category than in another; for example, the census yields a larger undercount of those who rent their homes than of those who own them. Undercounting primarily affects the data on low-income residents of inner cities. This is the case because the poor often move and are thus difficult to contact, are more likely to be illiterate or non-English speakers (there was no Spanish-language census form until 1990), and are more likely to be illegal immigrants afraid to respond to a government questionnaire. This count is significant because the Constitution requires a count of *all* the people in the United States, not just those who are citizens or legal residents. Because census data affect the distribution of billions of dollars of federal aid for "everything from feeding the poor to running mass transit systems" (Espiritu, 1992:116), undercounting has a significant impact on everyone. Indeed, the bureau's Census 2000 FAQ Web page notes that $182 billion will be distributed annually to state, local, and tribal governments based on formulas using Census 2000 data.

Census data had always been critical to the functioning of American government: the apportionment of seats in the U.S. House of Representatives and the distribution of federal funding to states and localities are based on census data. However, by the 1970s information on race was increasingly needed to document and eliminate discrimination. Such data, the newly formed U.S. Commission on Civil Rights argued, was necessary to monitor equal access in housing, education, and employment. In addition,

> There were the civil rights movement and its offshoots such as the Mexican-American Brown Power movement. In addition, the federal government initiated the War Against Poverty and the Great Society programs. These movements and programs stated clearly that poor minority groups had a legitimate claim to better conditions in cities. Several of the social welfare programs of President Johnson's Great Society distributed dollars by means of statistically driven grant-in-aid formulas. The proliferation of federal grants programs and the cities' increasing dependence upon them tended to heighten the political salience of census statistics. Such formulas often incorporated population size, as measured or estimated by the Census Bureau, as a major factor. By 1978 there were more than one hundred such programs, covering a wide range of concerns, from preschool education (Headstart) to urban mass transportation (U.S. Congress, 1978). . . . [T]he single most commonly used data source was the decennial census. (Choldin, 1994:27–8)

In all, the census offered an important source of information for the courts, Congress, and local entities to gauge the extent of discrimination and monitor civil rights enforcement. Data on race allowed for the monitoring of the Voting Rights Act, equal employment opportunity programs, and racial disparities in health, birth, and death rates.

To improve the collection of race data, the Commission on Civil Rights recommended that the Office of Management and Budget (OMB) develop government-wide standards. In developing its recommendation, the commission reviewed the race categorization practices of federal agencies and concluded that while "the designations do not refer strictly to race, color, national or ethnic origin," the categories were nonetheless what the general public understood to be *minority groups* (U.S. Commission on Civil Rights, 1973:39). "The federal emphasis was clearly on minority status in a legal sense. Minority group status did not derive from a specific race or ethnicity *per se,* but on the treatment of race and ethnicity to confer a privileged, disadvantaged, or equitable status and to gauge representation and underrepresentation" (Tamayo Lott, 1998:37). The aim of data collection was to pinpoint the extent of discrimination, not to identify all population categories.

Thus, in 1977 the OMB issued Statistical Directive No. 15, "Race and Ethnic Standards for Federal Statistics and Administrative Reporting," which established standard categories and definitions for all federal agencies, including the Bureau of the Census. Directive No. 15 defined four racial and one ethnic category: American Indian or Alaskan Native, Asian or Pacific Islander, Negro or Black, White, and Hispanic.

> The choice of four racial categories and one ethnic category [Hispanic] redefined the United States beyond a White and non-White classification and even beyond a White and

> Black classification. The new classification facilitated the enumeration of a multiracial and multicultural population. . . . The particular status of Hispanics was recognized in two ways. Hispanic was the only choice for the ethnic category. Furthermore . . . Black and White Hispanics were enumerated as Hispanics. To avoid duplicated counts, the Black and White categories excluded Hispanics. (Tamayo Lott, 1998:54)

The racial and ethnic diversity of the United States is more complex now than it was in the 1970s. Reading 4 provides the first 17 questions of the "long" version of the 2000 census. The long form, also called the "sample" version because it is sent to a sample of the population, is distributed to an average of one in six households; the "short" (or 100 percent) form goes to all other households. Both short and long versions ask for the name of each person in the household and their sex, age, race, and whether they are of Spanish/Hispanic/Latino ancestry—which means that these are the only questions asked of *all* those who take the census. The long form asks additional questions on the social and economic characteristics of householders (including their ethnicity, as in question 10), and on the physical and financial characteristics of their housing.

One of the most notable changes in the 2000 census is its recognition that a person may identify himself or herself as being a member of more than one racial group. For the first time in its 210-year history, the census's race question (question 6 on the long form) provides for the identification of mixed lineage—though it does not offer a category called *multiracial.* This change was one outcome of a comprehensive review and revision of OMB's Directive No. 15 begun in 1994. That review included public hearings, sample surveys of targeted populations, and collaboration among the more than 30 federal agencies that collect and use data on race and ethnicity. While this change was certainly spurred by activists who identified themselves as mixed-race, the bureau's pretesting also indicated that less than 2 percent of respondents would mark more than one race for themselves, and thus the historical continuity with previous censuses would not be compromised.

The 1990s revision of Directive No. 15 yielded a variety of other changes in the 2000 census:

- *Indian (Amer.)* was changed to *American Indian.*
- *Hawaiian* was changed to *Native Hawaiian.*
- *African Am.* was added to *Black* and *Negro.*
- The Hispanic origin question was placed before the race question in an effort to increase race reporting by showing that those of Hispanic origin may be of any race.
- *Latino* was added as a descriptor, making the question "Is this person Spanish/Hispanic/Latino?"
- While it is implicit in the questionnaire, the category *Asian and Pacific Islander* was split into *Asian* and *Native Hawaiian or Other Pacific Islander. Asian* is now defined as including any of the original peoples of the Far East, Southeast Asia, or the Indian subcontinent including, for example, Cambodia, China, India, Japan, Korea, Pakistan, the Philippine Islands, Thailand, and Vietnam. *Native Hawaiian*

or Other Pacific Islander includes the original peoples of Hawaii, Guam, Samoa, or other Pacific Islands, and the Pacific Islander groups reported in the 1990 census.

- One change that was not made, however, was inclusion of a race category called *Arab* or *Middle Eastern* because public comment did not indicate agreement on a definition for this category. Thus, in the 2000 census Arab or Middle Eastern peoples continue to be categorized as white.

As in previous censuses, undercounting remains an important fiscal and political issue, given the disproportionate underenumeration of people of color. Still, gay couples may well be the most undercounted group. Since the 1990 census, the form has provided "unmarried partner" as a possible answer to the question of how the people in the household are related to one another. The number of gay couples (not gay people) increased more than 300 percent between the 1990 and 2000 censuses, to 594,391 couples, but that number is likely less than a full count because of respondents' reluctance to report (Cohn, 2001).

Overall, however, the Census Bureau contends that the net *national* undercount for the 2000 census was smaller than it had been in 1990 (down to 0.06 percent from 1.6 percent) (U.S. Department of Commerce, October 18, 2001). For the 2000 census, the bureau had proposed supplementing the traditional head count with statistical sampling techniques such as those used in opinion polls. This would provide an estimate of the number and demographic characteristics of those who did not respond to the census. In a 5 to 4 decision in 1999, the Supreme Court barred use of these methods for determining the nation's population for congressional reapportionment. However, it left open the possibility of using these methods to allocate federal funds and to redistrict within the states.

We end this portion of our discussion with two cautions. First, on a personal level, many of us find census categorizations objectionable. But simultaneously as *citizens,* we seek the benefits and protections of policies based on these data—and as citizens we share the goal of eliminating discriminatory practices.

> [R]eliable racial data are crucial to enforcing our basic laws against intentional racial discrimination, which enjoy broad public support. For example, in order to demonstrate that an employer is engaging in a broad based "pattern or practice" of discrimination in violation of the Civil Rights Act of 1964, a plaintiff must rely on statistical proof that goes beyond the plight of an individual employee. Supreme Court precedent in such cases requires plaintiffs to show a statistically significant disparity between the proportion of qualified minorities in the local labor market and the proportion within the employer's work force. A disparity of more than two standard deviations creates a legal presumption that intentional discrimination is occurring, since a disparity of that magnitude almost never occurs by accident.
>
> Demographic information, in other words, provides the "big picture" that places individual incidents in context. Voting rights cases require similar proof, as do many housing discrimination cases and suits challenging the discriminatory use of federal funds. Without reliable racial statistics, it would be virtually impossible for courts or agencies to detect institutional bias, and antidiscrimination laws would go unenforced. More

fundamentally, we simply cannot know as a society how far we've come in conquering racial discrimination and inequality without accurate information about the health, progress and opportunities available to communities of different races (Jenkins, 1999:15–16).

Second, when considering official counts of the population, we must be careful not to assume that what is counted is real. While census data contribute to the essentialist view that the world is populated by distinct, scientifically defined categories of people, this brief history demonstrates that not even those who collect the data make that assumption; rather, census categories have been based on constructionist premises. As OMB warns,

> The racial and ethnic categories set forth in the standards should not be interpreted as being primarily biological or genetic in reference. Race and ethnicity may be thought of in terms of social and cultural characteristics as well as ancestry. (Office of Management and Budget, 1997:2)
>
> There are no clear, unambiguous, objective generally agreed-upon definitions of the terms "race" and "ethnicity." Cognitive research shows that respondents are not always clear on the differences between race and ethnicity. There are differences in terminology, group boundaries, attributes and dimensions of race and ethnicity. . . .
>
> [The Directive No. 15 categories] do not represent objective "truth" but rather are ambiguous social constructs and involve subjective and attitudinal issues. (Office of Management and Budget, 1995:44680)

Aggregating and Disaggregating Federal identification policies have collapsed various national-origin groups into four categories: Hispanics or Latinos, Native Americans, Blacks, and Asian or Pacific Islanders. This process *aggregated* categories of people; that is, it combined, or "lumped together," different groups. In their answers to the census questions, Puerto Ricans, Mexicans, and Cubans all became "Latino" in some sense. While *Latino* and *Hispanic* remain commonly used aggregate terms, the diversity of this population has increased dramatically. Data from the 2000 census show that the number of respondents identifying as "Other Spanish/Hispanic/Latino"—that is, who are neither Mexican, Mexican American, Chicano, Puerto Rican, or Cuban—has doubled from 5 million to 10 million since the 1990 census. "Other Spanish/Hispanic/Latino" is now the fastest growing group in the Spanish/Hispanic/Latino category (Population Reference Bureau, 2001).

The groups that are now lumped together have historically regarded one another as different, and thus in people's everyday lives the aggregate category is likely to *disaggregate,* or fragment, into its constituent national-origin elements. For example, one might think that *Latino* or *Asian American* are terms used for self-identification, but this is often not the case. In the United States, "Mexicans, Puerto Ricans, and Cubans have little interaction with each other, most do not recognize that they have much in common culturally, and they do not profess strong affection for each other" (de la Garza et al., 1992:14). Thus, it is not surprising that a survey of the Latino population concludes that "respondents do not primarily identify as members of an Hispanic or Latino community. . . . [Rather, they] overwhelmingly prefer to identify by national origin . . ." (de la Garza et al., 1992:13). While members of these groups share common positions on many domestic policy issues, they do not appear to share a commitment to Spanish-language maintenance, common cultural traditions, or religiosity (de la Garza et al., 1992). In short, the category *Latino/Hispanic* exists primarily, but not exclusively, from the perspective of non-Latinos.

While the classification *Latino/Hispanic* offers at least a commonality in Spanish as a shared language in the country of origin, among those sharing the category *Asian American* are groups with different languages, cultures, and religions and sometimes centuries of hostility. In contrast, the category *Asian American* is based on geography rather than on any cultural, racial, linguistic, or religious commonalities. "Asian Americans are those who come from a region of the world that *the rest of the world* has defined as Asia" (Hu-Dehart, 1994).[5]

Collective classifications such as Latino or Asian American were not simply the result of federal classifications, however. Student activists inspired by the Black Power and civil rights movements first proposed the terms. As Yen Le Espiritu describes in Reading 7, college students coined the identifier *Asian American* in response to "the similarity of [their] experiences and treatment." *Asian American* and *Latino* are examples of *panethnic* terms, that is, classifications that span national-origin identities. Panethnicity is "the development of bridging organizations and solidarities among subgroups of ethnic collectivities that are often seen as homogeneous by outsiders. . . . Those . . . groups that, from an outsider's point of view, are most racially homogeneous are also the groups with the greatest panethnic development" (Lopez and Espiritu, 1990:219–20).

Panethnicity is both useful and unstable. "The elites representing such groups find it advantageous to make political demands by using the numbers and resources panethnic formations can mobilize. The state, in turn, can more easily manage claims by recognizing and responding to large blocs as opposed to dealing with the specific claims of a plethora of ethnically defined interest groups" (Omi, 1996:180). At the same time, competition and historic antagonisms make such alliances unstable. "At times it is advantageous to be in a panethnic bloc, and at times it is desirable to mobilize along particular ethnic lines" (Omi, 1996:181).

---

[5]In census classification, the category *Asian* includes Asian Indian, Chinese, Filipino, Japanese, Korean, Vietnamese; *Other Asian* includes Bangladeshi, Bhutanese, Burmese, Cambodian, Hmong, Indo-Chinese, Indonesian, Iwo Jiman, Laotian, Malaysian, Maldivian, Mongolian, Nepalese, Okinawan, Pakistani, Singaporean, Sri Lankan, Thai, and Taiwanese. The category *Pacific Islander* includes Native Hawaiian, Guamanian or Chamorro, Samoan; *Other Pacific Islander* includes Carolinian, Chuukese, Fijian, Kirabati, Kosraean, Mariana Islander, Marshallese, Melanesian, Micronesian, New Hebrides, Palauan, Papua New Guinean, Pohnpeian, Polynesian, Saipanese, Solomon Islander, Tahitian, Tokelauan, Tongan, and Yapese (U.S. Census Bureau, 2001).

In 1980, Asian Indians successfully lobbied to change their census classification from white to Asian American by reminding Congress that historically immigrants from India had been classed as Asian. With other Asians, those from India had been barred from immigration by the 1917 Immigration Act, prohibited from becoming naturalized citizens until 1946, and denied the right to own land by the 1920 Alien Land Law. Indeed, in 1923 the U.S. Supreme Court (in *Thind*) ruled that Asian Indians were nonwhite, and could therefore have their U.S. citizenship nullified (Espiritu, 1992:124–25). Thus, for most of their history in the United States, Asian Indians had been classed as Asian.

The terms *Native American* and *African American* are also aggregate classifications, but in this case they are the result of conquest and enslavement.

> The "Indian," like the European, is an idea. The notion of "Indians" was invented to distinguish the indigenous peoples of the New World from Europeans. The "Indian" is the person on shore, outside of the boat. . . . There [were] hundreds of cultures, languages, ways of living in Native America. The place was a model of diversity at the time of Columbus's arrival. Yet Europeans did not see this diversity. They created the concept of the "Indian" to give what they did see some kind of unification, to make it a single entity they could deal with, because they could not cope with the reality of 400 different cultures. (Mohawk, 1992: 440)[6]

Conquest made "Indians" out of a heterogeneity of tribes and nations that had been distinctive on linguistic, religious, and economic grounds. It was not only that Europeans had the unifying concept of "Indian" in mind—after all, they were sufficiently aware of cultural differences to generate an extensive body of tribally specific treaties. It was also that conquest itself—encompassing as it did the appropriation of land, the forging and violation of treaties, and the implementation of policies that forced relocation—structured the lives of Native Americans along common lines. While contemporary Native Americans still identify themselves by tribal ancestry, just as those called Asian American and Latino identify themselves by national origin, their shared experience of conquest also forged the common identity reflected in the collective name, *Native American.*

Similarly, the capture, purchase, and forced relocation of Africans, and their experience of forcibly being moved from place to place as personal property, created the category now called *African American.* This experience forged a single people from a culturally diverse group; it produced an "oppositional racial consciousness," that is, a unity-in-opposition (Omi and Winant, 1994). "Just as the conquest created the 'native' where once there had been Pequot, Iroquois, or Tutelo, so too it created the 'black' where once there had been Asante or Ovimbundu, Yoruba or Bakongo" (Omi and Winant, 1994:66).

Even the categories of gay and straight, male and female, and poor and middle class are aggregations that presume a commonality by virtue of shared master status. For example, the category *gay and lesbian* assumes that sharing a sexual orientation binds people together despite all the issues that might divide them as men and women, people of different colors, or people of different social classes. And, just as in the cases we have previously discussed, alliances of gay and lesbian people can be expected to come together, but at times to separate in response to social circumstances.

---

[6]The idea of "Europe" and the "European" is also a constructed, aggregate category. "Physically, Europe is not a continent. Where is the water separating Europe from Asia? It is culture that separates Europe from Asia. Western Europe roughly comprises the countries that in the Middle Ages were Latin Christendom, and Eastern Europe consists of those countries that in the Middle Ages were Eastern Orthodox Christendom. It was about 1257 A.D. when the Pope claimed hegemony over the secular emperors in Western Europe and formulated the idea that Europeans, that Christians, were a unified ethnicity even though they spoke many different languages" (Mohawk, 1992:439–40).

Still, our analysis has so far ignored one category of people. From whose perspective do the categories of Native American, Asian American, African American, and Latino/Hispanic exist? Since "difference" is always "difference *from,*" from whose perspective is "difference" determined? Who has the power to define "difference"? If "we" are in the boat looking at "them," who precisely are "we"?

Every perspective on the social world emerges from a particular vantage point, a particular social location. Ignoring who the "us" is in the boat treats that place as if it were just the view "anyone" would take. Historically, the people in the boat were European; contemporarily, they are white Americans. As Ruth Frankenberg frames it in Reading 8, in America "whites are the nondefined definers of other people," "the unmarked marker of others' differentness." Failing to identify the "us" in the boat means that "white culture [becomes] the unspoken norm," a category that is powerful enough to define others while itself remaining invisible. Indeed, Frankenberg argues that those with the most power in a society are best positioned to have their own identities left unnamed, thus masking their power.

The term *androcentrism* describes the world as seen from a male-centered perspective. By analogy, one may also describe a *Eurocentric* and *heterocentric* perspective. To some extent, regardless of their sex, race, or sexual orientation, all Americans operate from an andro-, Euro-, and heterocentric perspective since these are the guiding assumptions of the culture. Recognizing these perspectives as historically and culturally located makes it possible to evaluate their adequacy.

Dichotomizing

Many forces promote the construction of aggregate categories of people. Frequently, these aggregates emerge as *dichotomies.* To dichotomize is not only to divide something into two parts; it is also to see those parts as mutually exclusive and in opposition. Dichotomization encourages the sense that there are only two categories, that everyone fits easily in one or the other, and that the categories stand in opposition to each other. In contemporary American culture, we appear to treat the master statuses of race, sex, class, and sexual orientation as if each embodied "us" and "them"—as if for each master status people could be easily sorted into two mutually exclusive, opposed groupings.[7]

Dichotomizing Race

The clearest example of dichotomization is provided by the "one-drop rule" discussed by F. James Davis in Reading 1. Despite the increasing number of people who are biracial (partly a consequence of the increase in the number of interracial marriages from 1 to 2 percent between 1970 and 1990 [Spencer, 1997]), many popular autobiographies by biracial people, and the census's introduction of the multiple checkoff for race, American social practices apparently remain governed by the "rule" that a person with any traceable African heritage is black. Indeed, one piece

[7]Springer and Deutsch (1981) coined the term *dichotomania* to describe the current belief that there are male and female sides of the brain. We think that term also fits our discussion.

of evidence that the "rule" persists is the fact that so few African Americans used the 2000 census to identify themselves as being of multiple races—even though a large portion would have Native American and/or white ancestry. While in other cultures people of mixed racial ancestry might be defined as *mixed,* the American one-drop rule specifically denies that possibility. As Davis describes, the one-drop rule is an informal social practice strongly supported by both blacks and whites, and reaffirmed by the Supreme Court as recently as 1986.

In the 2000 census, those who reported being of more than one race were likely to be "under 18, living in the West, and of Hispanic/Latino origin. Nearly two-thirds of all those who reported more than one race lived in just 10 states: California, New York, Texas, Florida, Hawaii, Illinois, New Jersey, Washington, Michigan, and Ohio" (U.S. Department of Commerce, November 29, 2001). The youth of the population identifying itself as biracial—and the life stories of biracial and multiracial celebrities such as Jasmine Guy, Jennifer Beals, Halle Berry, Derek Jeeter, Lenny Kravitz, Mariah Carey, Greg Louganis, and Tiger Woods—may well indicate the future unraveling of the rule.

The black/white dichotomy has been an abiding and rigidly enforced one, but different regions and historical periods have also produced their own two-part distinctions. In the Southwest the divide has been between Anglos and Latinos, and on parts of the West Coast it is between Asian Americans and whites. Each of these variations, however, is an instance of America's more encompassing and historic dichotomization: that of whites and nonwhites.

While three racial categories—*white, Negro,* and *Indian*—were identified throughout the 19th century (Omi and Winant, 1994), all were located within the white/nonwhite dichotomy. In 1854, the California Supreme Court in *People v. Hall* held that blacks, mulattos, Native Americans, and Chinese were "not white" and therefore could not testify for or against a white man in court (Takaki, 1993:205–6). (Hall, a white man, had been convicted of killing a Chinese man on the testimony of one white and three Chinese witnesses; the Supreme Court overturned the conviction.) Mexican residents of the southwest territories ceded to the United States in the 1848 Treaty of Guadalupe Hidalgo, however, "were defined as a white population and accorded the political-legal status of 'free white persons'" (Omi and Winant, 1994). European immigrants were initially treated as nonwhite, or at least not-yet-white. In turn, they lobbied for their own inclusion in American society on the basis of the white/nonwhite distinction.

> [Immigrants struggled to] equate whiteness with Americanism in order to turn arguments over immigration from the question of who was foreign to the question of who was white. . . . Immigrants could not win on the question of who was foreign. . . . But if the issue somehow became defending "white man's jobs" or "white man's government" . . . [they] could gain space by deflecting debate from nativity, a hopeless issue, to race, an ambiguous one. . . . After the Civil War, the new-coming Irish would help lead the movement to bar the relatively established Chinese from California, with their agitation for a "white man's government," serving to make race, and not nativity, the center of the debate and to prove the Irish white. (Roediger, 1994:189–90)

Historically, *American* has meant white, as many Americans of Asian ancestry learn when they are complimented on their English—a compliment that presumes that someone who is Asian could not be a native-born American.[8] A story from the 1998 Winter Olympics illustrates the same point. At the conclusion of the figure skating competition, MSNBC posted a headline that read "American Beats Out Kwan for Women's Figure Skating Title." The reference was to Michelle Kwan, who won the silver medal, losing the gold to Tara Lapinski. But both Kwan and Lapinsky are Americans. While Kwan's parents immigrated from Hong Kong, she was born and raised in the United States, is a U.S. citizen, and was a member of the U.S. team. The network attributed the mistake to overworked staff and apologized. But for Asian American activists, this was an example of how people of Asian descent have remained perpetual foreigners in American society.

Novelist Toni Morrison would describe this as a story about "how *American* means *white*":

> Deep within the word "American" is its association with race. To identify someone as South African is to say very little; we need the adjective "white" or "black" or "colored" to make our meaning clear. In this country it is quite the reverse. American means white, and Africanist people struggle to make the term applicable to themselves with . . . hyphen after hyphen after hyphen. (Morrison, 1992:47)

Because *American* means *white,* those who are not white are presumed to be recent arrivals and often told to go "back where they came from." Thus, we appear to operate within the dichotomized *racial* categories of American/non-American—these are racial categories, because they effectively mean white/nonwhite.

But what exactly *is* race? First, we need to distinguish *race* from *ethnicity.* Though common usage often muddies the two concepts, race and ethnicity have "very different consequences for social life, especially in terms of assimilation and achievement in the United States" (Fuller, personal communication, 2001). Social scientists define *ethnic groups* as categories of people who are distinctive on the basis of national origin, language, and cultural practices. "Members of an ethnic group hold a set of common memories that make them feel that their customs, culture, and outlook are distinctive" (Blauner, 1992). Thus, racial categories encompass different ethnic groups. For example, the racial category *white* includes ethnic groups such as Irish, Italian, and Polish Americans. Unfortunately, many fail to recognize ethnic distinctions among people of color. For example, not all blacks in the United States are African American; some are Haitian, Jamaican, or Nigerian.

The term *race* first appeared in the Romance languages of Europe in the Middle Ages to refer to breeding stock (Smedley, 1993). A "race" of horses described common ancestry and a distinctive appearance or behavior. *Race* appears to have been first applied to New World peoples by the Spanish in the 16th century. Later it was adopted by the English, again in reference to people of the New World, and

[8]Since the historic American ban on Asian immigration remained in place until 1965, it is nonetheless the case that a high proportion of Asian Americans are foreign born. The 1990 census indicated that 66 percent of the Asian American population was foreign born. This figure, however, masks a considerable range. Among Japanese Americans, only 32 percent were foreign born, while that was the case for 83 percent of Vietnamese Americans (Hirschman, 1996).

generally came to mean "people," "nation," or "variety." By the late 18th century, "when scholars became more actively engaged in investigations, classifications, and definitions of human populations, the term 'race' was elevated as the one major symbol and mode of human group differentiation employed extensively for non-European groups and even those in Europe who varied in some way from the subjective norm" (Smedley, 1993:39).

Though elevated to the level of science, the concept of race continued to reflect its origins in animal breeding. Farmers and herders had used the concept to describe stock bred for particular qualities; scholars used it to suggest that human behaviors could also be inherited. "Unlike other terms for classifying people . . . the term 'race' places emphasis on innateness, on the inbred nature of whatever is being judged" (Smedley, 1993:39). Like animal breeders, scholars also presumed that appearance revealed something about potential behavior. Just as the selective breeding of animals entailed the ranking of stock by some criteria, scholarly use of the concept of race involved the ranking of humans. Differences in skin color, hair texture, and the shape of head, eyes, nose, lips, and body were developed into an elaborate hierarchy of merit and potential for "civilization."

The idea of race emerged among all the European colonial powers, although their conceptions of it varied. However, only the British in North America and South Africa constructed a system of rigid, exclusive racial categories and a social order *based on race,* a "racialized social structure" (Omi and Winant, 1994). "[S]kin color variations in many regions of the world and in many societies have been imbued with some degree of social value or significance, but color prejudice or preferences do not of themselves amount to a fully evolved racial worldview . . ." (Smedley, 1993:25).

This racialized social structure—which in America produced a race-based system of slavery and subsequently a race-based distribution of political, legal, and social rights—was a historical first. "Expansion, conquest, exploitation, and enslavement have characterized much of human history over the past five thousand years or so, but none of these events before the modern era resulted in the development of ideologies or social systems based on race" (Smedley, 1993:25, 15). While differences of color had long been noted, societies had never before been built on those differences.

As scientists assumed that race differences involved more than simply skin color or hair texture, they sought the biological distinctiveness of racial categories—but with little success. In the early 20th century, anthropologists looked to physical features such as height, stature, and head shape to distinguish the races, only to learn that these are affected by environment and nutrition. Later the search turned to genetics, only to find that those cannot be correlated with conventional racial classifications. Even efforts to reach a consensus about how many races exist or what specific features distinguish them from one another are problematic. As one anthropologist has put it, "Classifying people by color is very much like classifying cars by color. Those in the same classification look alike . . . but the classification tells you nothing about the hidden details of construction or about how the cars or people will perform" (Cohen, 1998:12).

> If our eyes could perceive more than the superficial, we might find race in chromosome 11: there lies the gene for hemoglobin. If you divide humankind by which of two forms of the gene each person has, then equatorial Africans, Italians and Greeks fall into the "sickle-cell race"; Swedes and South Africa's Xhosas (Nelson Mandela's ethnic group) are in the healthy hemoglobin race. Or do you prefer to group people by whether they have epicanthic eye folds, which produce the "Asian" eye? Then the !Kung San (Bushmen) belong with the Japanese and Chinese. . . . [D]epending on which traits you pick, you can form very surprising races. Take the scooped-out shape of the back of the front teeth, a standard "Asian" trait. Native Americans and Swedes have these shovel-shaped incisors, too, and so would fall in the same race. Is biochemistry better? Norwegians, Arabians, north Indians and the Fulani of northern Nigeria . . . fall into the "lactase race" (the lactase enzyme digests milk sugar). Everyone else—other Africans, Japanese, Native Americans—form the "lactase-deprived race" (their ancestors did not drink milk from cows or goats and hence never evolved the lactase gene). How about blood types, the familiar A, B, and O groups? Then Germans and New Guineans, populations that have the same percentages of each type, are in one race; Estonians and Japanese comprise a separate one for the same reason. . . . The dark skin of Somalis and Ghanaians, for instance, indicates that they evolved under the same selective force (a sunny climate). But that's all it shows. It does *not* show that they are any more closely related in the sense of sharing more genes than either is to Greeks. Calling Somalis and Ghanaians "black" therefore sheds no further light on their evolutionary history and implies—wrongly—that they are more closely related to each other than either is to someone of a different "race." . . . If you pick at random any two "blacks" walking along the street, and analyze their 23 pairs of chromosomes, you will probably find that their genes have less in common than do the genes of one of them with that of a random "white" person. (Begley, 1995:67, 68)

The "no-race" theory now dominates the fields of physical anthropology and human genetics (Cohen, 1998). This perspective argues that "(1) Biological variability exists but this variability does not conform to the discrete packages labeled races. (2) So-called racial characteristics are not transmitted as complexes. (3) Races do not exist because isolation of groups has been infrequent; populations have always interbred" (Lieberman, 1968:128). Still, few scholars outside of anthropology seem to take this perspective into account.

> [I]t does not appear that this debate [about the existence of race] has had widespread impact on professionals in the fields of medicine, psychology, sociology, history, or political science. . . . [I]t will suffice to point out that virtually all scholars who write about "race and intelligence" assume that the "races" which they study are distinguished on the basis of biologically relevant criteria. So accepted is this fact that most scholars engaged in such research never consider it necessary to justify their assignment of individuals to this or that "race." . . . [Thus], the layman who reads the literature on race and racial groupings is justified in assuming that the existent typologies have been derived through the application of theories and methods current in disciplines concerned with the biological study of human variation. Since the scientific racial classifications which a layman finds in the literature are not too different from popular ones, he can be expected to feel justified in the maintenance of his views on race. (Marshall, 1993:117, 121)

In all, the primary significance of race is as a *social* concept: We "see" it, we expect it to tell us something significant about a person, and we organize social policy, law, and the distribution of wealth, power, and prestige around it. From the essentialist position, race is assumed to exist independently of our perception of it; it is assumed to significantly distinguish one group of people from another. From the constructionist perspective, race exists because we have created it as a meaningful category of difference among people.

Dichotomizing Sexual Orientation Many similarities exist in the construction of race and sexual orientation. First, both are often dichotomized—into black/white, white/nonwhite, or gay/straight—and individuals are expected to fit easily into one category or the other. While popular discussion of bisexuality is increasing and some gay organizations have added the term to their title, the depth of support for this third category is not yet clear. For example, many people publicly assert that bisexuals are "really" gay (Pope and Reynolds, 1991) or are heterosexuals who are merely experimenting with same-sex relationships. In either case, the acceptable options are still only gay or straight.

Scientists have sought biological differences between gay and straight people just as they have looked for such differences between the "races." In Reading 17, Barbara Sherman Heyl notes that such research is intrinsically suspect, since we are unlikely to find any biological structure or process that *all* gay people share but *no* straight people have. Still, the conviction that such differences must exist propels the search and leads to the naive acceptance of questionable findings (as Gilbert Zicklin describes in Reading 47).

As with race, sexual orientation appears more straightforward than it really is. Because sexuality encompasses physical, social, and emotional attraction, as well as fantasies, self-identity, and actual sexual behavior over a lifetime (Klein, 1978), determining one's sexual orientation may involve emphasizing one of these features over the others. Just as the system of racial classification asks people to pick *one* race, the sexual orientation system requires that all the different aspects of sexuality be distilled into one of two possible choices.

For example, an acquaintance described the process by which he came to self-identify as gay. In high school and college he had dated and been sexually active with women, but his relations with men had always been more important to him. He looked to men for emotional and social gratification and for relief from "gender games" he felt required to play with women. He had been engaged to be married, but when that ended he spent his time exclusively with other men. Eventually he established a sexual relationship with another man and came to identify himself as gay. His experience reflects the varied dimensions of sexuality and shows the resolution of those differences by choosing a single sexual identity. Rather than say "I used to be straight but I am now gay," he described himself as always "really" having been gay.

Alfred Kinsey's landmark survey of American sexual practices, described by Barbara Sherman Heyl in Reading 17,[9] showed that same-sex experience was more

[9]Heyl's article is titled "Homosexuality: A Social Phenomenon." The subtitle conveys Heyl's constructionist orientation, since in sociological theory the term *phenomenon* emphasizes the constructed dimension of social life. Heyl is not using the term to indicate something extraordinary or unusual.

common than had been assumed, and that sexual practices could change over the lifespan. Kinsey suggested that instead of thinking about "homosexuals" and "heterosexuals" as if these were two discrete categories of people, we should recognize that sexual behavior exists along a continuum from those who are exclusively heterosexual to those who are exclusively gay.

Further, there is no necessary correspondence between identity and sexual behavior. Someone who self-identifies as gay is still likely to have had some heterosexual experience; someone who self-identifies as straight may have had some same-sex experience; and even those who have had *no* sexual experience may lay claim to being gay or straight. Identity is not always directly tied to behavior. Indeed, a person who self-identifies as gay may have had *more* heterosexual experience than someone who self-identifies as straight. This distinction between identity and experience was underscored by the results of a 1994 survey, the most comprehensive American sex survey since Kinsey's. Only 2.8 percent of the men and 1.4 percent of the women identified themselves as gay, but an additional 7.3 percent and 7.2 percent, respectively, reported a same-sex experience or attraction (Michael, 1994).

One last analogy between the construction of race and sexual orientation bears discussion. Most Americans would not question the logic of this sentence: "Tom has been monogamously married for 30 years and had a dozen children, but I think he's *really* gay." In a real-life illustration of the same logic, a young man and woman were often seen kissing on our campus. When this became the subject of a class discussion, a suggestive ripple of laughter went through the room: Everyone "knew" that the young man was really gay.

How could they "know" that? For such conclusions to make sense, we must believe that someone could be gay irrespective of his or her actual behavior. Just as it is possible in this culture for one to be "black" even if one looks "white," apparently one may be gay despite acting straight. Just as "black" can be established by any African heritage, "gay" is apparently established by displaying any behavior thought to be associated with gays. Indeed, "gay" can be "established" by reputation alone, by a failure to demonstrate heterosexuality, or even by the demonstration of an overly aggressive heterosexuality. Therefore, "gay" can be assigned no matter what one actually does. Sociologist Jack Katz (1975) explains this as the imposition of an *essential identity,* that is, an identity assigned to an individual *irrespective of his or her actual behavior,* as in "I know she's a genius even though she's flunking all her courses." Because "gay" is understood as an essential identity in our culture, it can be assigned no matter what one's behavior. Because no behavior can ever conclusively prove one is *not* gay, this label is an extremely effective mechanism of social control.

In all, several parallels exist between race and sexual orientation classifications. With both, we assume there are a limited number of possibilities—usually two, but no more than three—and we assume individuals can be easily fit into one or another of these options. We treat both race and sexual orientation categories as encompassing populations that are internally homogeneous and profoundly dissimilar from each other. For both, this presumption of difference has prompted a wide-ranging search for the biological distinctiveness of the categories. Different races or sexual orientations are judged superior and inferior to one another, and members of each category historically have been granted unequal legal and social rights. Finally, we assume that sexual orientation, like color, tells us something meaningful about a person.

Dichotomizing Class Any discussion of social class in the United States must begin with the understanding that "American natives almost never speak of themselves or their society in class terms. In other words, class is not a central category of cultural discourse in America" (Ortner, 1991:169). Indeed, considering the time and attention Americans devote to sexual orientation, sex/gender, or race, it is hard not to conclude that social class is a taboo subject in our culture (Fussell, 1983). Because social class is so seldom discussed, the vocabulary for talking about it is not well developed. Still, as Sherry Ortner contends in Reading 13, divisions of social class that cannot be directly addressed may instead be displaced onto other relationships, for example, interactions between men and women or between parents and their children. Certainly it seems that we often substitute race for class. For example, the common assumption that people of color are poor and whites well-off applies the dichotomy of race to social class.

Even though American social class categories have not been as thoroughly constructed as our race, sex/gender, and sexual orientation categories, social class still exists. That is, there are clearly unequal distributions of income and wealth (described by Michael Zweig in Reading 14), differential rates of social mobility (described by Daniel McMurrer and Isabel Sawhill in Reading 15), and differences in the ownership of the means of production (as held by Marxist theory). Like the other master status categories, social class is also often dichotomized, in this case into "the poor" and "the middle class."

Americans often construct the poor/middle class dichotomy as if one's location in either category accurately reflected one's individual merit. More than people of other nationalities, Americans explain success and failure in terms of *individual merit* rather than economic or social forces (Morris and Williamson, 1982). This is, however, a relatively recent treatment. Before the Great Depression, those who were poor were understood to be "hardworking, low-wage workers, a group of people who in the public mind were at once numerous (perhaps the majority), the least well-off, economically productive, and impeded by socially contrived barriers to their advancement" (Cohen 1995 in Arrow, Bowles, and Durlauf, 2000:x). Today, however, "many of the least well off are not regarded as productive in any respect, and widespread understandings of their actions now serve more often to disqualify than to entitle them to a larger share of the social product" (Arrow et al., 2000:x). Now an emphasis on individual values, attributes, and lifestyle—rather than unemployment, discrimination, or a changing economy—characterizes popular opinion and social science research on social class (Kahlenberg, 1997; Mincy, 1994). Americans are prone to think that those who succeed financially do so on the basis of their own merit, and that those who don't succeed have failed because they lack merit. Indeed many talk about social class as if it were just the result of personal values or attitudes. Surveys indicate that over half of the American public believe "that lack of effort by the poor was the principal reason for poverty, or a reason at least equal to any that was beyond a person's control. . . . Popular majorities did not consider any other factor to be a very important cause of poverty—not low wages, or a scarcity of jobs, or discrimination, or even sickness" (Schwarz and Volgy, 1992:11).

This attribution of poverty and wealth to individual merit hides the complex reality of American social class. It ignores those who work but earn less than the poverty line—a group estimated to be between 7 and 9 million workers (Kim, 1999). It also defines those in the highest income brackets as "really just like the rest of us," that is, middle class. Although Americans are aware of a broad range of social class differences (Jackman and Jackman, 1983; Vanneman and Cannon, 1987), the widespread conviction that one's station in life reflects one's merit in many ways overshadows this awareness. In all, social class standing is taken to reveal one's essential nature and merit—a strikingly essentialist formulation.

Just as the American/non-American distinction functions to mean white/nonwhite, the middle class/poor dichotomy is often understood to mean white/nonwhite.

Dichotomizing Sex First, to distinguish the terms *sex* and *gender, sex* refers to females and males—that is, to chromosomal, hormonal, anatomical, and physiological differences—and *gender* describes the socially constructed roles associated with each sex. Gender is learned; it is the culturally and historically specific acting out of "masculinity" and "femininity." The term is often used erroneously as being synonymous with biological sex. For example, newspapers describe what are really sex differences in voting as "gender differences." In these Framework Essays, however, the distinction between the two terms will be maintained.

Indeed, even sex can be understood as a socially created dichotomy much like race, sexual orientation, or gender, although that approach can be unsettling. Readings 9, 10, and 11 by developmental geneticist Anne Fausto-Sterling and anthropoligist Walter Williams describe the belief in Western culture that there are two, and only two, sexes and that all individuals can be clearly identified as one or the other (Kessler and McKenna, 1978). But like sexual orientation, sex refers to a complex set of attributes—anatomical, chromosomal, hormonal, physiological—that may sometimes be inconsistent with one another or with individuals' sense of their own identity. This situation was illustrated by a Spanish athlete who is anatomically female, but in a pregame genetic test was classified as male. On the basis of that test, she was excluded from the 1985 World University Games. She was then reclassified as female in 1991, when the governing body for track-and-field contests abandoned genetic testing and returned to physical inspection. As the gynecologist for the sports federation noted, "about 1 in 20,000 people has genes that conflict with his or her apparent gender" (Lemonick, 1992).

Just as with race and sexual orientation, people are assigned to the categories of male or female irrespective of inconsistent or ambiguous evidence. In order to achieve consistency between the physical and psychological, some people are propelled into sex change surgery as they seek to produce a body consistent with their self-identities. Others will pursue psychotherapy to find an identity consistent with their bodies. In either case, it makes more sense to some people to use surgery and therapy to create consistency than to accept inconsistency: a man who feels like a woman must become a woman rather than just being a man who feels like a woman.

The Social Construction of Disability

Our discussion of race, sexual orientation, sex and gender, and social class has emphasized that each of these categories encompasses a continuum of behavior and characteristics rather than a finite set of discrete or easily separated groupings. It has also stressed that difference is a social creation—that differences of color or sex, for example, have no meaning other than what is attributed to them.

Can the same be said about ability and disability, which also qualify as master statuses? It is often assumed that people are easily classed as able-bodied or disabled, but that is no more true in this case than it is for the other master statuses. The comments of sociologist Irving Zola show how our use of statistics contributes to the misconception of ability/disability as fixed and dichotomous.

> The way we report statistics vis-à-vis disability and disease is generally misleading. If we speak of ratio figures for a particular disease as 1 in 8, 1 in 14, etc., we perpetuate what Rene Dubos (1961) once called "The Mirage of Health." For these numbers convey that if 1 person in 10 *does get* a particular disease, that 9 out of 10 *do not.* This means, however, only that those 9 people do not get *that* particular disease. It does not mean that they are disease-free, nor are they likely to be so. . . .
>
> Similarly deceptive is the now-popular figure of "43 million people with a disability" . . . for it implies that there are over 200 million Americans without a disability. . . . But the metaphor of being but a banana-peel slip away from disability is inappropriate. The issue of disability for individuals . . . is not *whether* but *when,* not so much *which one* but *how many* and *in what combination.* (Zola, 1993:18)

However, recognizing that the ability/disability dichotomy is illogical may be easier than understanding the case that disability is socially constructed. That point, which has emerged in the disability rights movement, is made by Michael Oliver in Reading 48. Rather than treating disability as a defect within an individual, this approach argues that disability is created by physical and social environments.

For example, disability is created by environments that lack the physical design or social supports that would make life worth living.

> Larry McAfee was aged 34 when a motorcycle accident resulted in complete paralysis and the need to use a ventilator. His insurance benefit (of $1 million) enabled him to employ personal care attendants in his own home for a period after his accident but when this ran out he was forced to enter a nursing home. He decided life wasn't worth living and tried turning his respirator off but couldn't cope with the feeling of suffocation. So he petitioned the courts to be allowed to be sedated while someone else unplugged his breathing apparatus. . . .
>
> Yet when, as a result of the publicity, McAfee received an outpouring of support from disability activists, he decided to delay the decision to take his own life. What he really wanted was to live in his own home and get a job. . . .
>
> It is not the physical disability itself but the social and economic circumstances of the experience which can lead to a diminished quality of life. (Morris, 1991:40–41)

Not only is disability the result of disabling environments, but the categories of disability are themselves socially constructed. "Epilepsy, illness, disease, and disability are not 'givens' in nature . . . but rather *socially constructed* categories that emerge from the interpretive activities of people acting together in social situations" (Schneider, 1988:65). Learning disabilities are an example of this process.

> Before the late 1800s when observers began to write about "word blindness," and, more significantly, before the mid-1960s when educators and others began to popularize learning disability, it did not exist. Learning disability did not exist as a means for making sense of difficulties people experienced in learning groups (Coles, 1987). Even the human variation (i.e., the learning difficulties) to which it refers has not existed for most of human history. However, today almost 2 million students are served as learning disabled, more than are served through any other disability category (U.S. Department of Education, 1990:12). (Higgins, 1992:9)

While both abled and disabled individuals participate in the social construction of disability, they do not do so on an equal basis. Cultural concepts such as dependence and independence—which bear heavily on judgments about what constitutes a disability—are most often imposed on disabled people by those not so identified.

> In terms of the physical world, none of us—whether disabled or not—is completely independent in the sense that we rely on nothing and nobody. However, the meaning of our dependence on others and on the physical world is determined by both its socio-economic and ideological context. For example, we all depend on water coming out of the tap when we turn it on, while a disabled person depends on someone to help her get dressed in the morning. However, when non-disabled people talk about water coming out of the tap, the issue is whether the water company is reliable; when they talk about [a disabled person] being dependent on an assistant, the issue for them is what they see as her helplessness created by her physical limitations. (Morris, 1991:137–38)

In both these ways—physical and conceptual—we create disability. "Through our beliefs and our behaviors, through our policies and our practices, we make disability (Albrecht, 1981:275; Ferguson, 1987). Through interpersonal, organizational, and social activities, we make disability (Bogdan and Biklen, 1977). In all areas of social life we make and remake disability" (Higgins, 1992:6).

Constructing the "Other"

We have seen how the complexity of a population may be reduced to aggregates and then to a simplistic dichotomy. Aggregation assumes that those who share a master status are alike in "essential" ways. It ignores the multiple and conflicting statuses an individual inevitably occupies. Dichotomization especially promotes the image of a mythical *Other* who is not at all like "us." Whether in race, sex, sexual orientation, social class, or disability, dichotomization yields a vision of "them" as profoundly different. Ultimately, dichotomization results in stigmatizing those who are less powerful. It provides the grounds for whole categories of people to become the objects of contempt.

Constructing "Others" as Profoundly Different The expectation that Others are profoundly different can be seen most clearly in the significance that has been attached to sex differences. In this case, biological differences between males and females have been the grounds from which to infer an extensive range of nonbiological differences. Women and men are assumed to differ from each other in behavior, perception, and personality, and such differences are used to argue for different legal, social, and economic roles and rights. The expectation that men and women are not at all alike is so widespread that we often talk about them as members of the "opposite" sex; indeed, it is not unusual to talk about the "war" between the sexes.

While this assumption of difference undergirds everyday life, few significant differences in behavior, personality, or even physical ability have been found between men and women of any age. As Cynthia Fuchs Epstein describes in Reading 12, "there are far more variations within each sex with regard to talents, interests, and intelligence than there are between each sex." Susan Basow illustrates this point in the following:

> The all-or-none categorizing of gender traits is misleading. People just are not so simple that they either possess all of a trait or none of it. This is even more true when trait dispositions for groups of people are examined. Part a of Figure 1 illustrates what such an all-or-none distribution of the trait "strength" would look like: all males would be strong, all females weak. The fact is, most psychological and physical traits are distributed according to the pattern shown in Part b of Figure 1 with most people possessing an average amount of that trait and fewer people having either very much or very little of that trait.
>
> To the extent that females and males may differ in the average amount of the trait they possess (which needs to be determined empirically), the distribution can be characterized

FIGURE 1

Three types of distribution for the trait "strength."

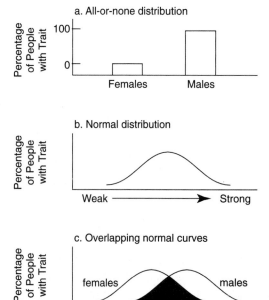

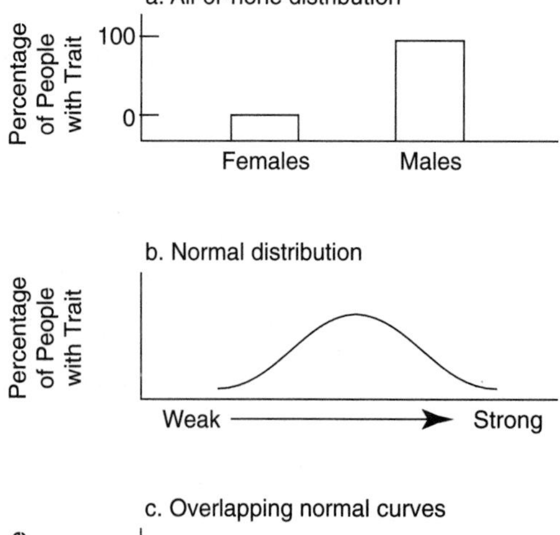

> by *overlapping normal curves,* as shown in Part c of Figure 1. Thus, although most men are stronger than most women, the shaded area indicates that some men are weaker than some women and vice versa. The amount of overlap of the curves generally is considerable. Another attribute related to overlapping normal curves is that differences within one group are usually greater than the differences between the two groups. Thus, more variation in strength occurs within a group of men than between the average male and the average female. (Basow, 1992:8)

This lack of difference between women and men is especially striking given the degree to which we are all socialized to produce such differences. Thus, while boys and girls, and men and women, are often socialized to be different as well as treated differently, this does not mean they inevitably *become* different. Even though decades of research have confirmed few sex differences, the search for difference continues and some suggest may even have been intensified by the failure to find many differences.

The same expectation that the Other differs in personality or behavior emerges in race, class, and sexual orientation classifications. Race differences are expected to involve more than just differences of color, those who are "gay" or "straight" are expected to differ in more ways than just their sexual orientation, and the poor and middle class are expected to differ in more than just economic standing. In each case, scientific research is often directed toward finding such differences.

Sanctioning Those Who Associate with the "Other" There are also similarities in the sanctions against those who cross race, sex, class, or sexual orientation boundaries. Parents sometimes disown children who marry outside of their racial or social class group, just as they often sever connections with children who are gay. Those who associate with the Other are also in danger of being labeled a member of that category.

For example, during Reconstruction the fear of invisible black ancestry was pervasive among southern whites, since that heritage would subject them to nascent segregation. "Concern about people passing as white became so great that even behaving like blacks or willingly associating with them were often treated as more important than any proof of actual black ancestry" (Davis, 1991:56). Thus, southern whites who associated with blacks ran the risk of being defined as black.

A contemporary parallel can be found in gay/straight relations. Those who associate with gays and lesbians or defend gay rights are often presumed—by gays and straights alike—to be gay. Many men report that when they object to homophobic remarks, they simply become the target of them. Indeed, the prestige of young men in fraternities and other all-male groups often rests on a willingness to disparage women and gays (Sanday, 1990).

Similarly, few contemporary reactions are as strongly negative as that against men who appear feminine. Because acting like a woman is so disparaged, boys learn at an early age to control their behavior or suffer public humiliation. This ridicule has its greatest effect on young men; the power and prestige usually available to older men reduces their susceptibility to such accusations. There is a long list of behavior young men must avoid for fear of being called feminine or gay: Don't be too emotional, watch how you sit, don't move your hips when you walk, take long strides, don't put your hands on your hips, don't talk too much, don't let your voice show emotion, don't be too compliant or eager to please, etc.

Because effeminate men are often assumed to be gay, they become targets for verbal and physical abuse. Indeed, as Laura Sessions Stepp describes in Reading 33, even elementary school boys are subject to this abuse. The popular linkage of effeminate behavior with a gay sexual orientation is so strong that it may be the primary criterion most Americans use to decide who is gay: A "masculine" man must be straight, a "feminine" man must be gay. But gender and sexual orientation are *separate* phenomena. Knowing that someone is a masculine man or a feminine woman does not tell us what that person's sexual orientation is—indeed, our guesses are most likely to be "false negatives"; that is, we are likely to falsely identify someone as straight. Since we do not know who around us is gay, we cannot accurately judge how gay people behave.

In the world of mutual Othering, being labeled one of "them" is a remarkably effective social control mechanism. Boys and men control their behavior so that they are not called gay. Members of racial and ethnic groups maintain distance from one another to avoid the criticism that might be leveled by members of their own and other groups. These social controls are effective because all parties continue to enforce them.

Stigma

In the extreme, those depicted as Other may be said to be *stigmatized.* Whole categories of people have been stigmatized as a result of the outcome of large-scale social and historical processes.

The term *stigma* comes from ancient Greece, where it meant a "bodily sign designed to expose something unusual and bad about the moral status of [an individual]" (Goffman, 1963:1). Such signs were "cut or burnt into the body to advertise that the bearer was a slave, a criminal, or a blemished person, ritually polluted, to be avoided, especially in public places" (Goffman, 1963:1). Stigmatized people are those "marked" as bad, unworthy, and polluted because of the category they belong to, for example, their race, sex, sexual orientation, or social class category. The core assumption behind stigma is that internal merit is revealed through external features—for the Greeks, that a brand or a cut showed the moral worth of the person. This is not an unusual linkage; for example, physically attractive people are often assumed to possess a variety of positive attributes (Adams, 1982). We assume that people who look good must *be* good.

Judgments of worth based on membership in certain categories have a self-fulfilling potential. Those who are judged superior by virtue of their membership in some acceptable category are given more opportunity to prove their worth; those who are judged less worthy by virtue of membership in a stigmatized category have difficulty establishing their merit no matter what they do. For example, social psychology data indicate that many whites perceive blacks as incompetent, regardless of evidence to the contrary: White subjects were "reluctant or unable to recognize that a black person is higher or equal in intelligence compared to themselves"

(Gaertner and Dovidio, 1986:75). This would explain why many whites react negatively to affirmative action programs. If they cannot conceive of black applicants as being *more* qualified than whites, they will see such programs as only mandates to hire the less qualified.

Stigma involves objectification as well as devaluation. *Objectification* means treating people as if they were objects, members of a category rather than possessors of individual characteristics. In objectification, the "living, breathing, complex individual" ceases to be seen or valued (Allport, 1958:175). In its extreme, those who are objectified are "viewed as having no other noteworthy status or identity. When that point is reached a person becomes *nothing* but 'a delinquent,' 'a cripple,' 'a homosexual,' 'a black,' 'a woman.' The indefinite article 'a' underlines the depersonalized nature of such response" (Schur, 1984:30–31).

Examples of Stigmatized Master Statuses: Women and the Poor Sociologist Edwin Schur argues that women are subject to both objectification and devaluation, with the result that they are discredited, that is, stigmatized, because they are female. First, considering objectification, Schur argues that women are seen

> as all alike, and therefore substitutable for one another; as innately passive and object-like; as easily ignored, dismissed, trivialized, treated as childlike, and even as a non-person; as having a social standing only through their attachments to men (or other non-stigmatized groups); and as a group which can be easily victimized through harassment, violence, and discrimination. (Schur, 1984:33)

Objectification occurs when women are thought of as generally indistinguishable from one another, as for example when someone says, "Let's get the woman's angle on this story"; or "Tonight I'm going to get one of these women in bed with me." In these statements, one woman stands for "any woman"; they are all the same, interchangeable.

African Americans, Latinos, Asian Americans, and gay/lesbian people are often similarly treated as indistinguishable from one another. Indeed, hate crimes have been defined by this quality of interchangeability, such as the attack on any black family that moves into a neighborhood or the assault on any woman or man who looks gay. Hate crimes are also marked by excessive brutality, personal violence rather than property destruction, and are likely to have been perpetrated by multiple offenders—all of which indicate that the victims have been objectified (Levin and McDevitt, 1993).

Some members of stigmatized categories objectify themselves in the same ways that they are objectified by others. Thus, women may evaluate their own worth in terms of physical appearance. In the process of self-objectification, a woman "joins the spectators of herself"; that is, she views herself as if from the outside, as if she were nothing more than what she looked like (Berger, 1963:50). This sense of making an object of oneself was captured by a cereal commercial where a bikini-clad woman posed before a mirror. She had lost weight for an upcoming vacation and was imagining herself as a stranger on the beach might see her. Thus, she succeeded in making an object of herself. While physical appearance is also valued for men, it rarely takes precedence over all other qualities. Rather, men are more likely to be objectified in terms of wealth and power.

In addition to being objectified, there is a strong case that American women as a category remain devalued, a conclusion drawn from the characteristics most frequently attributed to men and women. Research conducted over the last 40 years has documented a remarkable consistency in those attributes. Both sexes are described as possessing valued qualities, but the characteristics attributed to men are more valued in the culture as a whole. For example, the female-valued characteristics include being talkative, gentle, religious, aware of the feelings of others, security oriented, and attentive to personal appearance. Male-valued traits include being aggressive, independent, unemotional, objective, dominant, active, competitive, logical, adventurous, and direct (Basow, 1992).[10] (Remember that these attributes are only people's *beliefs* about sex differences.)

In many ways, the characteristics attributed to women are inconsistent with core American values. While American culture values achievement, individualism, and action—all understood as male attributes—women are expected to subordinate their personal interests to the family and to be passive and patient (Richardson, 1977). Therefore, "women are asked to become the kind of people that this culture does not value" (Richardson, 1977:11). Thus, it is more acceptable for women to display masculine traits, since these are culturally valued, than it is for men to display less-valued feminine characteristics. Men who are talkative, gentle, religious, aware of the feelings of others, security oriented, and attentive to personal appearance are much maligned. In contrast, women may be independent, unemotional, objective, dominant, active, competitive, logical, adventurous, and direct with less negative consequences. The characteristics we attribute to women are not valued for everyone, unlike the characteristics attributed to men.

Much of what we have described about the stigmatization of women applies to the poor as well. Indeed, being poor is a much more obviously shameful status than being female. The category *poor* is intrinsically devalued. It is presumed there is little commendable to be said about poor people; "they" are primarily constructed as a "problem." Poor people are also objectified; they are described as "*the* poor," as if they were all alike, substitutable for and interchangeable with one another.

> Most of the writing about poor people, even by sympathetic observers, tells us that they are different, truly strangers in our midst: Poor people think, feel, and act in ways unlike middle-class Americans. . . .
>
> We can think about poor people as "them" or as "us." For the most part, Americans have talked about "them." Even in the language of social science, as well as in ordinary

---

[10]"Compared with White women, Black women are viewed as less passive, dependent, status conscious, emotional and concerned about their appearance. . . . Hispanic women tend to be viewed as more 'feminine' than White women in terms of submissiveness and dependence. . . . [A] similar stereotype holds for Asian women, but with the addition of exotic sexuality. . . . Native-American women typically are stereotyped as faceless . . . drudges without any personality. . . . Jewish women are stereotyped as either pushy, vain 'princesses' or overprotective, manipulative 'Jewish mothers' . . . working-class women are stereotyped as more hostile, confused, inconsiderate and irresponsible than middle-class women . . . and lesbians are stereotyped as possessing masculine traits" (Basow, 1992:4).

> conversation and political rhetoric, poor people usually remain outsiders, strangers to be pitied or despised, helped or punished, ignored or studied, but rarely full citizens, members of a larger community on the same terms as the rest of us. They are . . . "those people," objects of curiosity, analysis, prurience, or compassion, not subjects who construct their own lives and history. Poor people seem cardboard cutouts, figures in single dimension, members of inferior categories, rarely complex, multifaceted, even contradictory in the manner of other persons. (M. Katz, 1989:6, 126)

Like women, poor people are not expected to display attributes valued in the culture as a whole.

Stereotypes about People in Stigmatized Master Statuses Finally, in an effort to capture the general features of what "we" say about "them," let us consider five common stereotypes about individuals in stigmatized master statuses.

First, they are presumed to lack the values the culture holds dear. Neither women nor those who are poor, gay, black, Asian American, or Latino are expected to be independent, unemotional, objective, dominant, active, competitive, logical, adventurous, or direct. Stigmatized people are presumed to lack precisely those values that nonstigmatized people are expected to possess.

Second, stigmatized people are likely to be seen as a problem (Adam, 1978; Wilson and Gutierrez, 1985). Certainly black, Latino, and Native American men and women, gay and lesbian people of all colors, white women, and people living in poverty are constructed as *having* problems and *being* problems. Often the implication is that they are also responsible for many of our national problems. While public celebrations often highlight the historic contributions of such groups to the culture, little in the public discourse lauds their current contributions. Indeed, those in stigmatized categories are often constructed as *nothing but a problem,* as if they did not exist apart from those problems. This was illustrated by a black student who described her shock at hearing white students describe her middle-class neighborhood as a "ghetto."

Ironically, this depiction of stigmatized people as nothing but a problem is often accompanied by the trivialization of those problems. For example, "a majority of voting Americans believe that Asian Americans are not discriminated against" (U.S. Commission on Civil Rights, 1992) despite evidence of racial harassment and employment discrimination (Feagin and Feagin, 1999). Despite the participation of thousands of people in annual Gay Pride marches throughout the country, television footage typically trivializes that population by focusing on the small number in drag. Whites' opinion that blacks prefer welfare to supporting themselves similarly trivializes the experience of poverty (Thornton and Whitman, 1992). The pervasive belief that women and men are now treated equally in employment dismisses the segregation and wage gap that continues to characterize the workforce, as Reskin and Padavic describe in Reading 45. Thus, the problems that stigmatized categories of people create for those in privileged statuses are highlighted, while the problems they experience are discounted.

Third, people in stigmatized master statuses are stereotyped as lacking self-control; they are characterized as being lustful, immoral, and carriers of disease

(Gilman, 1985, 1991). Currently, such accusations hold center stage in the depictions of gay men, but historically such charges have been leveled at African American, Latino, and Asian American men (e.g., Chinese immigrants in the late 19th century). Poor women and women of color have been and continue to be depicted as promiscuous, while poor men and women are presumed to be morally irresponsible.

Fourth, people in stigmatized categories are often marked as having too much or too little intelligence, and in either case as tending to deception or criminality. Many stigmatized categories of people have been assumed to use their "excessive" intelligence to unfair advantage. This was historically the case for Jews, and now appears to be the case for Asian American college students.

> [T]he educational achievement of Asian American students was, and continues to be, followed by a wave of reaction. The image of Asian Americans as diligent super-students has often kindled resentment in other students. Sometimes called "damned curve raisers," a term applied first to Jewish students at elite East Coast colleges during the 1920s and 1930s, Asian American students have increasingly found themselves taking the brunt of campus racial jokes. (Takagi, 1992:60)

Fifth, people in stigmatized categories are depicted as both childlike and savagely brutal. Historically, characterizations of Native Americans, enslaved Africans, and Chinese immigrants reflected these conceptions. Currently, the same is true for the poor in their representation as both pervasively violent and irresponsible. A related depiction of women as both "virgins and whores" has been well documented in scholarship over time.

Perhaps because people in stigmatized master statuses are stereotyped as deviant, it appears that those who commit violence against them are unlikely to be punished. For example in 1997, 82 percent of those convicted of killing a white person were sentenced to death, but only 12 percent of those convicted of murdering an African American were. When the victim was Asian, the percentage dropped to 4 percent; when the victim was Latino, the percentage dropped even further to 2 percent (Amnesty International, 1997). While a number of factors are operating here, one conclusion is that stigmatized minority victims are valued less than white victims. The same conclusion could be reached in terms of the punishment meted out to those accused of sexual assault. "Major offenses *against* women, which we *profess* to consider deviant, in practice have been responded to with much ambivalence" (Schur, 1984:7). Indeed, one way to recognize a stigmatized category of people is that the violence directed at them is not treated seriously (Schur, 1984).

Overall, individuals in stigmatized master statuses are represented as not only physically distinctive but also the antithesis of the culture's desired behaviors and attributes. They do not operate from cultural values. They are problems; they are immoral and disease ridden; their intelligence is questionable; they are childlike and savage. Such characterizations serve to dismiss claims of discrimination and unfair treatment, affirming that those in stigmatized categories deserve such treatment, that they are themselves responsible for their plight. Indeed, many of these stereotypes are also applied to teenagers, whom the media depict as violent, reckless, hypersexed, ignorant, out of control, and the cause of society's problems (Males, 1994).

A Final Comment

It is disheartening to think of oneself as a member of a stigmatized group, just as it is disheartening to think of oneself as thoughtlessly perpetuating stigma. Still, there are at least two important points of hopefulness here. First, the characteristics attributed to stigmatized groups are similar across a great variety of master statuses. Thus, there is the relief of impersonality because the stigmatized characteristics are not tied to the actual characteristics of any particular group. Second, people who are stigmatized have often formed alliances with those who are not stigmatized to successfully lobby against these attributions.

As we said at the outset of this essay, our hope is to provide you with a framework by which to make sense of what sex, race, social class, and sexual orientation mean in contemporary American society. Clearly, these categorizations are complex; they are tied to emotionally intense issues that are uniquely American; and they have consequences that are both mundane and dramatic. From naming, to aggregating, to dichotomizing, and ultimately to stigmatizing, difference has a meaning for us. The readings in Section I explore the construction of these categorizations; the readings in Section II examine how we experience them; and the readings in Section III address the meaning that is attributed to difference.

KEY CONCEPTS

aggregate To combine or lump together (verb); something composed of different elements (noun). (pages 12–15)

-centrism or -centric Suffix meaning centered around, focused around, taking the perspective of. Thus, **androcentric** means focused around or taking the perspective of men; **heterocentric** means taking the perspective of heterosexuals; and **eurocentric** means having a European focus. (page 15)

constructionism The perspective that reality cannot be separated from the way a culture makes sense of it—that meaning is "constructed" through social, political legal, scientific, and other practices. From this perspective, differences among people are created through social processes. (pages 2–5)

dichotomize To divide into two parts and to see those parts as mutually exclusive. (pages 15–24)

differential undercount In the census, undercounting more of one group than of another. (pages 8–12)

disaggregate To separate something into its constituent elements. (pages 12–15)

essential identity An identity that is treated as core to a person. Essential identities can be attributed to people even when they are inconsistent with actual behavior. (page 21)

essentialism The perspective that reality exists independently of our perception of it, that we perceive the meaning of the world rather than construct that meaning. From this perspective, there are real and important (essential) differences among categories of people. (pages 2–5)

ethnic group, ethnicity An ethnic group is composed of people with a shared national origin or ancestry and shared cultural characteristics, such as language. For example, Polish Americans, Italian Americans, Chinese Americans, and Haitian Americans are ethnic groups. "African American" can be considered a racial category, but also an ethnicity (given the shared history of slavery). (page 17)

gender Masculinity and femininity; the acting out of the behaviors thought to be appropriate for a particular sex. (page 23)

heterosexism The presumption that all people are heterosexual (in this sense, synonymous with heterocentric); the presumption that heterosexuality is the only acceptable form of sexual expression. (page 2)

master status A status that has a profound effect on one's life, that dominates or overwhelms the other statuses one occupies. In contemporary American society, race, sex, sexual orientation, social class, and ability/disability function as master statuses, but other statuses—such as religion—do not. For example, race strongly affects occupational status, income, health, and longevity. Religion may have a similar impact in other cultures. (page 2)

objectification Treating people as if they were objects, as if they were nothing more than the attributes they display. (page 29)

Other A usage designed to refer to those considered profoundly unlike oneself. (page 25)

panethnic An ethnic classification that spans national-origin identities. (page 13)

race The conception that people can be classified into coherent groups based on skin color, hair texture, shape of head, eyes, nose, and lips. (pages 15–20)

sex The categories of male and female. (page 23)

status A position in society. Individuals occupy multiple statuses simultaneously, such as occupational, kinship, and educational statuses. (page 2)

stigma An attribute for which someone is considered bad, unworthy, or deeply discredited. (pages 28–32)

REFERENCES

Adam, Barry. 1978. *The Survival of Domination.* New York: Elsevier.

Adams, Gerald R. 1982. Physical Attractiveness. *In the Eye of the Beholder: Contemporary Issues in Stereotyping,* edited by A. G. Miller, 253–304. New York: Praeger.

Albrecht, Gary L. 1981. Cross-National Rehabilitation Policies: A Critical Assessment. *Cross-National Rehabilitation Policies: A Sociological Perspective,* edited by G. Albrecht, 269–77. Beverly Hills, CA: Sage.

Allport, Gordon. 1958. *The Nature of Prejudice.* Garden City, NY: Doubleday Anchor.

Amnesty International. 1997. Amnesty International Death Penalty Developments in the U.S.A. in 1997. www.amnesty-usa/abolish/race.html.

Arrow, Kenneth, Samuel Bowles, and Steven Durlauf. 2000. Introduction. *Meritocracy and Economic Inequality,* edited by Kenneth Arrow, Samuel Bowles, and Steven Durlauf, ix–xv. Princeton, NJ: Princeton University Press.

Basow, Susan A. 1992. *Gender: Stereotypes and Roles.* 3d ed. Pacific Grove, CA: Brooks/Cole Publishing.

Begley, Sharon. 1995. Three Is Not Enough. *Newsweek,* February 13, 1995, 67–69.

Berger, Peter L. 1963. *Invitation to Sociology: A Humanistic Perspective.* Garden City, NY: Doubleday Anchor.

Blauner, Robert. 1992. Talking Past Each Other: Black and White Languages of Race. *The American Prospect,* 10.

Bogdan, Robert, and Douglas Biklen. 1977. Handicapism. *Social Policy,* 7:14–19.

Choldin, Harvey M. 1986. Statistics and Politics: The "Hispanic Issue" in the 1980 Census. *Demography,* 23:403–18.

———. 1994. *Looking for the Last Percent: The Controversy over Census Undercounts.* New Brunswick, NJ: Rutgers University Press.

Cohen, G. 1995. *Self, Ownership, Freedom, and Equality.* Cambridge: Cambridge University Press.

Cohen, Mark Nathan. 1998. *Culture of Intolerance: Chauvinism, Class, and Racism in the United States.* New Haven, CT: Yale University Press.

Cohn, D'Vera. 2001. Counting of Gay Couples Up 300%. *Washington Post,* August 22, A.

Coles, Gerald. 1987. *The Learning Mystique: A Critical Look at "Learning Disabilities."* New York: Pantheon.

Conrad, Peter, and Joseph W. Schneider. 1980. *Deviance and Medicalization: From Badness to Sickness.* Philadelphia: Temple University Press.

Davis, F. James. 1991. *Who Is Black? One Nation's Rule.* University Park, PA: Pennsylvania State University Press.

de la Garza, Rudolfo O., Louis DeSipio, F. Chris Garcia, John Garcia, and Angelo Falcon. 1992. *Latino Voices: Mexican, Puerto Rican, and Cuban Perspectives on American Politics.* Boulder, CO: Westview Press.

Dubos, Rene. 1961. *Mirage of Health.* Garden City, NY: Anchor Books.

Espiritu, Yen Le. 1992. *Asian American Panethnicity: Bridging Institutions and Identities.* Philadelphia: Temple University Press.

Faderman, Lillian. 1991. *Odd Girls and Twilight Lovers: A History of Lesbian Life in Twentieth-Century America.* New York: Penguin Books.

Feagin, Joe R., and Clairece Booher Feagin. 1999. *Racial and Ethnic Relations.* 6th ed. Upper Saddle River, NJ: Prentice-Hall.

Ferguson, Philip M. 1987. The Social Construction of Mental Retardation. *Social Policy,* 18:51–52.

Fuller, Jill E. 2001. Personal communication.

Fussell, Paul. 1983. *Class.* New York: Ballentine Books.

Gaertner, Samuel L., and John F. Dovidio. 1986. The Aversive Form of Racism. *Prejudice, Discrimination, and Racism,* edited by John F. Dovidio and Samuel L. Gaertner, 61–89. Orlando, FL: Academic Press.

Gilman, Sander. 1991. *The Jew's Body.* New York: Routledge.

———. 1985. *Difference and Pathology: Stereotypes of Sexuality, Race, and Madness.* Ithaca, NY: Cornell University Press.

Goffman, Erving. 1963. *Stigma: Notes on the Management of Spoiled Identity.* Englewood Cliffs, NJ: Prentice-Hall.

Gordon, Margaret T., and Stephanie Riger. 1989. *The Female Fear.* New York: The Free Press.

Henshel, Richard L., and Robert A. Silverman. 1975. *Perceptions in Criminology.* New York: Columbia University Press.

Higgins, Paul C. 1992. *Making Disability: Exploring the Social Transformation of Human Variation.* Springfield, IL: Charles C. Thomas.

Hilts, V. 1973. Statistics and Social Science. *Foundations of Scientific Method in the Nineteenth Century,* edited by R. Giere and R. Westfall, 206–33. Bloomington, IN: Indiana University Press.

Hirschman, Charles. 1996. Studying Immigrant Adaptation from the 1990 Population Census: From Generational Comparisons to the Process of "Becoming American." *The New Second Generation,* edited by A. Portes, 54–81. New York: Russell Sage Foundation.

Hu-Dehart, Evelyn. 1994. Asian/Pacific American Issues in American Education. Presentation at the 7th Annual National Conference on Race and Ethnicity in American Higher Education, Atlanta, sponsored by The Southwest Center for Human Relations Studies, University of Oklahoma, College of Continuing Education.

Jackman, Mary R., and Robert W. Jackman. 1983. *Class Awareness in the United States.* Berkeley, CA: University of California Press.

Jenkins, Alan. 1999. See No Evil. *The Nation,* June 28:15–19.

Kahlenberg, Richard D. 1997. *The Remedy: Class, Race, and Affirmative Action.* New York: Basic Books.

Katz, Jack. 1975. Essences as Moral Identities: Verifiability and Responsibility in Imputations of Deviance and Charisma. *American Journal of Sociology,* 80:1369–90.

Katz, Michael B. 1989. *The Undeserving Poor: From the War on Poverty to the War on Welfare.* New York: Pantheon Books.

Kessler, Suzanne J., and Wendy McKenna. 1978. *Gender: An Ethnomethodological Approach.* New York: John Wiley & Sons.

Kim, Marlene. 1999. The Working Poor: Lousy Jobs or Lazy Workers. *A New Introduction to Poverty: The Role of Race, Power, and Politics,* edited by Louis Kushnick and James Jennings, 307–19. New York: New York University Press.

Kinsey, Alfred, Wardell Pomeroy, and Clyde Martin. 1948. *Sexual Behavior in the Human Male.* Philadelphia: W. B. Saunders.

Klein, Fritz. 1978. *The Bisexual Option.* New York: Arbor House.

Lemonick, Michael. 1992. Genetic Tests under Fire. *Time,* February 24, 65.

LeVay, Simon. 1991. A Difference in Hypothalmic Structure between Heterosexual and Homosexual Men. *Science,* 253:1034–37.

Levin, Jack, and Jack McDevitt. 1993. *Hate Crimes.* New York: Plenum Press.

Lieberman, Leonard. 1968. A Debate over Race: A Study in the Sociology of Knowledge. *Phylon,* 29:127–41.

Lopez, David, and Yen Espiritu. 1990. Panethnicity in the United States: A Theoretical Framework. *Ethnic and Racial Studies,* 13:198–224.

Males, Mike. 1994. Bashing Youth: Media Myths about Teenagers. *Extra!,* March/April, 8–11.

Marshall, Gloria. 1993. Racial Classifications: Popular and Scientific. *The "Racial" Economy of Science: Toward a Democratic Future,* edited by Sandra Harding, 116–27. Bloomington, IN: Indiana University Press (Originally published 1968).

Marshall, Gordon. 1994. *The Concise Oxford Dictionary of Sociology.* Oxford: Oxford University Press.

Michael, Robert T. 1994. *Sex in America: A Definitive Survey.* Boston: Little, Brown.

Mills, Jane. 1989. *Womanwords: A Dictionary of Words about Women.* New York: Henry Holt.

Mincey, Ronald B. 1994. *Confronting Poverty: Prescriptions for Change.* Cambridge: Harvard University Press.

Mohawk, John. 1992. Looking for Columbus: Thoughts on the Past, Present and Future of Humanity. *The State of Native America: Genocide, Colonization, and Resistance,* edited by M. Annette Jaimes, 439–44. Boston: South End Press.

Morris, Jenny. 1991. *Pride against Prejudice: Transforming Attitudes to Disability.* Philadelphia: New Society Publishers.

Morris, Michael, and John B. Williamson. 1982. Stereotypes and Social Class: A Focus on Poverty. *In the Eye of the Beholder,* edited by Arthur G. Miller, 411–65. New York: Praeger.

Morrison, Toni. 1992. *Playing in the Dark.* New York: Vintage.

Newport, Frank. 2001. American Attitudes toward Homosexuality Continue to Become More Tolerant. *Gallup News Service,* June 4. www.gallup.com/poll/releases/pr010604.asp.

Office of Management and Budget. 1995. Standards for the Classification of Federal Data on Race and Ethnicity Notice. *Federal Register* 60:44674–693.

———. October 1997. *Revisions to the Standards for the Classification of Federal Data on Race and Ethnicity.* Washington, DC: U.S. Government Printing Office.

Omi, Michael. 1996. Racialization in the Post–Civil Rights Era. *Mapping Multiculturalism,* edited by A. Gordon and C. Newfield, 178–85. Minneapolis: University of Minnesota Press.

———, and Howard Winant. 1994. *Racial Formation in the United States.* New York: Routledge.

Ortner, Sherry B. 1991. Reading America. Preliminary Notes on Class and Culture. *Recapturing Anthropology: Working in the Present,* edited by Richard G. Fox, 163–89. Santa Fe, NM: School of American Research Press.

Pfuhl, Erdwin H. 1986. *The Deviance Process.* 2d ed. Belmont, CA: Wadsworth.

Pope, Raechele L., and Amy L. Reynolds. 1991. Including Bisexuality: It's More than Just a Label. *Beyond Tolerance: Gays, Lesbians, and Bisexuals on Campus,* edited by Nancy J. Evans and Vernon A. Wall, 205–11. Alexandria, VA: American College Personnel Association.

Population Reference Bureau. 2001. Increasing Diversity in the U.S. Hispanic Population. www.prb.org.

Richardson, Laurel. 1977. *The Dynamics of Sex and Gender: A Sociological Perspective.* New York: Harper and Row.

———. 1988. *The Dynamics of Sex and Gender: A Sociological Perspective.* 3d ed. New York: Harper and Row.

Rist, Darrell Yates. 1992. Are Homosexuals Born That Way? *The Nation,* 255:424–29.

Roediger, David. 1994. *Towards the Abolition of Whiteness.* London: Verso.

Sanday, Peggy Reeves. 1990. *Fraternity Gang Rape.* New York: New York University Press.

Schneider, Joseph W. 1988. Disability as Moral Experience: Epilepsy and Self in Routine Relationships. *Journal of Social Issues,* 44:63–78.

Schur, Edwin. 1984. *Labeling Women Deviant: Gender, Stigma, and Social Control.* New York: Random House.

Schwarz, John E., and Thomas J. Volgy. 1992. *The Forgotten Americans.* New York: W. W. Norton.

Shipman, Pat. 1994. *The Evolution of Racism: Human Differences and the Use and Abuse of Science.* New York: Simon and Schuster.

Shorris, Earl. 1992. *Latinos: A Biography of the People.* New York: W. W. Norton.

Smedley, Audrey. 1993. *Race in North America: Origin and Evolution of a Worldview.* Boulder, CO: Westview Press.

Smith, Tom W. 1992. Changing Racial Labels: From "Colored" to "Negro" to "Black" to "African American." *Public Opinion Quarterly,* 56:496–514.

Spelman, Elizabeth. 1988. *Inessential Woman.* Boston: Beacon Press.

Spencer, Michael Jon. 1997. *Colored People: The Mixed-Race Movement in America.* New York: New York University Press.

Springer, S. P., and G. Deutsch. 1981. *Left Brain, Right Brain.* San Francisco: Freeman.

Steinberg, Stephen. 1989. *The Ethnic Myth: Race, Ethnicity, and Class in America.* Boston: Beacon Press.

Takagi, Dana Y. 1992. *The Retreat from Race: Asian-American Admission and Racial Politics.* New Brunswick, NJ: Rutgers University Press.

Takaki, Ronald. 1990. *Iron Cages: Race and Culture in 19th-Century America.* New York: Oxford University Press.

———. 1993. *A Different Mirror.* Boston: Little Brown.

Tamayo Lott, Juanita. 1998. *Asian Americans: From Racial Category to Multiple Identities.* Walnut Creek, CA: Altamira Press.

Thornton, Jeannye, and David Whitman. 1992. Whites' Myths about Blacks. *U.S. News and World Report,* November 9: 41–44.

U.S. Census Bureau. 2001. *Census 2000 Summary File 2, Technical Documentation:* September 2001, SF2/01:G39-G41.

U.S. Commission on Civil Rights. 1973. *To Know or Not to Know: Collection and Use of Racial and Ethnic Data in Federal Assistance Programs.* Washington, DC: U.S. Government Printing Office.

———. 1992. *Civil Rights Issues Facing Asian Americans in the 1990s.* Washington, DC: U.S. Government Printing Office.

U.S. Department of Commerce. 2001. Census Bureau Says No to Adjustment: Review Finds Duplicates Wipe Out Most of Net Undercount. *United States Department of Commerce News,* October 18.

———. 2001. People Who Reported Two or More Races Are Young and Tend to Live in the West. *United States Department of Commerce News,* November 29.

U.S. Department of Education, 1990. *To Assure the Free Appropriate Public Education of All Handicapped Children: Twelfth Annual Report to Congress on the Implementation of the Education of the Handicapped Act.* Washington, DC: U.S. Government Printing Office.

Vanneman, Reeve, and Lynn Weber Cannon. 1987. *The American Perception of Class.* Philadelphia: Temple University Press.

Weinberg, George. 1973. *Society and the Healthy Homosexual.* Garden City, NY: Anchor.

Wilson, II, Clint, and Felix Gutierrez. 1985. *Minorities and the Media.* Beverly Hills, CA: Sage.

Zola, Irving K. 1993. Disability Statistics, What We Count and What It Tells Us: A Personal and Political Analysis. *Journal of Disability Policy Studies,* 4:10–37.

What Is Race?

READING 1

Who Is Black? One Nation's Definition

F. James Davis

In a taped interview conducted by a blind, black anthropologist, a black man nearly ninety years old said: "Now you must understand that this is just a name we have. I am not black and you are not black either, if you go by the evidence of your eyes. . . . Anyway, black people are all colors. White people don't look all the same way, but there are more different kinds of us than there are of them. Then too, there is a certain stage [at] which you cannot tell who is white and who is black. Many of the people I see who are thought of as black could just as well be white in their appearance. Many of the white people I see are black as far as I can tell by the way they look. Now, that's it for looks. Looks don't mean much. The things that makes us different is how we think. What we believe is important, the ways we look at life" (Gwaltney, 1980:96).

How does a person get defined as a black, both socially and legally, in the United States? What is the nation's rule for who is black, and how did it come to be? And so what? Don't we all know who is black, and isn't the most important issue what opportunities the group has? Let us start with some experiences of three well-known American blacks—actress and beauty pageant winner Vanessa Williams, U.S. Representative Adam Clayton Powell, Jr., and entertainer Lena Horne.

For three decades after the first Miss America Pageant in 1921, black women were barred from competing. The first black winner was Vanessa Williams of Millwood, New York, crowned Miss America in 1984. In the same year the first runner-up—Suzette Charles of Mays Landing, New Jersey—was also black. The viewing public was charmed by the television images and magazine pictures of the beautiful and musically talented Williams, but many people were also puzzled. Why was she being called black when she appeared to be white? Suzette Charles, whose ancestry appeared to be more European than African, at least looked like many of the "lighter blacks." Notoriety followed when Vanessa Williams resigned because of the impending publication of some nude photographs of her taken before the pageant, and Suzette Charles became Miss America for the balance of 1984. Beyond the troubling question of whether these young women could have won if they had looked "more black," the publicity dramatized the nation's definition of a black person.

Some blacks complained that the Rev. Adam Clayton Powell, Jr., was so light that he was a stranger in their midst. In the words of Roi Ottley, "He was white to all appearances, having blue eyes, an aquiline nose, and light, almost blond, hair" (1943:220), yet he became a bold, effective black leader—first as minister of the Abyssinian Baptist Church of Harlem, then as a New York city councilman, and finally as a U.S. congressman from the state of New York. Early in his activist career he led 6,000 blacks in a march on New York City Hall. He used his power in Congress to fight for civil rights legislation and other black causes. In 1966, in Washington, D.C., he convened the first black power conference.

In his autobiography, Powell recounts some experiences with racial classification in his youth that left a lasting impression on him. During Powell's freshman year at Colgate University, his roommate did not know that he was a black until his father, Adam Clayton Powell, Sr., was invited to give a chapel talk on Negro rights and problems, after which the roommate announced

---

F. James Davis is professor emeritus of sociology at Illinois State University.

that because Adam was a Negro they could no longer be roommates or friends.

Another experience that affected Powell deeply occurred one summer during his Colgate years. He was working as a bellhop at a summer resort in Manchester, Vermont, when Abraham Lincoln's aging son Robert was a guest there. Robert Lincoln disliked blacks so much that he refused to let them wait on him or touch his luggage, car, or any of his possessions. Blacks who did got their knuckles whacked with his cane. To the great amusement of the other bellhops, Lincoln took young Powell for a white man and accepted his services (Powell, 1971:31–33).

Lena Horne's parents were both very light in color and came from black upper-middle-class families in Brooklyn (Horne and Schickel, 1965; Buckley, 1986). Lena lived with her father's parents until she was about seven years old. Her grandfather was very light and blue-eyed. Her fair-skinned grandmother was the daughter of a slave woman and her white owner, from the family of John C. Calhoun, well-known defender of slavery. One of her father's great-grandmothers was a Blackfoot Indian, to whom Lena Horne has attributed her somewhat coppery skin color. One of her mother's grandmothers was a French-speaking black woman from Senegal and never a slave. Her mother's father was a "Portuguese Negro," and two women in his family had passed as white and become entertainers.

Lena Horne's parents had separated, and when she was seven her entertainer mother began placing her in a succession of homes in different states. Her favorite place was in the home of her Uncle Frank, her father's brother, a red-haired, blue-eyed teacher in a black school in Georgia. The black children in that community asked her why she was so light and called her a "yellow bastard." She learned that when satisfactory evidence of respectable black parents is lacking, being light-skinned implies illegitimacy and having an underclass white parent and is thus a disgrace in the black community. When her mother married a white Cuban, Lena also learned that blacks can be very hostile to the white spouse, especially when the "black" mate is very light. At this time she began to blame the confused color line for her childhood troubles. She later endured much hostility from blacks and whites alike when her own second marriage, to white composer-arranger Lennie Hayton, was finally made public in 1950 after three years of keeping it secret.

Early in Lena Horne's career there were complaints that she did not fit the desired image of a black entertainer for white audiences, either physically or in her style. She sang white love songs, not the blues. Noting her brunette-white beauty, one white agent tried to get her to take a Spanish name, learn some Spanish songs, and pass as a Latin white, but she had learned to have a horror of passing and never considered it, although Hollywood blacks accused her of trying to pass after she played her first bit part in a film. After she failed her first screen test because she looked like a white girl trying to play black-face, the directors tried making her up with a shade called "Light Egyptian" to make her look darker. The whole procedure embarrassed and hurt her deeply. . . .

Other light mulatto entertainers have also had painful experiences because of their light skin and other caucasoid features. Starting an acting career is never easy, but actress Jane White's difficulties in the 1940s were compounded by her lightness. Her father was NAACP leader Walter White. Even with dark makeup on her ivory skin, she did not look like a black person on the stage, but she was not allowed to try out for white roles because blacks were barred from playing them. When she auditioned for the part of a young girl from India, the director was enthusiastic, although her skin color was too light, but higher management decreed that it was unthinkable for a Negro to play the part of an Asian Indian (White, 1948:338). Only after great perseverance did Jane White make her debut as the educated mulatto maid Nonnie in the stage version of Lillian Smith's *Strange Fruit* (1944). . . .

THE ONE-DROP RULE DEFINED

As the above cases illustrate, to be considered black in the United States not even half of one's ancestry must be African black. But will one-fourth do, or one-eighth, or less? The nation's answer to the question "Who is black?" has long been that a black is any person with *any* known African black ancestry (Myrdal, 1944:113–18; Berry and Tischler, 1978:97–98; Williamson, 1980:1–2). This definition reflects the long experience with slavery and later with Jim Crow segregation. In the South it became known as the "one-drop rule," meaning that a single drop of "black blood" makes a person a black. It is also known as the "one black ancestor rule," some courts have called it the "traceable amount rule," and anthropologists call it the "hypo-descent rule," meaning that racially mixed persons are assigned the status of the subordinate group (Harris, 1964:56). This definition emerged from the American South to become the nation's definition, generally accepted by whites and blacks alike (Bahr, Chadwick, and Stauss, 1979:27–28). Blacks had no other choice. This American cultural definition of blacks is taken for granted as readily by judges, affirmative action officers, and black protesters as it is by Ku Klux Klansmen.

Let us not be confused by terminology. At present the usual statement of the one-drop rule is in terms of "black blood" or black ancestry, while not so long ago it referred to "Negro blood" or ancestry. The term "black" rapidly replaced "Negro" in general usage in the United States as the black power movement peaked at the end of the 1960s, but the black and Negro populations are the same. The term "black" is used [here] for persons with any black African lineage, not just for unmixed members of populations from sub-Saharan Africa. The term "Negro," which is used in certain historical contexts, means the same thing. Terms such as "African black," "unmixed Negro," and "all black" are used here to refer to unmixed blacks descended from African populations.

We must also pay attention to the terms "mulatto" and "colored." The term "mulatto" was originally used to mean the offspring of a "pure African Negro" and a "pure white." Although the root meaning of mulatto, in Spanish, is "hybrid," "mulatto" came to include the children of unions between whites and so-called "mixed Negroes." For example, Booker T. Washington and Frederick Douglass, with slave mothers and white fathers, were referred to as mulattoes (Bennett, 1962:255). To whatever extent their mothers were part white, these men were more than half white. Douglass was evidently part Indian as well, and he looked it (Preston, 1980:9–10). Washington had reddish hair and gray eyes. At the time of the American Revolution, many of the founding fathers had some very light slaves, including some who appeared to be white. The term "colored" seemed for a time to refer only to mulattoes, especially lighter ones, but later it became a euphemism for darker Negroes, even including unmixed blacks. With widespread racial mixture, "Negro" came to mean any slave or descendant of a slave, no matter how much mixed. Eventually in the United States, the terms mulatto, colored, Negro, black, and African American all came to mean people with any known black African ancestry. Mulattoes are racially mixed, to whatever degree, while the terms black, Negro, African American, and colored include both mulattoes and unmixed blacks. These terms have quite different meanings in other countries.

Whites in the United States need some help envisioning the American black experience with ancestral fractions. At the beginning of miscegenation between two populations presumed to be racially pure, quadroons appear in the second generation of continuing mixing with whites, and octoroons in the third. A quadroon is one-fourth African black and thus easily classed as black in the United States, yet three of this person's four grandparents are white. An octoroon has seven white great-grandparents out of eight and usually looks white or almost so. Most parents of black

American children in recent decades have themselves been racially mixed, but often the fractions get complicated because the earlier details of the mixing were obscured generations ago. Like so many white Americans, black people are forced to speculate about some of the fractions—one-eighth this, three-sixteenths that, and so on. . . .

PLESSY, PHIPPS, AND OTHER CHALLENGES IN THE COURTS

Homer Plessy was the plaintiff in the 1896 precedent-setting "separate-but-equal" case of *Plessy v. Ferguson* (163 U.S. 537). This case challenged the Jim Crow statute that required racially segregated seating on trains in interstate commerce in the state of Louisiana. The U.S. Supreme Court quickly dispensed with Plessy's contention that because he was only one-eighth Negro and could pass as white he was entitled to ride in the seats reserved for whites. Without ruling directly on the definition of a Negro, the Supreme Court briefly took what is called "judicial notice" of what it assumed to be common knowledge: that a Negro or black is any person with any black ancestry. (Judges often take explicit "judicial notice" not only of scientific or scholarly conclusions, or of opinion surveys or other systematic investigations, but also of something they just assume to be so, including customary practices or common knowledge.) This has consistently been the ruling in the federal courts, and often when the black ancestry was even less than one-eighth. The federal courts have thus taken judicial notice of the customary boundary between two sociocultural groups that differ, on the average, in physical traits, not between two discrete genetic categories. In the absence of proof of a specific black ancestor, merely being known as a black in the community has usually been accepted by the courts as evidence of black ancestry. The separate-but-equal doctrine established in the Plessy case is no longer the law, as a result of the judicial and legislative successes of the civil rights movement, but the nation's legal definition of who is black remains unchanged.

State courts have generally upheld the one-drop rule. For instance, in a 1948 Mississippi case a young man, Davis Knight, was sentenced to five years in jail for violating the anti-miscegenation statute. Less than one-sixteenth black, Knight said he was not aware that he had any black lineage, but the state proved his great-grandmother was a slave girl. In some states the operating definition of black has been limited by statute to particular fractions, yet the social definition—the one-drop rule—has generally prevailed in case of doubt. Mississippi, Missouri, and five other states have had the criterion of one-eighth. Virginia changed from one-fourth to one-eighth in 1910, then in 1930 forbade white intermarriage with a person with any black ancestry. Persons in Virginia who are one-fourth or more Indian and less than one-sixteenth African black are defined as Indians while on the reservation but as blacks when they leave (Berry, 1965:26). While some states have had general race classification statutes, at least for a time, others have legislated a definition of black only for particular purposes, such as marriage or education. In a few states there have even been varying definitions for different situations (Mangum, 1940:38–48). All states require a designation of race on birth certificates, but there are no clear guidelines to help physicians and midwives do the classifying.

Louisiana's latest race classification statute became highly controversial and was finally repealed in 1983 (Trillin, 1986:77). Until 1970, a Louisiana statute had embraced the one-drop rule, defining a Negro as anyone with a "trace of black ancestry." This law was challenged in court a number of times from the 1920s on, including an unsuccessful attempt in 1957 by boxer Ralph Dupas, who asked to be declared white so that a law banning "interracial sports" (since repealed) would not prevent him from boxing in the state. In 1970 a lawsuit was brought on behalf of a child whose ancestry was allegedly only one two-hundred-fifty-sixth black, and the legislature revised its law. The 1970 Louisiana statute defined a black as someone whose ancestry is more than one thirty-second black (La. Rev. Stat. 42:267). Adverse publicity about this law was widely disseminated during the Phipps trial in 1983 (discussed below), filed as *Jane Doe v. State of Louisiana.* This case was decided in a district court in May 1983, and in June the legislature abolished its one thirty-second statute and gave parents the right to designate the race of newborns, and even to change classifications on birth certificates if they can prove the child is white by a "preponderance of the evidence." However, the new statute in 1983 did not abolish the "traceable amount rule" (the one-drop rule), as demonstrated by the outcomes when the Phipps decision was appealed to higher courts in 1985 and 1986.

The history in the Phipps (Jane Doe) case goes as far back as 1770, when a French planter named Jean Gregoire Guillory took his wife's slave, Margarita, as his mistress (Model, 1983: 3–4). More than two centuries and two decades later, their great-great-great-great-granddaughter, Susie Guillory Phipps, asked the Louisiana courts to change the classification on her deceased parents' birth certificates to "white" so she and her brothers and sisters could be designated white. They all looked white, and some were blue-eyed blonds. Mrs. Susie Phipps had been denied a passport because she had checked "white" on her application although her birth certificate designated her race as "colored." This designation was based on information supplied by a midwife, who presumably relied on the parents or on the family's status in the community. Mrs. Phipps claimed that this classification came as a shock, since she had always thought she was white, had lived as white, and had twice married as white. Some of her relatives, however, gave depositions saying they considered themselves "colored," and the lawyers for the state claimed to have proof that Mrs. Phipps is three thirty-seconds black (Trillin, 1986:62–63, 71–74). That was more than enough "blackness" for the district court in 1983 to declare her parents, and thus Mrs. Phipps and her siblings, to be legally black.

In October and again in December 1985, the state's Fourth Circuit Court of Appeals upheld the district court's decision, saying that no one can change the racial designation of his or her parents or anyone else's (479 So. 2d 369). Said the majority of the court in its opinion: "That appellants might today describe themselves as white does not prove error in a document which designates their parents as colored" (479 So. 2d 371). Of course, if the parents' designation as "colored" cannot be disturbed, their descendants must be defined as black by the "traceable amount rule." The court also concluded that the preponderance of the evidence clearly showed that the Guillory parents were "colored." Although noting expert testimony to the effect that the race of an individual cannot be determined with scientific accuracy, the court said the law of racial designation is not based on science, that "individual race designations are purely social and cultural perceptions and the evidence conclusively proves those subjective perspectives were correctly recorded at the time the appellants' birth certificates were recorded" (479 So. 2d 372). At the rehearing in December 1985, the appellate court also affirmed the necessity of designating race on birth certificates for public health, affirmative action, and other important public programs and held that equal protection of the law has not been denied so long as the designation is treated as confidential.

When this case was appealed to the Louisiana Supreme Court in 1986, that court declined to review the decision, saying only that the court "concurs in the denial for the reasons assigned by the court of appeals on rehearing" (485 So. 2d 60). In December 1986 the U.S. Supreme Court was equally brief in stating its reason for refusing to review the decision: "The appeal is dismissed for want of a substantial federal question" (107 Sup. Ct. Reporter, interim ed. 638). Thus, both the final court of appeals in Louisiana and the highest court of the United States saw no reason to disturb the application of the one-drop rule in the lawsuit brought by Susie Guillory Phipps and her siblings.

CENSUS ENUMERATION OF BLACKS

When the U.S. Bureau of the Census enumerates blacks (always counted as Negroes until 1980), it does not use a scientific definition, but rather the one accepted by the general public and by the courts. The Census Bureau counts what the nation wants counted. Although various operational instructions have been tried, the definition of black used by the Census Bureau has been the nation's cultural and legal definition: all persons with any known black ancestry. Other nations define and count blacks differently, so international comparisons of census data on blacks can be extremely misleading. For example, Latin American countries generally count as black only unmixed African blacks, those only slightly mixed, and the very poorest mulattoes. If they used the U.S. definition, they would count far more blacks than they do, and if Americans used their definition, millions in the black community in the United States would be counted either as white or as "coloreds" of different descriptions, not as black.

Instructions to our census enumerators in 1840, 1850, and 1860 provided "mulatto" as a category but did not define the term. In 1870 and 1880, mulattoes were officially defined to include "quadroons, octoroons, and all persons having any perceptible trace of African blood." In 1890 enumerators were told to record the *exact* proportion of the "African blood," again relying on visibility. In 1900 the Census Bureau specified that "pure Negroes" be counted separately from mulattoes, the latter to mean "all persons with some trace of black blood." In 1920 the mulatto category was dropped, and black was defined to mean any person with any black ancestry, as it has been ever since.

In 1960 the practice of self-definition began, with the head of household indicating the race of its members. This did not seem to introduce any noticeable fluctuation in the number of blacks, thus indicating that black Americans generally apply the one-drop rule to themselves. One exception is that Spanish-speaking Americans who have black ancestry but were considered white, or some designation other than black, in their place of origin generally reject the one-drop rule if they can. American Indians with some black ancestry also generally try to avoid the rule, but those who leave the reservation are often treated as black. At any rate, the 1980 census count showed that self-designated blacks made up about 12 percent of the population of the United States.

No other ethnic population in the nation, including those with visibly non-caucasoid features, is defined and counted according to a one-drop rule. For example, persons whose ancestry is one-fourth or less American Indian are not generally defined as Indian unless they want to be, and they are considered assimilating Americans who may even be proud of having some Indian ancestry. The same implicit rule appears to apply to Japanese Americans, Filipinos, or other peoples from East Asian nations and also to Mexican Americans who have Central American Indian ancestry, as a large majority do. For instance, a person whose ancestry is one-eighth Chinese is not defined as just Chinese, or East Asian, or a member of the mongoloid race. The United States certainly does not apply a one-drop rule to its white ethnic populations either, which include both national and religious groups. Ethnicity has often been confused with racial biology and not just in Nazi Germany. Americans do not insist that an American with a small fraction of Polish ancestry be classified as a Pole, or that someone with a single remote Greek ancestor be designated Greek, or that someone with any trace of Jewish lineage is a Jew and nothing else.

It is interesting that, in *The Passing of the Great Race* (1916), Madison Grant maintained that the one-drop rule should be applied not only to blacks but also to all the other ethnic groups he considered biologically inferior "races," such as Hindus, Asians in general, Jews, Italians, and other Southern and Eastern European peoples. Grant's book went through four editions, and he and others succeeded in getting Congress to pass the national origins quota laws of the early 1920s. This racist quota legislation sharply curtailed immigration from everywhere in the world except Northern and Western Europe and the Western Hemisphere, until it was repealed in 1965. Grant and other believers in the racial superiority of their own group have confused race with ethnicity. They consider miscegenation with any "inferior" people to be the ultimate danger to the survival of their own group and have often seen the one-drop rule as a crucial component in their line of defense. Americans in general, however, while finding other ways to discriminate against immigrant groups, have rejected the application of the drastic one-drop rule to all groups but blacks.

UNIQUENESS OF THE ONE-DROP RULE

Not only does the one-drop rule apply to no other group than American blacks, but apparently the rule is unique in that it is found only in the United States and not in any other nation in the world. In fact, definitions of who is black vary quite sharply from country to country, and for this reason people in other countries often express consternation about our definition. James Baldwin relates a revealing incident that occurred in 1956 at the Conference of Negro-African Writers and Artists held in Paris. The head of the delegation of writers and artists from the United States was John Davis. The French chairperson introduced Davis and then asked him why he considered himself Negro, since he certainly did not look like one. Baldwin wrote, "He *is* a Negro, of course, from the remarkable legal point of view which obtains in the United States, but more importantly, as he tried to make clear to his interlocutor, he was a Negro by choice and by depth of involvement—by experience, in fact" (1962:19).

The phenomenon known as "passing as white" is difficult to explain in other countries or to foreign students. Typical questions are: "Shouldn't Americans say that a person who is passing as white is white, or nearly all white, and has previously been passing as black?" or "To be consistent, shouldn't you say that someone who is one-eighth white is passing as black?" or "Why is there so much concern, since the so-called blacks who pass take so little negroid ancestry with them?" Those who ask such questions need to realize that "passing" is so much more a social phenomenon than a biological one, reflecting the nation's unique definition of what makes a person black. The concept of "passing" rests on the one-drop rule and on folk beliefs about race and miscegenation, not on biological or historical fact.

The black experience with passing as white in the United States contrasts with the experience of other ethnic minorities that have features that are clearly non-caucasoid. The concept of passing applies only to blacks—consistent with the nation's unique definition of the group. A person who is one-fourth or less American Indian or Korean or Filipino is not regarded as passing if he or she intermarries and joins fully the life of the dominant community, so the minority ancestry need not be hidden. It is often suggested that the key reason for this is that the physical differences between these other groups and whites are less pronounced than the physical differences between African blacks and whites, and therefore are less threatening to whites. However, keep in mind that the one-drop rule and anxiety about passing originated during slavery and later received powerful reinforcement under the Jim Crow system.

For the physically visible groups other than blacks, miscegenation promotes assimilation, despite barriers of prejudice and discrimination during two or more generations of racial mixing. As noted above, when ancestry in one of these racial minority groups does not exceed one-fourth, a person is not defined solely as a member of that group. Masses of white European immigrants have climbed the class ladder not only through education but also with the help of close personal relationships in the dominant community, intermarriage, and ultimately full cultural and social assimilation. Young people tend to marry people they meet in the same informal social circles (Gordon, 1964:70–81). For visibly noncaucasoid minorities other than blacks in the United States, this entire route to full assimilation is slow but possible.

For all persons of any known black lineage, however, assimilation is blocked and is not promoted by miscegenation. Barriers to full opportunity and participation for blacks are still formidable, and a fractionally black person cannot escape these obstacles without passing as white and cutting off all ties to the black family and community. The pain of this separation, and condemnation by the black family and community, are major reasons why many or most of those who could pass as white choose not to. Loss of security within the minority community, and fear and distrust of the white world are also factors.

It should now be apparent that the definition of a black person as one with any trace at all of black African ancestry is inextricably woven into the history of the United States. It incorporates beliefs once used to justify slavery and later used to buttress the castelike Jim Crow system of segregation. Developed in the South, the definition of "Negro" (now black) spread and became the nation's social and legal definition. Because blacks are defined according to the one-drop rule, they are a socially constructed category in which there is wide variation in racial traits and therefore not a race group in the scientific sense. However, because that category has a definite status position in the society it has become a self-conscious social group with an ethnic identity.

The one-drop rule has long been taken for granted throughout the United States by whites and blacks alike, and the federal courts have taken "judicial notice" of it as being a matter of common knowledge. State courts have generally upheld the one-drop rule, but some have limited the definition to one thirty-second or one-sixteenth or one-eighth black ancestry, or made other limited exceptions for persons with both Indian and black ancestry. Most Americans seem unaware that this definition of blacks is extremely unusual in other countries, perhaps even unique to the United States, and that Americans define no other minority group in a similar way. . . .

REFERENCES

Bahr, Howard M., Bruce A. Chadwick, and Joseph H. Stauss. 1979. *American Ethnicity.* Lexington, MA: D.C. Heath & Co.

Baldwin, James. 1962. *Nobody Knows My Name.* New York: Dell Publishing Co.

Bennett, Lerone, Jr. 1962. *Before the Mayflower: A History of the Negro in America 1619–1962.* Chicago: Johnson Publishing Co.

Berry, Brewton. 1965. *Race and Ethnic Relations.* 3rd ed. Boston: Houghton Mifflin Co.

Berry, Brewton, and Henry L. Tischler. 1978. *Race and Ethnic Relations.* 4th ed. Boston: Houghton Mifflin Co.

Buckley, Gail Lumet. 1986. *The Hornes: An American Family.* New York: Alfred A. Knopf.

Gordon, Milton M. 1964. *Assimilation in American Life.* New York: Oxford University Press.

Grant, Madison. 1916. *The Passing of the Great Race.* New York: Scribner.

Gwaltney, John Langston. 1980. *Drylongso: A Self-Portrait of Black America.* New York: Vintage Books.

Harris, Melvin. 1964. *Patterns of Race in the Americas.* New York: W. W. Norton.

Horne, Lena, and Richard Schickel. 1965. *Lena.* Garden City, NY: Doubleday & Co.

Mangum, Charles Staples, Jr. 1940. *The Legal Status of the Negro in the United States.* Chapel Hill: University of North Carolina Press.

Model, F. Peter, ed. 1983. "Apartheid in the Bayou." *Perspectives: The Civil Rights Quarterly* 15 (Winter–Spring), 3–4.

Myrdal, Gunnar, assisted by Richard Sterner and Arnold M. Rose. 1944. *An American Dilemma.* New York: Harper & Bros.

Ottley, Roi. 1943. *New World A-Coming.* Cleveland: World Publishing Co.

Powell, Adam Clayton, Jr. 1971. *Adam by Adam: The Autobiography of Adam Clayton Powell, Jr.* New York: Dial Press.

Preston, Dickson J. 1980. *Young Frederick Douglass: the Maryland Years.* Baltimore: Johns Hopkins University Press.

Trillin, Calvin. 1986. "American Chronicles: Black or White." *New Yorker,* April 14, 1986, pp. 62–78.

White, Walter. 1948. *A Man Called White: The Autobiography of Walter White.* New York: Viking Press.

Williamson, Joel. 1980. *New People: Miscegenation and Mulattoes in the United States.* New York: The Free Press.

PERSONAL ACCOUNT

A Wonderful Opportunity

I was one among many—growing up and being educated in a stable, loving, supportive Black community—who was informed of a wonderful opportunity that lay ahead for me.

My neighborhood school would be closed and I, and others like me, would have the "honor" and "privilege" of being transported to the suburbs to go to school where everything would be "bigger and better": bigger gym, bigger lunchroom, better teachers, better equipment, better books, "better" people. It would be a great opportunity for me, and others like me, to "better" ourselves.

This land of "bigger and better" was located atop one of the many hills surrounding the city of Pittsburgh, Pennsylvania, a hill pregnant with fear, ignorance, and hate. It was not long after my arrival in this land that I, and others like me, would be greeted, verbally and visually, with that welcoming term of endearment, "nigger."

During my stay in this land of "bigger and better" (mid-seventies through early eighties, grades 6 through 12) this hill gave birth, on several occasions, to a human wall of hate brandishing weapons of intimidation: lead pipes, baseball bats, vicious dogs, and vicious racial epithets. Those of us who were targets of this intimidation did what anyone would do when an assault against one's humanity is launched. We masked our fear with anger-bravado-attitude and defiance. A hostile confrontation ensued. Some of us were chased by dogs, some were attacked with pipes and chains, some were injured when buses were turned over while occupied, some were hit and cut by rocks being thrown at buses as they attempted to descend the hill.

No one effectively intervened on our behalf. Our parents' response was to be defiant, to send us back up the hill determined not to have their children denied access to that "wonderful opportunity." The parents of our combatants responded by aligning themselves on the hill with their children. Thus, busing for integration was transformed into busing for confrontation. . . . Welcome to the Suburbs.

I would have liked for both groups of parents (Black and White) to have realized that the political, ideological, and social battle for and against integration left in the middle a group of kids battling (literally) each other. This physical battle strained and/or dissolved newly formed friendships. The mental battle shattered a child's sense of self and fostered feelings of inadequacy, inferiority, and hatred of others (and self) in a young person previously insulated from such a penetrating and devastating psychological ambush. What an "opportunity."

R.M.A.

READING 2

Race, Censuses, and Citizenship

Melissa Nobles

Obtaining racial data would seem to be a straightforward process: the census asks a question; statisticians, demographers, and other properly trained professionals tabulate the responses. To count by race presumes, however, that there is "something" there to be counted—but what exactly is it? Nor does counting by race necessarily reveal how racial data will be tabulated or what purposes they will serve. The answers to these questions are found in the actions of politicians, scientists, public-policy makers, organized advocates, and in particular political and historical circumstances. Counting by race is as much a political act as it is an enumerative one. Census bureaus are not simply producers of racial statistical data; they are also political actors.

This [discussion] analyzes the mutually reinforcing dynamic between concepts of race, censuses, and citizenship. It argues that censuses help form racial discourse, which in turn affects the public policies that either vitiate or protect the rights, privileges, and experiences commonly associated with citizenship. To support this argument, it makes four basic and related claims. The first is that race is not an objective category, which censuses simply count, but a fluid and internally contradicting discourse, partly created by and embedded in institutional processes, including those of the census itself. The second is that census bureaus are not politically neutral institutions, employing impartial methods, but state agencies that use census methods and data as instruments of governance. Third, racial discourse influences both the rationales for public policy and its outcomes. Public policies not only use racial census data; these data assist in the development of public policy. Fourth, and finally, individuals and groups seek to alter the terms of racial discourse in order to advance political and social aims, and have targeted censuses precisely because they help to make and sustain such discourse. At its broadest level, this [discussion] examines the interaction between ideas and institutions: ideas about race are partly created and enlivened by census bureaus, which thus structure political outcomes.

I should clarify at the outset what this [discussion] does *not* argue: that racial ideas and discourse are entirely reducible to more fundamental material interests and political power, or that they are wholly independent of larger political and economic arrangements. The same is true of census bureaus. Rather, this [discussion] contends that racial discourse is itself consequential, and that the existence of accompanying interests and power neither diminishes its power nor exhausts its meanings.[1] Similarly, census bureaus do not operate in a vacuum but within broad political and economic contexts.[2] The statement that racial ideas and discourse matter would seem to need little defense. Yet stating *that* they matter is not the same as showing *how* they matter or explaining *why* they matter. This [discussion] takes up that task and does so by way of census-taking. Finally, although census-taking is the focus, this does not mean that census bureaus are the only or the most important places where concepts of race are made and remade. The point is that census bureaus are typically overlooked as participants in the creation and perpetuation of race. This [discussion] seeks to remove the cloak of neutrality and social scientific objectivity to reveal their insider status.

It is no surprise that politics infuses census-taking. Public distrust of statistics is long-standing, a sentiment captured in a quip by Benjamin Disraeli: "[T]here are three kinds of lies: lies, damned lies, and statistics." Yet this distrust exists uneasily alongside a deep reliance

---

Melissa Nobles is associate professor of political science at the Massachusetts Institute of Technology.

on statistics and a strong belief in statistical methods, if not in any specific set of numbers.[3] This reliance is obvious; statistical data are used everywhere, in countless ways and for all conceivable purposes. Demographic and medical statistics provide information on virtually all stages of human existence: life expectancy, fecundity, morbidity, nutrition, and mortality. Economic statistics furnish similarly comprehensive information. Statistics provide a powerful and useful way of knowing the world. But we also come to know the world, in part, through the order that statistics and statistical methodology impose. Our dependence on numbers is linked to our "trust in numbers" and their ability to reveal truth, if not *the* truth.[4] The force of statistics in public life is not derived solely from their methods and truth claims, however. It is also derived from state authority. States have long relied on census statistics.[5] In the past, rulers have used censuses to spy on inhabitants, to conscript them into military service, and to levy taxes on them. Today, states more often use censuses to assess a country's population and resources, the enumerated being considered citizens to be served, not simply subjects to be watched, conscripted, or taxed. The state's production and use of census statistics enhance their influence in public life precisely because they thus become "official." The pall that state involvement casts over census-taking, however, extends beyond the political uses of this information to the political origins of certain categories. One of these is race.

Our thinking about race is conflicted. On the one hand, we are confused about it—is it a biological or a social construct?—and about what it means to be of "one race" or of "mixed race." On the other hand, we are convinced that there is something there, that we can know an individual's race by looking at him or her or by asking questions. Science has shaped our thinking on race in profound ways. Yet science has also raised as many questions about race as it has purported to answer. As historians of scientific racial thought have shown, ideas about what groups were or could be properly defined as "races" have changed over time, as have methods of determining racial membership. People with religious, linguistic, or physical characteristics in common, or who have simply shared geographical space, have at various times been defined as constituting a race.[6] Moreover, scientific determinants of racial membership have ranged from simple observation of skin complexion to elaborate and precise measurement of skull size (craniology and phrenology), shape of face and facial features, and body stature (anthropometry).[7] Today, many scientists and anthropologists call for the abandonment of the idea of discrete races.[8] Science's new stance on race is not that of census bureaus, however, which still count by race. In recent years, as in the past, census definitions of race have differed from scientific definitions, however much science has influenced census-taking. The interests of science and of social science in knowing about race differ too. The questions nonetheless remain, what are censuses counting today and why; what have they counted historically and why? Through examining census methods and policies, we come closer to understanding what race is and what it is not.

If race is a vexing but salient social identification, citizenship is the most fundamental political identification. A citizen is formally a member of a nation-state, but citizenship is more than a mere formality; it entitles a person to a set of rights, imposes obligations, and engenders lived experiences. To be sure, the road to the civil, political, and economic rights described by T. H. Marshall as the hallmarks of citizenship has always been a rocky and winding one.[9] Deciding who enjoys these rights has often been as contentious as establishing the rights themselves. As important as citizen status is, then, it does not stand alone. Other identifications, such as race, gender, class, and nativity, have often qualified citizenship, if not defined it explicitly. Across nations and historical epochs, political communities have included groups and excluded groups according to different, often shifting, criteria. In the United States, for example, race has been a fundamental qualifier of citizenship. During the antebellum period, citizenship depended on group membership: whites were citizens; slaves were not.[10] Free blacks were legally citizens until the Dred Scott Decision of 1857, "when the Supreme Court ruled that they were not citizens after all."[11] Yet, even as citizens, free blacks did not enjoy the same rights and privileges as whites. The passage of the Thirteenth, Fourteenth, and Fifteenth amendments after the Civil War formally extended citizenship and the franchise to black Americans, but it would be another 100 years before all black Americans could hope to enjoy the rights described and guaranteed in the Fourteenth and Fifteenth. To be a black in apartheid South Africa or a Jew in Nazi Germany was to be a non-citizen.[12] . . .

A discussion of citizenship and race would seem a far remove from census-taking, but it is not. Most simply, censuses register and reinforce the racial identifications germane to citizenship through the process of categorization itself. But their involvement goes much deeper. Justifications for racial exclusion in the United States have relied heavily on racial census data. As we shall see, nineteenth-century politicians and scientists marshaled racial census data as incontrovertible proof of the racial inferiority of black Americans and their unsuitability for full citizenship. Of course, political and economic forces more powerful than the census were ultimately responsible for undermining full citizenship for blacks, but racial ideas were essential to these justifications, and census data in turn became crucial to sustaining and advancing these ideas. Today, U.S. racial data are vital to a range of public policies and laws designed to address racial disadvantage and discrimination; indeed, the successful remedying of such disadvantage is viewed as essential in deepening the meanings and experiences of American citizenship. . . .

The story of censuses, race, and citizenship is larger than the sum of its parts. After all, censuses are conducted only once every ten years; and the census schedule is a form, albeit an official one. Taken together, however, census schedules have been used as the building blocks of social knowledge. State officials, scientists, politicians, and citizens have assigned great weight to censuses, with great political consequences. Racial categorization likewise tells us much and yet obscures much about the societies in which racial thought is prevalent. Censuses provide a lens for examining at close range how race is constructed. National citizenship is often taken for granted by everyone—except those who are excluded or disallowed from enjoying its full benefits. Who is considered a first-class citizen and what it means depends on who is considered a second-class citizen and what it means. Race has qualified citizenship. Examining race, censuses, and dimensions of citizenship together enhances our understanding of all three as separate components and as a working whole. . . .

RACE AS DISCOURSE

Counting by race is hardly a transparent process, because of the very conceptual ambiguities that surround race itself and the political stakes attached to it. These ambiguities are neither trivial nor simple, given the place of race in economic, political, and social life. Although the scholarship that refers to race in one way or another is vast, the portion of it that explains the concept of race is noticeably less so, albeit still substantial. The intellectual consensus today is that race has no objective existence. In the wake of this revelation, itself largely the result of scientific decree, scholars have set themselves the task of defining, explaining, describing, and analyzing race. Thus, according to the sociologists Michael Omi and Howard Winant, race is "a concept which signifies and symbolizes social conflicts and interests referring to different types of human bodies."[13] The historian Evelyn Brooks Higginbotham understands race to have various "faces"; it is at once a "social construction," "a highly contested representation of relations of power between social categories by which individuals are identified and identify themselves," "a myth," "a global sign," and a "metalanguage."[14] The philosopher David Theo Goldberg argues that race is an "irreducibly *political* category," in that "racial creation and management acquire import in framing and giving specificity to the body politic."[15] According to Ian Haney Lopez, the law constructs race legally by fixing the boundaries of races, by defining the content of racial identities, and by specifying their relative disadvantages and privileges in American society.[16] The literary critic Henry Louis Gates sees race as the "ultimate trope of difference because it is so very arbitrary in its application."[17] Historians of ideas have traced ideas of race and racial thought in various countries and different historical epochs.[18]

Scholars are a long way indeed from seeing race as fixed or objective, and, in significant ways, as deriving its existence from human bodies at all. Instead, its existence derives from and rests in language, in social practices, in legal definitions, in ideas, in structural arrangements, in the distribution of political and economic power, and in contests over such distribution. On these views, taken together, race is at once an empty category and a powerful instrument. Yet theoretical formulations that stress the radical plasticity of race, mostly correctly, I think, risk obscuring its concrete manifestations and the institutional sites of its construction and maintenance. These scholars may view race as political in some fundamental way, but they pay little close attention to state institutions and political processes.[19]

Building on this theoretical work, this [discussion] also interprets race as discourse. That is, race is not something that language simply describes, it is something that is created through language and institutional practices. As discourse, race creates and organizes human differences in politically consequential ways. The [discussion] advances this understanding of race by analyzing how census bureaus help to develop and maintain it.

Race has many, although not equally formative, sources. Science, religion, moral philosophy, law, politics, and economics have all contributed to a greater, and internally contradictory, discourse of race. Christianity, for example, has long nurtured belief in a cosmic order to which every race belongs and in which it is hierarchically ranked. God created human races, and the observable differences in appearance and in political, economic, and social standing are God's will.[20] National laws have also at times provided explicit definitions of racial membership. Slavery was, of course, a prime contributor to the entrenchment of racial thought in the Americas. Racial thought has accompanied, if not preceded, and been used to justify a range of economically exploitative arrangements. In both the United States and Brazil, the ongoing material consequences of racial memberships complicate how class inequalities are viewed and politically addressed.

The power of racial discourse derives from the mutually reinforcing dynamic among these separate foundations, with science, law, economics, religion, and politics coming together on a macro level to reinforce the positive consequences of some racial memberships and the negative consequences of others. Just as all these sources have not made equal contributions to racial discourse, the influence of each has also been unequal. The weight of scientific thought in racial discourse can hardly be overestimated. As the historian Nancy Stepan observes, during the period from 1800 to 1960, European and American scientists especially were "preoccupied by race," which was viewed as a principal determinant of human affairs.[21] It would be a mistake, too, to regard this science simply as "pseudoscience." Race science was not perceived as "pseudo" in its own time, and far from being regarded as "quacks," its practitioners were highly regarded and respected. Today, although scientists reject race as a scientifically meaningful concept, whether race was (or is) viewed as "natural" is, in certain ways, quite beside the point. Scientific racial thought has never simply meant "proving" the biological reality of race. Equally important has been the role of scientific ideas in shaping political discourse and public policies.

As we shall see, the nineteenth-century scientist Josiah Nott's interest in race was inextricably connected with his ideas about slavery, Negro citizenship, and the propriety of white economic, political, and social supremacy.

This formulation of race as discourse sets out to clarify what race is, but just as important and illuminating is what race is not. "Racial discourse," as referred to here, is not synonymous with racism. This distinction is a fine one, and it is intended to capture differences in degree, not in kind. Once dominant and still highly influential variants of racial discourse have themselves been profoundly racist. Yet there are also variants that attempt to define race in nonhierarchical ways, that purport merely to acknowledge human differences without according them undue significance. Whatever their impulses, however, these two broad variants constitute a discourse that variously creates race and imparts to it political and social salience.

Ethnicity is sometimes defined in terms of race, as well as of culture, language, ancestry, and religion, but racial discourse is not ethnic discourse.[22] Scholars treat ethnic categorization as a benignly descriptive marker—albeit one sometimes used for politically objectionable ends—but race has always had political meanings and uses. Nonetheless, whether ethnic identity is a matter of birth, of choice, or of some other factor, ethnicity indisputably resembles race in that it points to human similarities and differences. Ethnicity is a fluid designation, however, and, unlike race, it has never had the imprimatur of science: scholars have regarded it as socially made and subjective, and race as naturally created and objective. This [discussion] takes the opposite view, treating race as artificial, although not arbitrary, and subjective, although not inconsequential.

CENSUS BUREAUS AND RACE

Bureaucracies are not necessarily monolithic, omnipotent organizations; nor need they be entirely beholden to other, more powerful political bodies, such as legislatures, courts, or chief executives.[23] Their organization and their culture, as well as the motivations of bureaucrats and the capacities of leaders, are important in explaining their behavior and efficacy. The larger institutional and political context in which bureaucracies operate is also of great significance. This is as true for statistical bureaucracies as for any other kind. Yet, however obvious the claim, census bureaus are not always viewed as political bureaucracies. Rather, scholars present them as embattled state institutions that attempt to shield themselves (usually unsuccessfully) from political pressures that may impede their ability to produce impartial numbers. Somehow statistical methods are expected to cleanse the census-taking process of politics. History and politics cannot, however, be expunged from census-taking. Numbers without categories are useless, and the origins of categories require explanation. This view of census-taking as political in origin and consequence competes with concerted efforts by international bodies and national governments to ensure and demonstrate its political impartiality.

Most national census bureaus employ similar statistical methods and administrative procedures, and international guidelines have advanced this uniformity. Since 1946, the United Nations has sponsored four world population programs whose express purpose is to improve and standardize national censuses.[24] The push for standardization entrenches the view that census-taking methods, and, by extension, census bureaus, can transcend particular political and economic environments. Thus, census-taking can, in theory at least, be methodologically the same in democratic states and in authoritarian ones, in rich countries and in poor ones, in homogeneous and heterogeneous societies. Indeed, when censuses have been overtly tied to political regimes, they have been seen as the exceptions that prove the rule of impartiality. Soviet census data were completely suppressed in 1937, for example, because they revealed the unusually high mortality rates that resulted from the 1932–33 famine, brought on by forced collectivization.[25] Senior statisticians who had supervised the census were arrested and shot. The appearance of political noninvolvement is crucially important to the legitimacy of census bureaus and censuses, both domestically and internationally. Soviet census data were mistrusted internationally precisely because of their obviously close connection to the regime's political goals.[26] At the same time, this Soviet example reveals, albeit in an extreme way, the enduring connection between census-taking and statecraft in all countries. State officials have long used censuses to fulfill basic state "behavioral imperatives" to know and control their populations, consolidate political and economic power, and present national bills of health and wealth.[27] Today, state officials and international organizations consider census-taking an indispensable component of responsible governance. Yet censuses remain instruments at a state's disposal, not simply registers of performance and population.

Census bureau statisticians treat racial enumeration as the task of devising appropriate categories and counting by them. Race and its use as a counter have been regarded as self-evident in a way that belies the conceptual and political wrangling surrounding the production of racial data. Most scholarly and popular books on censuses present racial categorization as a technical procedure in need of little explanation. An institutional history of the U.S. Census Bureau written by a former bureau director never mentions racial categorization's contentious history.[28] . . . Until very recently, census officials and statisticians offered no clear public explanations of the racial categories employed and their definitions. Current explanations raise as many questions as they answer.

According to Sally Katzen, director of the Office of Information and Regulatory Affairs at the Office of Management and Budget, "[W]hen the OMB got into the business of establishing categories, it was purely statistical, not programmatic. . . . It was certainly never meant to *define* a race."[29] However, OMB's Statistical Directive No. 15 explicitly defines races, making her statement inconsistent with practice. Her point, however, is that races are out there in the world, waiting to be counted. Government officials reject any notion that OMB plays any role in creating race through categorization. . . .

It would be inaccurate to suggest, however, that those most closely connected to census-taking are the only ones who insist on the political disinterest of census bureaus and objectivity of statistical methods. Social scientists, who have long recognized the role of other state institutions in shaping racial politics, have all but ignored census bureaus and censuses. Instead, they have emphasized the ways in which state institutions distribute public goods along racial lines and/or manage racially based demands from civil society. The actions and policies of public institutions such as schools, courts, and social service agencies have been examined extensively, and the role of electoral systems in shaping racial politics has been analyzed. However, scholars have usually treated state agencies as managers of racial issues or referents for racial demands, not as places where race is constituted. An important exception is the work of critical race theorists in the United States, who examine, not only the ways in which the law treats persons categorized into different races differently, but how the law creates the racial categories themselves.[30]

When social scientists mention censuses, they refer to contention over numbers and over the distribution of political power, public goods, and rhetorical claims that hang in the balance. Census politics are, according to one scholar, an "entitlement" issue, where an ethnic group's anxiety about its own fecundity vis-à-vis that of another group combines with fear of political domination.[31] Majority group status effectively determines which group is entitled to political, economic, and social power. Much of the scholarly and public reaction to potential changes in race categories in the 2000 U.S. census has focused on the efforts of organized groups to protect their numbers and the benefits and protections that attach to racial categorization.[32] Undoubtedly, census politics overlap with racial/ethnic politics in matters of distribution, but the connection between race and censuses goes deeper. The Census Bureau has escaped inquiry both as a state institution that determines the benefits and penalties of racial memberships through the data it collects and as a place where racial categories themselves are constructed. The perception that census agencies and census categories are at some remove from politics ensures that a deeper theoretical appreciation of how the census supports racial discourse and how census racial data serve public policy is blunted.

NOTES

1. Goldstein and Keohane 1993, ch. 1, makes similar arguments in regard to the role of ideas in explaining foreign policy outcomes.
2. Here I draw on the insights of the "new institutionalism" (see Steinmo, Thelen, and Longstreth 1992), which asserts that institutions structure political action and thus influence political outcomes. At the same time, institutions are influenced by the broader political context. Institutions are defined as both "formal organizations and informal rules and procedures that structure conduct" (ibid., p. 2).
3. Here I use the term *statistics* in the generic sense of large numbers manipulated by prevailing methods. The development of statistics as a mathematical science has been a long and involved one. For a useful summary, see Feinberg 1992. See also Porter 1986; Stigler 1990; and Hacking 1990.
4. I borrow the phrase "trust in numbers" from Porter 1995, which argues and demonstrates that quantification is powerfully credible largely because of its claims to objectivity.
5. Woolf 1989; Patriarca 1996; Hacking 1991; and Scott 1998.
6. Stepan 1982, p. xvii.
7. Horsman 1981, ch. 3; Gould 1996; Jordan 1968.
8. See, e.g., "Race: What Is It Good For?" *Discover,* November 1994; Wheeler 1995; Goodman 1997; Lewontin, Rose, and Kamin 1984; Cavalli-Sforza, Menozzi, and Piazza 1994; American Anthropological Association 1997; Cartmill 1998; and Templeton 1998.
9. See Marshall and Bottomore 1992; Somers 1993; and Shklar 1991.
10. "Yet as long as slaves could be viewed in some sense as property, judges could avoid fitting them into established categories of membership or nonmembership. As chattels, slaves were neither aliens nor citizens: 'Persons in the status of slavery are, in contemplation of law, slaves,'" observes James H. Kettner (1978, p. 301).
11. Ibid., p. 315.
12. Under the apartheid regime, ten separate African "homelands" were created, and as these became "self-governing" and "independent," their citizens were deprived of their South African citizenship (Thompson 1995, p. 191). According to the Reich Citizenship Law of 1935, German Jews were redefined as "subjects," not citizens (Burleigh and Wipperman 1991, p. 45).
13. Omi and Winant 1994, p. 55
14. Higginbotham 1992, pp. 251–56.
15. Goldberg 1992, p. 563 (italics in original).
16. Haney-Lopez 1996, p. 10.
17. Gates 1986, p. 5.
18. See, e.g., Jordan 1968; Horsman 1981; Gould 1981; Barkan 1992; and Skidmore 1993a and b. It is important to note that many of the more influential works (in the United States at least) have not surprisingly focused on American ideas about race, and more specifically on the enduring preoccupation with "whiteness" and "blackness."
19. Recent work on the law is an important exception to this trend.
20. Mosse 1978; Gossett 1963.
21. Stepan 1982, p. x.
22. See, e.g., Horowitz 1985, esp. ch. 2; Isaacs 1975; and Weber 1968.
23. Wilson 1989; Starr 1987.
24. Goyer and Domschke 1983, pp. 6–7.
25. Merridale 1996.
26. Starr 1987, pp. 38–39.
27. I borrow the phrase "behavorial imperative" from Young 1994, ch. 2.
28. Eckler 1972.

29. Wright 1994, p. 54 (italics in original).
30. See, e.g., Crenshaw 1988; Gotanda 1991; Haney-Lopez 1996.
31. Horowitz 1985, pp. 194–96.
32. Hollinger 1995; Hartman 1997.

BIBLIOGRAPHY

American Anthropological Association. 1997. "Press Release/OMB 15." AAA web page, October.

Burleigh, Michael, and Wolfgang Wipperman. 1991. *The Racial State: Germany, 1933–1945.* New York: Cambridge University Press.

Cartmill, Matt. 1998. "The Status of the Race Concept in Physical Anthropology." *American Anthropologist* 100, no. 3 (September): 651–60.

Cavalli-Sforza, L. Luca, Paolo Menozzi, and Alberto Piazza. 1994. *The History and Geography of Human Genes.* Princeton, NJ: Princeton University Press.

Crenshaw, Kimberlé. 1988. "Race, Reform, and Retrenchment: Transformation and Legitimization in Antidiscrimination Law." *Harvard Law Review* 101, no. 7 (May):1331–87.

Eckler, A. Ross. 1972. *The Bureau of the Census.* New York: Praeger.

Feinberg, Stephen E. 1992. "A Brief History of Statistics in Three and One-Half Chapters: A Review Essay." *Statistical Science* 7, no. 2: 208–25.

Gates, Henry Louis, Jr. 1986. "Introduction: Writing 'Race' and the Difference It Makes." In *Race, Writing, and Difference,* ed. Henry Louis Gates, pp. 1–20. Chicago: University of Chicago Press.

———. 1996. "White Like Me." *New Yorker,* June 17, pp. 66–81.

Goldberg, David Theo. 1992. "The Semantics of Race." *Ethnic and Racial Studies* 15, no. 4 (October): 543–69.

Goldstein, Judith, and Robert Keohane. 1993. *Ideas and Foreign Policy: Beliefs, Institutions, and Political Change.* Ithaca, NY: Cornell University Press.

Goodman, Alan H. 1997. "Bred in the Bone?" *The Sciences,* March–April.

Gossett, Thomas. 1963. *Race: The History of an Idea in America.* Dallas, Texas: Methodist University Press.

Gotanda, Neil. 1991. "A Critique of 'Our Constitution Is Color-Blind.'" *Stanford Law Review* 44, no. 1 (November): 1–68.

Gould, Stephen Jay. [1981] 1996. *The Mismeasure of Man.* New York: Norton.

Goyer, Doreen S., and Elaine Domschke. 1983. *The Handbook of National Population Censuses: Latin America and the Caribbean, North America and Oceania.* Westport, CT: Greenwood Press.

Hacking, Ian. 1990. *The Taming of Chance.* Cambridge: Cambridge University Press.

———. 1991. "How Should We Do the History of Statistics?" In *The Foucault Effect: Studies in Governmentality,* ed. Graham Burchell, Colin Gordon, and Peter Miller, pp. 181–95. Chicago: University of Chicago Press.

Haney-Lopez, Ian. 1996. *White by Law: The Legal Construction of Race.* New York: New York University Press.

Hartman, Chester. 1997. *Double Exposure: Poverty and Race in America.* New York: M. E. Sharpe.

Higginbotham, Evelyn Brooks. 1992. "African-American Women's History and the Metalanguage of Race." *Signs: Journal of Women in Culture and Society* 17, no. 2: 251–74.

Hollinger, David. 1995. *Postethnic America: Beyond Multiculturalism.* New York: Basic Books.

Horowitz, Donald L. 1985. *Ethnic Groups in Conflict.* Berkeley and Los Angeles: University of California Press.

Horsman, Reginald. 1981. *Race and Manifest Destiny: The Origins of American Racial Anglo-Saxonism.* Cambridge, MA: Harvard University Press.

Jordan, Winthrop D. 1968. *White over Black: American Attitudes Toward the Negro, 1550–1812.* Chapel Hill, NC: University of North Carolina Press.

Kettner, James H.1978. *The Development of American Citizenship, 1608–1870.* Chapel Hill, NC: University of North Carolina Press.

Lewontin, R. C., Steven Rose, and Leon J. Kamin. 1984. *Not in Our Genes: Biology, Ideology, and Human Nature.* New York: Pantheon Books.

Marshall, T. H., and Tom Bottomore. [1950] 1992. *Citizenship and Social Class.* Concord, MA: Pluto Press.

Merridale, Catherine. 1996. "The 1937 Census and the Limits of Stalinist Rule." *Historical Journal* 39, no. I:225–40.

Mosse, George L. 1978. *Toward the Final Solution: A History of European Racism.* New York: Howard Fertig.

Omi, Michael, and Howard Winant. [1986] 1994. *Racial Formation in the United States: From the 1960s to the 1980s.* 2d ed. New York: Routledge.

Patriarca, Silvana. 1996. *Numbers and Nationhood: Writing Statistics in Nineteenth-Century Italy.* Cambridge: Cambridge University Press.

Porter, Theodore M. 1986. *The Rise of Statistical Thinking.* Princeton, NJ: Princeton University Press.

———. 1995. *Trust in Numbers: The Pursuit of Objectivity in Science and Public Life.* Princeton, NJ: Princeton University Press.

"Race: What Is It Good For?" 1994. *Discover: Special Issue on the Science of Race.* November.

Scott, James C. 1998. *Seeing Like a State: How Certain Schemes to Improve the Human Condition Have Failed.* New Haven, CT: Yale University Press.

Shklar, Judith N. 1991. *American Citizenship: The Quest for Inclusion.* Cambridge, MA: Harvard University Press.

Skidmore, Thomas. [1974] 1993a. *Black into White: Race and Nationality in Brazilian Thought.* Durham, NC: Duke University Press.

———. 1993b. "Bi-racial U.S.A./Multi-racial Brazil: Is the Contrast Still Valid?" *Journal of Latin American Studies* 25: 373–86.

Somers, Margaret R. 1993. "Citizenship and the Place of the Public Sphere: Law, Community, and Political Culture in the Transition to Democracy." *American Sociological Review* 58 (October): 587–620.

Steinmo, Sven, Kathleen Thelen, and Frank Longstreth, eds. 1992. *Structuring Politics: Historical Institutionalism in Comparative Analysis.* New York: Cambridge University Press.

Stepan, Nancy Leys. 1982. *The Idea of Race in Science: Great Britain, 1800–1960.* Hamden, CT: Archon Books.

Stigler, Stephen M. 1990. *The History of Statistics: The Measurement of Uncertainty before 1900.* Cambridge, MA: Harvard University Press.

Templeton, Alan R. 1998. "Human Races: A Genetic and Evolutionary Perspective." *American Anthropologist* 100, no. 3 (September): 632–50.

Thompson, Leonard. [1990] 1995. *A History of South Africa,* rev. ed. New Haven, CT: Yale University Press.

Wheeler, David L.1995. "A Growing Number of Scientists Reject the Concept of Race." *Chronicle of Higher Education,* February 17, pp. A-8–9, 15.

Woolf, Stuart. 1989. "Statistics and the Modern State." *Comparative Study of Society and History* 31: 588–604.

Wright, Lawrence. 1994. "One Drop of Blood." *New Yorker,* July 25, pp. 46–55.

Young, Crawford. 1994. *The African Colonial State in Comparative Perspective.* New Haven, CT: Yale University Press.

The Evolution of Identity

Decade to decade, the U.S. census has changed its classifications of race and ethnicity. Partially, this reflects the growing diversity of the country. It also reveals the nation's evolving politics and social mores. When the first census was taken in 1790, enumerators classified free residents as white or "other," while slaves were counted separately. By 1860, residents were classified as white, black or mulatto. Hispanic origin first became a category in 1970. Here are the categories used in the decennial counts from 1860 to 2000, as presented by AmeriStat (www.ameristat.org).

1860	1870	1880	1890[1]	1900[2]	1910	1920	1930	1940	1950	1960	1970	1980	1990	2000
White **Black** **Mulatto**	White Black Mulatto	White Black Mulatto	White Black Mulatto	White Black (Negro descent)	White Black Mulatto	White Black Mulatto	White Black	White Black	White Negro	White Negro	White Negro or Black	White Black or Negro	White Black or Negro	White Black, African American or Negro
	Chinese **Indian**	Chinese Indian	Chinese Indian **Quadroon** **Octoroon**	Chinese Indian	Chinese Indian	Chinese Indian	Chinese Indian	Chinese Indian	Chinese Amer. Indian	Chinese Amer. Indian	Chinese Indian (Amer.)	Chinese Indian	Chinese Indian (Amer.)	Chinese Amer. Indian or Alaska Native
			Japanese	Japanese	Japanese	Japanese **Filipino** **Hindu** **Korean**	Japanese Filipino Hindu Korean **Mexican**	Japanese Filipino Hindu Korean	Japanese Filipino	Japanese Filipino	Japanese Filipino Korean	Japanese Filipino Asian Indian Korean	Japanese Filipino Asian Indian Korean	Japanese Filipino Asian Indian Korean
										Aleut **Eskimo** **Hawaiian** **Part Hawaiian**	Hawaiian	Aleut Eskimo Hawaiian	Aleut Eskimo Hawaiian	Native Hawaiian
												Vietnamese **Guamanian** **Samoan**	Vietnamese Guamanian Samoan **Other Asian Pacific Islander**	Vietnamese Guamanian or Chamorro Samoan **Other Asian** **Other Pacific Islander**
					Other	Other	Other	Other	Other	Other	Other	Other	Other race	Some other race
										ETHNICITY	Mexican **Puerto Rican** **Central/So. American** **Cuban** **Other Spanish** **(None of these)**	Mexican, Mexican Amer. **Chicano** Puerto Rican Cuban Other Spanish/ Hispanic Not Spanish/ Hispanic	Mexican, Mexican Amer. Chicano Puerto Rican Cuban Other Spanish/ Hispanic Not Spanish/ Hispanic	Mexican, Mexican Amer. Chicano Puerto Rican Cuban Other Spanish/ Hispanic/Latino Not Spanish/ Hispanic/Latino

1 In 1890, mulatto was defined as a person who was three-eighths to five-eighths black. A quadroon was one-quarter black and an octoroon one-eighth black.

2 American Indians have been asked to specify their tribe since the 1900 Census.

Bold letters indicate first usage since 1860.

NOTE: Before the 1970 Census, enumerators wrote in the race of individuals using the designated categories. In subsequent censuses, respondents or enumerators filled in circles next to the categories with which the respondent identified. Also beginning with the 1970 Census, people choosing American Indian, other Asian, other race, or for the Hispanic question, other Hispanic categories, were asked to write in a specific tribe or group. Hispanic ethnicity was asked of a sample of Americans in 1970 and of all Americans beginning with the 1980 Census.

Sources: AmeriStat, "200 Years of U.S. Census Taking: Population and Housing Questions 1790–1990," U.S. Census Bureau.
FROM: *The Washington Post*, Federal Page, August 13, 2001.

Census 2000: Seventeen Questions from the Long Form

Person 1

Your answers are important! Every person in the Census counts.

1 What is this person's name? *Print the name of Person 1 from page 2.*

Last Name

First Name MI

2 What is this person's telephone number? *We may contact this person if we don't understand an answer.*

Area Code + Number

3 What is this person's sex? *Mark [X] ONE box.*

- [ ] Male
- [ ] Female

4 What is this person's age and what is this person's date of birth?

Age on April 1, 2000

Print numbers in boxes.

Month Day Year of birth

→ **NOTE: Please answer BOTH Questions 5 and 6.**

5 Is this person Spanish/Hispanic/Latino? *Mark [X] the* ***"No"*** *box if* ***not*** *Spanish/Hispanic/Latino.*

- [ ] **No**, not Spanish/Hispanic/Latino
- [ ] Yes, Mexican, Mexican Am., Chicano
- [ ] Yes, Puerto Rican
- [ ] Yes, Cuban
- [ ] Yes, other Spanish/Hispanic/Latino — *Print group.*

6 What is this person's race? ***Mark [X] one or more races*** *to indicate what this person considers himself/herself to be.*

- [ ] White
- [ ] Black, African Am., or Negro
- [ ] American Indian or Alaska Native — *Print name of enrolled or principal tribe.*
- [ ] Asian Indian
- [ ] Chinese
- [ ] Filipino
- [ ] Japanese
- [ ] Korean
- [ ] Vietnamese
- [ ] Other Asian — *Print race.*
- [ ] Native Hawaiian
- [ ] Guamanian or Chamorro
- [ ] Samoan
- [ ] Other Pacific Islander — *Print race.*
- [ ] Some other race — *Print race.*

7 What is this person's marital status?

- [ ] Now married
- [ ] Widowed
- [ ] Divorced
- [ ] Separated
- [ ] Never married

8 a. At any time since February 1, 2000, has this person attended regular school or college? *Include only nursery school or preschool, kindergarten, elementary school, and schooling which leads to a high school diploma or a college degree.*

- [ ] No, has not attended since February 1 → *Skip to 9*
- [ ] Yes, public school, public college
- [ ] Yes, private school, private college

☞ Question is asked of all persons on the short (100-percent) and long (sample) forms.

2043 Form D-61B

Person 1 (continued)

8 b. What grade or level was this person attending? *Mark ☒ ONE box.*

- ☐ Nursery school, preschool
- ☐ Kindergarten
- ☐ Grade 1 to grade 4
- ☐ Grade 5 to grade 8
- ☐ Grade 9 to grade 12
- ☐ College undergraduate years (freshman to senior)
- ☐ Graduate or professional school *(for example: medical, dental, or law school)*

9 What is the highest degree or level of school this person has COMPLETED? *Mark ☒ ONE box. If currently enrolled, mark the previous grade or highest degree received.*

- ☐ No schooling completed
- ☐ Nursery school to 4th grade
- ☐ 5th grade or 6th grade
- ☐ 7th grade or 8th grade
- ☐ 9th grade
- ☐ 10th grade
- ☐ 11th grade
- ☐ 12th grade, **NO DIPLOMA**
- ☐ **HIGH SCHOOL GRADUATE** — high school DIPLOMA or the equivalent *(for example: GED)*
- ☐ Some college credit, but less than 1 year
- ☐ 1 or more years of college, no degree
- ☐ Associate degree *(for example: AA, AS)*
- ☐ Bachelor's degree *(for example: BA, AB, BS)*
- ☐ Master's degree *(for example: MA, MS, MEng, MEd, MSW, MBA)*
- ☐ Professional degree *(for example: MD, DDS, DVM, LLB, JD)*
- ☐ Doctorate degree *(for example: PhD, EdD)*

10 What is this person's ancestry or ethnic origin?

(For example: Italian, Jamaican, African Am., Cambodian, Cape Verdean, Norwegian, Dominican, French Canadian, Haitian, Korean, Lebanese, Polish, Nigerian, Mexican, Taiwanese, Ukrainian, and so on.)

11 a. Does this person speak a language other than English at home?

- ☐ Yes
- ☐ No → *Skip to 12*

b. What is this language?

(For example: Korean, Italian, Spanish, Vietnamese)

c. How well does this person speak English?

- ☐ Very well
- ☐ Well
- ☐ Not well
- ☐ Not at all

12 Where was this person born?

- ☐ In the United States — *Print name of state.*
- ☐ Outside the United States — *Print name of foreign country, or Puerto Rico, Guam, etc.*

13 Is this person a CITIZEN of the United States?

- ☐ Yes, born in the United States → *Skip to 15a*
- ☐ Yes, born in Puerto Rico, Guam, the U.S. Virgin Islands, or Northern Marianas
- ☐ Yes, born abroad of American parent or parents
- ☐ Yes, a U.S. citizen by naturalization
- ☐ No, not a citizen of the United States

14 When did this person come to live in the United States? *Print numbers in boxes.*

Year

15 a. Did this person live in this house or apartment 5 years ago (on April 1, 1995)?

- ☐ Person is under 5 years old → *Skip to 33*
- ☐ Yes, this house → *Skip to 16*
- ☐ No, outside the United States — *Print name of foreign country, or Puerto Rico, Guam, etc., below; then skip to 16.*
- ☐ No, different house in the United States

Person 1 (continued)

15 **b. Where did this person live 5 years ago?**

Name of city, town, or post office

Did this person live inside the limits of the city or town?

☐ Yes
☐ No, outside the city/town limits

Name of county

Name of state

ZIP Code

16 **Does this person have any of the following long-lasting conditions:**

	Yes	No
a. Blindness, deafness, or a severe vision or hearing impairment?	☐	☐
b. A condition that substantially limits one or more basic physical activities such as walking, climbing stairs, reaching, lifting, or carrying?	☐	☐

17 **Because of a physical, mental, or emotional condition lasting 6 months or more, does this person have any difficulty in doing any of the following activities:**

	Yes	No
a. Learning, remembering, or concentrating?	☐	☐
b. Dressing, bathing, or getting around inside the home?	☐	☐
c. (Answer if this person is 16 YEARS OLD OR OVER.) Going outside the home alone to shop or visit a doctor's office?	☐	☐
d. (Answer if this person is 16 YEARS OLD OR OVER.) Working at a job or business?	☐	☐

READING 5

Federal Indian Identification Policy

M. Annette Jaimes

I'm forever being asked not only my "tribe," but my "percentage of Indian blood." I've given the matter a lot of thought, and find I prefer to make the computation based on all of me rather than just the fluid coursing through my veins. Calculated in this way, I can report that I am precisely 52.5 pounds Indian—about 35 pounds Creek and the remainder Cherokee—88 pounds Teutonic, 43.5 pounds some sort of English, and the rest "undetermined." Maybe the last part should just be described as "human." It all seems rather silly as a means of assessing who I am, don't you think?

Ward Churchill
Creek/Cherokee Métis, 1991

The question of my "identity" often comes up. I think I must be a mixed-blood. I claim to be male, although only one of my parents was male.

Jimmie Durham
Cherokee, 1991

By all accepted standards of international jurisprudence and human decency, American Indian peoples whose territory lies within the borders of the United States hold compelling legal and moral rights to be treated as fully sovereign nations. It is axiomatic that any such national entity is inherently entitled to exercise the prerogative of determining for itself the criteria by which its citizenry, or "membership," is to be recognized by other sovereign nations. This is a principle that applies equally to superpowers such as the U.S. and to non-powers such as Grenada and Monaco. In fact, it is a tenet so widely understood and imbedded in international law, custom, and convention that it bears no particular elaboration here.

Contrary to virtually universal practice, the United States has opted to preempt unilaterally the rights of many North American indigenous nations to engage in this most fundamental level of internal decisionmaking. Instead, in pursuit of the interests of their own state rather than those of the nations that are thereby affected, federal policymakers have increasingly imposed "Indian identification standards" of their own design. Typically centering upon a notion of "blood quantum"—not especially different in its conception from the eugenics code once adopted by nazi Germany in its effort to achieve "racial purity," or currently utilized by South Africa to segregate Blacks and "coloreds"—this aspect of U.S. policy has increasingly wrought havoc with the American Indian sense of nationhood (and often the individual sense of self) over the past century. This chapter offers a brief analysis of the motivations underlying this federal usurpation of the American Indian expression of sovereignty and points out certain implications of it.

FEDERAL OBLIGATIONS

The more than 370 formally ratified treaties entered into by the United States with various Indian nations represent the basic real estate documents by which the federal government now claims legal title to most of its land base. In exchange for the lands ceded by Indians, the United States committed itself to the permanent provision of a range of services to Indian populations (i.e., the citizens of the Indian nations with which the treaty agreements were reached), which would assist them in adjusting their economies and ways of life to their newly constricted territories. For example, in the 1794 Treaty with the Oneida (also affecting the Tuscarora and Stockbridge Indians), the United States guaranteed provision of instruction "in the arts of the miller and sawyer," as well as regular annuities paid in goods and cash, in exchange for a portion of what is now the state of New York.[1] Similarly, the 1804 Treaty with the Delaware extended

M. Annette Jaimes is a lecturer in American Indian studies at the University of Colorado, Boulder.

assurances of technical instruction in agriculture and the mechanical arts, as well as annuities.[2] As Evelyn C. Adams frames it:

> Treaties with the Indians varied widely, stipulating cash annuities to be paid over a specified period of time or perpetually; rations and clothing, farming implements and domestic animals, and instruction in agriculture along with other educational opportunities. . . . [And eventually] the school supplemented the Federal program of practical teaching.[3]

The reciprocal nature of such agreements received considerable reinforcement when it was determined, early in the 19th century, that "the enlightenment and civilization of the Indian" might yield—quite aside from any need on the part of the United States to honor its international obligations—a certain utility in terms of subordinating North America's indigenous peoples to Euroamerican domination. Secretary of War John C. Calhoun articulated this quite clearly in 1818:

> By a proper combination of force and persuasion, of punishment and rewards, they [the Indians] ought to be brought within the pales of law and civilization. Left to themselves, they will never reach that desirable condition. Before the slow operation of reason and experience can convince them of its superior advantages, they must be overwhelmed by the mighty torrent of our population. Such small bodies, with savage customs and character, cannot, and ought not, to be allowed to exist in an independent society. Our laws and manners ought to supersede their present savage manners and customs . . . their [treaty] annuities would constitute an ample school fund; and education, comprehending as well as the common arts of life, reading, writing, and arithmetic, ought not to be left discretionary with the parents. . . . When sufficiently advanced in civilization, they would be permitted to participate in such civil and political rights as the respective States.[4]

The utter cynicism involved in Calhoun's position—that of intentionally using the treaty instruments by which the United States conveyed recognition of Indian sovereignty as the vehicle with which to destroy that same sovereignty—speaks for itself. The more important point for purposes of this study, however, is that by 1820 U.S. strategic interests had congealed around the notion of extending federal obligations to Indians. The tactic was therefore continued throughout the entirety of the period of U.S. internal territorial conquest and consolidation.[5] By 1900, the federal obligations to Indian nations were therefore quite extensive.

FINANCIAL FACTORS

As Vine Deloria, Jr., has observed:

> The original relationship between the United States government and American Indian [nations] was one of treaties. Beginning with the establishment of federal policy toward Indians in the Northwest Ordinance of 1787, which pledged that the utmost good faith would be exercised toward the Indian [nations], and continuing through many treaties and statutes, the relationship has gradually evolved into a strange and stifling union in which the United States has become responsible for all the programs and policies affecting Indian communities.[6]

What this meant in practice was that the government was being required to underwrite the cost of a proliferating bureaucratic apparatus overseeing "service delivery" to Indians, a process initiated on April 16, 1818, with the passage of an act (*U.S. Statutes at Large,* 13:461) requiring the placement of a federal agent with each Indian nation, to serve as liaison and to "administer the discharge of Governmental obligations thereto." As the number of Indian groups with which the United States held relations had increased, so too had the number of "civilizing" programs and services undertaken, ostensibly in their behalf. This was all well and good during the time-span when it was seen as a politico-military requirement, but by the turn of the century this need had passed. The situation was compounded by the fact that the era of Indian population decline engendered by war and disease had also come to an end; the population eligible for per capita benefits, which had been reduced to a quarter-million by the 1890s, could be expected to rebound steadily in the 20th century. With its land base secured, the United States was casting about for a satisfactory mechanism to avoid paying the ongoing costs associated with its acquisition.

The most obvious route to this end, of course, lay in simply and overtly refusing to comply with the terms of the treaties, thus abrogating them.[7] The problems in this regard were, however, both two-fold and extreme. First, the deliberate invalidation of the U.S. treaties with the Indians would (obviously) tend to simultaneously invalidate the legitimacy which the country attributed to its occupancy of much of North America. Second, such a move would immediately negate the useful and carefully nurtured image the U.S. had cultivated of itself as a country of progressive laws rather than raw force. The federal government had to appear to continue to meet its commitments, while at the same time avoiding them, or at least containing them at some acceptable level. A devious approach to the issue was needed.

This was found in the so-called "blood quantum" or "degree of Indian blood" standard of American Indian identification which had been adopted by Congress in 1887 as part of the General Allotment Act. The function of this piece of legislation was to expedite the process of Indian "civilization" by unilaterally dissolving their collectively (i.e., nationally) held reservation land holdings. Reservation lands were reallocated in accordance with the "superior" (i.e., Euroamerican) concept of property: *individually* deeded land parcels, usually of 160 acres each. Each Indian, identified as being those documentably of *one-half or more Indian blood,* was entitled to receive title in fee of such a parcel; all others were simply disenfranchised altogether. Reserved Indian land which remained unallotted after all "blooded" Indians had received their individual parcels was to be declared "surplus" and opened up for non-Indian use and occupancy.

Needless to say, there were nowhere near enough Indians meeting the Act's genetic requirements to absorb by individual parcel the quantity of acreage involved in the formerly reserved land areas. Consequently, between 1887 and 1934, the aggregate Indian land base within the U.S. was "legally" reduced from about 138 million acres to about 48 million.[8] Moreover, the allotment process itself had been manipulated in such a way that the worst reservation acreage tended to be parceled out to Indians, while the best was opened to non-Indian homesteading and corporate use; nearly 20 million of the acres remaining in Indian hands by the latter year were arid or semi-arid, and thus marginal or useless for agricultural purposes.[9]

By the early 1900s, then, the eugenics mechanism of the blood quantum had already proven itself such a boon in the federal management of its Indian affairs that it was generally adapted as the "eligibility factor," triggering entitlement to any federal service from the issuance of commodity rations to health care, annuity payments, and educational benefits. If the government could not repeal its obligations to Indians, it could at least act to limit their number, thereby diminishing the cost associated with underwriting their entitlements on a per capita basis. Concomitantly, it must have seemed logical that if the overall number of Indians could be kept small, the administrative expenses involved in their service programs might also be held to a minimum. Much of the original impetus toward the federal preemption of the sovereign Indian prerogative of defining "who's Indian," and the standardization of the racist degree-of-blood method of Indian identification, derived from the budgetary considerations of a federal government anxious to avoid paying its bills.

OTHER ECONOMIC FACTORS

As the example of the General Allotment Act clearly demonstrates, economic determinants other than the mere outflow of cash from the federal treasury figure into the federal utilization of the blood quantum. The huge windfall of land expropriated by the United States as a result of the act was only the tip of the iceberg. For instance, in constricting the acknowledged size of Indian populations, the government could technically meet its obligations to reserve "first rights" to water usage for Indians while simultaneously siphoning off artificial "surpluses" to non-Indian agricultural, ranching, municipal, and industrial use in the arid west.[10] The same principle pertains to the assignment of fishing quotas in the Pacific Northwest, a matter directly related to the development of a lucrative non-Indian fishing industry there.[11]

By the 1920s, it was also becoming increasingly apparent that much of the agriculturally worthless terrain left to Indians after allotment lay astride rich deposits of natural resources such as coal, copper, oil, and natural gas; later in the century, it was revealed that some 60 percent of all "domestic" uranium reserves also lay beneath reservation lands. It was therefore becoming imperative, from the viewpoint of federal and corporate economic planners, to gain unhindered access to these assets. Given that it would have been just as problematic to simply seize the resources as it would have been to abrogate the treaties, another expedient was required. This assumed the form of legislation unilaterally extending the responsibilities of citizenship (though not all the rights; Indians are still regulated by about 5,000 more laws than other citizens) over all American Indians within the United States.

> Approximately two-thirds of the Indian population had citizenship conferred upon them under the 1877 Allotment Act, as a condition of the allotment of their holdings. . . . [In 1924] an act of Congress [8 U.S.C.A. 1402 (a) (2)] declared all Indians to be citizens of the United States and of the states in which they resided. . . .[12]

The Indian Citizenship Act greatly confused the circumstances even of many of the blooded and federally certified Indians insofar as it was held to bear legal force, and to carry legal obligations, whether or not any given Indian or group of Indians wished to be a U.S. citizen. As for the host of non-certified, mixed-blood people residing in the U.S., their status was finally "clarified"; they had been definitionally absorbed into the American mainstream at the stroke of the congressional pen. And, despite the fact that the act technically left certified Indians occupying the status of citizenship in their own indigenous nation as well as in the U.S. (a "dual form" of citizenship so awkward as to be sublime), the juridical door had been opened by which the weight of Indian obligations would begin to accrue more to the U.S. than to themselves. Resource negotiations would henceforth be conducted between "American citizens" rather than between representatives of separate nations, a context in which federal and corporate arguments "for the greater good" could be predicted to prevail.

In 1934, the effects of the citizenship act were augmented by the passage of the Indian Reorganization Act. The expressed purpose of this law was finally and completely to usurp the traditional mechanisms of American Indian governance (e.g., the traditional chiefs, council of elders, etc.), replacing them with a system of federally approved and regulated "tribal councils." These councils, in turn, were consciously structured more along the lines of corporate boards than of governmental entities. As Section 17 of the IRA, which spells out the council functions, puts the matter:

> [An IRA charter] may convey to the incorporated tribe the power to purchase, take by gift, or bequest, or otherwise, own, hold, manage, operate, and dispose of property of every description, real and personal, including the power to purchase restricted Indian lands and to issue in exchange for corporate property, and such further powers as may be incidental to the conduct of corporate business, not inconsistent with the law.

Indeed, since the exercise of such typical governmental attributes as jurisdiction over criminal law had already been stripped away from the councils by legislation such as the 1885 Major Crimes Act, there has been very little for the IRA form of Indian government to do *but* sign off on leasing and other business arrangements with external interests. The situation was and is compounded by the fact that grassroots Indian resistance to the act's "acceptance" on many reservations was overcome by federal manipulation of local referenda.[13] This has left the IRA governments in the position of owing Washington rather than their supposed constituents for whatever legitimacy they may possess. All in all, it was and is a situation made to order for the rubber-stamping of plans integral to U.S. economic development at the direct expense of Indian nations and individual Indian people. This is readily borne out by the fact that, as of 1984, American Indians received, on the average, less than 20 percent of the market royalty rates (i.e., the rates paid to non-Indians) for the extraction of minerals from their land. As Winona LaDuke observes:

> By official census counts, there are only about 1½ million Indians in the United States. By conservative estimates a quarter of all the low sulphur coal in the United States lies under our reservation land. About 15 percent of all the oil and natural gas lies there, as well as two-thirds of the uranium. 100 percent of all U.S. uranium production since 1955 has been on Indian land. And we have a lot of copper, timber, water rights and other resources too. By any reasonable estimation, with this small number of people and vast amount of resources, we should be the richest group in the United States. But we are the poorest. Indians have the lowest per capita income of any population group in the U.S. We have the highest rate of unemployment and the lowest level of educational attainment. We have the highest rates of malnutrition, plague disease, death by exposure and infant mortality. On the other hand, we have the shortest life-span. Now, I think this says it all. Indian wealth is going somewhere, and that somewhere is definitely not to Indians. I don't know your definition of colonialism, but this certainly fits into mine.[14]

In sum, the financial advantages incurred by the United States in its appropriation of the definition of Indian identity have been neatly joined to even more powerful economic motivators during this century. The previously noted reluctance of the federal government to pay its bills cannot be uncoupled from its desire to profit from the resources of others.

CONTEMPORARY POLITICAL FACTORS

The utilization of treaties as instruments by which to begin the subordination of American Indian nations to U.S. hegemony, as well as subsequent legislation, such as the Major Crime Act, the General Allotment Act, and the Termination Act, all carry remarkably clear political overtones. This, to be sure, is the language of the colonizer and the colonized, to borrow a phrase from Albert Memmi,[15] and in each case the federal manipulation of the question of American Indian identity has played its role. These examples, however, may rightly be perceived as being both historical and parts of the "grand scheme" of U.S. internal colonialism (or "Manifest Destiny," as it was once called).

Today, the function of the Indian identity question appears to reside at the less rarified level of maintaining the status quo. First, it goes to the matter of keeping the aggregate number of Indians at less than 1 percent of the overall U.S. population and thus devoid of any potential electoral power. Second, and perhaps of equal importance, it goes to the classic "divide and conquer" strategy of keeping Indians at odds with one another, even within their own communities. As Tim Giago, conservative editor of the *Lakota Times,* asks:

> Don't we have enough problems trying to unite without . . . additional headaches? Why must people be categorized as full-bloods, mixed-bloods, etc? Many years ago, the Bureau of Indian Affairs decided to establish blood quanta for the purpose of [tribal] enrollment. At that time, blood quantum was set at one-fourth degree for enrollment.

> Unfortunately, through the years this caused many people on the reservation to be categorized and labeled . . . [The] situation [is] created solely by the BIA, with the able assistance of the Department of Interior.[16]

What has occurred is that the limitation of federal resources allocated to meeting U.S. obligations to American Indians has become so severe that Indians themselves have increasingly begun to enforce the race codes excluding the genetically marginalized from both identification as Indian citizens and consequent entitlements. In theory, such a posture leaves greater per capita shares for all remaining "bona fide" Indians. But, as American Indian Movement activist Russell Means has pointed out:

> The situation is absurd. Our treaties say nothing about your having to be such-and-such a degree of blood in order to be covered . . . when the federal government made its guarantees to our nations in exchange for our land, it committed to provide certain services to us as we defined ourselves. As nations, and as a *people*. This seems to have been forgotten. Now we have Indian people who spend most of their time trying to prevent other Indian people from being recognized as such, just so that a few more crumbs—crumbs from the federal table—may be available to them, personally. I don't have to tell you that this isn't the Indian way of doing things. The Indian way would be to get together and demand what is coming to each and every one of us, instead of trying to cancel each other out. We are acting like colonized peoples, like subject peoples. . . .[17]

The nature of the dispute has followed the classic formulation of Frantz Fanon, wherein the colonizer contrives issues which pit the colonized against one another, fighting viciously for some presumed status within the colonial structure, never having time or audacity enough to confront their oppressors.[18] In the words of Stella Pretty Sounding Flute, a member of the Crow Creek band of Lakota, "My grandmother used to say that Indian blood was getting all mixed up, and some day there would be a terrible mess. . . . [Now] no matter which way we turn, the white man has taken over."[19]

The problem, of course, has been conscientiously exacerbated by the government through its policies of leasing individual reservation land parcels to non-Indians, increasingly "checkerboarding" tribal holdings since 1900. Immediate economic consequences aside, this has virtually ensured that a sufficient number of non-Indians would be residents in reservations, and that intermarriage would steadily result. During the 1950s, the federal relocation program—in which reservation-based Indians were subsidized to move to cities, where they might be anticipated as being subsumed within vastly larger non-Indian populations—accelerated the process of "biological hybridization." Taken in combination with the ongoing federal insistence that "Indianness" could be measured only by degree of blood, these policies tend to speak for themselves. Even in 1972 when, through the Indian Education Act (86 *Stat.* 334), the government seemed finally to be abandoning the blood quantum, there was a hidden agenda. As Lorelei DeCora (Means), a former Indian education program coordinator, put it:

> The question was really one of control, whether Indians would ever be allowed to control the identification of their own group members or citizens. First there was this strict blood quantum thing, and it was enforced for a hundred years, over the strong objections of a lot of Indians. Then, when things were sufficiently screwed up because of that, the feds suddenly reverse themselves completely, saying it's all a matter of self-identification. Almost anybody who wants to can just walk in and announce that he or she is Indian—no familiarity with tribal history, or Indian affairs, community recognition, or anything else really required—and, under the law, there's not a lot that Indians can do about it. The whole thing is suddenly just . . . really out of control. At that point, you really did have a lot of people showing up claiming that one of their ancestors, seven steps removed, had been some sort of "Cherokee princess." And we were obliged to accept that, and provide services. Hell, if all of

> that was real, there are more Cherokees in the world than there are Chinese.[20]

Predictably, Indians of all perspectives on the identity question reacted strongly against such gratuitous dilution of themselves. The result was a broad rejection of what was perceived as "the federal attempt to convert us from being the citizens of our own sovereign nations into benign members of some sort of all-purpose U.S. 'minority group,' without sovereign rights."[21] For its part, the government, without so much as a pause to consider the connotations of the word "sovereign" in this connection, elected to view such statements as an *Indian* demand for resumption of the universal application of the blood-quantum standard. Consequently, the Reagan administration, during the 1980s, set out to gut the Indian Education Act[22] and to enforce degree-of-blood requirements for federal services, such as those of the Indian Health Service.[23]

An even clearer example of the contemporary reassertion of eugenics principles in federal Indian identification policies came under the Bush administration. On November 30, 1990, Public Law 101-644 (104 *Stat.* 4662) went into effect. Grotesquely described as "an Act to promote development of Indian arts and crafts," the statute legally restricts definition of American Indian artists to those possessing a federally issued "Certificate of Degree of Indian Blood"—derogatorally referred to as "pedigree slips" by opponents—or those certified as such by "federally recognized tribes" or the "Alaska Native Corporation." Excluded are not only those who fall below blood-quantum requirements, but anyone who has, for politico-philosophical reasons, refused to cooperate with federal pretensions to define for itself who will and who will not be considered a member and citizen of a recognized indigenous nation. Further, the entire populations of federally unrecognized nations such as the populous Lumbees of North Carolina, Abenakis of Vermont, and more than 200 others, are simply written out of existence even in terms of their internal membership identification as Indians.

In order to put "teeth" into the legislation, Congress imposed penalties of up to $1 million in fines and as much as fifteen years in a federal prison for anyone not meeting its definition to "offer to display for sale or to sell any good, with or without a Government trademark, which . . . suggests it is Indian produced." For galleries, museums, and other private concerns to display as "Indian arts or crafts" the work of any person not meeting the federal definition of Indian-ness, a fine of up to $5 million is imposed. Under such conditions, the Cherokee National Museum in Muskogee, Oklahoma, was forced to close its doors when it was discovered that even the late Willard Stone—a talented sculptor, creator of the Great Seal of the Cherokee Nation, and a probable "full blood"—had never registered himself as a bona fide Indian according to federal standards.[24] At this juncture, things have become such a welter of confusion that:

> The Federal government, State governments and the Census Bureau all have different criteria for defining "Indians" for statistical purposes, and even Federal criteria are not consistent among Federal agencies. For example, a State desiring financial aid to assist Indian education receives the aid only for the number of people with one-quarter or more Indian blood. For preference in hiring, enrollment records from a Federally recognized tribe are required. Under regulations for law and order, anyone of "Indian descent" is counted as an Indian. If the Federal criteria are inconsistent, State guidelines are [at this point] even more chaotic. In the course of preparing this report, the Commission contacted several States with large Indian populations to determine their criteria. Two States accept the individual's own determination. Four accept individuals as Indian if they were "recognized in the community" as Native Americans. Five use residence on a reservation as criteria. One requires one-quarter blood, and still another uses the Census Bureau definition that Indians are who they say they are.[25]

This, without doubt, is a situation made to order for conflict, among Indians more than anyone else. Somehow, it is exceedingly difficult to imagine that the government would wish to see things turn out any other way.

IMPLICATIONS

The eventual outcome of federal blood-quantum policies can be described as little other than genocidal in their final implications. As historian Patricia Nelson Limerick recently summarized the process:

> Set the blood quantum at one-quarter, hold to it as a rigid definition of Indians, let intermarriage proceed as it had for centuries, and eventually Indians will be defined out of existence. When that happens, the federal government will be freed of its persistent "Indian problem."[26]

Already, this conclusion receives considerable validation in the experience of the Indians of California, such as the Juaneño. Pursuant to the "Pit River Consolidated Land Settlement" of the 1970s, in which the government purported to "compensate" many of the small California bands for lands expropriated during the course of non-Indian "settlement" in that state (at less than 50 cents per acre), the Juaneño and a number of other "Mission Indians" were simply declared to be "extinct." This policy was pursued despite the fact that substantial numbers of such Indians were known to exist, and that the government was at the time issuing settlement checks to them. The tribal rolls were simply ordered closed to any new additions, despite the fact that many of the people involved were still bearing children, and their population might well have been expanding. It was even suggested in some instances that children born after an arbitrary cutoff date should be identified as "Hispanic" or "Mexican" in order that they benefit from federal and state services to minority groups.[27]

When attempting to come to grips with the issues raised by such federal policies, the recently "dissolved" California groups, as well as a number of previously unrecognized ones such as the Gay Head Wampanoags (long described as extinct), confronted a Catch-22 situation worthy of Joseph Heller. This rested in the federal criteria for recognition of Indian existence to the present day:

1. An Indian is a member of any federally recognized Indian Tribe. To be federally recognized, an Indian Tribe must be comprised of Indians.
2. To gain federal recognition, an Indian Tribe must have a land base. To secure a land base, an Indian Tribe must be federally recognized.[28]

As Shoshone activist Josephine C. Mills put it in 1964, "There is no longer any need to shoot down Indians in order to take away their rights and land [or to wipe them out] . . . legislation is sufficient to do the trick legally."[29]

The notion of genocidal implications in all this receives firm reinforcement from the increasing federal propensity to utilize residual Indian land bases as dumping grounds for many of the more virulently toxic by-products of its advanced technology and industry.[30] By the early '70s, this practice had become so pronounced that the Four Corners and Black Hills regions, two of the more heavily populated locales (by Indians) in the country, had been semi-officially designated as prospective "National Sacrifice Areas" in the interests of projected U.S. energy development.[31] This, in turn, provoked Russell Means to observe that such a move would turn the Lakota, Navajo, Laguna, and other native nations into "national sacrifice peoples."[32]

AMERICAN INDIAN RESPONSE

Of late, there have been encouraging signs that American Indians of many perspectives and political persuasions have begun to arrive at common conclusions regarding the use to which the federal government had been putting their identity and the compelling need for Indians to finally reassert complete control over this vital aspect of their lives. For instance, Dr. Frank Ryan, a liberal and rather establishmentarian Indian who has served as the director of the federal

Office of Indian Education, began during the early 1980s to reach some rather hard conclusions about the policies of his employers. Describing the federal blood-quantum criteria for benefits eligibility in the educational arena as "a racist policy," Ryan went on to term it nothing more than "a shorthand method for denying Indian children admission to federal schools [and other programs]."[33] He concluded that, "The power to determine tribal membership has always been an essential attribute of inherent tribal sovereignty," and called for abolition of federal guidelines on the question of Indian identity without *any* lessening of federal obligations to the individuals and groups affected.[34] The question of the (re)adoption of blood-quantum standards by the Indian Health Service, proposed during the '80s by the Reagan administration, has served as even more of a catalyst. The National Congress of American Indians, never a bastion of radicalism, took up the issue at its 43rd Annual Convention, in October 1986. The NCAI produced a sharply worded statement rejecting federal identification policy:

> [T]he federal government, in an effort to erode tribal sovereignty and reduce the number of Indians to the point where they are politically, economically and culturally insignificant, [is being censured by] many of the more than 500 Indian leaders [attending the convention].[35]

The statement went on to condemn:

> . . . a proposal by the Indian Health Service to establish blood quotas for Indians, thus allowing the federal government to determine who is Indian and who is not, for the purpose of health care. Tribal leaders argue that *only* the individual tribe, not the federal government, should have this right, and many are concerned that this debate will overlap [as it has, long since] into Indian education and its regulation as well [emphasis added].[36]

Charles E. Dawes, Second Chief of the Ottawa Indian Tribe of Oklahoma, took the convention position much further at about the same time:

> What could not be completed over a three hundred year span [by force of arms] may now be completed in our life-span by administrative law. . . What I am referring to is the continued and expanded use of blood quantum to determine eligibility of Indian people for government entitlement programs . . . [in] such areas as education, health care, management and economic assistance . . . [obligations] that the United States government imposed upon itself in treaties with sovereign Indian nations. . . . We as tribal leaders made a serious mistake in accepting [genetic] limits in educational programs, and we must not make the same mistake again in health programs. On the contrary, we must fight any attempt to limit any program by blood quantum every time there is mention of such a possibility . . . we simply cannot give up on this issue—ever. . . . Our commitment as tribal leaders must be to eliminate any possibility of *genocide* for our people by administrative law. We must dedicate our efforts to insuring that . . . Native American people[s] will be clearly identified without reference to blood quantum . . . and that our sovereign Indian Nations will be recognized as promised [emphasis added].[37]

On the Pine Ridge Reservation in South Dakota, the Oglala Lakota have become leaders in totally abandoning blood quantum as a criterion for tribal enrollment, opting instead to consider factors such as residency on the reservation, affinity to and knowledge of, as well as service to the Oglala people.[38] This follows the development of a recent "tradition" of Oglala militancy in which tribal members played a leading role in challenging federal conceptions of Indian identity during the 1972 Trail of Broken Treaties takeover of BIA headquarters in Washington, and seven non-Indian members of the Vietnam Veterans Against the War were naturalized as citizens of the "Independent Oglala Nation" during the 1973 siege of Wounded Knee.[39] In 1986, at a meeting of the United Sioux Tribes in Pierre, South Dakota, Oglala representatives lobbied the leaders of other Lakota reservations to broaden their own enrollment criteria beyond federal norms. This is so, despite recognition that "in the past fifty years, since the Indian Reorganization Act of 1934, tribal leaders have been reluctant to recognize blood from individuals from other tribes [or any one else]."[40]

In Alaska, the Haida have produced a new draft constitution which offers a full expression of indigenous sovereignty, at least insofar as the identity of citizenry is concerned. The Haida draft begins with those who are now acknowledged as members of the Haida nation and posits that all those who marry Haidas will also be considered eligible for naturalized citizenship (just as in any other nation). The children of such unions would also be Haida citizens from birth, regardless of their degree of Indian blood, and children adopted by Haidas would also be considered citizens.[41] On Pine Ridge, a similar "naturalization" plank had surfaced in the 1983 TREATY platform upon which Russell Means attempted to run for the Oglala Lakota tribal presidency before being disqualified at the insistence of the BIA.[42]

An obvious problem that might be associated with this trend is that even though Indian nations have begun to recognize their citizens by their own standards rather than those of the federal government, the government may well refuse to recognize the entitlement of unblooded tribal members to the same services and benefits as any other. In fact, there is every indication that this is the federal intent, and such a disparity of "status" stands to heighten tensions among Indians, destroying their fragile rebirth of unity and solidarity before it gets off the ground. Federal policy in this regard is, however, also being challenged.

Most immediately, this concerns the case of Dianne Zarr, an enrolled member of the Sherwood Valley Pomo Band of Indians, who is of less than one-quarter degree of Indian blood. On September 11, 1980, Zarr filed an application for higher educational grant benefits, and was shortly rejected as not meeting quantum requirements. Zarr went through all appropriate appeal procedures before filing, on July 15, 1983, a suit in federal court, seeking to compel award of her benefits. This was denied by the district court on April 2, 1985. Zarr appealed and, on September 26, 1985, the lower court was reversed on the basis of the "Snyder Act" (25 U.S.C. S297), which precludes discrimination based solely on racial criteria.[43] Zarr received her grant, setting a very useful precedent for the future.

Still, realizing that the utility of the U.S. courts will necessarily be limited, a number of Indian organizations have recently begun to seek to bring international pressure to bear on the federal government. The Indian Law Resource Center, National Indian Youth Council, and, for a time, the International Indian Treaty Council have repeatedly taken Native American issues before the United Nations Working Group on Indigenous Populations (a component of the U.N. Commission on Human Rights) in Geneva, Switzerland, since 1977. Another forum that has been utilized for this purpose has been the Fourth Russell International Tribunal on the Rights of the Indians of the Americas, held in Rotterdam, Netherlands, in 1980. Additionally, delegations from various Indian nations and organizations have visited, often under auspices of the host governments, more than thirty countries during the past decade.[44]

CONCLUSION

The history of the U.S. imposition of its standards of identification upon American Indians is particularly ugly. Its cost to Indians has involved millions of acres of land, the water by which to make much of this land agriculturally useful, control over vast mineral resources that might have afforded them a comfortable standard of living, and the ability to form themselves into viable and meaningful political blocks at any level. Worse, it has played a prominent role in bringing about their generalized psychic disempowerment; if one is not allowed even to determine for one's self, or within one's peer group, the answer to the all-important question "Who am I?," what possible personal power can one feel s/he possesses? The negative impact, both physically and psychologically, of this process upon succeeding generations of Native Americans in the United States is simply incalculable.

The blood-quantum mechanism most typically used by the federal government to assign identification to individuals over the years is as racist as any conceivable policy. It has brought about the systematic marginalization and eventual exclusion of many more Indians from their own cultural/national designation than it has retained. This is all the more apparent when one considers that, while one-quarter degree of blood has been the norm used in defining *Indian-ness,* the quantum has varied from time to time and place to place; one-half blood was the standard utilized in the case of the Mississippi Choctaws and adopted in the Wheeler-Howard Act; one sixty-fourth was utilized in establishing the Santee rolls in Nebraska. It is hardly unnatural, under the circumstances, that federal policy has set off a ridiculous game of one-upmanship in Indian Country: "I'm more Indian than you" and "You aren't Indian enough to say (or do, or think) that" have become common assertions during the second half of the 20th century.

The restriction of federal entitlement funds to cover only the relatively few Indians who meet quantum requirements, essentially a cost-cutting policy at its inception, has served to exacerbate tensions over the identity issue among Indians. It has established a scenario in which it has been perceived as profitable for one Indian to cancel the identity of her/his neighbor as means of receiving her/his entitlement. Thus, a bitter divisiveness has been built into Indian communities and national policies, sufficient to preclude our achieving the internal unity necessary to offer any serious challenge to the status quo. At every turn, U.S. practice vis-à-vis American Indians is indicative of an advanced and extremely successful system of colonialism.

Fortunately, increasing numbers of Indians are waking up to the fact that this is the case. The recent analysis and positions assumed by such politically diverse Indian nations, organizations, and individuals as Frank Ryan and Russell Means, the National Congress of American Indians and the Indian Law Resource Center, the Haida and the Oglala are a very favorable sign. The willingness of the latter two nations simply to defy federal standards and adopt identification and enrollment policies in line with their own interests and traditions is particularly important. Recent U.S. court decisions, such as that in the *Zarr* case, and growing international attention and concern over the circumstances of Native Americans are also hopeful indicators that things may be at long last changing for the better.

We are currently at a crossroads. If American Indians are able to continue the positive trend in which we reassert our sovereign prerogative to control the criteria of our own membership, we may reasonably assume that we will be able to move onward, into a true process of decolonization and reestablishment of ourselves as functioning national entities. The alternative, of course, is that we will fail, continue to be duped into bickering over the question of "who's Indian" in light of federal guidelines, and thus facilitate not only our own continued subordination, expropriation, and colonization, but ultimately our own statistical extermination.

NOTES

1. Kappler, Charles J., ed., *Indian Treaties, 1778–1883,* Interland Publishing Co., New York, (Second Printing) 1973, pp. 3–5.
2. Ibid., pp. 7–9.
3. Adams, Evelyn C., *American Indian Education: Government Schools and Economic Progress,* King's Crown Press, New York, 1946, pp. 30–31.
4. Calhoun is quoted in *American State Papers: Indian Affairs* (Volume II), Wilmington, DE, 1972, pp. 183–84.
5. The bulk of the obligations in question were established prior to Congress' 1871 suspension of treaty-making with "the tribes" (Title 25, Section 71, U.S. Code). Additional obligations were

undertaken by the federal government thereafter by "agreement" and as part of its ongoing agenda of completing the socio-political subordination of Indians, with an eye toward their eventual "assimilation" into the dominant culture and polity.

6. Deloria, Vine, Jr., "The Place of Indians in Contemporary Education," *American Indian Journal,* Vol. 2, No. 21, February, 1976, p. 2.
7. This strategy was actually tried in the wake of the passage of the House Concurrent Resolution 108 in June 1953. Predictably, the federal dissolution of American Indian nations such as the Klamath and Menominee so tarnished the U.S. image that implementation of the policy was shortly suspended (albeit the law remains on the books).
8. Collier, John, *Memorandum, Hearings on H.B. 7902 Before the House Committee on Indian Affairs,* (73rd Cong., 2d Sess.), U.S. Department of the Interior, Washington, DC, 1934, pp. 16–18.
9. Deloria, Vine, Jr., and Clifford M. Lytle, *American Indians, American Justice,* University of Texas Press, Austin, 1983, p. 10.
10. See Hundley, Norris C., Jr., "The Dark and Bloody Ground of Indian Water Rights," in Roxanne Dunbar Ortiz and Larry Emerson, eds., *Economic Development in Indian Reservations,* University of New Mexico Press, Albuquerque, 1979.
11. See American Friends Service Committee, *Uncommon Controversy: Fishing Rights of the Muckleshoot, Puyallup, and Nisqually Indians,* University of Washington Press, Seattle, 1970. Also see Cohen, Fay G., *Treaties on Trial: The Continuing Controversy over Northwest Indian Fishing Rights,* University of Washington Press, Seattle, 1986.
12. League of Women Voters, *Indian Country,* Publication No. 605, Washington, DC, 1977, p. 24.
13. Probably the best overview of the IRA process may be found in Deloria, Vine, Jr., and Clifford M. Lytle, *The Nations Within: The Past and Future of American Indian Sovereignty,* Pantheon Press, New York, 1984; on referenda fraud, see chapter 11.
14. LaDuke, Winona, presentation at International Women's Week activities, University of Colorado at Boulder, March 13, 1984; tape on file.
15. Memmi, Albert, *The Colonizer and the Colonized,* Beacon Press, Boston, 1967.
16. Giago, Tim, "Blood Quantum Is a Degree of Discrimination," *Notes From Indian Country,* Vol. 1, State Publishing Co., Pierre, SD, 1984, p. 337.
17. Means, Russell, speech at the law school of the University of Colorado at Boulder, April 19, 1985; tape on file.
18. See Fanon, Frantz, *The Wretched of the Earth,* Grove Press, New York, 1966.
19. Quoted in Martz, Ron, "Indians decry verification plan for federally-funded health care," *Cox News Service,* Pierre, SD, October 7, 1986.
20. DeCora (Means), Lorelei, statement on radio station KILI, Porcupine, SD, October 12, 1986.
21. Means, Ted, statement before the South Dakota Indian Education Association, Pierre, SD, November 16, 1975.
22. See Jones, Richard, *American Indian Policy: Selected Major Issues in the 98th Congress,* Issue Brief No. 1B83083, Library of Congress, Government Division, Washington, DC (updated version, February 6, 1984), pp. 3–4.
23. Martz, op. cit.
24. Nichols, Lyn, "New Indian Art Regulations Shut Down Muskogee Museum," *San Francisco Examiner,* December 3, 1990.
25. American Indian Policy Review Commission, *Final Report,* Vol. 1, May 17, 1977, U.S. Government Printing Office, Washington, DC, 1977, p. 89.
26. Limerick, Patricia Nelson, *The Legacy of Conquest: The Unbroken Past of the American West,* W. W. Norton and Co., New York, 1987, p. 338.
27. The author is an enrolled Juaneño, as is her eldest son. Her younger son, born after the closing of the Juaneño rolls, is not "federally recognized" as an Indian, despite the fact that his genealogy, cultural background, etc., is identical to that of his brother. The "suggestions" mentioned in the text were made to the author by a federal employee in 1979. The Juaneño band in California, in the 1990s, is initiating federal recognition procedures.
28. Native American Consultants, Inc., *Indian Definition Study,* contracted pursuant to P.L. 95-561, Title IV, Section 1147, submitted to the Office of the Assistant Secretary of Education, U.S. Department of Education, Washington, DC, January 1980, p. 2.
29. Quoted in Armstrong, Virginia I., *I Have Spoken: American History Through the Voices of Indians,* Pocket Books, New York, 1975, p. 175.

PERSONAL ACCOUNT

Shopping with a Friend

My best friend and I decided that we wanted to take pictures together in the photo booth in our local mall. Taking pictures meant buying new outfits. So we decided to go shopping at a center downtown one day after school. We picked a store and began our search.

We browsed for a bit before deciding to try on two items each. That afternoon, there was only one sales associate working. My friend and I had to wait for what seemed like five minutes before we could get her attention to request to use the dressing room. She quickly checked what we had and handed us a ticket listing the number of clothing items. She motioned for us to go into the dressing room as she continued her telephone conversation.

While we were trying on our clothes, my friend suddenly realized that she had to be home within the next half-hour. That meant we had to hurry up because we had to catch the bus. We put the clothes back on the hangers and left the dressing room. We tried to get the sales associate's attention to show her that we had returned the clothes to the rack outside the dressing room, but she was too involved in her telephone conversation to notice us.

On our way out, my friend wanted to stop briefly in the adjoining store. Shortly after we entered, I felt a hand on *my* shoulder. A security guard was standing directly behind me. He said to me in a very authoritative voice, "Come with me, please." He brought me back to the store we had just left. My friend followed. The sales associate approached us and said to me in a very accusatory tone of voice, "Where are the clothes that you tried on?" At that point, my heart was pounding. She thinks I stole the clothes, I thought to myself. I just prayed that the clothes were still where I left them. Otherwise, it would be my word again against hers. I walked toward the rack. At first I did not see them. That happens sometimes in panicky situations. Thank God my best friend saw them and said, "They are right there." I handed the clothes to the sales associate, who snatched them away and left in a huff. No apology, no thank you, nothing.

I have often heard the saying "Nothing is a black-or-white issue." My situation was obviously the exception. In terms of black and white, I am black, my best friend appears to be white—although she is black and white—and the sales associate is white. That explains why I was questioned and not my friend.

What bothers me most is that the sales associate truly felt that she did not owe me an apology. She considered her actions to be completely justified. I would not have been as mad if she had told the security guard that *two* teenage girls might have stolen some clothing, but she did not do that. She singled me out simply because I am black. In addition, my best friend looked at the situation as merely a misunderstanding, Also, she could not be supportive in an empathetic way because she had never been subjected to that kind of treatment. Although it happened three years ago, retelling the story still brings back all the anger, embarrassment, and frustration that I felt on that day.

Rashonda Ambrose

30. See Churchill, Ward, "American Indian Lands: The Native Ethic amid Resource Development," *Environment,* Vol. 28, No. 6, July/August 1986, pp. 12–17, 28–33.
31. Ibid.
32. Means, Russell, "The Same Old Song," in Ward Churchill, ed., *Marxism and Native Americans,* South End Press, Boston, 1983, p. 25.
33. Ryan, Frank A., *A Working Paper Prepared for the National Advisory Committee on Indian Education,* Paper No. 071279, Harvard American Indian Education Program, Harvard University Graduate School of Education, Cambridge, MA, July 18, 1979, p. 3.
34. Ibid., pp. 41–44.
35. Quoted in Martz, Ron, "Indians maintain U.S. trying to erode tribal sovereignty: cultural insignificance said to be goal," *Cox News Service,* Pierre, SD, October 26, 1986.
36. Quoted in Martz, Ron, "Indians decry verification plan for federally-funded health care," *Cox News Service,* Pierre, SD, October 26, 1986.
37. Dawes, Charles E., "Tribal leaders see danger in use of blood quantum as eligibility standard," *The Uset Calumet,* Nashville, TN, February/March, 1986, pp. 7–8.
38. "Indians decry verification plan for federally-funded health care," op. cit.

39. On the Trail of Broken Treaties challenge, see Editors, *BIA, I'm Not Your Indian Any More, Akwesasne Notes,* Mohawk Nation via Rooseveltown, NY, 1973, p. 78. On VVAW naturalization, see Burnette, Robert, and John Koster, *The Road to Wounded Knee,* Bantam Books, New York, 1974, p. 238.
40. "Indians maintain U.S. trying to erode tribal sovereignty," op. cit.
41. Draft, Haida Constitution, circa 1982, xerox copy provided to the author by Pam Colorado.
42. *TREATY: The Campaign of Russell Means for the Presidency of the Oglala Sioux Tribe,* Porcupine, SD, 1982, p. 3.
43. *Zarr v. Barlow, et al.,* No. 85-2170, U.S. Ninth Circuit Court of Appeals, District Court for the Northern District of California, Judge John P. Vukasin presiding.
44. These have included Austria, Cuba, Nicaragua, Poland, East Germany, Hungary, Rumania, Switzerland, Algeria, Grenada, El Salvador, Colombia, Tunisia, Libya, Syria, Jordan, Iran, the Maori of New Zealand, New Aotara (Australia), Belize, Mexico, Costa Rica, Guinea, Kenya, Micronesia, the USSR, Finland, Norway, Sweden, Canada, Great Britain, Netherlands, France, Belgium, Japan, West Germany, Bulgaria, Yugoslavia, and Papua (New Guinea). The list here is undoubtedly incomplete.

READING 6

La Raza and the Melting Pot

A Comparative Look at Multiethnicity

Carlos A. Fernández

LATIN AMERICA: LA RAZA CÓSMICA[1]

. . . The year 1992 marks the 500th anniversary of the accidental discovery of the Americas by Columbus under the sponsorship of the Catholic Spanish monarchs Isabella and Fernando. In the United States, we refer to the commemoration of this discovery as Columbus Day. In parts of Latin America, however, they celebrate El Día de la Raza (the Day of the [New Mixed] Race). The different names for the same observance illustrate one of the most fundamental cultural, historical, and even philosophical differences between the United States and Latin America, namely, the way we view race and interracial mixture.[2]

Many Americans are unaware of the "racial" history of Latin America. Evidence for this can be found in the fact that people of Latin American origin or ancestry are included as "Whites" in the U.S. Census, and since about 1980 have come to be referred to as "Hispanic," that is, European (Muñoz, 1989). What is the truth of the matter?

MEXICO AND MEXICANS

. . . The racial history of Mexico out of which Mexican Americans have emerged starts with Native Americans. An estimated 25 million Native Americans, the largest concentration in the hemisphere, lived in the region of Mexico and Central America at the time of the Spanish invasion (MacLachlan & Rodríguez O, 1980). The Spanish eventually conquered the Mexica[3] (Aztec) capital city, Tenochtitlán, in 1522, not by superior arms, nor by disease, which took its heavy toll later, but by their ability to muster a huge army of non-Mexica indigenous peoples eager to rid themselves of their reputedly oppressive overlords. The conquest of the Aztec empire was not just a Spanish conquest, but also a Spanish-led indigenous revolt (White, 1971).

Upon the Spanish-Indian alliance's success, the Spanish soldiery and the Native American ruling classes, including what remained of the Mexicas, established mutually agreeable social and political ties, secured in many cases by intermarriage with noble families. The first mestizos born of these relationships were not products of rape; they were acknowledged as "Spanish" or "Creoles" by their Spanish fathers. Of course, the

---

No biographical material available.

ordinary Native Americans who constituted the masses of the people were not privy to any of these transactions. Indeed, rape and concubinage befell many indigenous commoner women; their children became the first "illegitimate" mestizos. During this early era, the "purely" Spanish constituted approximately 3–5% of the total population, and never grew beyond an estimated 10% throughout the subsequent history of Mexico (MacLachlan & Rodríguez O, 1980; Morner, 1970).

From the beginning of Spanish colonialism, Indian slaves in large numbers were employed in the silver mines. In 1523, the first foreign-origin slaves were introduced to Mexico, mainly as servants. These first slaves were a collection of Spanish Moslems—Arabs, Berbers, Moors (a mixed people of Arab, Berber, and Black African ancestry)—and *ladino* Blacks, that is, Blacks who had been slaves in Spain or one of its colonies prior to arriving in Mexico (MacLachlan & Rodríguez O, 1980). With the opening up of the large coastal plantations, however, the Spanish turned to the principal region in the world where slaves were being offered for sale in significant numbers at the time, the coast of Africa.

The number of African slaves increased dramatically in Mexico between 1530 and 1700. By the middle of the eighteenth century, African and part-African people were the second largest component of the Mexican population. Only the Native Americans had a larger population. Several individuals of acknowledged part-African ancestry played prominent roles in Mexican history; for example, the Independence hero Vicente Guerrero, for whom a state is named (MacLachlan & Rodríguez O, 1980).

Toward the end of the eighteenth century, the mestizo population began to increase more rapidly. By 1800, it overtook the African and part-African groups, who were increasingly absorbed into the mestizo population. By 1900, the mestizos had become the largest ethnic group in Mexico.

Although the 1921 census was the last in which racial classifications were used in Mexico, some estimates are that mestizos (which in practice became a catchall term for all mixtures) today constitute some 85–90% of the Mexican population and Native Americans some 8–10%, with Europeans, mainly Spanish, making up the rest of the total (Morner, 1970). These estimates are highly suspect, however, a fact generally acknowledged by Mexican demographers, because *Indian* has come to mean "someone who speaks an Indian language" or who "lives like an Indian," that is, who is poor. The fact is, many biological Indians have become cultural mestizos who speak Spanish, and hence are regarded as mestizos. There are also many "Indians" and "Spanish" who are actually of mixed ancestry (Morner, 1970). This ambiguity serves to highlight the absurdity and practical irrelevance of racial categories in Mexico today. . . .

LA RAZA CÓSMICA VERSUS THE MELTING POT

The prevailing attitude toward race among the masses throughout Latin America might be summarized as comparative indifference. Of course, this is far from concluding that the region is the exaggerated stereotype of a "racial paradise." Indeed, by observing the disproportion of darker people in the lower classes and of lighter people in the upper classes, one might be led to conclude that race is at least as much of an active principle in Latin America as it is in the United States. But this is not quite true. For example, how is it that the Mexicans could elect a full-blooded Indian, Benito Juárez, as their president around the time of the U.S. Civil War? How is it that Peruvians of today elected an Asian their president? Many Mexican and other Latin American leaders have been and are of mixed blood. Then what explains the apparent tie between race and class in Latin America?

Many sociologists have long noted that in the absence of effective countermeasures, poverty and wealth alike tend to be inherited (Harris, 1971, chap. 18). Thus in Latin America the caste form of racism that was the hallmark of its colonial past has become ensconced, even though legal racial discrimination has long since been done away with. Add to this the blurring of racial lines on a large scale over hundreds of years, such that customary forms of discrimination based on actual ancestry have been rendered impotent. Taken together, these factors are what is usually meant by the observation that the race question in Latin America has by and large been transformed into a socioeconomic issue (Morner, 1970).

It needs to be said, however, that active remnants of attitudinal racism persist. One of these presents itself as "colorism" or even "featurism," neither of which requires proof of actual ancestry to be operative. Professor G. Reginald Daniel of the University of California, Los Angeles, very aptly terms this phenomenon a "recapitulation of racism" (personal communication, February 1991). To what extent this attitude affects whatever social mobility is available to poor people of any phenotype in Latin America remains to be definitively measured. Some evidence for it can be seen in the disproportion of European-looking models and actors in the Latin American media, although another, probably coexistent, explanation for this is that, for socioeconomic reasons, access to the media is easier for the predominantly lighter elite. There is also a conservative tendency to ape the European and U.S. media.

Another remnant of racism can be heard in many derogatory expressions that include the term *indio* (or other, usually vulgar, terms for Black). Though originally directed at *indios,* these epithets have become generalized insults often used even by their supposed objects, the purely racist feeling having been muted or lost (as, for instance, we might use the expression "welshed"). However, in those districts where Native American communities remain relatively intact, such as in the Yucatán, the Andes, and the many isolated mountain settlements throughout Latin America, these expressions still carry their hard edge and reflect a real, present-day situation of unresolved interethnic conflict and outright oppression.

In the United States, it is the biological aspect of race and racial mixture that is essential to racist thinking, quite apart from any other consideration. This attitude finds expression in the failure of our society and its institutions officially to acknowledge racial mixture, potentially the basis for a unifying national identity and a crucial step for breaking down traditional lines of social separation. Such an important omission unnecessarily contributes to the perpetuation of ethnic divisiveness in U.S. society.

HISTORICALLY EVOLVED CULTURAL FACTORS

Since both the United States and Latin America came into existence from the same expansionary impulse of a Europe reawakening out of medievalism, what might explain the contrasting attitudes regarding race and race mixture?

Sex Ratio Differences

An important difference between the Anglo-dominated colonization of North America and the Iberian conquest of Central and South America was that the Spanish and Portuguese came primarily as soldiers and priests, while the British (and Dutch) came as religious rebels and farmers. That is to say, the Iberians had proportionally fewer of their countrywomen with them than did the Anglos. Thus sexual relations occurred more frequently between the Iberians and the indigenous and African slave women, and, consequently, the numbers of "mixed" people began to increase in Latin America relative to Anglo America right from the outset.

Because interracial unions were less common in Anglo America, their rare occurrence was regarded as aberrational and, hence, in a religiously puritanical milieu where anything unusual was cause for alarm, deeply sinful. On the other hand, while the Catholic church was not at all tolerant of any sexual relations outside of marriage, interracial sexual relations within the bounds of marriage were permitted and at times even encouraged. Nevertheless, the vast majority of interracial sexual relations occurred outside of marriage in Latin America, to the extent that the very terms for a mixed person, *mestizo* and *mulato,* became synonyms for *bastard.*[4] In Mexico, use of the term *mestizo* was not really legitimized until the Revolution of 1910. Today it is regarded by most Mexicans as an honorable badge of national identity (if it is given any thought at all) (Páz, 1950/1961).

Racial Classifications

Another striking difference between Anglo and Latin America can be seen in the systems of racial classification. In Anglo America, no mixed category has ever existed officially, except as a means for assigning all people of any discernible African ancestry to the status of "Negro." This principle of classifying Blacks has been referred to as the "one-drop rule." In common parlance, terms such as *mulatto, Eurasian,* and *half-breed* (or simply *breed*) have been used, but never adopted as ongoing racial categories.[5] This institutional refusal to make a place for a racially mixed identity is strong evidence for the visceral abhorrence of race mixture in U.S. culture. Further evidence can be seen in that peculiar rule of "check one box only" with which multiethnic children and adults are constantly confronted (which parent and heritage shall be denied today?).

In Latin America, on the other hand, elaborate racial taxonomies gained official recognition from the outset, drawing on Spain's own national experience. Some of these have already been mentioned. In the Spanish colonies, these *casta* designations became distinct identities unto themselves, with legal rights as well as disabilities attaching to each.[6] Most, if not all, of Spain's colonies abolished the *casta* system upon their independence. Classifications based on race persisted in some official documents, but discriminatory application of laws based on race was forbidden, something that did not occur in the United States until the middle of the twentieth century. Today, given the large degree of mixture in the Latin American countries, racial classifications are virtually meaningless and hence, for the most part, are no longer used. . . .

The Native Americans, North and South

The difference in the size and nature of the Native American populations in Anglo and Latin America also helps account for the emergence of different attitudes about race. In that part of North America in which the English, Dutch, and others settled, the indigenous peoples were by and large nomadic or seminomadic and not very numerous. Moreover, the socioeconomic and technological distance between the settlers and the indigenous peoples they encountered allowed the settlers from England and other parts of Northwestern Europe to regard surviving Native Americans as savages, mere objects of the wilderness to be moved out of the way. The Anglos, for the most part, felt they had little reason to respect Native Americans (notwithstanding later maudlin stories about the "noble savage"), nor did they feel any need to compromise with them, or to abide by the few compromises that were made.

Entire peoples were segregated, forcibly removed, or exterminated. The occasional exceptions to this history of genocide are few and far between. Although some intermarriage occurred, and some native peoples managed to survive in various desperate, ingenious, and often fortuitous ways, the major outcome was the virtual disappearance of Native Americans as a significant part of North American society.

In those parts of the Americas to which the Spanish came, particularly Mexico and Peru, the indigenous peoples lived a settled, advanced (even by European standards) agricultural life with large cities and developed class systems. They were also very numerous, despite the estimated disease mortality rate of nearly 90% following the first contacts with Europeans.

Eliminating them, even if the idea had occurred to the Spanish, would probably have been impossible. Instead, the Spanish found it advantageous to graft their feudal society onto the semifeudal structures of the Native American civilizations already in place. Spaniards, in the absence of their countrywomen, married into Indian ruling-class families, thereby acquiring key kinship ties to the various peoples composing the Mexican and Incan empires. In short, the Spanish integrated themselves and their culture into communities of civilized (defined as above, in terms of relative technological and socioeconomic development) peoples. Instead of genocide, they opted for a more profitable (and brutally exploitative) *modus vivendi.*

In contrast to the Anglo settlers, many, though not all, of the Spanish came to regard the Native Americans as people rather than savages.[7] The Catholic church itself eventually recognized this and, in theory at least, maintained that an Indian could become the spiritual equal of a Spaniard, if only he or she converted to Christianity. Of course, there was no question about who was superior in secular life, but the very idea of making a place for the Native American in Spanish colonial society demonstrated an attitude far different from the outright genocidal policies carried out further to the north. This difference resulted in a greater permissiveness in the Iberians regarding miscegenation, an attitude that was to some extent generalized to include Africans.

Race Consciousness and "Scientific" Racism

A major ideological difference between the United States and Latin America respecting race and race consciousness is a result of the development of "race theory," a pseudoscientific expression of social Darwinism in the nineteenth century. It is this theory and concept of race to which most Americans have become accustomed, particularly in the form of the "three-race theory" (King, 1981; Stepan, 1982). It is also the basis of modern racism.[8]

Whereas the idea that the human species might be divided up into distinct subspecies marked by skin color or other superficial features had occurred before, it was not until the scientific revolution that accompanied the Industrial Revolution in Europe and North America that such divisions were elevated to the status of "science." The first outstanding proponent of the race theory was the Count Gobineau, a petty French noble among whose occupations had been an ambassadorship in Rio de Janeiro from 1868 to 1870. Of that stay, he once wrote, revealingly: "This is not a country to my taste. An entirely Mulatto population, corrupted in body and soul, ugly to a terrifying degree" (quoted in Morner, 1967). His *Essay on the Inequality of the Human Races* became the starting point for a long line of intellectual racists, culminating in the atrocities of the Nazi death camps (Biddess, 1970). Other Europeans and Americans of European ancestry took up the race theory with relish, perhaps noting how conveniently it displaced onto "nature" human responsibility for discriminatory laws and practices, the drawing of territorial borders, the annexation and government of non-Europeans in the interests of overseas commercial empires, and so forth.

Today, most anthropologists reject traditional race theory, though their continued occasional use of its terminology betrays its stubborn influence, and remains a source of ongoing debate. Reputable anthropologists will typically use the alternative term *population* to refer to groupings of humans having various genetic frequencies. But these groups are predefined by the researcher, their boundaries changing depending on what it is that he or she wishes to study. When discussing the very real sociocultural distinctions that exist among human societies, terms such as *tribe, ethnic group, class,* and *religion* are preferred. These labels do not suffer from the disabilities of the term *race* because they are acknowledged to be artifices of humankind, with no pretense or implication of being "natural."

In the nineteenth century, pseudoscientific concepts of race had a decisive influence on the public mind in Europe and the United States, an influence that continues right down to the present. On the other hand, though race theory was disseminated and discussed among the intelligentsia in Latin America, it never caught on among the masses of the people in the same way as it did here. The reasons for this different receptivity have much to do with the various historically evolved cultural factors reviewed above.

Demographic Differences

The outcome of the differing conditions outlined above brings us finally to the most important difference between Latin and Anglo America with regard to race: the fact that people of mixed racial ancestry came to form a much greater proportion of the population in Latin America than in Anglo America. This simple fact meant that, in varying degrees, race was neutralized as a significant social issue (or at least transformed into a class issue) throughout much of Latin America while it remains one of the most salient features of North American life.

Mexican Americans in the Melting Pot

The United States is poised to integrate the greatest diversity of ethnic groups across all traditional "race" lines that the world has yet seen. As the "browning of America" accelerates through the course of the next few decades, the question of race in all its dimensions will have to be resolved. With their numbers rapidly growing, Mexican Americans, together with their Latino cousins, will undoubtedly exercise an increasing influence on the future development of U.S. culture. Indeed, that influence has already occurred in our folk culture—witness the all-American cowboy, originally the *vaquero,* the Mexican mestizo ranch hand of what is now the American Southwest.

But perhaps the most important contribution is yet to come, that is, in the reshaping of our attitudes about race and especially about race mixture. As the bearers of Latin America's historico-cultural experience and familiar with the ways of U.S. society, Mexican Americans are uniquely positioned to upset the traditional Anglo-American taboo against "race mixing" by merely reaffirming their heritage. Concretely, Chicanos and their Latino cousins are also favorably positioned to mediate alliances among the various racial and ethnic groups that make up the U.S. population, something the African American group, for all its accomplishments, could not do, defined as it was (and is still) by the dominant White culture. Latinos, and especially Mexican Americans, have been conditioned by their history, however imperfectly and unevenly, to accept racial ambiguity and mixture as "normal." This attitude might be of enormous benefit to all of us in the United States. First, the race question may be neutralized and energies redirected to other pressing socioeconomic issues. Second, the principle of *mestizaje,* or "multicultural synthesis," as a social norm, a truer expression of the old melting-pot thesis, can free us all from the limits of ethnocentrism by opening us up to a wider repertoire of cultural elements, thereby stimulating our creativity to the fullest. From this, we can reap economic as well as psychological benefits. As a society, we will then be especially well suited to shape the ongoing emergence of a truly global community.

Unfortunately, it must be noted here that the pervasiveness of U.S. culture in Latin America as well as the assimilation of Latin American immigrants into it within this country has had some effect of instilling U.S.-style race consciousness. Thus some Latin Americans will adopt views against intermarriage or repeat what racist Whites say about African and Asian Americans, or even Latin Americans of nationalities different from their own.[9] There are also some who will insist on the purity of their Spanish ancestry and culture, by which they mean White, European ancestry, especially if they are phenotypically light-skinned, even though, for most, such hoped-for purity is extremely dubious.[10] The self-proclaimed "Hispanic" who has definite

African or Native American features is particularly absurd and foolish.

Which way will the Latino community go? Nonracial ethnocentrism? Anglo conformity? *Hispanidad? Indigenismo?* Afrocentrism? Or *mestizaje?* The decision must be made. In this society, deeply scarred by racism, evading the issue will prove useless. Latinos cannot avoid the reality of their mixed identity without losing themselves. In the process of asserting their mixed identity, Mexican Americans and other Latinos will have little choice but to challenge traditional American race thinking.[11]

CONCLUSION

Whether we in the United States change our attitudes as a society or not, the numbers of "mixed," "blended," "brown," "cosmic," "melded," or simply *multiethnic* people will grow, in both numbers and complexity. Moreover, our global society is rapidly becoming a union of all cultures, the old cultures not dying, but living on in new forms. It is in the minds of the multiethnic children that the new culture of the future world society is being synthesized. There will be no place for racism or ethnocentrism in this new world, because the multiethnic children cannot hate or disrespect their parents and their heritage without sacrificing their own personal integrity and peace of mind.

What will happen in this future world of race or ethnic irrelevance? As many have speculated, national cultures may indeed disappear as independent entities, to be replaced not by the homogeneous-monotony specter we often hear about (really what narrow cultural nationalism is about—rigid, forced conformity to an ideal, monolithic cultural standard), but by a society that recognizes and respects diversity at the level of the individual.

The fulfillment of the melting-pot and *La Raza Cósmica*—ideals and realities on the continents of the Western Hemisphere—these will form the real New World for all humankind.

NOTES

1. *La Raza Cósmica* is the title of an essay by the Mexican philosopher and educator Jose Vasconcelos (1925/1979), in which he proclaims and extolls the spiritual virtues that may ensue from the fact that America—in particular, Latin America—has become the site of the first large-scale mixture of "races" in the world. As Minister of Education he took every opportunity to foster a unified Mexican identity. Vasconcelos was responsible for the motto of the National Autonomous University of Mexico (my father's alma mater): "Por mi raza, el espíritu se hablará" (Through my race [the mixed race], the spirit shall speak).
2. Of course, any discussion of race or racial mixing presumes the existence of "race" or, more specifically, the existence of the particular concept of race that holds sway in the popular consciousness.
3. *Mexica* (pronounced meshEEca), besides being the origin of the name for the country of Mexico, is also the probable origin of *Chicano,* a slang term for Mexican Americans popularized in the 1960s. In colonial times, many in the Spanish upper class did not consider themselves "Mexican," that is, Indian or mestizo. Thus they might refer to ordinary Mexicans derogatorily as *xicanos.* The usage was carried over into the United States, where Mexican American youths transformed *Chicano* into a term of pride and defiance.
4. The number of terms for the various mixtures of peoples in Latin America far exceeds the two mentioned here. In fact, the race terminology in popular usage and adopted into law by many states in the United States is directly derived from the Spanish: *Negro* (from the Spanish word for *black*), *mulatto* (from the Spanish *mulato,* which means mule, meaning half Black and half White), *quadroon* (from the Spanish *cuarterón,* or one-quarter Black), *octoroon* (from the Spanish *octorón,* or one-eighth Black), *zambo* (from the Spanish *zambo,* or Black and Indian), and *maroon* (from the Spanish *cimarrón,* or runaway Black slave). Many other terms were also used, including *coyote, pardo, castizo, morisco, lobo,* and *chino.* Collectively, the mixed groups were called *castas* (castes). See O'Crouley (1774/1972) and Woodbridge (1948).

5. The U.S. Census, for example, included mulatto and quadroon during some censuses, but not consistently, and certainly with no bearing on the legal rights of the people so designated.
6. *Casta* was a term midway in meaning between "estate" and "race." To the extent it meant race it had a spiritual or ethnic sense rather than the genetic sense to which we are accustomed (Castro, 1971).
7. The question of Native American humanity was the subject of a famous debate in Valladolid, Spain, between Bartolomé de las Casas and Juan Ginés de Sepúlveda during the sixteenth century. Sepúlveda invoked Aristotle's thesis that some people are naturally slaves. Las Casas argued that slavery and generally brutal treatment of Native Americans violated Christian principles. Las Casas won the debate, and the Laws of the Indies resulted. Unfortunately, Las Casas's solution to Native American slavery was African slavery, a view that he later apparently recanted. That any controversy existed at all during this early period says much about Spanish attitudes regarding race compared with those of other Europeans (including their fellow Iberians, the Portuguese) of that or subsequent times. For an excellent examination of this famous debate, see Hanke (1959/1970).
8. I contend that in its most essential sense, racism is a system of thinking, an *ideology,* based on the concept of race.
9. In March 1989, 82% of "Hispanic" men who got married married Hispanic women, while 85% of "Hispanic" women married Hispanic men. The Mexican intermarriage rate was nearly the same as the overall "Hispanic" rate, while it was actually higher (28%) for Puerto Rican men (see U.S. Bureau of the Census, 1990).
10. Even if this is true in any given instance, Spaniards and Spanish culture are a mixture anyway, including the ancestry of Black Africans, Gypsies (from India), and Semites (Jews, Arabs, and Phoenicians), as well as Romans, Celts, Germans, Greeks, Berbers, Basques, and probably more. Today, there are even many mestizo and *mulato* immigrants from Latin America resident in Spain.
11. Interestingly, more than 96% of the 9.8 million people who declined to choose a particular race by checking the "other race" box on the 1990 census forms were "Hispanics" (J. García, demographic analyst, U.S. Bureau of the Census, Ethnic and Hispanic Branch, personal communication, May 1991).

REFERENCES

Biddess, M. D. (1970). *Father of racist ideology: The social and political thought of Count Gobineau.* New York: Weybright & Talley.

Castro, A. (1971). *The Spaniards: An introduction to their history.* Berkeley: University of California Press.

Hanke, L. (1970). *Aristotle and the American Indians: A study in race prejudice in the modern world.* Bloomington: Indiana University Press. (Original work published 1959.)

Harris, M. (1971). *Culture, man and nature.* New York: Thomas Y. Crowell.

King, J. C. (1981). *The biology of race.* Berkeley: University of California Press.

MacLachlan, C. M., & Rodríguez O, J. E. (1980). *The forging of the cosmic race: A reinterpretation of colonial Mexico.* Berkeley: University of California Press.

Morner, M. (1967). *Race Mixture in the History of Latin America.* Boston: Little, Brown

Morner, M. (Ed.). (1970). *Race and class in Latin America.* New York: Columbia University Press.

Muñoz, C., Jr. (1989). *Youth, identity, power: The Chicano movement.* London: Verso.

O'Crouley, P. (1972). *A description of the kingdom of New Spain in 1774.* San Francisco: John Howell. (Original work published 1774.)

Páz, O. (1961). *The labyrinth of solitude: Life and thought in Mexico* (L. Kemp, Trans.). New York: Grove. (Original work published 1950.)

Stepan, N. (1982). *The idea of race in science.* Hamden, CT: Archon.

U.S. Bureau of the Census. (1990). *The Hispanic population in the United States: March 1989* (Current Population Reports, Series P-20, No. 444). Washington DC: Government Printing Office.

U.S. Bureau of the Census. (1991, March 11). *U.S. Department of Commerce News* (Publication No. CB91-100). Washington, DC: Government Printing Office.

Vasconcelos, J. (1979). *La raza cósmica* (D. T. Jaen, Trans.). Los Angeles: California State University,

Centro de Publicaciones. (Original work published 1925.)

White, J. M. (1971). *Cortés and the downfall of the Aztec empire.* New York: St. Martin's.

Woodbridge, H. C. (1948). Glossary of names in colonial Latin America for crosses among Indians, Negros and Whites. *Journal of the Washington Academy of Sciences,* 38, 353–362.

READING 7

Asian American Panethnicity

Yen Le Espiritu

Arriving in the United States, nineteenth-century immigrants from Asian countries did not think of themselves as "Asians." Coming from specific districts in provinces in different nations, Asian immigrant groups did not even consider themselves Chinese, Japanese, Korean, and so forth, but rather people from Toisan, Hoiping, or some other district in Guandong Province in China or from Hiroshima, Yamaguchi, or some other prefecture in Japan. Members of each group considered themselves culturally and politically distinct. Historical enmities between their mother countries further separated the groups even after their arrival in the United States. Writing about early Asian immigrant communities, Eliot Mears (1928:4) reported that "it is exceptional when one learns of any entente between these Orientals." However, non-Asians had little understanding or appreciation of these distinctions. For the most part, outsiders accorded to Asian peoples certain common characteristics and traits that were essentially supranational (Browne 1985:8–9). Indeed, the exclusion acts and quotas limiting Asian immigration to the United States relied upon racialist constructions of Asians as homogeneous (Lowe 1991:28).

Mindful that whites generally lump all Asians together, early Asian immigrant communities sought to "keep their images discrete and were not above denigrating, or at least approving the denigration of, other Asian groups" (Daniels 1988:113). It was not until the late 1960s, with the advent of the Asian American movement, that a pan-Asian consciousness and constituency were first formed. To build political unity, college students of Asian ancestry heralded their common fate—the similarity of experiences and treatment that Asian groups endured in the United States (Omi and Winant 1986:105). In other words, the pan-Asian concept, originally imposed by non-Asians, became a symbol of pride and a rallying point for mass mobilization by later generations. This [discussion] examines the social, political, and demographic factors that allowed pan-Asianism to take root in the 1960s and not earlier.

ETHNIC "DISIDENTIFICATION"

Before the 1960s, Asians in this country frequently practiced ethnic disidentification, the act of distancing one's group from another group so as not to be mistaken and suffer the blame for the presumed misdeeds of that group (Hayano 1981:162). Faced with external threats, group members can either intensify their solidarity or they can distance themselves from the stigmatized segment. Instead of uniting to fight anti-Asian forces, early Asian immigrant communities often disassociated themselves from the targeted group so as not to be mistaken for members of it and suffer any possible negative consequences (Hayano 1981:161; Daniels 1988:113). Two examples of ethnic disidentification among Asians in this country occurred during the various anti-Asian exclusion movements and during World War II. These incidents are instructive not only as evidence of ethnic disidentification but also as documentation of the pervasiveness of

Yen Le Espiritu is professor of ethnic studies, University of California, San Diego.

racial lumping. Precisely because of racial lumping, persons of Asian ancestry found it necessary to disassociate themselves from other Asian groups.

Exclusion Movements

Beginning with the first student laborers in the late nineteenth century, Japanese immigrants always differentiated themselves from Chinese immigrants. Almost uniformly, Japanese immigrants perceived their Chinese counterparts in an "unsympathetic, negative light, and often repeated harsh American criticisms of the Chinese" (Ichioka 1988:191). In their opinion, the Chinese came from an inferior nation; they also were lower-class laborers, who had not adapted themselves to American society. In 1892, a Japanese student laborer described San Francisco's Chinatown as "a world of beasts in which . . . exists every imaginable depravity, crime, and vice" (cited in Ichioka 1988:191).

Indeed, the Japanese immigrants were a more select group than their Chinese counterparts. The Japanese government viewed overseas Japanese as representatives of their homeland. Therefore, it screened prospective emigrants to ensure that they were healthy and literate and would uphold Japan's national honor (Takaki 1989:46).

More important, Japanese immigrants distanced themselves from the Chinese because they feared that Americans would lump them together. Aware of Chinese exclusion, Japanese immigrant leaders had always dreaded the thought of Japanese exclusion. To counteract any negative association, Japanese immigrant leaders did everything possible to distinguish themselves from the Chinese immigrants (Ichioka 1988:250). For example, to separate themselves from the unassimilable Chinese laborers, some Japanese immigrant leaders insisted that their Japanese workers wear American work clothes and even eat American food (Ichioka 1988:185). In 1901, the Japanese in California distributed leaflets requesting that they be differentiated from the Chinese (tenBroek, Barnhart, and Matson 1970:23).

However, under the general rubric Asiatic, the Japanese inherited the painful experiences of the Chinese.[1] All the vices attributed to the Chinese were transferred to these newest Asian immigrants (Browne 1985). Having successfully excluded Chinese laborers, organized labor once again led the campaign to drive out the Japanese immigrants. In 1904, the American Federation of Labor adopted its first anti-Japanese resolution. Charging that the Japanese immigrants were as undesirable as the Chinese, the unions' resolution called for the expansion of the 1902 Chinese Exclusion Act to include Japanese and other Asian laborers. By mid-1905, the labor unions of California had joined forces to establish the Asiatic Exclusion League (Hill 1973:52–54; Ichioka 1988:191–192).

Since the Japanese immigrants considered themselves superior to the Chinese, they felt indignant and insulted whenever they were lumped together with them. In 1892, a Japanese immigrant wrote in the *Oakland Enquirer* that he wished "to inveigh with all my power" against American newspapers that compared the Japanese to "the truly ignorant class of Chinese laborers and condemned them as bearers of some mischievous Oriental evils" (cited in Ichioka 1988:192). Instead of joining with the Chinese to fight the anti-Asian exclusion movement, some Japanese leaders went so far as to condone publicly the exclusion of the Chinese while insisting that the Japanese were the equals of Americans (Daniels 1988:113). Above all else, Japanese immigrant leaders wanted Japanese immigration to be treated on the same footing as European immigration (Ichioka 1988:250).

In the end, Japanese attempts at disidentification failed. With the passage of the 1924 Immigration Act, Japanese immigration was effectively halted. This act contained two provisions designed to stop Japanese immigration. The first barred the immigration of Japanese wives even if their husbands were United States citizens. The second prohibited the immigration of aliens ineligible for citizenship. Because the Supreme Court had ruled in 1922 that persons of

Japanese ancestry could not become naturalized citizens, this provision effectively closed the door on Japanese and most other Asian immigration (U.S. Commission on Civil Rights 1986:8–9). The Japanese immigrants felt doubly affronted by the 1924 act because it ranked them, not as the equals of Europeans, but on the same level as the lowly Chinese, the very people whom they themselves considered inferior (Ichioka 1988:250). Thus, despite all their attempts to disassociate themselves from the Chinese, with the passage of the act, the Japanese joined the Chinese as a people deemed unworthy of becoming Americans. Little did they foresee that, in less than two decades, other Asian groups in America would disassociate themselves from the Japanese.

World War II and Japanese Internment

Immediately after the bombing of Pearl Harbor, the incarceration of Japanese Americans began. On the night of December 7, the Federal Bureau of Investigation (FBI) began taking into custody persons of Japanese ancestry who had connections to the Japanese government. Working on the principle of guilt by association, the security agencies simply rounded up most of the Issei (first-generation) leaders of the Japanese community. Initially, the federal government differentiated between alien and citizen Japanese Americans, but this distinction gradually disappeared. In the end, the government evacuated more than 100,000 persons of Japanese ancestry into concentration camps, approximately two-thirds of whom were American-born citizens. It was during this period that the Japanese community discovered that the legal distinction between citizen and alien was not nearly so important as the distinction between white and yellow (Daniels 1988:ch. 6).

Like the Japanese, the Chinese understood the importance of the distinction between white and yellow. Fearful that they would be targets of anti-Japanese activities, many persons of Chinese ancestry, especially in the West, took to wearing buttons that proclaimed positively "I'm Chinese." Similarly, many Chinese shopkeepers displayed signs announcing, "This is a Chinese shop." Some Chinese immigrants even joined the white persecution with buttons that added "I hate Japs worse than you do" (Daniels 1988:205; Takaki 1989:370–371). The small Korean and Filipino communities took similar actions. Because of Japan's occupation of Korea at the time, being mistaken as Japanese particularly angered Koreans in the United States. Cognizant of Asian lumping, the United Korean Committee prepared identification cards proclaiming "I am Korean." During the early months of the war, women wore Korean dresses regularly to distinguish themselves from the Japanese (Melendy 1977:158; Takaki 1989:365–366). Similarly, persons of Filipino ancestry wore buttons proclaiming "I am a Filipino" (Takaki 1989:363).

Given the wars between their mother countries and Japan, it is not surprising that the Chinese, Koreans, and Filipinos distanced themselves from the Japanese. But their reactions are instructive not only as examples of ethnic disidentification but also as testimonies to the pervasiveness of racial lumping. Popular confusion of the various Asian groups was so prevalent that it was necessary for Chinese, Filipinos, and Koreans to don ethnic clothing and identification buttons to differentiate themselves from the Japanese. Without these *visible* signs of ethnicity, these three Asian groups would probably have been mistaken for Japanese by anti-Japanese forces. As Ronald Takaki (1989:370) reported, Asian groups "remembered how they had previously been called 'Japs' and how many whites had lumped all Asians together." But there are also examples of how Asian groups united when inter-Asian cooperation advanced their common interests.

Inter-Asian Labor Movements

The most notable example of inter-Asian solidarity was the 1920 collaboration of Japanese and Filipino plantation laborers in Hawaii. In the beginning, plantation workers had organized in terms of national origins. Thus, the Japanese belonged to the Japanese union and the Filipinos to the Filipino union. In the early 1900s, an ethnically based strike seemed sensible to Japanese plantation laborers because they represented about 70 percent of the entire work force. Filipinos constituted less than 1 percent. However, by 1920, Japanese workers represented only 44 percent of the labor force, while Filipino workers represented 30 percent. Japanese and Filipino union leaders understood that they would have to combine to be politically and economically effective (Johanessen 1950:75–83; Takaki 1989:152).

Because together they constituted more than 70 percent of the work force in Oahu, the 1920 Japanese-Filipino strike brought plantation operations to a sudden stop. Although the workers were eventually defeated, the 1920 strike was the "first major interethnic working-class struggle in Hawaii" (Takaki 1989:154).[2] Subsequently, the Japanese Federation of Labor elected to become an interethnic union. To promote a multiethnic class solidarity, the new union called itself the Hawaii Laborers Association (Takaki 1989:154–155).

Although the 1920 strike was a de facto example of pan-Asian cooperation, this cooperation needs to be distinguished from the post-1960 pan-Asian solidarity. The purported unifying factor in 1920 was a common class status, not a shared cultural or racial background (Takaki 1989:154). This class solidarity is different from the large-scale organization of ethnicity that emerged in the late 1960s. For most Asian Americans, the more recent development represents an enlargement of their identity system, a circle beyond their previous national markers of identity. True, like working-class unions, panethnic groups are interest groups with material demands (Glazer and Moynihan 1963; Bonacich and Modell 1980). However, unlike labor unions, panethnic groups couch their demands in ethnic or racial terms—not purely in class terms. In other words, their ethnicity is used as a basis for the assertion of collective claims, many but not all of which are class based.

SOCIAL AND DEMOGRAPHIC CHANGES: SETTING THE CONTEXT

. . . Before 1940, the Asian population in the United States was primarily an immigrant population. Immigrant Asians faced practical barriers to pan-Asian unity. Foremost was their lack of a common language. Old national rivalries were another obstacle, as many early Asian immigrants carried the political memories and outlook of their homelands. For example, Japan's occupation of Korea resulted in pervasive anti-Japanese sentiments among Koreans in the United States. According to Brett Melendy (1977:155), "Fear and hatred of the Japanese appeared to be the only unifying force among the various Korean groups through the years." Moreover, these historical enmities and linguistic and cultural differences reinforced one another as divisive agents.

During the postwar period, due to immigration restrictions and the growing dominance of the second and third generations, American-born Asians outnumbered immigrants. The demographic changes of the 1940s were pronounced. During this decade, nearly twenty thousand Chinese American babies were born. For the first time, the largest five-year cohort of Chinese Americans was under five years of age (Kitano and Daniels 1988:37). By 1960, approximately two-thirds of the Asian population in California had been born in the United States (Ong 1989:5–8). As the Asian population became a native-born community, linguistic and cultural differences began to blur. Although they had attended Asian-language schools, most American-born Asians possessed only a limited knowledge of their ethnic language (Chan 1991:115). By 1960, with English as the common language, persons from different Asian backgrounds were able to communicate with one another (Ling

1984:73), and in so doing create a common identity associated with the United States.

Moreover, unlike their immigrant parents, native-born and American-educated Asians could muster only scant loyalties to old world ties. Historical antagonisms between their mother countries thus receded in importance (Wong 1972:34). For example, growing up in America, second-generation Koreans "had difficulty feeling the painful loss of the homeland and understanding the indignity of Japanese domination" (Takaki 1989:292). Thus, while the older generation of Koreans hated all Japanese, "their children were much less hostile or had no concern at all" (Melendy 1977:156). As a native-born Japanese American community advocate explained, "By 1968, we had a second generation. We could speak English; so there was no language problem. And we had little feelings of historical animosity" (Kokubun interview).

As national differences receded in subjective importance, generational differences widened. For the most part, American-born Asians considered themselves to have more in common with other American-born Asians than they did with foreign-born compatriots.[3] According to a third-generation Japanese American who is married to a Chinese American, "As far as our experiences in America, I have more things in common than differences with a Chinese American. Being born and raised here gives us something in common. We have more in common with each other than with a Japanese from Japan, or a Chinese from China" (Ichioka interview). Much to their parents' dismay, young Asian Americans began to choose their friends and spouses from other Asian groups. . . .

Before World War II, Asian immigrant communities were quite distinct entities, isolated from one another and from the larger society. Because of language difficulties, prejudice, and lack of business opportunities elsewhere, there was little chance for Asians in the United States to live outside their ethnic enclaves (Yuan 1966:331). Shut out of the mainstream of American society, the various immigrant groups struggled separately in their respective Chinatowns, Little Tokyos, or Manilatowns. Stanford Lyman (1970:57–63) reported that the early Chinese and Japanese communities in the western states had little to do with one another—either socially or politically . . .

Economic and residential barriers began to crumble after World War II. The war against Nazism called attention to racism at home and discredited the notions of white superiority. The fifteen years after the war was a period of largely positive change as civil rights statutes outlawed racial discrimination in employment as well as housing (Daniels 1988:ch. 7). Popular attitudes were also changing. Polls taken during World War II showed a distinct hostility toward Japan: 74 percent of the respondents favored either killing off all Japanese, destroying Japan as a political entity, or supervising it. On the West Coast, 97 percent of the people polled approved of the relocation of Japanese Americans. In contrast, by 1949, 64 percent of those polled were either friendly or neutral toward Japan (Feraru 1950).

During the postwar years, Asian American residential patterns changed significantly. Because of the lack of statistical data,[4] a longitudinal study of the changing residential patterns of Asian Americans cannot be made. However, descriptive accounts of Asian American communities indicate that these enclaves declined in the postwar years. Edwin Hoyt (1974:94) reported that in the 1940s, second-generation Chinese Americans moved out of the Chinatowns. Although they still came back to shop or to see friends, they lived elsewhere. In 1940, Rose Hum Lee found twenty-eight cities with an area called Chinatown in the United States. By 1955, Peter Sih found only sixteen (Sung 1967:143–144). New York's Chinatown exemplifies the declining significance of Asian ethnic enclaves. In 1940, 50 percent of the Chinese in New York City lived in its Chinatown; by 1960, less than one-third lived there (Yuan 1966:331).

Similarly, many returning Japanese Americans abandoned their prewar settlement in old central cities and joined the migration to suburbia (Daniels 1988:294). In the early 1970s, Little Tokyo in Los Angeles remained a bustling Japanese American center, "but at night the shop owners [went] home to the houses in the suburbs" (Hoyt 1974:84). . . .

Moreover, recent research on suburban segregation indicates that the level of segregation between certain Asian American groups is often less than that between them and non-Asians. . . . Though not comprehensive, these studies together suggest that Asian residential segregation declined in the postwar years.

As various Asian groups in the United States interacted, they became aware of common problems and goals that transcended parochial interests and historical antagonisms. One recurrent problem was employment discrimination. According to a 1965 report published by the California Fair Employment Practices Commission, for every $51 earned by a white male Californian, Japanese males earned $43 and Chinese males $38—even though Chinese and Japanese American men had become slightly better educated than the white majority (Daniels 1988:315). Moreover, although the postwar period marked the first time that well-trained Chinese and Japanese Americans could find suitable employment with relative ease, they continued to be passed over for promotion to administrative and supervisory positions (Kitano and Daniels 1988:47). Asians in the United States began to see themselves as a group that shared important common experiences: exploitation, oppression, and discrimination (Uyematsu 1971).

Because inter-Asian contact and communication were greatest on college campuses, pan-Asianism was strongest there (Wong 1972: 33–34). Exposure to one another and to the mainstream society led some young Asian Americans to feel that they were fundamentally different from whites. Disillusioned with the white society and alienated from their traditional communities, many Asian American student activists turned to the alternative strategy of pan-Asian unification (Weiss 1974:69–70).

THE CONSTRUCTION OF PAN-ASIAN ETHNICITY

Although broader social struggles and internal demographic changes provided the impetus for the Asian American movement, it was the group's politics—confrontational and explicitly pan-Asian—that shaped the movement's content. Influenced by the internal colonial model, which stresses the commonalities among "colonized groups," college students of Asian ancestry declared solidarity with fellow Asian Americans—and with other Third World[5] minorities (Blauner 1972:ch. 2). Rejecting the label "Oriental," they proclaimed themselves "Asian American." Through pan-Asian organizations, publications, and Asian American studies programs, Asian American activists built pan-Asian solidarity by pointing out their common fate in American society. The pan-Asian concept enabled diverse Asian American groups to understand their "unequal circumstances and histories as being related" (Lowe 1991:30).

From "Yellow" to "Asian American"

Following the example of the Black Power movement, Asian American activists spearheaded their own Yellow Power movement to seek "freedom from racial oppression through the power of a consolidated yellow people" (Uyematsu 1971:12). In the summer of 1968, more than one hundred students of diverse Asian backgrounds attended an "Are You Yellow?" conference at UCLA to discuss issues of Yellow Power, identity, and the war in Vietnam (Ling 1989:53). In 1970, a new pan-Asian organization in northern California called itself the "Yellow Seed" because "Yellow [is] the common bond between Asian-Americans and Seed symboliz[es] growth as an individual and as an alliance" (Masada 1970). This "yellow" reference was dropped when Filipino Americans rejected the term, claiming that they were brown, not yellow

(Rabaya 1971:110; Ignacio 1976:84). At the first Asian American national conference in 1972, Filipino Americans "made it clear to the conferees that we were 'Brown Asians'" by forming a Brown Asian Caucus (Ignacio 1976:139–141). It is important to note, however, that Filipino American activists did not reject the term "yellow" because they objected to the pan-Asian framework. Quite the contrary, they rejected it because it allegedly excluded them from that grouping (Rabaya 1971:110).

. . . Asian American activists also rejected *Oriental* because the term conjures up images of "the sexy Susie Wong, the wily Charlie Chan, and the evil Fu Manchu" (Weiss 1974:234). It is also a term that smacks of European colonialism and imperialism: *Oriental* means "East"; Asia is "east" only in relationship to Europe, which was taken as the point of reference (Browne 1985). To define their own image and to claim an *American* identity, college students of Asian ancestry coined the term *Asian American* to "stand for all of us Americans of Asian descent" (Ichioka interview). While *Oriental* suggests passivity and acquiescence, *Asian Americans* connotes political activism because an Asian American "gives a damn about his life, his work, his beliefs, and is willing to do almost anything to help Orientals become Asian Americans" (cited in Weiss 1974:234).

The account above suggests that the creation of a new name is a significant symbolic move in constructing an ethnic identity. In their attempt to forge a pan-Asian identity, Asian American activists first had to coin a composite term that would unify and encompass the constituent groups. Filipino Americans' rejection of the term "yellow" and the activists' objection to the cliché-ridden *Oriental* forced the group to change its name to Asian American. . . .

Pan-Asian Organizations

Influenced by the political tempo of the 1960s, young Asian Americans began to join such organizations as the Free Speech Movement at the University of California at Berkeley, Students for a Democratic Society, and the Progressive Labor Party. However, these young activists "had no organization or coalition to draw attention to themselves as a distinct group" (Wong 1972:33). Instead, they participated as individuals—often at the invitation of their white or black friends (Chin 1971:285; Nakano 1984:3–4). While Asian American activists subscribed to the integrationist ideology of the 1960s and 1970s social movements, they also felt impotent and alienated. There was no structure to uphold their own identity. As an example, when the Peace and Freedom Party was formed on the basis of black and white coalitions, Asian American activists felt excluded because they were neither black nor white (Wong 1972:34; Yoshimura 1989:107).

In the late 1960s, linking their political views with the growth of racial pride among their ranks, Asian Americans already active in various political movements came together to form their own organizations (Nakano 1984:3–4). Most of the early pan-Asian organizations were college based. In 1968, activists at the University of California, Berkeley, founded one of the first pan-Asian political organizations: the Asian American Political Alliance (AAPA). According to a co-founder of the organization, its establishment marked the first time that the term "Asian American" was used nationally to mobilize people of Asian descent (Ichioka interview). . . .

By the mid-1970s, *Asian American* had become a familiar term (Lott 1976:30). Although first coined by college activists, the pan-Asian concept began to be used extensively by professional and community spokespersons to lobby for the health and welfare of Americans of Asian descent. In addition to the local and single-ethnic organizations of an earlier era, Asian American professionals and community activists formed national and pan-Asian organizations such as the Pacific/Asian Coalition and the Asian American Social Workers (Ignacio 1976:162; Kuo 1979:283–284). Also, Asian American caucuses could be found in national professional organizations such as the American Public Health Association, the American Sociological Association, the

American Psychological Association, the American Psychiatric Association, and the American Librarians Association (Lott 1976:31). Commenting on the "literally scores of pan-Asian organizations" in the mid-1970s, William Liu (1976:6) asserted that "the idea of pan-Asian cooperation [was] viable and ripe for development." . . .

THE LIMITS OF PAN-ASIANISM

Although pan-Asian consolidation certainly has occurred, it has been by no means universal. For those who wanted a broader political agenda, the pan-Asian scope was too narrow and its racial orientation too segregative (Wong 1972:33; Lowe 1991:39). For others who wanted to preserve ethnic particularism, the pan-Asian agenda threatened to remove second- and third-generation Asians "from their conceptual ties to their community" (R. Tanaka 1976:47). These competing levels of organization mitigated the impact of pan-Asianism.

Moreover, pan-Asianism has been primarily the ideology of native-born, American-educated, and middle-class Asians. Embraced by students, artists, professionals, and political activists, pan-Asian consciousness thrived on college campuses and in urban settings. However, it barely touched the Asian ethnic enclaves. When the middle-class student activists carried the enlarged and politicized Asian American consciousness to the ethnic communities, they encountered apprehension, if not outright hostility (Chan 1991:175). Conscious of their national origins and overburdened with their day-to-day struggles for survival, most community residents ignored or spurned the movement's political agenda (P. Wong 1972:34). Chin (1971:287) reported that few Chinatown residents participated in any of the pan-Asian political events. Similarly, members of the Nisei-dominated Japanese American Citizens League "were determined to keep a closed mind and maintain their negative stereotype" of the members of the Asian American Political Alliance (J. Matsui 1968:6). For their part, young Asian American activists accused their elders of having been so white-washed that they had deleted their experiences of prejudice and discrimination from their history (Weiss 1974:238). Because these young activists were not rooted in the community, their base of support was narrow and their impact upon the larger society often limited (Wong 1972:37; Nishio 1982:37).

Even among those who were involved in the Asian American movement, divisions arose from conflicting sets of interests as subgroups decided what and whose interests would be addressed. Oftentimes, conflicts over material interests took on ethnic coloration, with participants from smaller subgroups charging that "Asian American" primarily meant Chinese and Japanese American, the two largest and most acculturated Asian American groups at the time (Ignacio 1976:220; Ling 1984:193–195). For example, most Asian American Studies programs did not include courses on other Asian groups, but only on Chinese and Japanese. Similarly, the Asian American women's movement often subsumed the needs of their Korean and Filipina members under those of Chinese and Japanese women (Ling 1984:193–195). Chinese and Japanese Americans also were the instructors of Asian American ethnic studies directors and staff members of many Asian American projects,[6] and advisory and panel members in many governmental agencies (Ignacio 1976:223–224).

The ethnic and class inequality within the pan-Asian structure has continued to be a source of friction and mistrust, with participants from the less dominant groups feeling shortchanged and excluded. The influx of the post-1965 immigrants and the tightening of public funding resources have further deepened the ethnic and class cleavages among Asian American subgroups.

CONCLUSION

The development of a pan-Asian consciousness and constituency reflected broader societal developments and demographic changes, as well as the group's political agenda. By the late 1960s, pan-Asianism was possible because of the more amicable relationships among the Asian countries, the declining residential segregation among diverse Asian groups in America, and the large number of native-born, American-educated political actors. Disillusioned with the larger society and estranged from their traditional communities, third- and fourth-generation Asian Americans turned to the alternative strategy of pan-Asian unification. Through pan-Asian organizations, media, and Asian American Studies programs, these political activists assumed the role of "cultural entrepreneurs" consciously creating a community of culture out of diverse Asian peoples.[7] This process of pan-Asian consolidation did not proceed smoothly nor did it encompass all Asian Americans. Ethnic chauvinism, competition for scarce resources, and class cleavages continued to divide the subgroups. However, once established, the pan-Asian structure not only reinforced the cohesiveness of already existing networks but also expanded these networks. Although first conceived by young Asian American activists, the pan-Asian concept was subsequently institutionalized by professionals and community groups, as well as government agencies. The confrontational politics of the activists eventually gave way to the conventional and electoral politics of the politicians, lobbyists, and professionals, as Asian Americans continued to rely on the pan-Asian framework to enlarge their political capacities.

NOTES

1. On the other hand, due to the relative strength of Japan in the world order, Japanese immigrants at times received more favorable treatment than other Asian immigrants. For example, in 1905, wary of offending Japan, national politicians blocked an attempt by the San Francisco Board of Education to transfer Japanese students from the public schools reserved for white children to the "Oriental" school serving the Chinese (Chan 1991: 59).
2. Although many Korean laborers were sympathetic to the 1920 strike, because of their hatred for the Japanese, they did not participate. As the Korean National Association announced, "We do not wish to be looked upon as strikebreakers, but we shall continue to work in the plantation and we are opposed to the Japanese in everything" (cited in Melendy 1977: 164).
3. The same is true with other racial groups. For example, American-born Haitians are more like their African American peers than like their Haitian parents (Woldemikael 1989: 166).
4. Ideally, residential patterns should be analyzed at the census tract level. However, this analysis cannot be done because Asians were not tabulated by census tracts until the 1980 census.
5. During the late 1960s, in radical circles, the term *third world* referred to the nation's racially oppressed people.
6. For example, the staff of the movement publication *Gidra* were predominantly Japanese Americans.
7. For a discussion of the role of "cultural entrepreneurs," see Cornell (1988b).

REFERENCES

Blauner, Robert. 1972. *Racial Oppression in America.* New York: Harper & Row.

Bonacich, Edna, and John Modell. 1980. *The Economic Basis of Ethnic Solidarity: A Study of Japanese Americans.* Berkeley: University of California Press.

Browne, Blaine T. 1985. "A Common Thread: American Images of the Chinese and Japanese, 1930–1960." Ph.D. dissertation, University of Oklahoma.

Chan, Sucheng. 1991. *Asian Americans: An Interpretive History.* Boston: Twayne.

Chin, Rocky. 1971. "NY Chinatown Today: Community in Crisis." Pp. 282–295 in *Roots: An Asian American Reader,* edited by Amy Tachiki, Eddie Wong, and Franklin Odo. Los Angeles: UCLA Asian American Studies Center.

Cornell, Stephen. 1988a. *The Return of the Native: American Indian Political Resurgence.* New York: Oxford University Press.

———. 1988b. "Structure, Content, and Logic in Ethnic Group Formation." Working Paper series, Center for Research on Politics and Social Organization, Department of Sociology, Harvard University.

Daniels, Roger. 1971. *Concentration Camps USA: Japanese Americans and World War II.* Hinsdale, IL: Dryden Press.

———. 1988. *Asian America: Chinese and Japanese in the United States since 1850.* Seattle: University of Washington Press.

Feraru, Arthur N. 1950. "Public Opinions Polls on Japan." *Far Eastern Survey* 19 (10): 101–103.

Glazer, Nathan, and Daniel Patrick Moynihan. 1963. *Beyond the Melting Pot: The Negroes, Puerto Ricans, Jews, Italians, and Irish of New York City.* Cambridge, MA: M.I.T. Press.

Hayano, David M. 1981. "Ethnic Identification and Disidentification: Japanese-American Views of Chinese-Americans." *Ethnic Groups* 3 (2): 157–171.

Hill, Herbert. 1973. "Anti-Oriental Agitation and the Rise of Working-Class Racism." *Society* 10 (2): 43–54.

Hoyt, Edwin P. 1974. *Asians in the West.* New York: Thomas Nelson.

Ichioka, Yuji. 1988. *The Issei: The World of the First Generation Japanese Americans, 1885–1924.* New York: Free Press.

Ignacio, Lemuel F. 1976. *Asian Americans and Pacific Islanders (Is There Such an Ethnic Group?).* San Jose: Filipino Development Associates.

Johanessen, Edward L. H. 1950. *The Labor Movement in the Territory of Hawaii.* M.A. thesis, University of California, Berkeley.

Kitano, Harry H. L., and Roger Daniels. 1988. *Asian Americans: Emerging Minorities.* Englewood Cliffs, NJ: Prentice-Hall.

Kuo, Wen H. 1979. "On the Study of Asian-Americans: Its Current State and Agenda." *Sociological Quarterly* 20 (Spring): 279–290.

Ling, Susie Hsiuhan. 1984. "The Mountain Movers: Asian American Women's Movement in Los Angeles." M.A. thesis, University of California, Los Angeles.

———. 1989. "The Mountain Movers: Asian American Women's Movement in Los Angeles." *Amerasia Journal* 15 (1): 51–67.

Liu, William. 1976. "Asian American Research: Views of a Sociologist." *Asian Studies Occasional Report,* no. 2.

Lott, Juanita Tamayo. 1976. "The Asian American Concept: In Quest of Identity." *Bridge,* November, pp. 30–34.

Lowe, Lisa. 1991. "Heterogeneity, Hybridity, Multiplicity: Marking Asian American Differences." *Diaspora* 1: 24–44.

Lyman, Stanford M. 1970. *The Asian in the West.* Reno and Las Vegas: Desert Research Institute, University of Nevada.

Masada, Saburo. 1970. "Stockton's Yellow Seed." *Pacific Citizen,* 9 October.

Massey, Douglas S., and Nancy A. Denton. 1987. "Trends in the Residential Segregation of Blacks, Hispanics, and Asians, 1970–1980." *American Sociological Review* 52 (December): 802–825.

Matsui, Jeffrey. 1968. "Asian Americans." *Pacific Citizen,* 6 September.

Mears, Eliot Grinnell. 1928. *Resident Orientals on the American Pacific Coast.* New York: Arno Press.

Melendy, H. Brett. 1977. *Asians in America: Filipinos, Koreans, and East Indians.* Boston: Twayne.

Nakano, Roy. 1984. "Marxist Leninist Organization in the Asian American Community: Los Angeles, 1969–79." Unpublished student paper, UCLA.

Nishio, Alan. 1982. "Personal Reflections on the Asian National Movements." *East Wind,* Spring/Summer, pp. 36–38.

Omi, Michael, and Howard Winant. 1986. *Racial Formation in the United States: From the 1960s to the 1980s.* New York: Routledge and Kegan Paul.

Ong, Paul. 1989. "California's Asian Population: Past Trends and Projections for the Year 2000." Los Angeles: Graduate School of Architecture and Urban Planning.

Rabaya, Violet. 1971. "I Am Curious (Yellow?)." Pp. 110–111 in *Roots: An Asian American Reader,* edited by Amy Tachiki, Eddie Wong, and Franklin Odo. Los Angeles: UCLA Asian American Studies Center.

Sung, Betty Lee. 1967. *Mountain of Gold: The Story of the Chinese in America.* New York: Macmillan.

Takaki, Ronald. 1989. *Strangers from a Different Shore: A History of Asian Americans.* Boston: Little, Brown.

Tanaka, Ron. 1976. "Culture, Communication, and the Asian Movement in Perspective." *Journal of Ethnic Studies* 4 (1): 37–52.

tenBroek, J., E. N. Barnhart, and F. W. Matson. 1970. *Prejudice, War, and the Constitution.* Berkeley: University of California Press.

U.S. Commission on Civil Rights. 1986. *Recent Activities against Citizens and Residents of Asian*

Descent. Washington, DC: U.S. Government Printing Office.

Uyematsu, Amy. 1971. "The Emergence of Yellow Power in America." Pp. 9–13 in *Roots: An Asian American Reader,* edited by Amy Tachiki, Eddie Wong, and Franklin Odo. Los Angeles: UCLA Asian American Studies Center.

Weiss, Melford S. 1974. *Valley City: A Chinese Community in America.* Cambridge, MA: Schenkman.

Woldemikael, Tekle Mariam. 1989. *Becoming Black Americans: Haitians and American Institutions in Evanston, Illinois.* New York: AMS Press.

Wong, Paul. 1972. "The Emergence of the Asian-American Movement." *Bridge* 2 (1): 33–39.

Yoshimura, Evelyn. 1989. "How I Became an Activist and What It All Means to Me." *Amerasia Journal* 15 (I): 106–109.

Yuan, D. Y. 1966. "Chinatown and Beyond: The Chinese Population in Metropolitan New York." *Phylon* 23 (4): 321–332.

PERSONAL ACCOUNT

I Thought My Race Was Invisible

In a conversation with a close friend, I noticed that I am, to her, a representative of my entire racial category. To put things in perspective, my friend Janet and I have been friends for eight years. During this period, it has come up that I am a third-generation Japanese-American who has no ties to being Japanese other than a couple of sushi dishes I learned how to make from my grandmother. Nonetheless, whenever a question regarding "Asians" comes up, she comes to me as if I can provide the definitive answer to every Asian mystery.

Yesterday Janet asked me if there is a cultural reason why Asians "always drive so slow." Not having noticed that Asians drive slowly (in fact, I have noticed a number of Asians who actually exceed the speed limit), I commented that perhaps they are law-abiding citizens. She said that must explain it: "They are used to following the law." I thought, "Am I one of 'they'?" but didn't comment further. Before we switched subjects, she noted that she "knew there had to be a cultural reason" for their driving.

Janet then told me about a Vietnamese woman at the Hair Cuttery who cut her husband's hair. As is normal, her husband talked to the woman as she worked on his hair; he asked her what she did before working at the Hair Cuttery. She said that she used to work in the fields in California (i.e., she was a field hand). Janet told me of the healthy respect that she and her husband had for a woman who worked in the fields, put herself through cosmetology school, moved East, and became a professional hairstylist. She commented that "Blacks" should follow her example and work instead of complaining of their lot in life.

This conversation was interesting and a bit startling. Janet is a good friend who shares many interests with me. What I realized from this conversation, and in remembering others that were similar, is that she feels that I am a representative of the whole Asian race. Not only is this unrealistic, but it is surprising that she would imagine I could answer for my race given my lack of real cultural exposure. In relaying the story of the Vietnamese woman, I had a sense that she was complimenting me, and my race, for the industriousness "we" demonstrate. It seems to me that she approved of the "typically" Asian way of working (quietly, so as not to insult or offend), even though this woman was probably underpaid and overworked in her field hand job. While she approved of her reticence, Janet did not approve of "Black" complaints.

I realize that to Janet, I will always be Asian. I had not really thought about it before, but I never think of Janet as White; her race is invisible to me. I had thought that my race was invisible too; however, I realize now that I will always be the "marked" friend. This saddens me a bit, but I accept it with the knowledge that she is a close friend. Nonetheless, it is unfortunate to think that even between friends, race is an issue.

Sherri H. Pereira

READING 8

Whiteness as an "Unmarked" Cultural Category

Ruth Frankenberg

> America's supposed to be the melting pot. I know that I've got a huge number of nationalities in my blood, but how do I—what do I call myself? And hating this country as I do, I don't like to say I'm an American. Even though it is what I am. I hate identifying myself as only an American, because I have so much objections to Americans' place in the world. I don't know how I felt about that when I was growing up, but I never—I didn't like to pledge allegiance to the flag. . . . Still, at this point in my life, I wonder what it is that somebody with all this melting pot blood can call their own. . . .
>
> Especially growing up in the sixties, when people *did* say "I'm proud to be Black," "I'm proud to be Hispanic," you know, and it became very popular to be proud of your ethnicity. And even feminists, you know, you could say, "I'm a woman," and be proud of it. But there's still a majority of the country that can't say they are proud of anything!

Suzie Roberts's words powerfully illustrate the key themes . . . that stirred the women I interviewed as they examined their own identities: what had formed them, what they counted as (their own or others') cultural practice(s), and what constituted identities of which they could be proud.* This [discussion] explores perceptions of whiteness as a location of culture and identity, focusing mainly on white feminist . . . women's views and contrasting their voices with those of more politically conservative women. . . .

[M]any of the women I interviewed, including even some of the conservative ones, appeared to be self-conscious about white power and racial inequality. In part because of their sense of the links and parallels between white racial dominance in the United States and U.S. domination on a global scale, there was a complex interweaving of questions about race and nation—whiteness and Americanness—in these women's thoughts about white culture. Similarly, conceptions of racial, national, and cultural belonging frequently leaked into one another.

On the one hand, then, these women's views of white culture seemed to be distinctively modern. But at the same time, their words drew on much earlier historical moments and participated in long-established modes of cultural description. In the broadest sense, Western colonial discourses on the white self, the nonwhite Other, and the white Other too, were very much in evidence. These discourses produced dualistic conceptualizations of whiteness versus other cultural forms. The women thus often spoke about culture in ways that reworked, and yet remained tied to, "older" forms of racism.

For a significant number of young white women, being white felt like being cultureless. Cathy Thomas, in the following description of whiteness, raised many of the themes alluded to by other feminist and race-cognizant women. She described what she saw as a lack of form and substance:

> . . . the formlessness of being white. Now if I was a middle western girl, or a New Yorker, if I had a fixed regional identity that was something palpable, then I'd be a white New Yorker, no doubt, but I'd still be a New Yorker. . . . Being a Californian, I'm sure it has its hallmarks, but to me they were invisible. . . . If I had an ethnic base to identify from, if I was even Irish American, that would have been something formed, if I was a working-class woman, that would have been something formed. But to be a Heinz 57 American, a white, class-confused American, land of the Kleenex type American, is so formless in and of itself. It only takes shape in relation to other people.

Whiteness as a cultural space is represented here as amorphous and indescribable, in contrast with a range of other identities marked by race,

---

Ruth Frankenberg is associate professor of American studies at the University of California, Davis.

*Between 1984 and 1986 I interviewed 30 white women, diverse in age, class, region of origin, sexuality, family situation and political orientation, all living in California at the time of the interviews.

ethnicity, region, and class. Further, white culture is viewed here as "bad" culture. In fact, the extent to which identities can be named seems to show an inverse relationship to power in the U.S. social structure. The elisions, parallels, and differences between characterizations of white people, Americans, people of color, and so-called white ethnic groups will be explored [here].

Cathy's own cultural positioning seemed to her impossible to grasp, shapeless and unnameable. It was easier to know others and to know, with certainty, what one was *not.* Providing a clue to one of the mechanisms operating here is the fact that, while Cathy viewed New Yorkers and midwesterners as having a cultural shape or identity, women from the East Coast and the Midwest also described or mourned their own seeming lack of culture. The self, where it is part of a dominant cultural group, does not have to name itself. In this regard, Chris Patterson hit the nail on the head, linking the power of white culture with the privilege not to be named:

> I'm probably at the stage where I'm beginning to see that you can come up with a definition of white. Before, I didn't know that you could turn it around and say, "Well what *does* white mean?" One thing is, it's taken for granted. . . . [To be white means to] have some sort of advantage or privilege, even if it's something as simple as not having a definition.

The notion of "turning it around" indicates Chris's realization that, most often, whites are the nondefined definers of other people. Or, to put it another way, whiteness comes to be an unmarked or neutral category, whereas other cultures are specifically marked "cultural."

Many of the women shared the habit of turning to elements of white culture as the unspoken norm. This assumption of a white norm was so prevalent that even Sandy Alvarez and Louise Glebocki, who were acutely aware of racial inequality as well as being members of racially mixed families, referred to "Mexican" music versus "regular" music, and regular meant "white."

Similarly, discussions of race difference and cultural diversity at times revealed a view in which people of color actually embodied difference and whites stood for sameness. Hence, Margaret Phillips said of her Jamaican daughter-in-law that: "She *really* comes with diversity." In spite of its brevity, and because of its curious structure, this short statement says a great deal. It implicitly designates whiteness as norm, and Jamaicans as having or bearing with them "differentness." At the risk of being crass, one might say that in this view, diversity is to the daughter-in-law as "the works" is to a hamburger—added on, adding color and flavor, but not exactly essential. Whiteness, seen by many of these women as boring, but nonetheless definitive, could also follow this analogy. This mode of thinking about "difference" expresses clearly the double-edged sword of a color- and power-evasive repertoire, apparently valorizing cultural difference but doing so in a way that leaves racial and cultural hierarchies intact.

For a seemingly formless entity, then, white culture had a great deal of power, difficult to dislodge from its place in white consciousness as a point of reference for the measuring of others. Whiteness served simultaneously to eclipse and marginalize others (two modes of making the other inessential). Helen Standish's description of her growing-up years in a small New England town captured these processes well. Since the community was all white, the differences at issue were differences between whites. (This also enables an assessment of the links between white and nonwhite "marked" cultures.) Asked about her own cultural identity, Helen explained that "it didn't seem like a culture because everyone else was the same." She had, however, previously mentioned Italian Americans in the town, so I asked about their status. She responded as follows, adopting at first the voice of childhood:

> They are different, but I'm the same as everybody else. They speak Italian, but everybody else in the U.S. speaks English. They eat strange, different food, but I eat the same kind of food as everybody else in the U.S. . . . The way I was brought up was

to think that everybody who was the same as me were "Americans," and the other people were of "such and such descent."

Viewing the Italian Americans as different and oneself as "same" serves, first, to marginalize, to push from the center, the former group. At the same time, claiming to be the same as everyone else makes other cultural groups invisible or eclipses them. Finally, there is a marginalizing of all those who are not like Helen's own family, leaving a residual, core or normative group who are the true Americans. The category of "American" represents simultaneously the normative and the residual, the dominant culture and a nonculture.

Although Helen talked here about whites, it is safe to guess that people of color would not have counted among the "same" group but among the communities of "such and such descent" (Mexican American, for example). Whites, within this discursive repertoire, became conceptually the real Americans, and only certain kinds of whites actually qualified. Whiteness and Americanness both stood as normative and exclusive categories in relation to which other cultures were identified and marginalized. And this clarifies that there are two kinds of whites, just as there are two kinds of Americans: those who are truly or only white, and those who are white but also something more—or is it something less?

In sum, whiteness often stood as an unmarked marker of others' differentness—whiteness not so much void or formlessness as norm. I associate this construction with colonialism and with the more recent assymetrical dualisms of liberal humanist views of culture, race, and identity. For the most part, this construction views nonwhite cultures as lesser, deviant, or pathological. However, another trajectory has been the inverse: conceptualizations of the cultures of peoples of color as somehow better than the dominant culture, perhaps more natural or more spiritual. These are positive evaluations of a sort, but they are equally dualistic. Many of the women I interviewed saw white culture as less appealing and found the cultures of the "different" people more interesting. As Helen Standish put it:

[We had] Wonder bread, white bread. I'm more interested in, you know, "What's a bagel?" in other people's cultures rather than my own.

The claim that whiteness lacks form and content says more about the definitions of culture being used than it does about the content of whiteness. However, I would suggest that in describing themselves as cultureless these women are in fact identifying specific kinds of unwanted absences or presences in their own culture(s) as a generalized lack or nonexistence. It thus becomes important to look at what they *did* say about the cultural content of whiteness.

Descriptions of the content of white culture were thin, to say the least. But despite the paucity of signifiers, there was a great deal of consistency across the narratives. First, there was naming based on color, the linking of white culture with white objects—the clichéd white bread and mayonnaise, for example. Freida Kazen's identification of whiteness as "bland," together with Helen Standish's "blah," also signified paleness or neutrality. The images connote several things—color itself (although exaggerated, and besides, bagels are usually white inside, too), lack of vitality (Wonder bread is highly processed), and homogeneity. However, these images are perched on a slippery slope, at once suggesting "white" identified as a color (though an unappealing one) and as an absence of color, that is, white as the unmarked marker.

Whiteness was often signified in these narratives by commodities and brands: Wonder bread, Kleenex, Heinz 57. In this identification whiteness came to be seen as spoiled by capitalism, and as being linked with capitalism in a way that other cultures supposedly are not. Another set of signifiers that constructed whiteness as uniquely tainted by capitalism had to do with the "modern condition": Dot Humphrey described white neighborhoods as "more privatized," and Cathy Thomas used "alienated" to describe her cultural condition. Clare Traverso added to this theme, mourning her own feeling of lack of identity, in contrast with images of her husband's Italian American background (and here, Clare is again talking about perceived differences between whites):

> Food, old country, mama. Stories about a grandmother who can't speak English. . . . Candles, adobe houses, arts, music. [It] has emotion, feeling, belongingness that to me is unique.

In linking whiteness to capitalism and viewing nonwhite cultures as untainted by it, these women were again drawing on a colonial discourse in which progress and industrialization were seen as synonymous with Westernization, while the rest of the world is seen as caught up in tradition and "culture." In addition, one can identify, in white women's mourning over whiteness, elements of what Raymond Williams has called "pastoralism," or nostalgia for a golden era now gone by (but in fact, says Williams, one that never existed).[1]

The image of whiteness as corrupted and impoverished by capitalism is but one of a series of ways in which white culture was seen as impure or tainted. White culture was also seen as tainted by its relationship to power. For example, Clare Traverso clearly counterposed white culture and white power, finding it difficult to value the former because of the overwhelming weight of the latter:

> The good things about whites are to do with folk arts, music. Because other things have power associated with them.

For many race-cognizant white women, white culture was also made impure by its very efforts to maintain race purity. Dot Humphrey, for example, characterized white neighborhoods as places in which people were segregated by choice. For her, this was a good reason to avoid living in them.

The link between whiteness and domination, however, was frequently made in ways that both artificially isolated culture from other factors and obscured economics. For at times, the traits the women envied in Other cultures were in fact at least in part the product of poverty or other dimensions of oppression. Lack of money, for example, often means lack of privacy or space, and it can be valorized as "more street life, less alienation." Cathy Thomas's notion of Chicanas' relationship to the kitchen ("the hearth of the home") as a cultural "good" might be an idealized one that disregards the reality of intensive labor.

Another link between class and culture emerged in Louise Glebocki's reference to the working-class Chicanos she met as a child as less pretentious, "closer to the truth," more "down to earth." And Marjorie Hoffman spoke of the "earthy humor" of Black people, which she interpreted as, in the words of Langston Hughes, a means of "laughing to keep from crying." On the one hand, as has been pointed out especially by Black scholars and activists, the positions of people of color at the bottom of a social and economic hierarchy create the potential for a critique of the system as a whole and consciousness of the need to resist.[2] From the standpoint of race privilege, the system of racism is thus made structurally invisible. On the other hand, descriptions of this kind leave in place a troubling dichotomy that can be appropriated as easily by the right as by the left. For example, there is an inadvertent affinity between the image of Black people as "earthy" and the conservative racist view that African American culture leaves African American people ill equipped for advancement in the modern age. Here, echoing essentialist racism, both Chicanos and African Americans are placed on the borders of "nature" and "culture."

By the same token, often what was criticized as "white" was as much the product of middle-class status as of whiteness as such. Louise Glebocki's image of her fate had she married a white man was an image of a white-collar, nuclear family:

> Him saying, "I'm home, dear," and me with an apron on—ugh!

The intersections of class, race, and culture were obscured in other ways. Patricia Bowen was angry with some of her white feminist friends who, she felt, embraced as "cultural" certain aspects of African American, Chicano, and Native American cultures (including, for example, artwork or dance performances) but would reject as "tacky" (her term) those aspects of daily life that communities of color shared with working-class whites, such as the stores and supermarkets of poor neighborhoods. This, she felt, was tantamount to a selective expansion of middle-class aesthetic horizons, but not to true antiracism or to comprehension of the cultures of people of color. Having herself grown up in a white working-class family, Pat also felt that middle-class white feminists were able to use selective engagement to avoid addressing their class privilege.

I have already indicated some of the problems inherent in this kind of conceptualization, suggesting that it tends to keep in place dichotomous constructions of "white" versus Other cultures, to separate "culture" from other dimensions of daily life, and to reify or strip of history *all* cultural forms. There are, then, a range of issues that need to be disentangled if we are to understand the location of "whiteness" in the terrain of culture. It is, I believe, useful to approach this question by means of a reconceptualization of the concept of culture itself. A culture, in the sense of the set of rules and practices by means of which a group organizes itself and its values, manners, and worldview—in other words, culture as "a field articulating the life-world of subjects . . . and the structures created by human activity"[3]—is an indispensable precondition to any individual's existence in the world. It is nonsensical in terms of this kind of definition to suggest that anyone could actually have "no culture." But this is not, as I have suggested, the mode of thinking about culture that these women are employing.

Whiteness emerges here as inextricably tied to domination partly as an effect of a discursive "draining process" applied to both whiteness and Americanness. In this process, any cultural practice engaged in by a white person that is not identical to the dominant culture is automatically counted as either "not really white"—and, for that matter, not really American, either—(but rather of such and such descent), or as "not really cultural" (but rather "economic"). There is a slipperiness to whiteness here: it shifts from "no culture" to "normal culture" to "bad culture" and back again. Simultaneously, a range of marginal or, in Trinh T. Minh-ha's terminology, "bounded" cultures are generated. These are viewed as enviable spaces, separate and untainted by relations of dominance or by linkage to other structures or systems. By contrast, whiteness is conceived as axiomatically tied to dominance, to economics, to political structures. In this process, both whiteness and nonwhiteness are reified, made into objects rather than processes, and robbed of historical context and human agency. As long as the discussion remains couched in these terms, a critique of whiteness remains a double-edged sword: for one thing, whiteness remains normative because there is no way to name the cultural practices associated with it *as* cultural. Moreover, as I have suggested, whether whiteness is viewed as artificial and dominating (and therefore "bad") or civilized (and therefore "good"), whiteness and all varieties of nonwhiteness continue to be viewed as ontologically different from one another.

A genuine sadness and frustration about the meaning of whiteness at this moment in history motivated these women to decry white culture. It becomes important, then, to recognize the grains of truth in their views of white culture. It is important to acknowledge their anger and frustration about the meaning of whiteness as we reach toward a politicized analysis of culture that is freer of colonial and pastoral legacies.

The terms "white" and "American" as these women used them signified domination in international and domestic terms. This link is both accurate and inaccurate. While it is true that, by and large, those in power in the United States are white, it is also true that not all those who are white are in power. Nor is the axiomatic linkage between Americanness and power accurate, because not all Americans have the same access to power. At the same time, the link between whiteness, Americanness, and power *are* accurate because, as we have seen, the terms "white" and "American" both function discursively to exclude people from normativity—including white people "of such and such descent." But here we need to distinguish between the fates of people of color and those of white people. Notwithstanding a complicated history, the boundaries of Americanness and whiteness have been much more fluid for "white ethnic" groups than for people of color.

There have been border skirmishes over the meaning of whiteness and Americanness since the inception of those terms. For white people, however, those skirmishes have been resolved through processes of assimilation, not exclusion. The late nineteenth and early twentieth centuries in the United States saw a systematic push toward the cultural homogenization of whites carried out through social reform movements and the schools. This push took place alongside the expansion of industrial capitalism, giving rise to the sense that whiteness signifies the production and consumption of commodities under capitalism.[4] But recognition of this history should not be translated into an assertion that whites were stripped of culture (for to do that would be to continue to adhere to a colonial view of "culture"). Instead one must argue that certain cultural practices replaced others. Were one to undertake a history of this "generic" white culture, it would fragment into a thousand tributary elements, culturally specific religious observances, and class survival mechanisms as well as mass-produced commodities and mass media.

There are a number of dangers inherent in continuing to view white culture as no culture. Whiteness appeared in the narratives to function as both norm or core, that against which everything else is measured, and as residue, that which is left after everything else has been named. A far-reaching danger of whiteness coded as "no culture" is that it leaves in place whiteness as defining a set of normative cultural practices against which all are measured and into which all are expected to fit. This normativity has underwritten oppression from the beginning of colonial expansion and has had impact in multiple ways: from the American pioneers' assumption of a norm of private property used to justify appropriation of land that within their worldview did not have an owner, and the ideological construction of nations like Britain as white,[5] to Western feminism's Eurocentric shaping of its movements and institutions. It is important for white feminists not to continue to participate in these processes.

And if whiteness has a history, so do the cultures of people of color, which are worked on, crafted, and created, rather than just "there." For peoples of color in the United States, this work has gone on as much in the context of relationships to imperialism and capitalism as has the production of whiteness, though it has been premised on exclusion and resistance to exclusion more than on assimilation. Although not always or only forged in resistance, the visibility and recognition of the cultures of U.S. peoples of color in recent times *is* the product of individual and collective struggle. Only a short time has elapsed since those struggles made possible the introduction into public discourse of celebration and valorization of their cultural forms. In short, it is important not to reify any culture by failing to acknowledge its createdness, and not to view it as always having been there in unchanging form.

Rather than feeling "cultureless," white women need to become conscious of the histories and specificities of our cultural positions, and of the political, economic, and creative fusions that form all cultures. The purpose of such an exercise is not, of course, to reinvert the dualisms and valorize whiteness so much as to develop a clearer sense of where and who we are.

NOTES

1. Raymond Williams, *The Country and the City* (New York: Oxford University Press, 1978).
2. The classic statement of this position is W. E. B. Du Bois's concept of the "double consciousness" of Americans of African descent. Two recent feminist statements of similar positions are Patricia Hill Collins, *Black Feminist Thought: Knowledge, Consciousness, and the Politics of Empowerment* (Boston: Unwin Hyman, 1990); and Aida Hurtado, "Relating to Privilege: Seduction and Rejection in the Subordination of White Women and Women of Color," Signs 14, no. 4:833–55.
3. Paul Gilroy, *There Ain't No Black In The Union Jack.* London: Hutchinson, 1987.
4. See, for example, Winthrop Talbot, ed., *Americanization* (New York: H. W. Wilson, 1917), esp. Sophonisba P. Breckinridge, "The Immigrant Family," 251–52, Olivia Howard Dunbar, "Teaching the Immigrant Woman," 252–56, and North American Civic League for Immigrants, "Domestic Education among Immigrants," 256–58; and Kathie Friedman Kasaba, "'To Become a Person': The Experience of Gender, Ethnicity and Work in the Lives of Immigrant Women, New York City, 1870–1940," doctoral dissertation, Department of Sociology, State University of New York, Binghamton, 1991. I am indebted to Katie Friedman Kasaba for these references and for her discussions with me about working-class European immigrants to the United States at the turn of this century.
5. Gilroy, *There Ain't No Black In The Union Jack.*

What Is Sex? What Is Gender?

READING 9

The Five Sexes

Why Male and Female Are Not Enough

Anne Fausto-Sterling

In 1843 Levi Suydam, a twenty-three-year-old resident of Salisbury, Connecticut, asked the town board of selectmen to validate his right to vote as a Whig in a hotly contested local election. The request raised a flurry of objections from the opposition party, for reasons that must be rare in the annals of American democracy: it was said that Suydam was more female than male and thus (some eighty years before suffrage was extended to women) could not be allowed to cast a ballot. To settle the dispute a physician, one William James Barry, was brought in to examine Suydam. And, presumably upon encountering a phallus, the good doctor declared the prospective voter male. With Suydam safely in their column the Whigs won the election by a majority of one.

Barry's diagnosis, however, turned out to be somewhat premature. Within a few days he discovered that, phallus notwithstanding, Suydam menstruated regularly and had a vaginal opening. Both his/her physique and his/her mental predispositions were more complex than was first suspected. S/he had narrow shoulders and broad hips and felt occasional sexual yearnings for women. Suydam's "feminine propensities, such as a fondness for gay colors, for pieces of calico, comparing and placing them together, and an aversion for bodily labor, and an inability to perform the same, were remarked by many," Barry later wrote. It is not clear whether Suydam lost or

Anne Fausto-Sterling is professor of biology and women's studies at Brown University.

retained the vote, or whether the election results were reversed.

Western culture is deeply committed to the idea that there are only two sexes. Even language refuses other possibilities; thus to write about Levi Suydam I have had to invent conventions—*s/he* and *his/her*—to denote someone who is clearly neither male nor female or who is perhaps both sexes at once. Legally, too, every adult is either man or woman, and the difference, of course, is not trivial. For Suydam it meant the franchise; today it means being available for, or exempt from, draft registration, as well as being subject, in various ways, to a number of laws governing marriage, the family and human intimacy. In many parts of the United States, for instance, two people legally registered as men cannot have sexual relations without violating anti-sodomy statutes.

But if the state and the legal system have an interest in maintaining a two-party sexual system, they are in defiance of nature. For biologically speaking, there are many gradations running from female to male; and depending on how one calls the shots, one can argue that along that spectrum lie at least five sexes—and perhaps even more.

For some time medical investigators have recognized the concept of the intersexual body. But the standard medical literature uses the term *intersex* as a catch-all for three major subgroups with some mixture of male and female characteristics: the so-called true hermaphrodites, whom I call herms, who possess one testis and one ovary (the sperm- and egg-producing vessels, or gonads); the male pseudohermaphrodites (the "merms"), who have testes and some aspects of the female genitalia but no ovaries; and the female pseudohermaphrodites (the "ferms"), who have ovaries and some aspects of the male genitalia but lack testes. Each of those categories is in itself complex; the percentage of male and female characteristics, for instance, can vary enormously among members of the same subgroup. Moreover, the inner lives of the people in each subgroup—their special needs and their problems, attractions and repulsions—have gone unexplored by science. But on the basis of what is known about them I suggest that the three intersexes, herm, merm and ferm, deserve to be considered additional sexes each in its own right. Indeed, I would argue further that sex is a vast, infinitely malleable continuum that defies the constraints of even five categories.

Not surprisingly, it is extremely difficult to estimate the frequency of intersexuality, much less the frequency of each of the three additional sexes: it is not the sort of information one volunteers on a job application. The psychologist John Money of Johns Hopkins University, a specialist in the study of congenital sexual-organ defects, suggests intersexuals may constitute as many as 4 percent of births. As I point out to my students at Brown University, in a student body of about 6,000 that fraction, if correct, implies there may be as many as 240 intersexuals on campus—surely enough to form a minority caucus of some kind.

In reality though, few such students would make it as far as Brown in sexually diverse form. Recent advances in physiology and surgical technology now enable physicians to catch most intersexuals at the moment of birth. Almost at once such infants are entered into a program of hormonal and surgical management so that they can slip quietly into society as "normal" heterosexual males or females. I emphasize that the motive is in no way conspiratorial. The aims of the policy are genuinely humanitarian, reflecting the wish that people be able to "fit in" both physically and psychologically. In the medical community, however, the assumptions behind that wish—that there be only two sexes, that heterosexuality alone is normal, that there is one true model of psychological health—have gone virtually unexamined.

The word *hermaphrodite* comes from the Greek names Hermes, variously known as the messenger of the gods, the patron of music, the controller of dreams or the protector of livestock, and Aphrodite, the goddess of sexual love and beauty. According to Greek mythology, those two gods parented Hermaphroditus, who at age fifteen became half male and half female when his body fused with the body of a nymph he fell in love with. In some true hermaphrodites the testis and the ovary grow separately but bilaterally; in others they grow together within the same organ, forming an ovo-testis. Not infrequently, at least one of the gonads functions quite well, producing either sperm cells or eggs, as well as functional levels of the sex hormones—androgens or estrogens. Although in theory it might be possible for a true hermaphrodite to become both father and mother to a child, in practice the appropriate ducts and tubes are not configured so that egg and sperm can meet.

In contrast with the true hermaphrodites, the pseudohermaphrodites possess two gonads of the same kind along with the usual male (XY) or female (XX) chromosomal makeup. But their external genitalia and secondary sex characteristics do not match their chromosomes. Thus merms have testes and XY chromosomes, yet they also have a vagina and a clitoris, and at puberty they often develop breasts. They do not menstruate, however. Ferms have ovaries, two X chromosomes and sometimes a uterus, but they also have at least partly masculine external genitalia. Without medical intervention they can develop beards, deep voices and adult-size penises. . . .

Intersexuality itself is old news. Hermaphrodites, for instance, are often featured in stories about human origins. Early biblical scholars believed Adam began life as a hermaphrodite and later divided into two people—a male and a female—after falling from grace. According to Plato there once were three sexes—male, female and hermaphrodite—but the third sex was lost with time.

Both the Talmud and the Tosefta, the Jewish books of law, list extensive regulations for people of mixed sex. The Tosefta expressly forbids hermaphrodites to inherit their fathers' estates (like daughters), to seclude themselves with women (like sons) or to shave (like men). When hermaphrodites menstruate they must be isolated from men (like women); they are disqualified from serving as witnesses or as priests (like women), but the laws of pederasty apply to them.

In Europe a pattern emerged by the end of the Middle Ages that, in a sense, has lasted to the present day: hermaphrodites were compelled to choose an established gender role and stick with it. The penalty for transgression was often death. Thus in the 1600s a Scottish hermaphrodite living as a woman was buried alive after impregnating his/her master's daughter.

For questions of inheritance, legitimacy, paternity, succession to title and eligibility for certain professions to be determined, modern Anglo-Saxon legal systems require that newborns be registered as either male or female. In the U.S. today sex determination is governed by state laws. Illinois permits adults to change the sex recorded on their birth certificates should a physician attest to having performed the appropriate surgery. The New York Academy of Medicine, on the other hand, has taken an opposite view. In spite of surgical alterations of the external genitalia, the academy argued in 1966, the chromosomal sex remains the same. By that measure, a person's wish to conceal his or her original sex cannot outweigh the public interest in protection against fraud.

During this century the medical community has completed what the legal world began—the complete erasure of any form of embodied sex that does not conform to a male–female, heterosexual pattern. Ironically, a more sophisticated knowledge of the complexity of sexual systems has led to the repression of such intricacy.

In 1937 the urologist Hugh H. Young of Johns Hopkins University published a volume titled *Genital Abnormalities, Hermaphroditism and Related Adrenal Diseases.* The book is remarkable for its erudition, scientific insight and open-mindedness. In it Young drew together a wealth of carefully documented case histories to demonstrate and study the medical treatment of such "accidents of birth." Young did not pass judgment on the people he studied, nor did he attempt to coerce into treatment those intersexuals who rejected that option. And he showed unusual even-handedness in referring to those people who had had sexual experiences as both men and women as "practicing hermaphrodites."

One of Young's more interesting cases was a hermaphrodite named Emma who had grown up as a female. Emma had both a penis-size clitoris and a vagina, which made it possible for him/her to have "normal" heterosexual sex with both men and women. As a teenager Emma had had sex with a number of girls to whom s/he was deeply attracted; but at the age of nineteen s/he had married a man. Unfortunately, he had given Emma little sexual pleasure (though he had had no complaints), and so throughout that marriage and subsequent ones Emma had kept girlfriends on the side. With some frequency s/he had pleasurable sex with them. Young describes his subject as appearing "to be quite content and even happy." In conversation Emma occasionally told him of his/her wish to be a man, a circumstance Young said would be relatively easy to bring about. But Emma's reply strikes a heroic blow for self-interest:

> Would you have to remove that vagina? I don't know about that because that's my meal ticket. If you did that, I would have to quit my husband and go to work, so I think I'll keep it and stay as I am. My husband supports me well, and even though I don't have any sexual pleasure with him, I do have lots with my girlfriends.

Yet even as Young was illuminating intersexuality with the light of scientific reason, he was beginning its suppression. For his book is also an extended treatise on the most modern surgical and hormonal methods of changing intersexuals into either males or females. Young may have differed from his successors in being less judgmental and controlling of the patients and their families, but he nonetheless supplied the foundation on which current intervention practices were built.

By 1969, when the English physicians Christopher J. Dewhurst and Ronald R. Gordon wrote *The Intersexual Disorders,* medical and surgical approaches to intersexuality had neared a state of rigid uniformity. It is hardly surprising that such a hardening of opinion took place in the era of the feminine mystique—of the post-Second World War flight to the suburbs and the strict division of family roles according to sex. That the medical consensus was not quite universal (or perhaps that it seemed poised to break apart again) can be gleaned from the near-hysterical tone of Dewhurst and Gordon's book, which contrasts markedly with the calm reason of Young's founding work. Consider their opening description of an intersexual newborn:

> One can only attempt to imagine the anguish of the parents. That a newborn should have a deformity . . . [affecting] so fundamental an issue as the very sex of the child . . . is a tragic event which immediately conjures up visions of a hopeless psychological misfit doomed to live always as a sexual freak in loneliness and frustration.

Dewhurst and Gordon warned that such a miserable fate would, indeed, be a baby's lot should the case be improperly managed; "but fortunately," they wrote, "with correct management the outlook is infinitely better than the poor parents—emotionally stunned by the event—or indeed anyone without special knowledge could ever imagine."

Scientific dogma has held fast to the assumption that without medical care hermaphrodites are doomed to a life of misery. Yet there are few empirical studies to back up that assumption, and some of the same research gathered to build a case for medical treatment contradicts it. Francies Benton, another of Young's practicing hermaphrodites, "had not worried over his condition, did not wish to be changed, and was enjoying life." The same could be said of Emma, the opportunistic hausfrau. Even Dewhurst and Gordon, adamant about the psychological importance of treating intersexuals at the infant stage, acknowledged great success in "changing the sex" of older patients. They reported on twenty cases of children reclassified into a different sex after the supposedly critical age of eighteen months. They asserted that all the reclassifications were "successful," and they wondered then whether reregistration could be "recommended more readily than [had] been suggested so far."

The treatment of intersexuality in this century provides a clear example of what the French historian Michel Foucault has called biopower. The knowledge developed in biochemistry, embryology, endocrinology, psychology and surgery has enabled physicians to control the very sex of the human body. The multiple contradictions in that kind of power call for some scrutiny. On the one hand, the medical "management" of intersexuality certainly developed as part of an attempt to free people from perceived psychological pain (though whether the pain was the patient's, the parents' or the physician's is unclear). And if one accepts the assumption that in a sex-divided culture people can realize their greatest potential for happiness and productivity only if they are sure they belong to one of only two acknowledged sexes, modern medicine has been extremely successful.

On the other hand, the same medical accomplishments can be read not as progress but as a mode of discipline. Hermaphrodites have unruly bodies. They do not fall naturally into a binary classification; only a surgical shoehorn can put them there. But why should we care if a "woman," defined as one who has breasts, a vagina, a uterus and ovaries and who menstruates, also has a clitoris large enough to penetrate the vagina of another woman? Why should we care if there are people whose biological equipment enables them to have sex "naturally" with both men and women? The answers seem to lie in a cultural need to maintain clear distinctions between the sexes. Society mandates the control of intersexual bodies because they blur and bridge the great divide. Inasmuch as hermaphrodites literally embody both sexes, they challenge traditional beliefs about sexual difference: they possess the irritating ability to live sometimes as one sex and sometimes the other, and they raise the specter of homosexuality.

But what if things were altogether different? Imagine a world in which the same knowledge that has enabled medicine to intervene in the management of intersexual patients has been placed at the service of multiple sexualities. Imagine that the sexes have multiplied beyond currently imaginable limits. It would have to be a world of shared powers. Patient and physician, parent and child, male and female, heterosexual and homosexual—all those oppositions and others would have to be dissolved as sources of division. A new ethic of medical treatment would arise, one that would permit ambiguity in a culture that had overcome sexual division. The central mission of medical treatment would be to preserve life. Thus hermaphrodites would be concerned primarily not about whether they can conform to society but about whether they might develop potentially life-threatening conditions—hernias, gonadal tumors, salt imbalance caused by adrenal malfunction—that sometimes accompany hermaphroditic development. In my ideal world medical intervention for intersexuals would take place only rarely before the age of reason; subsequent treatment would be a cooperative venture between physician, patient and other advisers trained in issues of gender multiplicity.

I do not pretend that the transition to my utopia would be smooth. Sex, even the supposedly "normal," heterosexual kind, continues to cause untold anxieties in Western society. And certainly a culture that has yet to come to grips—religiously and, in some states, legally—with the ancient and relatively uncomplicated reality of homosexual love will not readily embrace intersexuality. No doubt the most troublesome arena by far would be the rearing of children. Parents, at least since the Victorian era, have fretted, sometimes to the point of outright denial, over the fact that their children are sexual beings.

All that and more amply explains why intersexual children are generally squeezed into one of the two prevailing sexual categories. But what would be the psychological consequences of taking the alternative road—raising children as unabashed intersexuals? On the surface that tack seems fraught with peril. What, for example, would happen to the intersexual child amid the unrelenting cruelty of the school yard? When the time came to shower in gym class, what horrors and humiliations would await the intersexual as his/her anatomy was displayed in all its nontraditional glory? In whose gym class would s/he register to begin with? What bathroom would s/he use? And how on earth would Mom and Dad help shepherd him/her through the mine field of puberty?

In the past thirty years those questions have been ignored, as the scientific community has, with remarkable unanimity, avoided contemplating the alternative route of unimpeded intersexuality. But modern investigators tend to overlook a substantial body of case histories, most of them compiled between 1930 and 1960, before surgical intervention became rampant. Almost without exception, those reports describe children who grew up knowing they were intersexual (though they did not advertise it) and adjusted to their unusual status. Some of the studies are richly detailed—described at the level of gym-class showering (which most intersexuals avoided without incident); in any event, there is not a psychotic or a suicide in the lot.

Still, the nuances of socialization among intersexuals cry out for more sophisticated analysis. Clearly, before my vision of sexual multiplicity can be realized, the first openly intersexual children and their parents will have to be brave pioneers who will bear the brunt of society's growing pains. But in the long view—though it could take generations to achieve—the prize might be a society in which sexuality is something to be celebrated for its subtleties and not something to be feared or ridiculed.

READING 10

The Five Sexes, Revisited

Anne Fausto-Sterling

As Cheryl Chase stepped to the front of the packed meeting room in the Sheraton Boston Hotel, nervous coughs made the tension audible. Chase, an activist for intersexual rights, had been invited to address the May 2000 meeting of the Lawson Wilkins Pediatric Endocrine Society (LWPES), the largest organization in the United States for specialists in children's hormones. Her talk would be the grand finale to a four-hour symposium on the treatment of genital ambiguity in newborns, infants born with a mixture of both male and female anatomy, or genitals that appear to differ from their chromosomal sex. The topic was hardly a novel one to the assembled physicians.

Yet Chase's appearance before the group was remarkable. Three and a half years earlier, the American Academy of Pediatrics had refused her request for a chance to present the patients' viewpoint on the treatment of genital ambiguity, dismissing Chase and her supporters as "zealots." About two dozen intersex people had responded by throwing up a picket line. The Intersex Society of North America (ISNA) even issued a press release: "Hermaphrodites Target Kiddie Docs."

It had done my 1960s street-activist heart good. In the short run, I said to Chase at the time, the picketing would make people angry. But eventually, I assured her, the doors then closed would open. Now, as Chase began to address the physicians at their own convention, that prediction was coming true. Her talk, titled "Sexual Ambiguity: The Patient-Centered Approach,"

Anne Fausto-Sterling is a professor of biology and women's studies at Brown University. Portions of this [essay] were adapted from her book *Sexing the Body* (Basic Books, 2000).

was a measured critique of the near-universal practice of performing immediate, "corrective" surgery on thousands of infants born each year with ambiguous genitalia. Chase herself lives with the consequences of such surgery. Yet her audience, the very endocrinologists and surgeons Chase was accusing of reacting with "surgery and shame," received her with respect. Even more remarkably, many of the speakers who preceded her at the session had already spoken of the need to scrap current practices in favor of treatments more centered on psychological counseling.

What led to such a dramatic reversal of fortune? Certainly, Chase's talk at the LWPES symposium was a vindication of her persistence in seeking attention for her cause. But her invitation to speak was also a watershed in the evolving discussion about how to treat children with ambiguous genitalia. And that discussion, in turn, is the tip of a biocultural iceberg—the gender iceberg—that continues to rock both medicine and our culture at large.

Chase made her first national appearance in 1993 . . . announcing the formation of ISNA in a letter responding to an essay I had written for *The Sciences,* titled "The Five Sexes" [March/April 1993]. In that article I argued that the two-sex system embedded in our society is not adequate to encompass the full spectrum of human sexuality. In its place, I suggested a five-sex system. In addition to males and females, I included "herms" (named after true hermaphrodites, people born with both a testis and an ovary); "merms" (male pseudohermaphrodites, who are born with testes and some aspect of female genitalia); and "ferms" (female pseudohermaphrodites, who have ovaries combined with some aspect of male genitalia).

I had intended to be provocative, but I had also written with tongue firmly in cheek. So I was surprised by the extent of the controversy the article unleashed. Right-wing Christians were outraged, and connected my idea of five sexes with the United Nations–sponsored Fourth World Conference on Women, held in Beijing in September 1995. At the same time, the article delighted others who felt constrained by the current sex and gender system.

Clearly, I had struck a nerve. The fact that so many people could get riled up by my proposal to revamp our sex and gender system suggested that change—as well as resistance to it—might be in the offing. Indeed, a lot has changed since 1993, and I like to think that my article was an important stimulus. As if from nowhere, intersexuals are materializing before our very eyes. Like Chase, many have become political organizers, who lobby physicians and politicians to change current treatment practices. But more generally, though perhaps no less provocatively, the boundaries separating masculine and feminine seem harder than ever to define.

Some find the changes under way deeply disturbing. Others find them liberating.

Who is an intersexual—and how many intersexuals are there? The concept of intersexuality is rooted in the very ideas of male and female. In the idealized, Platonic, biological world, human beings are divided into two kinds: a perfectly dimorphic species. Males have an X and a Y chromosome, testes, a penis and all of the appropriate internal plumbing for delivering urine and semen to the outside world. They also have well-known secondary sexual characteristics, including a muscular build and facial hair. Women have two X chromosomes, ovaries, all of the internal plumbing to transport urine and ova to the outside world, a system to support pregnancy and fetal development, as well as a variety of recognizable secondary sexual characteristics.

That idealized story papers over many obvious caveats: some women have facial hair, some men have none; some women speak with deep voices, some men veritably squeak. Less well known is the fact that, on close inspection, absolute dimorphism disintegrates even at the level of basic biology. Chromosomes, hormones, the internal sex structures, the gonads and the external genitalia all vary more than most people realize. Those born outside of the Platonic dimorphic mold are called intersexuals.

In "The Five Sexes" I reported an estimate by a psychologist expert in the treatment of intersexuals, suggesting that some 4 percent of all live births are intersexual. Then, together with a group of Brown University undergraduates, I set out to conduct the first systematic assessment of the available data on intersexual birthrates. We scoured the medical literature for estimates of the frequency of various categories of intersexuality, from additional chromosomes to mixed gonads, hormones and genitalia. For some conditions we could find only anecdotal evidence; for most, however, numbers exist. On the basis of that evidence, we calculated that for every 1,000 children born, seventeen are intersexual in some form. That number—1.7 percent—is a ballpark estimate, not a precise count, though we believe it is more accurate than the 4 percent I reported.

Our figure represents all chromosomal, anatomical and hormonal exceptions to the dimorphic ideal; the number of intersexuals who might, potentially, be subject to surgery as infants is smaller—probably between one in 1,000 and one in 2,000 live births. Furthermore, because some populations possess the relevant genes at high frequency, the intersexual birthrate is not uniform throughout the world.

Consider, for instance, the gene for congenital adrenal hyperplasia (CAH). When the CAH gene is inherited from both parents, it leads to a baby with masculinized external genitalia who possesses two X chromosomes and the internal reproductive organs of a potentially fertile woman. The frequency of the gene varies widely around the world: in New Zealand it occurs in only forty-three children per million; among the Yupik Eskimo of southwestern Alaska, its frequency is 3,500 per million.

Intersexuality has always been to some extent a matter of definition. And in the past century physicians have been the ones who defined children as intersexual—and provided the remedies. When only the chromosomes are unusual, but the external genitalia and gonads clearly indicate either a male or a female, physicians do not advocate intervention. Indeed, it is not clear what kind of intervention could be advocated in such cases. But the story is quite different when infants are born with mixed genitalia, or with external genitals that seem at odds with the baby's gonads.

Most clinics now specializing in the treatment of intersex babies rely on case-management principles developed in the 1950s by the psychologist John Money and the psychiatrists Joan G. Hampson and John L. Hampson, all of Johns Hopkins University in Baltimore, Maryland. Money believed that gender identity is completely malleable for about eighteen months after birth. Thus, he argued, when a treatment team is presented with an infant who has ambiguous genitalia, the team could make a gender assignment solely on the basis of what made the best surgical sense. The physicians could then simply encourage the parents to raise the child according to the surgically assigned gender. Following that course, most physicians maintained, would eliminate psychological distress for both the patient and the parents. Indeed, treatment teams were never to use such words as "intersex" or "hermaphrodite"; instead, they were to tell parents that nature intended the baby to be the boy or the girl that the physicians had determined it was. Through surgery, the physicians were merely completing nature's intention.

Although Money and the Hampsons published detailed case studies of intersex children who they said had adjusted well to their gender assignments, Money thought one case in particular proved his theory. It was a dramatic example, inasmuch as it did not involve intersexuality at all: one of a pair of identical twin boys lost his penis as a result of a circumcision accident. Money recommended that "John" (as he came to be known in a later case study) be surgically turned into "Joan" and raised as a girl. In time, Joan grew to love wearing dresses and having her hair done. Money proudly proclaimed the sex reassignment a success.

But as recently chronicled by John Colapinto, in his book *As Nature Made Him,* Joan—now known to be an adult male named David Reimer—eventually rejected his female assignment. Even without a functioning penis and testes (which had been removed as part of the reassignment) John/Joan sought masculinizing medication, and married a woman with children (whom he adopted).

Since the full conclusion to the John/Joan story came to light, other individuals who were reassigned as males or females shortly after birth but who later rejected their early assignments have come forward. So, too, have cases in which the reassignment has worked—at least into the subject's mid-twenties. But even then the aftermath of the surgery can be problematic. Genital surgery often leaves scars that reduce sexual sensitivity. Chase herself had a complete clitoridectomy, a procedure that is less frequently performed on intersexuals today. But the newer surgeries, which reduce the size of the clitoral shaft, still greatly reduce sensitivity.

The revelation of cases of failed reassignments and the emergence of intersex activism have led an increasing number of pediatric endocrinologists, urologists and psychologists to reexamine the wisdom of early genital surgery. For example, in a talk that preceded Chase's at the LWPES meeting, the medical ethicist Laurence B. McCullough of the Center for Medical Ethics and Health Policy at Baylor College of Medicine in Houston, Texas, introduced an ethical framework for the treatment of children with ambiguous genitalia. Because sex phenotype (the manifestation of genetically and embryologically determined sexual characteristics) and gender presentation (the sex role projected by the individual in society) are highly variable, McCullough argues, the various forms of intersexuality should be defined as normal. All of them fall within the statistically expected variability of sex and gender. Furthermore, though certain disease states may accompany some forms of intersexuality, and may require medical intervention, intersexual conditions are not themselves diseases.

McCullough also contends that in the process of assigning gender, physicians should minimize what he calls irreversible assignments: taking steps such as the surgical removal or modification of gonads or genitalia that the patient may one day want to have reversed. Finally, McCullough urges physicians to abandon their practice of treating the birth of a child with genital ambiguity as a medical or social emergency. Instead, they should take the time to perform a thorough medical workup and should disclose everything to the parents, including the uncertainties about the final outcome. The treatment mantra, in other words, should be therapy, not surgery.

I believe a new treatment protocol for intersex infants, similar to the one outlined by McCullough, is close at hand. Treatment should combine some basic medical and ethical principles with a practical but less drastic approach to the birth of a mixed-sex child. As a first step, surgery on infants should be performed only to save the child's life or to substantially improve the child's physical well-being. Physicians may assign a sex—male or female—to an intersex infant on the basis of the probability that the child's particular condition will lead to the formation of a particular gender identity. At the same time, though, practitioners ought to be humble enough to recognize that as the child grows, he or she may reject the assignment—and they should be wise enough to listen to what the child has to say. Most important, parents should have access to the full range of information and options available to them.

Sex assignments made shortly after birth are only the beginning of a long journey. Consider, for instance, the life of Max Beck: Born intersexual, Max was surgically assigned as a female and consistently raised as such. Had her medical team followed her into her early twenties, they would have deemed her assignment a success because she was married to a man. (It should be noted that success in gender assignment has traditionally been defined as living in that gender as a heterosexual.) Within a few years, however, Beck had come out as a butch lesbian; now in her mid-thirties, Beck has become a man and married his lesbian partner, who (through the miracles of modern reproductive technology) recently gave birth to a girl.

Transsexuals, people who have an emotional gender at odds with their physical sex, once described themselves in terms of dimorphic absolutes—males trapped in female bodies, or vice versa. As such, they sought psychological relief through surgery. Although many still do, some so-called transgendered people today are content to inhabit a more ambiguous zone. A male-to-female transsexual, for instance, may come out as a lesbian. Jane, born a physiological male, is now in her late thirties and living with her wife, whom she married when her name was still John. Jane takes hormones to feminize herself, but they have not yet interfered with her ability to engage in intercourse as a man. In her mind Jane has a lesbian relationship with her wife, though she views their intimate moments as a cross between lesbian and heterosexual sex.

It might seem natural to regard intersexuals and transgendered people as living midway between the poles of male and female. But male and female, masculine and feminine, cannot be parsed as some kind of continuum. Rather, sex and gender are best conceptualized as points in a multidimensional space. For some time, experts on gender development have distinguished between sex at the genetic level and at the cellular level (sex-specific gene expression, X and Y chromosomes); at the hormonal level (in the fetus, during childhood and after puberty); and at the anatomical level (genitals and secondary sexual characteristics). Gender identity presumably emerges from all of those corporeal aspects via some poorly understood interaction with environment and experience. What has become increasingly clear is that one can find levels of masculinity and femininity in almost every possible permutation. A chromosomal, hormonal and genital male (or female) may emerge with a female (or male) gender identity. Or a chromosomal female with male fetal hormones and masculinized genitalia—but with female pubertal hormones—may develop a female gender identity.

The medical and scientific communities have yet to adopt a language that is capable of describing such diversity. In her book *Hermaphrodites and the Medical Intervention of Sex,* the historian and medical ethicist Alice Domurat Dreger of Michigan State University in East Lansing documents the emergence of current medical systems for classifying gender ambiguity. The current usage remains rooted in the Victorian approach to sex. The logical structure of the commonly used terms "true hermaphrodite," "male pseudohermaphrodite" and "female pseudohermaphrodite" indicates that only the so-called true hermaphrodite is a genuine mix of male and female. The others, no matter how confusing their body parts, are really hidden males or females. Because true hermaphrodites are rare—possibly only one in 100,000—such a classification system supports the idea that human beings are an absolutely dimorphic species.

At the dawn of the twenty-first century, when the variability of gender seems so visible, such a position is hard to maintain. And here, too, the old medical consensus has begun to crumble. Last fall the pediatric urologist Ian A. Aaronson of the Medical University of South Carolina in Charleston organized the North American Task Force on Intersexuality (NATFI) to review the clinical responses to genital ambiguity in infants. Key medical associations, such as the American Academy of Pediatrics, have endorsed NATFI. Specialists in surgery, endocrinology, psychology, ethics, psychiatry, genetics and public health, as well as intersex patient-advocate groups, have joined its ranks.

One of the goals of NATFI is to establish a new sex nomenclature. One proposal under consideration replaces the current system with emotionally neutral terminology that emphasizes developmental processes rather than preconceived gender categories. For example, Type I intersexes develop out of anomalous virilizing influences; Type II result from some interruption of virilization; and in Type III intersexes the gonads themselves may not have developed in the expected fashion.

What is clear is that since 1993, modern society has moved beyond five sexes to a recognition that gender variation is normal and, for some people, an arena for playful exploration. Discussing my "five sexes" proposal in her book *Lessons from the Intersexed* (New Brunswick, N.J.: Rutgers University Press, 1998), the psychologist Suzanne J. Kessler of the State University of New York at Purchase drives this point home with great effect:

> The limitation with Fausto-Sterling's proposal is that . . . [it] still gives genitals . . . primary signifying status and ignores the fact that in the everyday world gender attributions are made without access to genital inspection. . . . What has primacy in everyday life is the gender that is performed, regardless of the flesh's configuration under the clothes.

I now agree with Kessler's assessment. It would be better for intersexuals and their supporters to turn everyone's focus away from genitals. Instead, as she suggests, one should acknowledge that people come in an even wider assortment of sexual identities and characteristics than mere genitals can distinguish. Some women may have "large clitorises or fused labia," whereas some men may have "small penises or misshapen scrota," as Kessler puts it, "phenotypes with no particular clinical or identity meaning."

As clearheaded as Kessler's program is—and despite the progress made in the 1990s—our society is still far from that ideal. The intersexual or transgendered person who projects a social gender—what Kessler calls "cultural genitals"—that conflicts with his or her physical genitals still may die for the transgression. Hence legal protection for people whose cultural and physical genitals do not match is needed during the current transition to a more gender-diverse world. One easy step would be to eliminate the category of "gender" from official documents, such as driver's licenses and passports. Surely attributes both more visible (such as height, build and eye color) and less visible (fingerprints and genetic profiles) would be more expedient.

A more far-ranging agenda is presented in the International Bill of Gender Rights, adopted in 1995 at the fourth annual International Conference on Transgender Law and Employment Policy in Houston, Texas. It lists ten "gender rights," including the right to define one's own gender, the right to change one's physical gender if one so chooses and the right to marry whomever one wishes. The legal bases for such rights are being hammered out in the courts as I write and, most recently, through the establishment, in the state of Vermont, of legal same-sex domestic partnerships.

No one could have foreseen such changes in 1993. And the idea that I played some role, however small, in reducing the pressure—from the medical community as well as from society at large—to flatten the diversity of human sexes into two diametrically opposed camps gives me pleasure.

Sometimes people suggest to me, with not a little horror, that I am arguing for a pastel world in which androgyny reigns and men and women are boringly the same. In my vision, however, strong colors coexist with pastels. There are and will continue to be highly masculine people out there; it's just that some of them are women. And some of the most feminine people I know happen to be men.

READING 11

The Berdache Tradition

Walter L. Williams

Because it is such a powerful force in the world today, the Western Judeo-Christian tradition is often accepted as the arbiter of "natural" behavior of humans. If Europeans and their descendant nations of North America accept something as normal, then anything different is seen as abnormal. Such a view ignores the great diversity of human existence.

This is the case for the study of gender. How many genders are there? To a modern Anglo-American, nothing might seem more definite than the answer that there are two: men and women. But not all societies around the world agree with Western culture's view that all humans are either women or men. The commonly accepted notion of "the opposite sex," based on anatomy, is itself an artifact of our society's rigid sex roles.

Among many cultures, there have existed different alternatives to "man" or "woman." An alternative role in many American Indian societies is referred to by anthropologists as *berdache*. . . . The role varied from one Native American culture to another, which is a reflection of the vast diversity of aboriginal New World societies. Small bands of hunter-gatherers existed in some areas, with advanced civilizations of farming peoples in other areas. With hundreds of different languages, economies, religions, and social patterns existing in North America alone, every generalization about a cultural tradition must acknowledge many exceptions.

This diversity is true for the berdache tradition as well, and must be kept in mind. My statements should be read as being specific to a particular culture, with generalizations being treated as loose patterns that might not apply to peoples even in nearby areas.

Briefly, a berdache can be defined as a morphological male who does not fill a society's standard man's role, who has a nonmasculine character. This type of person is often stereotyped as effeminate, but a more accurate characterization is androgyny. Such a person has a clearly recognized and accepted social status, often based on a secure place in the tribal mythology. Berdaches have special ceremonial roles in many Native American religions, and important economic roles in their families. They will do at least some women's work, and mix together much of the behavior, dress, and social roles of women and men. Berdaches gain social prestige by their spiritual, intellectual, or craftwork/artistic contributions, and by their reputation for hard work and generosity. They serve a mediating function between women and men, precisely because their character is seen as distinct from either sex. They are not seen as men, yet they are not seen as women either. They occupy an alternative gender role that is a mixture of diverse elements.

In their erotic behavior berdaches also generally (but not always) take a nonmasculine role, either being asexual or becoming the passive partner in sex with men. In some cultures the berdache might become a wife to a man. This male-male sexual behavior became the focus of an attack on berdaches as "sodomites" by the Europeans who, early on, came into contact with them. From the first Spanish conquistadors to the Western frontiersmen and the Christian missionaries and government officials, Western culture has had a considerable impact on the berdache tradition. In the last two decades, the most recent impact on the tradition is the adaptation of a modern Western gay identity.

To Western eyes berdachism is a complex and puzzling phenomenon, mixing and redefining the very concepts of what is considered male and

Walter L. Williams is professor of anthropology and the study of women and men in society at the University of Southern California, Los Angeles.

female. In a culture with only two recognized genders, such individuals are gender nonconformist, abnormal, deviant. But to American Indians, the institution of another gender role means that berdaches are not deviant—indeed, they do conform to the requirements of a custom in which their culture tells them they fit. Berdachism is a way for society to recognize and assimilate some atypical individuals without imposing a change on them or stigmatizing them as deviant. This cultural institution confirms their legitimacy for what they are.

Societies often bestow power upon that which does not neatly fit into the usual. Since no cultural system can explain everything, a common way that many cultures deal with these inconsistencies is to imbue them with negative power, as taboo, pollution, witchcraft, or sin. That which is not understood is seen as a threat. But an alternative method of dealing with such things, or people, is to take them out of the realm of threat and to sanctify them.[1] The berdaches' role as mediator is thus not just between women and men, but also between the physical and the spiritual. American Indian cultures have taken what Western culture calls negative, and made it a positive; they have successfully utilized the different skills and insights of a class of people that Western culture has stigmatized and whose spiritual powers have been wasted.

Many Native Americans also understood that gender roles have to do with more than just biological sex. The standard Western view that one's sex is always a certainty, and that one's gender identity and sex role always conform to one's morphological sex is a view that dies hard. Western thought is typified by such dichotomies of groups perceived to be mutually exclusive: male and female, black and white, right and wrong, good and evil. Clearly, the world is not so simple; such clear divisions are not always realistic. Most American Indian worldviews generally are much more accepting of the ambiguities of life. Acceptance of gender variation in the berdache tradition is typical of many native cultures' approach to life in general.

Overall, these are generalizations based on those Native American societies that had an accepted role for berdaches. Not all cultures recognized such a respected status. Berdachism in aboriginal North America was most established among tribes in four areas: first, the Prairie and western Great Lakes, the northern and central Great Plains, and the lower Mississippi Valley; second, Florida and the Caribbean; third, the Southwest, the Great Basin, and California; and fourth, scattered areas of the Northwest, western Canada, and Alaska. For some reason it is not noticeable in eastern North America, with the exception of its southern rim. . . .

AMERICAN INDIAN RELIGIONS

Native American religions offered an explanation for human diversity by their creation stories. In some tribal religions, the Great Spiritual Being is conceived as neither male nor female but as a combination of both. Among the Kamia of the Southwest, for example, the bearer of plant seeds and the introducer of Kamia culture was a man-woman spirit named Warharmi.[2] A key episode of the Zuni creation story involves a battle between the kachina spirits of the agricultural Zunis and the enemy hunter spirits. Every four years an elaborate ceremony commemorates this myth. In the story a kachina spirit called *ko'lhamana* was captured by the enemy spirits and transformed in the process. This transformed spirit became a mediator between the two sides, using his peacemaking skills to merge the differing lifestyles of hunters and farmers. In the ceremony, a dramatic reenactment of the myth, the part of the transformed *ko'lhamana* spirit, is performed by a berdache.[3] The Zuni word for berdache is *lhamana,* denoting its closeness to the spiritual mediator who brought hunting and farming together.[4] The moral of this story is that the berdache was created by the deities for a special purpose, and that this creation led to the improvement of society. The continual reenactment of this story provides a justification for the Zuni berdache in each generation.

In contrast to this, the lack of spiritual justification in a creation myth could denote a lack of tolerance for gender variation. The Pimas, unlike most of their Southwestern neighbors, did not respect a berdache status. *Wi-kovat,* their derogatory word, means "like a girl," but it does not signify a recognized social role. Pima mythology reflects this lack of acceptance, in a folk tale that explains male androgyny as due to Papago witchcraft. Knowing that the Papagos respected berdaches, the Pimas blamed such an occurrence on an alien influence.[5] While the Pimas' condemnatory attitude is unusual, it does point out the importance of spiritual explanations for the acceptance of gender variance in a culture.

Other Native American creation stories stand in sharp contrast to the Pima explanation. A good example is the account of the Navajos, which presents women and men as equals. The Navajo origin tale is told as a story of five worlds. The first people were First Man and First Woman, who were created equally and at the same time. The first two worlds that they lived in were bleak and unhappy, so they escaped to the third world. In the third world lived two twins, Turquoise Boy and White Shell Girl, who were the first berdaches. In the Navajo language the word for berdache is *nadle,* which means "changing one" or "one who is transformed." It is applied to hermaphrodites—those who are born with the genitals of both male and female—and also to "those who pretend to be *nadle,*" who take on a social role that is distinct from either men or women.[6]

In the third world, First Man and First Woman began farming, with the help of the changing twins. One of the twins noticed some clay and, holding it in the palm of his/her hand, shaped it into the first pottery bowl. Then he/she formed a plate, a water dipper, and a pipe. The second twin observed some reeds and began to weave them, making the first basket. Together they shaped axes and grinding stones from rocks, and hoes from bone. All these new inventions made the people very happy.[7]

The message of this story is that humans are dependent for many good things on the inventiveness of *nadle.* Such individuals were present from the earliest eras of human existence, and their presence was never questioned. They were part of the natural order of the universe, with a special contribution to make.

Later on in the Navajo creation story, White Shell Girl entered the moon and became the Moon Bearer. Turquoise Boy, however, remained with the people. When First Man realized that Turquoise Boy could do all manner of women's work as well as women, all the men left the women and crossed a big river. The men hunted and planted crops. Turquoise Boy ground the corn, cooked the food, and weaved cloth for the men. Four years passed with the women and men separated, and the men were happy with the *nadle.* Later, however, the women wanted to learn how to grind corn from the *nadle,* and both the men and the women had decided that it was not good to continue living separately. So the women crossed the river and the people were reunited.[8]

They continued living happily in the third world, until one day a great flood began. The people ran to the highest mountaintop, but the water kept rising and they all feared they would be drowned. But just in time, the ever-inventive Turquoise Boy found a large reed. They climbed upward inside the tall hollow reed, and came out at the top into the fourth world. From there, White Shell Girl brought another reed, and they climbed again to the fifth world, which is the present world of the Navajos.[9]

These stories suggest that the very survival of humanity is dependent on the inventiveness of berdaches. With such a mythological belief system, it is no wonder that the Navajos held *nadle* in high regard. The concept of the *nadle* is well formulated in the creation story. As children were educated by these stories, and all Navajos believed in them, the high status accorded to gender variation was passed down from generation to generation. Such stories also provided instructions for *nadle* themselves to live by. A spiritual explanation guaranteed a special place for a person who was considered different but not deviant.

For American Indians, the important explanations of the world are spiritual ones. In their view, there is a deeper reality than the here-and-now. The real essence or wisdom occurs when one finally gives up trying to explain events in terms of "logic" and "reality." Many confusing aspects of existence can better be explained by actions of a multiplicity of spirits. Instead of a concept of a single god, there is an awareness of "that which we do not understand." In Lakota religion, for example, the term *Wakan Tanka* is often translated as "god." But a more proper translation, according to the medicine people who taught me, is "The Great Mystery."[10]

While rationality can explain much, there are limits to human capabilities of understanding. The English language is structured to account for cause and effect. For example, English speakers say, "It is raining," with the implication that there is a cause "it" that leads to rain. Many Indian languages, on the other hand, merely note what is most accurately translated as "raining" as an observable fact. Such an approach brings a freedom to stop worrying about causes of things, and merely to relax and accept that our human insights can go only so far. By not taking ourselves too seriously, or overinflating human importance, we can get beyond the logical world.

The emphasis of American Indian religions, then, is on the spiritual nature of all things. To understand the physical world, one must appreciate the underlying spiritual essence. Then one can begin to see that the physical is only a faint shadow, a partial reflection, of a supernatural and extrarational world. By the Indian view, everything that exists is spiritual. Every object—plants, rocks, water, air, the moon, animals, humans, the earth itself—has a spirit. The spirit of one thing (including a human) is not superior to the spirit of any other. Such a view promotes a sophisticated ecological awareness of the place that humans have in the larger environment. The function of religion is not to try to condemn or to change what exists, but to accept the realities of the world and to appreciate their contributions to life. Everything that exists has a purpose.[11]

One of the basic tenets of American Indian religion is the notion that everything in the universe is related. Nevertheless, things that exist are often seen as having a counterpart: sky and earth, plant and animal, water and fire. In all of these polarities, there exist mediators. The role of the mediator is to hold the polarities together, to keep the world from disintegrating. Polarities exist within human society also. The most important category within Indian society is gender. The notions of Woman and Man underlie much of social interaction and are comparable to the other major polarities. Women, with their nurturant qualities, are associated with the earth, while men are associated with the sky. Women gatherers and farmers deal with plants (of the earth), while men hunters deal with animals.

The mediator between the polarities of woman and man, in the American Indian religious explanation, is a being that combines the elements of both genders. This might be a combination in a physical sense, as in the case of hermaphrodites. Many Native American religions accept this phenomenon in the same way that they accept other variations from the norm. But more important is their acceptance of the idea that gender can be combined in ways other than physical hermaphroditism. The physical aspects of a thing or a person, after all, are not nearly as important as its spirit. American Indians use the concept of a person's *spirit* in the way that other Americans use the concept of a person's *character*. Consequently, physical hermaphroditism is not necessary for the idea of gender mixing. A person's character, their spiritual essence, is the crucial thing.

THE BERDACHE'S SPIRIT

Individuals who are physically normal might have the spirit of the other sex, might range somewhere between the two sexes, or might have a spirit that is distinct from either women or men. Whatever category they fall into, they are seen as being different from men. They are accepted spiritually as "Not Man." Whichever option is chosen, Indian religions offer spiritual explanations. Among the Arapahos of the Plains, berdaches are called *haxu'xan* and are seen to be that way as a result of a supernatural gift from birds or animals. Arapaho mythology recounts the story of Nih'a'ca, the first *haxu'xan.* He pretended to be a woman and married the mountain lion, a symbol for masculinity. The myth, as recorded by ethnographer Alfred Kroeber about 1900, recounted that "These people had the natural desire to become women, and as they grew up gradually became women. They gave up the desires of men. They were married to men. They had miraculous power and could do supernatural things. For instance, it was one of them that first made an intoxicant from rainwater."[12] Besides the theme of inventiveness, similar to the Navajo creation story, the berdache role is seen as a product of a "natural desire." Berdaches "gradually became women," which underscores the notion of woman as a social category rather than as a fixed biological entity. Physical biological sex is less important in gender classification than a person's desire—one's spirit.

The myths contain no prescriptions for trying to change berdaches who are acting out their desires of the heart. Like many other cultures' myths, the Zuni origin myths simply sanction the idea that gender can be transformed independently of biological sex.[13] Indeed, myths warn of dire consequences when interference with such a transformation is attempted. Prince Alexander Maximilian of the German state of Wied, traveling in the northern Plains in the 1830s, heard a myth about a warrior who once tried to force a berdache to avoid women's clothing. The berdache resisted, and the warrior shot him with an arrow. Immediately the berdache disappeared, and the warrior saw only a pile of stones with his arrow in them. Since then, the story concluded, no intelligent person would try to coerce a berdache.[14] Making the point even more directly, a Mandan myth told of an Indian who tried to force *mihdacke* (berdaches) to give up their distinctive dress and status, which led the spirits to punish many people with death. After that, no Mandans interfered with berdaches.[15]

With this kind of attitude, reinforced by myth and history, the aboriginal view accepts human diversity. The creation story of the Mohave of the Colorado River Valley speaks of a time when people were not sexually differentiated. From this perspective, it is easy to accept that certain individuals might combine elements of masculinity and femininity.[16] A respected Mohave elder, speaking in the 1930s, stated this viewpoint simply: "From the very beginning of the world it was meant that there should be [berdaches], just as it was instituted that there should be shamans. They were intended for that purpose."[17]

This elder also explained that a child's tendencies to become a berdache are apparent early, by about age nine to twelve, before the child reaches puberty: "That is the time when young persons become initiated into the functions of their sex. . . . None but young people will become berdaches as a rule."[18] Many tribes have a public ceremony that acknowledges the acceptance of berdache status. A Mohave shaman related the ceremony for his tribe: "When the child was about ten years old his relatives would begin discussing his strange ways. Some of them disliked it, but the more intelligent began envisaging an initiation ceremony." The relatives prepare for the ceremony without letting the boy know of it. It is meant to take him by surprise, to be both an initiation and a test of his true inclinations. People from various settlements are invited to attend. The family wants the community to see it and become accustomed to accepting the boy as an *alyha.*

On the day of the ceremony, the shaman explained, the boy is led into a circle: "If the boy showed a willingness to remain standing in the circle, exposed to the public eye, it was almost certain that he would go through with the ceremony. The singer, hidden behind the crowd, began singing the songs. As soon as the sound reached the boy he began to dance as women do." If the boy is unwilling to assume *alyha* status, he would refuse to dance. But if his character—his spirit—is *alyha,* "the song goes right to his heart and he will dance with much intensity. He cannot help it. After the fourth song he is proclaimed." After the ceremony, the boy is carefully bathed and receives a woman's skirt. He is then led back to the dance ground, dressed as an *alyha,* and announces his new feminine name to the crowd. After that he would resent being called by his old male name.[19]

Among the Yuman tribes of the Southwest, the transformation is marked by a social gathering, in which the berdache prepares a meal for the friends of the family.[20] Ethnographer Ruth Underhill, doing fieldwork among the Papago Indians in the early 1930s, wrote that berdaches were common among the Papago Indians, and were usually publicly acknowledged in childhood. She recounted that a boy's parents would test him if they noticed that he preferred female pursuits. The regular pattern, mentioned by many of Underhill's Papago informants, was to build a small brush enclosure. Inside the enclosure they placed a man's bow and arrows, and also a woman's basket. At the appointed time the boy was brought to the enclosure as the adults watched from outside. The boy was told to go inside the circle of brush. Once he was inside, the adults "set fire to the enclosure. They watched what he took with him as he ran out and if it was the basketry materials, they reconciled themselves to his being a berdache."[21]

What is important to recognize in all of these practices is that the assumption of a berdache role was not forced on the boy by others. While adults might have their suspicions, it was only when the child made the proper move that he was considered a berdache. By doing woman's dancing, preparing a meal, or taking the woman's basket he was making an important symbolic gesture. Indian children were not stupid, and they knew the implications of these ceremonies beforehand. A boy in the enclosure could have left without taking anything, or could have taken both the man's and the woman's tools. With the community standing by watching, he was well aware that his choice would mark his assumption of berdache status. Rather than being seen as an involuntary test of his reflexes, this ceremony may be interpreted as a definite statement by the child to take on the berdache role.

Indians do not see the assumption of berdache status, however, as a free will choice on the part of the boy. People felt that the boy was acting out his basic character. The Lakota shaman Lame Deer explained:

> They were not like other men, but the Great Spirit made them *winktes* and we accepted them as such. . . . We think that if a woman has two little ones growing inside her, if she is going to have twins, sometimes instead of giving birth to two babies they have formed up in her womb into just one, into a half-man/half-woman kind of being. . . . To us a man is what nature, or his dreams, make him. We accept him for what he wants to be. That's up to him.[22]

While most of the sources indicate that once a person becomes a berdache it is a lifelong status, directions from the spirits determine everything. In at least one documented case, concerning a nineteenth-century Klamath berdache named Lele'ks, he later had a supernatural experience that led him to leave the berdache role. At that time Lele'ks began dressing and acting like a man, then married women, and eventually became one of the most famous Klamath chiefs.[23] What is important is that both in assuming berdache status and in leaving it, supernatural dictate is the determining factor.

DREAMS AND VISIONS

Many tribes see the berdache role as signifying an individual's proclivities as a dreamer and a visionary. . . .

Among the northern Plains and related Great Lakes tribes, the idea of supernatural dictate through dreaming—the vision quest—had its highest development. The goal of the vision quest is to try to get beyond the rational world by sensory deprivation and fasting. By depriving one's body of nourishment, the brain could escape from logical thought and connect with the higher reality of the supernatural. The person doing the quest simply sits and waits for a vision. But a vision might not come easily; the person might have to wait for days.

The best way that I can describe the process is to refer to my own vision quest, which I experienced when I was living on a Lakota reservation in 1982. After a long series of prayers and blessings, the shaman who had prepared me for the ceremony took me out to an isolated area where a sweat lodge had been set up for my quest. As I walked to the spot, I worried that I might not be able to stand it. Would I be overcome by hunger? Could I tolerate the thirst? What would I do if I had to go to the toilet? The shaman told me not to worry, that a whole group of holy people would be praying and singing for me while I was on my quest.

He had me remove my clothes, symbolizing my disconnection from the material world, and crawl into the sweat lodge. Before he left me I asked him, "What do I think about?" He said, "Do not think. Just pray for spiritual guidance." After a prayer he closed the flap tightly and I was left in total darkness. I still do not understand what happened to me during my vision quest, but during the day and a half that I was out there, I never once felt hungry or thirsty or the need to go to the toilet. What happened was an intensely personal experience that I cannot and do not wish to explain, a process of being that cannot be described in rational terms.

When the shaman came to get me at the end of my time, I actually resented having to end it. He did not need to ask if my vision quest were successful. He knew that it was even before seeing me, he explained, because he saw an eagle circling over me while I underwent the quest. He helped interpret the signs I had seen, then after more prayers and singing he led me back to the others. I felt relieved, cleansed, joyful, and serene. I had been through an experience that will be a part of my memories always.

If a vision quest could have such an effect on a person not even raised in Indian society, imagine its impact on a boy who from his earliest years had been waiting for the day when he could seek his vision. Gaining his spiritual power from his first vision, it would tell him what role to take in adult life. The vision might instruct him that he is going to be a great hunter, a craftsman, a warrior, or a shaman. Or it might tell him that he will be a berdache. Among the Lakotas, or Sioux, there are several symbols for various types of visions. A person becomes *wakan* (a sacred person) if she or he dreams of a bear, a wolf, thunder, a buffalo, a white buffalo calf, or Double Woman. Each dream results in a different gift, whether it is the power to cure illness or wounds, a promise of good hunting, or the exalted role of a *heyoka* (doing things backward).

A white buffalo calf is believed to be a berdache. If a person has a dream of the sacred Double Woman, this means that she or he will have the power to seduce men. Males who have a vision of Double Woman are presented with female tools. Taking such tools means that the male will become a berdache. The Lakota word *winkte* is composed of *win,* "woman," and *kte,* "would become."[24] A contemporary Lakota berdache explains, "To become a *winkte,* you have a medicine man put you up on the hill, to search for your vision. You can become a *winkte* if you truly are by nature. You see a vision of the White Buffalo Calf Pipe. Sometimes it varies. A vision is like a scene in a movie."[25] Another way to become a *winkte* is to have a vision given by a *winkte* from the past.[26]. . .

By interpreting the result of the vision as being the work of a spirit, the vision quest frees the person from feeling responsible for his transformation. The person might even claim that the change was done against his will and without his control. Such a claim does not suggest a negative attitude about berdache status, because it is common for people to claim reluctance to fulfill their spiritual duty no matter what vision appears to them. Becoming any kind of sacred person involves taking on various social responsibilities and burdens.[27] . . .

A story was told among the Lakotas in the 1880s of a boy who tried to resist following his vision from Double Woman. But according to Lakota informants "few men succeed in this effort after having taken the strap in the dream." Having rebelled against the instructions given him by the Moon Being, he committed suicide.[28] The moral of that story is that one should not resist spiritual guidance, because it will lead only to grief. In another case, an Omaha young man told of being addressed by a spirit as "daughter," whereupon he discovered that he was unconsciously using feminine styles of speech. He tried to use male speech patterns, but could not. As a result of this vision, when he returned to his people he resolved himself to dress as a woman.[29] Such stories function to justify personal peculiarities as due to a fate over which the individual has no control.

Despite the usual pattern in Indian societies of using ridicule to enforce conformity, receiving instructions from a vision inhibits others from trying to change the berdache. Ritual explanation provides a way out. It also excuses the community from worrying about the cause of that person's difference, or the feeling that it is society's duty to try to change him.[30] Native American religions, above all else, encourage a basic respect for nature. If nature makes a person different, many Indians conclude, a mere human should not undertake to counter this spiritual dictate. Someone who is "unusual" can be accommodated without being stigmatized as "abnormal." Berdachism is thus not alien or threatening; it is a reflection of spirituality.

NOTES

1. Mary Douglas, *Purity and Danger* (Baltimore: Penguin, 1966), p. 52. I am grateful to Theda Perdue for convincing me that Douglas's ideas apply to berdachism. For an application of Douglas's thesis to berdaches, see James Thayer, "The Berdache of the Northern Plains: A Socioreligious Perspective," *Journal of Anthropological Research* 36 (1980): 292–93.
2. E. W. Gifford, "The Kamia of Imperial Valley," *Bureau of American Ethnology Bulletin* 97 (1931): 12.
3. By using present tense verbs in this text, I am not implying that such activities are necessarily continuing today. I sometimes use the present tense in the "ethnographic present," unless I use the past tense when I am referring to something that has not continued. Past tense implies that all such practices have disappeared. In the absence of fieldwork to prove such disappearance, I am not prepared to make that assumption, on the historic changes in the berdache tradition.
4. Elsie Clews Parsons, "The Zuni La' Mana," *American Anthropologist* 18 (1916): 521; Matilda Coxe Stevenson, "Zuni Indians," *Bureau of American Ethnology Annual Report* 23 (1903): 37; Franklin Cushing, "Zuni Creation Myths," *Bureau of American Ethnology Annual Report* 13 (1894): 401–3. Will Roscoe clarified this origin story for me.
5. W. W. Hill, "Note on the Pima Berdache," *American Anthropologist* 40 (1938): 339.
6. Aileen O'Bryan, "The Dine': Origin Myths of the Navaho Indians," *Bureau of American Ethnology Bulletin* 163 (1956): 5; W. W. Hill, "The Status of the Hermaphrodite and Transvestite in Navaho Culture," *American Anthropologist* 37 (1935): 273.
7. Martha S. Link, *The Pollen Path: A Collection of Navajo Myths* (Stanford, CA: Stanford University Press, 1956).
8. O'Bryan, "Dine'," pp. 5, 7, 9–10.
9. Ibid.
10. Lakota informants, July 1982. See also William Powers, *Oglala Religion* (Lincoln: University of Nebraska Press, 1977).
11. For this admittedly generalized overview of American Indian religious values, I am indebted to traditionalist informants of many tribes, but especially those of the Lakotas. For a discussion of native religions see Dennis Tedlock, *Finding the Center* (New York: Dial Press, 1972); Ruth Underhill, *Red Man's Religion* (Chicago: University

of Chicago Press, 1965); and Elsie Clews Parsons, *Pueblo Indian Religion* (Chicago: University of Chicago Press, 1939).
12. Alfred Kroeber, "The Arapaho," *Bulletin of the American Museum of Natural History* 18 (1902–7): 19.
13. Parsons, "Zuni La' Mana," p. 525.
14. Alexander Maximilian, *Travels in the Interior of North America, 1832–1834,* vol. 22 of *Early Western Travels,* ed. Reuben Gold Thwaites, 32 vols. (Cleveland: A. H. Clark, 1906), pp. 283–84, 354. Maximilian was quoted in German in the early homosexual rights book by Ferdinand Karsch-Haack, *Das Gleichgeschlechtliche Leben der Naturvölker* (The same-sex life of nature peoples) (Munich: Verlag von Ernst Reinhardt, 1911; reprinted New York: Arno Press, 1975), pp. 314, 564.
15. Oscar Koch, *Der Indianishe Eros* (Berlin: Verlag Continent, 1925), p. 61.
16. George Devereux, "Institutionalized Homosexuality of the Mohave Indians," *Human Biology* 9 (1937): 509.
17. Ibid., p. 501.
18. Ibid.
19. Ibid., pp. 508–9.
20. C. Daryll Forde, "Ethnography of the Yuma Indians," *University of California Publications in American Archaeology and Ethnology* 28 (1931): 157.
21. Ruth Underhill, *Social Organization of the Papago Indians* (New York: Columbia University Press, 1938), p. 186. This story is also mentioned in Ruth Underhill, ed., *The Autobiography of a Papago Woman* (Menasha, WI: American Anthropological Association, 1936), p. 39.
22. John Fire and Richard Erdoes, *Lame Deer, Seeker of Visions* (New York: Simon and Schuster, 1972), pp. 117, 149.
23. Theodore Stern, *The Klamath Tribe: A People and Their Reservation* (Seattle: University of Washington Press, 1965), pp. 20, 24; Theodore Stern, "Some Sources of Variability in Klamath Mythology," *Journal of American Folklore* 69 (1956): 242ff; Leshe Spier, *Klamath Ethnography* (Berkeley: University of California Press, 1930), p. 52.
24. Clark Wissler, "Societies and Ceremonial Associations in the Oglala Division of the Teton Dakota," *Anthropological Papers of the American Museum of Natural History* 11, pt. 1 (1916): 92; Powers, Oglala Religion, pp. 57–59.
25. Ronnie Loud Hawk, Lakota informant 4, July 1982.
26. Terry Calling Eagle, Lakota informant 5, July 1982.
27. James S. Thayer, "The Berdache of the Northern Plains: A Socioreligious Perspective," *Journal of Anthropological Research* 36 (1980): 289.
28. Fletcher, "Elk Mystery," p. 281.
29. Alice Fletcher and Francis La Flesche, "The Omaha Tribe," *Bureau of American Ethnology Annual Report* 27 (1905–6): 132.
30. Harriet Whitehead offers a valuable discussion of this element of the vision quest in "The Bow and the Burden Strap: A New Look at Institutionalized Homosexuality in Native North America," in *Sexual Meanings,* ed. Sherry Ortner and Harriet Whitehead (Cambridge: Cambridge University Press, 1981), pp. 99–102. See also Erikson, "Childhood," p. 329.

READING 12

Similarity and Difference

The Sociology of Gender Distinctions

Cynthia Fuchs Epstein

. . . Today, social scientists and the lay public are interested in the extent to which sex and gender distinctions are basic (e.g., part of their "essential" nature) because of biology or psychological processes set early in life, or result primarily from structural and cultural boundaries, and are therefore amenable to alteration through changes in law, policy, and opportunity. The essentialist belief in basic sex differences has consequences for women's position in life and has justified

Cynthia Fuchs Epstein is professor of sociology at the Graduate Center, City University of New York.

men's dominance and women's subordination in most spheres of social life, yet it is unsupported empirically. There are far more variations within each sex with regard to talents, interests, and intelligence than there are between each sex, although it often does not look that way. The small gender differences that show up in tests measuring certain cognitive abilities (including math and verbal skills) are perceived to be representative of the entire population of males or females, rather than the small percentages difference they are, while within-gender differences are minimized or overlooked (Baumeister, 1988; Feingold, 1988; Hyde, 1981, cited in Briton & Hall, 1995). Furthermore, men and women are often forced to display the qualities of behavior, interest, or appearance that a person of their sex is supposed to possess naturally (Goffman, 1977), which may situate them differently (or segregate them) in the family (Goode, 1964) and at work (Reskin & Hartmann, 1986). For example, women do smile and laugh more than men according to one study (Hall, 1984), but this may be because women receive positive feedback when they smile, and elicit anger when they do not.

Unlike other categories of people who are regarded as "other," such as people of color, females and males do not live in different residential communities but often cluster in separate domains within them, such as workplaces and places of recreation (Epstein, 1992; Huffman & Velasco, 1997; Bielby & Buron, 1984). Not only is gender segregation often not seen as problematic to men or women, but many people believe that a higher order, a higher morality, the good of society, or the good of each sex is served by such differentiation (e.g., advocates of single-sex schools for girls, and segregated male military schools) (Epstein, 1997; Vojdik, 1997).

Such perspectives often come from a cultural bias toward simple explanations and a bias toward consistency between ideals and behavior. Thus, most people believe there is common agreement with regard to what they mean by "man" or "woman." Yet, as with all broad categories, popular definitions and perceptions may vary considerably.

Interpretations of the "typical" male and female (as is the case with other broadly defined categories) also vary according to age, class, and the special circumstances of interaction. Assessments of what is typical and appropriate may be perceived differently in different settings. For example, in all-female groups women may act in a bawdy manner without fear of being perceived as unfeminine, although bawdiness is usually regarded as male behavior, as Westwood (1985) illustrates in her study of British hosiery company workers. Yet, in some all-male groups (e.g., in some sports and war), men often demonstrate tender and caring behavior that might be interpreted as unmanly in mixed groups. When atypical gendered behavior becomes public, however, redefinition or reinterpretation about what is "normal" for a particular category of people may occur.

Women are not only different within their gender but they may also manifest different behaviors and traits in their private lives. That is, aspects of the "selves" may include differing and even contradictory components (Crosby, 1987; Haraway, 1991; Nicholson, 1990; Spence, 1984, 1985; Thoits, 1983); or, they may show different personalities in playing different roles. Those scholars who write as if there were a single feminine self assume that women and men play out their roles with reliable consistency, as if they possessed monotone personalities. They, like many laypeople, prefer the idea of a whole person with a body and personality that match. Some believe it to be an indicator of integrity. The notion of oneness not only also fits cultural stereotypes but fits neatly into scientific categories that one can run through a computer or code on a data sheet (such as running "sex" as a variable with the underlying assumption that being male or female accounts for a behavior). Sometimes, of course, roles are consistent, or people may highlight one dimension of their "self" for political or personal purposes (e.g., Hispanic or senior citizen) to differentiate themselves from others. Thus, people may concentrate on the traits that differentiate themselves from others, not those they share, a common problem in the politics of many institutions such as the family and the workplace.

EXPLAINING THE ORIENTATION TOWARD DIFFERENCES

The persistent emphasis on differences between women and men with regard to their basic nature (cognitive and emotional)—whether it comes from scholars who identify themselves as feminists or nonfeminists—may be attributed to various factors: (1) inattention to the evidence that shows similarities rather than differences between the sexes; (2) incomplete and inappropriate models, such as those assuming a sex-differentiated "human nature"; (3) an ideological agenda; (4) confusion between cause and effect, such as regarding sex segregation at work as "natural" rather than the result of biases that force men and women into sex-labeled occupations; and (5) focus on sex as the primary determining variable that explains behavior. Many of these overlap (Epstein, 1991). . . .

The explanatory frameworks used to account for observed differences and gender inequality have evoked contentious debate. These debates have been engaged in within an historical context in which the reporting of sex differences is often biased in the direction of differences rather than similarities in characteristics and behavior between the sexes. Scholars, as well as journalists, proclaim difference (no matter how small) in ways that imply mutually exclusive qualities between women and men. Sometimes this work suggests support for the perspective that women are inferior to men because they are not capable of engaging in the activities with which men are associated (such as working as engineers and scientists), but more recently it has been used to suggest women's superiority in some attributes such as morality (see Epstein, 1988, for a discussion of this). Further, studies that report support for conventional views of women's personalities and abilities are more often reported by the press (James, 1997), but those indicating positive outcomes of women's unconventional behavior (such as superior mental health of employed women compared to homemakers) have been given short shrift by the media. The journalist and scholar Susan Faludi (1991) reports that the press failed (and continues to fail) to report paradigms and studies showing gender similarity and the positive outcomes of the changing social roles of women and men. Yet, in recent years, "difference" has been accepted by some feminist scholars and used to evaluate women as better than men on issues of "connection" or empathy (Gilligan, 1982), or to suggest that they have alternative modes of understanding (Belenky, Clinchy, Goldberger, & Tarule, 1986; Tannen 1990). I have detailed the evidence elsewhere (Epstein, 1988) for rejecting the view that women have basically different abilities than men. This view is also supported by comprehensive reviews by Aries (1996), Hyde (1990a), Feingold (1992), and by Tavris (1992), who wisely concluded in her book *The Mismeasure of Woman,* ". . . women are not the better sex, the inferior sex, or the opposite sex." Yet there has been an enormous spillover effect from the work of Gilligan (1982), who suggested that women are predisposed to an ethic of "care," into many fields, including legal studies and educational theory. The idea that women have "different ways of knowing" has been developed also by social philosophers, such as Harding (1986), and by the historian of science Keller (1978) (see also Belenky et al., 1986). . . .

Meaningful Differences

The magnitude of difference in behavior preferences of men and women is also important to consider when establishing how meaningful a quality might be in differentiating the sexes. Usually, large differences would be the measure of meaningful sex variation. However, studies might show *statistically* significant differences when the actual differences might be quite tiny, and thus *socially* insignificant. Thus, the purpose of the inquiry ought to determine social and not merely statistical "significance." As an example, politicians are usually concerned with otherwise insignificant differences between groups because a tiny difference can determine the results of an election. From a social science point of view, it is the case that between-sex differences are far smaller than within-sex differences. For example, in the 1996 congressional race, 55% of women voted for Democrats compared to 46% of men, according to a *New York Times* poll (*New York Times,* November 11, 1996)—the notable "gender gap." The focus is on the 9% who voted differently and not the 91% who voted the same. In the 1992 Presidential race the disparity between males and females was even less—6%. As Hout and his colleagues point out (Hout, Brooks, & Manza, 1995), class differences in voting patterns are twice as large as gender difference.

Most reporting that refers to "women" and "men" as unitary collectivities does not make note of the spread of preferences or capacities found within each category and is usually based on very small percentage differences. The reporting indicates an ignorance of how to interpret a statistical distribution. It refers to categories as if they were mutually exclusive, such as "black" and "white." As in the case of sex, in defining a racial category, many of the same kinds of conceptualizations are understood to be real representations that are in fact not descriptive of individuals within a group (e.g., racial laws in some states classified individuals as black when they had one-sixteenth black "blood," and could have more easily described such an individual as "white"). Similarly, using small differences to distinguish "male" or "female" behavior (often not more than a two or three percentage point difference) or any observed characteristic is enough to convince people that a particular man or woman can be located at the end of the distribution where those small differences lie (Sherif, 1979).

The problem of the method used to assess difference is great, as can be illustrated through examination of the research in two areas, leadership and aggression.

It is widely believed that women and men have different styles of leadership (Rosener, 1995), although subordinates of women leaders (Aries, 1996, p. 67) and colleagues (Dobbins & Platz, 1986; Nieva & Gutek, 1982; Powell, 1988) indicate that they exhibit the same range of behaviors as men. However, some studies show differences whereas other studies show great similarities in the behavior of women and men. Some studies also indicate that individuals' reports on their own behavior are inconsistent with the reports of observers. For example, in one study women reported that they demonstrated less dominant and competitive behavior than men, but the researcher observed no difference (Snodgrass & Rosenthal, 1984). Other studies found no gender differences in dominance and competitive behavior (Chanin & Schneer, 1984; Rahim, 1983). In another study (Korabik, Baril, & Watson, 1993) experienced managers of both sexes failed to reveal differences in self-reported conflict management style. However, *self-reports* about preferred conflict management style are poor predictors of actual behaviors (Baril, Korabik, Watson, Grencavage, & Gutkowski, 1990; Bass, 1990; Korabik et al., 1993). It is interesting that among 374 studies of leadership styles, only 37 were observation studies and the rest were self-reports (Aries, 1996).

Even when the management styles of women and men are similar, there may be a perception, and consequent evaluation of that style based on gender. For example, the study of gender differences in management style and leadership effectiveness by Korabik et al. (1993) revealed that although there were no gender differences in their management styles, male and female supervisors were evaluated differently.

Thus we see that although some men and women leaders report similar styles, others do not. Moreover, in many cases individuals report behaviors that conform to stereotypes for their sex, although observers report that they behave quite differently than their self-descriptions suggest. Because there is widespread belief in difference, many books and conferences are devoted to women's presumed different styles (see Belenky et al., 1986; Gilligan, 1982; Harding, 1986; Keller, 1978; Rosener, 1995; Smith, 1990; Tannen, 1990). Furthermore, male superiors believe women behave differently and thus offer them jobs in human resources and exclude them from staff jobs that would give them the experience to rise in a corporation (Kanter, 1977).

Aggression has been identified as a trait found to occur more in males than in females (Maccoby & Jacklin, 1974). It is important to examine this concept because aggression is supposed to account for the domination of men in the power structure of society and in their relations with women.[1] Yet the very term "aggression" refers to a loose collection of behaviors and attitudes that are often unrelated to one another [as a review by Brinkerhof and Booth (1984) points out]. Predation, initiative, competition, dominance, territorial behavior, and hostility are among the behaviors considered in studies of aggression. A comprehensive review of hundreds of experimental studies on adult female and male aggression by Frodi, Macaulay, and Thome (1977) shows that it is difficult to make a clear assessment of differences on all these dimensions. First, the studies are not all comparative and over half are studies of men only. Many studies tend to be of children or college students; however, it has been found that differences noted between boys and girls, especially preschoolers, tend to become small by adulthood (Hyde, 1990a). An overview (McKenna & Kessler, 1974) shows that of more than 80 general and theoretical discussions of aggression in books and journals, references to studies do not specify the magnitude of differences and whether they are large enough to warrant characterizing women as less aggressive than men. Using a meta-analysis, Eagly (1987), has shown that aggressive and nonaggressive behaviors are tied to social roles (see also Hyde, 1990a); men are required to show aggression, when, for example, they work as soldiers or even bonds tradesmen, but women are required *not* to be aggressive as teachers or nurses. Nonetheless, men working as social workers are required to be nonaggressive and women firefighters are supposed to charge into dangerous situations. Other studies show that women are often the same or harsher than men with regard to verbal aggression or hostility (Epstein, 1988).

Choice of Indicators

"Male" and "female" or "masculine" and "feminine" are general concepts. How they are defined, however, varies in different groups and different cultures. Definitions of male and female often follow stereotypes and may not accurately reflect the actual behavior of men and women or the range of behaviors exhibited by each sex. For example, women are regarded as emotional and men as unemotional in American society, yet the opposite is true in Iran (Epstein, 1970). Probably both sexes, in all societies, manifest "emotion" publicly according to the norms that encourage or discourage such behavior and may not reflect their internal states.

"Male" and "female" are usually based on a composite of factors that seem to go together. For example, women are believed to be nurturant, self-sacrificing, and sociable. There is an underlying assumption that these are stable characteristics and consistent across situations. Many researchers assume stability when they study people at a particular point in time. This constitutes a bias in perspective that reflects the fact that individuals may vary over the course of a day, or a lifetime. It fails to recognize that individuals are complicated, and their behaviors are not necessarily consistent.

Attributes as Interactional

Most behavior identified as male and female is seen in interactional settings (Deaux & Major, 1987; Ridgeway, 1997). Individuals in interaction may put pressure on each other to conform to an expected behavior that is in line with a stereotype. For example, in my research on women in the legal profession, some women attorneys reported that male judges ordered them to smile. Of course, they had to respond to the order. This shows how the status and rank of the person with whom a female or male is interacting will cause adjustments in behavior. Females and males may therefore act quite differently when alone; with an age peer; or with a person who is older, with more power, and in a normatively defined role relationship. How "female" or "male" one is may very much depend on one's interactional partner. Thus, research centered on single events rarely captures the complexity created by the feedback effects of individuals in social settings.

Inattention to Variables Other Than Sex

Power, age, social status, and ethnicity all structure how gender-related behaviors play out, and how they also vary in particular situations and historical periods. Therefore, researchers need to go beyond identifying the sex of a person and note the other characteristics that may account for his or her behavior. For example, women who hold positions of authority are usually more assertive than women in powerless jobs. This is not because they become "like men," but because the positions require assertiveness and women learn to act in that manner. Similarly, men in subordinate positions are not "like women" when they defer to a boss; they are playing their role according to the rules. Characteristics thought of as "male" or "female" are also embedded in a life cycle and time framework. In any concrete situation in which maleness and femaleness are being assessed or observed, females and males of particular ages are being observed. Yet women and men often exhibit very different characteristics at young, middle, and older ages, women often gaining in authority, and men often demonstrating more nurturing qualities after retirement or during child rearing years if they take on child care responsibility (Brody, 1997).

The issue of the life course is of great interest because, as noted previously, many studies that define male and female behavior are based on studies conducted in schools or laboratory settings (using school-aged children or young adults). Yet youngsters may change their "character" either through maturity, developmental changes, socialization, or acquisition of different roles.

Impact of Social Change on Gendered Behavior

Many views about females and males are tied to particular time periods. Tastes change in popular culture and with them, men's and women's behavior. Some practices change because legal changes open women's options. Other practices change because social conditions permit or repress certain kinds of activity. This phenomenon is too extensive to document in this [discussion], but a few examples illustrate the social construction of what are believed to be immutable sex-related behaviors.

As noted earlier, aggression is taken to be a defining characteristic of males and not females, yet its expression changes in form and incidence in different time periods. Norms regarding the appropriateness of women expressing aggression also change in societies (Zuckerman, Cole, & Bruer, 1991). Many feminist historians have documented women's assertiveness in labor union activity at certain points and places in history (Costello, 1991; Turbin, 1992; Vallas, 1993), yet traditionally public collective action was associated with men and not women.

Interest in and use of guns may be a good indicator of aggression and assertiveness. The use of firearms has been considered a natural prerogative of men, and people look to its sources in the play behavior of boys who often "turn" objects into guns and play "cops and robbers." This is used as an example of men's "natural" aggression and women's "natural" passivity. Nonetheless, girls and women now are more interested in guns than in the past. A significant number take target practice and they comprise 15% to 20% of the National Rifle Association membership (Epstein, 1995). That organization even elected its first woman president in 1995 (*Wall Street Journal,* May 22, 1995). In Israel, women, who are conscripted into the army, commonly train with guns (unless they are religiously orthodox, in which case they are not required to join the army).

In the United States, women and men choose to go to medical and law schools in almost equal numbers (Epstein, 1993), a radical change from the time when it was believed that women did not enjoy the conflict of the courtroom (Epstein, 1993) or the challenge of the operating room (Lorber, 1984). In 1963 women constituted only 3.8% of entering classes in professional schools (Epstein, 1981) and it was believed that women had no interest in medicine or the law. Today, they constitute more than 40% of students in these professional schools.

Conversations between men and women have received much attention recently, partly because of Deborah Tannen's (1990) popular book, *You Just Don't Understand,* which was on the best seller lists for many weeks. This book implies that basic differences lead to a "two worlds" approach to gender interaction. However, studies of speech show that men's and women's voices are influenced by social expectations and social control. For example, a recent article in the *Wall Street Journal* reported that "elevator girls" in Japan who had been required to speak in a high-pitched voice deemed essentially feminine are now permitted to speak in a more natural, lower-moderated tone. . . .

CONCLUSION

Men and women are adaptable, but their adaptability is not random. Members of some social groups or categories are permitted more diversity and change. The last few decades have provided the perfect "field experiment" to indicate how variable women and men can be. More dramatically today than at any time in history, American women (and unfortunately to a lesser extent, men) are recognized as publicly and personally complex creatures. The ambivalence that greets these changes also indicates the extent to which cultural and social controls determine the ability to change and to accept the notion of change in oneself.

Sociological studies of gender should more directly relate to this experience and we should derive our models from it, not from the armchair or the paradigmatic legacies of theorists who had a stake in the status quo. The more one goes into the field to do actual research on women's behavior, the more one finds that the concepts we call male and female—or gender—comprise multiple realities for the individual and for society. Researchers should note that "male" and "female" are concepts, not things. What they are is always in question; they are not steady states. The theory and research methodology that label gender characteristics and define them according to custom without checking them against reality cheat women and men of their right to be evaluated as individuals, with an array of human characteristics.

Acknowledgments

I would like to acknowledge the research assistance of Marie Mark, Elizabeth Wissinger and Barry Davison in the preparation of this [essay]. I would also like to thank Carol Crane, who helped produce this manuscript while I was in residence at the Stanford Law School, 1997–98.

NOTE

1. For a fuller discussion see "It's all in the mind," Chapter 4 in Epstein (1988).

REFERENCES

Aries, E. (1996). *Men and women in interaction: Reconsidering the differences.* New York: Oxford University Press.

Baril, G. L., Korabik, K., Watson, C., Grencavage, L. M., & Gutkowksi, J. M. (1990, June). Manager's conflict resolution behaviors as predictors of leadership effectiveness. A paper presented at the meeting of the International Association for Conflict Management, Vancouver, BC.

Bass, B. M. (1990). *Bass and Stogdill's handbook of leadership* (3rd ed.). New York: The Free Press.

Baumeister, R. F. (1988). Should we stop studying sex differences altogether? *American Psychologist,* 43, 1092–1095.

Belenky, M. F., Clinchy, B. M., Goldberger, N. R., & Tarule, J. M. (1986). *Women's ways of knowing: The development of self, voice, and mind.* New York: Basic Books.

Bielby, W. T., & Baron, J. N. (1984). A woman's place is with other women: Sex segregation within organizations. In B. Reskin (ed.), *Sex segregation in the workplace: Trends, explanations, remedies* (pp. 27–55). Washington, DC: National Academy Press.

Brinkerhof, D. B., & Booth, A. (1984). Gender dominance and stress. *Journal of Social Biological Structure,* 7 (2), 159–177.

Briton, N. J., & Hall, J. A. (1995). Beliefs about female and male nonverbal communication. *Sex Roles: A Journal of Research,* 32, 79–91.

Brody. L. (1997). Gender and emotion: Beyond stereotypes. *Journal of Social Issues,* 53, 369–394.

Chanin, M. N., & Schneer, J. A. (1984). A study of the relationship between Jungian personality dimensions and conflict-handling behavior. *Human Relations,* 37, 863–879.

Costello, C. (1991). *We're worth it! Women and collective action in the insurance workplace.* Chicago: University of Illinois Press.

Crosby, F. (1987). *Spouse, parent, worker: On gender and multiple roles.* New Haven, CT: Yale University Press.

Deaux, K., & Major, B. (1987). Putting gender into context: An interactive model of gender-related behavior. *Psychological Review,* 94, 369–389.

Dobbins, G. H., & Platz, S. J. (1986). Sex differences in leadership: How real are they? *Academy of Management Review,* 11, 118–127.

Eagly, A. H. (1987). *Sex differences in social behavior: A social role interpretation.* Hillsdale, NJ: Erlbaum.

Epstein, C. F. (1970). *Woman's place: Options and limits in professional careers.* Berkeley: University of California Press.

Epstein, C. F. (1988). *Deceptive distinctions: Sex, gender and the social order.* New Haven, CT: Yale University Press.

Epstein, C. F. (1991). What's right and what's wrong with the research on gender. *Sociological Viewpoints,* 5, 1–14.

Epstein, C. F. (1992). Tinkerbells and pinups: The construction and reconstruction of gender boundaries at work. In M. Lamont & M. Fournier, *Cultivating differences: Symbolic boundaries and the making of inequality* (pp. 232–256). Chicago: University of Chicago Press.

Epstein, C. F. (1993). *Women in law* (2nd ed.). Chicago: University of Illinois Press.

Epstein, C. F. (1995). Pistol-packing mamas. *Dissent,* Fall, 536–537.

Epstein, C. F. (1997). Myths and justifications of sex segregation in higher education: VMI and the Citadel. *Duke Journal of Gender Law & Policy,* 4, 101–118.

Epstein, C. F., & Coser, R. L. (1981). *Access to power: Cross-national studies of women and elites.* London: George Allen & Unwin.

Faludi, S. (1991). *Backlash: The undeclared war against American women.* New York: Crown.

Feingold, A. (1988). Cognitive gender differences are disappearing. *American Psychologist,* 43, 95–103.

Feingold, A. (1992). Sex differences in variability in intellectual abilities: A new look at an old controversy. *Review of Educational Research,* 62, 61–84.

Frodi, A., Macaulay, J., & Thome, P. R. (1977). Are women always less aggressive than men? A review of the experimental literature. *Psychological Bulletin* 84, 634–660.

Gilligan, C. (1982). *In a different voice.* Cambridge, MA: Harvard University Press.

Goffman, E. (1977). Arrangements between the sexes. *Theory and Society,* 4, 301–331.

Goode, W. J. (1964). *The family* (2nd ed.). Englewood Cliffs, NJ: Prentice-Hall.

Hall, J. A. (1984). *Nonverbal sex differences: Communication accuracy and expressive style.* Baltimore, MD: The Johns Hopkins University Press.

Haraway, D. (1991). *Simians, cyborgs, and women.* New York: Routledge.

Harding, S. (1986). *The science question in feminism.* Ithaca: Cornell University Press.

Hout, M., Brooks, C., & Manza, J. (1995). The democrative class struggle in the United States,

1948–1992. *American Sociological Review,* 60, 805–828.

Huffman, M. L., & Velasco, S. C. (1997). When more is less: Sex composition, organizations and earning in U.S. firms. *Work and Occupations,* 24, 214–244.

Hyde, J. S. (1981). How large are cognitive gender differences? *American Psychologist,* 36, 892–901.

Hyde, J. S. (1990a). Meta-analysis and the psychology of gender differences. *Signs,* 16, 55–73.

Hyde, J. S. (1990b). *Understanding human sexuality.* New York: McGraw Hill.

James, J. B. (1997). What are the social issues involved in focusing on difference in the study of gender? *Journal of Social Issues,* 53, 213–232.

Kanter, R. M. (1977). *Men and women of the corporation.* New York: Basic Books.

Keller, E. F. (1978). Gender and science. *Psychoanalysis and Contemporary Thought,* September, 409–433.

Korabik, K., Baril, G. L., & Watson, C. (1993). Managers' conflict management style and leadership effectiveness: The moderating effects of gender. *Sex Roles: A Journal of Research,* 29, 405–421.

Lorber, J. (1984). *Women physicians: Careers, status and power.* New York: Methuen.

Maccoby, E., & Jacklin, C. (1974). *The psychology of sex differences.* Stanford, CA: Stanford University Press.

McKenna, W., & Kessler, S. (1974, August). *Experimental design as a source of sex bias in social psychology.* Paper presented at the meeting of the American Psychological Association, New Orleans, LA.

New York Times, November 11, 1996. Who voted for whom in the house? B3.

Nicholson, L. (1990). *Feminism/postmodernism.* New York: Routledge.

Nieva, V. F., & Gutek, B. A. (1982). *Women and work: A psychological perspective.* New York: Praeger.

Powell, G. N. (1988). *Women and men in management.* Beverly Hills, CA: Sage.

Rahim, M. A. (1983). A measure of styles of handling interpersonal conflict. *Academy of Management Journal,* 26, 368–375.

Reskin, B., & Hartmann, H. (1986). *Women's work, men's work: Sex segregation on the job.* Washington, DC: National Academy Press.

Ridgeway, C. (1997). Interaction and the conservation of gender inequality. *American Sociological Review,* 62, 218–235.

Rosener, J. (1995). *America's competitive secret: Utilizing women as a management strategy.* New York: Oxford University Press.

Sherif, C. W. (1979). Bias in psychology. In J. A. Sherman & E. T. Beck (eds.), *The prism of sex: Essays in the sociology of knowledge* (pp. 93–133). Madison: University of Wisconsin Press.

Smith, D. E. (1990). *The conceptual practices of power: A feminist sociology of knowledge.* Boston: Northeastern University Press.

Snodgrass, S. E., & Rosenthal, R. (1984). Females in charge: Effects of sex of subordinate and romantic attachment status upon self-ratings of dominance. *Journal of Personality,* 52, 355–371.

Spence, J. T. (1984). Masculinity, femininity, and gender-related traits: A conceptual analysis and critique of current research. *Progress in Experimental Personality Research,* 13, 1–97.

Spence, J. T. (1985). Gender identity and its implications for concepts of masculinity and femininity. In T. Sondregger (ed.), *Nebraska Symposium on Motivation* (pp. 59–95). Lincoln: University of Nebraska Press.

Tannen, D. (1990). *You just don't understand: Women and men in conversation.* New York: Morrow.

Tavris, C. (1992). *The mismeasure of woman.* New York: Simon and Schuster.

Thoits, P. (1983). Multiple identities and psychological well-being: A reformulation and test of the social isolation hypothesis. *American Sociological Review,* 48, 174–87.

Turbin, C. (1992). *Working women of Collar City: Gender, class, and community in Troy, New York, 1864–86.* Urbana: University of Illinois Press.

Vallas, S. (1993). *Power in the workplace: The politics of production at AT&T.* Albany: State University of New York Press.

Vojdik, V. K. (1997). Girls' schools after VMI: Do they make the grade? *Duke Journal of Gender Law & Policy,* 4, 69–100.

Westwood, S. (1985). *All day every day: Factory and family in the making of women's lives.* Champaign: University of Illinois Press.

Zuckerman, H., Cole, J., & Bruer, J. (1991). *The outer circle: Women in the scientific community.* New York: Norton.

PERSONAL ACCOUNT

He Hit Her

I was raised in Charleston, South Carolina, a city where racial and class lines are both evident and defined by street address. I had been taught all my life that black people were different than "us" and were to be feared, particularly in groups.

One summer afternoon when I was eighteen or nineteen, I was sitting in my car at a traffic light at the corner of Cannon and King streets, an area on the edge of the white part of the peninsular city, but progressively being inhabited by more and more blacks. It was hot, had been for weeks, and the sticky heat of South Carolina can be enraging by itself.

As I waited at the light, a young black couple turned the corner on the sidewalk and began to walk towards where I was sitting. The man was yelling and screaming and waving his arms about his head. The woman, a girl really, looked scared and was walking and trying to ignore his tirade. Perhaps it was her seeming indifference that finally did it, perhaps the heat, I don't know. As they drew right up next to my car though, he hit her. He hit her on the side of her head, open palmed, and her head bounced off the brick wall of the house on the corner and she sprawled to the ground, dazed and crying. The man stood over her, shaking his fist and yelling.

I looked around at the other people in cars around me, mostly whites, and at the other people on the sidewalks, mostly blacks, and I realized as everyone gaped that no one was going to do anything, no one was going to help, and neither was I. I don't think it was fear of the man involved that stopped me; rather, I think it was fear generated by what I had been told about the man that stopped me. Physically I was bigger than he was and I knew how to handle myself in a fight: I worked as a bouncer in a nightclub. What I was afraid of was what I had been told about blacks: that *en masse,* they hated whites, and that given the opportunity they would harm me. I was afraid getting out of the car in that neighborhood would make me the focus of the fight and in a matter of time I would be pummeled by an angry black crowd. Also in my mind were thoughts of things I had heard voiced as a child: "They are different. Violence is a part of life for them. They beat, stab, and shoot each other all the time, and the women are just as bad as the men." So I sat and did nothing. The light changed and I pulled away.

The incident has haunted me over the last almost fifteen years. I have often thought about it and felt angry when I did. I believe that as I examined it over time the woman who had been hit, the victim, became less and less prominent, and the black man and myself more prominent. Then I had an epiphany about it.

What bothered me about the incident was not that a man had hit a woman and I had done nothing to intervene, not even to blow my horn, but that a man had hit a woman and I had done nothing to intervene and that this reflected on me as a man. "Men don't hit women, and other men don't let men hit women," was also part of my masculinity training as a boy. There was a whole list of things that "real" men did and things that "real" men didn't do, and somewhere on there was this idea that men didn't let other men hit women. I realized that the incident haunted me not because a man had hit a woman, but because my lack of response was an indictment of *my* masculinity. The horror had become that I was somehow less of a man because of my inaction. Part of the dichotomy that this set up was the notion that the black man had done something to *me,* not to the woman he hit, and it was here that my anger lay. I wonder how this influenced my perception of black men I encountered in the future.

Tim Norton

What Is Social Class?

READING 13

Reading America

Preliminary Notes on Class and Culture

Sherry B. Ortner

It is important to note here that I take the position that class is not the only "objective" structure of domination, that it is no more or less real than a number of others, and that it should not be construed as more fundamental.[1] Further it is not distinguished from other such structures as being somehow more "material"; all structures of domination are simultaneously material and cultural. Nonetheless, it is real in the sense that one can speak of its existence and its constraints even when it is not directly articulated in native discourse. In fact, as I shall argue in this [discussion], it does appear in native discourse (no "reality" could fail to do so), but not in terms that we would immediately recognize as a discourse "about class."

But if the constraints of class are real, so too, apparently, are the high rates of social mobility in the American system. There are literally hundreds of studies of mobility, done at different times and with different assumptions over the course of the twentieth century, but the statistical findings seem to be relatively consistent with one another, and I will use the one provided in Lipset and Bendix's *Social Mobility in Industrial Society* (1957). The authors do an exhaustive survey of mobility studies and come up with the following figures: The average for upward mobility (narrowly defined as a shift from manual to nonmanual labor), drawn from studies done with different assumptions, and at different historical moments, runs around 33 percent, with a range from 20 percent to 40 percent. The average for downward mobility runs around 26 percent, with a range from 15 percent to 35 percent (Lipset and Bendix 1957: 25, and chapter 2 passim). These rates are quite high. On average, one out of three male Americans (only males were studied) will personally experience upward mobility in his lifetime; on average, one out of four will personally experience downward mobility. (The rate of upward mobility always seems to be slightly ahead of the rate for downward mobility. Much has been written about this, but the general, though not uncontested, point is that the middle class has been gradually expanding over time.) Even if the specific figures are disputed, no one seems to disagree with the general statement that there are high rates of social mobility in America.

According to Lipset and Bendix, the United States is not unique in having these high rates of mobility. The central point of this [discussion] is that such rates are characteristic of all the class societies, including Europe as well as the United States. What is unique about the American system is its ideology. Where European cultures have tended to emphasize traditional ranks and statuses, and to present themselves as more rigid in class terms than they really are, the United States has glorified opportunity and mobility, and has presented itself as more open to individual achievement than it really is. There is nothing terribly new about this point, but it is, I think, one of many strands feeding into what is probably a massively overdetermined phenomenon: the absence of class discourse in American culture. The deeply individualistic grounding of American social thought no doubt also plays a role in generating this absence, in that classes are social categories that cannot be understood in terms of individual motives and desires. . . . Because hegemonic American culture takes both the ideology of mobility and the ideology of individualism seriously, explanations for

Sherry B. Ortner is a professor of anthropology at Columbia University.

nonmobility not only focus on the failure of individuals (because they are said to be inherently lazy or stupid or whatever), but shift the domain of discourse to arenas that are taken to be "locked into" individuals—gender, race, ethnic origin, and so forth.

Whatever the explanation (and again, this is a highly overdetermined phenomenon), one of the effects of jamming the cultural airwaves with respect to class is to be seen in what Richard Sennett and Jonathan Cobb have called "the hidden injuries of class" (1972). Poorer and less successful Americans tend to blame themselves for their failures, and not to recognize the ways in which their chances for success were circumscribed from the outset. Another of the effects, I suggest, is the one to be documented in this paper: a displacement of class strain and friction into other arenas of life, a displacement not without its costs for experience in those other arenas.

CLASS AND THE SOCIAL GEOGRAPHY OF GENDER AND SEXUAL PRACTICES

The particular pattern I want to focus on here is the displacement of class frictions into the discourse and practices of gender and sexual relations. The basic point, which emerged for me more or less accidentally as I read a set of American community studies with, initially, no particular agenda, is this: gender relations for both middle-class and working-class Americans (I have only glanced at elites at this point) carry an enormous burden of quite antagonistic class meaning. To turn the point around, class discourse is submerged within, and spoken through, sexual discourse, taking "sex" here in the double English sense of pertaining to both gender and the erotic (see Ortner and Whitehead 1981). And while the general point of displacement holds for both middle-class and working-class discourse, it works differently in each case. I start with the working class.

(I should note here that I will use the present tense throughout this [discussion], though the examples to be discussed run from the early fifties through the early eighties. The patterns in question seem to have been, with only minor variations, impressively durable.)

Working Class Discourses of Sex and Class

I begin with the assumption that the classes are relationally constituted, that they define themselves always in implicit reference to the other(s). Thus, while we normally think of class relations as taking place *between* classes, in fact each class contains the other(s) within itself, though in distorted and ambivalent forms. This is particularly visible in the working class, where the class structure of the society is introjected into the culture of the working class itself, appearing as a problematic choice of "life-styles" for working-class men and women—a choice between a lifestyle modeled essentially on middle-class values and practices and one modeled on more distinctively working- or lower-class values and practices.[2] This split, which is given different names by different ethnographers and different ethnographees, shows up in virtually every study of both white and black working-class communities. One example may be seen in Herbert Gans's classic study (1962) of an urban working-class community in Boston. Gans sees two major styles of working-class life, which he labels the styles of the "routine seekers" and the "action seekers" (1962:28). To this basic split he adds two more extreme types, the "maladapteds" at the very bottom of the working class, and the "middle-class mobiles" at the top of the class. The general pattern of these styles will be intuitively comprehensible to any American native. Routine seekers follow a relatively settled life-style centered on family and work. Action seekers, on the other hand, live the "fast" life, centered importantly on relations with "the boys," the male peer group; family and work are avoided or minimized as much as possible. Of the two more extreme versions of this basic split, middle-class mobiles are similar to routine seekers except that they are more oriented, as the label suggests, toward actual upward mobility. Maladaptives are similar to action seekers, but generally have a problem such as alcoholism or drug abuse that renders them more irredeemable.

To characterize the split within working-class culture in terms of activity (as in "action seekers") and passivity (as in "routine seekers") is reminiscent of Paul Willis's account of the culture of British working-class high school students (1977). Willis focused on the "lads," or the nonconformists, who divided the school between themselves and what they called the "ear'oles": "The term 'ear'ole' itself connotes the passivity and absurdity of the school conformists for 'the lads.' It seems that they are always listening, never *doing;* never animated with their own internal life, but formless in rigid reception" (1977:14; see also Sennett and Cobb 1972:82).

The same pattern of life-style split, between a "middle-class" life-style (whether oriented toward actual upward mobility or not) and a working- or lower-class lifestyle, shows up in the black ghetto neighborhood studied by the Swedish anthropologist Ulf Hannerz:

> The people of Winston Street often describe themselves and their neighbors in the community as comprising two categories distinguished according to way of life. . . . Some refer to one category—in which they usually include themselves—as respectable, "good people," or, more rarely and somewhat facetiously, as "model citizens." More seldom do they refer to this category as "middle class.". . . They use these labels to distinguish themselves from what they conceive of as their opposites, people they describe as "undesirables," "no good," "the rowdy bunch," "bums," or "trash." (1969:34–35).

In sum, there is a general tendency for working- or lower-class culture to embody *within* itself the split in society *between* the working and the middle class. This split appears as a subcultural typology of "styles": the action-seekers versus the routine-seekers, the lads versus the ear'oles, the respectables versus the undesirables.

From the actor's point of view, the split in turn appears as a set of choices, a set of life possibilities between which a young man growing up within the working class will consciously or unconsciously choose. Here is where class, now translated as "life-style," intersects with the discourses and practices of gender and sexuality. For it appears overwhelmingly the case in working-class culture that women are symbolically aligned, from both the male point of view and, apparently, their own, with the "respectable," "middle-class" side of those oppositions and choices. Thus every sexual choice is symbolically also a class choice, for better or worse.

This pattern is again seen in virtually every ethnography of working-class culture. Gans describes it for the neighborhood he studied in Boston: "Marriage is a crucial turning point in the life of the West End boy. It is then that he must decide whether he is going to give up the boys on the corner for the new peer group of related siblings and in-laws—a decision related to and reflected in his choice of a mate" (1962: 70). In the extreme instance, which is to say the instance of (would-be) mobility, the couple will move to the suburbs. Such a move is generally blamed (by "the boys") on the wife's ambitions (Gans 1962: 53), and this may indeed be the case. Gans goes on to say that these kinds of pulls create a great deal of strain between husband and wife (1962:70).

David Halle, in his ethnography of chemical workers in Elizabeth, New Jersey (1984), reports much the same patterns and explores them with great insight. His fine-grained ethnography shows that the perception of women as more "middle class" than men, and as aligned with middle-class values and practices, extends into (or emerges from) the workplace as well as the domestic situation. Within the single plant studied, the men normally work in the production areas, while the women normally work in the office. The men's jobs are dirty and physical, while the women's jobs both allow and require them to be more dressed up and to remain clean throughout the day. Further, women in the office work more closely and directly with management. For all these reasons, they are apparently symbolically associated with management (Halle 1984: 61).

As Halle explored with male workers their own cultural category of "working man," he found that the term contained several meanings: it meant quite literally working, as opposed to not working (the very rich and the "welfare bums" are similar in not working at all); it meant hard, physical labor as opposed to soft, easy work; and it meant productive labor as opposed to purposeless paper pushing. To the male workers, even women with paid employment, including the clerical and office workers in the men's own plant, were not seen as "working" (Halle 1984:206):

> Researcher: How about secretaries? [i.e., are they "working persons"?]
> Worker: No! They often spend half the afternoon reading magazines. I've seen them through the window.

And in another interview (Halle 1984:207):

> Researcher: How about secretaries?
> Worker: No, they work in an office . . . They just answer the phone and type letters.

Let me return to the issue of women as not merely displaying middle-class patterns (as in the cleanly dressed secretary) but of actually seeming to enforce such patterns on men. While it is the perception of "the boys" that it is women, as wives, who exert a middle-class pull on their husbands, this perception may have some basis in women's actual practice. Although Halle's information comes mostly from male informants, their claims are specific enough to have the ring of true reporting. Thus, many men say that their wives complain about their social status being too low and exert pressure on them to change their kinds of work, or at least their behavioral styles, in a more "middle-class" direction (Halle 1984: 59). Husbands found this irritating, to say the least. Issues of behavioral style—how a man eats or speaks, for example—connect to (or are perceived as being connected to) lack of education, and are "particularly explosive since the overwhelming majority of workers are very sensitive about their lack of formal education" (Halle 1984:60).

The pattern is essentially identical in the black neighborhood studied by Ulf Hannerz, who did talk to women as well as men. He found that while women recognized variation among men in terms of life-style, there was a general tendency to lump all men in the "nonrespectable" pool, and themselves implicitly in the respectable group (Hannerz 1969:97, 99).

Nor are these symbolic alignments simply matters of "discourse" abstracted from lived experience. Both Halle and Hannerz discuss at some length the ways in which men's and women's perceptions of each other articulate with a pattern of often highly conflictful and unhappy gender relations. Although some of Halle's male informants (one suspects that Gans would have classified them as "routine seekers") felt that their wives' (real or imagined) middle-class inclinations "rescued them from the wild life-style of the male culture, a life-style they believe would in the end have been their downfall" (Halle 1984:64), this feeling was less common than its opposite—that women's real or supposed identification with middle-class ideals placed their husbands under a great deal of strain.

At this point, class no longer appears as a choice of lifestyle, but as an imposed pressure and constraint. Yet the imposition appears to come not from class "enemies"—the rich, the politicians, the pampered sons of the middle class—but from the men's own girlfriends and wives. I will return to this point below.

Middle-Class Discourses of Class and Sex

Given both the high rates of social mobility in America and the strong cultural emphasis on its possibility and desirability, each class has a characteristic stance on the question. Moreover, each class views the others not only, or even primarily, as antagonistic groups but as images of their hopes and fears for their own lives and futures. For the white working class, it is the black working class (which is poorer and less secure than the white) that represents their worst fears for themselves; this, as much as any putative threat of economic competition, underlies much of white working-class racism. The middle class, in contrast, is a source of tremendous ambivalence from a working-class perspective. Middle-class status is highly desirable for its greater material affluence and security, but undesirable for all the ways in which its patterns are culturally "other," and for the ways in which upward mobility would pull one away from kin, friends, or neighborhood.

For the middle class, the pattern of fears and desires is different. There is much less ambivalence about upward social mobility, since much of it would not involve significant changes of "culture." The "fear of falling," however (to borrow a phrase from Barbara Ehrenreich's study of middle-class culture [1989]), is intense. This may be true particularly at the lower edge of the class, and particularly for new arrivals, but it seems to be a general and pervasive substrate of middle-class thought. If much of working-class culture can be understood as a set of discourses and practices embodying the ambivalence of upward mobility, much of middle-class culture can be seen as a set of discourses and practices embodying the terror of downward mobility.

In both cases the complex attitudes held about adjacent classes derive from the classes' functioning as mirrors of these possibilities. Although the middle class and the working class may be inherently antagonistic as a result of their positioning within the capitalist productive order, in the phenomenology of class cultures the frictions between them seem largely to derive from this mirroring function. And for each class, the frictions are introjected into, and endlessly replayed through, social relations internal to the class itself.

My sense is that it is parent-child relations in the middle class that carry much of the burden of introjected "class struggle" and even class "war," comparable to the ways in which gender carries this burden in the working class. There is no doubt that gender carries a lot of this for the middle class as well, and I will come back to that in a moment. But it seems to me—and at this point I speak more from my experience as a native than from anything I have seen yet in ethnographies—that there is the kind of both chronic friction and explosive potential in middle-class parent-child relations that one sees in working-class gender relations (see especially Ehrenreich 1989: ch. 2).

At a practical level, there is always the question of whether middle-class children will successfully retain the class standing the parents have provided them. As a result of this practical question, which revolves around issues of education, occupation, and (here is the intersection with gender) marriage choice, there are tremendous parental attempts to control their children's behavior, over a much longer span of time and to a much later age than in the working class. (Both Willis [1977:21–22] and Gans [1962:56–57] indicate that working-class parents do not attempt to impose, and especially to extend, these kinds of controls.) But if middle-class parents see their children as embodying the threat of a working-class future (for the children if not for themselves), and attempt to control them accordingly, adolescent children respond in kind. They criticize their parents' values, which is to say essentially class values, and they resist their parents' controls precisely through representations of lower-class affiliation—language, hairstyle, clothing, music, and sometimes cross-class friendships and cross-class dating or sexual relationships. It is hardly a novel observation that much of middle-class adolescent culture is drawn both from "real" lower-class culture (e.g., by way of the lower-class origins of many rock groups) and from marketing fantasies of what lower-class culture looks like. In any event, it is clear that the discourse of parent-child relations (specifically parent-child conflict) in the middle class, like the discourse of gender in the working class, is simultaneously a class discourse. It draws on and feeds the fears and anxieties that make sense if we assume that the classes view each other as their own pasts and possible futures.

But although parent-child relations carry a good bit of the burden of class antagonism or fear in the middle class, discourses on gender and sexuality are not without their own significant freight of class meanings. Here, however, the pattern is quite different from that seen in the working class. Where for the working class, class is, in effect, pulled into the subculture and mapped onto internal relations of gender and sexuality, for the middle class, gender and sexuality are projected out onto the world of class relations.[3] Specifically, the working class is cast as the bearer of an exaggerated sexuality, against which middle-class respectability is defined.

One of the best places to see these patterns is in predominantly middle-class high schools. They almost always contain at least some kids from working-class backgrounds, and the high-school ethnosociology tends to build distinctions around these differences, reproducing the split between respectable and nonrespectable that is so central to working-class culture. This split is called by endlessly different names in different schools. In my high school in the fifties, the terminology was inconsistent—the respectables were largely merged with the dominant ethnic category (Jews), while the nonrespectables were usually called "hoods," a term that was apparently of near-national scope at that time. In the school studied by Gary Schwartz and Don Merten in the early seventies, the terms were "socies" and hoods (1975). In the school studied by Eckert in the early eighties, the terms were jocks and burnouts (1989). Whatever the labels, the social category split marked by these terms is almost never recognized by the students as a class split, and the terms used for it almost never refer to class or even money differences—a good example of the taboo on class discourse in America. Nonetheless, the split tends to map rather accurately onto differences that adults or parents or social scientists would recognize as class differences.

The distinctions between the two groups are marked in a whole range of ways—clothing; language; haircuts; attitudes toward teachers, school work, and school citizenship; and all the rest. But for the middle-class adolescents, one of the key dimensions of difference is a supposed difference in attitudes toward and practices of sexual behavior. Middle-class kids, both male and female, define working-class kids as promiscuous, highly experienced, and sexually unconstrained. I give one ethnographic example; the pattern is so well known that it does not require extensive illustration. Schwartz and Merten studied sorority initiation rites in a middle-class American high school (1975). The high-school social system was divided by the sorority girls (who were at the top of it) into "socialites," or "socies," and "hoods" or "greasers." (The authors identify a middle category that is neither really "hoody" nor cool enough to be among the "socies," but which is said generally to approve of "socie" values.)[4]

While the bulk of Schwartz and Merten's article focuses on interpreting the sorority hazings as initiation rites that facilitate identity transformations of various kinds (which is doubtless true), the authors move into a discussion of the class dimensions of the categories toward the end. Here we see the ways in which class differences are largely represented as sexual differences:

> For socie girls, those who subscribe to the adolescent version of a middle-class way of life are morally acceptable; girls who follow the adolescent variant of a working-class way of life are morally contemptible. All of our socie informants felt that hoody girls tended to be promiscuous, sloppy, stupid, and unfriendly. (Schwartz and Merten 1975:207)

Clothing and cosmetic differences are taken to be indexes of the differences in sexual morals between the girls of the two classes:

> The act of smearing [socie sorority] pledges with lipsticks on hell night [of the initiation rites] is a veiled reference to what socies believe is a most salient feature of the hoody cosmetic style, the use of makeup in ways that resemble the appearance of a slut. . . . Socies interpret hoody hairstyles, in which the hair is worn massed on top of the head and is held together by a liberal application of hair spray, as a sign of a lack of sexual restraint. (Schwartz and Merten 1975:210)[5]

It is painfully ironic that the same girls who are taken to be "sluts" by middle-class sorority girls will be taken by their own men to be agents of middle-class values and resented as such. Here truly is a "hidden injury of class."[6]

As in the case of the working class, this kind of sexual mapping of classes will also appear, at least to some middle-class actors, as a set of choices or possibilities for their own lives. There is both a similarity with and a difference from working-class patterns. For both groups, there is a sense that different women will pull men in different directions in class terms. For the working class, the pattern, or at least the threat, tends to be generalized to all women, and men do not represent themselves as having a great deal of agency in the matter. For middle-class men, however, there seems to be more of a notion of choice. Women of various class positions appear as kind of a smorgasbord of sexual-cum-class possibilities, most of which are not likely to be realized, but all of which are apparently "good to think."[7]. . .

In the past there has been a strong tendency on the part of many anthropologists studying America to "ethnicize" (the domestic version of "orientalize") the various groups, classes, and even institutions (e.g., corporations) under study, to treat them as if they were in effect separate tribes. There are exceptions to this tendency, as discussed earlier, but in general, anthropologists studying America have mirrored anthropologists studying other peoples in this respect. There are indications now that the anthropology of America is shifting on this point (this study is part of that shift), and beginning to recognize the importance of studying the relationships between whatever unit one undertakes to study and the larger social and cultural universe within which it operates. This includes recognizing both the ways in which various pieces of the society or culture may be mutually constituting (as in the arguments about the middle class and the working class in this paper), and the ways in which all the pieces are at the same time constituted by the larger histories and structures that encompass them. . . .

However much we now recognize that cultures are riddled with inequality, differential understanding, and differential advantage, and however much we now recognize that cultures are at least partly constituted by forces external, and often inimical, to them, nonetheless they remain for the people who live within them sources of value, meaning, and ways of understanding—and resisting—the world. This is as true for disadvantaged groups in, say, a class system as for the far-flung people we more often went off to study in the past. As we study the ways in which the cultures of dominant and subordinate groups shape one another, or the ways in which a particular culture is reshaped through colonial encounters, capitalist penetration, or class domination, we must at the same time work against the denial of cultural authenticity that this may imply, and the related implication that the ethnography of meaningful cultural worlds is no longer a significant enterprise.[8]

NOTES

This paper was written while I was a visiting member at the Institute for Advanced Study in Princeton, New Jersey, supported by funds from the University of Michigan and the National Endowment for the Humanities. Arjun Appadurai, Nicholas B. Dirks, and Elliot Shore read the first draft on short notice, and gave me extremely useful comments. Later drafts were read by Nancy Chodorow, Salvatore Cucchiari, Richard Fox, Abigail Stewart, and Peter van der Feer, all of whom provided excellent insights and suggestions. There was also very constructive and stimulating discussion of the paper in the Thursday night seminar of the Program in the Comparative Study of Social Transformations, which has been both nourishing and provoking me intellectually at the University of Michigan for the past three years.

1. This is the so-called multiple domination position, with which I am in basic agreement. One of the clearest statements of this position is to be found in Cohen (1982). Another version is developed in Laclau and Mouffe (1985). Feminist theory in general also tends toward a multiple domination position; see, for example, Sacks (1989).
2. There is a problem of terminology here. The terms for the lower end of the class structure seem to be racially coded. The term "working class" seems normally to refer to whites. For blacks, one more often sees "lower class." I will use the terms interchangeably for both.
3. There seems to have been more introjection in the nineteenth century, where the split between the middle class and the working class was played out *within* middle-class gender relations (see Smith-Rosenberg 1986).
4. The authors also identify an important ethnographic category: "nobody," as in, "Her? Oh, she's nobody." More work needs to be done on nobodies. For example, the organizers for my high-school reunion did not locate about 50 percent of the addresses in the class. This included all the blacks and virtually all of the non-Jews. It also included some percentage of the Jewish kids, and I suspect that those not located were distinguished from those who were, as "nobodies" are to "somebodies."
5. In Willis's account of the discourse of the nonconformist (i.e., the most "hoody") working-class lads, they claim this greater sexual experience and knowledgeability for themselves, and Willis thinks it is probably true that they have more active sexual lives than the ear'oles.
6. I am indebted to Arjun Appadurai for putting these particular pieces together. Some of my students at Michigan think that this sexual-cum-class division no longer applies, because even middle-class kids are having a lot of sex in high school. Although I accept my students as valid informants, the question needs to be investigated more closely. I suspect that the situation is similar to that described by Eckert in her high-school study with respect to drugs: both middle-class and working-class kids do drugs, but the use of drugs plays an entirely different role in their respective symbolic economies (Eckert 1989).
7. The phrase is from Claude Lévi-Strauss (1966).
8. After this paper had gone to press, a student brought to my attention the 1990 book by Benjamin DeMott, *The Imperial Middle: Why Americans Can't Think Straight about Class* (New York: William Morrow and Company). As the subtitle indicates, the book makes arguments very similar to those made in this paper. I regret not having had access to it before the paper reached the point of editorial untouchability.

REFERENCES

Eckert, Penelope. 1989. *Jocks and Burnouts: Social Categories and Identity in the High School.* New York: Teachers College Press.

Ehrenreich, Barbara. 1989. *Fear of Falling: The Inner Life of the Middle Class.* New York: Pantheon.

Gans, Herbert. 1962. *Urban Villagers: Group and Class in the Life of Italian-Americans.* New York: The Free Press.

Halle, David. 1984. *America's Working Man: Work, Home, and Politics among Blue Collar Property Owners.* Chicago: University of Chicago Press.

Hannerz, Ulf. 1969. *Soulside: Inquiries into Ghetto Culture and Community.* New York: Columbia University Press.

Lévi-Strauss, Claude. 1966. *The Savage Mind.* Chicago: University of Chicago Press.

Lipset, Seymour Martin, and Reinhard Bendix. 1957. *Social Mobility in Industrial Society.* Berkeley: University of California Press.

Ortner, Sherry B., and Harriet Whitehead, eds. 1981. *Sexual Meanings: The Cultural Construction of Gender and Sexuality.* Cambridge: Cambridge University Press.

Sacks, Karen Brodkin. 1989. Toward a unified theory of class, race, and gender. *American Ethnologist* 16(3):534–50.

Schwartz, Gary, and Don Merten. 1975. Social identity and expressive symbols. In *The Nacirema: Readings on American Culture.* J. P. Spradley and M. A. Rynkiewich, eds. Boston: Little, Brown.

Sennett, Richard, and Jonathan Cobb. 1972. *The Hidden Injuries of Class.* New York: Vintage Books.

Smith-Rosenberg, Carroll. 1986. Writing history: language, class and gender. In *Feminist Studies, Critical Studies.* T. de Lauretis, ed. Bloomington: University of Indiana Press.

Willis, Paul. 1977. *Learning to Labor: How Working Class Kids Get Working Class Jobs.* New York: Columbia University Press.

READING 14

Why Is Class Important?

Michael Zweig

. . . Let's consider three widely reported developments of the last twenty-five years and see how our understanding of them changes when we look at them through the lens of class: the widespread decline in real wages and the increasing inequality in the distributions of income and of wealth.

Falling Real Wages

Back in 1983, Jim Ramey earned $11.83 an hour assembling ATM machines at the Diebold Corporation in Canton, Ohio. By 1996, his pay had dropped to $9.93—in 1996 dollars.[1] He was not alone. Since 1972, median weekly earnings for all private sector workers adjusted for inflation had fallen nearly 20 percent, from $315 to $225 in 1982 dollars (the median is the point at which half make more, half less). This experience was common to workers in nearly every sector of the economy, from manufacturing to services, construction, and transportation.[2] Low unemployment at the end of the 1990s ended the wage decline, at least temporarily, but did not come close to recouping the losses.

Through the last quarter of the twentieth century, family incomes remained nearly unchanged despite falling wages. This was possible only because the number of wage earners in the average family increased sharply, especially for families with children at home. By 1992, 57 percent of all families had two or more wage earners, while three out of four married-couple families with children at home had both parents working. In 1972, that had been true for only half of such families. Between 1972 and 1992, the percentage of "traditional families" (Dad working, Mom at home with the kids) fell from 23 percent of all U.S. families to 9 percent.[3]

For most working people, life has gotten harder. Families are working longer hours and have less time for one another. Parents can't be home for the children. Stress levels are high. On top of falling incomes and extra jobs, companies making record profits keep laying off more workers. Increasingly, working people feel that no one is safe in their jobs, no matter how hard they work or how much they contribute to the success of their company. Economic insecurity permeates life for tens of millions of people, more than at any time since the Great Depression three generations ago. Business is booming, but workers do not share the proceeds.

In 1995, 22 million people worked part-time jobs in the United States, over 4 million of them only because they couldn't find full-time work. Even those who prefer to work part-time pay a heavy price. For every hour they work, on average a part-timer makes only 62 cents for every dollar a full-time worker gets. Only 10 percent of part-timers receive any employer contribution to a pension plan beyond Social Security (the figure is fewer than half of all full-time private sector workers). And only 10 percent of part-timers have employer-provided health care coverage (65 percent of full-timers).[4] As employers have

Michael Zweig is professor of economics at the State University of New York at Stony Brook.

moved increasingly to part-time work forces, the conditions of millions of working people have deteriorated.

To help maintain living standards during the period of declining real income, Americans have resorted to debt. Since the mid-1970s personal debt has risen steadily as a percentage of disposable income (income after taxes). Most of the increase was in home mortgage debt, but installment debt rose from 17.5 percent of disposable income in 1975 to 21 percent in 1996.[5] In the same period the real interest rate that consumers pay rose (after taking into account the impact of inflation), so the burden of the debt went up even faster than the debt itself.

The broad decline in living standards has been well reported, but not in terms of working class experience. A typical example is a *New York Times* story under the headline "The Middle Class: Winning in Politics, Losing in Life."[6] The article talks mostly about workers, but not at all about the working class. As usual, class is reported in terms of income alone, and workers are said to be in the middle class, the middle three-fifths of the income distribution. The middle class is "winning in politics," according to the writer, because everyone from Newt Gingrich to President Clinton is trying to help them with "middle class tax cuts," but they are "losing in life" because their earnings are down.

The fall in real wages has occurred in spite of continuing increases in output and productivity (output per hour of work). Figure 1 presents a dramatic picture: The top line shows increases in output per nonsupervisory worker hour, a measure of productivity. The lower line shows what happened to weekly earnings for nonsupervisory workers, after taking inflation into account.

After World War II, and continuing until 1972, workers' wages increased about as fast as productivity did. Workers shared in the growing wealth. But since 1972, as Figure 1 shows, wages have been falling even though productivity and output have continued to rise.[7] Workers have been producing more and getting less. Even taking benefits into account doesn't change that fact.[8]

In the last half of the 1990s, real wages (wages adjusted for inflation) began to rise

FIGURE 1 WORKERS STOPPED SHARING ECONOMIC GROWTH AFTER 1972.
Source: Author's calculations based on data from the U.S. Department of Labor, *Employment, Hours, and Earnings, United States,* Vol. 1, Bulletin 2445, September 1994; Bulletin 2481, August 1966; *Employment and Earnings,* January 1999; *Economic Report of the President,* 1999.

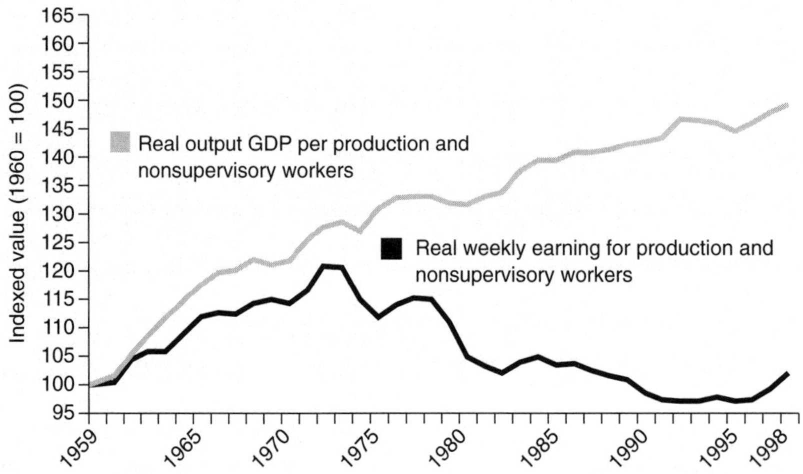

again. By 1999, the strong labor market and the increase in the minimum wage finally brought up the incomes of the bottom 20 percent.[9] The improvement led many to believe good times were back. But it wasn't until 1998 that real weekly earnings returned to the level of 1989 for the average worker, who is still far away from the peak earnings of the early 1970s. Perhaps more important, workers are far from regaining their share of total output.*

Where did the increased income and wealth go? The stark picture of workers unable to benefit from their own increased productivity has another side: spectacular increases in income and wealth for capitalists and for those most closely associated with them in business dealings.

Changes in the Distribution of Income

Between 1977 and 1989, production of all goods and services in the United States increased 42 percent (after correcting for inflation). You might think, therefore, that the average person improved his or her living standards by that amount. But it didn't happen. That's because 60 percent of all the gains in after-tax income from 1977 to 1989 went to the richest 1 percent of families. The bottom 80 percent of the population got just 5 percent of the increase.

That top 1 percent of the population, with an average income of $559,800 in 1989, did very well indeed. Their incomes went up 77 percent (after adjusting for inflation) compared with 1977. Meanwhile, the bottom 20 percent of the population, with an average 1989 income of $8,400, experienced a 9 percent *reduction* in their incomes.[10]

Contrary to myth, it's not that low-income people weren't working hard. The poorest fifth of the population worked 4.6 percent more in 1989 than at the beginning of the go-go eighties decade, but they got 4.1 percent less for their efforts.[11] A Miller beer ad in the late eighties promised "more taste, less filling" to people whose life experience was "more work, less money."

The distribution of income in the United States has become steadily more unequal since 1968, and especially after 1980. Economists commonly divide the population into five layers based on income: the highest-earning 20 percent, the next-highest 20 percent, and so on (these are called "quintiles").[12] . . .

Compared with 1968, every layer of the population has lost ground except the top. In 1968, the poorest 20 percent of the population (in 1997 dollars this would be households with income of less than $15,400) received 4.2 percent of all income. But by 1997 their share had fallen to just 3.6 percent. This amounted to a 14 percent decline in their share. The next 20 percent layer (household income less than $29,200 in 1997) experienced the greatest decline, their share falling by 20 percent (from 11.1 percent of all income in 1968 to 8.9 percent in 1997). In every case, the trend to greater inequality that characterized the Reagan and Bush years continued and even accelerated during the Clinton presidency. Even the next-to-highest quintile (household

---

*It may seem that at times when both productivity and wages are increasing by the same percentage, workers are getting the whole increase in their output. But this is not the case, because output is always divided between workers and capitalists.

To see this, suppose that total output is 100 and workers get 70 while capitalists get 30. Now suppose that output increases by 10 percent, to 110. If wages go up 10 percent, too, then out of the 10 units of increased output workers will get 7 more (not 10 more), and the capitalists will get 3 more. The new, larger output will be divided 77 to 33, and the share of the total going to workers will remain unchanged. But if workers do not get a raise to match their increase in productivity, the distribution of income will change. Suppose workers get a raise of only 5 instead of 7. Their income will rise to 75, which is a smaller share of the 110 total than they had before, while the capitalists will get 35, an increase in their share.

In other words, workers can receive a smaller share of total income even if their wages are going up, if the wage increases don't match productivity gains. Between 1972 and 1996, as productivity and output went up, workers' wages actually went down, which corresponded to the dramatic changes in distribution of income in the period. In the strong labor markets of 1997 to 1999, this trend ended, at least temporarily, as real wages sometimes increased more quickly than productivity.

income less than $71,500 in 1997) lost ground, especially after 1992. It's only when we come to the top 20 percent (household income over $71,500 in 1997), and especially to the top layers of the elite, that we find the people who made out like bandits during this period. . . .

One especially galling sign of the growing inequality is the explosion in executive compensation since the early 1980s. In the year Ronald Reagan was elected, *Business Week* reported that the average large-corporation CEO was paid 42 times an average factory worker's wage. By 1995, the ratio had risen to 141: $3.75 million for the CEO and $26,652 for the worker. And that counts only direct compensation, not income from investments. Executive pay continued to explode during the Clinton years, so that by 1998, the CEO earned 419 times the pay of the average blue collar worker.[13] In other words, if in 1994 workers making $25,000 a year had gotten this rate of pay increase, in 1998 they would have been making $138,350. Instead, by then the average big-time CEO was making more in a day than the average worker made in a year.

This is the kind of thing that gets people mad. While Jim Ramey's pay at Diebold in Ohio was going down, and the company laid off hundreds of workers, Robert Mahoney, Diebold's CEO, was doing fine. He pulled down $2.37 million in 1995, up from $464,250 in 1990. Mr. Ramey didn't like it. "I begrudge Mahoney his big salary. I begrudge his bonuses when workers are hurting." But the Diebold board had other concerns. They gave Mahoney and other top executives these huge raises to keep up with increases in executive pay at competing companies.[14]

It doesn't have to be this way. U.S. executives are the highest paid and lowest taxed of any in the industrial world.[15] And, more generally, income is distributed far more unequally in the United States than in any other industrial country.[16]

Changes in the Distribution of Wealth

So far, we have been looking at income: what people make in a year. Personal wealth is something different: the value of money and other assets someone has managed to accumulate up to a given point in time. A person who makes $50,000 a year in income may have some wealth in the form of savings, or accumulations in a 401K plan, or equity in a house. The components of wealth are valued on a balance sheet reflecting the situation on a specific date, like December 31 of a given year. Many people who have incomes have no wealth, especially low-income people. People at higher levels of income tend to have more wealth, and their wealth is in a greater variety of assets, such as real estate and corporate bonds.

Wealth is distributed even more unequally than income. People with low incomes spend all they get and have very little assets. Those with wealth tend to be people with higher incomes, so as income has become more unequally distributed, it is not surprising that wealth, too, has become even more concentrated in the hands of a relative few.

In the words of one headline, "Rich Control More of U.S. Wealth, Study Says, as Debts Grow for Poor."[17] In 1994, the wealthiest 10 percent of families owned 66.8 percent of all wealth, up from 61.6 percent in 1989. The poorest 10 percent had no wealth at all, in either year, but their average debt had increased by 49 percent (after correcting for inflation), from $4,744 in 1989 to $7,075 in 1994. Wealth is now more concentrated at the top than at any time since the Great Depression. After decades of slowly increasing equality, inequality jumped in the last quarter century.[18]

Between 1983 and 1989, after adjusting for inflation, the top 1 percent of households received 62 percent of all new wealth. The next 19 percent received 37 percent of all new wealth. The rest of the population, 80 percent of the country, got 1 percent.

If we leave aside the value of housing and other real estate and look at financial assets alone, the picture becomes even more skewed. The top 1 percent got two-thirds of new net financial wealth

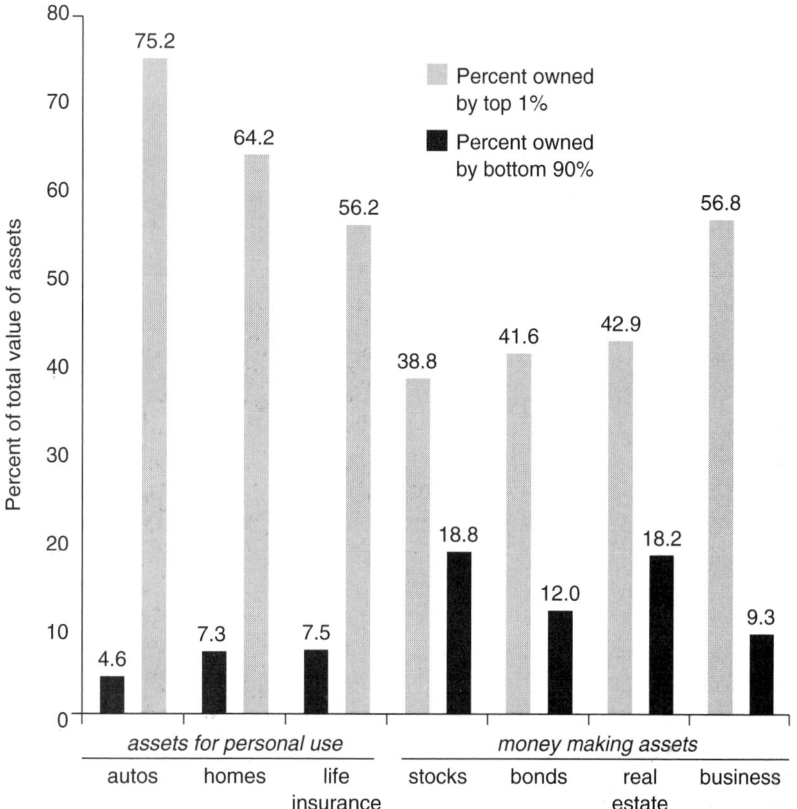

FIGURE 2 DISTRIBUTION OF WEALTH IN THE UNITED STATES, 1992
(*Source:* Arthur Kennickell, Douglas McManus, and R. Louise Woodburn, "Weighted Design for the 1992 *Survey of Consumer Finances,*" unpublished technical paper quoted in *Left Business Observer,* No. 72, April 3, 1996, 5.)

(after accounting for any changes in people's debts). The bottom 80 percent of people actually lost ground because of the sharp increase in their debt. On average they had 3 percent less wealth in 1989, compared with 1983.[19]

By 1992, the top 1 percent of the population owned 30.5 percent of all personal assets in the country (as net worth, after taking into account any outstanding debts). They owned 38.1 percent of all assets other than homes; this was more than half again as much as was owned by the bottom 90 percent of the population. Even among the very wealthy, wealth is unequally distributed. In 1992 the top *one half* of 1 percent owned 29.1 percent of all nonresidential net worth in the country, which was more than three quarters of the amount held by the whole top 1 percent.[20]

Figure 2 shows us how the different kinds of wealth are distributed.[21] For each type of asset shown at the bottom, the chart shows what percentage of the total value of that asset belonging to all households in the country was owned by the wealthiest 1 percent and by the bottom 90 percent. On the left are assets for personal use: automobiles, homes, and life insurance.

Looking at cars, for example, the top 1 percent own more than their share (4.6 percent of the value of all cars in 1992), while the bottom 90 percent own less than their share (75.2 percent). The same is true for other personal assets. But the inequality is nowhere near as dramatic as what we find for money-making assets.

Money-making assets are stocks, bonds, real estate (other than personal residence), and business assets. The right side of Figure 2 shows that the top 1 percent own many times more than the bottom 90 percent put together. For example, the wealthiest 1 percent of households own 43 percent of all income-producing real estate owned by individuals (rather than by corporations), two-and-a-half times what the bottom 90 percent own).

But it is business assets that are most highly concentrated in the hands of the super-wealthy. This isn't surprising, since owning these assets is what allows the rich to accumulate wealth in the first place. These assets are types of capital, and they are concentrated not just among "the rich" but among the capitalists. For all the talk about widespread individual business ownership in the United States (remember that there are over 15 million unincorporated businesses), the top 1 percent of households own 57 percent of business assets, six times the value in the hands of the bottom 90 percent. A very minor fraction of business assets is in the hands of working class families who own a small business on the side.

Even within the top 1 percent, wealth is concentrated among the most rich, the top half of one percent of the population. This is the part of the population with names like Rockefeller, Gates, Kennedy, Carnegie, Mellon, and a few thousand others who seldom make it into the news. If we look at the business assets owned just by the top 1 percent, 85 percent of them are in the hands of the top half of that 1 percent. The same for stock: the top half of 1 percent of households own 72 percent of the stock owned by the entire richest 1 percent.[22]

The concentration of stock ownership is particularly revealing. As Figure 2 shows, in 1992 the top 1 percent of households owned 39 percent of all individually owned stock (stock not owned by corporations), double the 19 percent in the hands of the bottom 90 percent. But not everyone in the bottom 90 percent owns stock. In fact, only about 40 percent of all households in the United States include even a single person who owns any stock at all in any form, whether directly as shares of individual companies (including where they work) or in mutual funds, or through a personal or company pension plan with money invested in stocks on behalf of the individual.[23] Pension plans are far from universal. In 1996, only 42 percent of all employees had a company- or union-provided pension plan.[24]

One would think that stocks were important to almost everyone, given the market reports every half hour on all-news radio and the daily price movements featured on every nightly TV news show. Without question, stock ownership is more widespread now than it was thirty years ago, before financial deregulation and the spread of Keogh and 401(k) plans. But the skyrocketing stock prices of the 1990s left 60 percent of the population entirely untouched in their personal finances. Working class people do own scattered shares of stock and mutual funds, but this hardly amounts to "people's capitalism."

The business press occasionally lets us know who they consider the little guy "everyman" involved in the market. In a story about the stock market turmoil of August 1998, the *New York Times* reported that the flighty actions of institutional investors were being tempered by the steady confidence of the "small investor." The article tells us that a small investor is someone who trades fewer than ten thousand shares at a time![25]

When the market had recovered and was reaching new highs in spring 1999, the *Wall Street Journal* also focused on the growing role of individuals in the market. Without explicitly mentioning class, of course, the story acknowledged that 60 percent of the population owns no stock whatsoever, but that "ordinary people" were more deeply involved than ever. The ordinary people described were high-level corporate executives and investment managers, Washington lawyers and lobbyists, a senior U.S. Marshal, and a fitness trainer for the wealthy—"ordinary" only among the readers of the *Wall Street Journal.* The one working class person in the story, a cafeteria cook who was standing in line at the Department of Motor Vehicles, owned no stock. She expressed some annoyance at the airs some people put on with their new wealth. "It's not like people earned all that stock market money. It, like, happened while they slept."[26]

Working class people often do have personal assets in a house and car and some savings. This is especially true at middle age, in peak earning years, before major health and retirement expenses start. But even paid-off houses are now being re-mortgaged in ever greater numbers to pay the expenses of the elderly, eating up the most common form of working class asset.

By the time workers die, there is usually nothing left. We can get a sense of this by looking at the number of households who receive inheritances. In 1993, 90 percent of Hispanic households with a person aged 51–61 had received no financial inheritance. For blacks, it was 89 percent; for whites, 66 percent.[27]

Except for rare cases where parents disinherit their children, lack of inheritance means either that both parents have not yet died, or that they died but had nothing left to pass on. Taking into account different life expectancies at different incomes (people with lower incomes die younger), and factoring in the proportion of people who are white, black, and Hispanic, I calculate that about 45 percent of the population receives no financial inheritance from their parents. Most of these people are in lower-income families, part of the 62 percent of the population who are the working class.

In other words, well over half of American working class families have nothing left to give when the last parent dies. Maybe they were able to help their kids buy a car or some furniture or contribute to a down payment on a house when they were in their prime earning years. But that basically just allows the kids to get by these days, when real wages have fallen. The sad fact is that after a lifetime of work, most working class people have no assets left to show for it, only their kids to take their place.

In the last decades of the twentieth century, then, production and worker productivity continued their historic climb. But real wages for working class people fell, and both income and wealth shifted away from workers to capitalists. These experiences show starkly that economic growth alone is no guarantee of a more prosperous country for all. A rising tide does not lift all boats in a world with such differences in class power. To switch metaphors, it is not enough just to make a larger pie. We have to ask, who gets to eat it? And that's a question of power.

UNDERSTANDING POWER

Analyzing class [also] allows us a better understanding of power. The econonic trends just discussed reflect shifts in the relative power of workers and their bosses, labor and capital, both at work and in the political process.

Although most people do not look at social issues in class terms, many business leaders have a keen appreciation of the matter. For twenty-five years they have mounted a deliberate and public attack on working class wages and power. While working and middle class people have been disregarding class, others have been astutely conducting class struggle—on behalf of capitalists.

Since the 1970s, employers have argued continuously that workers get paid too much, that unions put too many restrictions on management (either directly or through their influence in politics), that workers have to give up past gains to help business regain competitiveness. Politicians complain that labor is a "special interest" that threatens the middle class; any talk of the working class and class conflict is considered a ridiculous throwback to outworn dogma. These are all direct attacks on labor by capital. It is class struggle, but only one side seems to know it.

In fact, the long decline in working class living standards coincides with the gradual and now almost total disappearance of the working class as a subject of public discussion. As part of the attack on labor, the working class has been disappeared. As part of a renewed and vigorous defense of labor, the working class must reappear.

My insistence on identifying a working class is not a word game. It is not just a matter of semantics to say that workers are in the working class, not the middle class; it is a question of power.

To exercise power, you need to know who you are. You also need to know who your adversary is, the target in the conflict. When the working class disappears into the middle class, workers lose a vital piece of their identity. In political, social, and cultural terms, they don't know who they are any more. To make matters worse, they also lose a sense of the enemy, as the capitalist class vanishes among "the rich." As the capitalist class disappears from view, the target of struggle disappears, too.

Rich people are not the problem working and middle class people face. Real wages haven't fallen, unions aren't weaker, multiple wage earners aren't a necessity in almost every working class household because Sylvester Stallone and Madonna are rich. If we look at the movie stars, big-name athletes, and rock musicians among the rich (although they are hardly typical, either of the rich or of all actors, athletes, and musicians), we find that most of them are rich because, through their talent and work, they have made other people even richer—the team owners, the owners of studios and recording companies, in short, the *capitalists* among the rich. (Of course, some of these stars become capitalists themselves.) Thinking of class in terms of "rich, middle, and poor" or "upper, middle, and lower" wipes out this vital distinction. Capitalists tend to be rich, yes, but more important is the fact that they are capitalists.

When the capitalist class disappears, the middle class, and particularly workers, who are thought to be middle class, seem to confront . . . whom? The rich? It is relatively easy to trivialize and ridicule class politics when it appears to be a knee-jerk attack on the rich. Not least, this is because most people would like to become rich themselves, to live the good life with ease. To attack the rich is to attack what many people hope for in their own futures. It seems to rob people of their aspirations.

Thinking about class in a more appropriate way helps clarify the proper target of struggle. Economic problems arise not because some people are rich but because private profit and the power of capital are the highest priorities in the economic system. Then, as history and current experience show us, the pursuit of profit leads too many business owners to too easily abuse workers, ruin the environment, and corrupt the political process. Economic problems come from the economic system, and the structure of power within it, that favors one class and disfavors others. Too few people have too much power over culture, education, the economy, and the institutions that affect the life chances of us all.

With the disappearance of the terms "capitalist" and "working class" from public discussion, politics in the late twentieth century meant the substitution of a host of targets other than the capitalists for the wrath of working and middle class people. As the capitalists disappeared, we saw the poor, the immigrant, the foreigner, the government, and even the workers themselves and their unions proposed as targets for our anger. The results have been bad for workers, good for capitalists. . . .

NOTES

1. Michael Winerip, "Canton's Economic Seesaw: Managers' Fortunes Rise as Workers Get Bumpy Ride," *New York Times,* July 7, 1996, 7.
2. U.S. Department of Labor, *Employment, Hours, and Earnings, United States, 1909–94,* Vol. 1, Bulletin 2445, September 1994; *Employment, Hours, and Earnings, United States, 1988–96,* Bulletin 2481, August 1996; *Employment and Earnings,* January 1999.
3. U.S. Department of Commerce, Bureau of the Census, *Current Population Reports, Series P-60,* various issues.
4. Ann Crittenden, "Temporary Solutions," *Working Woman,* Vol. 19, No. 2, February 1994, 32; "Contingent and Alternative Employment Arrangements, February, 1997," U.S. Department of Labor 97-422, http://stats.bls.gov/newsrels.htm.
5. Calculated from data in *Economic Report of the President, 1998,* Tables B-30, 75, 77.
6. Louis Uchitelle, *New York Times,* July 19, 1998, Section 4, 1.
7. Production worker earnings and employment data from U.S. Department of Labor, *Employment, Hours, and Earnings, United States,* Vol. 1, Bulletin 2445, September 1994; Bulletin 2481, August 1996; *Employment and Earnings,* January 1999. Output data from *Economic Report of the President, 1999.*
8. Lawrence Mishel, Jared Bernstein, and John Schmitt, *The State of Working America, 1996–1997* (Armonk, NY: M. E. Sharpe, 1996), 139.
9. Jacob M. Schlesinger, "Low-Wage Workers Make Strong Gains," *Wall Street Journal,* February 5, 1999, A2.
10. Sylvia Nasar, "The 1980s: A Very Good Time for the Very Rich," *New York Times,* March 5, 1992, A1, citing Congressional Budget Office data and analysis by economist Paul Krugman.
11. Jason deParle, "House Data on U.S. Income Sets Off Debate on Fairness," *New York Times,* May 22, 1992, A16, citing U.S. House of Representatives Committee on Ways and Means, *Green Book,* May 21, 1992.
12. U.S. Department of Commerce, Bureau of the Census, *Money Income in the United States: 1997, Current Population Reports, Series P-60,* No. 200, September 1998, Table B-3.
13. "Executive Pay: Special Report," *Business Week,* April 19, 1999, 78.
14. Michael Winerip, "Canton's Economic Seesaw."
15. Graef F. Crystal, *In Search of Excess: The Overcompensation of American Executives* (New York: W. W. Norton, 1991), chapter 13.
16. Keith Bradsher, "Widest Gap in Incomes? Research Points to U.S.," *New York Times,* October 27, 1995, D2, citing data from the Luxembourg Income Study.
17. Keith Bradsher, *New York Times,* June 22, 1996, 22, citing a new study of wealth from the University of Michigan's Panel Survey of Income Dynamics.
18. Edward Wolff, *Top Heavy* (New York: Twentieth Century Fund, 1996), Figure 3.4.
19. Ibid., Figure 3.1.
20. Arthur Kennickell, Douglas McManus, and R. Louise Woodburn, "Weighted Design for the 1992 *Survey of Consumer Finances,*" unpublished Federal Reserve Board technical paper quoted in Doug Henwood, *Left Business Observer,* No. 72, April 3, 1996, 5.
21. Ibid.
22. Ibid.
23. *Barron's,* May 11, 1998. Similar results were found by PSI Global Corporation's Financial Services Research Program Survey, conducted March to May 1998.
24. U.S. Department of Commerce, *Statistical Abstract of the United States: 1998,* Table 702.
25. David Barboza, "Amid Market Turmoil, Small Investor Is Steadfast," *New York Times,* August 13, 1998, D1.
26. Ron Suskind, "Ordinary People Show Extraordinary Faith, Reaping Rich Rewards," *Wall Street Journal,* March 30, 1999, A1.
27. James P. Smith, *Unequal Wealth and Incentives to Save* (Santa Monica, CA: RAND Corporation, 1995), 15.

READING 15

Getting Ahead

Economic and Social Mobility in America

Daniel P. McMurrer

Isabel V. Sawhill

The half century since World War II can be divided into two periods. In the first period—from 1947 to 1973—family incomes rose at a healthy clip and the gains were more or less equally shared. Between 1973 and 1994, however, incomes rose more slowly and the gains were heavily tilted toward the top of the distribution (Chart 1).

This part of the story is hardly new. The disappointing rate of economic growth and the growing income gap between rich and poor in recent decades is by now well documented.[1] But there is another chapter in this story.

Income Growth Has Been Unequally Distributed Since 1973

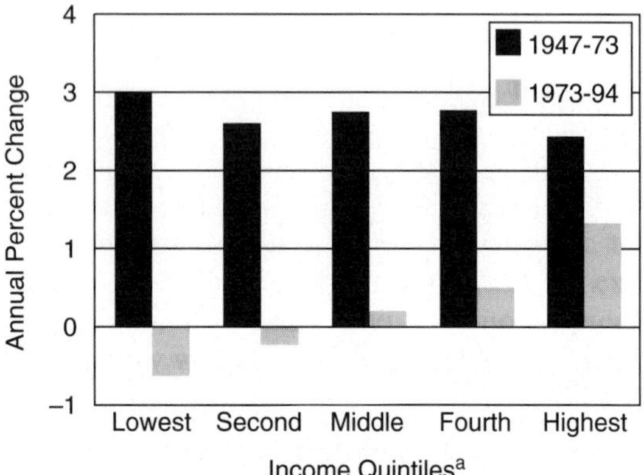

Source: Lawrence Mishel and Jared Bernstein, *The State of Working America 1996-97* (Economic Policy Institute, 1997).

[a]The lowest income quintile consists of the 20 percent of all families with the lowest income as measured by the Census Bureau. The second quintile consists of the second-poorest 20 percent, and so forth.

CHART 1

INEQUALITY AND MOBILITY

Most people would look at the trend depicted in Chart 1 and conclude that America is becoming a bifurcated society. That is too hasty a conclusion. Although the distribution of income among individuals may be unequal in any given year, this does not necessarily mean it is unequal over their lifetimes. For various reasons, many individuals move up in the distribution over time, while many others move down. And the reasons for movement vary. A poor single mother who marries an accountant, for example, may move up substantially in the year of the marriage. A well-to-do farmer whose crop fails may move way down that year. A young computer programmer who works hard may move up steadily year by year as she acquires more job experience.

Economic historian Joseph Schumpeter compared the income distribution to a hotel—full of rooms that are always occupied, but often by different people.[2] In order to have an accurate picture of an individual's experience over a lifetime, therefore, we must know not only the size of the different rooms but also the rate at which individuals switch rooms.

This switching goes on all the time and makes it difficult to interpret the standard statistics showing how the top (or bottom) 20 percent of the population has fared over some period of time.

Economists now understand that the amount of mobility is just as important as the distribution of economic rewards in any given year, because it determines the extent to which inequality in the short term translates into inequality over the long term. For example, a very unequal distribution of income in any one year would be of little consequence in a society in which individuals were

Daniel P. McMurrer is a senior researcher specializing in the effects of human capital investments at the American Society for Training and Development in Alexandria, Virginia. Isabel V. Sawhill is a senior fellow in economic studies at the Brookings Institute in Washington, DC.

constantly moving up or down the economic ladder, resulting in each receiving an equal share of the rewards over a lifetime. Conversely, a society in which there was very little mobility would have a very different character than the previous one—*even if their annual income distributions looked exactly the same.* Thus a crucial question is: How much economic mobility is there?

MOBILITY IN THE UNITED STATES

Much less is known about mobility than about inequality. In recent years, however, a number of studies have used survey data to track the incomes of the same individuals over time.[3] The most commonly used technique for analyzing their mobility is to rank their incomes from highest to lowest in a beginning year. Typically, this ranking breaks the sample into five equal-sized groups (quintiles). This is done again for the incomes of these same individuals in a later year. The percentage of individuals who change income quintiles between these two years is then used as an indicator of mobility. Because the focus is on relative position within the distribution, in order for one individual to move up it is necessary for someone else to move down.[4]

How Much Mobility?

These studies of relative mobility have produced remarkably consistent results, with regard to both the degree of mobility and the extent of changes in mobility over time.[5] Mobility in the United States is substantial, according to this evidence. Large proportions of the population move into a new income quintile, with estimates ranging from about 25 to 40 percent in a single year. As one would expect, the mobility rate is even higher over longer periods—about 45 percent over a 5-year period and about 60 percent over both 9-year and 17-year periods.[6]

Who Moves Up?

Which groups are most likely to be *upwardly* mobile in the income distribution? Evidence suggests that, in recent years, individuals with at least a college education are more likely to move up than any other group (Chart 2).[7] This is a significant change from the 1970s, when income increases were more evenly distributed across educational levels.

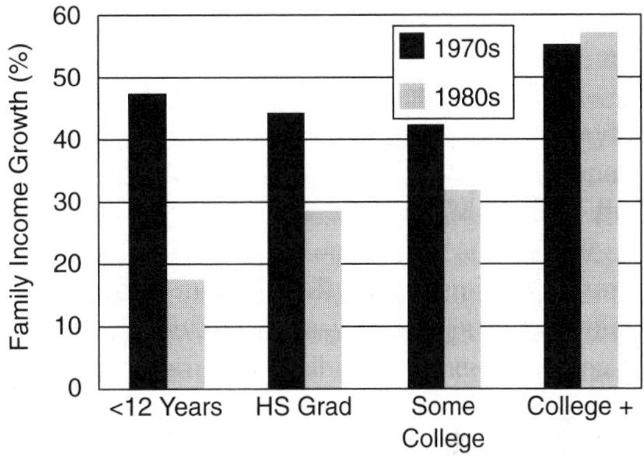

Source: Rose (1993), cited in endnote 7. Rose used the Panel Study of Income Dynamics to calculate growth in real family income, after adjusting for family size, for adults ages 22 to 48 at the beginning of each decade.

CHART 2

International Comparisons

Although mobility in the United States is substantial, evidence indicates that it is no higher in this country than elsewhere. Indeed, the few studies that have directly compared mobility across countries have concluded that, despite significant differences in labor markets and government policies across countries, mobility rates are surprisingly similar.[8]

Other Measures of Mobility

Two widely reported recent studies of mobility in the United States found extremely high rates of mobility—rates that are much higher than those cited above.[9] This results from differences in analytical approach.[10] Most importantly, these studies examined absolute (rather than relative) mobility.[11] Under this definition of mobility, anyone who moves across a fixed threshold (established in the base year or for the population as a whole) is considered mobile regardless of his or her relative position within the distribution. As a result, factors such as economic growth and the natural tendency of incomes to increase with age can cause almost everyone to appear mobile.

Mobility over Time

Although mobility in the United States is neither higher than it is in other countries nor as high (in our view) as suggested by studies of absolute mobility, there is nevertheless broad agreement among researchers that the year-by-year movement of individuals between income quintiles is substantial and that lifetime earnings are more evenly distributed than annual earnings. But what about changes in mobility over time? In particular, what has happened to mobility since the early 1970s, when annual inequality began to increase?

The evidence on this point is clear: Mobility has not changed significantly over the last 25 years. Indeed, a number of different studies indicate that relative mobility rates in the United States—both short term and long term—have been remarkably stable (Chart 3 displays the results of two out of six mobility studies cited in endnote 5). Thus, Americans continue to move up and down in the income distribution at the same rate as they did in the past.

As a result, the recent increases in annual inequality have proceeded unchecked by any increase in mobility. An individual's income in any one year is always a poor predictor of lifetime income, but it is not a worse predictor now than it was in the past.

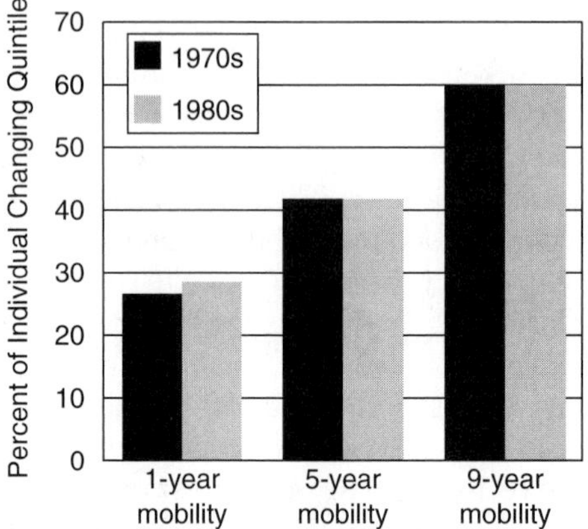

Sources: Data for one-year and five-year mobility are from Burkhauser, Holtz-Eakin, and Rhody (1996), cited in endnote 5; data for nine-year mobility are from Sawhill and Condon (1992), cited in endnote 2. Time periods are slightly different. For one-year and five-year mobility, average rates for 1970–79 and 1980–89 are used; for nine-year mobility, 1967–76 is used for the "1970s" and 1977–86 is used for the "1980s."

CHART 3

SUMMING UP

The incomes of American families change frequently. Some of the poor get richer, some of the rich get poorer, and for a variety of reasons: accumulation of job skills and experience, marriage and divorce, job change, addition or loss of a second paycheck, and business success or failure.

But despite this churning, overall rates of mobility in the United States have not changed over time. Thus, it is fair to conclude that increases in annual inequality have worsened the distribution of lifetime incomes. Although the disparity in economic rewards has increased, the availability of those rewards—the probability of success or failure—has remained unchanged.

There has been one notable development within this broader picture, however. The mobility of those with little education has declined. Increasingly, a college education is the ticket to upward mobility.

The question of how much inequality is acceptable or appropriate in the United States, as noted earlier, is an issue on which there is no agreement. Still, it is somewhat disturbing to learn that the seemingly relentless growth in the inequality of economic rewards has been unmitigated by any increase in access to those rewards, especially for those with the fewest skills.

CLASS AND OPPORTUNITY

Americans are more likely than individuals in other nations to believe in the importance of talent and effort in shaping a person's life prospects. They are also more likely to reject social class as an acceptable determinant of whether someone succeeds or fails.[12] Given such a strong consensus on the goal of equal opportunity, the American public has paid remarkably little attention to how close society is to achieving it.

Evidence suggests that family background matters quite a bit—that this society is still far from providing everyone an equal chance to succeed. At the same time, real progress has been made. Inherited advantages of class play a smaller role than they used to in shaping the success of individual Americans, with larger numbers now moving beyond their origins. In this sense, opportunity has increased.

But in another sense, it has not. In the past, the dynamism of the U.S. economy ensured that each generation's prospects were better than those of the last one, irrespective of social origins. Almost all Americans were able to achieve more than their parents. As economic growth has slowed in recent decades, however, so has opportunity. The depressing effect of this growth slowdown has almost completely offset the opportunity gains that have come from the declining importance of class.

Class Still Matters

Opportunity is here defined as the extent to which an individual's economic and social status is determined by his or her own skills and effort rather than by class of origin. It is typically measured as the relationship between parents and their offspring[13] on various indicators of class—occupational status and income are common ones.[14] The more closely the status of individuals reflects the status of their parents, the less opportunity exists in a society and the more class matters. Conversely, the more independent the overall parent-offspring relationship, the less class matters.

In today's America, the socioeconomic class into which individuals are born significantly affects their status as adults. Even in an open, fair, and dynamic society, of course, some relationship between the status of parents and their adult children would be expected.[15] Genetic inheritance alone is likely to account for some of this (although estimates suggest that it would be an extremely small fraction). Further, there will always be a tendency for parents who occupy positions of high status—whether through their own achievements or for other reasons—to try to extend their advantages to their children. This is a tendency for which public policy can probably never fully compensate as long as children are reared within their own families. Thus, it is almost impossible to imagine a society in which parents' and children's outcomes are completely independent.

The link between the incomes and occupations of parents and offspring in the United States, however, is stronger than would be expected even given these considerations. Recent studies have found an observed correlation between the incomes of fathers and sons of about 0.4.[16] This means, for example, that an adult son whose father's income was a quarter of the way from the bottom of the income distribution (at the 25th percentile) would have a 50 percent chance of having an income in the bottom two-fifths (Chart 4). Conversely, a son whose father's income was at the 95th percentile (not shown) would have a 76 percent chance of being above the median, including a 42 percent chance of being in the top 20 percent.

Occupations are similarly correlated across generations, with children of professionals significantly more likely to become professionals as adults, and children of blue collar workers significantly more likely to work in blue collar occupations (Chart 5). For example, men with

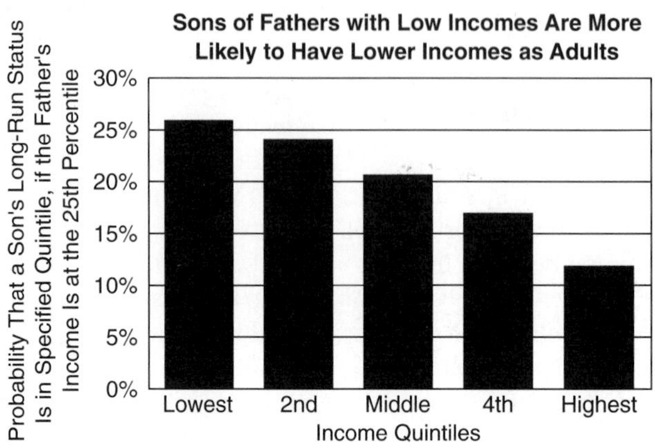

Source: Solon (1989, 1992), cited in endnote 16.
Note: Assumes an intergenerational income correlation of 0.4 and normal income distribution.

CHART 4

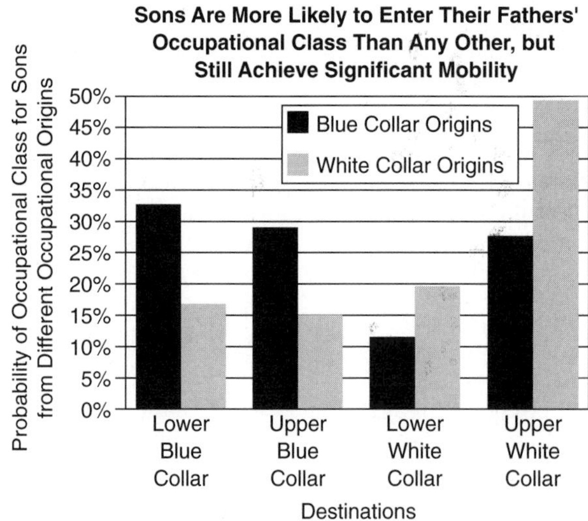

Source: Authors' calculations of Hout's (1988) data, cited in endnote 17, excluding farm origins and destinations.

CHART 5

white collar origins are almost twice as likely as those with blue collar origins to end up in upper white collar jobs.

Thus, origins continue to matter. Children from advantaged backgrounds are likely to do well as adults, and children from disadvantaged backgrounds are more likely to do badly. But this is not the end of the story.

Class Matters Less Than Previously

Class may still matter in the United States, but not as much as it used to. The effect of parents' occupational status on that of their offspring declined by about one-third in less than a generation, according to one study.[17] Other studies have confirmed this decline and have shown that it is a continuing one, evident for at least the last three generations and probably longer.[18] One ambitious study finds that the decline dates back to the mid-19th century.[19]

The decline has been driven by the growth of meritocratic practices in the hiring process, the decline of self-employment, and the growing number of Americans with access to higher education. The percentage of adults who are college graduates, for example, increased from 8 percent in 1960 to 23 percent in 1995. Attainment of a college degree has been shown to greatly attenuate the link between occupational origins and occupational destinations.

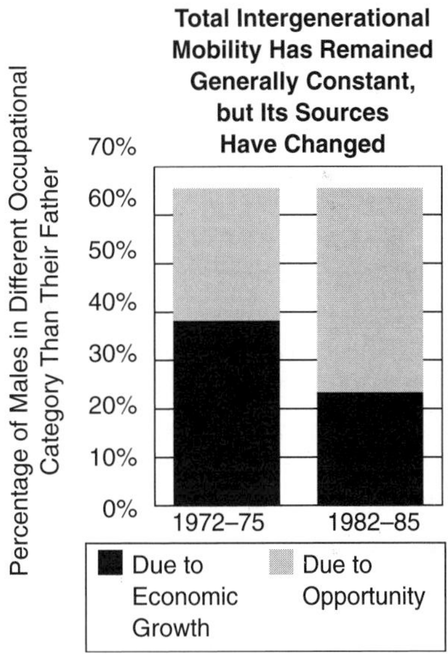

Source: Authors' calculations of Hout's (1988) data, cited in endnote 17, using five occupational categories.

CHART 6

The Offsetting Effect of Slower Economic Growth

The vigorous economic growth that fueled continuing change in the occupational structure of the U.S. economy for most of our history has declined, slowing the pace of occupational change along with it. The economy itself is no longer creating as many chances for individuals to move up the economic ladder as used to be the case—a trend that has largely offset the declining importance of background. One study finds that the two trends have almost completely offset one another, resulting in little overall change in the rates at which individuals move from the class into which they were born.[20] The only difference has come in the composition of upward mobility. A larger proportion of upward mobility across generations is attributable to the declining importance of class and a smaller proportion to economic growth (Chart 6). (If individual opportunity increases in an economy that is not growing at all, intergenerational churning between the socioeconomic classes will increase, but there may be no net improvement for younger generations over their parents.)[21]

This change in the composition of upward mobility—growing individual opportunity and lagging economic growth—is important, because it will be felt differently by different groups, depending on where they start. Everyone is hurt by slower growth. But individuals from more-modest backgrounds will benefit from a more open, less class-based social structure. On balance, according to the data, they should come out ahead. For individuals from more-privileged backgrounds, in contrast, the increased individual "opportunity" implied by the declining importance of class represents an increased likelihood of moving down the social scale. They are more likely than before to experience a drop in status relative to their parents. Both trends (economic growth and individual opportunity) represent losses for them.

Summing Up

The United States remains a society in which class matters. Children who grow up in privileged families are more likely to become highly paid professionals, for example, than are children raised in less-advantaged households. Still, the effects of family background have declined in recent years. Success is less likely to be inherited than it was in earlier years, suggesting that the American playing field is becoming more equal.

The role of higher education in increasing individual opportunity is notable. Educational attainment in the United States has improved significantly, suggesting that opportunity may continue to grow as a result.

The failure of the economy to grow as rapidly as in the past is equally notable, however. Even as individual opportunity has increased, the slowing of economic growth and the related stagnation of occupational prospects have almost offset this gain. While individuals are increasingly free to move from their roots, fewer destinations represent improvements.

NOTES

1. Attempts to adjust the data for changes in family size, for different measures of inflation, for the receipt of capital gains, or for income transfers and taxes have not markedly changed the basic trends described above.
2. For further discussion of this analogy, see Isabel V. Sawhill and Mark Condon, "Is U.S. Income Inequality Really Growing? Sorting Out the Fairness Question," Urban Institute, *Policy Bites* 13 (1992).
3. For a more detailed analysis of these studies, see Daniel P. McMurrer and Isabel V. Sawhill, "Economic Mobility in the United States," Research paper 6722 (Washington, DC: Urban Institute, 1996).
4. Thus, if average incomes are increasing over time as a result of economic growth, an individual's income must rise more quickly than the rest of the sample in order to move up to a higher quintile. Movement between quintiles is a relatively crude measure of mobility, as it only roughly captures the magnitude of the change in an individual's income.
5. These studies include Richard V. Burkhauser, Douglas Holtz-Eakin, and Stephen E. Rhody, "Labor Earnings Mobility in the United States and Germany during the Growth Years of the 1980s," mimeograph (Syracuse, NY: Syracuse University, 1996); Mark Condon and Isabel V. Sawhill, "Income Mobility and Permanent Income Inequality," Research paper 6723 (Washington, DC: Urban Institute, 1992); Maury Gittleman and Mary Joyce, "Earnings Mobility in the United States, 1967–91," *Monthly Labor Review,* 3–13 (September 1995); Peter Gottschalk, "Notes on 'By Our Own Bootstraps: Economic Opportunity and the Dynamics of Income Distribution,' by Cox and Alm," mimeograph (Boston: Boston College, 1996); Thomas Hungerford, "U.S. Income Mobility in the Seventies and Eighties," *Review of Income and Wealth,* 403–417 (1993); and Sawhill and Condon (1992).
6. Over any period longer than one year, some individual movement between quintiles is not captured by the analysis. For example, an individual who is in the same quintile in both years examined (say, the first and ninth years) may still have moved between quintiles in the intervening years, although he or she would appear to have been "immobile" over the nine-year period.
7. Stephen Rose, "Declining Family Incomes in the 1980s: New Evidence from Longitudinal Data," *Challenge,* 29–36 (November–December 1993).
8. Rolf Aaberge et al., "Income Inequality and Income Mobility in the Scandinavian Countries Compared to the United States," mimeograph, Statistics Norway (1996); Burkhauser et al. (1996); Greg J. Duncan et al., "Poverty Dynamics in Eight Countries," *Journal of Population Economics*, 215–234 (1993).
9. U.S. Department of the Treasury, Office of Tax Analysis, "Household Income Mobility during the 1980s: A Statistical Analysis Based on Tax Return Data" (Washington, DC: U.S. Department of the Treasury, 1992); and W. Michael Cox and Richard Alm, "By Our Own Bootstraps: Economic Opportunity and the Dynamics of Income Distribution," *Federal Reserve Bank of Dallas Annual Report 1995* (Dallas: Federal Reserve Bank of Dallas, 1995).
10. For additional discussion of these methodological questions, see Gottschalk (1996) and Paul Krugman, "The Right, the Rich, and the Facts: Deconstructing the Income Distribution Debate," *American Prospect,* 19–31 (Fall 1992).
11. Absolute mobility is the movement of an individual in relation to an external standard, usually

PERSONAL ACCOUNT

I Am a Pakistani Woman

I am a Pakistani woman, raised in the U.S. and Canada, and often at odds with the Western standard of beauty.

As a child in Nova Scotia and later growing up in New York and Indiana, I was proud of my uniqueness. On traditional Pakistani and Muslim holidays, I got to wear bright, fun clothes from my country and colorful jewelry. I had a whole rich tradition of my own to celebrate in addition to Christmas and Easter. However, as I started school, I somehow came to realize that being different wasn't so great—that in other people's viewpoint, I looked strange and acted funny. I learned the importance of fitting in and behaving like the other girls. This involved dressing well, giggling a lot, and having a superior, but flirtatious attitude toward boys. I was very outgoing and had very good grades, so outwardly I was able to "assimilate" with some success. But my sister, who was quiet and reticent, often took the brunt of other children's cruelty. I realize how proud and ashamed I was of my heritage when I look at my relationship with my family.

A lesson I learned early on in the U.S. was that being beautiful took a lot of money. It is painful, as an adult, for me to consider the inexorable, never-ending pressure that my father was under to embody the dominant, middle-class cultural expressions of masculinity, as in success at one's job, making a big salary, and owning status symbols. I resented him so much then for being a poor, untenured professor and freelance writer. I wanted designer clothes, dining out at nice restaurants, and a big allowance. Instead, I had a deeply spiritual thinker, writer, and theologian for a dad. I love(d) him and am so very grateful for what he's taught me, but as a child I didn't think of him as a success.

The prettiest girls in school all had a seemingly endless array of outfits, lots of makeup and perfume, and everything by the "right" designers. I hated my mom for making many of my clothes and buying things on sale (and my mom was a great seamstress). I hungrily read about Brooke Shields's seemingly perfect life, with her excursions to expensive restaurants and appointments with personal trainers at exclusive spas. I felt a sense of hopelessness that I could never have the resources or opportunities necessary to compete, to be beautiful.

Instead I found safety in conformity. When I was in high school, the WASPy, preppy look was hot; it represented the epitome of success and privilege in America. I worked hard to purchase a wardrobe of clothes with a polo-horse insignia, by many hours at an after-school job. I tried to hide my exotic look behind Khakis, boat shoes, hair barrettes, and pearl studs. There was comfort in conformity. I saw the class "sex symbol" denigrated for wearing tight dresses and having a very well-developed body for a sixteen-year-old, and the more unique dressers dismissed as frivolous, trendy, and more than a little eccentric. You couldn't be too pretty, too ugly, too different—you had to just blend in.

Though I did it well, I perpetually felt like an imposter. This rigidly controlled, well-dressed preppy going through school with good grades in advanced placement classes in no way represented what I felt to be my true essence.

Hoorie I. Siddique

defined by averages among the population as a whole. Thus, it is possible for all individuals in a fixed group to move up in relation to this external standard. Absolute mobility does not measure change in an individual's relative position within a given sample, and is therefore not comparable to relative mobility.

12. See, e.g., Seymour Martin Lipset, *American Exceptionalism* (New York: W.W. Norton, 1996).
13. Because of data limitations, many of the studies in this area have excluded women, focusing on the relationship between fathers and sons.
14. To analyze income relationships, researchers compare the incomes of parents (frequently only fathers) at a certain age with the incomes of their children at a similar age. Analysis of occupational relationships is more complicated. This comparison also requires ranking occupations on a hierarchical scale, which is usually based on a combination of the average income and average years of schooling associated with each occupation.
15. For a more complete discussion of how much opportunity might exist in an open society, see Daniel P. McMurrer, Mark Condon, and Isabel V. Sawhill, "Intergenerational Mobility in the United States," Research paper 6796 (Washington, DC: Urban Institute, 1997).

16. Gary Solon, "Intergenerational Income Mobility in the United States," *American Economic Review* 82:393–408 (1992); Gary Solon, "Intergenerational Income Mobility in the United States," Discussion paper no. 894–89 (Madison, WI: University of Wisconsin Institute for Research on Poverty, 1989); and David J. Zimmerman, "Regression toward Mediocrity in Economic Stature," *American Economic Review* 82:409–429 (1992).
17. Michael Hout, "More Universalism, Less Structural Mobility: The American Occupational Structure in the 1980s," *American Journal of Sociology* 93:1358–1400 (1988).
18. Timothy Biblarz, Vern Bengston, and Alexander Bucur, "Social Mobility across Three Generations," *Journal of Marriage and the Family* 58:188–200 (1996). See also David Grusky and Thomas DiPrete, "Recent Trends in the Process of Stratification," *Demography* 27:617–637 (1990).
19. David Grusky, "American Social Mobility in the 19th and 20th Centuries," Working paper no. 86–28 (Madison, WI: University of Wisconsin Center for Demography and Ecology, 1989).
20. Hout (1988).
21. Different rates of fertility can also affect overall levels of mobility. If less-privileged individuals reproduce more rapidly than the more privileged, more people will be able to experience upward mobility—even in the absence of economic growth.

What Is Sexual Orientation?

READING 16

The Invention of Heterosexuality

Jonathan Ned Katz

In the United States, in the 1890s, the "sexual instinct" was generally identified as a *procreative* desire of men and women. But that reproductive ideal was beginning to be challenged, quietly but insistently, in practice and theory, by a new *different-sex pleasure* ethic. According to that radically new standard, the "sexual instinct" referred to men's and women's erotic desire for each other, *irrespective of its procreative potential.* Those two, fundamentally opposed, sexual moralities informed the earliest American definitions of "heterosexuals" and "homosexuals." Under the old procreative standard, the new term *heterosexual* did not, at first, always signify the normal and good.

The earliest-known use of the word *heterosexual* in the United States occurs in an article by Dr. James G. Kiernan, published in a Chicago medical journal in May 1892.[1]

Heterosexual was not equated here with normal sex, but with perversion—a definitional tradition that lasted in middle-class culture into the 1920s. Kiernan linked heterosexual to one of several "abnormal manifestations of the sexual appetite"—in a list of "sexual perversions proper"—in an article on "Sexual Perversion." Kiernan's brief note on depraved heterosexuals attributed their definition (incorrectly, as we'll see) to Dr. Richard von Krafft-Ebing of Vienna.

These heterosexuals were associated with a mental condition, "psychical hermaphroditism." . . . Heterosexuals experienced so-called male erotic attraction to females *and* so-called female erotic attraction to males. That is, these heterosexuals periodically felt "inclinations to both sexes."[2] The hetero in these heterosexuals referred *not* to their interest in *a different sex,* but to their desire for *two different sexes.* Feeling desire inappropriate, supposedly, for their sex,

---

Jonathan Ned Katz has written for the *Village Voice,* the *Nation,* and the *Advocate.*

these heterosexuals were guilty of what we now think of as gender and erotic deviance.

Heterosexuals were also guilty of reproductive deviance. That is, they betrayed inclinations to "abnormal methods of gratification"—modes of ensuring pleasure without reproducing the species. They also demonstrated "traces of the normal sexual appetite"—a touch of the desire to reproduce.

Dr. Kiernan's article also included the earliest-known U.S. publication of the word *homosexual.* The "pure homosexuals" he cited were persons whose "general mental state is that of the opposite sex." These homosexuals were defined explicitly as gender benders, rebels from proper masculinity and femininity. In contrast, his heterosexuals deviated explicitly from gender, erotic, and procreative norms. In their American debut, the abnormality of heterosexuals appeared to be thrice that of homosexuals.[3]. . .

KRAFFT-EBING'S *PSYCHOPATHIA SEXUALIS*

The new term *hetero-sexual* next appeared early in 1893, in the first U.S. publication, in English, of *Psychopathia Sexualis, with Especial Reference to Contrary Sexual Instinct: A Medico-Legal Study,* by Richard von Krafft-Ebing, "Professor of Psychiatry and Neurology at the University of Vienna."[4] This book would appear in numerous later U.S. editions, becoming one of the most famous, influential texts on "pathological" sexuality.[5] Its disturbing (and fascinating) examples of a sex called sick began quietly to define a new idea of a sex perceived as healthy.[6]

In this primer, the "pathological sexual instinct" and "contrary sexual instinct" are major terms referring to non-procreative desire. Their opposite, called, simply, "sexual instinct," is reproductive. But that old procreative norm was no longer as absolute for Krafft-Ebing as it was for Kiernan. . . .

In the heat of different-sex lust, declares Krafft-Ebing, men and women are not usually thinking of baby making: "In sexual love the real purpose of the instinct, the propagation of the species, does not enter into consciousness."[7] An unconscious procreative "purpose" informs his idea of "sexual love." . . . Placing the reproductive aside in the unconscious, Krafft-Ebing created a small, obscure space in which a new pleasure norm began to grow.

Krafft-Ebing's procreative, sex-differentiated, and erotic "sexual instinct" was present by definition in his term *hetero-sexual*—his book introduced that word to many Americans. A hyphen between, Krafft-Ebing's "hetero" and "sexual" newly spliced sex-difference and eroticism to constitute a pleasure defined explicitly by the different sexes of its parties. His hetero-sexual, unlike Kiernan's, does not desire two sexes, only one, different, sex.

Krafft-Ebing's term *hetero-sexual* makes no *explicit* reference to reproduction, though it always implicitly includes reproductive desire. Always, therefore, his hetero-sexual implicitly signifies erotic normality. His twin term, *homosexual,* always signifies a same-sex desire, pathological because non-reproductive.

Contrary to Kiernan's earlier attribution, Krafft-Ebing consistently uses hetero-sexual to mean normal sex. In contrast, for Kiernan, and some other late-nineteenth- and early-twentieth-century sexologists, a simple reproductive standard was absolute: The hetero-sexuals in Krafft-Ebing's text appeared guilty of procreative ambiguity, thus of perversion.

These distinctions between sexual terms and definitions are historically important, but complex, and may be difficult for us to grasp. Our own society's particular, dominant heterosexual norm also helps to cloud our minds to other ways of categorizing.

Readers such as Dr. Kiernan might also understand Krafft-Ebing's hetero-sexuals to be perverts by association. For the word *hetero-sexual,* though signifying normality, appears often in the Viennese doctor's book linked with the non-procreative perverse—coupled with "contrary sexual instinct," "psychical hermaphroditism," "homo-sexuality," and "fetichism."

For example, Krafft-Ebing's first use of "hetero-sexual" occurs in a discussion of several case histories of "hetero- and homo-sexuality" in which "a certain kind of attire becomes a fetich."[8] The hetero-sexual premieres, with the homo-sexual, as clothes fetishist. . . .

Krafft-Ebing's use of the word *hetero-sexual* to mean a normal different-sex eroticism marked in discourse a first historic shift away from the centuries-old procreative norm. His use of the terms *hetero-sexual* and *homo-sexual* helped to make sex difference and eros the basic distinguishing features of a new linguistic, conceptual, and social ordering of desire. His hetero-sexual and homo-sexual offered the modern world two sex-differentiated eroticisms, one normal and good, one abnormal and bad, a division which would come to dominate our twentieth-century vision of the sexual universe. . . .

NOTES

1. Dr. James G. Kiernan, "Responsibility in Sexual Perversion," *Chicago Medical Recorder* 3 (May 1892), 185–210; "Read before the Chicago Medical Society, March 7, 1892," but it's difficult to imagine him reading his footnote on Krafft-Ebing. Kiernan's note on 197–98 cites Krafft-Ebing's classifications in *Psychopathia Sexualis,* "Chaddock's translation" (no date). The U.S. publication in 1893 of C. G. Chaddock's translation of Krafft-Ebing's *Psychopathia Sexualis* followed Kiernan's article (see note 4 below). So there's some confusion about the exact source of Kiernan's brief note on Krafft-Ebing's terms "hetero-sexual" and "homo-sexual." Perhaps Kiernan saw a prepublication version of Chaddock's translation. It's also possible that Kiernan had seen some earlier article by Krafft-Ebing or the English translation by F. J. Rebman of the 10th German edition of Krafft-Ebing's *Psychopathia Sexualis,* published in London in 1889 (I have not inspected that edition). Kiernan seems to have based his brief gloss on Krafft-Ebing's definition of the heterosexual and homosexual on a superficial reading of pages 222–23 of the 1893 edition of Chaddock's translation of *Psychopathia Sexualis,* paragraphs numbered 1–4.
2. Mental hermaphrodites experienced, sometimes, the "wrong" feelings for their biological sex; their erotic desire was improperly inverted. A moral judgment founded the ostensibly objective, scientific concept of psychical hermaphroditism.

   Kiernan's idea of "psychical hermaphroditism" is not exactly the same as the attraction we now label "bisexual," referring as we do to the sex of the subject and the two different sexes to which he or she is attracted. Psychical hermaphroditism referred to mental gender, while our bisexuality refers to the sex of a sex partner. Mental hermaphroditism might lead to both sexes as erotic partners, but the term laid the cause in the mental gender of the subject (like the concept of inversion). Our bisexuality does not involve any necessary link to mental gender. I am grateful to Lisa Duggan for this clarification.
3. But heterosexuals' appearance of triple the abnormality of homosexuals was deceiving. For Kiernan, the gender deviance of homosexuals *implied* that they were also, simultaneously, rebels from a procreative norm and an erotic norm. But it's significant that Kiernan explicitly stresses homosexuals' gender rebellion, not their erotic or reproductive deviancy. George Chauncey, Jr., discusses the late-nineteenth-century stress on gender inversion in "From Sexual Inversion to Homosexuality: Medicine and the Changing Conceptualization of Female Deviance," *Salmagundi* 56–59 (Fall–Winter 1983), 114–46.
4. R. von Krafft-Ebing, *Psychopathia Sexualis, with Especial Reference to Contrary Sexual Instinct: A Medico-Legal Study,* trans. Charles Gilbert Chaddock (Philadelphia: F. A. Davis, 1893), from the 7th and revised German ed.; preface dated November 1892. Hereafter cited as Krafft-Ebing. The U.S. Copyright Office received and registered this edition on February 16, 1893 (Copyright Office to Katz, May 25, 1990).

This book's year of publication is confused, because its copyright page and its preface are dated 1892, while its title page lists the year of publication as 1893. *The National Union Catalogue of Pre-1956 Publications* says this edition was first published in 1892, and the first citation of "hetero-sexual" listed in the *Oxford English Dictionary* (1976 Supplement, p. 85) is to this edition of Krafft-Ebing, attributed to 1892. That year is incorrect. Although it was evidently prepared by November 1892, the date of its preface, it was not officially published until 1893.

For Krafft-Ebing and his *Psychopathia* see Peter Gay, *The Bourgeois Experience: Victoria to Freud,* Volume II, *The Tender Passion* (New York: Oxford University Press, 1986), 221, 223–24, 226, 229, 230–32, 286, 338, 350; Gert Hekma, "A History of Sexology: Social and Historical Aspects of Sexuality," in Jan Bremmer, ed., *From Sappho to De Sade: Moments in the History of Sexuality* (first published 1989; New York: Routledge, 1991), 173–93; and Arnold I. Davidson, "Closing Up the Corpses: Diseases of Sexuality and the Emergence of the Psychiatric Style of Reasoning," in George Boolos, ed., *Meaning and Method: Essays in Honor of Hilary Putnam* (New York: Cambridge University Press, 1990), 295–325. I am also greatly indebted to talks with Harry Oosterhuis and an advance copy of his paper "Richard von Krafft-Ebing's Step-Children of Nature: Psychiatry and the Making of Modern Sexual Identity," presented as a talk at the Second Carleton Conference on the History of the Family, May 12, 1994, in Ottawa, Canada.

5. Krafft-Ebing's focus, as a psychiatrist, on disturbed mental states contrasts with the earlier nineteenth-century focus of neurologists on disturbed brains. I thank Lisa Duggan for this comment.
6. In this text the doctor's descriptions of sex sickness and sex health replaced the old, overtly moral judgments about bad sex and good sex, introducing the modern medical model of sexuality to numbers of Americans.
7. Krafft-Ebing 9.
8. Krafft-Ebing 169.

READING 17

Homosexuality: A Social Phenomenon

Barbara Sherman Heyl

. . . This [essay] focuses primarily on the theoretical debates over how best to explain the "condition" of homosexuality, once Western culture had conceptualized it that way. Is there something "essential" that makes homosexuals who they are, or has the identity grown out of social interaction? The sociological view tends to see homosexuality as a social construction, both at the macro level—where society defines what homosexual behavior means within its cultural boundaries, and at the micro level—where the individual, in interaction with others, acquires his or her own personal sense of a sexual identity.

VIEWING HOMOSEXUAL BEHAVIOR IN ITS SOCIETAL CONTEXT

Cross-Cultural Variations

If patterns of sexual behavior and the meanings given to them are products of the social, cultural, and historical context out of which they developed, then we can expect them to vary cross-culturally. Recently published research has documented homosexual behavior in different parts of the world and in different time periods; the behavior was found to be interconnected with the social relationships and cultural beliefs of the societies under study (Callender & Kochems, 1983; Dover, 1978; Herdt, 1981; Whitam & Mathy, 1986). These cross-cultural data allow us

Barbara Sherman Heyl is professor of sociology at Illinois State University.

to compare different types of social organization and division of labor, and how they promote particular forms of homosexual behavior, as well as affect social responses to such behavior (Adam, 1985; Herdt, 1984).

. . . The kinship-structured society of Sambia in New Guinea included homosexual relations between older men and younger boys; the relations are ritualized and in a sense obligatory. This pattern was found in other societies on the eastern islands of Melanesia, as well as in southern New Guinea, and has been termed the "Melanesian" model by Barry Adam (1985). There are several characteristics of Melanesian-model societies that are influential in shaping the ritualized homosexuality that exists in those cultures. For example, these societies exhibit a high degree of gender separation and inequality (Herdt, 1984). Adam (1985) notes that "men and women have separate residences, pathways, crops, foods and rites" (see Allen, 1967). Women are viewed as important for reproductive and labor purposes, but are considered by males to have a polluting influence on young males. As a result of this belief, males "develop a complex and extended system of magical practices to rescue boys from impure contact with their mothers and convert them into men. This conversion is not easy and typically involves the seclusion of youths during which time they are fed and 'grown' by older men" (Adam, 1985, pp. 25, 26).

Thus, in Melanesian societies the homosexual patterns are age-graded, with the older males contributing their semen to the younger males as a way of giving them "manhood," initiating them into warrior groups, and making them strong (Herdt, 1984, pp. 59–64, 181–183). Semen is highly valued as necessary not only in creating life but also as a way of "binding the male line" (Adam, 1985, p. 27). The young men are required to ingest semen from older males in order to become part of the lineage of their past male ancestors. A related but different method of masculinizing boys is practiced among the Sambia of New Guinea. These people segregate young boys from women by sending them to forest lodges for ten to fifteen years. During this seclusion the boys pass through a series of rites, including frequent fellatio practiced between the younger and older boys (Herdt, 1984). After the initiation procedures are completed the males are expected to marry women and to end homosexual behavior.

Separating the young males from any contact with women produces a stage of enforced bachelorhood that all Melanesian males must pass through in order to become adult males. Adam (1985) notes that this separation allows the adult males exclusive rights to "use women's productive and reproductive power for their own use" (p. 20). Thus, the bachelorhood status and its accompanying rituals facilitate the maintenance of social control by the older males over both the young men and the women. Since homosexual behavior in Melanesian societies is routine and obligatory as part of the social organization of these societies, it is not perceived as deviant or abnormal behavior. Clearly, we cannot label this behavior according to our norms or view these men as "homosexuals"—a term that derives from our Western culture (see Herdt, 1984; Stoller, 1980).

Western Culture: Developing a Category of Homosexuality

Most Western cultures have not built overt homosexual behavior into their accepted and obligatory social roles; indeed homosexual behavior has long been discouraged and repressed. Not only has the Judeo-Christian religion taken a strong stand against homosexual behavior, but secular laws have prohibited acts of sodomy as well. There have been variations in this generally negative history; for example, the famous French Penal Code of 1791 did decriminalize homosexual acts between consenting adults (Greenberg & Bystryn, 1984). However, public opinion in nineteenth century Europe and the United States remained hostile to overt homosexual behavior.

In the late eighteenth and early nineteenth centuries the category of homosexuality emerged as a way of describing a condition and the homosexual as a type of person (Foucault, 1978; Richardson, 1984, p. 80). Until that time the moral and legal debates on homosexual behavior had centered on just that—behavior. The shift in focus defined homosexuality as a "state of being" that could exist prior to and without any overt homosexual act and, from somewhere inside the person, compelled a lifelong habitual preference for same-sex partners. Homosexuals became a highly stigmatized category of persons. (It should become clear now why it is inappropriate to use this term to describe the Melanesian males.)

Greenberg and Bystryn (1984) propose that one explanation for this conceptual development was the new capitalism of nineteenth century Europe and the United States which increased competition among men, sharpened the sexual division of labor, and strengthened the ideology of the family. Foucault (1978) and Weeks (1981) relate the conceptual development to the rise in the early nineteenth century of a "scientific" interest in sexual behavior. The medical profession, as part of the scientific community of this period, played a significant role in defining homosexuality by depicting it as a medical pathology or abnormality (Greenberg & Bystryn, 1984; Richardson, 1984).

EFFORTS SINCE THE NINETEENTH CENTURY TO EXPLAIN HOMOSEXUALITY

Shifts in the Major Theoretical Approaches to Homosexuality

The category of "homosexual," once it had been created, demanded an explanation. The first theoretical approach came from the biological/medical model, well established by the late nineteenth century and viewed as the key to understanding homosexuality as well as a wide variety of other perceived social problems, such as crime, alcoholism, retardation, and insanity. Physicians helped instill the idea that homosexuals were stricken by something beyond their control. The medicalization of homosexuality meant that homosexuals were subjected to efforts to cure them with such "therapeutic" interventions as castration, sterilization, and commitment to mental health facilities (Greenberg & Bystryn, 1984, p. 41). These developments launched the debates that continued into 1950s and 1960s over how one could define the biological or mental characteristic that placed "homosexuals" in a different category from the rest of the population; "was homosexuality congenital or acquired, ineradicable or susceptible to cure?" (Weeks, 1981, p. 86).

A second theoretical approach emerged in the early twentieth century that shifted attention to the psychological state of the individual and conceptualized homosexuality as a *sexual orientation* toward members of the same sex as sexual and love objects. Sigmund Freud's (1905; 1931) writings influenced this shift. His theory of homosexuality included the premise that humans came into the world with a capacity to be sexually attracted to both sexes. Richardson (1984) notes that Freud's "concept of bisexuality was based on evidence that embryological remnants of the anatomical characteristics of the opposite sex, however rudimentary, are present in all individuals" (p. 81). Freud's theory of psychosexual development assumed that the normal process of libidinal development resulted in a heterosexual orientation. Homosexuality resulted from the development in the individual, beginning in early childhood, of a fixed and fundamental "sexual orientation" guiding the individual into later homosexual behavior. Thus, both the biological/medical model and the psychological/sexual orientation model posit that there is some "essential" trait about the person that explains his or her homosexuality.

An important turning point in these discussions came from the 1948 Kinsey studies of sexuality in the United States. This nationwide survey of self-reported sexual behavior revealed a much wider involvement in homosexual behavior in the male population than had been previously thought. The study also documented shifting patterns of such involvement over the life span of individual men. As Kinsey and his co-authors note (Kinsey, Pomeroy, & Martin, 1948), "The histories which have been available in the present study make it apparent that the heterosexuality or homosexuality of many individuals is not an all-or-none proposition" (p. 638). This conclusion supported Kinsey's decision to propose a continuum of categories to describe experience in a given age period in the individual's life, ranging from exclusively heterosexual experiences (category 0) to exclusively homosexual experiences (category 6), with five categories in between reflecting varying proportions of same-sex and opposite-sex sexual experiences.

The Kinsey continuum would allow researchers to more accurately describe the experiences of the population with respect to sexual partners than was allowed by the previous assumption that one could easily divide the population into two groups—the heterosexuals and the homosexuals. If behavior was to be an indicator of who could be considered "the homosexuals," then where on the continuum do we draw the line? Were the homosexuals only those who fit into category 6 (exclusively homosexual experiences), or did they include anyone from category 1 (had had only incidental homosexual contact, while having predominantly heterosexual experiences) through category 6? Additionally, Kinsey's data included reports by individuals of their psychic responses to members of the same and opposite sex, and these feelings varied across a continuum and across the life span of the respondents as well.

Kinsey's research posed a major challenge to both previous theoretical approaches. If either the biological or sexual orientation theories were true, how was one to explain changing patterns of homosexual behavior over the life span of one individual? By documenting diversity in lifestyles, sexual behavior patterns, and emotions, Kinsey promoted consideration by other researchers of the individual's own definition of self as relevant data in the debate on how to identify "the homosexual." This new consideration focuses attention again on homosexuality as a state of being—but this time, as Richardson (1984) states, "It is, however, a different form of 'being' than previously conceived where the fundamental question was what caused a person to develop into a homosexual. The new question is: How does the state of being a person who *self-identifies as homosexual* come about?" (p. 83).

A third theoretical approach to homosexuality focused on this new question and was dominant in sociology in the United States and Britain from the 1960s to the present. It is known as the labeling interactionist perspective and derives from symbolic interactionism (Weeks, 1981, p. 94). It views the category of homosexuality as a product of the meanings we give the term in our Western culture (social process at the macro level), and sees the individuals who fit the category as those who have come to identify themselves as homosexuals (the result of social process at the micro level). This interactionist or social constructionist perspective allows for considering identity separate from behavior, which proved helpful in interpreting the Kinsey data. For example, since the Kinsey data documented gradations of heterosexual and homosexual experiences within the lives of individuals, then if sexual identity was a direct result of sexual behavior, we would expect all those who had engaged in both homosexual and heterosexual sexual activities to identify themselves as bisexual. Data indicate that such is not the case (Blumstein & Schwartz 1976; Humphreys, 1975; Paul, 1984). One explanation is that an identity as a bisexual is stigmatized by both the heterosexual and homosexual populations, so that many fewer people consider themselves "bisexual" than would be expected given their actual sexual behavior (Golden, 1987, pp. 30–31). Explaining homosexuality from the third perspective meant understanding how individuals arrived at a point where they identified themselves as homosexuals.

Research on the Causes of Homosexuality

Each of the three theoretical approaches discussed above has generated research designed to test the proposed explanation of homosexuality. Much of the resulting research was designed to reveal the ultimate causal explanation of homosexuality. Such a search is based on a belief that the category of "homosexual" consists of people who have some essential characteristic in common that differentiates them from "the heterosexuals" in the society. Just phrasing the problem in this way points to the difficulty a researcher would have locating such a characteristic. Both homosexual and heterosexual categories include people of very diverse backgrounds, personalities, and lifestyles. Even if researchers were able to divide the total population into two distinct and separate groups—homosexual and heterosexual—and discover a common characteristic of all homosexuals that was not characteristic of any heterosexual, the researcher still would have to be careful about announcing that this factor explained the "homosexuality" of the one group. The factor, depending on its nature, might well have developed as a *result* of living out a homosexual lifestyle. But in spite of the difficulties, such research has continued on the premise that something definite will emerge to explain why "homosexuals" are who they are.

Research from the biological or medical model has enjoyed particularly strong appeal since, if a particular gene or hormonal pattern could be found to explain homosexuality, then everyone could know definitively who the homosexuals were and why. The factor would solve issues of who or what is responsible for the condition, and the medical profession might even be able to "help" those found with this condition. Such is the seduction of the biological model. Indeed, biologists and geneticists have for decades searched for the biological key to homosexuality, but such an answer has been elusive.

First, the scientific basis of the research has changed. Biological research on homosexuality conducted during the 1940s or earlier has been thoroughly discredited now on grounds of incomplete understanding of genes and hormones, as well as faulty research designs (Richardson, 1981). Scientific understanding of human biology has developed significantly in recent decades, and technological developments have also facilitated more precise measurement of the sex hormones. However, in spite of these advances, a second set of methodological problems remain. For example, there continues to be a lack of data on the standards of biological characteristics that can appropriately be used as a basis for measurement of differences or deviations, repeated failure to find statistical differences between the "homosexuals" and the control groups, problems in identifying who belongs appropriately in what group (often the heterosexual sample is composed of men the researcher assumes to be heterosexual), failure to include any data on women, while still drawing conclusions about women, and the fact that hormones are influenced by many factors in the subject's world, including stress.

A third problem with the medical model is that it is based on the unwarranted assumption that biology can explain sexuality. Ricketts (1984) notes, that "explanations of a direct cause-and-effect relationship between biological factors and sexual orientation falter because they cannot embrace the complexity and variety of human sexual behavior" (p. 88). Given the diversity of ways in which humans can and do experience their sexuality, including changes in sexual behavior, attractions, and fantasies, it is not surprising that the careful assessment of the biological research results in the conclusion that this research has contributed little to our understanding of sexual identity (Hoult, 1984; Ricketts, 1984; Richardson, 1981). In spite of these research conclusions, the belief that there is a genetic or biochemical explanation for homosexuality still appears frequently in today's media and among the general population.

Research from the second theoretical approach views "sexual orientation" as "a relatively enduring psychological characteristic of the individual, largely determined in early life" (Richardson, 1984, p. 84). Researching the cause of a homosexual "sexual orientation" required documenting early learning experiences and the influences of family relationships on the young "pre-homosexual." Psychologists and psychoanalysts conducted such research by using their homosexual clients in psychotherapy as their source of data. Critics of such research have noted a number of methodological difficulties (see Browning, 1984; Richardson, 1981). First, when researchers draw samples solely from therapy clients, their data come from homosexuals who are likely different from other homosexuals who have not sought out psychotherapy. Second, research conclusions were reached without comparing the data on homosexuals with a control group of heterosexuals. Third, since the psychological researchers attempted to document the existence of a deep-seated, family-oriented sexual orientation, the data came from retrospective accounts. Not only is it difficult for adults to recall accurately events they experienced as children, but the retelling of those events, as well as descriptions of family relationships, can be influenced by their present circumstances and identity, the therapy process itself, and available knowledge about homosexuality. Fourth, most research was conducted with male clients only.

As the criticisms noted above gained recognition, research was conducted that included homosexuals not in therapy and compared their family backgrounds and personality data to heterosexuals, also not in therapy, who were interviewed and given the same questionnaires and standard personality tests as the homosexuals. One hypothesis had been that a homosexual orientation developed from a particular family structure involving a "dominant" mother and a "weak" or absent father. The use of the comparison group of heterosexuals was important in undermining this "explanation" of homosexuality, since there were heterosexuals whose family histories also revealed this pattern (e.g., see Marmor, 1965). Indeed, no single "family constellation" or other pattern, such as the child having identified more with one parent than the other, could be found to explain the adult lifestyle of homosexuality (Bell, Weinberg, & Hammersmith, 1981a; Hooker, 1969; Siegelman, 1974).

Gradually a body of research data accumulated, based on nonpatient and noninstitutionalized homosexual populations that showed that "most lesbians and gay men were remarkably similar to heterosexuals with the exception of their sexual preference" (Browning, 1984, p. 20). Researchers found that homosexuals did not constitute a clinical category. These conclusions led the American Psychiatric Association in 1973 to remove homosexuality from its manual that lists the known pathological clinical conditions. In 1974 the American Psychological Association took the same step.

Since the research from the first two theoretical perspectives failed to identify any biological or psychological factors that could differentiate homosexuals as a separate category from heterosexuals, then homosexuality could not be explained as a biological or psychological phenomenon. The third theoretical approach suggested that homosexuality was a social phenomenon—in that both the category and its contents, "the homosexuals," developed out of social process. The researcher from this approach acknowledges that the individual comes packaged with specific biological characteristics and, in the process of living through early childhood and adolescence, the individual has many experiences that contribute to his or her psychosexual development and individual personality. To develop a sexual identity, however, the individual picks out certain personal characteristics and past experiences as significant, while excluding others. The responses of other people to the individual are an integral part of the process. The individual takes these responses, as well as his or her own feelings about the experiences, into account when he or she assesses the experiences later for clues as to who he or she "really" is. Research from this approach to homosexuality focused on the social process of acquiring a sexual identity, and the next section is devoted to examining these efforts.

HOMOSEXUALITY AS A STATE OF IDENTITY

The question of how and when and under what conditions someone would or could acquire an identity as a homosexual was posed as a genuinely sociological question, and the research into this question benefited greatly from the interactionist perspective in sociology during the 1960s and 1970s. Proponents of this perspective assert that the development of one's personal identity (how an individual answers privately the question of "Who am I?") is an ongoing life process and takes place in a social context. The individual develops a sense of self in relation to major aspects of life, such as work and sex. For example, we develop an occupational or professional identity out of our experiences related to work and our interpretations, utilizing feedback from others, regarding who we are in our work roles. We develop a sexual identity out of all the experiences we have had involving sexuality and the meanings we attach to these experiences. Sexual identity summarizes our sense of self as sexual beings. Sexual orientation or sexual preference is one component of sexual identity that expresses our attraction to members of the same or opposite sex.

From this perspective sexual identity is a social construction. This is not the same as saying one's identity is freely chosen. We are, from this perspective, a product of all we have been through, including experiences which we may not have enjoyed or chosen, but experienced nonetheless. Out of these events and our feelings about them, we try to make sense out of what our life has been and who we are. The process may seem complicated but is remarkably ordinary. Gagnon (1977) notes "people become sexual in the same way they become everything else. Without much reflection, they pick up directions from their social environment" (p. 2). If this is descriptive of sexuality generally, then it also applies to homosexuality more specifically.

Given the premise of a gradual learning of sexual behavior patterns and identities, how does the social scientist conduct research on such a long drawn-out process involving interaction between the personal and the social? And how, if one perceives the culture as providing strong encouragement for heterosexuality (some view it as "compulsory heterosexuality"; see Adrienne Rich, 1980), can one gradually develop a homosexual identity?

One research strategy that derived from the labeling/interactionist tradition focuses on efforts to discover and document what stages of development an individual goes through in the process of acquiring a sexual identity. Beginning in the mid-1970s researchers used intensive interviews with self-acknowledged gay males and lesbians to attempt to identify crucial stages or turning-point experiences in the process of reaching a homosexual identity. Following other developmental models, these models typically have an assumption of linear development. The process begins with no sexual identity or a presumption of heterosexuality and passes through experiences in a middle phase that could include some or all of the following: increasing awareness of attraction to members of the same sex, increasing knowledge about the category of "homosexual," sexual involvement with same-sex partners, and self-labeling as homosexual. The final stage of development consists of the individual's acceptance of a strong lesbian or gay male identity. (See especially, Plummer, 1975; Troiden, 1979, 1988; Gramick, 1984; Sophie, 1986.)

One of the problems with a linear model is that it is assumed that those who reach the final stage have all passed through the same series of steps. Research designed to document "stage-sequential models," however, revealed diversity as well as patterns; the more specific the stages or steps were in a given model, the less likely the stages matched the experiences of the different individuals under study (Sophie, 1986, p. 50). . . .

Multiple Dimensions of a Homosexual Identity

The research on identity development documented not only that individuals followed different paths for reaching new identities, but also that identities, once formed, were not always as stable and permanent as people had thought they would be. Golden (1987) concludes "that the assumption that we inherently strive for congruence between our sexual feelings, activities, and identities may not be warranted, and that given the fluidity of sexual feelings, congruence may not be an achievable state" (p. 31). Thus, behavior, emotions, and identities do not necessarily develop into stable packages that can be easily labeled as heterosexual, gay or lesbian, or even bisexual, even though the individual or the society or the gay community might desire such consistency. Both researchers and therapists should be cautious about categorizing under familiar labels people who may in fact be growing and changing their identities. This is not to say that all identities are unstable; many individuals develop a strong and stable sense of self that serves as a guide and source of comfort to their behavior and life choices. But others continue to consider new information about themselves and may be more or less aware that where they are at any point in time is just one step in an ongoing developmental process. Thus, undergoing periods of questioning one's sexual identity may occur at various points in the life cycle. . . .

As researchers and therapists alike are acknowledging the different combinations of components of identity, they can watch for patterns. One pattern that was expected from Freudian theory and one which still shows up in views among the general population is not a pattern at all. The expected pattern was that gender identity—one's own sense of being male or female—would predict one's sexual preference. Freud's theory assumed that "gender inversion" helped explain homosexuality. Consequently, researchers have looked to see if homosexual males had acquired female gender identities, and if lesbians had male gender identities. Although the research has found that a small proportion of homosexual respondents indicate cross-gender identity, Luria (1979) notes, "Male homosexuals almost universally feel they are males, and female homosexuals virtually all feel they are women" (p. 179; see also Storms, 1980; Harry, 1982; Bell, Weinberg, & Hammersmith, 1981a, p. 188). . . .

Sexual Preference and Gender Role Behavior

Gender role behavior, or simply gender role, refers to patterns of behavior or activities routinely expected of a particular gender. Thus, males are expected to engage in masculine behavior patterns, thereby assuming a male gender role. However, individuals may develop a preference for the traditional activities of the opposite gender, and gender role preference may vary separately from either gender identity or sexual identity. Harry (1982) has diagrammed the various combinations, noting, for example, that a heterosexual male with a male gender identity could have a feminine gender role preference. He is, thus, biologically male, views himself as a male, but has a preference for activities routinely associated with women. Since this is behavior, it could be expressed in many different ways, such as through a pattern of effeminate behavior, cross-dressing, or by taking a job in a traditionally female occupation.

Cross-dressing and interest in cross-gender activities during childhood have been reported by adult homosexuals significantly more often than by adult heterosexuals. For example, in the Bell, Weinberg, and Hammersmith (1981b) study, 68 percent of the white homosexual males reported that they were "Not at all" or "Very little" interested in "boys' activities (e.g., baseball, football)" during grade school compared with 11 percent of the white heterosexual males. The matching statistics for black homosexual males were 37 percent compared with 4 percent for black heterosexual males. The homosexual males, more often than heterosexual males, reported that they had enjoyed stereotypical girls' activities, such as playing house, hopscotch, and jacks. Harry (1982) saw these results as replicating his own research findings. Similar differences were found for the female respondents. Seventy-one percent of the white homosexual women reported they "Very much" enjoyed playing typical boys' activities (e.g., baseball, football) compared with 28 percent of the white heterosexual women. The homosexual respondents also reported having cross-dressed and pretending to be the opposite gender more often than the heterosexual respondents did (Bell, Weinberg, & Hammersmith, 1981a). The Bell et al. (1981a) research concludes that "a child's display of gender nonconformity greatly increases the likelihood of that child's becoming homosexual regardless of his or her family background and regardless of how much the child identifies with either parent" (p. 189). The researchers note, however, that gender nonconformity was not characteristic of most of the homosexual respondents and was reported by a minority of heterosexuals (Bell et al., 1981a, p. 188).

. . . We are unable to draw a straight line from behavior patterns or even gender role preferences to sexual preference. . . . Clearly, the environment of prejudice and hostility towards homosexuality has an impact on the process of acquiring a sexual identity—be it homosexual or heterosexual. Herek (1985) notes that the influence may also flow the other way—that the process of developing an identity helps reinforce hostility; thus, "individuals also may gain a sense of who they are by clarifying what they are not" (p. 149). Particularly as homosexuals have developed a stronger sense of themselves as a group, heterosexuals may have developed more of an identity as well. Indeed, as lesbian and gay communities have become more visible and organized, the opposition to them has also become more visible and organized. The in-group gets its identity by contrasting itself with the out-group, and the conflict promotes cohesion within both groups. This fundamental social process is one which sociology has documented as one of its earliest contributions to understanding society. In the case of homosexuality, however, we must recall that the negative label from society came long before persons so labeled organized themselves into a group. . . .

CONCLUSION

. . . I have argued here that the meanings given to behavior and to people who engage in that behavior derive from the culture and structure of the society involved. The major theoretical debate discussed in [this essay] is whether or not those who fit our cultural category of "homosexuals" have something that defines their essence as homosexuals or are very much like everyone else except for their sexual preference, which was acquired over their lifespan in the same way as their other identities and in the same way as heterosexual identities. At least one theorist, Kenneth Plummer, proposes that we consider both positions to be quite possibly correct. For example, a sexual orientation may be a kind of "essence," formed early in childhood and affecting later choices. Plummer (1981) notes,

> while some people develop restrictive and rigid orientations, others may be open and flexible, while still others may develop no "orientations" at all. . . . Likewise identities are—in all likelihood—highly variable throughout social encounters; but while for some people this may mean drastic restructuring of self-conceptions at critical turning

> points in life, others may develop relatively stable identities at early moments in life and use these as foci to orientate most future contact. (p. 72)

Thus, diversity of experience is a key here; individuals have different ways of coping with life's experiences and different routes for arriving at a place where they feel comfortable with who they are and what they like best. But through it all, the learning and becoming take place within a social environment highly affected by the rules and guidelines of the culture at hand. And it should be remembered that cultural expectations can and do change. The process of forming and maintaining a positive homosexual identity can be especially complex and problematic in the face of conflicting pressures, definitions and attitudes, as the concerns and priorities of the gay community and the surrounding culture change over time.

REFERENCES

Adam, B. D. (1985). Age, structure, and sexuality: Reflections on the anthropological evidence on homosexual relations. *Journal of Homosexuality,* 11 (3/4), 19–33.

Adam, B. D. (1987). *The rise of a gay and lesbian movement.* Boston: Twayne Publishers.

Allen, M. R. (1967). *Male cults and secret initiations in Melanesia.* Melbourne, Australia: Melbourne University Press.

Bell, A. P., Weinberg, M. S., & Hammersmith, S. K. (1981a). *Sexual preference: Its development in men and women.* Bloomington: Indiana University Press.

Bell, A. P., Weinberg, M. S., & Hammersmith, S. K. (1981b). *Sexual preference: Statistical appendix.* Bloomington: Indiana University Press.

Blumstein, P. W. & Schwartz, P. (1976). Bisexuality in women. *Archives of Sexual Behavior,* 5, 171–181.

Browning, C. (1984). Changing theories of lesbianism: Challenging the stereotypes. In T. Darty & S. Potter (Eds.), *Women-identified women* (pp. 11–30). Palo Alto, CA: Mayfield.

Callendar, C., & Kochems, L. (1983). The North American berdache. *Current Anthropology,* 24, 443–470.

Dover, K. J. (1978). *Greek homosexuality.* New York: Vintage Books.

Foucault, M. (1978). *The history of sexuality.* Volume 1: *An introduction.* New York: Random House.

Freud, S. (1905/1953). Three essays on the theory of sexuality. *Standard edition of the complete psychological works of Sigmund Freud,* 7, 136. London: Hogarth Press. (Originally published 1905.)

Freud, S. (1931/1961). Female sexuality. *Standard edition of the complete psychological works of Sigmund Freud,* 21, 223. London: Hogarth Press. (Originally published 1931.)

Gagnon, J. H. (1977). *Human sexualities.* Glenview, IL: Scott, Foresman.

Golden, C. (1987). Diversity and variability in women's sexual identities. In Boston Lesbian Psychologies Collective (Eds.), *Lesbian psychologies: Explorations and Challenges* (pp. 18–34). Urbana: University of Illinois Press.

Gramick, J. (1984). Developing a lesbian identity. In T. Darty & S. Potter (Eds.), *Women-identified women* (pp. 31–44). Palo Alto, CA: Mayfield.

Greenberg, D. F., & Bystryn, M. H. (1984). Capitalism, bureaucracy and male homosexuality. *Contemporary Crises,* 8, 33–56.

Harry, J. (1982). *Gay children grown up. Gender culture and gender deviance.* New York: Praeger.

Herdt, G. H. (1981). *Guardians of the flutes.* New York: McGraw-Hill.

Herdt, G. H. (Ed.). (1984). *Ritualized homosexuality in Melanesia.* Berkeley: University of California Press.

Herek, G. M. (1985). On doing, being and not being: Prejudice and the social construction of sexuality. *Journal of Homosexuality,* 12(1), 135–151.

Hooker, E. (1969). Parental relations and male homosexuality in patient and nonpatient samples. *Journal of Consulting and Clinical Psychology,* 33, 140–142.

Hoult, T. F. (1984). Human sexuality in biological perspective: Theoretical and methodological considerations. *Journal of Homosexuality,* 9(2/3), 137–155.

Hudson, W. W., & Ricketts, W. A. (1980). A strategy for the measurement of homophobia. *Journal of Homosexuality,* 5(4), 357–372.

Humphreys, L. (1975). *Tearoom trade.* Chicago: Aldine.

King, D. (1981). Gender confusions: Psychological and psychiatric conceptions of transvestism and transsexualism. In K. Plummer (Ed.), *The making of the modern homosexual* (pp. 155–184). Totowa, NJ: Barnes and Noble.

Kinsey, A. C., Pomeroy, W. B., & Martin, C. E. (1948). *Sexual behavior in the human male.* Philadelphia: W. B. Saunders.

Luria, Z. (1979). Psychosocial determinants of gender identity, role, and orientation. In H. A. Katchadourian (Ed.), *Human sexuality: A comparative and developmental perspective* (pp. 163–193). Berkeley: University of California Press.

Paul, J. P. (1984). The bisexual identity: An idea without social recognition. *Journal of Homosexuality,* 9(2/3), 45–63.

Plummer, K. (1975). *Sexual stigma: An interactionist account.* London: Routledge & Kegan Paul.

Plummer, K. (Ed). (1981). *The making of the modern homosexual.* Totowa, NJ: Barnes and Noble.

Rich, A. (1980). Compulsory heterosexuality and lesbian experience. *Signs,* 5, 631–660.

Richardson, D. (1981). Theoretical perspectives of homosexuality. In J. Hart & D. Richardson (Ed.), *The theory and practice of homosexuality.* London: Routledge & Kegan Paul.

Richardson, D. (1984). The dilemma of essentiality in homosexual theory. *Journal of Homosexuality,* 9(2/3), 79–90.

Richardson, D., & Hart, J. (1981). The development and maintenance of a homosexual identity. In J. Hart & D. Richardson (Eds.), *The theory & practice of homosexuality* (pp. 73–92). London: Routledge & Kegan Paul.

Ricketts, W. (1984). Biological research on homosexuality: Ansell's cow or Occam's razor? *Journal of Homosexuality,* 9(2/3), 45–63.

Siegelman, M. (1974). Parental background of male homosexuals and heterosexuals. *Archives of Sexual Behavior,* 3, 3–18.

Sophie, J. (1986). A critical examination of stage theories of lesbian identity development. *Journal of Homosexuality,* 12(2), 39–51.

Stoller, R. J. (1980). Problems with the term "homosexuality." *The Hillside Journal of Clinical Psychiatry,* 2, 3–25.

Storms, M. D. (1980). Theories of sexual orientation. *Journal of Personality and Social Psychology,* 38, 783–792.

Troiden, R. R. (1988). *Gay and lesbian identity: A sociological analysis.* Dix Hills, NY: General Hall.

Weeks, J. (1981). Discourse, desire and sexual deviance: Some problems in a history of homosexuality. In K. Plummer (Ed.), *The making of the modern homosexual* (pp. 76–111). London: Hutchinson.

Whitam, F. L., & Mathy, R. M. (1986). *Male homosexuality in four societies.* New York: Praeger.

READING 18

The Development of Gay, Lesbian, and Bisexual Identities

Heidi Levine

Nancy J. Evans

To understand the issues faced by gay, lesbian, and bisexual people on college campuses, we must first examine the life experiences of these individuals. What it means to be gay, lesbian, or bisexual is unique to each person; but some commonalities exist as individuals become aware of their attraction to others of the same sex and integrate these feelings into other aspects of their identity.

The research that considers timing and age factors in the gay and lesbian identity development process suggests that many developmental issues occur during the traditional undergraduate years (Bell, Weinberg, & Hammersmith, 1981; McDonald, 1982). As student development professionals, we know that this is a key time for identity development in general (Chickering, 1969; Erikson, 1968; Moore & Upcraft, 1990). College and university students are faced with many areas in which they need to reconsider

Heidi Levine is the director of the Lauderdale Center for Student Health and Counseling at Geneseo State University of New York. Nancy J. Evans is associate professor of educational leadership and policy studies at Iowa State University.

their self-perceptions, develop new skills, and master developmental tasks. The possibility or certainty that one is gay, lesbian, or bisexual complicates these developmental challenges and adds an additional set of complicated issues that must be resolved. . . .

[Before we proceed,] a distinction must be made between the terms *homosexual identity* and *gay identity.* Homosexual identity is a narrower term, referring to sexual behavior only, whereas gay identity suggests the total experience of being gay (Warren, 1974). The use of the term *homosexual identity* is often viewed negatively by the gay and lesbian community because it has been used as a diagnostic label by many clinicians and is often associated with a negative self-image. *Gay identity,* however, has a positive connotation within the gay and lesbian communities and is seen as encompassing emotional, lifestyle, and political aspects of life rather than being exclusively sexual (Beane, 1981).

Jandt and Darsey (1981) noted that all definitions of homosexual or gay identity have in common a shift in perception of self as a member of the majority to self as a member of the minority. Along with this change in perception comes adoption of a new set of values and a redefinition of acceptable behavior. As such, development of a gay, lesbian, or bisexual identity is mainly an internal, psychological process. . . .

LESBIAN IDENTITY DEVELOPMENT

Differences in Identity Development between Gay Men and Lesbians

Largely because of differences in the way men and women are socialized in Western society, a number of variations are evident in the patterns of identity development and lifestyles of gay men and lesbians (Cass, 1979).

The timing of events associated with the process of developing a gay or lesbian identity is different for men and women. Lesbians exhibit more variation than gay men in age at which awareness of attraction to individuals of the same sex occurs (Moses & Hawkins, 1986), and evidence suggests that gay men become aware of same-sex attractions, act on those attractions, and self-identify as gay at earlier ages than do lesbians. Men also disclose their homosexual identity earlier than women (DeMonteflores & Schultz, 1978; Sohier, 1985–1986; Troiden, 1988). Henderson (1984) proposed two hypotheses in reference to these timing variations: (1) women's sexual orientation may be more variable than men's and more tied to particular relationships, or (2) women are more likely to be influenced by societal norms that expect everyone to be heterosexual and so adhere longer to heterosexual behavior patterns and a heterosexual identity. Gramick (1984) concurred with the latter point of view.

Lesbians tend to establish ongoing love relationships earlier than gay men (Troiden, 1988) and are more likely to commit to a homosexual identity within the context of an intense emotional relationship, whereas gay men do so within the context of their sexual experiences (Groves & Ventura, 1983; Sohier, 1985–1986; Troiden, 1988). In general, emotional attachment is the most significant aspect of relationship for lesbians, but sexual activity is most important for gay men (DeMonteflores & Schultz, 1978; Gramick, 1984). As a result, lesbians tend to look for and maintain more stable, long-term relationships than do gay men (Gramick, 1984).

Although this pattern may be changing because of concern arising from the spread of AIDS, historically, gay men have been involved with many more one-time-only sexual partners than have lesbians (Kimmel, 1978; Marmor, 1980). This pattern, again, can be related to differences in the manner in which men and women are socialized; men are expected to be interested in sex before love, whereas women look for love before sex (Henderson, 1984; Westfall, 1988). Men are also encouraged to experiment sexually more than women (Coleman, 1981–1982). As one might expect given these socialization patterns, "tricking" (picking up unknown individuals for brief sexual liaisons) has been much more common among gay men than among lesbians who tend to meet others and interact in more intimate, private settings (Cronin, 1974; Gramick, 1984; Nuehring, Fein, & Tyler, 1974).

DeMonteflores and Schultz (1978) suggested that lesbians often use feelings to avoid thinking of themselves as homosexual whereas men use denial of feelings as a way to avoid self-labeling as gay. Women use the rationale that they merely love one particular woman, but men view their homosexual activity as insignificant because they are not emotionally involved with their partners.

Some researchers (Bell & Weinberg, 1978; Sohier, 1985–1986) have suggested that acceptance of homosexuality is easier for women than for men since sexual relationships between women are less stigmatized than those between men (DeMonteflores & Schultz, 1978; Marmor, 1980; Paul, 1984). The women's movement may have assisted lesbians to come out; there has been no comparable movement for men (DeMonteflores & Schultz, 1978). Also, since many lesbians become aware of their identity at later ages, they may have resolved other identity issues and be more adept at handling the coming out process than gay men who generally self-identity during their teens (Paul, 1984).

A number of writers have suggested that lesbians are more likely to view their sexuality as a choice, whereas gay men see it as a discovery (Henderson, 1984; Kimmel, 1978; Westfall, 1988). This distinction is particularly true for feminist lesbians. Feminist lesbians also identify more strongly with the political-philosophical aspects of their lifestyle, whereas gay men are more concerned with the physical-social aspects (Jandt & Darsey, 1981).

With regard to relationship development, lesbians more closely resemble other women than they do gay men (Marmor, 1980). Women, in general, are more concerned with the relational aspects of their attachments to other people and focus on establishing intimate, long-term relationships. Because they fear displeasing others, they may have difficulty breaking norms and acknowledging that they cannot accept the roles family, friends, and society have identified for them. Men, however, are taught to be independent, competitive, and autonomous. These factors appear to play an important role in the differences exhibited between lesbians and gay men.

Relational versus Political Lesbians

Great variation exists in the way lesbians describe themselves and how they come to identify themselves as lesbian (Miller & Fowlkes, 1980). And as Golden (1987) noted, feelings, behaviors, and self-identification do not always agree nor do they always remain the same over time. Two major philosophical approaches to lesbianism can be identified in the literature, however; a traditional relational viewpoint that focuses on emotional and sexual attraction to other women (Moses, 1978; Ponse, 1980) and a radical feminist perspective that views the lesbian lifestyle as a political statement (Faraday, 1981; Lewis, 1979).

A number of theorists note that a distinction must be made between women who view their lesbianism as beyond their control and those who see it as a choice (Golden, 1987; Richardson, 1981b). Generally, lesbian feminists adhere to the latter viewpoint, but relational lesbians take the former position (Richardson, 1981; Sophie, 1987).

In a small study of 20 self-identified lesbians, Henderson (1979) distinguished three groups: (1) *ideological lesbians,* women who can be viewed as radical feminists for whom a lesbian lifestyle is politically correct; (2) *personal lesbians,* women concerned with establishing an independent identity who find homosexuality supportive of this goal and who view lesbianism as a choice; and (3) *interpersonal lesbians,* women who find themselves involved with another woman, often to their chagrin, and who experience their involvement as a discovery rather than a choice.

Development of a Lesbian Identity

Although a number of writers believe that sexual activity between women has become more acceptable as a result of the women's movement and the freeing of sexual norms (Blumstein & Schwartz, 1974; Henderson, 1979), the developmental process of identifying oneself as a lesbian is still difficult.

Many lesbians recall being "tomboys" as youngsters: a preference for "masculine" rather than "feminine" activities as a child is often the first indication that they do not fit the heterosexual pattern (Lewis, 1979). This awareness intensifies during puberty when the adolescent finds herself attracted to women rather than men. This discovery can lead to intense feelings of loneliness. Because of the difficulty young lesbians experience in finding a support group of other lesbians or identifying positive role models, this period is particularly difficult in the person's life (Sophie, 1982).

Most lesbians have a history of sexual involvement with men and, contrary to popular belief, become involved with women not because of unsatisfactory relationships with men but rather because they experience greater emotional and sexual satisfaction from women (Groves & Ventura, 1983). Indeed, women frequently identify themselves as bisexual prior to adopting a lesbian identity.

It needs to be noted that most lesbians go through a period during which they reject their identity because they are unable to deal with the stigma associated with the label *lesbian* (Groves & Ventura, 1983). Often they seek security and an escape from their feelings of isolation and anxiety in heterosexual activity or marriage (Lewis, 1979; Sophie, 1982).

Usually involvement in an intense, all-encompassing love relationship with another woman is the decisive factor in embracing a lesbian identity (Groves & Ventura, 1983; Lewis, 1979). Such an involvement often develops slowly, starting out as a friendship.

Sophie (1982) noted that it is difficult for lesbians to feel good about themselves until they reconceptualize the term *lesbian* into positive terms. This process rarely occurs in isolation. Interaction with other lesbians and other sources of information about positive aspects of a lesbian lifestyle are helpful.

Coming out, both to other lesbians and to accepting heterosexuals, is also supportive of establishment of a lesbian identity (Richardson, 1981; Sophie, 1982). Often the individual decides to come out because it takes too much energy to maintain a heterosexual image. Usually the individual comes out first to close friends who appear trustworthy (Lewis, 1979). As the woman becomes involved in the lesbian community, pressure is often applied to come out publicly (Lewis, 1979). Doing so can be viewed as the final step in the solidification of a lesbian identity.

Identity Development Models

A number of theorists have proposed models of identity development specific for lesbians. Ponse (1980) noted three steps in lesbian identity development: becoming aware of feeling different because of sexual-emotional attraction to other women, becoming involved in a lesbian relationship, and seeking out other lesbians. This model differs from many of the gay male models in that a serious relationship is formed *before* the individual becomes involved in the lesbian community.

Gramick (1984) pointed out that in attempting to make meaning of their experiences, many lesbians reinterpret past events, feelings, and behaviors as sexual that were not perceived as such at the time they occurred. She suggested that the process of developing a lesbian identity first involves strong emotional attachment to other women leading to a feeling of "differentness" within the context of the social environment but without a recognition that this difference might be labeled as lesbian. In adolescence, heterosexual socialization patterns strongly influence all young women and often delay development of homosexual identity. Meeting other lesbians and becoming emotionally and sexually involved with another woman are usually key events in confirming and accepting a lesbian identity. In Gramick's model, supportive others, as well as sexual involvements, play a crucial role in identity development.

Lewis (1979) identified five stages in the development of a lesbian identity and focused more on the political aspects of lesbianism. Her stages include (1) experience of discomfort with the heterosexual and patriarchal nature of socialization, (2) labeling self as different from other women, (3) becoming aware of lesbianism, (4) finding and becoming involved in a lesbian community, and (5) educating self about the lesbian lifestyle.

Also writing from a feminist perspective, Faderman (1984) suggested that . . . the first step for lesbian feminists involves rejection of societal norms concerning the role of women and acceptance of a lesbian identity. This step is followed by experiences of prejudice and discrimination resulting in feelings of aloneness outside of the community of radical feminists and, finally, by sexual experiences with other women. Faderman suggested that because lesbian feminists are exposed to and accept the movement's political philosophy prior to their first homosexual experience they may not experience the guilt and shame felt by other lesbians and gay men. . . .

BISEXUAL IDENTITY

The gay rights movement has generally ignored bisexual men and women. Although Kinsey and his colleagues (Kinsey, Pomeroy, & Martin, 1948; Kinsey, Pomeroy, Martin, & Gebhard, 1953) discovered that more individuals are bisexual than strictly homosexual, later researchers and theorists have held to a rigid dichotomization of sexual behavior as either heterosexual or homosexual (Klein, Sepekoff, & Wolf, 1985). Acknowledging and attempting to understand the variation and fluidity of sexual attraction and behavior are important if we are to advance our knowledge of human sexuality and sexual identity development (Paul, 1985). . . .

Bisexuality comes in many forms. MacDonald (1982) identified four areas of variation: (1) individuals may have a preference for one gender over the other or may have no preference; (2) they may have partners of both sexes either simultaneously or sequentially; (3) they may be monogamous or have several partners; and (4) their bisexuality may be transitory, transitional, a basis for homosexual denial, or an enduring pattern. Zinik (1985) proposed the following criteria for assuming a bisexual identity: (1) being sexually aroused by both males and females, (2) desiring sexual activity with both, and (3) adopting bisexuality as a sexual identity label.

Two contrasting theories have been offered to account for bisexuality (Zinik, 1985): The conflict model suggests that bisexuality is associated with conflict, confusion, ambivalence, and an inability to determine one's sexual preference; the flexibility model hypothesizes that bisexuality is characterized by flexibility, personal growth, and fulfillment. The media tends to adhere to the former view, presenting bisexuality as a confused or conflicted lifestyle, as retarded sexual development, or as a denial of a true heterosexual or homosexual identity (Hansen & Evans, 1985).

Because the stigma attached to bisexuality is greater in many ways than that associated with homosexuality, many people who are bisexual in behavior do not identify themselves as such (Blumstein & Schwartz, 1974; Golden, 1987; Hansen & Evans, 1985; Paul, 1984; Zinik, 1985). Although some individuals are quite open about their identity, others hide it from both the heterosexual and the homosexual communities (Blumstein & Schwartz, 1977a). MacDonald (1981) suggested that bisexuals are less willing to disclose their identity than any other group because they believe that neither gays nor heterosexuals will accept them.

Bisexuals experience the same type of oppression as gay men and lesbians because society tends to group bisexuals with homosexuals. Heterosexuals assume that individuals are trying to excuse their homosexual inclinations by labeling themselves as bisexual (Blumstein & Schwartz, 1977a).

Because they do not conform to heterosexist culture, many bisexuals tend to align themselves with the gay and lesbian communities (Shuster, 1987). However, an individual's self-identification as bisexual is frequently met with skepticism in the homosexual community as well and viewed as an attempt to avoid the stigma of, or commitment to, a gay or lesbian lifestyle (Paul, 1984). The lesbian community, in particular, seems to have difficulty accepting bisexuality (Golden, 1987). Bisexuals are faced with considerable pressure to identify as homosexual and to behave in an exclusively homosexual manner (Blumstein & Schwartz, 1974; Hansen & Evans, 1985; Paul, 1985). Frequently, bisexuals respond to this pressure by pretending to be either exclusively homosexual or heterosexual depending on the social situation (Zinik, 1985).

Results of a study of 156 bisexuals conducted in the early 1970s (Blumstein & Schwartz, 1976, 1977a, 1977b) suggested that no identifiable bisexual life script exists and that identity and partner preferences change over the life course. Sexual experience and identity are not necessarily synonymous. The researchers identified several conditions that they saw as necessary for assumption of a bisexual identity: labeling, conflicting homosexual and heterosexual experiences, and contact with other bisexuals.

Zinik (1985) suggested that bisexual identity development may occur in stages similar to those proposed by Cass (1979) for homosexual identity formation. As with gay men and lesbians, the coming out process is one of both self-acknowledgment and disclosure to others (Shuster, 1987). Wide variation exists, however, in the timing and ordering of sexual experiences leading to a bisexual identification. In addition, because bisexuality lacks societal and scientific affirmation, acceptance of such an identity requires a high tolerance for ambiguity and is even harder than acceptance of a homosexual identity (MacDonald, 1981, Richardson & Hart, 1981). In most cases, bisexuals tend to identify in terms of particular relationships in which they are involved rather than with the abstract label bisexual (Shuster, 1987).

Although gay men and lesbians have formed support groups and political organizations, few such groups of bisexuals exist (Paul, 1985). As MacDonald (1981) noted, there is no "bisexual liberation movement" (p. 21). As a result, no clear bisexual identity exists, and little scientific research has examined the life experiences of bisexual men and women.

REFERENCES

Beane, J. (1981). "I'd rather be dead than gay": Counseling gay men who are coming out. *Personnel and Guidance Journal,* 60, 222–226.

Bell, A. P., & Weinberg, M. S. (1978). *Homosexualities: A study of diversity among men and women.* New York: Simon and Schuster.

Bell, A. P., Weinberg, M. S., & Hammersmith, S. K. (1981). *Sexual preference: Its development in men and women.* Bloomington: Indiana University.

Blumstein, P. W., & Schwartz, P. (1974). Lesbianism and bisexuality. In E. Goode & R. R. Troiden (Eds.), *Sexual deviance and sexual deviants* (pp. 278–295). New York: Morrow.

Blumstein, P. W., & Schwartz, P. (1976). Bisexuality in women. *Archives of Sexual Behavior,* 5, 171–181.

Blumstein, P. W., & Schwartz, P. (1977a). Bisexuality in men. In C. A. B. Warren (Ed.), *Sexuality: Encounters, identities, and relationships* (pp. 79–98). Beverly Hills, CA: Sage.

Blumstein, P. W., & Schwartz, P. (1977a). Bisexuality: Some social psychological issues. *Journal of Social Issues,* 33, 30–45.

Cass, V. C. (1979). Homosexual identity formation: A theoretical model. *Journal of Homosexuality,* 4, 219–235.

Chickering, A. W. (1969). *Education and identity.* San Francisco: Jossey-Bass.

Coleman, E. (1981–1982). Developmental stages of the coming out process. *Journal of Homosexuality,* 7, 31–43.

Cronin, D. M. (1974). Coming out among lesbians. In E. Goode & R. R. Troiden (Eds.), *Sexual deviance and sexual deviants* (pp. 268–277). New York: Morrow.

DeMonteflores, C., & Schultz, S. (1978). Coming out: Similarities and differences for lesbians and gay men. *Journal of Social Issues,* 34(3), 59–72.

Erikson, E. H. (1968). *Identity: Youth and crisis.* New York: Norton.

Faderman, L. (1984). The "new gay" lesbians. *Journal of Homosexuality,* 10(3/4), 85–95.

Faraday, A. (1981). Liberating lesbian research. In K. Plummer (Ed.), *The making of the modern homosexual* (pp. 112–129). Totowa, NJ: Barnes & Noble.

Golden, C. (1987). Diversity and variability in women's sexual identities. In Boston Lesbian Psychologies Collective (Eds.), *Lesbian psychologies: Explorations and challenges* (pp. 19–34). Urbana: University of Illinois Press.

Gramick, J. (1984). Developing a lesbian identity. In T. Darty & S. Potter (Eds.), *Women-identified women* (pp. 31–44). Palo Alto, CA: Mayfield.

Groves, P. A., & Ventura, L. A. (1983). The lesbian coming out process: Therapeutic considerations. *Personnel and Guidance Journal,* 62, 146–149.

Hansen, C. E., & Evans, A. (1985). Bisexuality reconsidered: An idea in pursuit of a definition. In F. Klein & T. J. Wolf (Eds.), *Bisexualities: Theory and research* (pp. 1–6). New York: Haworth.

Henderson, A. F. (1979). College age lesbianism as a developmental phenomenon. *Journal of American College Health,* 28(3), 176–178.

Henderson, A. F. (1984). Homosexuality in the college years: Development differences between men and women. *Journal of American College Health,* 32, 216–219.

Jandt, F. E., & Darsey, J. (1981). Coming out as a communicative process. In J. W. Chesebro (Ed.), *Gayspeak* (pp. 12–27). New York: Pilgrim.

Kimmel, D. C. (1978). Adult development and aging: A gay perspective. *Journal of Social Issues,* 34, 113–130.

Kinsey, A. C., Pomeroy, W. B., & Martin, C. E. (1948). *Sexual behavior in the human male.* Philadelphia: Saunders.

Kinsey, A. C., Pomeroy, W. B., Martin, C. E., & Gebhard, P. H. (1953). *Sexual behavior in the human female.* Philadelphia: Saunders.

Klein, F., Sepekoff, B., & Wolf, T. J. (1985). Sexual orientation: A multivariable dynamic process. In F. Klein & T. J. Wolf (Eds.), *Bisexualities: Theory and research* (pp. 35–49). New York: Haworth.

Lewis, S. G. (1979). *Sunday's women: A report on lesbian life today.* Boston: Beacon.

MacDonald, Jr., A. P. (1981). Bisexuality: Some comments on research and theory. *Journal of Homosexuality,* 6(3), 21–35.

MacDonald, Jr., A. P. (1982). Research on sexual orientation: A bridge that touches both shores but doesn't meet in the middle. *Journal of Sex Education and Therapy,* 8, 9–13.

Marmor, J. (1980). Overview: The multiple roots of homosexual behavior. In J. Marmor (Ed.), *Homosexual behavior: A modern reappraisal* (pp. 3–22). New York: Basic Books.

McDonald, G. J. (1982). Individual differences in the coming out process for gay men: Implications for theoretical models. *Journal of Homosexuality,* 8(1), 47–90.

Miller, P. Y., & Fowlkes, M. R. (1980). Social and behavior constructions of female sexuality. *Signs,* 5, 783–800.

Moore, L. V., & Upcraft, M. L. (1990). Theory in student affairs: Evolving perspectives. In L. V. Moore (Ed.), *Evolving theoretical perspectives on students* (pp. 3–23). *New Directions for Student Services,* No. 51. San Francisco: Jossey-Bass.

Moses, A. E. (1978). *Identity management in lesbian women.* New York: Praeger.

Moses, A. E., & Hawkins, R. O. (1986). *Counseling lesbian women and gay men: A life issues approach.* Columbus, OH: Merrill.

Nuehring, E., Fein, S. B., & Tyler, M. (1974). The gay college student: Perspectives for mental health professionals. *The Counseling Psychologist,* 4, 64–72.

Paul, J. P. (1984). The bisexual identity: An idea without social recognition. In J. P. DeCecco & M. G. Shively (Eds.), *Bisexual and homosexual identities: Critical theoretical issues* (pp. 45–63). New York: Haworth.

Paul, J. (1985). Bisexuality: Reassessing our paradigms of sexuality. In F. Klein & T. J. Wolf (Eds.), *Bisexualities: Theory and research* (pp. 21–34). New York: Haworth.

Ponse, B. (1980). Lesbians and their worlds. In J. Marmor (Ed.), *Homosexual behavior: A modern reappraisal* (pp. 157–175). New York: Basic Books.

Richardson, D. (1981). Lesbian identities. In J. Hart & D. Richardson (Eds.), *The theory and practice of homosexuality* (pp. 111–124). London: Routledge & Kegan Paul.

Richardson, D., & Hart, J. (1981). The development and maintenance of a homosexual identity. In J. Hart & D. Richardson (Eds.), *The theory and practice of homosexuality* (pp. 73–92). London: Routledge & Kegan Paul.

Shuster, R. (1987). Sexuality as a continuum: The bisexual identity. In Boston Lesbian Psychologies Collective (Eds.), *Lesbian psychologies: Explorations and challenges* (pp. 56–71). Urbana: University of Illinois Press.

Sohier, R. (1985–1986). Homosexual mutuality: Variation on a theme by E. Erikson. *Journal of Homosexuality,* 12(2), 25–38.

Sophie, J. (1982). Counseling lesbians. *Personnel and Guidance Journal,* 60(6), 341–344.

Sophie, J. (1987). Internalized homophobia and lesbian identity. *Journal of Homosexuality,* 14, 53–65.

Troiden, R. R. (1988). Homosexual identity development. *Journal of Adolescent Health Care,* 9(2), 105–113.

Warren, C. A. B. (1974). *Identity and community in the gay world.* New York: Wiley.

Westfall, S. B. (1988). Gay and lesbian college students: Identity issues and student affairs. *Journal of the Indiana University Student Personnel Association,* 1–6.

Zinik, G. (1985). Identity conflict or adaptive flexibility? Bisexuality reconsidered. In F. Klein & T. J. Wolf (Eds.), *Bisexualities: Theory and research* (pp. 7–19). New York: Haworth.

PERSONAL ACCOUNT

An Opportunity to Get Even

When I was a freshman in high school, my parents sent me to a private school. I got harassed a lot by a few of the sophomore guys there because I wore pants with the uniform (instead of the pleated mini-skirts), I didn't wear makeup, and probably most important, I would not date any of them (and couldn't give a reason for that). Most of this harassment was anti-gay slurs with specific references to me on the bathroom walls. One of the guys often yelled comments such as "Hey Dyke, I got what you need right here" while grabbing his crotch. My name was written on many of the bathroom stalls (both male and female), with my sexual orientation, and a rhyme about a gang bang.

After about six weeks of this, I confided in my soccer coach. I told her about the harassment and came out to her. I don't know what I expected, but I did not expect any positive reaction. She told me she was glad I came out to her, and she promised to keep my confidentiality. She also offered me an opportunity to get back at the three guys who were harassing me the most. She told me that this was my battle and that I was going to have to learn how to fight.

She knew that the three guys were part of the boys' soccer team, and made arrangements so that, as part of the homecoming festivities, our soccer team would play theirs. By doing this she gave me the opportunity to "show them up" and make them look bad in front of the school. I did my best to accomplish that. For example, every time any of them came near me, I would run into them or trip them. My goal was to embarrass them in front of the school. It did not look good for the guys because a "dyke" challenged and defeated the "jocks."

What my soccer coach did for me meant a lot. First, she was literally the only person I was out to at that time, so she was a source of support. Further, she went out of her way to help me get even with the harassers. Because of what she did for me, the harassment stopped.

Carol A. Mabry

PERSONAL ACCOUNT

Living Invisibly

For me, coming out is a Sisyphean task. Because of my invisible differences, I constantly have to reveal different parts of my identity. It's not an easy task, either. When I come out as a lesbian/queer woman, people are often surprised because I don't "look" queer. I can count on one hand the number of times I have been recognized by a stranger as part of the LGBT "family." Some people are also surprised to learn that I'm half Taiwanese. I am also half-white, and often assumed to be white, making my race another invisible identity. Because of this, there have been times when people have made racist jokes—either about Asians or other groups—because they thought I was white, and thus thought that these were "acceptable" jokes to tell in my presence.

Invisible identities work differently from other differences. I am lucky not to be harassed on the street because of my race, and since I don't appear queer to your average passerby, I don't usually get harassed for that. I benefit from the privilege of passing as a straight and white, but most days I wish that I could give up that privilege. It is extremely difficult to live your life where some of the most important things about you are hidden. For example, I never know when it is appropriate to come out as queer in class, and almost feel guilty if I never do, even though it may not always be necessary or appropriate. Because I am invisible, I bear the burden of disclosure. When someone assumes that I'm heterosexual, I have to correct her or him (my mother still doesn't believe that I'm queer). When someone assumes that I'm white, I do the same. Regardless, I come out all the time to new people in my life, and each time I do, I hope that they will be able to handle the information with care and respect.

Most people respond well when I come out to them, and I can breathe another sigh of relief when my peers accept me. College, especially, has been a (mostly) safe space for me to be out and proud about my race and sexuality. Living with my multiple invisible identities has taught me to be more assertive in all areas of my life, and I have learned to take risks. I know quite well how privilege works, and how that privilege can be taken away in an instant. I am also proud of all of my identities. The difficulty of coming out is well worth the satisfaction and pride I have of living my life the way that I have always wanted to.

Tara S. Ellison

SECTION II

EXPERIENCING DIFFERENCE

FRAMEWORK ESSAY

In the first framework essay, we considered the social construction of difference as master statuses were named, aggregated, dichotomized, and stigmatized. Now we turn to *experiencing* these statuses. Two examples illustrate this point.

Some years ago, a friend suggested renting the video *Willow* for her children. The eldest, a seven-year-old, had seen the opening scenes on television and was horrified at the prospect: "They kill the mom and steal the baby. There's dead bodies and blood everywhere." The man working in the video store, however, had seen the movie several times and vouched that it was not violent. Indeed, he did not remember the scenes the child described.

If you have seen *Willow,* you may recall that the movie opens as the soldiers of an evil queen round up all the pregnant women in the empire so that they can slay the enchanted baby when she is born. The soldiers kill the child's mother, but a midwife saves the baby and carries her into the forest. Then the midwife is attacked and killed by a pack of wild animals, and the baby floats downstream in a basket.

This offers a small lesson about social status. What one notices in the world depends in large part on the statuses one occupies; in this way one may be said to *experience* one's social status. The child noticed the violence both because of the unique person he is and because of his age, a master status. That the man in the video store did not see the movie as violent may be attributed, at least in part, to the same master status: age.

Although we do not specifically address age in *MOD*, it operates in ways that are analogous to race, sex, class, sexual orientation, and disability. Being young affects one's treatment in innumerable ways: at a minimum, restrictions on driving, employment, military enlistment, marriage, abortion, admission to movies, and alcohol and cigarette consumption; insurance rates; mandatory school attendance; and "status offenses" (acts that are illegal only for minors). In addition, minors are excluded from voting and other legal rights because they are presumed to be untrustworthy and irresponsible.

In these ways, those defined as "young" are treated differently from those who are not so defined. Because of that treatment, the world looks different to them than to those who are older and no longer operating within these constraints. The young notice things that older people need not notice, because they are not subject to the same rules. One's experiences are tied to the statuses one occupies.

The second example of experiencing one's status comes from the autobiography of one of the first black students in an exclusive white prep school. She recalls what it was like to hear "one [white] girl after another say, 'It doesn't matter to me if somebody's white or black or green or purple. I mean people are just people.'" While she appreciates the girls' intentions, she also hears her own *real* experience being trivialized by the comparison with green and purple creatures. Her status helps to explain what she noticed in these conversations (Cary, 1991:83–84).

In all, you experience your social statuses; you live through them. They are the filters through which you see and make sense of the world, and in large measure they account for how you are treated and what you notice. In the sections that follow, we will focus on the experiences of privilege and stigma associated with master statuses.

THE EXPERIENCE OF PRIVILEGE

Just as status helps to explain what we notice, it also explains what we *don't* notice. In the following classroom discussion between a black and a white woman, the white woman argues that because she and the black woman are both female, they should be allied. The black woman responds,

> "When you wake up in the morning and look in the mirror what do you see?"
> "I see a woman," replied the white woman.
> "That's precisely the issue," replied the black woman. "I see a black woman. For me, race is visible every day, because it is how I am *not* privileged in this culture. Race is invisible to you [because it is how you are privileged]." (Kimmel and Messner, 1989:3; emphasis added)

Thus, we are likely to be fairly unaware of the statuses that *privilege* us, that is, provide us with advantage, and acutely aware of those that are the source of trouble—those that yield negative judgments and unfair treatment. The mirror metaphor used by the black woman in this conversation emerges frequently among those who are stigmatized: "I looked in the mirror and saw a gay man." These moments of suddenly realizing one's social position with all of its life-shaping ramifications are usually about recognizing how one is stigmatized and underprivileged, but rarely about how one is privileged or advantaged, by the statuses one occupies.

Examples of Privilege

This use of the term *privilege* was first developed by Peggy McIntosh (1988) from her experience teaching women's studies courses. She noticed that while many men were willing to grant that women were disadvantaged (or "underprivileged") because of sexism, it was far more difficult for them to acknowledge that they were themselves advantaged (or "overprivileged") because of it. Extending the analysis to race, McIntosh generated a list of the ways in which she, as a white woman, was overprivileged by virtue of racism. Her list of over 40 white privileges included the following:

> I can turn on the television or open to the front page of the paper and see people of my race widely represented.
>
> When I am told about our national heritage or about "civilization," I am shown that people of my color made it what it is.
>
> I do not have to educate my children to be aware of systemic racism for their own daily protection.
>
> I can worry about racism without being seen as self-interested or self-seeking.
>
> I can think over many options, social, political, imaginative, or professional, without asking whether a person of my race would be accepted or allowed to do what I want to do. (McIntosh, 1988:5–8)

As she talked to people about her list, McIntosh learned about other white privileges: "A black woman said she was glad to hear me 'working on my own people,' because if she said these things about white privilege, she would be seen as a militant." Someone else noted that one privilege of being white was being able to be oblivious to those privileges. "Those in privileged groups are educated [to be oblivious] about what it is like for others, especially for others who have to be in their presence" (McIntosh, 1988).

One feature of privilege is that it makes life easier: it is easier to get around, to get what one wants, and to be treated in an acceptable manner. This is illustrated by the experience of a white newspaper columnist traveling with an African American colleague. Both were using complimentary airline tickets. The white columnist presented his ticket and was assigned a seat; then he watched the same white ticket agent ask his companion for some identification:

> The black man handed over his ticket. The female agent glanced at it and asked, "Do you have some identification?" [The columnist had not been asked for any identification.]
>
> "Yes, I do," the black man said, and he reached for his wallet. "But just out of curiosity, do you mind telling me why you want to see it?"
>
> The agent grinned in embarrassment.
>
> She said nothing in response.
>
> "How about a credit card?" the black man said, and he pulled one out of his wallet.
>
> "Do you have a work ID?" she asked, apparently hoping to see something with the black man's photo on it.
>
> "No," he said, and whipped out another credit card.
>
> "A driver's license would be fine," she said, sounding trapped.
>
> "I don't have my driver's license with me," he said. "I'm taking the plane, not the car. . . ."
>
> "That's fine sir, thank you," the agent finally said, shrinking a bit with each successive credit card. "Enjoy the flight."
>
> The men rode the escalator up to the gate area in silence.
>
> The white man shook his head. "I've probably watched that a hundred times in my life," he said. "But that's the first time I've ever *seen* it."
>
> The black man nodded. He'd seen it more times than he cared to count. "You don't ever need to remind yourself that you're black," he said, "because every day there's somebody out there who'll remind you."
>
> They walked on for a while, and the black man started to laugh to himself. Pirouetting, he modeled his outfit, an Italian-cut, double-breasted suit with a red rose in his lapel for Mother's Day. "I really can't look any better than this," he said sardonically. Then, he looked into his friend's eyes and said, "I had my driver's license. But if I show it, we may as well be in Soweto." (Kornheiser, 1990)

In reading about this exchange, one black student was particularly angered: "Whites will stand by and watch this happen, and either be oblivious to the slight or sympathize with you afterward, but they won't go to the mat and fight for you."

The columnist noted for the first time a privilege that he had as a middle-class white: he was not assumed to be a thief. By contrast, his black colleague was presumed to have potentially stolen the ticket no matter how upper-class or professional he looked. Similarly, many black and Latino students describe being closely monitored for shoplifting when they are in department stores, just as the students who work in department store security confirm that they are given explicit instructions to watch black and Latino customers more closely. On hearing this, one black student realized why she had the habit of walking through stores with her hands out, palms open, in front of her: it was a way to prove she was not stealing. Oddly, one of the privileges of being white is that shoplifting is easier, since the security people in stores are busy watching the black and Latino customers.

Just as whites are not assumed to be thieves, they are not assumed to be poor. Michael Patrick MacDonald in Reading 34 describes how neither his Irish neighbors in South Boston nor social welfare activists acknowledged the area's poverty, crime, and drugs. "Those were black things that happened in the ghettos of Roxbury. Southie was Boston's proud Irish neighborhood."

Perhaps even more important in the realm of white privilege is the presumption that one is not aggressive. This is especially worth noting because if a person or group of people are assumed to be violent, acting against them to preemptively ward off that violence is seen as somehow legitimate. While whites do not generally assume that other whites are a threat, they do assume that of blacks. While the percentage appears to be declining, about half of whites think blacks are aggressive or violent (Smith, 2001; National Opinion Research Center, 1990). A mundane example of the consequence of this belief is provided by law professor and author Patricia J. Williams:

> My best friend from law school is a woman named C. For months now I have been sending her drafts of this book, filled with many shared experiences, and she sends me back comments and her own associations. Occasionally we speak by telephone. One day, after reading the beginning of this chapter, she calls me up and tells me her abiding recollection of law school. "Actually, it has nothing to do with law school," she says.
>
> "I'll be the judge of that," I respond.
>
> "Well," she continues, "It's about the time I was held at gunpoint by a SWAT team."
>
> It turns out that during one Christmas vacation C. drove to Florida with two friends. Just outside Miami they stopped at a roadside diner. C. ordered a hamburger and a glass of milk. The milk was sour, and C. asked for another. The waitress ignored her. C. asked twice more and was ignored each time. When the waitress finally brought the bill, C. had been charged for the milk and refused to pay for it. The waitress started to shout at her, and a highway patrolman walked over from where he had been sitting and asked what was going on. C. explained that the milk was sour and that she didn't want to pay for it. The highway patrolman ordered her to pay and get out. When C. said he was out of his jurisdiction, the patrolman pulled out his gun and pointed it at her.
>
> ("Don't you think," asks C. when I show her this much of my telling of her story, "that it would help your readers to know that the restaurant was all white and that I'm black?" "Oh, yeah," I say. "And six feet tall.")
>
> Now C. is not easily intimidated and, just to prove it, she put her hand on her hip and invited the police officer to go ahead and shoot her, but before he did so *he* should try to drink the damn glass of milk, and so forth and so on for a few more descriptive rounds. What cut her off was the realization that, suddenly and silently, she and her two friends had been surrounded by eight SWAT team officers, in full guerrilla gear, automatic weapons drawn. Into the pall of her ringed speechlessness, they sent a local black

> policeman, who offered her twenty dollars and begged her to pay and be gone. C. describes how desperately he was perspiring as he begged and, when she didn't move, how angry he got—how he accused her of being an outside agitator, that she could come from the North and go back to the North, but that there were those of "us" who had to live here and would pay for her activism.
>
> C. says she doesn't remember how she got out of there alive or why they finally let her go; but she supposes that the black man paid for her. But she does remember returning to the car with her two companions and the three of them crying, sobbing, all the way to Miami. "The damnedest thing about it," C. said, "was that no one was interested in whether or not I was telling the truth. The glass was sitting there in the middle of all this, with the curdle hanging on the side, but nobody would taste it because a black woman's lips had touched it." (Williams, 1991:56–57)

Several front-page cases have shown dramatically how whites' fear of blacks has prompted aggression toward them—and then been used after the fact to legitimate the violence. Among the more notorious cases are Bernard Goetz's 1984 New York subway shooting of four unarmed black teenagers (two in the back), for which Goetz was found innocent of attempted murder; the 1989 Boston case of Charles Stuart who murdered his pregnant wife but so convinced the police that she had been shot by a black gunman that they failed to pursue an investigation that would have led to the plot hatched by Stuart and his brother; or the 1991 beating of Rodney King by white Los Angeles police, all of whom were acquitted. Thus every day, African Americans, especially men, must always be vigilant about becoming the targets of preemptive violence. Freedom from this kind of life-altering experience is one privilege of being white.[1]

The *racial profiling* described by John Lamberth in Reading 30 must be understood against this background of whites' presumption of black aggression and criminality. Racial profiling means singling out particular racial groups for heightened levels of police surveillance or investigation. The profiling Lamberth uncovered in his research in Maryland appears to be the case for police departments across the country as well as in the U.S. Customs Service's body searches for contraband. At least 13 states have laws requiring the collection of data that would indicate whether racial profiling was taking place, several federal agencies are now required to collect similar data, and some agencies (such as the Customs Service) have dramatically changed their practices to curtail profiling (Montgomery, 2001).

The September 11 terrorist attacks, however, have reopened the profiling debate, this time in terms of the profiling of Arab Americans and noncitizens from the Middle East. The public consensus that had come to oppose the profiling of African Americans and Latinos seems much less solidified in this case. The likelihood is that several lawsuits will emerge regarding the constitutionality of targeting Middle Eastern–looking men for investigation, detention, and deportation.

Another privilege likely to be invisible to those in single-race families is the privilege of being recognized as a family. The following account by a mother illustrates how the failure to perceive a family is linked to the expectation of black criminality.

[1]Despite whites' fear of violence at the hands of African Americans, crime is predominately *intra*racial.

> When my son was home visiting from college, we met in town one day for lunch. . . . On the way to the car, one of us thought of a game we'd often played when he was younger.
>
> "Race you to the car!"
>
> I passed my large handbag to him, thinking to more equalize the race since he was a twenty-year-old athlete. We raced the few blocks, my heart singing with delight to be talking and playing with my beloved son. As we neared the car, two young white men yelled something at us. I couldn't make it out and paid it no mind. When we arrived at the car, both of us laughing, they walked by and mumbled "Sorry" as they quickly passed, heads down.
>
> I suddenly understood. They hadn't seen a family. They had seen a young Black man with a pocketbook, fleeing a pursuing middle-aged white woman. My heart trembled as I thought of what could have happened if we'd been running by someone with a gun.
>
> Later I mentioned the incident in a three-day diversity seminar I was conducting at a Boston corporation. A participant related it that evening to his son, a police officer, and asked the son what he would have done if he'd observed the scene.
>
> The answer: "Shot out his kneecaps." (Lester, 1994:56–7)

Let us turn now from the privileges of race to the privileges of sexual orientation. The most obvious privilege enjoyed by heterosexuals is that they are free to talk to virtually anyone about their relationships and to display affection anywhere publicly. Those in same-sex relationships, however, can neither talk openly about their relationships nor display affection in public. Indeed, doing so puts them at risk for unemployment, ostracism, verbal abuse, loss of child custody, and potentially life-threatening physical assault.

Even the ability to display a picture of one's partner on a desk at work stands as an invisible privilege of heterosexuality.

> Consider, for example, an employee who keeps a photograph on her desk in which she and her husband smile for the camera and embrace affectionately. . . . [T]he photo implicitly conveys information about her private sexual behavior. [But] . . . most onlookers (if they even notice the photo) do not think of her partner primarily in sexual terms. . . .
>
> [But] if the photograph instead shows the woman in the same pose with a same-sex partner, everyone is likely to notice. As with the first example, the photograph conveys the information that she is in a relationship. But the fact that the partner is a woman overwhelms all other information about her. The *sexual* component of the relationship is not mundane and implicit as with the heterosexual spouse. . . . (Herek, 1992:95–6; emphasis added)

Because heterosexual public affection is so commonplace, it rarely conjures up images of sexual activity. But that is exactly what we may think of when we see a same-sex couple embrace. This is why gay and lesbian people are often accused of "flaunting" their sexuality: *any* display of affection between them is understood by many heterosexuals as virtually a display of the sex act.

In the realm of class privilege, several readings in this text address the considerable differences in health, life span, educational access, and quality of life that accompany American class differences. But these are perhaps the more visible privileges of being middle- and upper-class. Less apparent is the privilege of being treated as a competent member of the community. To get that treatment in his university, one of our working-class students described how he had to change out of his work clothes before going to campus; otherwise, staff and faculty treated him as though he did not belong at the university. "Competence" is also something disabled people are rarely assumed to possess.

Two privileges in particular shape the experience of those in nonstigmatized statuses: entitlement and the privilege of being "unmarked." *Entitlement* is the belief that one has the right to be respected, acknowledged, protected, and rewarded. This is so much taken for granted by those in nonstigmatized statuses that they are often shocked and angered when it is denied them.

> [After the lecture, whites in the audience] shot their hands up to express how excluded they felt because [the] lecture, while broad in scope, clearly was addressed first and foremost to the women of color in the room. . . . What a remarkable sense of entitlement must drive their willingness to assert their experience of exclusion! If I wanted to raise my hand every time I felt excluded, I would have to glue my wrist to the top of my head. (Ettinger, 1994:51)

Like entitlement, the privilege of occupying an "unmarked" status is shared by most of those in nonstigmatized categories. *Doctor* is an *unmarked* status; *woman* doctor is *marked.* Unmarked categories convey the usual and expected distribution of individuals in social statuses—the distribution that does not require any special comment. Thus, the unmarked category tells us what a society takes for granted.

Theoretically, the unmarked category *doctor* might include anyone, but in truth it refers to white males. How do we know that? Because other occupants of that status are usually marked: woman doctor, black doctor, and so on. While the marking of a status signals infrequency—there are few female astronauts or male nurses—it may also imply inferiority. A "woman doctor" or a "black doctor" may be considered less qualified.

Thus, a privilege of those who are not stigmatized is that their master statuses are not used to discount their accomplishments or imply that they serve only special interests. Someone described as "a politician" is presumed to operate from a universality that someone described as "a white male politician" is not. Because white male politicians are rarely described as such, their anchoring in the reality of their own master statuses is hidden. In this way, those in marked statuses appear to be always operating from an "agenda," or "special interest" (e.g., a black politician is often presumed to represent only black constituents), while those in unmarked statuses can appear to be agenda-free. Being white and male thus becomes invisible, since it is not regularly identified as important. For this reason, some recommend identifying *everyone's* race and sex as a way to recognize that we are all grounded in our master statuses.

This use of marked statuses also applies to classroom interactions. At white-dominated universities, white students are unlikely to be asked what white people think or asked to explain the "white experience." In this way, those who are white, male, heterosexual, and middle class appear to have no race, sex, sexual orientation, or social class, and thus have the privilege of escaping classroom discussions about the problems of "their people."

Stigmatized People and Their Experience of Privilege; Privileged People and Their Experience of Stigma

We have described some of the privileges enjoyed by those in nonstigmatized statuses. However, those with stigma also have some experience of privilege—it is just less frequent. For example, in 1991 the Urban Institute investigated racial discrimination in employment by sending previously coached pairs of black and white male college students to apply for jobs in Washington, D.C., and Chicago. They had virtually identical appearance, personal styles, dialects, educations, and job histories.

> In 20 percent [of the 576 job applications], the white applicant advanced farther in the hiring process [from obtaining a job application, to interview, to hiring] than his black counterpart, and in 15 percent the white applicant was offered a job while his equally qualified black partner was not. Blacks were favored over comparable white applicants in a much smaller share of cases; in 7 percent of the audits the black advanced farther in the hiring process, and in 5 percent only the black received the job offer. (Turner, Fix, and Struyk, 1991:18)

Black and white applicants both had some experience of preferential hiring, but the white applicant had about three times more. A similar study of job discrimination against Latino males conducted in Chicago and San Diego indicated an even larger gap between the level of privilege experienced by Anglos and Latinos (Cross, Kenney, Mell, and Zimmermann, 1990).

Thus, concerns about "reverse discrimination" often miss the mark. While blacks, Latinos, Asian Americans, or white women are sometimes favored in hiring, they are not favored as *frequently* as white males. Discrimination continues in its historic direction as evidenced in the constancy of race and sex differences in income. In 1975, black per capita median annual income was 58.5 percent that of whites. Over 20 years later, in 1997, the figure was only 60.5 percent. In 1975, the same measure for Latinos was 56.1 percent of whites; by 1997, it was down to 52.7 percent (U.S. Department of Commerce, 1993:454; U.S. Bureau of the Census, 1997).[2]

Because the focus is so frequently on how stigma affects those who bear it, it is easy to assume that only the targets of racism, sexism, homophobia, or classism are affected by it. But that is not the case. Those who are not themselves the targets of discrimination may still be affected by it. For example,

> Think of white slaveowners and their wives: the meaning of the sexual difference between them was constructed in part by the alleged contrast between them as whites and other men and women who were Black; what was supposed to characterize their relationship was not supposed to characterize the relationship between white men and Black women, or white women and Black men. . . . So even though the white men and women

---

[2]Income figures exclude "money income received before payments for personal income, taxes, Social Security, union dues, Medicare deductions, food stamps, health benefits, subsidized housing, or rent-free housing and goods produced and consumed on the farm" (U.S. Department of Commerce, 1993:425).

> were of the same race, and even though they were not the victims of racism, this does not mean that we can understand the relationship between them without reference to their race and to the racism that their lives enacted. (Spelman, 1988:104–5)

Similarly, interactions between men are affected by sexism, even though the men themselves are not subject to it.

> For example, we can't understand the racism that fueled white men's lynching of Black men without understanding its connection to the sexism that shaped their protective and possessive attitudes toward white women. The ideology according to which whites are superior and ought to dominate Blacks is nested with the ideology according to which white men must protect their wives from attack by Black men. . . . That men aren't subject to sexism doesn't mean sexism has no effect on their relationships to each other. . . . (Spelman, 1988:106)

Similar examples apply to sexual orientation, social class, and disability. Certainly, homophobia shapes heterosexual relations, treatment of those who are disabled affects those who are "temporarily able-bodied," and the stereotypes about poor people affect interactions among those in the middle class. Thus, the most obvious privilege of those in nonstigmatized statuses—that they are not affected by stigma—is not as straightforward as one might think.

Because privilege is usually invisible to those who possess it, they may assume that everyone is treated as they are. When they learn otherwise, they may think that the incident was exceptional rather than routine, that the victim was overreacting or misinterpreting, or that the victim must have provoked the encounter. Such responses do not necessarily deny that the incident took place; rather, they deny that the event carries any negative or special meaning.

Through such dismissals, those operating from positions of privilege can deny the experience of those without privilege. For example, college-age students often describe university administrators as unresponsive until they have had their parents call to complain. If the parents later said, "I don't know why *you* had such a problem with those people, they were very nice to *me*. Did you do something to antagonize them?" that would indicate they were oblivious to their privileged status in the university setting as well as unaware of their child's underprivileged status in it.

Dismissals like these treat the stigmatized person like a child inadequate to judge the world. Often such dismissals are framed in terms of the very stigma about which people are complaining. In this way, what stigmatized people say about their status is discounted precisely because they are stigmatized. The implication is that those who occupy a stigmatized status are somehow the ones *least* able to assess its consequence. The effect is to dismiss precisely those who have had the most experience with the problem.

This process, called *looping* or *rereading,* is described by many who have studied the lives of patients in psychiatric hospitals (Rosenhan, 1973; Schur, 1984; Goffman, 1961, 1963). If a patient says, "The staff here are being unfair to me," and the staff respond, "Of course he would think that—he's crazy," they have reread, or looped, his words through his status. His words have been heard in light of his stigma and dismissed for exactly that reason.

These dismissals serve a function. Dismissing another's experience of status-based mistreatment masks the possibility that one has escaped such treatment precisely because of one's privilege. If we do not acknowledge that *their* status affects *their* treatment, we need not acknowledge that *our* status affects *our* treatment. Thus, we avoid the larger truth that those who are treated well, those who are treated poorly, and all the rest in between are always evaluated both as individuals and as occupants of particular esteemed and disesteemed categories.

Hierarchies of Stigma and Privilege

While it may appear that people can be easily separated into two categories—privileged and stigmatized—every individual occupies several master statuses. The privilege or stigma that might be associated with one status emerges in the context of *all* of one's other statuses. For example, a middle-class, heterosexual Mexican American male may be privileged in terms of class, sex, and sexual orientation, but stigmatized by virtue of being Latino. Given the invisibility of privilege, he is more likely to notice the ways in which his status as Latino stigmatizes him than to notice the privileges that follow from his other statuses. Nonetheless, he is simultaneously all of his statuses; the privileges and disadvantages of each emerge in the context of all the others. An Anglo male and a Latino male may both be said to experience the privilege of sex, but they do not experience the *same* privilege.

While individuals may experience both privilege and stigma, some stigmas are so strong that they cancel out the privileges that one's other statuses might provide. For example, there is much evidence that the stigma of being black in America cancels any privileges that might be expected to follow from being middle-class.

> The first large-scale study of treatment decisions made by primary care physicians found that, when faced with identical complaints of chest pain, doctors were much more likely to recommend further cardiac testing for their white male patients than any others. Black and female patients were referred to heart specialists only 60 percent as often. (Goldstein, 1999:1)

> Blacks also remain about half as likely as Latinos or Asians to live in the suburbs. And despite their consistent preference for residential integration, blacks in almost all central cities remain highly segregated from non-Hispanic whites. They are more racially isolated from whites than are Latinos and Asians, and high incomes or levels of education make it no easier for African Americans to move into white neighborhoods. (Hochschild, 1995:42)

> A [*Los Angeles*] *Times* analysis found that while African Americans remain the most segregated group in the nation's top 25 metropolitan areas, Latinos and Asians are beginning to close this gap. . . . Demographers define a place as moderately segregated if more than 50% of a group's population would have to move to become evenly distributed in that place. Some 21 of the nation's 25 largest metropolitan areas registered as moderately segregated or worse for blacks in 2000. Eleven now meet this criterion for Latinos, up from 6 a decade earlier. There are 7 areas for Asians, an increase from 5 in 1990. (Fields and Herndon, 2001:A1–A17)

> In 1999 the U.S. Department of Agriculture agreed to settle a class-action lawsuit filed in 1997 by black farmers who claimed they had been denied government loans or given

> smaller and more restrictive loans than those awarded to white farmers with similar credit histories and assets. "Discrimination by USDA officials has been cited as a major reason why the ranks of black farmers have dwindled at three times the rate of white farmers. Blacks, who were 14 percent of the nation's farmers in the 1920s, now account for less than 1 percent." (Fletcher, 1999:10)

> *Roberts v. Texaco,* the class action filed in June 1994, charged the company with persistent failure to hire, promote or even treat with decency its African-American staffers. It cited numbers: in 1994 only four of Texaco's top 498 executives were black. And it included stunning affidavits of abuse and insult. . . . The case languished in court until late 1996, when a downsized Texaco executive, in an act of revenge or repentance, turned over tapes that caught top officials at the company—including him—making racist remarks . . . and plotting to purge the documents in the discrimination case. Texaco agreed to pay more than $115 million in racial reparations. (Solomon, 1996:48–49)

> [In a finding] by the Association of Community Organizations for Reform Now, or ACORN, discrimination is not only not getting any better, it's worsening. And not just in mortgages to buy homes but in refinancings, too. And not just in some jurisdictions but throughout the country as well. The ACORN investigation was released at a Department of Housing and Urban Development news conference, along with a second report by the Urban Institute for HUD that found minorities are less likely than whites to obtain mortgage financing. And when they do, it also discovered, they tend to receive less money at terms that aren't as favorable. . . . The ACORN and Urban Institute reports found that Blacks were denied mortgages 217 percent more often than whites in 1998, up from 206 in 1997. Hispanics were rejected 183 percent as often, up from 169. [The studies also found that] minority testers were less likely to receive information about loan products than their white counterparts. Loan officers also took less time with minorities than with whites and quoted higher rates. (Sichelman, 1999)

> Coca-Cola Co. agreed [in November 2000] to pay a record $192.5 million to settle a racial-discrimination lawsuit brought by black workers and agreed to make significant changes in the way it manages, promotes and treats its minority employees. . . . In the suite the employees accused Coca-Cola of discriminating against black employees in pay, promotions and evaluations. (Schafer, 2000:A1)

> The Center for the Study of Sport in Society at Northeastern University reports that U.S. colleges continue to provide the fewest opportunities for people of color at the top management level. In Division I, African-Americans make up only 2.4 percent of athletic directors while women hold 9 percent. The percentage of African-Americans coaching Division I men's basketball increased to 21.6 percent while falling in Division IA football to 4.7 percent, the lowest level since the Racial and Gender Report Card first published results for college sports. (Lapchick and Matthews, 2001)

Research on the effects of other stigmatized racial statuses has not been as thorough, nor are its findings as consistent, but it is clear that for African Americans, middle-class standing provides little protection against racism.

Does the stigma of being an out-of-the-closet gay or lesbian cause one to lose the privilege that comes from being middle-class, white, or both? Sexual orientation is not covered by federal civil rights legislation. While the proportion of Americans who believe gays should have equal job opportunities has increased—

from 56 percent in 1977 to 84 percent in 1996 (Berke, 1998)—there is still no federal protection barring discrimination against gays in employment, housing, or health care. In 1998, President Clinton issued an executive order barring federal agencies from such discrimination, but the House of Representatives denied funding to carry out the order (Berke, 1998). Thus, it often looks as though gays are predominately white and at least middle-class; in the absence of federal protection, few others can afford to publicly identify themselves as gay (Lester, 1994). While some jurisdictions enact protections, many of those ordinances are later challenged and repealed. In 2000, several state and local referendums barring discrimination against gays were defeated. At present, it appears that the stigma of being gay often overwhelms the privileges that one's other statuses might afford. The 1998 beating death of gay University of Wyoming student Matthew Shepard, like other hate crimes directed at gays and lesbians, offers horrifying evidence to that effect.

But which status is most important: one's race, sex, sexual orientation, or social class? For the sizable population that occupies multiple stigmatized statuses, it makes little sense to argue which status presents the greatest obstacle since most people live in the *intersection* of their master statuses. This experience is the subtext of many of the readings included in *MOD*. It is captured by high school teacher Patrick Welsh in Reading 27, as he describes the schisms among Latino students because of their differences in social class and national origin. Rosemarie Garland-Thomson identifies the intersection between sex and disability in Reading 51, and Barbara Reskin and Irene Padavic consider the joint impact of race, sex, and ethnicity on people's work experience. The intersection of master statuses is also one way to understand the anguish Lydia Minatoya in Reading 25 sees in the white husband of a Japanese American woman attending a remembrance ceremony. While people are often asked to make alliances based on one status being more significant than another, their real experience is not often that unidimensional.

Philosopher Elizabeth Spelman (1988), however, suggests a way to assess the relative priority of each of these statuses. If each master status is imagined as a room we will enter, we can consider which sequential ordering of these rooms most accurately reflects our experience. If the first rooms we encounter are labeled black, white, or Asian, we will find ourselves in a room with those who share our "race" but are different in terms of sex, social class, ethnicity, and sexual orientation. If the second set of rooms is labeled male and female, we will find ourselves with people of the same race and sex. Other rooms might be labeled with sexual orientation or social class categorizations.

Many white feminists have presumed that the first rooms we encounter are sex categorizations, thus arguing that the statuses of female and male have priority over race or class designations; that one is discriminated against first by virtue of one's sex and then by race. Latino, black, and some white feminists have countered that the first rooms are race classifications. In this case, it is argued that racism so powerfully affects people that men and women within racial categories have more in common with one another than they do with those of the same sex but of a different race. Alliances of gay and lesbian people by implication assume that the first doors are marked gay and straight, with sex, race, and class following; disability rights activists would argue that that status takes precedence over everything else. In addition to the orderings that correspond to the historical experience of categories of people, each of us likely maintains an ordering based on our personal experience of these statuses.

THE EXPERIENCE OF STIGMA

The previous section considered the privileges conferred by some master statuses; now we examine the stigma conferred by other master statuses.

In his classic analysis of stigma, sociologist Erving Goffman (1963) distinguished between the *discredited,* whose stigma is immediately apparent to an observer (for example, race, sex, some physical disabilities), and the *discreditable,* whose stigma can be hidden (for example, sexual orientation, social class). Since stigma plays out differently in the lives of the discredited and the discreditable, each will be examined separately.

The Discreditable: "Passing"

The discreditable are those who are *passing,* that is, not publicly acknowledging the stigmatized statuses they occupy. (Were they to acknowledge that status, they would become discredited.) The term *passing* comes from "passing as white," which emerged as a phenomenon after 1875 when southern states re-established racial segregation through hundreds of "Jim Crow"[3] laws. At that point, some African Americans passed as a way to get decent jobs.

> [S]ome who passed as white on the job lived as black at home. Some lived in the North as white part of the year and as black in the South the rest of the time. More men passed than women . . . the vast majority who could have passed permanently did not do so, owing to the pain of family separation, condemnation by most blacks, their fear of whites, and the loss of the security of the black community. . . . Passing as white probably reached an all-time peak between 1880 and 1925. (Davis, 1991:56–57)

"Passing as white" is now quite rare and strongly condemned by African Americans, a reaction that "indicate[s] the resolute insistence that anyone with even the slightest trace of black ancestry is black, and a traitor to act like a white" (Davis, 1991:138). We will use the term *passing* here to refer to those who have not made their stigmatized status evident; it is similar to the phrase "being in the closet" which is usually applied to gays. Because passing is now most frequent among gays—as well as most vehemently debated—many of our examples will focus on that stigmatized status.

One may engage in passing by chance as well as by choice. For example, the presumption that everyone is heterosexual can have the effect of putting gay people in

---

[3]"Jim Crow" was "a blackface, signing-dancing-comedy characterization portraying black males as childlike, irresponsible, inefficient, lazy, ridiculous in speech, pleasure-seeking, and happy, [and was] a widespread stereotype of blacks during the last decades before emancipation . . ." (Davis, 1991:51). "Jim Crow" laws were laws by which whites imposed segregation following the Civil War.

the closet even when they had not intended to be. During a series of lectures on marriage and the family, one of our colleagues realized that he had been making assignments, lecturing, and encouraging discussion assuming that all of the students in the class had, or wanted to have, heterosexual relationships. Unless his gay and lesbian students specifically countered his assumption, they were effectively passing. His actions forced them to choose between announcing or remaining silent about their status. Had he assumed that students would be involved only with others of the same race, he would have created a similar situation for those in interracial relationships. Thus, assumptions about others' private lives—for example, asking whether someone is married—may have the effect of making them choose between silence or an announcement of something they may consider private.

Since most heterosexuals assume that everyone else is heterosexual, many social encounters either put gay people in the closet or require they announce their status.

> Every encounter with a new classful of students, to say nothing of a new boss, social worker, loan officer, landlord, doctor, erects new closets [that] . . . exact from at least gay people new surveys, new calculations, new draughts and requisitions of secrecy or disclosure. Even an *out* gay person deals daily with interlocutors about whom she doesn't know whether they know or not [or whether they would care]. . . . The gay closet is not a feature only of the lives of gay people. But for many gay people it is still the fundamental feature of social life; there can be few gay people . . . in whose lives the closet is not a shaping presence. (Sedgwick, 1990:68)

Inadvertent passing is also experienced by those whose racial status is not immediately apparent. An African American acquaintance of ours who looks white is often in settings in which others do not know that she is African American—or in which she does not know if they know. Thus, she must regularly decide how and when to convey that information. This is important to her as a way to discourage racist remarks, since whites often assume it is acceptable to make racist remarks to one another (as men often assume it is acceptable to make sexist remarks to other men, or as straights presume it acceptable to make homophobic remarks to those they think are also straight). It is also important to her that others know she is black so that they understand the meaning of her words—so that they will hear her words through her status as an African American woman. Those whose stigma is not apparent must go to some lengths to avoid being in the closet by virtue of others' assumptions. Those with relatively invisible disabilities also face the tension of inadvertent passing. One of our students arrived in class in tears following an encounter with someone she had not realized was disabled. Seeing the young woman trip, the student had asked if she could help—and was angrily rebuffed. The offer to help had been taken as a show of pity.

But passing may also be an intentional choice. For example, one of our students, who was in the process of deciding that he was gay, had worked for many years at a local library, where he became friends with several of his coworkers. Much of the banter at work, however, involved disparaging gay, or presumably gay, library patrons. As he grappled with a decision about his own sexual identity, his social environment reminded him that being gay is a stigmatized status in American society.

The student did not so much face prejudice personally (since he was not "out" to his work friends) as he faced an "unwilling acceptance of himself by individuals who are prejudiced against persons of the kind he can be revealed to be" (Goffman, 1963:42). Thus, he was not the person his friends took him to be. While survey data indicate that those who personally know a gay man hold consistently more positive feelings about gays in general (Herek and Glunt, 1993), the decision to publicly reveal a stigma that others have gone on record as opposing is not made lightly.

Revealing stigma changes one's interactions with "normals," even with those who are not particularly prejudiced. Such revelations are likely to alter important relationships. Parents sometimes disown gay children, just as they do children involved in interracial relationships. Thus, the decision to pass or be "out" is not easily made. For the discreditable, what Goffman euphemistically described as "information management" is at the core of one's life. "To tell or not to tell; to let on or not to let on; to lie or not to lie; and in each case, to whom, how, when, and where" (Goffman, 1963:42). Such choices are faced daily by those who are discreditable—not just those who are gay and lesbian, but also those who are poor, have been imprisoned, attempted suicide, terminated a pregnancy through abortion, are HIV-positive, are drug or alcohol dependent, or have been the victims of incest or rape. By contrast, those who do not occupy stigmatized statuses don't have to invest emotional energy in monitoring information about themselves; they can choose to talk openly about their personal history.

Passing has both positive and negative aspects. On the positive side, passing lets the stigmatized person exert some power over the situation; the person controls the information, the flow of events, and their privacy. By withholding his or her true identity until choosing to reveal it, the person may create a situation in which others' prejudices are challenged. Passing forces one to be judged as an individual rather than be discounted by virtue of a stigma. Passing also limits one's exposure to verbal and physical abuse, allows for the development of previously forbidden relationships, and improves employment security by minimizing one's exposure to discrimination.

On the negative side, passing consumes a good deal of time, energy, and emotion in the management of personal information. It introduces deception and secrecy even into close relationships. Passing also denies others the opportunity to prove themselves unprejudiced, and it makes one vulnerable to blackmail by those who do know about one's stigma.

The Discredited: Flaming

While the discreditable face problems of invisibility, *visibility* is the problem for those who are discredited. Those who are discredited suffer from undue attention and are subject to being stereotyped.

Being discredited means that one's stigma is immediately apparent to others. As essayist bell hooks describes below, those who are discredited often have little patience for those who at least have the option of passing.

> Many of us have been in discussions where a non-white person—a black person—struggles to explain to white folks that while we can acknowledge that gay people of all colors

> are harassed and suffer exploitation and domination, we also recognize that there is a significant difference that arises because of the visibility of dark skin. . . . While it in no way lessens the severity of such suffering for gay people, or the fear that it causes, it does mean that in a given situation the apparatus of protection and survival may be simply not identifying as gay. In contrast, most people of color have no choice. No one can hide, change, or mask dark skin color. White people, gay and straight, could show greater understanding of the impact of racial oppression on people of color by not attempting to make these oppressions synonymous, but rather by showing the ways they are linked and yet differ. (hooks, 1989:125)

For the discredited, stigma is likely to always shape interaction with those who are not stigmatized. However, its effect does not necessarily play out in ways one can easily determine. For those whose stigma is visible, every situation forces them to decide whether the world is responding to them or their stigma. Florynce Kennedy, a black activist in the civil rights and women's movements, once commented that the problem with being black in America was that you never knew whether what happened to you, good or bad, was because of your talents or because you were black (Kennedy, 1976). This situation was described in 1903 by sociologist W. E. B. Du Bois as the "double consciousness" of being black in America. The concept was key to Du Bois's classic, *The Souls of Black Folk,* for which he was rightfully judged "the father of serious black thought as we know it today" (Hare, 1982:xiii). Du Bois described double consciousness this way:

> the Negro . . . [is] gifted with a second-sight in this American world—a world which yields him no true self-consciousness, but only lets him see himself through the revelation of the other world. It is a peculiar sensation, this double consciousness, this sense of always looking at one's self through the eyes of others, of measuring one's soul by the tape of a world that looks on in amused contempt and pity. One ever feels his twoness. . . . (1982:45)

This is the sense of seeing oneself through the eyes of a harshly critical other, and it relates to our discussion of objectification in Framework Essay I. When those who are stigmatized view themselves from the perspective of the nonstigmatized, they have reduced themselves to objects. This theme of double or "fractured" consciousness can also be found in contemporary analyses of women's experience.

The greatest effect of being visibly stigmatized is on one's life chances—literally, one's chances for living. Thus, the readings in this book detail differences in income, employment, health, lifespan, education, targeting for violence, and the likelihood of arrest and imprisonment. In this essay, however, we will consider the more mundane difficulties created by stigmatization, particularly the sense of being "on stage."

The discredited often have the feeling of being watched or on display when they are in settings dominated by nonstigmatized people. For example, when women walk through male-dominated settings, they often feel they are on display in terms of their physical appearance. Asian, black, and Latino students in white/Anglo-dominated universities often describe a sense of being on display in campus dining facilities. In such cases, the discredited are likely to feel that others are judging them in terms of their stigma.

As sociologist Rosabeth Moss Kanter (1980, 1993) has shown, this impression is likely to be accurate. When Kanter studied corporate settings in which there was one person visibly different from the others, that person was likely to get a disproportionate share of attention. In fact, people in the setting were likely to closely monitor what the minority person did, which meant his or her mistakes were more likely to be noticed—and the mistakes of those in the rest of the group were more likely to be overlooked, since everyone was watching the minority person. Even in after-work socializing, the minority member was still subject to disproportionate attention.

Kanter also found that the minority person's behavior was likely to be interpreted in terms of the prevailing stereotypes about the members of that category. For example, when there were only a few men in a setting dominated by women, the men were subject to intense observation and their behavior was filtered through the stereotypes about men. Perceptions were distorted to fit the pre-existing beliefs.

Without the presence of a visibly different person, members of a setting are likely to see themselves as different from one another in various ways. Through contrast with the visibly different person, however, they notice their own similarities. In this way, majority group members may construct dichotomies—"us" and "them"—out of settings in which there are a few who are different. It is not surprising that those who are visibly different sometimes isolate themselves in response.

Still, none of this is inevitable. Kanter argues strongly that once minority membership in a setting reaches 15 percent, these processes abate. Until that point, however, those who are in the minority (or visibly stigmatized) are the subject of a good deal of attention. As a consequence, they are often accused of "flaming." *Flaming* usually means acting in an effeminate manner, with the intention of letting observers know that one is gay. Most likely, the term originated as a criticism of gay men but has since been appropriated more positively by that community. We use the term here to describe an unabashed display of any stigmatized status.

Flaming is a charge that the nonstigmatized often level at those who are stigmatized. Although there are certainly occasions on which the discredited may deliberately make a show of their status, Kanter's work indicates that when their numbers are low in a setting, they are likely to be charged with flaming no matter what they do. Subjected to a disproportionate amount of attention and viewed through the lenses of stereotypes, almost anything the discredited do is likely to be noticed and attributed to the category to which they belong. Thus, one charge frequently leveled at those in discredited groups is that they are "so" black, Latino, gay, and so on—that is, that they make too big a show of their status.

This charge may affect those who are visibly stigmatized in various ways. Many are careful to behave in ways contrary to expectations. At other times, however, flaming may be deliberate. In the first session of one class, a student opened his remarks by saying, "Well, you all know I am a gay man, and as a gay man I think. . . ." The buzz of conversation stopped, other students stared at him, and one asked, "How would we know you were gay?" The student pointed to a pink triangle he had pinned to his book bag and explained that he thought they knew that someone wearing it would be gay. (Pink triangles were assigned to gay men during the Nazi era, black triangles to lesbians and other "unwanted" women. Both have been adopted as badges of pride among gay activists. Still, his logic was questionable: Anyone supportive of gay rights might wear the button.)

This announcement—which moved the student from a discreditable to a discredited status—may have been intended to keep his classmates from making overtly anti-gay comments in his presence. His strategy was designed to counter the negative consequences of passing. To avoid being mistakenly identified as straight, he decided to flame.

Similarly, light-skinned African Americans are required to "flame" as black, lest they be accused of trying to pass. In adolescence, light-skinned black men are often derided by their black and white peers as not "really" black and so they go to great lengths to counter that charge. As an example, the writer Itaberi Njeri offered a moving description of her cousin Jeffrey, who looked like singer Ricky Nelson, spent his brief life trying to demonstrate that he was black and tough, and died violently as a result (Njeri, 1991). While many light-skinned black men indicate that, when they are older, their skin color puts them at an advantage in both the black and white communities, in adolescence that is certainly not the case and thus they must "flame" their identity (Russell, Wilson, and Hall, 1992).

But flaming need not have this tragic side. For example, many bilingual Latino students talk about how much they enjoy a loud display of Spanish when Anglos are present; some Asian American students have described their pleasure in pursuing extended no-English-used card games in public spaces on campus. Black students and gay students sometimes entertain themselves by loudly affecting stereotypical behavior and then watching the disapproving looks from observers. Those who do not occupy stigmatized statuses may better appreciate these displays by remembering their experience of deliberate flaming as "obnoxious teenagers" in public settings. Thus, for some flaming may also be fun.

In all, those who are visibly stigmatized—who cannot or will not hide their identity—generate a variety of mechanisms to try to neutralize that stigma. Flaming is one of those mechanisms. It both announces one's stigmatized status and proclaims one's disregard for those who judge it negatively. Flaming neutralizes stigma by denying there is anything to be ashamed of. Thus, it functions as a statement of group pride.

European Ethnic Groups and Flaming

Whites of European ancestry sometimes envy the ethnic "flaming" of African Americans, Hispanics, and Asian Americans. As one student said, "It makes me feel like I just don't have anything." While his ancestry was a mix of Russian Jew, Italian Catholic, and Scotch-Irish Protestant, none of these identities seemed as compelling as the black, Asian, and Hispanic identities he saw around him.

This student's reaction reflects the transformed ethnic identity of the grandchildren and great-grandchildren of people who arrived in the peak immigration period of 1880 to 1920. At that time, Hungarians, Bohemians, Slovaks, Czechs, Poles, Russians, and Italians differed culturally and linguistically from one another and from the Irish, German, Scandinavian, and English immigrants who preceded them.

Over the generations—and through intermarriage—this ethnic distinctiveness has been replaced by a socioeconomic "convergence" (Alba, 1990). Among non-Hispanic whites, ethnic ancestry no longer shapes occupation, residence, or political interest, nor is it the basis of the creation of communities of interest. While many enjoy ethnic food and celebrations or have strong feelings attached to stories of immigration, the attachment is not likely to be deep or have much impact on behavior. Most important, the attachment is understood in terms of the history of one's family rather than of a particular culture or nationality (Alba, 1990; Schaefer, 1990).[4]

Thus, it is possible that "European American" is emerging as a panethnic identity much like Asian American (Omi, 1996); both are identities that span a wide range of ancestries. It is also possible that as ethnic identities disappear for whites, they will be replaced by heightened attention to race. "[M]ost whites do not experience their ethnicity as a definitive aspect of their social identity. . . . The 'twilight of white ethnicity' in a racially defined, and increasingly polarized, environment means that white racial identity will grow in salience" (Omi, 1996:182).

The Expectations of Those Who Share One's Stigma

Stigma also affects interaction among those *within* the stigmatized category. From others in the category one learns a sense of group pride and cues about how to behave, what to expect from those in and outside the category, and how to protect one's self. For those stigmatized by color, sex, or social class, such coping lessons likely come from family members. For those who are gay or lesbian, the lessons are usually provided later in life by members of the gay community.

Particularly for those with visible stigma, there are also frequent reminders that one will be seen as a representative of *all* members of the category. Thus, many in stigmatized categories must factor in virtually everyone's opinion: What will others in my category think? What will those who are not stigmatized think? Indeed, one may even be criticized for failing to deal with oneself as a stigmatized person—"After all, who do you think you are?" In a sense, members of stigmatized categories may monitor one another much as they are policed by those outside the category, with the difference that those within one's category can at least claim to be operating for one's defense.

This point is illustrated in a story by the late tennis champion Arthur Ashe (1993). Ashe described watching his daughter play with a gift she had just

---

[4]An exception to the process of convergence among European-originated groups may be white, urban, Catholic ethnics. Throughout the 19th century, American Catholic churches were established as specifically ethnic churches (called "nationality churches"). These mostly urban churches were tailored to serve a particular ethnic group, which often included sending a priest from the home country who spoke the immigrants' native language. Thus, within a single urban area one might find separate Irish, Italian, and Polish Catholic churches, as well as effectively separate Catholic schools. The formation of ethnic churches meant that parishes also became ethnically segregated. On occasion, those parishes came to constitute stable, distinctive, working-class ethnic enclaves. In these cases ethnic identity continues as an active, viable reality.

received—a white doll—as they sat in the audience of a televised match in his honor. When the cameras panned his section of seats, he realized that he needed to get the doll away from his daughter or risk the anger of some black viewers who would argue that by letting his child play with a white doll, he appeared to be a bad role model for the black community.

A different example is provided by a Mexican American acquaintance who worked in an office with only a few other Hispanics, most of whom felt that the routes to upward mobility were closed to them. Together they drafted a letter to the firm's president detailing their concerns and seeking some corrective action. Although he had qualms about signing the letter, our acquaintance felt there was no alternative. Because he worked for management, he was then called in to explain his behavior, which his supervisor saw as disloyal. Thus, he was put in the position of having to explain that, as a Chicano, he could not have refused to sign the letter.

Codes of conduct for those in stigmatized categories often require loyalty to the group, a fact of life that in this case the supervisor was unaware of. Indeed, the operating rule for many in stigmatized categories is to avoid public disagreement with one another or public airing of the group's "dirty laundry." Such codes are not trivial, because when violated members of stigmatized categories risk ostracism from a critical support network. The reality of discrimination makes it foolhardy to reject those who share one's stigma. What would it have meant to Arthur Ashe to lose the support of other African Americans? To whom would our acquaintance have turned in that organization had he refused to sign the letter? When they are unaware of these pressures, those in privileged categories may make impossible demands of those who are stigmatized; when aware of these pressures, however, such requests are clear tests of loyalty.

POINTS OF CONTENTION, STAGES OF CONTENTIOUSNESS

This essay focused on how privilege and stigma yield different treatment and different world views. In this final section we will examine the differing conceptions of racism. Then we will consider the stages of identity development within which privilege and stigma are experienced.

As we said earlier, flaming sometimes leaves those who are not members of the stigmatized category feeling excluded. For example, when Latino students talked about their enjoyment of using Spanish, an Anglo friend immediately responded with a description of how excluded she felt on those occasions. While aware of this, the Latino students nonetheless made it clear that they were not willing to forgo these opportunities. Their non-Spanish-speaking friends would just have to understand that it wasn't anything personal. This may well mark the bottom line: Those who are not stigmatized will sometimes feel and be excluded by their friends.

But another question is implied here: If the Hispanics exclude the Anglos, can the Anglos similarly exclude the Hispanics? As a way to approach this, consider the following two statements about gays and straights. In what ways are they similar, and in what ways different?

A heterosexual says, "I can't stand gays. I don't want to be anywhere around them."

A gay says, "I can't stand straights. I don't want to be anywhere around them."

While the statements are almost identical, the speakers come from very different positions of power. The heterosexual could likely structure his or her life so as to rarely interact with anyone gay, or at least anyone self-identified as gay. Most important, however, the heterosexual's attitude is consistent with major social, political, legal, and religious practices. Thus, the heterosexual in this example speaks from a position of some power, if only that derived from alignment with dominant cultural practices.

This is not the case for the gay person in this example, who is unlikely to be able to avoid contact with straights—and who would probably pay a considerable economic cost for self-segregation if that were attempted. There are no powerful institutional supports for hatred of straights. Similarly, the pleasure of exclusiveness enjoyed by bilingual Latino students exists against a backdrop of relative powerlessness, discrimination, stigmatization, and the general necessity of speaking English. The same might be said of men's disparagement of women compared to women's disparagement of men. As one student wrote, "As a male I have at times been on the receiving end of comments like, 'Oh, you're just like all men,' or 'Why can't men show more emotion?' but these comments or the sentiments behind them do not carry any power to affect my status. Even in the instance of a black who sees me as a representative of all whites, his vision of me does not change my privileged status."

Thus, the exclusiveness of those in nonstigmatized statuses has as its backdrop relative powerfulness, a sense of entitlement, infrequent discrimination based on master status, and a general ability to avoid those who might be prejudiced against people like themselves. The forms of exclusion available to minority group members are unlikely to tangibly affect the lives of those in privileged statuses. Being able to exclude someone from a dance or a club is not as significant as being able to exclude that person from employment, residence, or educational institution. This is what is meant when it is said that members of stigmatized categories may be prejudiced but not racist, or sexist, etc.; they do not have access to the institutional power by which to significantly affect the lives of those in nonstigmatized groups.

The term *racist* also carries different connotations for blacks and whites. For whites being color conscious is taken as evidence of racism; those who are not color conscious are not racists (Blauner, 1992). This understanding of what it means to be a racist has its basis in the civil rights movement. If, as the civil rights movement taught, color should not make a difference in the way people are treated, whites who make a point of *not* noticing race argue that they are being polite and not racist (Frankenberg, 1993).

But given America's historical focus on race, it seems unrealistic for any of us to claim that we are oblivious to it. While many consider it impolite to mention race, differential treatment does not disappear as a consequence. Further, a refusal to notice race conveys that being black, Asian, or Latino is a "defect" that is indelicate (for whites) to mention. Thus, it can be argued that colorblindness is not really a strategy of politeness; rather, it is a strategy of power evasion. Since race clearly makes a difference in people's lives, pretending not to see it is a way to avoid noticing its effect. The alternative would be a strategy of race cognizance, that is, of paying systematic attention to the impact of race on oneself and others (Frankenberg, 1993).

Different conceptions of racism also emerge in the course of *racial and ethnic identity development,* which is the "understanding shared by members of ethnic groups, of what it means to be black, white, Chicano, Irish, Jewish, and so on" (White and Burke, 1987:311). We offer here a brief composite sketch of what appear to be the stages of this development (Cross, 1971, 1978; Hazen, 1992, 1994; Helms, 1990; Morton and Atkinson, 1983; Thomas, 1970; Thomas and Thomas, 1971). This framework might also be extended to the sex, class, disability, and sexual orientation identities we have focused on in this text. One important caution is necessary, however: Not everyone necessarily goes through each of these stages. For example, it is argued that African Americans are rarely found in the first of the stages we detail (Hazen, 1992).

For those who are stigmatized, the first stage of identity development involves an internalization of the culture's negative imagery. This stage may include the disparagement of others in one's group and a strong desire to be accepted by dominant group members. For women, this might mean being highly critical of other women. For those who are low income or gay, this stage might entail feelings of shame. For people of color, it might involve efforts to lighten one's skin, straighten one's hair, or have an eye tuck.

In the second stage, anger at the dominant culture emerges, usually as the result of specific encounters with discrimination. Philosopher Sandra Bartky (1990), focusing on women's discovery of the extent of sexism, describes this as a period in which sexism appears to be everywhere. Events and objects that previously had been neutral are discovered to be sexist; it becomes impossible to get through the day without becoming enraged—and the injustices one discovers are communicated to everyone within earshot. One's own behavior is also subject to scrutiny: "Am I being sexist to buy a doll for my niece?" Situations that used to be straightforward become moral tests.

The third stage is sometimes called an immersion stage, because it involves total involvement in one's own culture. In the previous stage, the individual is focused on evaluating and reacting to the dominant culture. In this stage, however, the focus shifts to one's own group. Dominant group members and the dominant group culture become less relevant to one's pursuits. This is often a period of participation in segregated activities and organizations as one seeks distance from dominant group members. While anger is somewhat lessened here, the process of re-evaluating one's old identity continues.

The final stage is described as a period of integration as one's stigmatized status becomes integrated with the other aspects of one's life rather than taking precedence over them. Still, an opposition to prejudice and discrimination continues. At this point, one can distinguish between supportive and unsupportive dominant group members and thus is more likely to establish satisfying relations with them.

For those who do not occupy stigmatized statuses, the first stage of race or ethnic identity development is identified as an unquestioning acceptance of dominant group values. This acceptance might take shape as being oblivious to discrimination or as espousing supremacist ideologies. In Reading 29, Thandeka posits that whiteness is produced when the white child submits to the threats of family members to obey the racial divides.

In the second stage, one becomes aware of stigmatization, often through an eye-opening encounter with discrimination. Such an experience may produce a commitment to social change or a sense of powerlessness. As is the case for those in stigmatized statuses, in this stage those in privileged statuses also find themselves overwhelmed by all the forms of discrimination they see, often accompanied by a sense of personal guilt. In an attempt to affiliate and offer assistance, they are likely to seek alliances with those in stigmatized statuses. On college campuses this timing couldn't be worse, since many of those in stigmatized statuses are at their peak level of anger at those in privileged groups.

In stage three, those in privileged statuses focus less on trying to win the approval of those in stigmatized groups and instead explore the history of privileged and stigmatized statuses. Learning how privilege has affected one's own life is often a central question in this period.

The final stage involves integrating one's privileged statuses with all the other aspects of one's life, recognizing those in stigmatized categorizations as distinctive individuals rather than romanticizing them as a category ("just because oppressors are bad, doesn't mean that the oppressed are good" [Spivak, 1994]), and understanding that many with privilege have worked effectively against discrimination.

The research on cognitive development in higher education bears interestingly on the stages of race and ethnic identity development and on the diversity of the college population. For example,

> Our analyses suggest that diversity experiences in the first year of college seem to be particularly important in developing critical thinking. Indeed, diversity experiences at the beginning of college may positively affect a student's cognitive growth throughout his or her entire college career. Finally . . . racially oriented diversity experiences may be particularly important for the critical-thinking growth of white students. Indeed, experiences like making friends with students from a different race and attending a racial or cultural awareness workshop had positive impacts on growth in critical thinking only for white men and women. (Pascarella, 2001:25)

> It is interesting that perceptions about balkanization and self-segregation are shared by many [college] students, even when the evidence suggests that students are often part of diverse networks. In his dissertation on "The Impact of Friendship Groups in a Multicultural University," Anthony Antonio found that although the students he surveyed perceived the campus to be segregated, their friendship groups tended to be racially and ethnically mixed. It appears that students see ethnic clusters but do not see the increasingly diverse peer groups that are emerging of which they are a part. It may also be

> that students on our campuses are reflecting some disappointment with the campuses' inability to capitalize fully on the potential created by increasing diversity on campus. These findings underscore the fact that individuals, groups, and institutions thrive under campus conditions that acknowledge multiple affiliations and identities and facilitate their engagement. (Smith and Schonfeld, 2000:19)

Movement through the stages of ethnic or racial identity is positively related to self-esteem for all American race and ethnic groups, but the relationship is stronger for those who are Asian American, African American, and Latino than for those who are white (Hazen, 1994:55). Indeed, on various measures of self-esteem, African Americans score significantly higher than those in other race or ethnic groups (Hazen, 1992).

We once observed an African American student explain to his white classmates that he and his sister both self-identified as black, even though their mother was white. At that point a white student asked why he didn't call himself white since he looked white and that status would yield him more privilege. In response, he detailed all the qualities he prized in the black community and said he would never give up that status to be white. Much of what he said was new to the white students; many had never thought there was anything positive about being black in America.

The student's question reflected the common assumption that those who are stigmatized wish they belonged to the privileged group. Yet the woman who asked the question was clear that she never wanted to be a male, which was equally surprising to the men in the class. Thus, many men presume there is nothing positive about being female, many straights assume there is nothing positive about being gay, many able-bodied people assume that being disabled guarantees misery and loneliness (French, 1996), and many in the middle and upper classes assume there is nothing positive in life for those who are poor. But most people value and appreciate the statuses they occupy. We may wish those statuses weren't stigmatized or overprivileged, but that does not mean we would want to be other than who we are.

THE READINGS IN THIS SECTION

Our goal in this essay was to provide you with a framework by which to make sense of people's experience of privilege and stigma. Because there is a great deal of material that illustrates privilege and stigma, the readings in this section raise general issues or concepts applicable to those in various stigmatized or privileged statuses.

KEY CONCEPTS

discredited and discreditable The discredited are those whose stigma is known or apparent to others. The discreditable are those whose stigma is unknown or invisible to others; they are not yet discredited. (pages 188–93)

double consciousness A concept first offered by W. E. B. Du Bois to describe seeing oneself (or members of one's group) through the eyes of a critical, dominant group member. (pages 191–92)

entitlement The belief that one has the right to respect, protection, reward, and other privileges. (page 182)

flaming As used in this text, a flagrant display of one's stigmatized status; more often used to refer to gay men acting effeminately. (pages 190–93)

looping or rereading Interpreting (and usually dismissing) someone's words or actions because of the status that the person occupies. (page 184)

marked and unmarked statuses A marked status is one identified as "special" in some way, for example, a *blind* musician or a *woman* doctor. Unmarked statuses, such as musician or doctor, do not have such qualifiers. (page 182)

passing Not revealing a stigmatized identity. (pages 188–90)

privilege The advantages provided by some statuses. (pages 177–85)

REFERENCES

Alba, Richard D. 1990. *Ethnic Identity: The Transformation of White America.* New Haven, CT: Yale University Press.

Amnesty International. 1997. *Amnesty International Death Penalty Developments in the U.S.A. in 1997.* www.amnesty-usa/abolish/race.html.

Ashe, Arthur. 1993. *Days of Grace.* New York: Ballantine.

Bartky, Sandra. 1990. *Femininity and Domination: Studies in the Phenomenology of Oppression.* New York: Routledge.

Berke, Richard. 1998. Chasing the Polls on Gay Rights. *New York Times,* August 2, 4:3.

Blauner, Bob. 1992. Talking Past Each Other: Black and White Languages of Race. *The American Prospect,* Summer.

Cary, Lorene. 1991. *Black Ice.* New York: Knopf.

Cross, H., G. Kenney, J. Mell, and W. Zimmerman. 1990. *Employer Practices: Differential Treatment of Hispanic and Anglo Job Seekers.* Washington, DC: The Urban Institute.

Cross, W. E., Jr. 1971. The Negro-to-Black Conversion Experience: Toward a Psychology of Black Liberation. *Black World,* 20 (9):13–17.

———. 1978. The Thomas and Cross Models of Psychological Nigresence: A Review. *The Journal of Black Psychology,* 5 (1):13–31.

Davis, F. James. 1991. *Who Is Black? One Nation's Definition.* University Park, PA: Pennsylvania University Press.

Du Bois, W. E. B. 1982. *The Souls of Black Folk.* New York: Penguin. (Originally published in 1903.)

Ettinger, Maia. 1994. The Pocahontas Paradigm, or Will the Subaltern Please Shut Up? *Tilting the Tower,* edited by Linda Garber, 51–55. New York: Routledge.

Fields, Robin, and Ray Herndon. 2001. Segregation of a New Sort Takes Shape. *Los Angeles Times,* July 5, A1–A17.

Fletcher, Michael A. 1999. USDA Settlement Too Little, Too Late for Many Black Farmers. *Washington Post,* January 10, A:10.

Frankenberg, Ruth. 1993. *White Women, Race Matters: The Social Construction of Whiteness.* Minneapolis: University of Minnesota Press.

French, Sally. 1996. Simulation Exercises in Disability Awareness Training: A Critique. *Beyond Disability: Towards an Enabling Society,* edited by Gerald Hales, 114–23. London: Sage Publications.

Goffman, Erving. 1961. *Asylums.* New York: Doubleday Anchor.

———. 1963. *Stigma: Notes on the Management of Spoiled Identity.* Englewood Cliffs, NJ: Prentice-Hall.

Goldstein, Auram. 1999. G.U. Study Finds Disparity in Heart Care. *Washington Post,* February 25, A:1, 13.

Hare, Nathan. 1982. W. E. Burghart Du Bois: An Appreciation, pp. xiii–xxvii in *The Souls of Black Folk.* New York: Penguin. (Originally published in 1969.)

Hazen, Sharlie Hogue. 1992. *The Relationship between Ethnic/Racial Identity Development and Ego Identity Development.* Ph.D. proposal, Department of Psychology, George Mason University.

———. 1994. *The Relationship between Ethnic/Racial Identity Development and Ego Identity Development.* Ph.D. dissertation, Department of Psychology, George Mason University.

Helms, J. E. 1990. An Overview of Black Racial Identity Theory. *Black and White Racial Identity: Theory, Research, and Practice,* edited by J. E. Helms, 9–33. New York: Greenwood Press.

Herek, Gregory M. 1992. The Social Context of Hate Crimes. *Hate Crimes: Confronting Violence against Lesbians and Gay Men,* edited by Gregory Herek and Kevin Berrill, 89–104. Newbury Park, CA: Sage.

———, and Eric K. Glunt. 1993. Heterosexuals Who Know Gays Personally Have More Favorable Attitudes. *The Journal of Sex Research,* 30:239–44.

Hochschild, Jennifer L. 1995. *Facing Up to the American Dream.* Princeton, NJ: Princeton University Press.

hooks, bell. 1989. *Talking Back: Thinking Feminist, Thinking Black.* Boston: South End Press.

Kanter, Rosabeth Moss. 1993. *Men and Women of the Corporation.* New York: Basic Books. (Originally published in 1976.)

———, with Barry A. Stein. 1980. *A Tale of 'O': On Being Different in an Organization.* New York: Harper and Row.

Kennedy, Florynce. 1976. *Color Me Flo: My Hard Life and Good Times.* Englewood Cliffs, NJ: Prentice-Hall.

Kimmel, Michael S., and Michael A. Messner, eds. 1989. *Men's Lives.* New York: Macmillan.

Kornheiser, Tony. 1990. The Ordinary Face of Racism. *Washington Post,* May 16, F:1, 9.

Lapchick, Richard E., and Kevin J. Matthews. 2001. *2001 Racial and Gender Report Card.* Northeastern University, Center for Sport in Society. www.sportinsociety.org/rgrc2001.html.

Lester, Joan. 1994. *The Future of White Men and Other Diversity Dilemmas.* Berkeley, CA: Conari Press.

McIntosh, Peggy. 1988. White Privilege and Male Privilege: A Personal Account of Coming to See Correspondences through Work in Women's Studies. Working Paper Number 189, Wellesley College, Center for Research on Women, Wellesley, MA.

Montgomery, Lori, 2001. New Police Policies Aim to Discourage Racial Profiling. *Washington Post,* June 28, A1.

Morton, G., and D. R. Atkinson. 1983. Minority Identity Development and Preference for Counselor Race. *Journal of Negro Education,* 52(2):156–61.

National Opinion Research Center. 1990. *An American Profile: Opinions and Behavior 1972–1989.* Detroit: Gale Research.

Njeri, Itaberi. 1991. Who Is Black? *Essence,* September, 64–66, 114–16.

Omi, Michael. 1996. Racialization in the Post–Civil Rights Era. *Mapping Multiculturalism,* edited by Avery F. Gordon and Christopher Newfield, 178–86. Minneapolis: University of Minnesota Press.

Pascarella, Ernest T. 2001. Cognitive Growth in College. *Change,* November–December, 21–27.

Rosenhan, D. L. 1973. On Being Sane in Insane Places. *Science,* 179:250–58.

Russell, Kathy, Midge Wilson, and Ronald Hall. 1992. *The Color Complex: The Politics of Skin Color among African Americans.* New York: Harcourt Brace Jovanovich.

Schaefer, Richard T. 1990. *Racial and Ethnic Groups.* 4th ed. Glenview, IL: Scott, Foresman/Little, Brown Higher Education.

Schafer, Sarah. 2000. Coke to Pay $193 Million in Bias Suit. *Washington Post,* November 17, A1–A17.

Schur, Edwin. 1984. *Labeling Women Deviant: Gender, Stigma, and Social Control.* New York: Random House.

Sedgwick, Eve Kosofsky. 1990. *The Epistemology of the Closet.* Berkeley: University of California Press.

Sichelman, Lew. 1999. Mortgage Discrimination Is Alive and Well. *Realty Times,* October 4. www.realtytimes.com/.

Smith, Daryl G., and Natalie B. Schonfeld. 2000. The Benefits of Diversity: What the Research Tells Us. *About Campus,* November–December, 16–23.

Smith, Tom W. 2001. *Intergroup Relations in a Diverse America: Data from the 2000 General Social Survey.* The American Jewish Committee. www.ajc.org.

Sniderman, Paul M., and Edward G. Carmines. 1997. *Reaching beyond Race.* Cambridge, MA: Harvard University Press.

Solomon, Jolie. 1996. Texaco's Troubles. *Newsweek,* November 25, 48–50.

Spelman, Elizabeth. 1988. *Inessential Woman.* Boston: Beacon Press.

Spivak, Gayatre. 1994. George Mason University Cultural Studies presentation.

Thomas, C. 1970. Different Strokes for Different Folks. *Psychology Today* 4(4):48–53, 78–80.

——, and S. Thomas. 1971. Something Borrowed, Something Black. In *Boys No More: A Black Psychologist's View of Community,* edited by C. Thomas. Beverly Hills, CA: Glencoe Press.

Turner, Margery Austin, Michael Fix, and Raymond J. Struyk. 1991. *Opportunities Denied, Opportunities Diminished: Discrimination in Hiring.* Washington, DC: The Urban Institute.

U.S. Bureau of the Census. 1997. *Money Income in the United States.* Washington, DC: U.S. Government Printing Office.

U.S. Department of Commerce. 1993. *Statistical Abstract of the United States, 1992.* Washington, DC: U.S. Government Printing Office.

U.S. Department of Labor, Bureau of Labor Statistics. 1993. *Employment and Earnings.* Washington, DC: U.S. Government Printing Office

White, C. L., and P. J. Burke. 1987. Ethnic Role Identity among Black and White College Students: An Interactionist Approach. *Sociological Perspectives,* 30(3):310–31.

Williams, Patricia J. 1991. Teleology on the Rocks. *The Alchemy of Race and Rights.* Cambridge, MA: Harvard University Press.

READING 19

What Are You?

Joanne Nobuko Miyamoto

when I was young
kids used to ask me
what are you?
I'd tell them what my mom told me
I'm an American
chin, chin, Chinaman
you're a Jap!
flashing hot inside
I'd go home
my mom would say
don't worry
he who walks alone
walks faster

people kept asking me
what are you?
and I would always answer
I'm an American
they'd say
no, what nationality
I'm an American!
that's where I was born
flashing hot inside

and when I'd tell them what they wanted to know
Japanese
. . . Oh, I've been to Japan

I'd get it over with
me they could catalogue and file me
pigeon hole me
so they'd know just how
to think of me
priding themselves
they could guess the difference
between Japanese and Chinese

they had me wishing
I was American
just like them
they had me wishing I was what I'd
been seeing in movies and on TV
on bill boards and in magazines
and I tried

while they were making laws in California
against us owning land
we were trying to be american
and laws against us intermarrying with white people
we were trying to be american
our people volunteered to fight against
their own country
trying to be american
when they dropped the atom bomb
Hiroshima and Nagasaki
we were still trying

finally we made it
most of our parents
fiercely dedicated to give us
a good education
to give us everything they never had
we made it

now they use us as an example
to the blacks and browns
how we made it
how we overcame

but there was always
someone asking me
what are you?

Now I answer
I'm an Asian
and they say
why do you want to separate yourselves
now I say
I'm Japanese
and they say
don't you know this is the greatest country
in the world
Now I say in america
I'm part of the third world people
and they say
if you don't like it here
why don't you go back.

No biographical material available.

READING 20

Oppression

Marilyn Frye

It is a fundamental claim of feminism that women are oppressed. The word "oppression" is a strong word. It repels and attracts. It is dangerous and dangerously fashionable and endangered. It is much misused, and sometimes not innocently.

The statement that women are oppressed is frequently met with the claim that men are oppressed too. We hear that oppressing is oppressive to those who oppress as well as to those they oppress. Some men cite as evidence of their oppression their much-advertised inability to cry. It is tough, we are told, to be masculine. When the stresses and frustrations of being a man are cited as evidence that oppressors are oppressed by their oppressing, the word "oppression" is being stretched to meaninglessness; it is treated as though its scope includes any and all human experience of limitation or suffering, no matter the cause, degree or consequence. Once such usage has been put over on us, then if ever we deny that any person or group is oppressed, we seem to imply that we think they never suffer and have no feelings. We are accused of insensitivity; even of bigotry. For women, such accusation is particularly intimidating, since sensitivity is one of the few virtues that has been assigned to us. If we are found insensitive, we may fear we have no redeeming traits at all and perhaps are not real women. Thus are we silenced before we begin: the name of our situation drained of meaning and our guilt mechanisms tripped.

But this is nonsense. Human beings can be miserable without being oppressed, and it is perfectly consistent to deny that a person or group is oppressed without denying that they have feelings or that they suffer.

We need to think clearly about oppression, and there is much that mitigates against this. I do not want to undertake to prove that women are oppressed (or that men are not), but I want to make clear what is being said when we say it. We need this word, this concept, and we need it to be sharp and sure.

The root of the word "oppression" is the element "press." *The press of the crowd; pressed into military service; to press a pair of pants; printing press; press the button.* Presses are used to mold things or flatten them or reduce them in bulk, sometimes to reduce them by squeezing out the gasses or liquids in them. Something pressed is something caught between or among forces and barriers which are so related to each other that jointly they restrain, restrict or prevent the thing's motion or mobility. Mold. Immobilize. Reduce.

The mundane experience of the oppressed provides another clue. One of the most characteristic and ubiquitous features of the world as experienced by oppressed people is the double bind situations in which options are reduced to a very few and all of them expose one to penalty, censure or deprivation. For example, it is often a requirement upon oppressed people that we smile and be cheerful. If we comply, we signal our docility and our acquiescence in our situation. We need not, then, be taken note of. We acquiesce in being made invisible, in our occupying no space. We participate in our own erasure. On the other hand, anything but the sunniest countenance exposes us to being perceived as mean, bitter, angry or dangerous. This means, at the least, that we may be found "difficult" or unpleasant to work with, which is enough to cost one one's livelihood; at worst, being seen as mean, bitter, angry or dangerous has been known to result in rape, arrest, beating and murder. One can only choose to risk one's preferred form and rate of annihilation.

Marilyn Frye is a professor of feminist philosophy at Michigan State University.

Another example: It is common in the United States that women, especially younger women, are in a bind where neither sexual activity nor sexual inactivity is all right. If she is heterosexually active, a woman is open to censure and punishment for being loose, unprincipled or a whore. The "punishment" comes in the form of criticism, snide and embarrassing remarks, being treated as an easy lay by men, scorn from her more restrained female friends. She may have to lie and hide her behavior from her parents. She must juggle the risks of unwanted pregnancy and dangerous contraceptives. On the other hand, if she refrains from heterosexual activity, she is fairly constantly harassed by men who try to persuade her into it and pressure her to "relax" and "let her hair down"; she is threatened with labels like "frigid," "uptight," "manhater," "bitch" and "cocktease." The same parents who would be disapproving of her sexual activity may be worried by her inactivity because it suggests she is not or will not be popular, or is not sexually normal. She may be charged with lesbianism. If a woman is raped, then if she has been heterosexually active she is subject to the presumption that she liked it (since her activity is presumed to show that she likes sex), and if she has not been heterosexually active, she is subject to the presumption that she liked it (since she is supposedly "repressed and frustrated"). Both heterosexual activity and heterosexual nonactivity are likely to be taken as proof that you wanted to be raped, and hence, of course, weren't *really* raped at all. You can't win. You are caught in a bind, caught between systematically related pressures.

Women are caught like this, too, by networks of forces and barriers that expose one to penalty, loss or contempt whether one works outside the home or not, is on welfare or not, bears children or not, raises children or not, marries or not, stays married or not, is heterosexual, lesbian, both or neither. Economic necessity; confinement to racial and/or sexual job ghettos; sexual harassment; sex discrimination; pressures of competing expectations and judgments about *women, wives* and *mothers* (in the society at large, in racial and ethnic subcultures and in one's own mind); dependence (full or partial) on husbands, parents or the state; commitment to political ideas; loyalties to racial or ethnic or other "minority" groups; the demands of self-respect and responsibilities to others. Each of these factors exists in complex tension with every other, penalizing or prohibiting all of the apparently available options. And nipping at one's heels, always, is the endless pack of little things. If one dresses one way, one is subject to the assumption that one is advertising one's sexual availability; if one dresses another way, one appears to "not care about oneself" or to be "unfeminine." If one uses "strong language," one invites categorization as a whore or slut; if one does not, one invites categorization as a "lady," one too delicately constituted to cope with robust speech or the realities to which it presumably refers.

The experience of oppressed people is that the living of one's life is confined and shaped by forces and barriers which are not accidental or occasional and hence avoidable, but are systematically related to each other in such a way as to catch one between and among them and restrict or penalize motion in any direction. It is the experience of being caged in: all avenues, in every direction, are blocked or booby trapped.

Cages. Consider a birdcage. If you look very closely at just one wire in the cage, you cannot see the other wires. If your conception of what is before you is determined by this myopic focus, you could look at that one wire, up and down the length of it, and be unable to see why a bird would not just fly around the wire any time it wanted to go somewhere. Furthermore, even if, one day at a time, you myopically inspected each wire, you still could not see why a bird would have trouble going past the wires to get anywhere. There is no physical property of any one wire, *nothing* that the closest scrutiny could discover, that will reveal how a bird could be inhibited or harmed by it except in the most accidental way. It is only when you step back, stop looking at the wires one by one, microscopically, and take a macroscopic view of the whole cage, that you can see why the bird does not go anywhere; and then you will see it in a moment. It will require no great subtlety of mental powers. It is perfectly *obvious* that the bird is surrounded by a network of systematically related barriers, no one of which would be the least hindrance to its flight, but which, by their relations to each other, are as confining as the solid walls of a dungeon.

It is now possible to grasp one of the reasons why oppression can be hard to see and recognize: one can study the elements of an oppressive structure with great care and some good will without seeing the structure as a whole, and hence without seeing or being able to understand that one is looking at a cage and that there are people there who are caged, whose motion and mobility are restricted, whose lives are shaped and reduced.

The arresting of vision at a microscopic level yields such common confusion as that about the male door opening ritual. This ritual, which is remarkably widespread across classes and races, puzzles many people, some of whom do and some of whom do not find it offensive. Look at the scene of the two people approaching a door. The male steps slightly ahead and opens the door. The male holds the door open while the female glides through. Then the male goes through. The door closes after them. "Now how," one innocently asks, "can those crazy womenslibbers say that is oppressive? The guy *removed* a barrier to the lady's smooth and unruffled progress." But each repetition of this ritual has a place in a pattern, in fact in several patterns. One has to shift the level of one's perception in order to see the whole picture.

The door-opening pretends to be a helpful service, but the helpfulness is false. This can be seen by noting that it will be done whether or not it makes any practical sense. Infirm men and men burdened with packages will open doors for able bodied women who are free of physical burdens. Men will impose themselves awkwardly and jostle everyone in order to get to the door first. The act is not determined by convenience or grace. Furthermore, these very numerous acts of unneeded or even noisome "help" occur in counterpoint to a pattern of men not being helpful in many practical ways in which women might welcome help. What *women* experience is a world in which gallant princes charming commonly make a fuss about being helpful and providing small services when help and services are of little or no use, but in which there are rarely ingenious and adroit princes at hand when substantial assistance is really wanted either in mundane affairs or in situations of threat, assault or terror. There is no help with the (his) laundry; no help typing a report at 4:00 a.m.; no help in mediating disputes among relatives or children. There is nothing but advice that women should stay indoors after dark, be chaperoned by a man, or when it comes down to it, "lie back and enjoy it."

The gallant gestures have no practical meaning. Their meaning is symbolic. The door-opening and similar services provided are services which really are needed by people who are for one reason or another incapacitated—unwell, burdened with parcels, etc. So the message is that women are incapable. The detachment of the acts from the concrete realities of what women need and do not need is a vehicle for the message that women's actual needs and interests are unimportant or irrelevant. Finally, these gestures imitate the behavior of servants toward masters and thus mock women, who are in most respects the servants and caretakers of men. The message of the false helpfulness of male gallantry is female dependence, the invisibility or insignificance of women, and contempt for women.

One cannot see the meanings of these rituals if one's focus is riveted upon the individual event in all its particularity, including the particularity of the individual man's present conscious intentions and motives and the individual woman's conscious perception of the event in the moment. It seems sometimes that people take a deliberately myopic view and fill their eyes with things seen microscopically in order not to see macroscopically. At any rate, whether it is deliberate or not, people can and do fail to see the oppression of women because they fail to see macroscopically and hence fail to see the various elements of the situation as systematically related in larger schemes.

As the cageness of the birdcage is a macroscopic phenomenon, the oppressiveness of the situations in which women live our various and different lives is a macroscopic phenomenon. Neither can be *seen* from a microscopic perspective. But when you look macroscopically you can see it a network of forces and barriers which are systematically related and which conspire to the immobilization, reduction and molding of women and the lives we live. . . .

It seems to be the human condition that in one degree or another we all suffer frustration and limitation, all encounter unwelcome barriers, and all are damaged and hurt in various ways. Since we are a social species, almost all of our behavior and activities are structured by more than individual inclination and the conditions of the planet and its atmosphere. No human is free of social structures, nor (perhaps) would happiness consist in such freedom. Structure consists of boundaries, limits and barriers; in a structured whole, some motions and changes are possible, and others are not. If one is looking for an excuse to dilute the word "oppression," one can use the fact of social structure as an excuse and say that everyone is oppressed. But if one would rather get clear about what oppression is and is not, one needs to sort out the sufferings, harms and limitations and figure out which are elements of oppression and which are not.

From what I have already said here, it is clear that if one wants to determine whether a particular suffering, harm or limitation is part of someone's being oppressed, one has to look at it *in context* in order to tell whether it is an element in an oppressive structure: one has to see if it is part of an enclosing structure of forces and barriers which tends to the immobilization and reduction of a group or category of people. One has to look at how the barrier or force fits with others and to whose benefit or detriment it works. As soon as one looks at examples, it becomes obvious that not everything which frustrates or limits a person is oppressive, and not every harm or damage is due to or contributes to oppression.

If a rich white playboy who lives off income from his investments in South African diamond mines should break a leg in a skiing accident at Aspen and wait in pain in a blizzard for hours before he is rescued, we may assume that in that period he suffers. But the suffering comes to an end; his leg is repaired by the best surgeon money can buy and he is soon recuperating in a lavish suite, sipping Chivas Regal. Nothing in this picture suggests a structure of barriers and forces. He is a member of several oppressor groups and does not suddenly become oppressed because he is injured and in pain. Even if the accident was caused by someone's malicious negligence, and hence someone can be blamed for it and morally faulted, that person still has not been an agent of oppression.

Consider also the restriction of having to drive one's vehicle on a certain side of the road. There is no doubt that this restriction is almost unbearably frustrating at times, when one's lane is not moving and the other lane is clear. There are surely times, even, when abiding by this regulation would have harmful consequences. But the restriction is obviously wholesome for most of us most of the time. The restraint is imposed for our benefit, and does benefit us; its operation tends to encourage our *continued* motion, not to immobilize us. The limits imposed by traffic regulations are limits most of us would cheerfully impose on ourselves given that we knew others would follow them too. They are part of a structure which shapes our behavior, not to our reduction and immobilization, but rather to the protection of our continued ability to move and act as we will.

Another example: The boundaries of a racial ghetto in an American city serve to some extent to keep white people from going in, as well as to keep ghetto dwellers from going out. A particular white citizen may be frustrated or feel deprived because s/he cannot stroll around there and enjoy the "exotic" aura of a "foreign" culture, or shop for bargains in the ghetto swap shops. In fact, the existence of the ghetto, of racial segregation, does deprive the white person of knowledge and harm her/his character by nurturing unwarranted feelings of superiority. But this does not make the white person in this situation a member of an oppressed race or a person oppressed because of her/his race. One must look at the barrier. It limits the activities and the access of those on both sides of it (though to different degrees). But it is a product of the intention, planning and action of whites for the benefit of whites, to secure and maintain privileges that are available to whites generally, as members of the dominant and privileged group. Though the existence of the barrier has some bad consequences for whites, the barrier does not exist in systematic relationship with other barriers and forces forming a structure oppressive to whites; quite the contrary. It is part of a structure which oppresses the ghetto dwellers and thereby (and by white intention) protects and furthers white interests as dominant white culture understands them. This barrier is not oppressive to whites, even though it is a barrier to whites.

Barriers have different meanings to those on opposite sides of them, even though they are barriers to both. The physical walls of a prison no more dissolve to let an outsider in than to let an insider out, but for the insider they are confining and limiting while to the outsider they may mean protection from what s/he takes to be threats posed by insiders—freedom from harm or anxiety. A set of social and economic barriers and forces separating two groups may be felt, even painfully, by members of both groups and yet may mean confinement to one and liberty and enlargement of opportunity to the other.

The service sector of the wives/mommas/assistants/girls is almost exclusively a woman-only sector; its boundaries not only enclose women but to a very great extent keep men out. Some men sometimes encounter this barrier and experience it as a restriction on their movements, their activities, their control or their choices of "lifestyle." Thinking they might like the simple nurturant life (which they may imagine to be quite free of stress, alienation and hard work), and feeling deprived since it seems closed to them, they thereupon announce the discovery that they are oppressed, too, by "sex roles." But that barrier is erected and maintained by men, for the benefit of men. It consists of cultural and economic forces and pressures in a culture and economy controlled by men in which, at every economic level and in all racial and ethnic subcultures, economy, tradition—and even ideologies of liberation—work to keep at least local culture and economy in male control.*. . .

*Of course this is complicated by race and class. Machismo and "Black manhood" politics seem to help keep Latin or Black men in control of more cash than Latin or Black women control; but these politics seem to me also to ultimately help keep the larger economy in *white* male control.

READING 21

"Can You See the Rainbow?" The Roots of Denial

Sally French

CHILDHOOD

Some of my earliest memories are of anxious relatives trying to get me to see things. I did not understand why it was so important that I should

Sally French is a lecturer in health and social welfare at the Open University in England.

do so, but was acutely aware of their intense anxiety if I could not. It was aesthetic things like rainbows that bothered them most. They would position me with great precision, tilting my head to precisely the right angle, and then point to the sky saying "Look, there it is; look, there, there . . . THERE!" As far as I was concerned there was nothing there, but if I said as much their anxiety grew even more intense; they would rearrange my position and the whole scenario would be repeated.

In the end, despite a near total lack of colour vision and a complete indifference to the rainbow's whereabouts, I would say I could see it. In that way I was able to release the mounting tension and escape to pursue more interesting tasks. It did not take long to learn that in order to avert episodes such as these and to protect the feelings of the people around me, I had to deny my disability.

The adults would also get very perturbed if ever I looked "abnormal." Being told to open my eyes and straighten my face, when all I was doing was trying to see, made me feel ugly and separate. Having adults pretend that I could see more than I could, and having to acquiesce in the pretence, was a theme throughout my childhood.

Adults who were not emotionally involved with the issue of whether or not I could see also led me along the path of denial. This was achieved by their tendency to disbelieve me and interpret my behavior as "playing up" when I told them I could not see. Basically they were confused and unable to cope with the ambiguities of partial sight and were not prepared to take instruction on the matter from a mere child. One example of this occurred in the tiny country primary school that I attended. On warm, sunny days we had our lessons outdoors where, because of the strong sunlight, I could not see to read, write or draw. It was only when the two teachers realized I was having similar difficulties eating my dinner that they began to doubt their interpretation that I was a malingerer. On several occasions I was told off by opticians when I failed to discriminate between the different lenses they placed before my eyes. I am not sure whether they really disbelieved me or whether their professional pride was hurt when nothing they could offer seemed to help; whatever it was I rapidly learned to say "better" or "worse," even though all the lenses looked the same.

It was also very difficult to tell the adults, when they had scraped together the money and found the time to take me to the pantomime or wherever, that it was a frustrating and boring experience. I had a strong sense of spoiling other people's fun, just as a sober person among a group of drunken friends may have. As a child, explaining my situation without appearing disagreeable, sullen and rude was so problematic that I usually denied my disability and suffered in silence. All of this taught me from a very early age that, while the adults were working themselves up about whether or not I could see rainbows, my own anxieties must never be shared.

These anxieties were numerous and centered on getting lost, being slow, not managing and, above all, looking stupid and displaying fear. I tried very hard to be "normal," to be anonymous and to merge with the crowd. Beaches were a nightmare; finding my way back from the sea to specific people in the absence of landmarks was almost impossible, yet giving in to panic was too shameful to contemplate. Anticipation of difficulties could cause even greater anguish than the difficulties themselves and was sufficient to ruin whole days. The prospect of outings with lots of sighted children to unfamiliar places was enough to make me physically ill, and with a bewildering mix of remorse and relief, I would stay at home.

Brownie meetings were worrying if any degree of independent movement was allowed; in the summer when we left the confines and safety of our hut to play on the nearby common, the other children would immediately disperse, leaving me alone among the trees, feeling stupid and frightened and wondering what to do next. The adults were always adamant that I should join in, that I should not miss out on the fun, but how much they or the other children noticed my difficulties I do not know; I was never teased or blamed for them, they were simply never discussed, at least not with me. This lack of communication gave me a powerful unspoken message that my disability must be denied.

By denying the reality of my disability I protected myself from the anxiety, disapproval, frustration and disappointment of the adults in my life. Like most children I wanted their acceptance, approval and warmth, and quickly learned that this could best be gained by colluding with their perceptions of my situation. I denied my disability in response to their denial, which was often motivated by a benign attempt to integrate me in a world which they perceived as fixed. My denial of disability was thus not a psychopathological reaction, but a sensible and rational response to the peculiar situation I was in.

Special School

Attending special school at the age of nine was, in many ways, a great relief. Despite the crocodile walks,[1] the bells, the long separations from home, the regimentation and the physical punishment, it was an enormous joy to be with other partially sighted children and to be in an environment where limited sight was simply not an issue. I discovered that many other children shared my world and, despite the harshness of institutional life, I felt relaxed, made lots of friends, became more confident and thrived socially. For the first time in my life I was a standard product and it felt very good. The sighted adults who looked after us were few in number with purely custodial roles, and although they seemed to be in a permanent state of anger, provided we stayed out of trouble we were basically ignored. We lived peer-orientated, confined and unchallenging lives where lack of sight rarely as much as entered our heads.

Although the reality of our disabilities was not openly denied in this situation, the only thing guaranteed to really enthuse the staff was the slightest glimmer of hope that our sight could be improved. Contact lenses were an innovation at this time, and children who had previously been virtually ignored were nurtured, encouraged and congratulated, as they learned to cope with them, and were told how good they looked without their glasses on. After I had been at the school for about a year, I was selected as one of the guinea-pigs for the experimental "telescopic lenses" which were designed, at least in part, to preserve our postures (with which there was obsessive concern) by enabling us to read and write from a greater distance. For most of us they did not work.

I remember being photographed wearing the lenses by an American man whom I perceived to be very important. First of all he made me knit while wearing them, with the knitting held right down on my lap. This was easy as I could in any case knit without looking. He was unduly excited and enthusiastic and told me how much the lenses were helping. I knew he was wrong. Then he asked me to read, but this changed his mood completely; he became tense, and before taking the photograph he pushed the book, which was a couple of inches from my face, quite roughly to my knees. Although I knew he had cheated and that what he had done was wrong, I still felt culpable for his displeasure and aware that I had failed an important test.

We were forced to use equipment like the telescopic lenses even though it did not help, and sometimes actually made things worse; the behavior of the adults clearly conveyed the message, "You are not acceptable as you are." If we dared to reject the equipment we were reminded of the cost, and asked to reflect on the clever and dedicated people who were tirelessly working for the benefit of ungrateful creatures like ourselves. No heed was ever taken of our own suggestions; my requests to try tinted lenses were always ignored and it was not until I left school that I discovered how helpful they would be.

The only other times that lack of sight became an issue for us at the school were during the rare and clumsy attempts to integrate us with able-bodied children. The worst possible activity, netball,[2] was usually chosen for this. These occasions were invariably embarrassing and humiliating for all concerned and could lead to desperate maneuvers on the part of the adults to deny the reality of our situation—namely that we had insufficient sight to compete. I am reminded of one netball match, with the score around 20/nil, during which we overheard the games mistress[3] of the opposing team anxiously insisting that they let us get some goals. It was a mortifying experience to see the ball fall through the net while they stood idly by. Very occasionally local Brownies would join us for activities in our extensive grounds. We would be paired off with them for a treasure hunt through the woods, searching for milk-bottle tops—the speed at which they found them was really quite amazing. They seemed to know about us, though, and would be very kind and point the "treasure" out, and even let us pick it up ourselves sometimes, but relying on their bounty spoiled the fun and we wished we could just talk to them or play a different game.

Whether the choice of these highly visual activities was a deliberate denial of our disabilities or simply a lack of imagination on the part of the adults, I do not know. Certainly we played such games successfully among ourselves, and as we were never seen in any other context, perhaps it was the latter. It was only on rare occasions such as these that our lack of sight (which had all but been forgotten) and the artificiality of our world became apparent.

As well as denying the reality of their disabilities, disabled children are frequently forced to deny painful feelings associated with their experiences because their parents and other adults simply cannot cope with them. I am reminded of a friend who, at the age of six or seven, was repeatedly promised expensive toys and new dresses provided she did not cry when taken back to school; we knew exactly how we must behave. Protecting the feelings of the adults we cared about became an arduous responsibility which we exercised with care.

Bravery and stoicism were demanded by the institution too; any outward expression of sadness was not merely ridiculed and scorned, it was simply not allowed. Any hint of dejection led to stern reminders that, unlike most children, we were highly privileged to be living in such a splendid house with such fantastic grounds—an honor which was clearly not our due. There was no one to turn to for comfort or support, and any tears which were shed were, of necessity, silent and private. In contrast to this, the institution, normally so indifferent to life outside its gates, was peculiarly concerned about our parents' states of mind. Our letters were meticulously censored to remove any trace of despondency and the initial letter of each term had a compulsory first sentence: "I have settled down at school and am well and happy." Not only were we compelled to deny our disabilities, but also the painful feelings associated with the lifestyles forced upon us because we were disabled.

Such was our isolation at this school that issues of how to behave in the "normal" world were rarely addressed, but at the next special school I attended, which offered a grammar school education and had an entirely different ethos, much attention was paid to this. The headmaster, a strong, resolute pioneer in the education of partially sighted children, appeared to have a genuine belief not only that we were as good as everyone else, but that we were almost certainly better, and he spent his life tirelessly battling with people who did not share his view.

He liked us to regard ourselves as sighted and steered us away from any connection with blindness; for example, although we were free to go out by ourselves to the nearby town and beyond, the use of white canes was never suggested although many of us use them now. He delighted in people who broke new, visually challenging ground, like acceptance at art school or reading degrees in mathematics, and "blind" occupations, like physiotherapy, were rarely encouraged. In many ways his attitudes and behaviour were refreshing, yet he placed the onus to achieve and succeed entirely on ourselves; there was never any suggestion that the world could adapt, or that our needs could or should be accommodated. The underlying message was always the same: "Be superhuman and deny your disability."

ADULTHOOD

In adulthood, most of these pressures to deny disability persist, though they become more subtle and harder to perceive. If disabled adults manage to gain control of their lives, which for many is very difficult, these pressures may be easier to resist. This is because situations which pose difficulties, create anxieties or cause boredom can be avoided, or alternatively adequate assistance can be sought; many of the situations I was placed in as a child I now avoid. As adults we are less vulnerable and less dependent on other people, we can more easily comprehend our situation, and our adult status makes the open expression of other people's disapproval, frustration and disbelief less likely. In addition, disabled adults arouse less emotion and misplaced optimism than disabled children, which serves to dilute the insatiable drive of many professionals to cure or "improve" us. Having said this, many of the problems experienced by disabled adults are similar to those experienced by disabled children.

Disabled adults frequently provoke anxiety and embarrassment in others simply by their presence. Although they become very skillful at dealing with this, it is often achieved at great cost to themselves by denying their disabilities and needs. It is not unusual for disabled people to endure boredom or distress to safeguard the feelings of others. They may, for example, sit through lectures without hearing or seeing rather than embarrass the lecturer, or endure being carried rather than demanding an accessible venue. In situations such as these reassuring phrases such as "I'm all right" or "Don't worry about me" become almost automatic.

One of the reasons we react in this way, rather than being assertive about our disabilities, is to avoid the disapproval, rejection and adverse labeling of others, just as we did when we were children. Our reactions are viewed as resulting from our impairments rather than from the ways we have been treated. Thus being "up front" about disability and the needs which emanate from it can easily lead us to be labeled "awkward," "selfish" or "warped." Such labeling is very difficult to endure without becoming guilty, anxious and depressed; it eats away at our confidence, undermining our courage and leading us to deny our disabilities.

Disbelief remains a common response of able-bodied people when we attempt to convey the reality of our disabilities. If, for example, I try to explain my difficulty in coping with new environments, the usual response is, "Don't worry we all get lost" or "It looks as if you're doing fine to me." Or when I try to convey the feelings of isolation associated with not recognizing people or not knowing what is going on around me, the usual response is "You will in time" or "It took me ages too." This type of response renders disabled people "just like everyone else." For those of us disabled from birth or early childhood, where there is no experience of "normality" with which to compare our situation, knowing how different we really are is problematic and it is easy to become confused and to have our confidence undermined when others insist we are just the same.

An example of denial through disbelief occurred when I was studying a statistics component as part of a course in psychology. I could see absolutely nothing of what was going on in the lectures and yet my frequent and articulate requests for help were met with the response that all students panic about statistics and that everything would work out fine in the end. As it happens it did, but only after spending many hours with a private tutor. As people are generally not too concerned about how we "got there," our successes serve to reinforce the erroneous assumption that we really are "just like everyone else." When I finally passed the examination, the lecturer concerned informed me, in a jocular and patronizing way, that my worries had clearly been unfounded! When people deny our disabilities they deny who we really are.

This tendency to disbelieve is exacerbated by the ambiguous nature of impairments such as partial sight. It is very hard for people to grasp that although I appear to manage "normally" in many situations, I need considerable help in others. The knowledge of other people's perceptions of me is sufficiently powerful to alter my behavior in ways which are detrimental to myself; for example, the knowledge that fellow passengers have seen me use a white cane to cross the road, can be enough to deter me from reading a book on the train. A more common strategy among people with limited sight is to manage roads unaided, thereby risking life and limb to avoid being labeled as frauds.

A further reaction, often associated with the belief that we are really no different, is that because our problems are no greater than anyone else's we do not deserve any special treatment or consideration. People who react in this way view us as whining and ungrateful complainers whenever we assert ourselves, explain our disabilities, ask that our needs be met or demand our rights. My most recent and overt experience of this reaction occurred during a visit to Whitehall to discuss the lack of transport for disabled people. Every time I mentioned a problem which disabled people encounter, such as not being able to use the underground system or the buses, I was told in no uncertain terms that many other people have transport problems too; what about old people, poor people, people who live in remote areas? What was so special about disabled people, and was not a lot being done for them anyway? I was the only disabled person present in this meeting and my confidence was undermined sufficiently to affect the quality of my argument. Reactions such as this can easily give rise to feelings of insecurity and doubt; it is, of course, the case that many people do have problems, but disabled people are among them and cannot afford to remain passive or to be passed by.

College

At the age of 19, after working for two years, I started my physiotherapy training at a special segregated college for blind and partially sighted students. For the first time in my life my disability was, at least in part, defined as blindness. Although about half the students were partially sighted, one of the criteria for entry to the college was the ability to read and write braille (which I had never used before) and to type proficiently, as, regardless of the clarity of their handwriting, the partially sighted students were not permitted to write their essays or examinations by hand, and the blind students were not permitted to write theirs in braille. No visual teaching methods were used in the college and, for those of us with sight, it was no easy matter learning subjects like anatomy, physiology and biomechanics without the use of diagrams.

The institution seemed unable to accept or respond to the fact that our impairments varied in severity and gave rise to different types of disability. We were taught to use special equipment which we did not need and were encouraged to "feel" rather than "peer" because feeling, it was thought, was aesthetically more pleasing, especially when dealing with the poor, unsuspecting public. There was great concern about the way we looked in our professional roles; white canes were not allowed inside the hospitals where we practiced clinically, even by totally blind students, and guide dogs were completely banned. It appeared that the blind students were expected to be superhuman whereas the partially sighted students were expected to be blind. Any attempt to defy or challenge these rules was very firmly quashed so, in the interests of "getting through," we outwardly denied the reality of our disabilities and complied.

Employment

Deciding whether or not to deny disability probably comes most clearly to the fore in adult life when we attempt to gain employment. Until very recently it was not uncommon to be told very bluntly that, in order to be accepted, the job must be done in exactly the same way as everyone else. In many ways this was easier to deal with than the situation now, where "equal opportunity" policies have simultaneously raised expectations and pushed negative attitudes underground, and where, in reality, little has changed. Although I have no way of proving it, I am convinced that the denial of my disability has been absolutely fundamental to my success in gaining the type of employment I have had. I have never completely denied it (it is not hidden enough for that) but rather, in response to the interviewers' skeptical and probing questions, I have minimized the difficulties I face and portrayed myself in a way which would swell my headmaster's pride.

Curiously, once in the job, people have sometimes decided that certain tasks, which I can perform quite adequately, are beyond me, while at the same time refusing to relieve me of those I cannot do. At one college where I worked it was considered impossible for me to cope with taking the minutes of meetings, but my request to be relieved of invigilating large numbers of students, on the grounds that I could not see them, was not acceded to; once again the nature of my disability was being defined by other people. On the rare occasions I have been given "special" equipment or consideration at work it has been regarded as a charitable act or donation for which I should be grateful and beholden. This behavior signals two distinct messages: first that I have failed to be "normal" (and have therefore failed), and second that I must ask for nothing more.

In these more enlightened days of "equal opportunities," we are frequently asked and expected to educate others at work about our disabilities. "We know nothing about it, you must teach us" is the frequent cry. In some ways this is a positive development but, on the other hand, it puts great pressure on us because few formal structures have been developed in which this educative process can take place. In the absence of proactive equal opportunity policies, we are rarely taken seriously and what we say is usually forgotten or ignored. Educating others in this way can also mean that we talk of little else but disability, which, as well as becoming boring to ourselves, can lead us to be labeled adversely or viewed solely in terms of problems. Challenging disabling attitudes and structures, especially as a lone disabled person, can become frustrating and exhausting, and in reality it is often easier and (dare I say) more functional, in the short term at least, to cope with inadequate conditions rather than fight to improve them. We must beware of tokenistic gestures which do little but put pressure on us.

CONCLUSION

The reasons I have denied the reality of my disability can be summarized as follows:

1. To avoid other people's anxiety and distress.
2. To avoid other people's disappointment and frustration.
3. To avoid other people's disbelief.
4. To avoid other people's disapproval.
5. To live up to other people's ideas of "normality."
6. To avoid spoiling other people's fun.
7. To collude with other people's pretences.

I believe that from earliest childhood denial of disability is totally rational given the situations we find ourselves in, and that to regard it as a psychopathological reaction is a serious mistake. We deny our disabilities for social, economic and emotional survival and we do so at considerable cost to our sense of self and our identities; it is not something we do because of flaws in our individual psyches. For those of us disabled from birth or early childhood, denial of disability has deeply penetrating and entangled roots; we need

PERSONAL ACCOUNT

I Am Legally Blind

Like approximately 1.1 million people in the United States, I am legally blind, which means that I have some remaining vision. Therefore, I have the option to "come out" as a blind person or "pass" as someone who is fully sighted.

When I am passing, I avoid using my magnifier or my reading glasses, which have an obviously protruded lens and require me to hold items close to my face. By not asking for assistance, I avoid having to tell anyone I am blind. In restaurants, I order without consulting the menu. If I go out walking, I leave my white cane at home. I get on buses and subway trains without asking anyone to identify which line I'm boarding. I purchase items in stores without using my pocket magnifier to read labels or prices. On elevators that have not been adapted to meet ADA (Americans with Disabilities Act of 1990) guidelines of "reasonable accommodation," I take my best shot at hitting the right button. Therefore, I am never quite sure if I am exiting on the floor that I want. I wander through unfamiliar neighborhoods and buildings that are invariably marked with small print signs that are placed above doorways.

There is a price I pay for passing as a sighted person. I give away ten-dollar bills when I mean to pay one dollar. I come home from grocery stores with brands or flavors of items that I don't like or that cost too much. But, the highest cost is freedom: I relinquish my rights to life, liberty and the pursuit of happiness. Here's what happens when I don't ask for help.

When I don't solicit information about buses, trains, and elevators, I waste a lot of time trying to find specific destinations and end up feeling frustrated, angry, and exhausted. When I leave my white cane at home, I give up my right to travel freely because I can't navigate in unfamiliar places or go anywhere at all after dark: I jeopardize my own safety because I trip and fall on curbs, stairs, bumps, and potholes. I surrender my freedom of choice when, in fast food restaurants where the menus are inaccessible to me, I order the same food time and time again. I limit my choice of products when I don't use my visual aids because I have to choose by label color rather than to read the print, and I don't learn about new products, either. If I hadn't identified myself as a blind person at the university, I would have relinquished my right to pursue an education because I would have had no adaptive equipment nor would I have made use of the university's Disability Support Services. I would have failed in school, which is exactly what I did, both in high school and the first time I attended college.

So, why in the world would I ever choose to pass? Because sometimes, I get sick of people's stares, whispers, ignorant comments, and nosy questions. When I ask for directions or for someone to read something to me, I am often responded to as if I am stupid or a child. People often answer my questions in irritated or condescending tones. More times than not, they don't answer verbally, but point at the object instead, which forces me to have to ask again or to explain why I am asking. This happens a lot at checkout stands.

I have had people grab my arm and try to pull me where I don't want to go. Recently, at a concert, my companion and I, with my white cane in hand, were easing our way through the aisle to our seats when a woman jumped up, grabbed my arm, knocking me off balance, then pushed me toward my seat. She didn't even ask if I wanted help. It really was an assault. Indeed, to a mugger or rapist, my white cane identifies me as a potential victim.

When I go shopping, I behave differently than fully sighted people do. I must juggle my list, purse, magnifier, reading glasses as well as the product and shopping basket or cart. I hold items very close to my face to read product labels, tags, and prices. A surprising number of people have asked "What are you looking for?" Sometimes, I reply, "Why do you ask?" I don't like having to explain my methods of adaptation. I have been followed by security guards and even stopped once in a drug store. The guard said that I was "acting suspiciously." He felt pretty bad when I told him that I was trying to see the prices. After that, whenever I went into that store, he was right there asking me if I needed any help finding things. Even though he meant well, the end result was that he still was following me. Ever since that experience, I stay alert to the possibility that I might look suspicious and I stand in open areas when I go into my purse for my glasses. I don't like having to be concerned about this, but I like the idea of being nabbed for shoplifting even less.

These are the paradoxical consequences of passing or coming out. Both cause me trouble, although I have learned the hard way that the more I use adaptive techniques and aids, and the more often I ask for help, the more efficient and independent I become. Thus, when I am "out," I am true to my own needs and desires.

Beth Omansky Gordon

support and encouragement to make our needs known, but this will only be achieved within the context of genuine structural and attitudinal change.

In this paper I have drawn upon my life experiences and personal reactions to elucidate the pressures placed upon disabled people to deny the reality of their experience of disability. This approach is limited inasmuch as personal experiences and responses can never be divorced from the personality and biography of the person they concern. In addition these pressures will vary according to the individual's impairment. But with these limitations in mind, I am confident that most disabled people will identify with what I have described and that only the examples are, strictly speaking, mine.

NOTES

1. Walking two-by-two in a long file.
2. Girls' basketball.
3. Physical education teacher.

READING 22

How Long Must We Wait?

Unmet Promises of Disability Law and Policy

Beth Omansky Gordon and Michael Oliver

ALL WE REALLY WANT TO DO

In the fall of 2000 we were invited to attend a prestigious international conference in Washington, D.C., to launch the discipline of disability studies onto the academic world. We eagerly accepted the invitation and looked forward to a stimulating few days in interaction with academic colleagues from around the globe. This is a scenario not unknown to many thousands of international academics. However, we would argue, our experiences as disabled academics set us apart from those of our nondisabled colleagues because of the discriminatory treatment we face in doing ordinary things that our nondisabled colleagues take for granted; in this case, using public transportation.

We recognize that using public transportation can be a difficult experience for all concerned, but our experiences as disabled travelers go far beyond what the nondisabled traveler has to endure. When millions of disabled people all over the world still have their basic human rights denied to them, we feel uneasy about highlighting the personal difficulties of a few relatively privileged ones from the minority world. But as academics working in a discipline where personal experience is seen as pivotal to our understanding of the world and the ways it operates, we make no apologies for describing our own discriminatory and degrading treatment though we will try to use these personal experiences as a framework for broader analysis. In so doing, initially Mike will describe his experiences of flying to Washington, D.C., for the conference and then Beth will discuss her attempts to use the local transportation system to socialize with academic colleagues. We will end by considering some of the general issues raised.

LEAVING ON A JET PLANE [MIKE]

When I received an invitation to attend the conference in Washington, D.C., I was unsure whether or not to accept because it would mean that I would have to fly from Britain to the United States and I have had many unpleasant travel experiences in the past. I have been ignored, abused, patronized, dropped on the floor, and often handled worse than the dead meat that is served to the passengers on the flight, all because I use an electric wheelchair and require manual assistance. It seems incredible that when we have the technology to send people into

Beth Omansky Gordon is a disability studies scholar/author, professional counselor, and disability advocate.
Michael Oliver is professor of disability studies at the University of Greenwich in the United Kingdom.

space, we still find it difficult to enable disabled people to get on and off airplanes with their dignity and self-respect still intact. However, I decided that the promise of the conference plus the opportunity to socialize with other academics with interests similar to mine was too good to miss.

The first hassle, I knew from experience, would be in trying to find an airline that would permit me to prebook seats that would give me enough legroom to sit comfortably and safely. "It's not allowed," "IATA regulations don't permit it," "It's up to the Captain," "We don't know how the plane will be loaded," "You're not allowed to block exits," "We don't know what plane we will be using" are all excuses I have been given in the past. After several angry phone calls and an exchange of letters, I am eventually allowed to book seats that will give me the legroom I require and I know that the first battle is over.

When I check in at Heathrow, London—one of the world's busiest airports—the staff insist that I transfer out of my electric wheelchair and into one of their manual ones. I explain that that will mean me sitting in an uncomfortable chair for at least three hours as well as restricting my personal mobility. The equivalent for a nondisabled traveler would be the enforced wearing of someone else's shoes while being denied access to refreshments, duty-free shopping, and so on. My request that I be allowed to remain in my own wheelchair until I board the plane is turned down on health and safety grounds. I am told that the ground crew will not lift my wheelchair down the stairs from the gate to the tarmac for stowing in the hold.

Reluctantly I agree to get out of my chair and, after a few minutes' wait, two men turn up with a manual wheelchair and proceed to lift me bodily into it, in full view of those queuing for the flight as well as anyone else who wants to watch. This was managed competently, but it is hardly appropriate treatment for anyone to endure. The two men then try to dismantle my electric wheelchair and disconnect the batteries. I explain that the chair does not dismantle and the batteries are dry cell and do not need to be disconnected. They tell me that they must disconnect the batteries anyway, and I insist that it is unnecessary.

At this point my wife, Joy, who is traveling with me as my personal assistant, intervenes and calls the supervisor. After a heated argument and several phone calls, it is agreed that dry cell batteries do not need to be disconnected and the men and my wheelchair disappear into the bowels of the airport. As I watch it go, there is no guarantee that they, or the ground crew who will lift it into the hold, will not disconnect the batteries or, indeed, remove them altogether. The experience of a friend of mine briefly comes to mind. She flew from Heathrow only to notice that her chair was still on the ground as the plane took off: Not only had they refused to load it but they had also neglected to tell her.

Some two hours later I am taken to the gate for boarding and told I will be loaded before the rest of the passengers, which would at least preserve my privacy, if not my dignity. Unfortunately, however, the two men designated to carry me onto the plane are late and only arrive as other passengers are being boarded. This means a further delay until I am taken to the door of the aircraft. On reaching this point, a small lifting chair is produced and I am transferred from the airport wheelchair onto it. It is wholly unsuitable because it has no arms and does not take into account the fact that I have no balance. Eventually I am strapped to it and carried onto the aircraft, which is now full.

I am carried past row after row of passengers until I reach my seat. I am then lifted bodily into the aircraft seat, but the space is very confined and does not give the lifters much room and the arms of the aircraft seat are not detachable. As a consequence of this, I am virtually dragged over the arm. What physical damage this is causing I don't know as I have no sensation in that part of my body, but the dragging does pull my trousers down and exposes large amounts of naked flesh to the rest of the passengers. Eventually I am placed in the seat, and my wife helps me to rearrange my clothing. I now settle down for the nine-hour flight but realize that I must moderate my food and liquid intake for it is impossible for me to get to the toilet on the aircraft.

We arrive in the Washington, D.C., airport, and a row breaks out between airport staff and cabin crew as to whose responsibility it is to get me off the aircraft. This causes delays and clearly angers a tired cabin crew who want, quite rightly, to get off the aircraft themselves and end their shift. The situation is eventually resolved when a member of the cabin crew and the flight engineer agree to lift me off the aircraft. This they do, but they are not trained to do so and once again I am dragged across the seats and my clothing again comes adrift.

In the terminal, I am informed that I must now transfer into one of the airport wheelchairs before proceeding to the collection point for our suitcases and my wheelchair. There are two problems with this: their wheelchair does not have detachable arms and there is no one to lift me. Another row breaks out and eventually two airport staff volunteer to lift me into the airport's chair. Again this is managed with great difficulty and some danger to all of us as they are willing but untrained.

Eventually I am reunited with my own chair and I begin to relax. I decide to complain formally and demand to see someone in charge. A supervisor appears and informs me that getting on and off the aircraft is my responsibility and that I should have been lifted off by my wife and two colleagues who are traveling with us; one [colleague] is himself disabled and the other has a history of chronic back problems. At this point I leave as I desperately need a drink and to get to the hotel to survey any damage that may have been inflicted. Once I am in bed, I find that I have severe lacerations and bruising to my buttocks. It takes me several hours before I am able to stop shaking. Still I am here and I look forward to the next four days, though in the back of my mind I know I have to go through it all again in order to get home.

EVERYTHING IS BROKEN [BETH]

Knowing that my British colleagues have a predilection for American blues, I make reservations at a supper club where we will meet. I first met Mike and his colleague, Len, briefly at a conference in Chicago earlier in the year, and I found much in common with them. I am excited at the prospect of spending Sunday evening socializing and exchanging ideas with internationally renowned scholars on the first night of their visit to Washington, D.C.

Mike calls my home at about three o'clock on the Sunday afternoon of their arrival to say they are finally settled in at the hotel. He sounds perturbed, apparently due to mistreatment by airport employees, but still wishes to get together. We decide to meet at the blues club at seven o'clock that evening. Mike will contact the D.C. taxicab company to arrange for a wheelchair-accessible van.

About half an hour later, Mike calls back with our first piece of bad news: there is no wheelchair-accessible taxicab service to travel from one location to another within the District of Columbia. While you can go from D.C. into the Virginia or Maryland suburbs and back into D.C., the taxi service will not take you between locations within the District. I am astonished and baffled by the logic of this policy. I wonder if this is just a means to charge more by forcing disabled people to take lengthy detours into the suburbs and back again, or to discourage them from riding taxis altogether. We forgo any plan to find another music club that is both wheelchair and distance accessible, and choose instead to find a restaurant near the hotel where Mike, Joy, and Len are staying.

I plan to take the nine-mile ride from my home into the District via MetroAccess, the D.C. metropolitan area's paratransit system for disabled people. The Americans With Disabilities Act of 1990 (ADA) is a civil rights law designed to prohibit discrimination and to ensure equal access to transportation, employment, public accommodations, public services, and telecommunications. The law mandates paratransit service, usually consisting of a fleet of wheelchair-accessible vans and perhaps some cars. The Washington Metropolitan Area Transit Authority (WMATA) sponsors MetroAccess paratransit service, but subcontracts the work out to local governments and other local fixed-route transit systems, including privately owned for-profit companies in the metropolitan area.

Being considered disabled under the ADA is not enough to be considered eligible for paratransit ridership; disabled people must go through a certification process. Applicants must complete a lengthy, two-part form, to be filled out by the applicant and a physician. Eligibility is based on a person's "functional limitation," assessed by an occupational therapist or other medical professional who is determined (and paid) by MetroAccess officials as qualified to judge each applicant's ability to ride public fixed-route transit. In the main, able-bodied medical professionals determine who is eligible and who is denied access to paratransit. They are gatekeepers who lack personal expertise about what it is like to be disabled by an inaccessible environment.

Applicants are judged on their ability to walk or travel up to one-quarter of a mile, travel independently to and from bus stops, identify the correct bus or bus stop to board or get off, get on or off a bus or train using a lift, and ask for and understand instructions to board, ride, and disembark. Disabled people often encounter a well-crafted double-bind in the assessment process: if assessors determine that applicants' "mobility skills" are adequate, they are deemed able to ride public fixed-route transit, and thus declared ineligible for MetroAccess. But if assessors decide that applicants lack good mobility skills, they may be denied MetroAccess services and told to get additional mobility training.

Like hundreds of other disabled workers, I rely on MetroAccess to take me to and from work. I rely on it to get me to school at least twice a week, to out-of-office work-related appointments, to medical appointments, and to social engagements. MetroAccess has caused me to be more than one hour late for work appointments, school, and doctors' appointments more times than I can count, and I have missed some of these obligations altogether when my rides failed to show up. During my first semester in school, MetroAccess failed to pick me up after class one time, and I was left stranded in D.C., at ten-thirty at night, in freezing cold weather, with locked school buildings all around me and with no way home.

Routing has little or no logic. Passengers are forced to share rides that take them in opposite directions than intended. While MetroAccess policy states that passengers are not supposed to be on the van for twenty minutes longer than it would normally take for them to go from one particular destination to another, policy often differs from practice. Once, I rode on the van around the District exactly one hour, for what should have been a twenty-minute ride had we taken a direct route. At the end of that hour, I looked out the window and saw the exact location where I had been picked up. I had been driven around in one big circle, no closer to home than I was before I boarded the van.

Once, when the van came to take me to school, I asked if I would be ride-sharing and, if so, how long the trip would take. Learning that my shared ride would take an hour and a half—time I didn't have—I asked to be let off the van. The driver refused, saying "You are already on the van. You must stay on the van until we reach your destination. Go sit down and buckle your seat belt." I said, "We are still at my house. The van is not moving. Let me off." Again he refused and ordered me to sit down. I refused. He radioed the dispatch office to find out what he should do with me. The dispatcher said he would have to check with a supervisor. The minutes ticked by. Finally, after ten minutes, they agreed to let me off the van. Other times, when I protested circuitous routing and unjustifiable amounts of time riding around, drivers scolded me, saying such things as "Just sit there and be quiet. Your ride costs only $2.20, so you should be grateful for it." But MetroAccess is not a charity-based service. I am a taxpayer who contributes to the system, including to its employee salaries. Sometimes, I feel that they treat me as if I were a sack of groceries, as something less than human. My MetroAccess experiences are not unique. When I ride with other disabled people, we often swap MetroAccess horror stories.

Because my MetroAccess reservations have "disappeared" from manifests so often, I have learned to check and recheck with the scheduling office to make sure my ride is still listed. Nevertheless, this is no guarantee that the driver will arrive on time, or at all for that matter. Therefore, I made sure to call the reservation and dispatch center earlier in the day to confirm that I was, indeed, on the manifest for a six o'clock pickup to travel into D.C. to meet Mike, Joy, and Len, and then to go back home four hours later.

Now it's six o'clock and the van is not here. Tension vaguely gnaws at the back of my neck, causing the muscles to stiffen and ache. I know that MetroAccess allows itself a fifteen-minute window on either side of my pickup time, so I wait until six-fifteen before I call the office. The dispatcher reassures me that the van is scheduled to pick me up at six p.m. and that it should be there momentarily. By six-thirty my anxiety has given way to frustration. I call the dispatch office again. A man answers. I say, "My ride was supposed to be here a half hour ago. Would you please radio the driver?" After placing me on hold for ten minutes, he tells me, "I think we have a mix-up. I'll call you back in a few minutes." Twenty minutes later, he calls to say, "We booked you on Fastran (one of the local government's services), but Fastran doesn't run on weekends."

I know that by now my colleagues are expecting me to meet them at the hotel bar. I call their room repeatedly and leave messages. I call the hotel to have them paged at the bar, but there is no paging system there. There is nothing I can do but wait to hear from them. Upset and disappointed, I resign myself to the fact that I will not have my long-awaited evening with my British colleagues.

MAY THE LIGHT SHINE ON THE TRUTH SOMEDAY

We have recounted our own personal experiences of global and local transport systems, and we feel crushed by them. We can (and do) complain vociferously, campaign for the law to be changed, demonstrate on the streets, take our stories to the media, and so on, but complaints are easily managed by large organizations. Laws take a long time to change, and while taking to the streets is personally empowering, it will not enable us to go to the next conference, let alone socialize together when we are there.

There are things we need to understand from these experiences. To begin with, it is testament to the global power of the airlines that, even though there is civil rights legislation in both Britain and America, air travel is exempt from those laws. Clearly, the airline industry pays little or no attention to the needs of disabled travelers. As each new generation of aircraft comes off the drawing board, we continue to be designed out, rather than included in. With regard to ground transportation, government subcontracting of public services to for-profit companies dramatically shifts priorities away from democratic principles of inclusion and toward the bottom line of profit margins instead.

It is a fact that American civil rights legislation is the most comprehensive and enforceable in the world. Still it fails to ensure that disabled American citizens and their guests can move around their communities when and how they choose. This failure suggests that such legislation promises much more than it delivers. Indeed, we even begin to wonder whether such legislation is nothing more than a confidence trick, actually protecting the interests of the rich and powerful rather than ensuring that the rights of all citizens are actually being properly addressed.

Finally, and most importantly, we would like to return to a point we made earlier. If these are the kinds of everyday experiences that we, as relatively privileged and empowered disabled people, have to endure, what is life really like for those millions of underprivileged and disempowered disabled people who exist in all parts of the world? In talking about our own personal experiences, we hope we have shone some light on the truth of just how far we have to go in order to build a world that fully includes all disabled people.

READING 23

Please Ask Me Who, Not "What," I Am

Jordan Lite

I've been thinking a lot about that "Seinfeld" episode where Elaine is dating this guy and it's driving her nuts because she doesn't know "what" he is. They ultimately discover that neither is exotic enough for the other and they're so disappointed that they stop seeing each other.

It's the story of my life these days. Each new guy I meet, it seems, is fascinated by my ostensible failure to fall into an obvious racial category. Last year we could opt out of defining ourselves to the Census Bureau, but that option doesn't seem to have carried over into real life. I've lost track of how many flirty men have asked me what I am.

Jordan Lite worked in Ghana as an AIDS educator.

The first time, I was in Iowa and snobbishly dismissed the inquiry as rural provincialism. Then it happened again while I was on a date in San Francisco, a city that prides itself on its enlightenment.

Isn't is rude to ask "what" someone is when you've just met? Common courtesy would suggest so. But many people seem to feel uncomfortable if they can't immediately determine a new person's racial or ethnic background.

Of course, I've mused over "what" a stranger might be. But it's never occurred to me that asking "What are you?" of someone I've just met would elicit anything particularly revealing about him. I ask questions, but not that one.

So when a potential boyfriend asks me "What are you?" I feel like he wants to instantly categorize me. If he'd only let the answer come out naturally, he'd get a much better sense of what I'm about.

Perhaps acknowledging explicitly that race and ethnicity play a role in determining who we are is just being honest. But I'm not sure that such directness is always well intended. After I grouchily retorted "What do you mean, 'What am I?'" to one rather bewildered date, he told me his dad was African-American and his mom Japanese, and that he ruminated all the time over how to reconcile such disparate influences. I realized then that he believed my being "different" would magically confer upon me an understanding of what it was like to be like him.

If you're looking for your soulmate, maybe it's only natural to want a person who has shared your experience. But for some people, "What you are?" is just a line. "You're exotic-looking," a man at a party explained when I asked him why he wanted to know. In retrospect, I think he probably meant his remark as a compliment. As a Hispanic friend pointed out, when all things Latin became the new craze, it's trendy to be exotic. But if someone wants to get to know me, I wish he would at least pretend it's not because of my looks.

Still, this guy's willingness to discuss my discomfort was eye-opening. He told me that he was part Korean, part white. Growing up in the Pacific Northwest, he wasn't the only biracial kid on the block. One could acknowledge race, he said, and still be casual about it.

Although I spent by childhood in a town lauded for its racial diversity, discussing race doesn't often feel easy to me. Maybe my Japanese classmate in the first grade could snack on seaweed without being hassled, but I can readily recall being 11 years old and watching a local TV news report about a pack of white boys who beat, then chased a terrified black teen onto a highway, where he was struck by a car and killed. The violence on TV silenced me. It seemed better not to risk asking questions that might offend.

Years after we graduated from our private high school, one of my good friends told me how out of place she felt as one of the few black students. Her guardedness had kept me from probing; but there's a part of me that wonders if talking with her then about her unease at school would have made me more comfortable now when people ask me about my place in the world.

But as it is, I resent being pressed to explain myself upfront, as if telling a prospective date my ethnicity eliminates his need to participate in a real conversation with me. "What are you?" I am asked, but the background check he's conducting won't show whether we share real interests that would bring us together in a genuine give-and-take.

In a way, I enjoy being unclassifiable. Though there are people who try to peg me to a particular ethnic stereotype, I like to think others take my ambiguous appearance as an opportunity to focus on who I am as a person. So I haven't figured out why being myself should kill any chance of a relationship. Not long ago, a man asked me about my background when we met for a drink.

"Just a Jewish girl from New Jersey," I said truthfully.

I never heard from him again.

READING 24

The Accidental Asian

Eric Liu

The Asian American identity was born, as I was, roughly thirty years ago. In those three decades it has struggled to find relevance and a coherent voice. As I have. It has tried to adapt itself to the prevailing attitudes about race—namely, that one matters in this society, if one is colored, mainly to the extent that one claims a race for oneself. I, too, have tried to accommodate these forces. The Asian American identity, like me, renounces whiteness. It draws strength from the possibility of transcending the fear and blindness of the past. So do I. It is the so very American product of a rejection of history's limitations, rooted in little more than its own creation a generation ago. As I am.

What I am saying is that I can identify with the Asian American identity. I understand why it does what it does. It is as if this identity and I were twin siblings, separated at birth but endowed with uncanny foreknowledge of each other's motives. The problem is, I disagree with it often. I become frustrated by it, even disappointed. The feeling is mutual, I suspect. We react to the same world in very different ways.

And yes, I do think of this identity as something that reacts, something almost alive, in the way that a shadow, or a mirror image—or a conscience—is almost alive. It has, if not a will of its own, then at least a highly developed habit of asserting its existence. It is like a storm, a beautiful, swirling weather pattern that moves back and forth across my mind. It draws me in, it repulses me. I am ever aware of its presence. There is always part of me that believes I will find

Eric Liu is a correspondent and commentator for MSNBC. He also worked as a speechwriter for President Bill Clinton.

deliverance if I merge with this identity. Yet still I hold it at a remove. For I fear that in the middle of this swirl, this great human churn, lies emptiness.

What must it be like to be told you are Asian American? Imagine that you are an immigrant, young, but old enough to get by, and you have been in America for only a few months. Imagine that you come from Korea. Imagine that you speak Korean, read Korean newspapers, eat Korean food. Imagine that you live in East Flushing or in South Central and you see only the Korean faces. There are other faces, yes, brown and black and yellow and white, but the ones you see, the ones you can read, are Korean. Imagine that time passes, and you realize now that you see the other faces. Imagine that the order of life in this city, the invisible grid, has become visible to you. More than that, it has affected you. What was Korean before is not exactly Korean anymore: your speech is interspersed now with fragments of English, Spanish; your daily paper you must find at a crowded, strange-smelling newsstand, tucked among bundles of other scripts and shades of print; your strong, salty food, supplemented now by frosted cereal and cookies, you eat while quietly absorbed by a television program you cannot understand except in mime. Imagine that you are becoming a Korean American. Is that not shock enough? To know that what was once the noun is becoming the adjective? And so perhaps you retreat, you compensate, you remind yourself every night before you pray that you are Korean so that you and your Maker will not forget. But imagine that the forgetting is relentless. That more time passes, and a knock on the door of your apartment brings you face-to-face with a Japanese, and something deep inside you, a passing sneer or a cautionary tale, a history, twinges. And imagine that this Japanese begins speaking to you in English, the kind of English the television produces, and you understand perfectly what she is saying. Imagine that what she is saying is that she needs your help. That you are invited to a rally (or is it a party?). That we—you and this Japanese and so many unseen others—must stand together against a common foe. Imagine that what she is saying is that you are Asian American. What must it be like? What do you think about when you close the door and walk to the window and realize, while peering out over a scene of so many unknowable lives but four knowable colors, how faint the aroma of your own kitchen has become, how strong the scent of the street?

I find myself in a cavernous television studio, seated beside the anchorwoman. The cameras are on us, lights are burning overhead. I am nervous, although I shouldn't be: this is my job. I do commentary for a cable news network and I come to this studio often. This day, I have been called in as a "special guest" to discuss a recent and controversial cover of the *National Review* magazine depicting the president, vice president, and first lady in yellowface—that is, in stereotypical Oriental caricature. "The Manchurian Candidate," reads the cover text, referring, of course, to Bill Clinton and his role in the "Asian money" scandal that has been brewing since the 1996 election.

The news package leading up to my entrance describes the brouhaha that has arisen over the cover, and as the tape comes to a close a red light comes on, signaling that we are on the air. The anchor turns to me, her brow knit at the appropriate angle of concern: "What about this cover do you find offensive, Eric?"

Truth be told, I was not deeply offended when I first saw the cover. (My mother, in fact, was much angrier.) I mainly thought it was juvenile, sophomoric. And I didn't think about it again until a few days later, when my producer waved it at me and asked for a reaction. I knew what answer he was looking for; what answer any self-respecting Asian would give.

"Well," I say, turning now to the camera, "these caricatures play off a long history of demeaning anti-Asian stereotypes—the buck-teeth, the slanted eyes, the bamboo hat. They are racist in their effect." And on I go. I play, in other words, the Asian spokesman, ever vigilant against affronts to my race. The anchor nods understandingly as I speak.

Soon a staff writer from the *Review* joins the discussion via satellite. He, too, is Asian American, South Asian. "We didn't think this cover would be particularly controversial," I hear this other Asian say. "Normal people aren't offended by it."

Normal people? The more this other Asian talks, the more heated I become in my responses. At first I assume it's the adrenaline rush of verbal combat. But as he goes on mouthing his disingenuous party line—something like, "We would've used leprechauns if this scandal was about Irish money"—I become more than just irked, more than angry, until suddenly I realize that I am outraged. I am sending a searing look into my own reflection in the camera as I argue. And I am shouting now: I have raised my voice to defend *my people.*

"Somehow, we have gotten to the point where those who protest bias and insensitivity are *demonized* more than those who commit it!" I boom.

"I'm not demonizing you," the other Asian offers.

The segment ends shortly afterward, the red light goes off. An Asian American employee comes over to shake my hand. I feel pleased with myself, pumped up. But even before I've removed my mike, I realize something unusual has happened. When the debate began I was playing a part, because I felt I should. Eight minutes later I had merged completely with my role. Almost by chance, it seemed, I'd become a righteous, vocal Asian American. All it had taken was a stage and a villain.

That's how it is with Asian American identity—nothing brings it out like other people's expectations and a sense of danger. Until recently, I rarely self-identified as "Asian American." I might say "Chinese American," if asked. Otherwise, pointedly, "American." But there are times when what you choose to call yourself becomes irrelevant. Ask Tiger Woods, whose insistence that he was "Cablinasian" didn't keep the media from blackening him, when he first arrived, into golf's Jackie Robinson. There are times when other people *need* to think of you as X even if you believe you are Y. This was one of those times. I was in the studio to speak *as an Asian American.*

Of course, I was complicit in this casting; I chose to take the role. What was curious to me, however, is how I managed, if even for a moment, to lose myself in it. Here is where the sense of danger came into play. I may not have started out being terribly exercised about the perils of Yellow Peril stereotyping. But once I perceived the smarmy hypocrisy of this fellow—once I heard his intransigent insistence that the fault lay only with whiny, race-peddling Asians like me—I was chilled by the sense that maybe there is a danger out there. Maybe it *is* true, as I was then asserting on camera, that what separates insulting caricatures from more troubling forms of anti-Asian sentiment is only a slippery slope. At that moment I began to comprehend the most basic rationale for pan-Asian solidarity: self-defense.

I still understand that rationale, and many others. I understand, that is, why so many Americans of various ethnic origins have chosen, over the last generation, to adopt a one-size-fits-all "Asian American" identity. It is an affirming counterstatement to the narrative in which yellow people are either foreigners or footnotes. It is a bulwark against bigotry. It is, perhaps most important, a community. I can recount the ways, over the years, that I've become more Asian American myself. I've learned the appropriate cultural and political references. I've become familiar with the history. And of course, I've spoken out against Asian-bashing on national television.

Nevertheless, the fact remains: I am not an Asian American activist; I just play one on TV. Even though I have a grasp of why this identity matters, I cannot escape the feeling that it is contrived and, in a more profound way, unnecessary. In a way, I envy those who choose to become wholeheartedly Asian American: those who believe. At least they have a certain order to their existence. I, on the other hand, am an accidental Asian. Someone who has stumbled onto a sense of race; who wonders now what to do with it.

We are inventors, all. We assemble our selves from fragments of story.

Every identity is a social construction, a drawing of arbitrary lines. But are all identities *equally* arbitrary—and equally necessary? It's worthwhile to compare a racial identity like "Asian American" with what might be said to exist "within" it (ethnicity) and "around" it (nation).

An ethnic identity like "Chinese" matters because it is a medium of cultural continuity and meaning. "Chineseness," to be sure, is not an easy thing to delineate. It is a simplified marker for a complex reality. But the fact is that when I speak of my heritage—or when I speak of losing my heritage—I am referring to sounds and stories and customs that are *Chinese* American.

National identity, in the American case, is more problematic. It is far-flung and often contradictory. It is more reliant on myth and paradox than many other national identities. It is not, however, empty of meaning. America matters in both a civic sense and a cultural one. As a state, it is a guarantor of unmatched freedoms. As a place, it is an unrivaled incubator of ambition. The syntheses that America generates are, for better and worse, what pushes humanity forward today.

Race matters, too, of course. The difference is, race matters mainly because race matters. It's undeniable, in other words, that society is still ordered by the random bundle of traits we call "race"—and that benefits and penalties are often assigned accordingly. But it is this persistent social fact, more than any *intrinsic* worth, that makes racial identity deserving of our moral attention.

Don't get me wrong: it's not that I wish for a society without race. At bottom, I consider myself an identity libertarian. I wish for a society that treats race as an option, the way white people today are able to enjoy ethnicity as an option. As something cost-free, neutral, fluid. And yet I know that the tendency of race is usually to solidify: into clubs, into shields.

To a great degree, then, my misgivings about racial identity flow from a fear of ethnosclerosis: the hardening of the walls between the races. But perhaps my worries, like the pageants of difference that prompted them, belong to a time that is already passing. Perhaps over the horizon, beyond multiculturalism, awaits the cosmopolitan realm that David Hollinger calls "postethnic America." And perhaps there is no way to call forth this horizon but with the stories we have at hand.

I have a friend from college who used to be a deracinated East Coast suburban ABC—someone, in other words, quite like me. When he moved to the West Coast for graduate school, though, he got religion. He was, for the first time, in a place where Asian Americans were not few and far between. He joined the Asian student union, began reading Asian American journals and literature anthologies, spent more and more of his days with Asian friends, entered into his first relationship with a girl who wasn't white (she was Japanese, to the vexation of his parents). Soon he was speaking to me in earnest about the importance

of being Asian. And he seemed genuinely happy, at ease.

It's not hard to see why my friend became what I call a "born-again Asian." He had found fellowship and, with the fellowship, meaning. He had found a place where he would always fit in, always be recognized. He had found a way to fill a hole, the gnawing sense of heritage deficit that plagues many a second-generation banana. And the mortar he was using was not anything so ancient and musty as Chinese civilization; it was a new, synthetic, made-in-the-U.S.A. adhesive called "Asianness." For my friend, this was *exciting* as well as fulfilling.

My own conversion, if I can call it that, is far from complete. Having spent so much of my life up through college soft-pedaling my Asianness, I began afterward to realize how unnecessary that had been. I began, tentatively, to peel back the topmost layers of my anti-race defenses. Did I have an epiphany? No; I think I simply started to grow up. I became old enough to shed the mask of perpetual racelessness; old enough, as well, to sense in myself a yearning for affinity, for *affiliation.* So I joined a couple of Asian American organizations, began going to their meetings and conventions. And I was welcome. Nobody questioned my authenticity, my standing. Mainly I encountered people quite like me: second-generation, mainstream, in search of something else. Soon I was conversant in the patois of "the community." Soon I was calling myself, without hesitation, "Asian American."

Don't give me too much credit, though. The truth is, I was mainly exploring the public, institutional, side of Asian America. The private side, the realm of close friendships formed through race, I have entered only lately. Perhaps the most you could say of me is that I am an assimilist in recovery: once in denial, now halfway up the twelve-step to full, self-actualized Asian Americanness. I am glad to have climbed this far and to have left behind some insecurities. I am not sure, however, how much farther I should go.

Thirty-some years ago, there were no "Asian Americans." Not a single one. There were Japanese Americans, Chinese Americans, Filipino Americans, and so on: a disparate lot who shared only yellow-to-brown skin tones and the experience of bigotry that their pigmentation provoked. Though known to their countrymen, collectively, as "Orientals," and assumed to share common traits and cultures, they didn't think of themselves at all as a collective. It really wasn't until the upheavals of the late 1960s that some of them began to.

Stirred by the precedent of Black Power, a cadre of Asian student activists, mostly in California, performed an act of conceptual jujitsu: they would create a positive identity out of the unhappy fact that whites tend to lump all Asians together. Their first move was to throw off the "Oriental" label, which, to their thinking, was the cliché-ridden product of a colonial European gaze. They replaced it with "Yellow," and after protests from their darker-hued constituents, they replaced "Yellow" with "Asian American." In their campaign for semantic legitimacy, the ex-Orientals got an unlikely assist from bean-counting federal bureaucrats. Looking to make affirmative action programs easier to document, the Office of Management and Budget in 1973 christened the term *Asian and Pacific Islander* for use in government forms. In the eyes of the feds, all Asians now looked alike. But this was a *good* thing.

The greatest problem for "Asian America," at least initially, was that this place existed mostly in the arid realm of census figures. It was a statistical category more than a social reality. In the last few decades, though, Asian American activists, intellectuals, artists, and students have worked, with increasing success, to transform their label into a lifestyle and to create, by every means available, a truly pan-ethnic identity for their ten million members. They have begun to build a nation.

The scholar Benedict Anderson has aptly defined the nation as an "imagined community," a grouping that relies for cohesion on an intangible, exclusive sense of connection among its far-flung members. Sometimes a nation has a state to enforce its will, sometimes it does not. But it must *always* have a mythology, a quasi-official culture that is communicated to all who belong, wherever they may be.

The Asian American narrative is rooted deeply in threat. That is one of the main things polyglot Americans of Asian descent have had in common: the fear of being discriminated against simply on account of being, metaphorically if not genetically, Chinamen. It is no accident that an early defining skirmish for Asian American activists was the push for Asian American Studies programs at San Francisco State and Berkeley in 1968. For what these programs did, in part, was to record and transmit the history of mistreatment that so many immigrants from Asia had endured over the centuries. Today, in the same vein, one of the most powerful allegories in Asian American lore is the tale of Vincent Chin, a Chinese American beaten to death in 1982 by two laid-off white auto workers who took him to be Japanese. The Chin story tells of a lingering strain of vicious, indiscriminate racism that can erupt without warning.

Yet no race can live on threat alone. To sustain a racial identity, there must be more than other people's racism, more than a negation. There must also be an affirmative sensibility, an aesthetic that emerges through the fusing of arts and letters with politics. Benedict Anderson again, in *Imagined Communities,* points to vernacular "print-capitalism"—books, newspapers, pamphlets—as the driving force of an incipient national consciousness. On the contemporary scene, perhaps no periodical better epitomizes the emerging aesthetic than the New York–based bimonthly *A. Magazine: Inside Asian America.*

Founded eight years ago by a Harvard graduate and entrepreneurial dynamo named Jeff Yang, *A. Magazine* covers fashion, politics, film, books, and trends in a style one might call Multiculti Chic. To flip through the glossy pages of this publication is to be swept into a cosmopolitan, cutting-edge world where Asians *matter.* It is to enter a realm populated by Asian and Asian American luminaries: actors like Jackie Chan and Margaret Cho, athletes like Michael Chang and Kristi Yamaguchi. It is to see everyday spaces and objects—sporting events, television shows, workplaces, bookstores, boutiques—through the eyes of a well-educated, socially conscious, politically aware, media-savvy, left-of-center, twenty-to-thirty-something, second-generation Asian American. It is to create, and be created by, an Ideal Asian.

There is something fantastic about all this, and I mean that in every way. That the children of Chinese and Japanese immigrants, or Korean and Japanese, or Indian and Pakistani, should so heedlessly disregard the animosities of their ancestors; that they should prove it possible to reinvent themselves as one community; that they should catalog their collective contributions to society so very sincerely: what can you say, really, but "Only in America"? There is an impressive, defiant ambition at work here: an assertion of ownership, a demand for respect. But there is also, on occasion, an under-oxygenated air of fantasy, a shimmering mirage of whitelessness and Asian self-sufficiency. A *dream.*

The dream of a nation-race called Asian America makes the most sense if you believe that the long-discredited "melting pot" was basically replaced by a "quintuple melting pot." This is the multicultural method at its core: liquefy the differences *within* racial groups, solidify those *among* them. It is a method that many self-proclaimed Asian Americans, with the most meliorative of intentions, have applied to their own lives. They have thrown the *chink* and the *jap* and the *gook* and the *flip* into the same great bubbling cauldron. Now they await the emergence of a new and superior being, the *Asian American.* They wish him into existence. And what's troubling about this, frankly, is precisely what's inspiring: that it is possible.

The invention of a race testifies not only to the power of the human imagination but also to its limits. There is something awesome about the coalescence of a sprawling conglomerate identity. There is something frustrating as well, the sense that all this creativity and energy could have been harnessed to a greater end. For the challenge today is not only to announce the arrival of color. It is also to form combinations that lie beyond color. The creators of Asian America suggest that racial nationalism is the most meaningful way of claiming American life. I worry that it defers the greater task of confronting American life.

Power. Race, in the guise of whiteness, has always been about power. Now, in the masks of color, it is also about countervailing power. To call yourself a minority today is not only to acknowledge that you are seen by whites as nonwhite. It can also be to choose, as a matter of vocation, to sustain the dichotomy.

Frank Wu, a law professor and correspondent for *Asian-Week,* once wrote a candid and elegant essay in which he confessed to becoming a Professional Asian American. "Much like someone who becomes famous for being famous," he wrote, "I am making a career out of my race." He is not alone, of course, in his career choice. Over the last twenty years, there has been a proliferation of pan-Asian associations, advocacy groups, and political lobbies. These groups offer their members connections, capital, standing, protection. They do important work on behalf of those without a voice. Together, they represent the bureaucratization—the mechanization, really—of the race. The Professional Asian Americans who run these groups have learned well from their black and Hispanic counterparts that *if you build it, they will come*: if you construct the institutions that a "legitimate" race is supposed to have, then people will treat your race as legitimate.

One thing Professional Asian Americans are quick to point out is that they are not honorary whites. Fair enough: one would like to be able to do well in this country without being called white. And one should be able to address the fact that plenty of Asian Americans, unlike "real" whites, still pay a social penalty for their race. But something Professional Asian Americans sometimes overlook is that they are not honorary blacks either. African Americans created the template for minority politics in this country. That template, set in the heavy type of protest and opposition, is not always the best fit for Asian Americans. For Asian Americans haven't the moral purchase that blacks have upon our politics.

Asian Americans belong not to a race so much as to a confederation, a big yellow-and-brown tent that covers a panoply of interests. And while those interests converge usefully on some points—antidiscrimination, open immigration—they diverge on many others. This is a "community," after all, that consists of ten million people of a few dozen ethnicities, who have roots all across America and around the globe, whose families have been here anywhere from less than a week to more than a century, whose political beliefs run the ideological gamut, who are welfare mothers and multimillionaires, soldiers and doctors, believers and pagans. It would take an act of selective deafness to hear, in this cacophony, a unitary voice.

Without a unitary voice, however, there can never be maximum leverage in the bargaining for benefits. There can be no singular purpose for the Professional Asian American, no stable niche in the marketplace of identities. It will grow ever harder to speak of "the race." So be it. What will remain is the incalculable diversity of a great and growing mass of humanity. And there, in the multitudes, will lie a very different kind of power.

What maketh a race?

To people in China, the Chinese constitute a single race. Except, that is, for those Chinese who aren't Chinese; those who aren't of the dominant Han group, like the Miao or Yao or Zhuang or whatever. They belong to separate races.

To the Chinese, Indians are a single, and separate, race. But "Indian" to many Indians, is like "Asian American" to me: an artificial, monochrome label. The distinctions that matter in India are between Bengalis and Punjabis and Gujeratis and others.

To the Japanese, who certainly think of themselves as a race, the Chinese, Indians, and Koreans are all separate races. To the Koreans, the Filipinos are; to the Filipinos, the Vietnamese. And so on.

To the Anglos who founded the United States, the Irish who arrived in great waves in the early nineteenth century were a separate race. To the Germans who killed Jews in this century and the French who watched, the Jews were a separate race. To the blacks of America, the Anglos and the Irish and the Germans and French and the Jews have always ended up being part of the same, and separate, race.

To the judiciary system of the United States, Asian Indians were held to be: probably not white (1909), white (1910), white again (1913), not white (1917), white (1919 and 1920), not white (1923), still not white (1928), probably never again white (1939 and 1942).

To those who believe in race, the spaces in between are plugged tight with impurities: quadroons, octoroons, mulattoes, morenas, mutts, mongrels, half-castes, half-breeds, halfies, hapas.

To those who do not believe, there is only this faith: the mixed shall inherit the earth.

What maketh a race is not God but man. What maketh a race is only the sin of self-love.

Last May, I received in the mail a calendar of events and exhibits "celebrating Asian Pacific American Heritage Month." Here is what it included: A Celebration of APA Women's Leadership into the Twenty-first Century. An APA Spring Benefit. An APA Scholarship Dinner. An APA Performance Series. An APA Writers' Reading. A Performance of Music in the Lives of APAs. An APA Heritage Festival. (The theme this year: "One Vision, One Mission, One Voice.")

When I read the calendar the first time, I took all the information at face value, noted a few events that sounded interesting. When I read it a second time, a question pressed its way through the hazy membrane of multiculturalism in my brain and presented itself starkly, even rudely: What the heck is an "APA"?

If "Asian Pacific American" is an overbroad generalization, then what is "APA" but a soulless distillation of an overbroad generalization? I know it's a typographical and linguistic convenience, like the "USA" in *USA Today.* But the truncation and abbreviation of *experience* that the label perpetrates reflects the truncation and abbreviation of *reasoning* that you'll find in the call for celebration.

I agree that in the form of a coalition—that is, as a set of political alliances among organized groups—the Asian American identity can be quite important. But it is not a coalition that I am being asked to celebrate. It is a *race:* a discrete entity with "one vision, one mission, one voice." A race, which is supposed to be more primordial than any temporary, tactical alliance. A race, which apparently does not need justification for its existence but merely is. One celebrates the race as a matter of tradition, because it is there. Moreover, to celebrate the race is to nourish it, to sustain it. And that is precisely what gives me pause.

In a provocative book called *The Rise and Fall of Gay Culture,* Daniel Harris describes the way that the longtime isolation of the gay community inspired an intensely creative and pointedly oppositional gay culture. Now that intolerance and ostracism are declining, Harris says, elements of that subculture are being coopted by the mainstream: assimilated. He laments this fact, because in his view, a real cultural legacy is disappearing. But he does not lament it so much that he wishes for a return to the kind of homophobia that had yielded the subculture in the first place. Gay culture is no longer so necessary, Harris reluctantly acknowledges, and this is a triumph as much as it is a tragedy.

The case of gay culture is relevant because it raises the big questions of identity politics: After discrimination subsides, is it still necessary for a minority group to keep the cultural wagons circled? Should walls that once existed to keep a minority group *out* now be maintained to keep them *in?* Should a prison of identity be converted, upon liberation, into a home? It seems that many who cheer Asian Pacific American Heritage Month are saying "yes" to these questions.

I don't mean to suggest that Asian Americans are able to live bigotry-free lives today, or that most Asian American activists are cultural segregationists, or that the gay community provides a perfect parallel to the Asian community. What I am saying, simply, is that more than ever before, Asian Americans are only as isolated as they want to be. They—we—do not face the levels of discrimination and hatred that *demand* an enclave mentality, particularly among the second generation, which, after all, provides most of the leadership for the nation-race. The choice to invent and sustain a pan-Asian identity is just that: a choice, not an imperative.

When you think about it, though, this choice seems almost like a reflex, a compensatory reaction to a derogatory action. What troubles me about becoming Asian American is not that it entails associating with a certain kind of person who, in some respects, is like me. What troubles me is associating with a certain kind of person whose similarity to me is defined on the primary basis of pigmentation, hair color, eye shape, and so forth. On the basis, that is, of the very badge that was once the source of stigma. This progression is natural, perhaps even necessary. But it lends a fragile quality to calls for "Asian American pride." For what is such pride, in this light, but shame turned upside down?

There are, of course, many ways to be Asian American: single-mindedly, offhandedly, out of conviction, out of convention. Racial identity needn't be an all-or-none proposition. But the more I have had occasion to let out my "inner Asian," the more I have felt a tinge of insincerity. For it is as if I were applying a salve to a wound I am not even sure I have, nursing a memory of exclusion and second-class treatment that people who look like me are presumed to suffer. Is this memory of wounds, this wounded memory, really mine? Is there anything more to my "APA-ness"?

What's missing from Asian American culture is culture.

The idea seems absurd at first. No Asian American culture? What about Zen Buddhism, feng shui, karaoke bars? Well, yes. The problem, though, is that these and other forms of culture inherited by Asian Americans are *ethnic* in origin. The folkways are Chinese, for example, not "Asian." The holidays are Vietnamese, the language Korean, the dress Japanese. As far as an organically pan-Asian culture is concerned, there isn't much there. As one Asian American activist once said tellingly, "I think Asian American culture is anything that Asian Americans are doing. Just that."

Does the same logic apply to "Asian American history"? There is something undeniably powerful about a work like *Strangers from a Different Shore,* Ronald Takaki's synoptic history of Asian Americans. Chinese laborers built the railroads and challenged discriminatory laws, Japanese Americans fought for principle and for country in World War II. More people should know about these and other legacies. But herding such facts under the heading of "Asian American history" feels faintly like anachronism. In a subtle way, it ascribes to distinct ethnic communities of the past the pan-ethnic mind-set of the present. It serves to create collective memory *retroactively.*

Collective memory, like individual memory, can of course be constructed after the fact. But it has greater force in the world when it derives from a past of collective action and shared experience. And that is something that Asian Americans—*as* Asian Americans—have had for only two or three decades. That's why, compared with the black or Jewish or even Latino identity, the Asian American identity seems so awfully incoherent. Unlike blacks, Asians do not have a cultural idiom that arose from centuries of thinking of themselves as a race; unlike Jews, Asians haven't a unifying spiritual and historical legacy; unlike Latinos, another recently invented community, Asians don't have a linguistic basis for their continued apartness. While the Asian American identity shares with these other identities the bones of collective victimization, it does not have their flesh of cultural content.

It is more meaningful, I think, to celebrate Korean or Vietnamese or Chinese heritage—something with an identifiable cultural core. Something deeper than a mere label. Ultimately, though, my objection is not only to the APA label; it is to the labeling mind itself. The hunger for ethnic heritage is a hunger for classification, for the nostalgic certainty of place. "Heritage" offers us a usable past, coded easily by color. It does not tell us enough about how we—we of every color—should fashion a workable future.

Let me admit: When I read accounts of growing up Nisei in the middle of the century, when I read short stories by Indian immigrants about the struggle of life here, or when I read poems by the children of those immigrants, poems of loss and discovery, I feel connected to something. I find it easy to see in these characters and to hear in their diction the faces and voices of my own family. The scents, textures, and rhythms of my childhood come speeding into vibrant immediacy. This, the knowledge of cross-cultural connection, the possibility of pan-Asian empathy, is something to be valued.

But why, in the end, should empathy be skin-deep? Experiences like migration, generational conflict, language barriers, and ostracism are not the sole province of Asians or any other "race." I admire many Asian American writers who deal in such themes. I cannot get enough of Chang-Rae Lee's work. I quite enjoy Gish Jen. I find David Mura and Shawn Wong powerful. But at the same time, some of the most resonant scenes of youthful acculturation I ever read were to be found in Philip Roth's *Portnoy's Complaint.* Or *Colored People,* by Henry Louis Gates, Jr. Or Richard Rodriguez's *Hunger of Memory.* Or Norman Podhoretz's *Making It.*

I define my identity, then, in the simplest way possible: according to those with whom I identify. And I identify with whoever moves me.

No identity is stable in today's wild, recombinant mix of culture, blood, and ideas. Things fall apart; they make themselves anew. Every race carries within it the seeds of its own destruction.

Today, close to 50 percent of Asian Americans under thirty-five are marrying non-Asians, which promises rather quickly to change the meaning of the race. At the same time, growing numbers are reconstituting themselves into subcommunities of ethnicity, spurred by the Indian, Filipino, Korean, and other "Asian" Americans who have at times felt like extras in this Chinese- and Japanese-dominated show. Meanwhile, mass immigration has made for an Asian American population that is now two-thirds foreign-born, and among many recent arrivals, a pan-Asian identity seems uncomfortable and unnecessary. Finally, the accelerating whirl of global capitalism now means that the most noteworthy kind of Asian American culture may be Asian/American culture: fads and fashions that arrive directly from Asia; things you don't have to be Asian American to enjoy or to claim.

To put it simply: the Asian American identity as we now know it may not last another generation. Which makes doubters like me grow more doubtful—and more hopeful. There was something about the creation of this race, after all, that embodied the spirit of the times: compensatory, reactive, consumed with what Charles Taylor calls "the politics of recognition." There is something now about the mutation of the race that reflects a change in that spirit. If whiteness was once the thesis of American life, and colored cults of origin the antithesis, what remains to be written is the synthesis. From the perspective of my children and their children, from the perspective, that is, of those who will be the synthesis, it may seem that "Asian American" was but a cocoon: something useful, something to outgrow. And in this way, the future of the race may reflect the future of race itself. A future beyond recognition.

I am speaking now to a group of students, mostly freshmen and sophomores, at a small midwestern college. It is Asian Pacific American Heritage Month, and the students are members of the Asian Student Association. I have come to implore them to get more involved in politics, in public life.

College is supposed to be where Americans of Asian descent become Asian Americans, where the consciousness is awakened. But not this college. The students, improbably, are looking to me for guidance. Though they haven't said it in so many words, they want to know why it is they gather. They want to know what it is, besides the fact that there are so few of them on this white prairie campus, that should bring and hold them together; what, besides great potluck dinners, there is for them to *do*.

I am tempted for a moment to preach the gospel of The Individual, of the "unencumbered self" who has transcended such trivialities as race. I consider telling them that the Asian American identity is a leaky raft and that they had better learn to swim. But I don't have the heart to say any of this. For I, too, am of two minds. Instead, I tell them they should search for meaning as Asian Americans, if they so choose, or as whatever variety of self they feel free to express. So long as they feel free.

Afterward, I join a few students for dinner at a local Japanese restaurant. It is a nice place, spare and serene. We order, and then the oldest among them thanks me formally for coming to their school. For a few minutes, their attention is focused on me; they ask questions about my work, my opinions. Pretty soon, though, they're just talking to one another, in two or three different conversations, laughing, telling tales, flirting. That's all right with me. I am a stranger to them, after all, an outsider who doesn't know their stories. I am here by accident. And so I sit back, quietly, as they share their meal.

READING 25

The Day of Remembrance Ceremony

Lydia Minatoya

I am awakened by the sound of a ringing telephone. It is Sunday, raining, winter. Steve is on the telephone, telling me that today is the Day of Remembrance Ceremony—the day to commemorate the fortieth anniversary of the wartime Japanese Relocation Act. He tells me that this is the first time Japanese Americans across the nation will be gathering in recognition that such a think did take place, in recognition that they cannot forget, in recognition that internment is a

---

Lydia Minatoya is a writer living in Seattle, Washington. She has won the Pacific Northwest Booksellers' Award and the PEN American Center's Jerard Fund Award.

wound that still aches. "Can we count on you to be with us?" he asks.

The "we" is intentional. It implies a duty to my parents, my family, my people. Involuntarily, I recall a scene when I was eight years old: I have returned from school and stand in anger before my mother. "Liar, liar!" I shriek. "You made me look stupid in front of the whole class!" "*Nani,* Yuri-chan? What is it?" asks my mother with concern. "You told me you were sent to camp because America made a mistake. Teacher says no. You were sent because you are a traitor." My mother pulls me close to her, she kisses and soothes my brow. "I am so sorry Yuri-chan," she says, "for all the sadnesses like this that you will face." I tear free. "Liar," I sob. "Lousy Jap traitor."

I stop myself. There are things I do not want to remember.

"Can we count on you?" Steve is repeating.

"Yes," I whisper. I am surprised at how frightened I feel.

It is a chilling, colorless day as I cross Harvard Yard. The Remembrance Ceremony auditorium contains about sixty people. On the East Coast, it is unusual to see so many Japanese Americans congregated in one place. Only at weddings, only at funerals, only when they are kin, I think to myself. Poems and journal excerpts are read aloud. A woman my age reads a letter that her mother had written from camp. Although the mother is long dead, her voice comes through her daughter with youth, confusion, and loss.

In the bright auditorium the audience sits: erect, attentive, and self-contained. A young white husband sits next to his Japanese American wife. He wears a navy blue blazer and a school tie. His glance swerves, in panic, from her profile to the stage and back again. His posture strains crazily both toward her and away from her. His wife leans forward, like an alert student enrapt in a lecture. Her expression is composed. Her shoulders slightly shake. Tears roll steadily down her cheeks, and her husband does not know what to do. Should he put his arm around her? Rigidly, his arm grips the back of her chair. Would that be intrusive? Should he leave her alone with her thoughts? He leans away, trying to achieve enough distance so that he can keep her entire face in focus. Would that be abandoning? He has never seen her like this before. Never knew that this was important. What will this mean in their marriage? His wife is oblivious. She crosses her arms. Enfolded in her own embrace, she shifts forward and away. . . .

READING 26

Diversity and Its Discontents

Arturo Madrid

My name is Arturo Madrid. I am a citizen of the Unites States, as are my parents and as were my grandparents and my great-grandparents. My ancestors' presence in what is now the United States antedates Plymouth Rock, even without taking into account any American Indian heritage I might have.

I do not, however, fit those mental sets that define America and Americans. My physical appearance, my speech patterns, my name, my profession (a professor of Spanish) create a text that confuses the reader. My normal experience is to be asked, "And where are *you* from?" My response depends on my mood. Passive-aggressive, I answer, "From here." Aggressive-passive, I ask, "Do you mean where am I originally from?" But ultimately my answer to those follow-up questions that ask about origins will be that we have always been from here.

Overcoming my resentment I try to educate, knowing that nine times out of ten my words fall

---

Arturo Madrid is the Murchison Distinguished Professor of the Humanities at Trinity University in San Antonio, Texas.

on inattentive ears. I have spent most of my adult life explaining who I am not. I am exotic, but—as Richard Rodriguez of *Hunger of Memory* fame so painfully found out—not exotic enough . . . not Peruvian, or Pakistani, or whatever. I am, however, very clearly the *other,* if only your everyday, garden-variety, domestic *other.* I will share with you another phenomenon that I have been a part of, that of being a missing person, and how I came late to that awareness. But I've always known that I was the *other,* even before I knew the vocabulary or understood the significance of otherness.

I grew up in an isolated and historically marginal part of the United States, a small mountain village in the state of New Mexico, the eldest child of parents native to that region, whose ancestors had always lived there. In those vast and empty spaces, people who look like me, speak as I do, and have names like mine predominate. But the *americanos* lived among us: the descendants of those nineteenth-century immigrants who dispossessed us of our lands; missionaries who came to convert us and stayed to live among us; artists who became enchanted with our land and humanscape and went native; refugees from unhealthy climes, crowded spaces, unpleasant circumstances; and, of course, the inhabitants of Los Alamos, whose socio-cultural distance from us was accentuated by the fact that they occupied a space removed from and proscribed to us. More importantly, however, they—*los americanos*—were omnipresent (and almost exclusively so) in newspapers, newsmagazines, books, on radio, in movies and, ultimately, on television.

Despite the operating myth of the day, school did not erase my otherness. It did try to deny it, and in doing so only accentuated it. To this day what takes place in schools is more socialization than education, but when I was in elementary school—and given where I was—socialization was everything. School was where one became an American, because there was a pervasive and systematic denial by the society that surrounded us that we were Americans. That denial was both explicit and implicit.

Quite beyond saluting the flag and pledging allegiance to it (a very intense and meaningful action, given that the United States was involved in a war and our brothers, cousins, uncles, and fathers were on the frontlines), becoming American was learning English, and its corollary: not speaking Spanish. Until very recently ours was a proscribed language, either *de jure*—by rule, by policy, by law—or *de facto*—by practice, implicitly if not explicitly, through social and political and economic pressure. I do not argue that learning English was not appropriate. On the contrary. Like it or not, and we had no basis to make any judgments on that matter, we were Americans by virtue of having been born Americans, and English was the common language of Americans. And there was a myth, a pervasive myth, to the effect that if we only learned to speak English well—and particularly without an accent—we would be welcomed into the American fellowship.

Sam Hayakawa and the official English movement folks notwithstanding, the true text was not our speech, but rather our names and our appearance, for we would always have an accent, however perfect our pronunciation, however excellent our enunciation, however divine our diction. That accent would be heard in our pigmentation, our physiognomy, our names. We were, in short, the *other.*

Being the *other* involves a contradictory phenomenon. On the one hand being the *other* frequently means being invisible. Ralph Ellison wrote eloquently about that experience in his magisterial novel *Invisible Man.* On the other hand, being the *other* sometimes involves sticking out like a sore thumb. What is she/he doing here?

For some of us being the *other* is only annoying; for others it is debilitating; for still others it is damning. Many try to flee otherness by taking on protective colorations that provide invisibility, whether of dress or speech or manner or name.

Only a fortunate few succeed. For the majority of us otherness is permanently sealed by physical appearance. For the rest, otherness is betrayed by ways of being, speaking, or doing.

The first half of my life I spent downplaying the significance and consequences of otherness. The second half has seen me wrestling to understand its complex and deeply ingrained realities; striving to fathom why otherness denies us a voice or visibility or validity in American society and its institutions; struggling to make otherness familiar, reasonable, even normal to my fellow Americans.

I spoke earlier of another phenomenon that I am part of: that of being a missing person. Growing up in northern New Mexico I had only a slight sense of us being missing persons. *Hispanos,* as we called (and call) ourselves in New Mexico, were very much a part of the fabric of the society and there were *hispano* professionals everywhere about me: doctors, lawyers, schoolteachers, and administrators. My people owned businesses, ran organizations, and were both appointed and elected public officials.

My awareness of our absence from the larger institutional life of society became sharper when I went off to college, but even then it was attenuated by the circumstances of history and geography. The demography of Albuquerque still strongly reflected its historical and cultural origins, despite the influx of Midwesterners and Easterners. Moreover, many of my classmates at the University of New Mexico were *hispanos,* and even some of my professors. I thought that would obtain at UCLA, where I began graduate studies in 1960. Los Angeles had a very large Mexican population and that population was visible even in and around Westwood and on the campus. Many of the groundskeepers and food-service personnel at UCLA were Mexican. But Mexican-American students were few and mostly invisible, and I do not recall seeing or, knowing a single Mexican-American (or, for that matter, black, Asian, or American Indian) professional on the staff or faculty of that institution during the five years I was there. Needless to say, persons like me were not present in any capacity at Dartmouth College, the site of my first teaching appointment, and of course were not even part of the institutional or individual mind-set I knew then that we—a we that had come to encompass American Indians, Asian-Americans, African-Americans, Puerto Ricans, and women—were truly missing persons in American institutional life.

Over the past three decades, the *de jure* and *de facto* types of segregation that have ironically characterized American institutions have been under assault. As a consequence, minorities and women have become part of American institutional life. Although there are still many areas where we are not to be found, the missing persons phenomenon is not as pervasive as it once was. However, the presence of the *other,* particularly minorities, in institutions and institutional life resembles what we call in Spanish a *flor de tierra* (a surface phenomenon): we are spare plants whose roots do not go deep, vulnerable to inclemencies of an economic, or political, or social nature.

Our entrance into and our status in institutional life are not unlike a scenario set forth by my grandmother's pastor when she informed him that she and her family were leaving their mountain village to relocate to the Rio Grande Valley. When he asked her to promise that she would remain true to the faith and continue to involve herself in it, she asked why he thought she would do otherwise. "Doña Trinidad," he told her, "in the Valley there is no Spanish church. There is only an American church." "But," she protested, "I read and speak English and would be able to worship there." The pastor responded, "It is possible that they will not admit you, and even if they do, they might not accept you. And that is why I want you to promise me that you are going to go to church. Because if they don't let you in through the front door, I want you to go in through the back door. And if you can't get in through the back door, go in the side door. And if you are unable to enter through the side door I want you to go in through the window. What is important is that you enter and stay."

Some of us entered institutional life through the front door; others through the back door; and still others through side doors. Many, if not most of us, came in through windows, and continue to come in through windows. Of those who entered through the front door, some never made it past the lobby; others were ushered into corners and niches. Those who entered through back and side doors inevitably have remained in back and side rooms. And those who entered through windows found enclosures built around them. For, despite the lip service given to the goal of the integration of minorities into institutional life, what has frequently occurred instead is ghettoization, marginalization, isolation.

Not only have the entry points been limited, but in addition the dynamics have been singularly conflictive. Gaining entry and its corollary, gaining space, have frequently come as a consequence of demands made on institutions and institutional officers. Rather than entering institutions more or less passively, minorities have of necessity entered them actively, even aggressively. Rather than waiting to receive, they have demanded. Institutional relations have thus been adversarial, infused with specific and generalized tensions.

The nature of the entrance and the nature of the space occupied have greatly influenced the view and attitude of the majority population within those institutions. All of us are put into the same box; that is, no matter what the individual reality, the assessment of the individual is inevitably conditioned by a perception that is held of the class. Whatever our history, whatever our record, whatever our validations, whatever our accomplishments, by and large we are perceived unidimensionally and dealt with accordingly. I remember an experience I had in this regard, atypical only in its explicitness. A few years ago I allowed myself to be persuaded to seek the presidency of a well-known state university. I was invited for an interview and presented myself before the selection committee, which included members of the board of trustees. The opening question of that brief but memorable interview was directed at me by a member of that august body. "Dr. Madrid," he asked, "why does a one-dimensional person like you think he can be the president of a multi-dimensional institution like ours?"

Over the past four decades America's demography has undergone significant changes. Since 1965 the principal demographic growth we have experienced in the United States has been of peoples whose national origins are non-European. This population growth has occurred both through birth and through immigration. A few years ago discussion of the national birthrate had a scare dimension: the high—"inordinately high"—birthrate of the Hispanic population. The popular discourse was informed by words such as "breeding." Several years later, as a consequence of careful tracking by government agencies, we now know that what has happened is that the birthrate of the majority population has decreased. When viewed historically and comparatively, the minority populations (for the most part) have also had a decline in birthrate, but not one as great as that of the majority.

There are additional demographic changes that should give us something to think about. African-Americans are now to be found in significant numbers in every major urban center in the nation. Hispanic-Americans now number over 15 million people, and although they are a regionally concentrated (and highly urbanized) population, there is a Hispanic community in almost every major urban center of the United States. American Indians, heretofore a small and rural population, are increasingly more numerous and urban. The Asian-American population, which has historically consisted of small and concentrated communities of Chinese-, Filipino-, and Japanese-Americans, has doubled over the past decade, its complexion changed by the addition of Cambodians, Koreans, Hmongs, Vietnamese, et al.

Prior to the Immigration Act of 1965, 69 percent of immigration was from Europe. By far the largest number of immigrants to the United States since 1965 have been from the Americas and from Asia: 34 percent are from Asia; another 34 percent are from Central and South America; 16 percent are from Europe; 10 percent are from the Caribbean; the remaining 6 percent are from other continents and Canada. As was the case with previous immigration waves, the current one consists principally of young people: 60 percent are between the ages of 16 and 44. Thus, for the next few decades, we will continue to see a growth in the percentage of non-European-origin Americans as compared to European-Americans.

To sum up, we now live in one of the most demographically diverse nations in the world, and one that is increasingly more so.

During the same period social and economic change seems to have accelerated. Who would have imagined at mid-century that the prototypical middle-class family (working husband, wife as homemaker, two children) would for all intents and purposes disappear? Who could have anticipated the rise in teenage pregnancies, children in poverty, drug use? Who among us understood the implications of an aging population?

We live in an age of continuous and intense change, a world in which what held true yesterday does not today, and certainly will not tomorrow. What change does, moreover, is bring about even more change. The only constant we have at this point in our national development is change. And change is threatening. The older we get the more likely we are to be anxious about change, and the greater our desire to maintain the status quo.

Evident in our public life is a fear of change, whether economic or moral. Some who fear change are responsive to the call of economic protectionism, others to the message of moral protectionism. Parenthetically, I have referred to the movement to require more of students without in turn giving them more as academic protectionism. And the pronouncements of E. D. Hirsch and Allan Bloom are, I believe, informed by intellectual protectionism. Much more serious, however, is the dark side of the populism which underlies this evergoing protectionism—the resentment of the *other.* An excellent and fascinating example of that aspect of populism is the cry for linguistic protectionism—for making English the official language of the United States. And who among us is unaware of the tensions that underlie immigration reform, of the underside of demographic protectionism?

A matter of increasing concern is whether this new protectionism, and the mistrust of the *other* which accompanies it, is not making more significant inroads than we have supposed in higher education. Specifically, I wish to discuss the question of whether a goal (quality) and a reality (demographic diversity) have been erroneously placed in conflict, and, if so, what problems this perception of conflict might present.

As part of my scholarship I turn to dictionaries for both origins and meanings of words. Quality, according to the *Oxford English Dictionary,* has multiple meanings. One set defines quality as being an essential character, a distinctive and inherent feature. A second describes it as a degree of excellence, of conformity to standards, as superiority in kind. A third makes reference to social status, particularly to persons of high social status. A fourth talks about quality as being a special or distinguishing attribute, as being a desirable trait. Quality is highly desirable in both principle and practice. We all aspire to it in our own person, in our experiences, in our acquisitions and products, and of course we all want to be associated with people and operations of quality.

But let us move away from the various dictionary meanings of the word and to our own sense of what it represents and of how we feel about it. First of all we consider quality to be finite; that is, it is limited with respect to quantity; it has very few manifestations; it is not widely distributed. I have it and you have it, but they don't. We associate quality with homogeneity, with uniformity, with standardization, with order, regularity, neatness. All too often we equate it with smoothness, glibness, slickness, elegance. Certainly it is always expensive. We tend to identify it with those who lead, with the rich and famous. And, when you come right down to it, it's inherent. Either you've got it or you ain't.

Diversity, from the Latin *divertere,* meaning to turn aside, to go different ways, to differ, is the condition of being different or having differences, is an instance of being different. Its companion word, diverse, means differing, unlike, distinct; having or capable of having various forms; composed of unlike or distinct elements. Diversity is lack of standardization, of regularity, of orderliness, homogeneity, conformity, uniformity. Diversity introduces complications, is difficult to organize, is troublesome to manage, is problematical. Diversity is irregular, disorderly, uneven, rough. The way we use the word diversity gives us away. Something is too diverse, is extremely diverse. We want a little diversity.

When we talk about diversity, we are talking about the *other,* whatever that other might be: someone of a different gender, race, class, national origin; somebody at a greater or lesser distance from the norm; someone outside the set; someone who possesses a different set of characteristics, features, or attributes; someone who does not fall within the taxonomies we use daily and with which we are comfortable; someone who does not fit into the mental configurations that give our lives order and meaning.

In short, diversity is desirable only in principle, not in practice. Long live diversity . . . as long as it conforms to my standards, my mind set, my view of life, my sense of order. We desire, we like, we admire diversity, not unlike the way the French (and others) appreciate women; that is, *Vive la difference!*—as long as it stays in its place.

What I find paradoxical about and lacking in this debate is that diversity is the natural order of things. Evolution produces diversity. Margaret Visser, writing about food in her latest book, *Much Depends on Dinner,* makes an eloquent statement in this regard:

> Machines like, demand, and produce uniformity. But nature loathes it: her strength lies in multiplicity and in differences. Sameness in biology means fewer possibilities and therefore weakness.

The United States, by its very nature, by its very development, is the essence of diversity. It is diverse in its geography, population, institutions, technology; its social, cultural, and intellectual modes. It is a society that at its best does not consider quality to be monolithic in form or finite in quantity, or to be inherent in class. Quality in our society proceeds in large measure out of the stimulus of diverse modes of thinking and acting; out of the creativity made possible by the different ways in which we approach things; out of diversion from paths or modes hallowed by tradition.

One of the principal strengths of our society is its ability to address, on a continuing and substantive basis, the real economic, political, and social problems that have faced and continue to face us. What makes the United States so attractive to immigrants is the protections and opportunities it offers; what keeps our society together is tolerance for cultural, religious, social, political, and even linguistic difference; what makes us a unique, dynamic, and extraordinary nation is the power and creativity of our diversity.

The true history of the United States is one of struggle against intolerance, against oppression, against xenophobia, against those forces that have prohibited persons from participating in the larger life of the society on the basis of their race, their gender, their religion, their national origin, their linguistic and cultural background. These phenomena are not consigned to the past. They remain with us and frequently take on virulent dimensions.

If you believe, as I do, that the well-being of a society is directly related to the degree and extent to which all of its citizens participate in its institutions, then you will have to agree that we have a challenge before us. In view of the extraordinary changes that are taking place in our society, we need to take up the struggle again, irritating, grating, troublesome, unfashionable, unpleasant as it is. As educated and educator members of this society we have a special responsibility for ensuring that all American institutions, not just our elementary and secondary schools, our juvenile halls, or our jails, reflect the diversity of our society. Not to do so is to risk greater alienation on the part of a growing segment of our society; is to risk increased social tension in an already conflictive world; and, ultimately, is to risk the survival of a range of institutions that, for all their defects and deficiencies, provide us the opportunity and the freedom to improve our individual and collective lot.

Let me urge you to reflect on these two words—quality and diversity—and on the mental sets and behaviors that flow out of them. And let me urge you further to struggle against the notion that quality is finite in quantity, limited in its manifestations, or is restricted by considerations of class, gender, race, or national origin; or that quality manifests itself only in leaders and not in followers, in managers and not in workers, in breeders and not in drones; or that it has to be associated with verbal agility or elegance of personal style; or that it cannot be seeded, nurtured, or developed.

Because diversity—the *other*—is among us, will define and determine our lives in ways that we still do not fully appreciate, whether that other is women (no longer bound by tradition, house, and family); or Asians, African-Americans, Indians, and Hispanics (no longer

PERSONAL ACCOUNT

Going Home

It was the end of July on a day when the temperature climbed, yet again, into the middle 90s. Hot, hazy, and humid. I had just finished a summer program and was moving my things out of the college dormitory. My friend gathered my belongings on the sidewalk while I stood partially in the street to flag down a cab. When an empty cab *finally* stopped, I opened the door with the intention of putting my things into the trunk of the cab. However, before I could complete a full pivot, the cab driver asked me where I was going. I gave him my home address in the African-American neighborhood. "Where's that?" was his response. "Off of Shamut Avenue and Ruggles Street," I said. "No, sorry, I don't go there."

It actually took me a few minutes to collect myself afterward. There are countless nights when I must rely on cabs to get around the city. Surprisingly, I had grown accustomed to cab drivers ignoring my attempt to catch a taxi, but I had never had a brazen refusal after stopping. In this situation, it was hard for me to politely close the cab door without doing some damage by slamming it. I wanted the cab driver to know that I didn't appreciate his refusal, but words were hard to come by at that time. Action seemed more appropriate. At the sidewalk, my friend just shook his head.

In this and similar situations, one is forced to confront the issue of privilege. Since the cab driver did stop for me, my race could not have been a negative factor, or was it? I am giving him my money, so I should call the shots. Would he have dared to ask additional questions or refused to drive a middle-class man in a business suit? Or an elderly woman? I am an inner-city, young, Black woman. It's a shame that I cannot depend on a cab to take me home safely. No, I must stand partially in front of an oncoming cab so that it must stop. Is this even a Black or White issue? If so, would it surprise you to know that the cab driver who refused to transport me was himself Black?

Keeva Haynes

invisible, regional, or marginal); or our newest immigrants (no longer distant, exotic, alien). Given the changing profile of America, will we come to terms with diversity in our personal and professional lives? Will we begin to recognize the diverse forms that quality can take? If so, we will thus initiate the process of making quality limitless in its manifestations, infinite in quantity, unrestricted with respect to its origins, and more importantly, virulently contagious.

I hope we will. And that we will further join together to expand—not to close—the circle.

READING 27

Our Classroom Barrios

Patrick Welsh

"All the time American kids tell me, 'You're not from here; you don't belong. Go back to your own country.' Once a bunch of guys chased me and a friend with sticks, hollering at us to go back where we came from," says 10th-grader Walter Zelaya, who came to Alexandria from El Salvador two years ago.

The kids who scream "go home" are merely voicing what many adults not only hope, but believe: that the Central American "problem" in the Washington area will disappear, that "these people" will go home to their countries, and their friends and relatives will stop coming.

This summer, as I talked to Central American kids, I began to realize that the overt hostility Walter encountered is only the most blatant of the pressures Latino children endure in our schools. Despite their growing numbers, too many of us within the education system—myself included—haven't taken the time to understand the special isolation of these children who are set apart not only by language and appearance, but by the hardships and even horror many have seen and experienced.

Now that I have managed to look more closely, I have seen in these young immigrants a commitment to family that would shame most Americans. I have seen courage in the face of suffering that makes my preppy students' usual worries over cars, clothes and correct colleges look pathetic. I have seen families who, through sheer hard work and frugality, rose out of destitution to be contributing members of society.

My own education began with Jose Herrera, a senior at T. C. Williams. Sitting in the cafeteria during a break in summer school, I asked him how he got here from his native El Salvador. He replied casually, "I swam the Big River." Herrera paid $600 to a "coyote"—a mercenary specializing in smuggling Central Americans into the United States—to transport him into Guatemala in the back of a truck. Other coyotes guided him through Mexico to the spot where he swam the Rio Grande with four other Salvadorans. He was caught by immigration officers and kept in a detention center for several weeks, until a family friend sponsored him.

I heard many variants of the same story. Bartolome Paz had an easier time. When he swam the Rio Grande, "There was a coyote waiting on the other side: a friend had paid him," says Paz. Leon Soto had a less fortunate passage. In the Mexican desert coyotes beat and robbed him. Finally a coyote "put [us] in a big truck with a cover—it was hard to breathe. They drove us to Los Angeles. My brother sent the money and I flew to Washington," says Soto.

If there is romance and daring in these young people's flights to the Washington area, once here their lives are filled with the humdrum of hard work.

Now 15, Soto works more than 40 hours a week at an Alexandria fast-food restaurant. "I have to pay rent, gas, light, clothes, food. It's very hard. Look at me; I look like an old man. I

Patrick Welsh teaches English at T. C. Williams High School in Alexandria, Virginia.

miss my family all the time," he says. Herrera works a similar week as a cook, and sends half of what he makes to his mother in El Salvador. His teacher told me he missed two weeks of school when he took a second job to earn extra money because his mother was sick.

When Paz arrived in Alexandria at 15, he worked for a year and a half before registering for school. "I washed dishes but could hardly pay the bills. I got a job at Armand's bussing tables. People would say nasty words to me: 'That spic—he can't even speak English.' The manager was nice; he helped me learn English," says Paz, who just graduated from T. C.

After school every day, T. C. senior Allendis Morena takes the subway into Washington where he cleans offices. He gets home at 11:30 and is up the next morning at 6. Teachers say that the hands of Central American boys are often full of cracks and rashes from washing floors in area buildings at night. The problems Hispanic immigrants have adjusting to this country are compounded by jealousy, suspicion and class snobbery among Hispanics themselves.

T. C. graduate Janeth Soto, last year's Miss Latino America, said it was "very hard to keep both Spanish and white friends. When I was with Americans, Hispanics would say 'look at her; she wants to be *una gringa.*' "

First-generation Americans of Hispanic descent often feel embarrassed by the newcomers. One such young woman, now in a top college, described her social situation at Fairfax's J. E. B. Stuart High School as follows: "Most of my friends were white. There were a huge number of immigrants from Nicaragua and El Salvador. They dress differently and don't do well in school. It seemed like the Central Americans would come to school to start trouble; they are so insecure that they have to put up a front."

Even those first-generation Latinos who make an effort to befriend the newcomers often find themselves rebuffed. Marco Silva says he tried hard to get to know Hispanic immigrants at T. C. Williams. "I went so far as to change my schedule so I could get in classes with Hispanics. I thought about going into lower-phase [ability grouped] classes. I even tried out for soccer, but the Hispanics dogged [rejected] me," says Silva.

Class snobbery can be an even more potent factor than immigrant status in dividing Hispanics against themselves—even, according to Edgar Campos, more divisive than race is in the United States. "[In Latin America] the upper class won't even speak to the lower class. The Hispanic kids come here with an us versus them mentality; I had it when I came here," says Campos, who came here at 12 and is now a Cornell engineering student.

The daughter of a South American diplomat who attends J. E. B. Stuart told me through an interpreter that "the kids who come here from South America are shocked when they see the Central Americans. We are not used to associating with that class of people. Seeing all these low class [kids] makes you feel you don't want to be Hispanic. When I saw the Hispanics and blacks fighting at Stuart, I realized what a big mess this country is in," she said. . . .

"There is a reality to the stereotype," says Madelyn Marquez, special assistant to the president of Mount Holyoke College. "In Latin countries it is culturally acceptable to publicly recognize beauty."

But recent T. C. graduate Gustavo Rodriguez has a less philosophical explanation. "Most of my friends do it. I don't like it when they say things to non-Spanish speaking girls. They think the guys are saying worse things than they are and get scared. A Spanish-speaking girl can defend herself in the language. In our culture it is typical. When I see them doing it to another culture I feel bad. That's why I don't do it," says Rodriguez.

While middle-class students, black and white, often ignore the Hispanic kids, lower-class blacks have been known to be openly hostile. "Whenever we speak Spanish, the blacks think we are talking about them," says one junior high school student who resorted to carrying a knife to protect himself "One day at a locker after gym class I was talking to a guy who just got here from El Salvador. The black guys came over and punched me in the eye just because I was speaking Spanish."

But there is another side to the tension between black and Central American kids. "Many Salvadorans have all these ugly stereotypes about blacks," says Alexandria social worker Magda Leon. "When I worked with a class and told them about the history of slavery and segregation in this country, you could see their mouths drop. They had no idea of what blacks have gone through. Both groups need to be educated about the other. When they are they are very receptive," says Leon.

T. C. Williams teacher Vida Johnson, who is black and immigrated from the Dominican Republic as a teenager, is often called in to interpret when an Hispanic and a black American get in a fight. "When you got those kids together and they could talk back and forth, they started to understand. There were some touching moments," she says. "Both groups have irrational fears of the other. Each wants to think the other is lower than they are. We are not doing enough to get them to communicate better." For ESL teachers, their students often are illiterate in their own language; some have never held a pencil in their hands; many are grieving over family members left behind in their war-torn countries.

Spitting on the floor and grabbing girls' buttocks are not uncommon behaviors in the ESL classroom. ("Many have never been in a classroom, and think that what is acceptable in the village plaza is acceptable there," one ESL teacher told me.) And often just as ESL teachers have gotten their charges whipped into shape, an insurrection in some country sends new kids flooding into their classes and they have to start all over again.

In spite of all the problems, ESL teachers are, as a group, the most dedicated and fulfilled teachers I know. "You see children come from such poverty and go so far. It's so exhilarating to be part of it," says Barbara Elbeze, of George Washington Junior High School. Adds another ESL teacher: "With foreign students I always feel I am accomplishing something. The kids from Africa, Central America, Afghanistan all have a certain amount of drive just to be here. . . ."

Though ESL classes are crucial in helping immigrant kids connect to U.S. society, they can also be traps. ESL classes are often bunched together in one hall, isolating the immigrants from other students and further fostering stereotypes. When Isis Castro, a Cuban who has been in this country 30 years, asked if her daughter had met any Hispanics at her Fairfax elementary school, the girl replied, "Mom, I only see them in the hall or at gym; they are different; the other kids don't like them; even the school doesn't like them—they have them in a different hall."

A new program just instituted by the central office in Alexandria has created more ESL requirements. "Kids will now be isolated in the ESL ghetto even more. They can't take electives like drama. They hardly have any time to be with native speakers except in gym classes," says an Alexandria ESL teacher.

The social isolation of ESL classes impedes their very purpose—learning English. "The kids learn English faster in classes where they have native role models. In ESL classes, the major source of input is only one person—the teacher," says linguist Andrea Vincent of the Network of Educators on Central America.

But ESL teachers who are anxious to do the best for their students are caught in a bind. For foreign students in Alexandria, and, I am sure, in many other systems, getting into the mainstream can often mean going downstream. Campos recalls that after he arrived here, he got out of ESL as quickly as he could. "But I got in low phase [track] classes where there were constant discipline problems. I did everything I could to get moved up," he says.

One enormous deficit in my school and many others is the lack of bilingual guidance counselors. "I have friends who get in trouble and go to the guidance counselor for help. The counselors just say 'It will be all right; go back to class.' He leaves the student alone because trying to communicate is so frustrating for both of them. Then the kid gets screwed up more," says Gustavo Rodriguez.

Bilingual counselors can be as important in dealing with parents as with students. "Kids are embarrassed when their parents don't speak English," says Rodriguez. "My parents never came to meet my teachers because they couldn't speak English."

Arlington County is light years ahead of other area school systems in reaching out to parents of immigrant students. Many Arlington schools have bimonthly parenting workshops presented in Spanish, Vietnamese, Lao or Khmer. "In 1982 no one on our staff spoke Spanish. Now nine can," says Barrett Elementary Principal Herbert Ware. "It makes all the difference when kids feel that their parents are welcomed in the school. On parents night the auditorium is jammed because parents can now understand what is going on," says Ware. . . .

READING 28

Stumbling Blocks in Intercultural Communication

LaRay M. Barna

Why is it that contact with persons from other cultures is so often frustrating and fraught with misunderstanding? Good intentions, the use of what one considers to be a friendly approach, and even the possibility of mutual benefits don't seem to be sufficient to ensure success—to many people's surprise. A worse scenario is when rejection occurs just because the group to which a person belongs is "different." It's appropriate at this time of major changes in the international scene to take a hard look at some of the reasons for the disappointing results of attempts at communication. New proximity and new types of relationships are presenting communication challenges that few people are ready to meet.

THE SIX STUMBLING BLOCKS

Assumption of Similarities

One answer to the question of why misunderstanding and/or rejection occurs is that many people naively assume there are sufficient similarities among peoples of the world to make communication easy. They expect that simply being human and having common requirements of food, shelter, security, and so on makes everyone alike. Unfortunately, they overlook the fact that the forms of adaptation to these common biological and social needs and the values, beliefs, and attitudes surrounding them are vastly different from culture to culture. The biological commonalities are not much help when it comes to communication, where we need to exchange ideas and information, find ways to live and work together, or just make the kind of impression we want to make.

Another reason many people are lured into thinking that "people are people" is that it reduces the discomfort of dealing with difference, of not knowing. The thought that everyone is the same, deep down, is comforting. If someone acts or looks "strange" (different from them), it is then possible to evaluate this as wrong and treat everyone ethnocentrically.

The assumption of similarity does not often extend to the expectation of a common verbal language but it does interfere with caution in decoding nonverbal symbols, signs, and signals.

LaRay M. Barna is associate professor emeritus at Portland State University.

No cross-cultural studies have proven the existence of a common nonverbal language except those in support of Darwin's theory that facial expressions are universal.[1] Paul Ekman found that "the particular visible pattern on the face, the combination of muscles contracted for anger, fear, surprise, sadness, disgust, happiness (and probably also for interest) is the same for all members of our species."[2]

This seems helpful until we realize that a person's cultural upbringing determines whether or not the emotion will be displayed or suppressed as well as on which occasions and to what degree.[3] The situations that bring about the emotional feeling also differ from culture to culture; for example, the death of a loved one may be a cause for joy, sorrow, or some other emotion, depending upon the accepted cultural belief.

Since there seem to be no universals of "human nature" that can be used as a basis for automatic understanding, we must treat each encounter as an individual case, searching for whatever perceptions and communication means are held in common and proceed from there. This is summarized by Vinh The Do:

> If we realize that we are all culture bound and culturally modified, we will accept the fact that, being unlike, we do not really know what someone else "is." This is another way to view the "people are people" idea. We now have to find a way to sort out the cultural modifiers in each separate encounter to find similarity.[4]

Persons from the United States seem to hold this assumption of similarity more strongly than some other cultures do. The Japanese, for example, have the reverse belief that they are distinctively different from the rest of the world. This notion brings intercultural communication problems of its own. Expecting no similarities, they work hard to figure out the foreign stranger but do not expect foreigners to be able to understand them. This results in exclusionary attitudes and only passive efforts toward mutual understanding.[5]

As Western trappings permeate more and more of the world, the illusion of similarity increases. A look-alike facade deceives representatives from contrasting cultures when each wears Western dress, speaks English, and uses similar greeting rituals. It is like assuming that New York City, Tokyo, and Tehran are all alike because each has the appearance of a modern city. But without being alert to possible underlying differences and the need to learn new rules for functioning, persons going from one city to the other will be in immediate trouble, even when taking on such simple roles as pedestrian or driver. Also, unless a foreigner expects subtle differences, it will take a long time of noninsulated living in a new culture (not in an enclave of his or her own kind) before he or she can adjust to new perceptual and nonevaluative thinking.

The confidence that comes with the myth of similarity is much stronger than with the assumption of differences, the latter requiring tentative assumptions and behaviors and a willingness to accept the anxiety of not knowing. Only with the assumption of differences, however, can reactions and interpretations be adjusted to fit what is happening. Without it one is likely to misread signs and symbols and judge the scene ethnocentrically.

The stumbling block of assumed similarity is a "troublem," as one English learner expressed it, not only for the foreigner but for the people in the host country (United States or any other) with whom the international visitor comes into contact. The native inhabitants are likely to be lulled into the expectation that since the foreign person is dressed appropriately and speaks some of the native language, he or she will also have similar nonverbal codes, thoughts, and feelings. In the United States nodding, smiling, and affirmative comments will probably be confidently interpreted by straightforward, friendly Americans as meaning that they have informed, helped, and pleased the newcomer. It is likely, however, that the foreigner actually understood very little of the verbal and nonverbal content and was merely indicating polite interest or trying not to embarrass himself or herself or the host by trying to verbalize questions. The conversation may even have confirmed a stereotype that Americans are insensitive and ethnocentric.

In instances like this, parties seldom compare impressions and correct misinterpretations. One place where opportunities for achieving insights do occur is in an intercultural classroom. Here, for example, U.S. students often complain that international student members of a discussion or project group seem uncooperative or uninterested. One person who had been thus judged offered the following explanation:

> I was surrounded by Americans with whom I couldn't follow their tempo of discussion half of the time. I have difficulty to listen and speak, but also with the way they handle the group. I felt uncomfortable because sometimes they believe their opinion strongly. I had been very serious about the whole subject but I was afraid I would say something wrong. I had the idea but not the words.[6]

The classroom is also a good place to test whether one common nonverbal behavior, the smile, is actually the universal people assume it to be. The following enlightening comments came from international students newly arrived in the United States.[7]

Japanese student: On my way to and from school I have received a smile by non-acquaintance American girls several times. I have finally learned they have no interest for me; it means only a kind of greeting to a foreigner. If someone smiles at a stranger in Japan, especially [at] a girl, she can assume he is either a sexual maniac or an impolite person.

Korean student: An American visited me in my country for one week. His inference was that people in Korea are not very friendly because they didn't smile or want to talk with foreign people. Most Korean people take time to get to be friendly with people. We never talk or smile at strangers.

Arab student: When I walked around the campus my first day, many people smiled at me. I was very embarrassed and rushed to the men's room to see if I had made a mistake with my clothes. But I could find nothing for them to smile at. Now I am used to all the smiles.

Vietnamese student: The reason why certain foreigners may think that Americans are superficial—and they are, some Americans even recognize this—is that they talk and smile too much. For people who come from placid cultures where nonverbal language is more used, and where a silence, a smile, a glance have their own meaning, it is true that Americans speak a lot. The superficiality of Americans can also be detected in their relations with others. Their friendships are, most of the time, so ephemeral compared to the friendships we have at home. Americans make friends very easily and leave their friends almost as quickly, while in my country it takes a long time to find out a possible friend and then she becomes your friend—with a very strong sense of the term.

Statements from two U.S. students follow.[8] The first comes from someone who has learned to look for differing perceptions and the second, unfortunately, reflects the stumbling block of assumed similarity.

U.S. student: I was waiting for my husband on a downtown corner when a man with a baby and two young children approached. Judging by small quirks of fashion [I guessed] he had not been in the U.S. long. I have a baby about the same age and in appreciation of his family and obvious involvement as a father I smiled at him. Immediately I realized I did the wrong thing as he stopped, looked me over from head to toe and said, "Are you waiting for me? You meet me later?" Apparently I had acted as a prostitute would in his country.

U.S. student: In general it seems to me that foreign people are not necessarily snobs but are very unfriendly. Some class members have told me that you shouldn't smile at others while passing them by on the street. To me I can't stop smiling. It's just natural to be smiling and friendly. I can see now why so many foreign people stick together. They are impossible to get to know. It's like the Americans are big bad wolves. How do Americans break this barrier? I want friends from all over the world but how do you start to be friends without offending them or scaring them off—like sheep?

The discussion thus far threatens the popular expectation that increased contact with representatives of diverse cultures through travel, student exchange programs, joint business ventures, immigration, and so on will result in better understanding and friendship. Indeed, tests of that assumption have been disappointing.[9] For example, research has found that Vietnamese immigrants who speak English well and have the best jobs suffer more from psychosomatic complaints and psychological disorders and are less optimistic about the future than their counterparts who remain in ethnic enclaves without attempts to adjust to their new homeland. One explanation given by the researcher is that these persons, unlike the less acculturated immigrants, "spend considerable time in the mainstream of society, regularly facing the challenges and stresses of dealing with American attitudes."[10]

After twenty-four years of listening to conversations between international and U.S. students and professors and seeing the frustrations of both groups as they try to understand each other, I am inclined to agree with Charles Frankel, who says, "Tensions exist within nations and between nations that never would have existed were these nations not in such intensive cultural communication with one another."[11] Recent world events have proven this to be true.

From a communicative perspective, it doesn't have to be that way. Just as more opportunities now exist for cross-cultural contact, so does more information about how to meet this challenge. We now have access to more orientation and training programs around the world, more courses in intercultural communication in educational institutions, and more published material.[12] Until people can squarely face the likelihood of meeting up with difference and misunderstanding, however, they will not be motivated to take advantage of these resources.

Many potential travelers who do try to prepare for out-of-country travel (for business conferences, government negotiations, study tours, or whatever) might gather information about the customs of the other country and a smattering of the language. Behaviors and attitudes of its people are sometimes researched, but necessarily from a secondhand source, such as a friend who has "been there." Experts realize that information gained in this fashion is general, seldom sufficient, and may or may not be applicable to the specific situation a traveler encounters or an area that he or she visits. Also, knowing exactly "what to expect" often blinds the observer to all but that which confirms his or her image. Any contradictory evidence that does filter through the screens of preconception is likely to be treated as an exception and thus discounted.

A better approach is to begin by studying the history, political structure, art, literature, and language of the country as time permits. This provides a framework for on-site observations. It is even more important to develop an investigative, nonjudgmental attitude and a high tolerance for ambiguity—all of which require lowered defenses. Margaret Mead suggests sensitizing people to cross-cultural variables instead of developing behavior and attitude stereotypes. She reasons that there are individual differences in each encounter and that changes occur regularly in cultural patterns, making research information obsolete.[13]

Edward C. Stewart and Milton J. Bennett also warn against providing lists of "dos and don'ts" for travelers, mainly because behavior is ambiguous—the same action can have different meanings in different situations—and no one can be armed with prescriptions for every contingency. Instead they encourage people to learn to understand the assumptions and values on which their own behavior rests. This knowledge can then be compared with what is found in the other culture, and a "third culture" can be adopted based on expanded cross-cultural understanding.[14]

The remainder of this [Reading] will examine some of the variables of the intercultural communication process itself and point out danger zones therein.

Language Differences

The first stumbling block has already been discussed at length—the hazard of *assuming similarity instead of difference.* A second danger will surprise no one—*language difference.* Vocabulary, syntax, idioms, slang, dialects, and so on all cause difficulty, but the person struggling with a different language is at least aware of being in trouble.

A greater language problem is the tenacity with which some people will cling to just one meaning of a word or phrase in the new language, regardless of connotation or context. The variations in possible meaning, especially when inflection and tone are varied, are so difficult to cope with that they are often waved aside. This complacency will stop a search for understanding. The nationwide misinterpretation of Khrushchev's sentence "We will bury you" is a classic example. Even "yes" and "no" cause trouble. When a nonnative speaker first hears the English phrase, "Won't you have some tea?" he or she listens to the literal meaning of the sentence and answers, "No," meaning that he or she wants some. The U.S. hostess, on the other hand, ignores the double negative because of common usage, and the guest gets no tea. Also, in some cultures it is polite to refuse the first or second offer of refreshment. Many foreign guests have gone hungry because they never got a third offer. This is another case of where "no" means "yes."

There are other language problems, including the different styles of using language such as direct, indirect; expansive, succinct; argumentative, conciliatory; instrumental, harmonizing; and so on. These different styles can lead to wrong interpretations of intent and evaluations of insincerity, aggressiveness, deviousness, or arrogance, among others.

Nonverbal Misinterpretations

Learning the language, which most visitors to foreign countries consider their only barrier to understanding, is actually only the beginning. As Frankel says, "To enter into a culture is to be able to hear, in Lionel Trilling's phrase, its special 'hum and buzz of implication.'"[15] This suggests the third stumbling block, *nonverbal misinterpretations.* People from different cultures inhabit different sensory realities. They see, hear, feel, and smell only that which has some meaning or importance for them. They abstract whatever fits into their personal world of recognition and then interpret it through the frame of reference of their own culture. An example follows:

> An Oregon girl in an intercultural communication class asked a young man from Saudi Arabia how he would nonverbally signal that he liked her. His response was to smooth back his hair, which to her was just a common nervous gesture signifying nothing. She repeated her question three times. He smoothed his hair three times. Then, realizing that she was not recognizing this movement as his reply to her question, he automatically ducked his head and stuck out his tongue slightly in embarrassment. This behavior *was* noticed by the girl and she expressed astonishment that he would show liking for someone by sticking out his tongue.

The misinterpretation of observable nonverbal signs and symbols—such as gestures, postures, and other body movements—is a definite communication barrier. But it is possible to learn the meanings of these observable messages, usually in informal rather than formal ways. It is more difficult to understand the less obvious unspoken codes of the other cultures, such as the handling of time and spatial relationships and the subtle signs of respect of formality.

Preconceptions and Stereotypes

The fourth stumbling block is the presence of *preconceptions and stereotypes.* If the label "inscrutable" has preceded the Japanese guests, their behavior (including the constant and seemingly inappropriate smile) will probably be seen as such. The stereotype that Arabs are "inflammable" may cause U.S. students to keep their distance or even alert authorities when an animated and noisy group from the Middle East gathers. A professor who expects everyone from Indonesia, Mexico, and many other countries to "bargain" may unfairly interpret a hesitation or request from an international student as a move to manipulate preferential treatment.

Stereotypes help do what Ernest Becker says the anxiety-prone human race must do—reduce the threat of the unknown by making the world predictable.[16] Indeed, this is one of the basic functions of culture: to lay out a predictable world in which the individual is firmly oriented. Stereotypes are overgeneralized, secondhand beliefs that provide conceptual bases from which we make sense out of what goes on around us, whether or not they are accurate or fit the circumstances. In a foreign land their use increases our feeling of security. Stereotypes are psychologically necessary to the degree that we cannot tolerate ambiguity or the sense of helplessness resulting from our inability to understand and interact with people and situations beyond our comprehension.

Stereotypes are stumbling blocks for communicators because they interfere with objective viewing of stimuli—the sensitive search for cues to guide the imagination toward the other person's reality. They are not easy to overcome in ourselves or to correct in others, even with the presentation of evidence. Stereotypes persist because they are firmly established as myths or truisms by one's own national culture and because they sometimes rationalize prejudices. They are also sustained and fed by the tendency to perceive selectively only those pieces of new information that correspond to the image held. For example, a visitor who is accustomed to privation and the values of self-denial and self-help cannot fail to experience American culture as materialistic and wasteful. The stereotype for the visitor becomes a reality.

Tendency to Evaluate

The fifth stumbling block and deterrent to understanding between persons of differing cultures or ethnic groups is the *tendency to evaluate,* to approve or disapprove, the statements and actions of the other person or group. Rather than try to comprehend thoughts and feelings from the worldview of the other, we assume our own culture or way of life is the most natural. This bias prevents the open-mindedness needed to examine attitudes and behaviors from the other's point of view. A midday siesta changes from a "lazy habit" to a "pretty good idea" when someone listens long enough to realize the midday temperature in that country is 115 degrees Fahrenheit.

Fresh from a conference in Tokyo where Japanese professors had emphasized the preference of the people of Japan for simple natural settings of rocks, moss, and water and of muted greens and misty ethereal landscapes, I visited the Katsura Imperial Gardens in Kyoto. At the appointed time of the tour a young Japanese guide approached the group of twenty waiting Americans and remarked how fortunate it was that the day was cloudy. This brought hesitant smiles to the group, who were less than pleased at the prospect of a shower. The guide's next statement was that the timing of the summer visit was particularly appropriate in that the azalea and rhododendron blossoms were gone and the trees had not yet turned to their brilliant fall colors. The group laughed loudly, now convinced that the young man had a fine sense of humor. I winced at his bewildered expression, realizing that had I come before attending the conference, I would have shared the group's belief that he could not be serious.

The miscommunication caused by immediate evaluation is heightened when feelings and emotions are deeply involved; yet this is just the time when listening with understanding is most needed. As stated by Carolyn W. Sherif, Musafer Sherif, and Roger Nebergall, "A person's commitment to his religion, politics, values of his family, and his stand on the virtue of his way of life are ingredients in his self-picture—intimately felt and cherished."[17] It takes both an awareness of this tendency to close our minds and the courage to risk changing our own perceptions and values to dare to comprehend why someone thinks and acts differently from us. Religious wars and negotiation deadlocks everywhere are examples of this.

On an interpersonal level there are innumerable illustrations of the tendency to evaluate which result in a breach in intercultural relationships. Two follow:[18]

U.S. student: A Persian friend got offended because when we got in an argument with a third party, I didn't take his side. He says back home you are supposed to take a friend's or family's side even when they are wrong. When you get home then you can attack the "wrongdoer" but you are never supposed to go against a relative or friend to a stranger. This I found strange because even if it is my mother and I think she is wrong, I say so.

Korean student: When I call on my American friend he said through window, "I am sorry. I have no time because of my study." Then he shut the window. I couldn't understand through my cultural background. House owner should have welcome visitor whether he likes or not and whether he is busy or not. Also the owner never speaks without opening his door.

The admonition to resist the tendency to immediately evaluate does not mean that one should not develop one's own sense of right and wrong. The goal is to look and listen empathically rather than through the thick screen of value judgments that impede a fair and total understanding. Once comprehension is complete, it can be determined whether or not there is a clash in values or ideology. If so, some form of adjustment or conflict resolution can be put into place.

High Anxiety

High anxiety or *tension* also known as *stress,* is common in cross-cultural experiences due to the number of uncertainties present. The two words, *anxiety* and *tension,* are linked because one cannot be mentally anxious without also being physically tense. Moderate tension and positive attitudes prepare one to meet challenges with energy. Too much anxiety or tension requires some form of relief, which too often comes in the form of defenses, such as the skewing of perceptions, withdrawal, or hostility. That's why it is considered a serious stumbling block. As stated by Young Y. Kim,

> Stress, indeed, is considered to be inherent in intercultural encounters, disturbing the internal equilibrium of the individual system. Accordingly, to be interculturally competent means to be able to manage such stress, regain internal balance, and carry out the communication process in such a way that contributes to successful interaction outcomes.[19]

High anxiety or tension, unlike the other five stumbling blocks (assumption of similarity, language, nonverbal misinterpretations, preconceptions and stereotypes, and the practice of immediate evaluation), is not only distinct but often underlies and compounds the other stumbling blocks. The use of stereotypes and evaluations are defense mechanisms in themselves, used to alleviate the stress of the unknown. If the person were tense or anxious to begin with, these mechanisms would be used even more. Falling prey to the aura of similarity is also a protection from the stress of recognizing and accommodating to differences. Different language and nonverbal patterns are difficult to use or interpret under the best of conditions. The distraction of trying to reduce the feeling of anxiety (sometimes called "internal noise") makes mistakes even more likely. Jack R. Gibb remarks,

> Defense arousal prevents the listener from concentrating upon the message Not only do defensive communicators send off multiple value, motive, and affect cues, but also defensive recipients distort what they receive. As a person becomes more and more defensive, he becomes less and less able to perceive accurately the motives, the values, and the emotions of the sender.[20]

Anxious feelings usually permeate both parties in an intercultural dialogue. The host national is uncomfortable when talking with a foreigner because he or she cannot maintain the normal flow of verbal and nonverbal interaction. There are language and perception barriers; silences are too long or too short; proxemic and other norms may be violated. He or she is also threatened by the other's unknown knowledge, experience, and evaluation—the visitor's potential for scrutiny and rejection of the person and/or the country. The inevitable question, "How do you like it here?" which the foreigner abhors, is a quest for reassurance or at least a "feeler" that reduces the unknown. The reply is usually more polite than honest, but this is seldom realized.

The foreign members of dyads are even more threatened. They feel strange and vulnerable, helpless to cope with messages that swamp them. Their own normal reactions are inappropriate. Their self-esteem is often intolerably undermined unless they employ such defenses as withdrawal into their own reference group or into themselves, screen out or misperceive stimuli, use rationalization or overcompensation, or become aggressive or hostile. None of these defenses leads to effective communication.

Culture Shock If a person remains in a foreign culture over time, the stress of constantly being on guard to protect oneself against making "stupid mistakes" takes its toll and he or she will probably be affected by "culture fatigue," usually called *culture shock.* According to LaRay M. Barna,

> the innate physiological makeup of the human animal is such that discomfort of varying degrees occurs in the presence of alien stimuli. Without the normal props of one's own culture, there is unpredictability, helplessness, a threat to self-esteem, and a general feeling of "walking on ice"—all of which are stress producing.[21]

The result of several months of this sustained anxiety or tension (or excitation if the high activation is perceived positively) is that reserve energy supplies become depleted, the person's physical capacity is weakened, and a feeling of exhaustion, desperation, or depression may take over.[22] He or she consciously or unconsciously is then more likely to use psychological defenses, such as those described previously. If this temptation is resisted, the sojourner suffering from the strain of constant adjustment may find his or her body absorbing the stress in the form of stomach- or backaches, insomnia, inability to concentrate, or other stress-related illnesses.[23]

The following account by a sojourner to the United States illustrates the trauma of culture shock:

> Soon after arriving in the United States from Peru, I cried almost every day. I was so tense I heard without hearing, and this made me feel foolish. I also escaped into sleeping more than twelve hours at a time and dreamed of my life, family, and friends in Lima. After three months of isolating myself in the house and speaking to no one, I ventured out. I then began to have severe headaches. Finally I consulted a doctor, but she only gave me a lot of drugs to relieve the pain. Neither my doctor nor my teachers ever mentioned the two magic words that could have changed my life: culture shock! When I learned about this, I began to see things from a new point of view and was better able to accept myself and my feelings.
>
> I now realize most of the Americans I met in Lima before I came to the U.S. were also in one of the stages of culture shock. They demonstrated a somewhat hostile attitude toward Peru, which the Peruvians sensed and usually moved from an initially friendly attitude to a defensive, aggressive

> attitude or to avoidance. The Americans mostly stayed within the safe cultural familiarity of the embassy compound. Many seemed to feel that the difficulties they were experiencing in Peru were specially created by Peruvians to create discomfort for "gringos." In other words, they displaced their problem of adjustment and blamed everything on Peru.[24]

Culture shock is a state of dis-ease, and, like a disease, it has different effects, different degrees of severity, and different time spans for different people. It is the least troublesome to those who learn to accept cultural diversity with interest instead of anxiety and manage normal stress reactions by practicing positive coping mechanisms, such as conscious physical relaxation.[25]

Physiological Reactions Understanding the physiological component of the stumbling block of anxiety/tension helps in the search for ways to lessen its debilitating effects.[26] It is hard to circumvent because, as human animals, our biological system is set so that anything that is perceived as being "not normal" automatically signals an alert.[27] Depending on how serious the potential threat seems to be, extra adrenaline and noradrenaline pour into the system; muscles tighten; the heart rate, blood pressure, and breathing rate increase; the digestive process turns off; and other changes occur.[28]

This "fight or flight" response was useful—actually a biological gift for survival or effective functioning—when the need was for vigorous action. However, if the danger is to one's social self, which is more often the case in today's world, too much anxiety or tension just gets in the way. This is particularly true in an intercultural setting, where the need is for understanding, calm deliberation, and empathy in order to untangle misperceptions and enter into smooth relationships.

All is not doom and gloom, however. As stated by Holger Ursin, "The bodily response to changes in the environment and to threatening stimuli is simply activation."[29] Researchers believe that individuals control their emotional response to that activation by their own cognitions.[30] If a person expects something to be exciting rather than frightening, he or she is more likely to interpret the somatic changes of the body as excitement. Hans Selye would label that "the good stress," which does much less harm unless it continues for some time without relief.[31] Feeling "challenged" facilitates functioning as opposed to feeling "threatened."[32]

People also differ in their stress tolerance. Everyone knows people who, for whatever the reasons, "fall apart at the least thing" and others who seem unflappable in any crisis. If you are one of the former, there are positive ways to handle the stress of intercultural situations, whether these be one-time encounters or frequent dialogues in multicultural settings. For starters, you can find opportunities to become familiar with many types of people so that differences become normal and interesting instead of threatening. And you can practice body awareness so that changes that signify a stress reaction can be identified and counteracted.

CONCLUSION

Being aware of the six stumbling blocks is certainly the first step in avoiding them, but it isn't easy. For most people it takes insight, training, and sometimes an alteration of long-standing habits or thinking patterns before progress can be made. The increasing need for global understanding, however, gives all of us the responsibility for giving it our best effort.

We can study other languages and learn to expect differences in nonverbal forms and other cultural aspects. We can train ourselves to meet intercultural encounters with more attention to situational details. We can use an investigative approach rather than stereotypes and preconceptions. We can gradually expose ourselves to differences so that they become less threatening.

We can even learn to lower our tension level when needed to avoid triggering defensive reactions.

The overall goal should be to achieve *intercultural communication competence,* which is defined by Kim as "overall internal capability of an individual to manage key challenging features of intercultural communication: namely, cultural differences and unfamiliarity, intergroup posture, and the accompanying experience of stress."[33]

Roger Harrison adds a final thought:

> The communicator cannot stop at knowing that the people he is working with have different customs, goals, and thought patterns from his own. He must be able to feel his way into intimate contact with these alien values, attitudes, and feelings. He must be able to work with them and within them, neither losing his own values in the confrontation nor protecting himself behind a wall of intellectual detachment.[34]

NOTES

1. See Charles Darwin, *The Expression of Emotions in Man and Animals* (New York: Appleton, 1872); Irenaus Eibl-Eibesfeldt, *Ethology: The Biology of Behavior* (New York: Holt, Rinehart & Winston, 1970); Paul Ekman and Wallace V. Friesen, "Constants across Cultures in the Face and Emotion," *Journal of Personality and Social Psychology* 17 (1971): 124–29.
2. Paul Ekman, "Movements with Precise Meanings," *Journal of Communication* 26 (Summer 1976): 19–20.
3. Paul Ekman and Wallace v. Friesen, "The Repertoire of Nonverbal Behavior—Categories, Origins, Usage, and Coding," *Semiotica* 1 (1969): 1.
4. Personal correspondence. Mr. Do is a multicultural specialist, Portland Public Schools, Portland, Oregon.
5. E. Tai, "Modification of the Western Approach to Intercultural Communication for the Japanese Context," master's thesis, Portland State University, Portland, Oregon, 1986: 45–47.
6. Taken from student papers in a course in intercultural communication taught by the author.
7. Ibid.
8. Ibid.
9. See, for example, Bryant Wedge, *Visitors to the United States and How They See Us* (Princeton, NJ: D. Van Nostrand, 1965); and Milton Miller et al., "The Cross-Cultural Student: Lessons in Human Nature," *Bulletin of Menninger Clinic* (March 1971).
10. Jack D. Horn, "Vietnamese Immigrants: Doing Poorly by Doing Well," *Psychology Today* (June 1980): 103–4.
11. Charles Frankel, *The Neglected Aspect of Foreign Affairs* (Washington, DC: Brookings Institution, 1965): 1.
12. For information see newsletters and other material prepared by the Society for Intercultural Education, Training and Research (SIETAR), 1444 I Street NW, Suite 700, Washington, DC, 20005. Sources are also listed in the *International and Intercultural Communication Annual,* published by the National Communication Association, 5105 Backlick Rd., Suite E, Annandale, VA, 22003; the *International Journal of Intercultural Relations,* Department of Psychology, University of Mississippi, University, MS, 38677.
13. Margaret Mead, "The Cultural Perspective," in *Communication or Conflict,* edited by Mary Capes (New York: Association Press, 1960).
14. Edward C. Stewart and Milton J. Bennett, *American Cultural Patterns: A Cross-Cultural Perspective,* rev. ed. (Yarmouth, ME: Intercultural Press, 1991).
15. Frankel, *The Neglected Aspect of Foreign Affairs,* 103.
16. Ernest Becker, *The Birth and Death of Meaning* (New York: Free Press, 1962), 84–89.
17. Carolyn W. Sherif, Musafer Sherif, and Roger Nebergall, *Attitude and Attitude Change* (Philadelphia: W. B. Saunders, 1965), vi.
18. Taken from student papers in a course in intercultural communication taught by the author.
19. Young Y. Kim, "Intercultural Communication Competence: A Systems-Theoretic View," in *Cross-Cultural Interpersonal Communication,* vol. 15, edited by Stella Ting-Toomey and Felipe Korzenny, *International and Intercultural Communication Annual* (Newbury Park, CA: Sage, 1991).

20. Jack R. Gibb, "Defensive Communication," *Journal of Communication* 2 (September 1961): 141–48.
21. LaRay M. Barna, "The Stress Factor in Intercultural Relations," in *Handbook of Intercultural Training,* vol. 2, edited by Dan Landis and Richard W. Brislin (New York: Pergamon Press, 1983), 42–43.
22. Hans Selye, "Stress: It's a G.A.S.," *Psychology Today* (September 1969).
23. Barna, "Stress Factor," 29–30.
24. Personal correspondence.
25. Barna, "Stress Factor," 33–39.
26. Hans Selye, *Stress without Distress* (New York: J. B. Lippincott, 1974); Hans Selye, *The Stress of Life* (New York: McGraw-Hill, 1976).
27. Alvin Toffler, *Future Shock* (New York: Bantam, 1970), 334–42; Holger Ursin, "Activation, Coping and Psychosomatics," in *Psychobiology of Stress: A Study of Coping Men,* edited by Eirind Baade, Seymour Levine, and Holger Ursin (New York: Academic Press, 1978).
28. Donald Oken, "Stress—Our Friend, Our Foe," in *Blue Print for Health* (Chicago: Blue Cross, 1974).
29. Ursin, "Activation, Coping and Psychosomatics," 219.
30. B. B. Brown, "Perspectives on Social Stress," in *Selye's Guide to Stress Research,* vol. 1, edited by Hans Selye (New York: Van Nostrand Reinhold, 1980); J. P. Keating, "Environmental Stressors: Misplaced Emphasis Crowding as Stressor," in *Stress and Anxiety,* vol. 6, edited by Irwin G. Sarason and Charles D. Spielberger (Washington, DC: Hemisphere, 1979); Stanley Schachter and J. E. Singer, "Cognitive, Social and Physiological Determinants of Emotional State," *Psychological Review* 69 (1962).
31. Hans Selye, "On the Real Benefits of Eustress," *Psychology Today* (March 1978).
32. Richard S. Lazarus, "Positive Denial: The Case for Not Facing Reality," *Psychology Today* (November 1979).
33. Kim, "Intercultural Communication Competence," 259.
34. Roger Harrison, "The Design of Cross-Cultural Training: An Alternative to the University Model," in *Explorations in Human Relations Training and Research*, NEA, no. 2 (Bethesda, MD: National Training Laboratories, 1966), 4.

PERSONAL ACCOUNT

Where Are You From?

As a freshman at a predominantly white private college, I was confronted with a number of unusual situations. I was extremely young for a college freshman (I was sixteen), I was African American, and I was placed in upper-division courses, because of my academic background. So being accepted and fitting in were crucial to me.

I was enrolled in a course, Political Thought, with approximately thirty other students, mostly juniors and seniors who had taken courses with this professor before. I was the only African American in the class. During introductions for the first class, he never got around to letting me speak, even though he went alphabetically on the list (my last name begins with a "C"). Later, I began to be aware of his exclusion of me from class discussion. By the third class, I guess he felt there was no longer any way he could avoid speaking to me. He asked me a few questions about myself—where I was from, what high school had I attended, and what was my major. His questions began to seem like a personal attack, and then finally he asked, "Why are you here?" "Where are you from?" I was quite taken aback by his line of questioning, when one of the upperclassmen (a white man) responded for me. "She's a freshman, Dr. B. Any more questions?" That guy became one of my closest friends. We have maintained contact ever since college. His response to Dr. B. totally changed the professor's way of treating me.

C.C.

READING 29

The Cost of Whiteness

Thandeka

Most white Americans believe they were born white. Yet their own stories of early racial experiences describe persons who were bred white. Which is it—nature or nurture? Neither. The social process that creates whites produces persons who must think of their whiteness as a biological fact.

The process begins with a rebuke. A parent or authority figure reprimands the child because it's not yet white. The language used by the adult is racial, but the content of the message pertains to the child's own feelings and what the child must do with feelings the adult doesn't like. Stifle them. Philosopher Martha Nussbaum, in her book *Cultivating Humanity: A Classical Defense of Reform in Liberal Education,* tells how she learned to do this as a child being taught to be white.

Nussbaum's reflections begin with a description of the incident that provoked her father's racial rebuke: "In Bryn Mawr, Pennsylvania, in the early 1960s, I encountered black people only as domestic servants. There was a black girl my age named Hattie, daughter of the live-in help of an especially wealthy neighbor. One day, when I was about ten, we had been playing in the street and I asked her to come in for some lemonade. My father, who grew up in Georgia, exploded, telling me that I must never invite a black person into the house again." Nussbaum's first lessons ended at school where the only African Americans present were "kitchen help." Here, she and her classmates learned how to "efface them from our minds when we studied." The target of Nussbaum's first lessons in whiteness was her own sentient awareness of the surrounding environment. She had to learn how to disengage her own feelings, how to dissociate herself from them.

Most discussions of the creation of whites overlook this stage in the development of a white racial consciousness and thus assume that whites are insensitive to blacks by nature. White supremacist and anti-racist groups seem to hold this belief in common—that whites are born racist with a biologically predetermined disposition to hate blacks. To begin elsewhere, we have to pay attention to the feelings the child learns to squelch. I was able to listen in on these feelings when I conducted interviews for my book, *Learning to Be White.* An adult I call "Jay," for example, described the rationale for his parents' decision to take him on a car tour of the "black ghetto" when he was four. His parents knew he had never seen black people before and did not want him to embarrass the family by staring at "them" when the family went to New York on vacation the following month. The adult motivation for this mini tour of black America was to pre-empt a parental rebuke that would have occurred if Jay had indeed stared at "them" while on vacation. Jay thus learned something about what to do with his own natural curiosity. Suppress it. The protocol associated with this new knowledge was self-evident: Don't stare at them. The deeper implications of the message Jay received would develop over time: Don't even notice that they are there. Such behavior, of course, is described by Ralph Ellison's protagonist in *Invisible Man:* "I am invisible, understand, simply because people refuse to see me." Jay had begun to learn not to see what he saw.

Another example. "Sally's" parents, strong civil rights supporters, preached racial equality both at home and in the streets. She was thus flabbergasted when her parents prevented her from going out with a high school friend who came to pick her up for a Friday night date. He was black. The parents sent him away and

---

Thandeka, associate professor of theology and culture, Meadville/Lombard Theological School, is author of *Learning to Be White: Money, Race, and God in America* (Continuum 1999). Her name, "lovable" in Xhosa, was given to her by Archbishop Desmond Tutu.

forbade her to date him. "What will our neighbors say if they see you on the arms of a black man?" Sally was furious with them and thought them hypocrites. But she submitted to their dictates. "What was I going to do?" she asked rhetorically. "Rebel? Not in my household. They would have disowned me." So she suppressed her feelings.

Then there's "Dan." In college during the late 1950s, Dan joined a fraternity. With his prompting, his chapter pledged a black student. When the chapter's national headquarters learned of this first step toward the integration of its ranks, headquarters threatened to rescind the local chapter's charter unless the black student was expelled. The local chapter caved in to the pressure and Dan was elected to tell the black student member he would have to leave. Dan did it. "I felt so ashamed of what I did," he told me. "I have carried this burden for forty years," he said. "I will carry it to my grave." And he began to cry. Why? Because as psychoanalytic theorist Judith Lewis Herman reminds us in the opening pages of her book, *Trauma and Recovery,* the unspeakable will out.

"Sarah." At age sixteen, Sarah brought her best friend home with her from high school. After the friend left, Sarah's mother told her not to invite her friend home again. "Why?" Sarah asked, astonished and confused. "Because she's colored," her mother responded. That was not an answer, Sarah thought to herself. It was obvious that her friend was colored, but what kind of reason was that for not inviting her? So Sarah persisted, insisting that her mother tell her the real reason. None was forthcoming. The indignant look on her mother's face, however, made Sarah realize that if she persisted, she would jeopardize her mother's affection toward her. Horrified by what she had just glimpsed, Sarah severed her friendship with the girl. Sarah told me she had not thought of this incident in twenty years. She also said that until now, she had never consciously said to herself that for her the deepest tragedy in this incident was her loss of trust in her mother's love. Sarah, like Dan, began to cry.

Every European American I interviewed could tell me a tale about how they learned as youth to blunt positive feelings toward persons beyond the pale. These aren't the kinds of tales I had expected when I asked them to recount stories of their earliest racial incidents. To my astonishment, instead of describing interracial incidents, they described intra-racial conflicts. The message they learned was repress, deny, and split off from consciousness feelings that, if expressed, would provoke racial attacks from the adults in their own community. From these stories, I learned that becoming white is the product of a child's siege mentality. It's a defense mechanism to stop racial rebukes from one's own kith and kin.

Few accounts reveal this white siege mentality better than a story by writer Don Wallace in his *New York Times,* October 11, 1995, op-ed piece, "How I Learned to Fear the Cops." Wallace, in this essay, describes several incidents in which he was accosted by cops. The first altercation occurred when Wallace was ten. Wallace uses the third-person singular to tell this tale in the opening paragraphs of his essay:

> The 10-year-old boy skipped down the sidewalk a few steps ahead of his parents in the warmth of a Los Angeles night in 1962. Behind him glowed Olvera Street, a slice of the old California's Mexican heritage. . . . He heard the screech of brakes but paid no mind until a police officer seized him by the shoulder and pushed him against a wall. Another officer shoved his 12-year old brother. Then the boy saw something even more terrifying: the gun in the cop's hand.

Wallace's father spoke up, berating the cop and demanding an apology for pointing a gun at his sons, who were church-goers, Boy and Cub Scout members, and good students. The cops stood their ground, demanding that he get out of the way or face arrest. Wallace, who until this point has not told the reader the "race" of the family, now teases the reader, asking: "What do you think happened next? You've read the papers. You followed the Rodney King case. If the family in this true story were black, what odds would you give on the father staying out of jail? Or staying alive?" But he and his family are white, Wallace tells us, and they "got to go home to [their] all-white suburb."

As a teenager, Wallace continued to play on the wrong side of town. He attended a large inner-city high school in Long Beach and would often visit his first girlfriend, "a biology whiz" who had a Spanish surname and lived on the west side. To visit her, Wallace had to go through a Checkpoint Charlie consisting of a concrete levee, oil fields, and two eight-lane boulevards marking a racial change from all-white to brown, black, and yellow. The few streets which led in or out of the area created choke points and were usually "guarded by a squad car at each one, day and night." In his sophomore year, almost every night as he drove from his girlfriend's house, a squad car would swing behind him and tail him. "I got used to it," Wallace says with the determination of a teenage Rambo. He treated "each drive home as if it were a mission through hostile territory: my signals perfect, my turns crisp, my speed steady and always five miles per hour below the limit." Nevertheless, in spite of his white, "preppie look," he was stopped eleven times "with nary a ticket to show for it." The policemen's message was clear: Whites were not allowed to socialize in a non-white zone. Recounting an incident in which he and two friends were caught in the wrong zone, Wallace writes: "The police marched three of us into a field behind a screen of oil wells and then separated and handcuffed us. For an hour, we were threatened with a beating and arrest, yet no infraction was mentioned. The police were delivering their message of intimidation, insuring the crackle of fear, the walking-on-eggshells feeling, everytime we entered the nonwhite zone." Similarly, when Wallace, who was president of the student body and a football letterman, chose to sit with black friends during a basketball game, two police officers "waded into the bleachers and hauled me out to the floor to be searched, in full view of my teachers and friends."

Such incidents made it clear not only that race mixing was prohibited by these cops, but that neither whites nor non-whites are safe from police brutality when they enter a racial zone off limits to their kind. There is, however, another story being told. Wallace, in the process of recounting his youthful escapades with the police, also sings a different tune. He tells us how "this white boy [who] got the message long ago" grew up to "fear the cops." Wallace recounts this adult tale of submission to authority in another key.

Wallace's journalistic eye focuses our attention on the fact that as a youth, in spite of his ostensibly rebellious nature, he did not rebel. The boy did not protest his harassment but adjusted. Writes Wallace: "I am astonished how we adjusted to this state of constant siege." This adult astonishment forces us to set aside his teenage bravado and focus on a fact that neither the teenager nor the adult could state directly: Both the white youth and white adult civilians in Wallace's recollections submitted to the policemen's harassment. That he submitted to authority is clear. We simply must pay attention to the unsaid. Absent from Wallace's account is a description of complaints to his parents or schoolteachers. Nor does he report having gone to either the local police station or to the District Attorney's office to file a complaint. Such acts would have been made less likely by the fact that both his parents and the adults at his school were models of submission to police abuse rather than rebellion. Even Wallace's father, after an initial dismayed protest against the officer who had pulled a gun on white boys who were good (Scouts, Christian, and smart), relented and took his family home to their "all-white suburb." This, of course, was what the cops had wanted in the first place.

Wallace is recounting the antics of a teenager who grandstanded rather than rebelled. He is describing more than members of a police force out of control. He is also exposing a pervasive white adult submission to the threatening presence of its own police force, which is dead set on preventing so-called race mixing. The adult submission to this threat, in the boy's eyes, was the same as consent. Police harassment, together with the massive submission of adults to this brute force, taught the boy and the adult he grew up to be what he must do to act like a white person: Submit to the unwritten race laws of his policed state. This demand for submission to white race laws created a zone of fear and timidity within Wallace, the adult. As he writes: "Layer upon layer of incidents like these build a foundation of mistrust. It's why I'm a very cautious driver today." Wallace, in effect, has described the origins of his present siege mentality.

He had learned through experience that in a *de jure* and/or *de facto* system of racial apartheid, every member of the community is under siege. Instead of inspiring his rebellious rage, however, this siege mentality actually prevents Wallace from expressing his rage toward the police force. Even in his essay, instead of calling for more civilian oversight of an out-of-control police force, Wallace muffles his impulse to protest by cloaking it in blackness and concludes his essay with the moral tepidity of an interracial truism: "I firmly believe there will be no peace until black people can walk the same streets as white people without fearing the sound of the squad car's brakes, as I learned to do that night on Olvera Street." By referring to the risk African Americans run when they enter white zones, Wallace expresses in blackface his own fears as a European American caught in the wrong racial zone. Albeit unwittingly, this gesture towards tolerance ends up confirming the system Wallace criticizes.

After the siege mentality is in place, race talk by the newly created white usually follows. Such talk, however, often distracts attention from what produced it: white adult abuse against their own kids. The story of Dorothy, a middle-aged woman I met at a dinner party in an Upper West Side Manhattan apartment, shows how race talk about racism begins as a distraction from the emotional pain entailed in becoming white.

Dorothy and I were introduced by the host of the dinner party. Dorothy was a "poet," whose most recent volume of poetry was prominently displayed on the coffee table in front of the couch on which we were seated. I was a "writer" working on white identity issues. After our host departed, Dorothy wanted to know what a "white identity" was. She did not have one, she assured me. She was simply an American. I could help her find hers, I responded, if she wanted to know what it looked like. Her interest piqued, she accepted the offer. True to form, I asked her to recollect her earliest memory of knowing what it means to be white.

After a little excavation, she finally found the memory: When Dorothy was five, she and her family lived in Mexico for a year. Although her family's housekeeper brought her daughter, who was also five, to work, Dorothy's parents forbade her to play with the little girl. Dorothy, in fact, was never allowed to play with any Mexican children, and she and her two brothers were forbidden to venture beyond the gates of their backyard. Dorothy remembered her feelings of sadness and regret. The Mexican children and their parents seemed so much more at ease with themselves and each other. They seemed warm and tactile, unlike her own family, whose manners and expressions were cold and constrained.

Dorothy told me she had not thought of these feelings in years. She confessed that she now recalled how often, during that year, she wished to be brown. I suggested that the term "white" might not mean anything consciously to her today because it had too much negative meaning for her when she was five. She agreed and now expressed surprise that she had not written about these feelings, memories, or experiences in her work. She said much of her life had been devoted to freeing herself from the emotional strictures imposed on her by her parents. Most of her poetry was about them and the way they had drained life out of her. She reiterated her astonishment that this set of memories had not surfaced in her work. As she blushed, the resurrected feelings of the child seemed to disappear.

I now watched Dorothy transfer her own dis-ease to me and I braced myself for an attack. She was no longer the object of her painful racial memories. Now, I was. "You know," Dorothy now said pointedly, "you are the first black I've ever felt comfortable with talking about racism." To which I responded, "Why is it so easy for you to think of me as a 'black,' and yet until a few minutes ago you could not make any sense out of thinking about yourself as a 'white'?" Further—"Were we really talking about racism? And if so, whose? Your parents'? Yours? That of the five-year-old girl who wanted to be brown?"

Dorothy was silent for a long moment. "I now understand what I've just done, and I'm horrified," she finally confessed. She realized that if I were a black, she, too, must have a race: the one that had enraged her as a child. Not surprisingly, Dorothy now confessed that she was afraid to say anything else—not because I might condemn her, but much more tellingly because, as she put it, "I might not like what I hear myself saying." If she'd been forced to listen to herself continue to talk, she would have had to listen to a white woman speak in ways that the five-year-old child would have despised. She did not want to listen to such talk. Nor did I. Our conversation very quickly came to an end.

Dorothy had recalled the feelings of the child whose parents wanted to love a *white* child. The parts of her that were not "white"—her positive feelings toward Mexicans—had to be set aside as unloved and therefore unlovable. This sense of being unlovable is the core content of shame, psychoanalyst Léon Wurmser reminds us in his book, *The Mask of Shame.* Shame, Wurmser suggests, "forces one to hide, to seek cover and to veil or mask oneself." Such feelings, self psychologist Heinz Kohut notes in *The Search for the Self,* actually result from the failure of the parents or caretakers to adequately love the child, but the child blames itself rather than its parent or caretaking environment. Guilt, by contrast with shame, Helen Merrell Lynd notes in her book, *On Shame and the Search for Identity,* results from a wrongful deed, a self-condemnation for what one has done. A penalty can be exacted for this wrongful act. Recompense can be made and restitution paid. Not so with shame. Nothing can be done because shame results not from something one did wrong but rather from something wrong with oneself. Split-off feelings can create this feeling of personal shame. . . .

What can we conclude from these various examples of the processes entailed in becoming white in America? Two things. Whites like to think of themselves as biologically white in order to hide what they'd like to forget: Once upon a time they were attacked by whites in their own community because they weren't yet white. To stop the attack, they learned to disdain their own feelings. Who wants to remember such attacks? Who wants to know that they were once racial outsiders to their own racial group? Who wants to unearth denied feelings? Better to blame the blacks (and other so-called "colored groups"—"so-called" because I've never met anyone who didn't have a color!) than face the truth: whites are race victims of their own community's racial codes of conduct.

Most whites suffer from a survivor complex. They are products of a race war that rages within white America. The fact that there's a racial pecking order among ethnic groups in white America exacerbates this problem. As social psychologist Gordon Allport notes in his classic 1954 study *The Nature of Prejudice,* this race rating-scheme is widespread and remarkably uniform in judgments "concerning the relative acceptability [that is, whiteness] of various ethnic stocks: Germans, Italians, Armenians, and the like. Each of these can in sequence look down upon all groups lower in the series." Such racial abuse meted out to the "ethnics" who are too far away from the Anglo-Saxon Protestant ethnic ideal can have devastating effects not only on one's personality but also on one's paycheck.

This economic penalty is difficult to grasp because Americans have been taught to think only of the benefits—the "privileges"—of whiteness accorded to Europeans who immigrated to America and became white. W. E. B. Du Bois called the race privileges given to these workers and their progeny "the wages of whiteness." Whiteness, as Du Bois notes in his book *Black Reconstruction in America: 1860–1880,* meant "public deference and titles of courtesy"; access to "public functions, public parks and the best schools"; jobs as policemen; the right to sit on juries; voting rights; flattery from newspapers while Negro news was "almost utterly ignored except in crime and ridicule." These privileges also included the right, based on legal indifference and social approval, to taunt, police, humiliate, mob, rape, lynch, jibe, rob, jail, mutilate, and burn Negroes, which became a sporting game, "a sort of permissible Roman holiday for the entertainment of vicious whites." During the late 1800s, for example, "practically all white southern men went armed and the South reached the extraordinary distinction of being the only modern civilized country where human beings were publicly burned alive."

The price exacted for these privileges, however, was also considerable. Du Bois summarizes the main cost in the nineteenth century antebellum South: no major labor movement to protect the region's five million poor whites, who owned no slaves, from the 8,000 largest slaveholders who, in effect, ruled the South. Hatred of the Negro, slave and free, blocked furtive attempts by the lower classes to fight their own race's class exploiters. By playing the labor costs of both whites and Negroes against each other, contractors kept the earnings of both groups low. Both before and after the civil war, white privileges functioned as a kind of "public and psychological wage," supplementing the low-paying jobs that whites could easily lose to a lower-paid black worker.

I am not denying "white privilege." "All whites," as legal scholar Cheryl J. Harris notes in her essay "Whiteness as Property"—regardless of class position—"benefit from their wage of whiteness." Such talk of privilege, however, is incomplete unless we also speak of its penalty. For poorer wage earners "without power, money or influence," their wage of whiteness functions as a kind of workers' "compensation." It is a "consolation prize" to persons who, although not wealthy, do not have to consider themselves losers because they are, at least, white.

The irony, of course, is that neither in the past nor today are low-paid wage earners held in high esteem by their own white bosses who exploit their labor. These workers are, in effect, exploited twice: first as workers and then as "whites." Their "race" is used to distract them from their diminishing value as wage earners. Diminished as workers, they feel shame. Inflated as whites, they feel white supremacist pride. This is the double jeopardy of whiteness Martin Luther King, Jr., pointed to in his 1967 book *Where Do We Go from Here: Chaos or Community?* when noting that racial prejudice put poorer whites in the ironic position of fighting not only against the Negro, but also against themselves. White supremacy, King wryly noted, can feed the egos of poor whites but not their stomachs.

Today's "poor whites" are the working poor, the "over-spent Americans" be they lower- or middle-class—all the white Americans who are living from paycheck to paycheck. Whiteness functions as a distraction from the pervasive class problem of the white American worker. Talk of white privilege from this class perspective is really talk about the privileges entailed in being and remaining poor and exploited in America. Such talk is cheap. Too cheap.

We can do better than this—but only if we attend to the way in which most "whites" are broken by the persons who ostensibly made them white "for their own good": their parents, caretakers, and bosses.

In his September/October 1996 essay "Can the Left Learn to Take Yes for an Answer?" TIKKUN editorial board member Michael Bader describes a repeated pattern among white American progressives: "an unconscious belief that they're somehow not supposed to have a happier and healthier life than their loved ones, past and present." To explain this syndrome, Bader talks about "survivor guilt." We must begin to talk about survivor shame in Americans who are forced to become white. Without such discourse, the fact that European Americans racially abuse their own children, suffer from class exploitation under the guise of "white-skin privilege," mask their own racialized feelings of shame, and then download their self-contempt on the rest of us will remain America's invisible race problem.

READING 30

Driving While Black

A Statistician Proves That Prejudice Still Rules the Road

John Lamberth

In 1993, I was contacted by attorneys whose clients had been arrested on the New Jersey Turnpike for possession of drugs. They told me they had come across 25 African American defendants over a three-year period, all arrested on the same stretch of turnpike in Gloucester County, but not a single white defendant. I was asked whether, and how much, this pattern reflected unfair treatment of blacks.

They wanted to know what a professional statistician would make of these numbers. What were the probabilities that this pattern could occur naturally, that is, by chance? Since arrests for drug offenses occurred after traffic stops on the highway, was it possible that so many blacks were arrested because the police were disproportionately stopping them? I decided to try to answer their questions and embarked on one of the most intriguing statistical studies of my career: a census of traffic and traffic violators by race on Interstate 95 in New Jersey. It would require a careful design, teams of researchers with binoculars and a rolling survey.

To relieve your suspense, the answer was that the rate at which blacks were stopped was greatly disproportionate to their numbers on the road and to their propensity to violate traffic laws. Those findings were central to a March 1996 ruling by Judge Robert E. Francis of the Superior Court of New Jersey that the state police were de facto targeting blacks, in violation of their rights under the U.S. and New Jersey constitutions. The judge suppressed the evidence gathered in the stops. New Jersey is now appealing the case.

The New Jersey litigation is part of a broad attack in a number of states, including Maryland, on what has been dubbed the offense of "DWB"—driving while black. While this problem has been familiar anecdotally to African Americans and civil rights advocates for years, there is now evidence that highway patrols are singling out blacks for stops on the illegal and incorrect theory that the practice, known as racial profiling, is the most likely to yield drug arrests. Statistical techniques are proving extremely helpful in proving targeting, just as they have been in proving systemic discrimination in employment.

This was not my first contact with the disparate treatment of blacks in the criminal justice system. My academic research over the past 25 years had led me from an interest in small group decision-making to jury selection, jury composition and the application of the death penalty. I became aware that blacks were disproportionately charged with crimes, particularly serious ones; that they were underrepresented on jury panels and thus on juries; and that they were sentenced to death at a much greater rate than their numbers could justify.

As I began the New Jersey study, I knew from experience that any research that questioned

John Lamberth is in the psychology department of Temple University.

police procedures was sensitive. I knew that what I did must stand the test of a court hearing in which every move I made would be challenged by experts.

First, I had to decide what I needed to know. What was the black "population" of the road—that is, how many of the people traveling on the turnpike over a given period of time were African American? This task is a far cry from determining the population of a town, city or state. There are no Census Bureau figures. The population of a roadway changes all day, every day. By sampling the population of the roadway over a given period, I could make an accurate determination of the average number of blacks on the road.

I designed and implemented two surveys. We stationed observers by the side of the road, with the assignment of counting the number of cars and the race of the occupants in randomly selected three-hour blocks of time over a two-week period. The New Jersey Turnpike has four lanes at its southern end, two in each direction. By the side of the road, we placed an observer for each lane, equipped with binoculars to observe and note the number of cars and the race of occupants, along with a person to write down what the observers said. The team observed for an hour and a half, took a 30-minute break while moving to another observation point, and repeated the process.

In total, we conducted more than 21 sessions between 8 A.M. and 8 P.M. from June 11 to June 24, 1993, at four sites between Exits 1 and 3 of the turnpike, among the busiest highway segments in the nation. We counted roughly 43,000 cars, of which 13.5 percent had one or more black occupants. This was consistent with the population figures for the 11 states from which most of the vehicles observed were registered.

For the rolling survey, Fred Last, a public defender, drove at a constant 60 mph (5 mph above the speed limit at the time). He counted all cars that passed him as violators and all cars he passed as nonviolators. Speaking into a tape recorder, he also noted the race of the driver of each car. At the end of each day, he collated his results and faxed them to me.

Last counted 2,096 cars. More than 98 percent were speeding and thus subject to being stopped by police. African Americans made up about 15 percent of those drivers on the turnpike violating traffic laws. Utilizing data from the New Jersey State Police, I determined that about 35 percent of those who were stopped on this part of the turnpike were African Americans.

To summarize: African Americans made up 13.5 percent of the turnpike's population and 15 percent of the speeders. But they represented 35 percent of those pulled over. In stark numbers, blacks were 4.85 times as likely to be stopped as were others.

We did not obtain data on the race of drivers and passengers searched after being stopped or on the rate at which vehicles were searched. But we know from police records that 73.2 percent of those arrested along the turnpike over a 3½-year period by troopers from the area's Moorestown barracks were black—making them 16.5 times more likely to be arrested than others.

Attorneys for the 25 African Americans who had been arrested on the turnpike and charged with possessing drugs or guns filed motions to suppress evidence seized when they were stopped, arguing that police stopped them because of their race. Their motions were consolidated and heard by Judge Francis between November 1994 and May 1995. My statistical study, bolstered by an analysis of its validity by Joseph B. Kadane, professor of statistics at Carnegie Mellon University, was the primary exhibit in support of the motions.

But Francis also heard testimony from two former New Jersey troopers who said they had been coached to make race-based "profile" stops to increase their criminal arrests. And the judge reviewed police in-service training aids such as videos that disproportionately portrayed minorities as perpetrators.

The statistical disparities, Francis wrote, are "indeed stark. . . . Defendants have proven at least a de facto policy on the part of the State

Police . . . of targeting blacks for investigation and arrest." The judge ordered that the state's evidence be suppressed.

My own work in this field continues. In 1992, Robert L. Wilkins was riding in a rented car with family members when Maryland State Police stopped them, ordered them out, and conducted a search for drugs, which were not found. Wilkins happened to be a Harvard Law School trained public defender in Washington. With the support of the Maryland ACLU, he sued the state police, who settled the case with, among other things, an agreement to provide highway-stop data to the organization.

I was asked by the ACLU to evaluate the Maryland data in 1996 and again in 1997. I conducted a rolling survey in Maryland similar to the one I had done before and found a similar result. While 17.5 percent of the traffic violators on I-95 north of Baltimore were African American, 28.8 percent of those stopped and 71.3 percent of those searched by the Maryland State Police were African American. U.S. District Judge Catherine Blake ultimately ruled in 1997 that the ACLU made a "reasonable showing" that Maryland troopers on I-95 were continuing to engage in a "pattern and practice" of racial discrimination. Other legal actions have been filed in Pennsylvania, Florida, Indiana and North Carolina. Police officials everywhere deny racial profiling.

Why, then, are so many more African American motorists stopped than would be expected by their frequency on the road and their violation of the law? It seems clear to me that drugs are the issue.

The notion that African Americans and other minorities are more likely than whites to be carrying drugs—a notion that is perpetuated by some police training films—seems to be especially prevalent among the police. They believe that if they are to interdict drugs, then it makes sense to stop minorities, especially young men. State police are rewarded and promoted at least partially on the basis of their "criminal programs," which means the number of arrests they make. Testimony in the New Jersey case pointed out that troopers would be considered deficient if they did not make enough arrests. Since, as Judge Francis found, training points to minorities as likely drug dealers, it makes a certain sort of distorted sense to stop minorities more than whites.

But there is no untainted evidence that minorities are more likely to possess or sell drugs. There is evidence to the contrary. Indirect evidence in statistics from the National Institute of Drug Abuse indicates that 12 percent to 14 percent of those who abuse drugs are African American, a percentage that is proportionate to their numbers in the general population.

More telling are the numbers of those people who are stopped and searched by the Maryland State Police who have drugs. This data, which has been unobtainable from other states, indicates that of those drivers and passengers searched in Maryland, about 28 percent have contraband, whether they are black or white. The same percentage of contraband is found no matter the race.

The Maryland data may shed some light on the tendency of some troopers to believe that blacks are somehow more likely to possess contraband. This data shows that for every 1,000 searches by the Maryland State Police, 200 blacks and only 80 non-blacks are arrested. This could lead one to believe that more blacks are breaking the law—until you know that the sample is deeply skewed. Of those searched, 713 were black and only 287 were non-black.

We do not have comparable figures on contraband possession or arrests from New Jersey. But if the traffic along I-95 there is at all similar to I-95 in Maryland—and there is a strong numerical basis to believe it is—it is possible to speculate that black travelers in New Jersey also were no more likely than non-blacks to be carrying contraband.

The fact that a black was 16.5 times more likely than a non-black to be arrested on the New

Jersey Turnpike now takes on added meaning. Making only the assumption that was shown accurate in Maryland, it is possible to say even more conclusively that racial profiling is prevalent there and that there is no benefit to police in singling out blacks. More important, even if there were a benefit, it would violate fundamental rights. The constitution does not permit law enforcement authorities to target groups by race.

Fundamental fairness demands that steps be taken to prohibit profiling in theory and in practice. There is legislation pending at the federal level and in at least two states, Rhode Island and Pennsylvania, that would require authorities to keep statistics on this issue. This is crucial legislation and should be passed.

Only when the data are made available and strong steps are taken to monitor and curtail profiling, will we be able to assure minorities, and all of us who care about fundamental rights, that this practice will cease.

READING 31

A Day in the Life of Two Americas

Leonard Steinhorn

Barbara Diggs-Brown

Some people simply call it "the box." It's usually a large cardboard box found hidden away in a walk-in closet or down in the basement next to the washing machine. It contains diplomas, artwork, books, music, and especially all the family photos—anything that can identify the family as black. If a black family living in a predominantly white neighborhood wants to sell their house, they are often advised by friends or their real estate agent to put everything identifiably black—any vestige of who they are—in the box. Otherwise, white people may not buy the house.

For understandable reasons, real estate agents are often unwilling to acknowledge this practice. Nor are black homeowners very effusive about something so tinged with shame and regret. But walk into an open house any Saturday or Sunday, and if there are no family photos or mementos around, rest assured they're in the box. It happened once to the man who would become the highest-ranking civil rights official in America, former Assistant Attorney General Deval Patrick: "Yes. Actually, one time in one city, and I'll leave it at that. The realtor asked my wife and me to put all of our family photos away." It happened to a *Wall Street Journal* editor, who, after his house was appraised significantly below market value, decided not only to replace all the family photos with those of his white secretary but asked her and her blond son to be in the house when a new appraiser came by. The strategy worked. Black families are also advised to clear out when prospective white buyers want to see the house. Too many times a white family will drive up to a house, see the black homeowner working in the garden or garage, and quickly drive away.[1]

The box is a very small part of the daily commerce between blacks and whites, and its use is by nature limited to the relatively rare black family living in an overwhelmingly white community. But as a metaphor for race relations it looms very large, because it shows the lengths to which many whites will go to avoid intimate contact with anything black, and the degree to which blacks accept and grudgingly accommodate this reality. For blacks to succeed in the predominantly white world, they must—figuratively—carry this box around with them every day.

On a typical day in America, the lives of blacks and whites may intersect. but rarely do

Leonard Steinhorn is an assistant professor at the American University School of Communication.

Barbara Diggs-Brown is an associate professor of public communication at the American University School of Communication.

they integrate. In the matters most intimate and important to our lives—our neighborhoods, schools, work, faith, entertainment, and social life—we either go separate ways or, when forced together, follow what seems like a shadow dance of polite interaction. This by no means denies the real and meaningful contacts between some blacks and whites, but these instances are infrequent enough to be the conspicuous exceptions that prove the rule. Black and white Americans wake up in separate neighborhoods, send their kids off to separate schools, listen to different radio stations during the morning commute, briefly interact on the job but rarely as equals, return to their own communities after work, socialize in separate environments, and watch different television shows before going to sleep and starting the same process all over again. This is a day in the life of two Americas.

SEPARATE NEIGHBORHOODS

Most days begin the same for everyone, with the fresh morning air and the hustle to get out for work. But for black and white Americans, our lives begin to diverge after that. Chances are that a black family leaving home in the morning will see other black faces leaving their homes, and that a white family will see almost exclusively whites. Where we live defines so much of our lives—how we get to work, where our kids go to school, where we shop, whom we chat with, and who our friends will be. And where we live is more often than not determined by race.

About a third of all black Americans live in neighborhoods that are 90 percent or more black, and most other blacks live in neighborhoods disproportionately or predominantly black. Scholars Douglas Massey and Nancy Denton write in their book *American Apartheid* that "blacks remain the most spatially isolated population in U.S. history."[2] The isolation of blacks in central cities is as well documented as it is tragic. As Massey and Denton have pointed out, many blacks in these areas would have to go clear across town simply to find a white family. In cities like Chicago, Detroit, New York, Cleveland, St. Louis and Birmingham, blacks and whites are as divided and in some cases more divided than they were 40 years ago. Most whites lead parallel lives, living in virtually all-white neighborhoods, though often with a smattering of Hispanics and Asians. We may live in a nominally multiracial society, but millions upon millions of white Americans have no regular contact in their neighborhoods with blacks.

Years ago the suburbs were seen as the integration panacea, fresh fields for color-blind Americans to live together. More Americans now live in suburbs than anywhere else. But with the rise of black suburban migration over the last generation—close to a third of all blacks now live in the suburbs—the same pattern of separation has taken hold there as well. Most typical is the white suburb that stays virtually all white, the established black suburb that becomes more black, or the previously white suburb that in due time becomes all black once the color line has been broken. Very few suburbs boast a stable racial balance similar to the mix of middle-class blacks and whites in the metropolitan area, and even in these communities, residents still tend to cluster by race.

Consider the case of Bloomfield, Connecticut, which in 1971 was honored as an All-American City by *Look* magazine and the National Municipal League for its commitment to racial harmony and integrated schools. A small town with barely two thousand inhabitants, Bloomfield sits outside Hartford in pristine New England splendor, complete with a town green, church steeples, and well-appointed single-family homes. But with each passing year, Bloomfield has slowly become less and less white, and more and more black, first five percent black, then 10, then 20, and now nearing 50. First to change were the public schools, which by 1996 were nearly 85 percent black, despite a lingering white majority in town. It won't be long before the actual population follows suit. While many communities in the 1960s turned from all white to all black in a matter of months and years, today the transformation is more gradual. But it is a transformation nonetheless. Bloomfield is indeed an all-American city.

Bloomfield may be different from most communities because it tries to maintain a certain degree of integration, but it is no different in the inexorable residential process taking place there. It is a process that occurs in almost any region of the country where there is a substantial enough black population for whites to feel potentially threatened. The first harbinger of change in a community is the public school—much like the proverbial canary in the coal mine. As black students begin to populate the schools in more than token amounts, white flight from the schools begins to accelerate. White families either send their children to private schools or move out altogether—usually to an established white community or to a new development they call "a nice place to raise kids." In this beginning stage, the number of blacks in public schools is always higher than the number of blacks in the community. Usually the black and white neighbors are cordial and will stop each other to talk and say hello. As years go by and white families move out, few white families will move in. In some communities not a single white person will move in after the first black person calls the area home. Blocks and neighborhoods soon become racially identifiable. Eventually the only whites in the community are those who can't afford to move out, those with no children in school—empty-nesters—or those who can afford private school. Ultimately the remaining whites move out and the community turns predominantly black. This process is not always evident from the beginning, as the presence of one or two black families is often celebrated by most white neighbors as evidence of tolerance and diversity rather than feared as a sign of change. But once the welcome mat is put out for blacks, all it takes is a few white families to worry and move away and a few black families to take their place, and the domino effect begins.

Call it black humor if you wish, but the joke among blacks living in neighborhoods like these is to ask each other what the most popular vehicle is among the remaining white residents. The answer is a U-Haul. Humor is certainly a defense against disappointment, as it is indeed dispiriting to see neighbors move simply because of the color of one's skin. Study after study has shown that blacks would prefer to live in well-integrated neighborhoods between one-third and two-thirds black. All-black and especially all-white neighborhoods are the least desirable locations.[3] The reason is simple: A well-integrated neighborhood would be black enough to buffer against prejudice and isolation, but diverse enough to expose their children to people of all backgrounds. The problem for blacks is that a neighborhood that appears integrated will attract more blacks, which then accelerates white flight and the changeover to a predominantly black neighborhood. And so what many hail as racially mixed neighborhoods are actually neighborhoods undergoing racial transition. Seeing this, a number of blacks have simply stopped trying to integrate and are increasingly opting for identifiably black communities.

Whites see it very differently. Although public opinion surveys show considerable white support for residential integration, what actually happens in the neighborhoods is quite the opposite. If whites could be guaranteed that the number of blacks in their neighborhood would not rise above, say, five or six percent, few would move. But there are no such guarantees, so the white discomfort level begins to rise with each new black face on the block, and the neighborhood begins to tip. With the image of black crime and urban blight so formidable and pervasive, middle-class whites don't want to take what they perceive as a risk. It doesn't seem to matter if the new black residents have equal-status jobs or higher incomes. Whites still move away. It doesn't matter if the schools remain good, if crime doesn't increase, or if home values continue to rise. Whites still say the neighborhood will eventually go bad. Nor does it matter that homes in all-white areas tend to cost more than homes in racially diverse neighborhoods. Whites will pay the extra. For most whites, integration really means managed tokenism, and anything beyond that evokes anxiety and fear. . . .

Three fairly recent phenomena reinforce the residential separation of the races. First is the rapid growth of the gated community, where an estimated four million Americans—mostly white—currently live. With private security guards, visitor passes, locked entry gates, and tightly run residential associations, these communities have become, according to a 1995 article in the *Yale Law Journal,* "homogeneous enclaves undisturbed by the undesirably different." For many of these communities, the residential association serves as community gatekeeper and is often "a powerful tool for segregation," according to the *Yale Law Journal* article. One gated community described itself in marketing materials as a place that makes you "secure within the boundaries of your own neighborhood." It's unclear how much irony was intended when the gated communities on South Carolina's Hilton Head Island were officially called "plantations," but the message of most gated communities is clear to blacks: These are walled-off, peaceful oases for whites, and no matter how much you've accomplished in life, you are not welcome as a purchaser or guest.[4]

Whereas gated communities enable white Americans to live in isolation close to the city, the second phenomenon sees whites exiting the city to more distant suburbs and outlying communities relatively far from the urban core—so-called exurbs—that are attracting high-tech industries and an increasing number of residents. States especially popular for this white exodus are Nevada, Idaho, Utah, Colorado, and Washington. Between 1990 and 1994, more than one million Americans left the suburbs for these exurbs, and the trend is growing rapidly. The search for a more basic, pastoral life is nothing new in American history, so it is perfectly possible to ascribe this phenomenon to a desire for innocence, peace, and simplicity. But it would be naïve not to acknowledge that part of what whites want to escape is proximity to blacks. As one Utah executive candidly explained: "One thing people don't want to worry about is race relations. Companies think if they go to a neighborhood where everyone is like me, it makes it easier. It takes away from stress. People want to remove some of the variables of their lives.[5]

The third phenomenon reinforcing separation is the stabilization and growth of identifiably black middle-class communities, which are increasingly becoming the neighborhoods of choice for upwardly mobile blacks who want a secure place to raise families and are tired of rejection by whites. These are often urban enclaves or inner-ring suburbs just outside the city that years ago housed the first wave of white suburban migrants but have long since turned predominantly black. In Chicago, for example, nearly nine in ten black middle-class households with incomes above $35,000 live in predominantly black neighborhoods in just two parts of town, a pattern also found in other cities with a substantial black middle-class population.[6] Many blacks are also setting down roots deeper into the suburbs and moving to predominantly black communities such as Mitchellville outside Washington, D.C., Brook Glen outside Atlanta, and Rolling Oaks outside Miami. Builders in these areas understand what's going on and market these communities specifically to blacks. As *Los Angeles Times* reporter Sam Fulwood III writes in his compelling autobiography: "Without fully comprehending why, I was smitten by the model home with its subtle, subliminal persuasions aimed at racial pride and feelings of estrangement from white neighborhoods. . . . Indeed, I had never before seen a model home that featured decorations aimed at middle-income black buyers. The book with Dr. King's image on the cover was one item . . . on the bookshelf along with storybooks and a black-faced rag doll.[7]

Marketing isn't the only reason this is happening. It's a matter of living with dignity and respect. "We're flocking to mostly black suburbs partly because we still can't readily integrate with white society," said an editor of the black-oriented magazine *Emerge*. "We work in these corporations, law firms, hospitals, what have you, but we see what the limitations are. You also want to make sure your children can function without the stings of racism penetrating them all the time. . . . If I locked myself out of my house one night in a mostly white neighborhood, my neighbor might hesitate to open his door because of the color of my skin. That happened to me recently. But in an all-black area, I'd merely be inconveniencing my neighbors. They'd let me in."[8] . . .

SEPARATE SCHOOLS

It may be the most honest public high school in America. Just off Interstate 55 in the northwest corner of Mississippi is Hernando High School. Actually, it is two high schools in one building. There are black and white principals, black and white class presidents, black and white yearbook honors, and a black and white Mr. and Miss Hernando High. The students share the school's facilities and resources, but behave as separate student bodies. Like many Mississippi schools, Hernando lost most of its white students soon after the school was desegregated. But unlike other schools, Hernando gained many of them back after the district created the dual school structure, and it is now 70 percent white. In many ways Hernando offends our integrationist sensibilities, deeply so. It has recently made news because one student decided to challenge the status quo. But strip away the dual administrative layers and Hernando resembles countless other desegregated high schools throughout the country. Their administrators may not be as candid as Hernando's, and the racial division may not be quite as bald-faced, but the reality is pervasive nonetheless: two student worlds in one building, intersecting but not integrating.

On a typical day in America black and white parents pack lunches for their kids, send them off to school, and hope with all their hearts that their children receive a quality education. But the similarity largely ends there. Just as our neighborhoods are separated by race, so too are our schools. Millions of black children attend schools with few or no whites. Millions more white children attend schools with few or no blacks. Whites rarely constitute more than 15 percent of the students in our nation's largest urban school districts, and most of the time they attend predominantly white schools in their own corner of the city. In the South, nearly two-thirds of blacks attend majority-black schools, a proportion that has remained about the same for twenty-five years. Kansas City has spent nearly $2 billion in a court-ordered effort to rebuild and integrate the public schools. There are magnet schools now with broadcast studios, state-of-the-art computers, Olympic-sized swimming pools, and even a planetarium—but few whites. In Prince George's County, Maryland, where 62 percent of the residents are black, but about 80 percent of the schoolchildren are, integration has meant busing black students from 95 percent–black schools to schools only 70 percent black, ostensibly to achieve a better racial balance. The county also holds a number of seats empty in its well-regarded magnet schools in the vain hope that white youngsters will take the spots reserved for them, even if it means keeping hundreds of frustrated black students on waiting lists. One cash-poor district in South Carolina spent one million dollars to expand an all-white elementary school rather than send white students to a predominantly black school that was one-third empty and only 800 yards away. It is a litany that can go on and on.[9]

The situation isn't much better in racially mixed schools, though the separation is less obvious, more subtle. Students attending the same school are sometimes as divided as students attending separate schools. We like to think of racially balanced schools as integrated, but they are not. Race simply becomes the central organizing principle at these schools, often determining the social and educational lives of the students. Youngsters of both races may pass each other and even talk a bit in the hall, but their contact in the lunchroom, the classroom, and the schoolyard is frequently defined by race. These schools differ from Hernando only in that they do not have the dual administrative structure that makes the separation blatant. After almost three decades of busing, magnet schools, court orders, reassignment plans, and even state troopers guarding schoolhouse doors, America's public schools are barely more integrated than they were a generation ago. And while the rare success story deserves applause, the trend toward separation, according to Harvard's Project on School Desegregation, is in fact getting worse.[10]

When the civil rights movement broke the back of segregation, most people assumed that putting black and white students together at school would help us solve the nation's racial divide. It hasn't happened that way. The good news is that through grade school, younger kids tend to get along well in mixed settings. They are indeed color-blind. But it begins to break down soon after that. For students who attend racially mixed schools, the social separation of the races usually begins in middle school and all but ossifies by high school, when students become acutely aware of what it means to—as they put it—act one's color. Black kids who spend time with whites are accused of "acting white" or "bleaching out." White kids who hang out with blacks are derided as "wiggers" and "wannabes." Most evident is the invisible seating chart that divides cafeterias by race. "At lunch we're around the people that we want to be with," said a black high school girl during a focus group discussion of black teenage girls in Montgomery County, Maryland, and all the other girls in the group nodded in agreement.

But the separation is not just a lunchtime phenomenon. It filters to almost every aspect of school life. In some schools there are bathrooms blacks use and bathrooms whites use. In other schools the two groups use and congregate around different school entrances. Black kids wear Morehouse and Spelman sweatshirts, whites wear shirts from Harvard and Yale. Given the choice, blacks and whites often choose separate buses when going on field trips, separate sections of the stands when watching the basketball team, and even separate parts of the classroom in which to sit. School clubs and extracurricular activities, ranging from the drama club to the yearbook staff to the environmental club, rarely are mixed beyond the token member of the other race. As we will discuss in more detail later . . . , even high school sports teams, widely seen as the great racial leveler, have begun to divide by race, with blacks involved more in basketball, football, and sprinting while whites tend to play tennis, soccer, baseball and field hockey, and run cross-country.

Even when schools attempt to address racially relevant issues or celebrate Black History Month, the racial division festers under the programmatic veneer. While black students often express a proprietary attitude toward these events, white students quietly express their alienation. A Kansas City school that decided to have a "racial harmony day" on Martin Luther King's birthday was met with open resistance from black students who wanted the day devoted solely to King. A black history lecture in a Pittsburgh area school attracted enthusiastic black students but not a single white. Seating at Black History Month school assemblies is often divided by race, as is the level of interest. When given the chance to speak confidentially, as in a focus group, white students will complain about a Black History Month curriculum that includes books like Richard Wright's *Black Boy* or the film *Raisin in the Sun,* or express resentment at blacks who act "righteous" and "snobby" during the month. "They expect us to kiss their feet," said one white student in a focus group. Black students in these confidential settings say they are tired of educating white peers about black culture and often express anger that some whites provocatively call for a white history month.[11]

Most students from racially mixed schools make no integration pretense after school because they don't really have to—they rarely see each other. If black and white kids get together, it's often when school work is involved, little more. Groups that are not all white or all black usually have only one white or one black, seldom more. Interracial dating is rare, especially between black girls and white boys, and some of the most socially isolated children in America are black girls attending predominantly white high schools. For the sake of appearing racially tolerant, kids might say there's enough interracial dating, but probe further—as in a focus group—and the charade begins to fall away.

Music is another dividing line, with blacks tending toward rap or hip-hop and whites toward rock. Even when music crosses over and white kids listen to urban sounds, which is not uncommon, the closest most get to blacks is by watching *MTV Jams* in the comfort of their suburban homes, and when dancing is involved, the parties still tend to be all black or all white. The months of April, May, and June rarely pass without a news story on a student body that's holding two proms, one for blacks and one for whites. Although there are plenty of instances of true interracial friendship among young blacks and whites, these are still atypical. Most of the time the two worlds simply coexist in relative peace, while any tensions are kept under the surface. But not always. In one small Indiana town, a small breach of the dividing line was so threatening that the largely white high school nearly erupted when a group of white girls began dressing in urban hip-hop style. Act your color, they were told. One reporter who visited the town found a sweet irony when the same angry white students who threatened the girls were busy dancing with their classmates to the rhythm of gansta rapper Dr. Dre.[12]

What concerns educators is not necessarily the social divide but the pull it is having on the academic performance of blacks. So intense is the sense of alienation and separation felt among many young blacks that anyone perceived as "acting white" is frequently stigmatized, belittled, and ostracized—and "acting white" often includes academic success. Black students tell of camouflaging their schoolwork, of rarely talking with peers about their studies, and of never sharing their grades with friends. Some blacks even report avoiding honors courses for fear of the resulting social isolation. And while it is true that young people of all races exert peer pressure against academic achievement—no one wants to be called teacher's pet, brown nose, or nerd—in the case of blacks the stigma has become racialized. For many blacks a refusal to "act white"—expressed as an anti-achievement ethic—has become a point of racial pride.

RACIAL TRACKING

Perhaps even more alarming is that self-destructive attitudes may be partially spawned by the unintentional if not insidious practice of tracking black students into classes that isolate them from whites and create a culture of low expectations. Various studies suggest that tracking begins as early as kindergarten and first grade, when five- or six-year-olds are labeled gifted, average, or below average—and intensifies in middle school and beyond. "It was horrendous to automatically relegate a kindergarten kid to one of those low-level sections and to leave them there forever," said a white superintendent from rural southwest Georgia who has been threatened for his stance against racial tracking. In racially mixed schools, honors and accelerated classes tend to be mostly white, and special-education, basic-skills, and vocational classes tend to be mostly black. For example, in one Cleveland suburb blacks make up only 10 percent of the advanced-placement classes, even though the school district overall is 50 percent black. Some school districts have found that even regular classes tend to be racially imbalanced, as if the students were assigned by race even though no such policy was in place. A College Board study found that black students are steered away from college preparatory courses—geometry, algebra and laboratory sciences—and into the less demanding "general" track, in which math consists of consumer arithmetic and foreign languages and science are rarely taught.

According to the College Board's president, black eighth-graders with testing levels and grades similar to whites "were being shunted into remedial courses in high school." One federal magistrate found the racial tracking in Rockford, Illinois, so disturbing that he said it raised "discrimination to an art form." It is not unusual to hear a story like the one told by Harvard Law School professor Christopher Edley, Jr., who was so astonished by an elementary school's classification of his son that he spent $2,000 on tests that proved the school woefully wrong and then put his son in a private school in midyear.[13]

While some observers suggest that white students are tracked into predominantly white honors classes as a way to stem further white flight from racially mixed public schools, the practice of racial tracking is so widespread and apparent that we must assume no more than an ingrained and unconscious bias is at work. How else could a well-regarded teacher choose a white student over a black student for the gifted class when the two had identical test scores, grades, and attitudes? How else could some schools routinely hand white parents information packets on gifted classes and black parents information on regular classes? It has gotten to the point that white kids express surprise when they find out their black peers get good grades. In the end, whether tracking creates or merely reinforces separation, the result is the same: even blacks and whites who attend the same schools very rarely integrate in the classroom. This fact alone may help to explain why some black leaders are now rethinking the traditional focus on integration and are instead calling for a greater emphasis on school quality, regardless of the racial mix.[14] . . .

NOTES

1. Personal interview with Assistant Attorney General Deval Patrick, December 13, 1996; the appraisal experience is described in Joseph Boyce, "L.A. Riots and the 'Black Tax,'" *Wall Street Journal*, May 12, 1992, p. A24. See also Jean Bryant, "For Blacks and Whites in the Region, It's Still a House Divided," *Pittsburgh Post-Gazette*, April 14, 1996, p. A1, and NBC's *Dateline*, "Why Can't We Live Together," June 27, 1997, and Kevin Helliker, "To Sell to Whites, Blacks Hide Telltale Ethnic Touches," *Wall Street Journal*, March 26, 1998, pp. B1–2.
2. Douglas S. Massey and Nancy A. Denton, *American Apartheid* (Cambridge, MA: Harvard University Press, 1993), p. 114.
3. The best and most comprehensive study of racial housing preferences is the University of Michigan's Detroit Area Study. See also the *Detroit Free Press*, October 10, 1992.
4. David J. Kennedy, "Residential Associations as State Actors: Regulating the Impact of Gated Communities on Nonmembers," *Yale Law Journal*, December 1995, pp. 761–793. See also Dale Maharidge, "Walled Off," *Mother Jones*, November–December 1994, pp. 26–33.
5. On the exurbs, see Joel Kotkin, "White Flight to the Fringes," *Washington Post*, March 10, 1996, pp. C1–2. The Utah executive is quoted in Kotkin's article.
6. For the Chicago information, see an analysis by Ron Grossman and Byron P. White, "Poverty Surrounds Black Middle Class," *Chicago Tribune*, February 2, 1997, p. 1.
7. Sam Fulwood III, *Waking from the Dream* (New York: Anchor, 1996), p. 189.
8. Susan McHenry, executive editor of *Emerge* magazine, interviewed in *Fortune*, November 2, 1992, p. 128.
9. See Peter Applebome, "Schools See Re-emergence of 'Separate But Equal,'" *New York Times*, April 8, 1997, p. A10; the cash-poor district is in Darlington, South Carolina.
10. For recent trends in school desegregation, see Gary Orfield, Mark D. Bachmeier, David R. James, and Tamela Eitle, "Deepening Segregation in American Public Schools: A Special Report from the Harvard Project on School Desegregation," *Equity & Excellence in Education*, September 1997, pp. 5–24. The Harvard Project on School Desegregation is considered the leading authority on school desegregation issues.
11. See Arlynn Leiber Presser, "Broken Dreams," *ABA Journal*, May 1991, pp. 60–64; Bill Schackner, "For Blacks and Whites in Our Region,

School Desegregation Gets a Failing Grade," *Pittsburgh Post-Gazette*, April 21, 1996, p. A1; Ovetta Wiggins, "Symbols of Segregation Endure," *Bergen Record*, April 11, 1995, p. B1; Focus Group Transcripts and Focus Group Report to the Montgomery County Hate/Violence Committee, Montgomery County, Maryland, November 1993; Walt Harrington, "Black and White and the Future," *Washington Post Magazine*, November 24, 1991, pp. 25–39.

12. E. Jean Carroll, "The Return of the White Negro," *Esquire*, June 1994, pp. 100–107; see also Marjorie Rosen and Leah Eskin, "Wardrobe Wars," *People* magazine, January 31, 1994, p. 60.
13. For the information on Cleveland, see Julian E. Barnes, "Segregation, Now," *U.S. News & World Report*, September 22, 1997, p. 28. The College Board study is detailed in *Redeeming the American Promise*, a 1995 report by the Atlanta-based Southern Education Foundation, pp. xx, 28. The Georgia superintendent is quoted in "Georgia Superintendent Battles a Subtle Racism," *New York Times*, February 2, 1995, p. A10; Harvard Law professor Christopher Edley, Jr., related his son's story in a private correspondence with Leonard Steinhorn; see also "Racial Harm Is Found in Schools' 'Tracking,'" *New York Times*, September 20, 1990; Neal Thompson, "Tale of Two Schools," *Bergen Record*, April 10, 1995, p. A1; Debra Lynn Vial, "School Integration's Failed Promise: How North Jersey Parents and Towns See the Issue," *Bergen Record*, April 16, 1995, p. A1; Ovetta Wiggins, "Symbols of Segregation Endure," *Bergen Record*, April 11, 1995, p. B1; William Celis, III, "School System Found to Be Biased Against Bright Minority Students," *New York Times*, November 5, 1993, p. A22.
14. For an example of a teacher choosing the white student over the black, see Vial, "School Integration's Failed Promise"; for the packets handed to white and black parents, see Ellis Cose, "The Realities of Black and White," *Newsweek,* April 29, 1996, p. 36, in which he describes a New York City experiment by the activist group ACORN to test how black and white parents would be received in the schools. For white surprise when black students get good grades, see Montgomery County, Maryland, Focus Group Transcripts and Focus Group Report.

PERSONAL ACCOUNT

Play Some Rolling Stones

I left my favorite tavern late on a Friday night. On my way home I stopped to listen to the acoustic reggae of a black street musician. I threw a few dollars into a jar and he asked me what I would like to hear. He spoke with a heavy Jamaican accent and said he could only play reggae. As he began to play my request, several other white males gathered around. As my song ended, a member of the group told the street musician to stop playing that "nigger music" and play some Rolling Stones. The musician replied that he only knew the words to reggae songs. With that, the white male kicked the musician's money jar from his stool, shattering it on the sidewalk. When I objected, the white guy turned on me. Luckily he had spent several hours in the tavern, because his first punch missed its mark. Unfortunately, the other five punches were on target.

At night in the hospital and twenty-two sutures later, I wondered if it was worth it. But when I went back down to the same area the following weekend, the musician thanked me graciously. Then he began to play a classic Rolling Stones song.

Mark Donald Stockenberg

READING 32

Of Race and Risk

Patricia J. Williams

Several years ago, at a moment when I was particularly tired of the unstable lifestyle that academic careers sometimes require, I surprised myself and bought a real house. Because the house was in a state other than the one where I was living at the time, I obtained my mortgage by telephone. I am a prudent little squirrel when

Patricia J. Williams is a professor of law at the Columbia University Law School in New York.

it comes to things financial, always tucking away stores of nuts for the winter, and so I meet the criteria of a quite good credit risk. My loan was approved almost immediately.

A little while later, the contract came in the mail. Among the papers the bank forwarded were forms documenting compliance with the Fair Housing Act, which outlaws racial discrimination in the housing market. The act monitors lending practices to prevent banks from redlining—redlining being the phenomenon whereby banks circle certain neighborhoods on the map and refuse to lend in those areas. It is a practice for which the bank with which I was dealing, unbeknownst to me, had been cited previously—as well as since. In any event, the act tracks the race of all banking customers to prevent such discrimination. Unfortunately, and with the creative variability of all illegality, some banks also use the racial information disclosed on the fair housing forms to engage in precisely the discrimination the law seeks to prevent.

I should repeat that to this point my entire mortgage transaction had been conducted by telephone. I should also note that I speak a Received Standard English, regionally marked as Northeastern perhaps, but not easily identifiable as black. With my credit history, my job as a law professor and, no doubt, with my accent, I am not only middle class but apparently match the cultural stereotype of a good white person. It is thus, perhaps, that the loan officer of the bank, whom I had never met, had checked off the box on the fair housing form indicating that I *was* white.

Race shouldn't matter, I suppose, but it seemed to in this case, so I took a deep breath, crossed out "white" and sent the contract back. That will teach them to presume too much, I thought. A done deal, I assumed. But suddenly the transaction came to a screeching halt. The bank wanted more money, more points, a higher rate of interest. Suddenly I found myself facing great resistance and much more debt. To make a long story short, I threatened to sue under the act in question, the bank quickly backed down and I procured the loan on the original terms.

What was interesting about all this was that the reason the bank gave for its newfound recalcitrance was not race, heaven forbid. No, it was all about economics and increased risk: The reason they gave was that property values in that neighborhood were suddenly falling. They wanted more money to buffer themselves against the snappy winds of projected misfortune.

Initially, I was surprised, confused. The house was in a neighborhood that was extremely stable. I am an extremely careful shopper; I had uncovered absolutely nothing to indicate that prices were falling. It took my realtor to make me see the light. "Don't you get it," he sighed. "This is what always happens." And even though I suppose it was a little thick of me, I really hadn't gotten it: For of course, I was the reason the prices were in peril.

The bank's response was driven by demographic data that show that any time black people move into a neighborhood, whites are overwhelmingly likely to move out. In droves. In panic. In concert. Pulling every imaginable resource with them, from school funding to garbage collection to social workers who don't want to work in black neighborhoods. The imagery is awfully catchy, you had to admit: the neighborhood just tipping on over like a terrible accident, whoops! Like a pitcher, I suppose. All that nice fresh wholesome milk spilling out, running away . . . leaving the dark, echoing, upended urn of the inner city.

In retrospect, what has remained so fascinating to me about this experience was the way it so exemplified the problems of the new rhetoric of racism. For starters, the new rhetoric of race never mentions race. It wasn't race but risk with which the bank was so concerned.

Second, since financial risk is all about economics, my exclusion got reclassified as just a consideration of class. There's no law against class discrimination, goes the argument, because that would represent a restraint on that basic American freedom, the ability to contract or not. If schools, trains, buses, swimming pools and neighborhoods remain segregated, it's no longer a racial problem if someone who just happens to be white keeps hiking up the price for someone who accidentally and purely by the way happens to be black. Black people end up paying higher prices for the attempt to integrate, even as the integration of oneself threatens to lower the value of one's investment.

By this measure of mortgage-worthiness, the ingredient of blackness is cast not just as a social toll but as an actual tax. A fee, an extra contribution at the door, an admission charge for the high costs of handling my dangerous propensities, my inherently unsavory properties. I was not judged based on my independent attributes or financial worth; not even was I judged by statistical profiles of what my group actually does. (For in fact, anxiety-stricken, middle-class black people make grovelingly good cake-baking neighbors when not made to feel defensive by the unfortunate historical strategies of bombs, burnings or abandonment.) Rather, I was being evaluated based on what an abstraction of White Society writ large thinks we—or I—do, and that imagined "doing" was treated and thus established as a self-fulfilling prophecy. It is a dispiriting message: that some in society apparently not only devalue black people but devalue *themselves* and their homes just for having us as part of their landscape.

"I bet you'll keep your mouth shut the next time they plug you into the computer as white," laughed a friend when he heard my story. It took me aback, this postmodern pressure to "pass," even as it highlighted the intolerable logic of it all. For by these "rational" economic measures, an investment in my property suggests the selling of myself.

READING 33

Anti-Gay Slurs Common at School

A Lesson in Cruelty

Laura Sessions Stepp

Emmett English, a cheerful, easygoing boy, started third grade last year at a new school, Chevy Chase Elementary in Bethesda, Maryland. On his first day he proudly wore a new red Gap sweatshirt and almost immediately wished he had chosen something else.

"A girl called me 'gay,'" he remembered. "I didn't know what that meant but I knew it was something bad." His mother, Christina Files, confirmed this. "He came home quite upset," she said.

"That's soooo gay." "Faggot." Or "lesbo." For all the outcry over harassment of gays following the murder of college student Matthew Shepard two years ago, anti-gay insults are still the slang of choice among children and teenagers, according to teachers, counselors and youths themselves. Some say the insults are increasing in school classrooms and hallways—among children as young as 8 or 9—partly because gay youths and their supporters have become more visible and more active.

"Schools are seen as a safe place to say things and get away with it," said Jerry Newberry, director of health information for the National Education Association, a teachers' union. A recent survey of students in seven states backs up his impression. Human Rights Watch, an international research and advocacy group, reported last month that 2 million U.S. teenagers were having serious problems in school because they were taunted with anti-gay slurs.

Laura Sessions Stepp is a staff writer for the *Washington Post.*

Young people use these slurs in two different ways, one generally derogatory and one referring insultingly to sexual orientation. Schools have a hard time policing either use.

Taunts and slurs, particularly the words "fag" and "faggot," were cited in more than half of the publicized schoolyard shootings of the last three years, according to Newberry. Columbine shooters Eric Harris and Dylan Klebold were called fags. So was Andy Williams, who sprayed a San Diego high school with gunfire last March, killing two people.

Anti-gay language first appears on elementary school playgrounds. "Kids at our school say, 'That kid is sooo gay,'" said Julia Pernick, a classmate of Emmett's in fourth grade at Chevy Chase Elementary. "They think it means stupid or unusual or strange."

The insults multiply in the emotionally precarious years of early adolescence. "If you're too short, too tall, too fat, too skinny, you get targeted in middle school," said David Mumaugh, now a junior at Walter Johnson High School in Bethesda. "Kids sign their yearbooks, 'See you next year, fag.'"

Sarah Rothe, an eighth-grader at Lake Braddock Middle School in Burke, [Virginia,] said such words "are as common as the word 'like'" at her school. Classmate Christina Jagodnick said "there's a big difference" between anti-gay slurs and other derogatory terms. "If we were to say other words which we all know are wrong," she said, "someone would stop us."

At Lake Braddock this year, according to students, a boy was targeted by classmates who glued his locker shut, writing the word "gay" on the outside. No one knew the boy's sexual orientation, but the bullies called him names until, recently, he transferred to another school. The school would not comment on the situation.

Gay teens are reluctant to discuss personal harassment on the record for fear of attracting more. But when they're offered anonymity, they won't stop talking.

A junior at Magruder High School in Rockville, [Maryland,] said: "I have a lot of friends who say, 'Oh, that's so gay.' They don't associate it with homosexuality. You could plant that word in the dictionary for 'stupid.' Do I face a whole life of this?"

At Herndon High School in Herndon, [Virginia,] a junior said, "I was walking with a friend down the hall and this kid yells, 'Faggot.' How am I supposed to defend who I am?"

When straight students are bullied, they usually can count on an adult coming to their aid, counselors say. Gays don't have that assurance. According to several surveys, four out of five gay and lesbian students say they don't know one supportive adult at school.

"Teachers are aware they may offend someone if they speak about homosexuality in anything other than negative terms," said Deborah Roffman, who teaches sex education in the Baltimore and Washington areas. "They don't know how to cross that street safely, so they don't even step off the curb."

A LONELY CAMPAIGN

Jerry Newberry and other educators suggest that anti-gay insults are increasing partly because gay youths and their supporters have become more assertive in trying to stop them. Justen Deal, 16, has fought such a campaign alone.

A cherubic-looking blond kid from south of Charleston, W.Va., Justen heard anti-gay words from the time he could talk, even used them himself on occasion. But by the age of 12, when he first suspected he was gay, "they made my skin crawl," he said.

Unlike children in other minority groups, he had no natural support group to comfort him. His parents had relinquished custody of him to his paternal grandmother, Patty Deal, when he was born, and her only knowledge of homosexuals was what she had seen on the TV comedy "Ellen."

She did her best once she found out in his eighth-grade year that he was gay. He had written a letter to his school counselor that Patty Deal read. She immediately sought psychiatric help for him, took him to a hospital on the night he overdosed on antidepressants, [and] enrolled him in a new middle school in Boone County.

Neither she nor Justen knows how, but rumors started flying at Sherman Junior High. "I was asked eight times a day if I was gay," Justen remembered. "I'd say no, or not say anything. That year is when I learned for sure that the things you hear about words not hurting is a fairy tale."

Justen thought he'd be safe from gay-bashing once he reached Sherman Senior High. He knew principal Theresa Lonker, a tough-looking administrator who sends students to detention for cursing. When she told Justen, "We'll look out for you," she seemed to mean it.

But she couldn't be everywhere. Name-calling started slowly in his freshman year and picked up this year, according to Justen's friend Lindsey Light. Fed up this past spring, Justen tried to do something about language in a very visible way.

He drafted a new harassment policy for Sherman High to include sexual orientation and left it on Lonker's desk. He lobbied the county school superintendent, Steve Pauley, to rewrite the county's harassment policy.

He visited West Virginia Gov. Robert Wise's office asking the governor to convene a task force to investigate harassment. He testified before the legislature on an amendment to the state's hate crime bill that would have included protection based on sexual orientation. His comments made both Charleston newspapers, including the front page of the *Daily Mail.*

Some of his classmates were not exactly thrilled with the attention. They threw coins and paper wads at him on a school bus during a field trip and also one afternoon in a science class. "Everyone [in the class] heard me tell them to stop, but the teacher was in his own little world," Justen said.

The science teacher, Robert Britton, said he didn't realize at the time there was any harassment going on. "I heard [Justen] say something about stuff being thrown at him but I thought he was just talking about words," Britton said.

Justen's one-person language crusade was rebuffed at every turn. Principal Lonker said she never saw the recommendation for changing the school's harassment policy. Superintendent Pauley said he was reluctant to single out gay students for special mention. Gov. Wise's office declined to appoint a task force on the needs of gay students. The legislature voted against adding sexual orientation to its anti-harassment statute. By mid-April, Justen, feeling defeated, decided to change what he could: his school.

He transferred to Huntington High, about 90 miles north. The school has a sizable population of openly gay students, and friends found a gay couple with whom he could live.

On his last day at Sherman High, his grandmother waited for him in her blue Chevy Impala. She appeared both nervous and sad.

"I've always taught Justen to tell the truth," she said. "I reckon he just listened too good. I knew he'd leave one day—I just didn't know it would be so soon."

Justen didn't want to leave his grandma. But despite Lonker's efforts to keep him safe at school, he said, he didn't *feel* safe and thus had a hard time keeping his mind on equations and Civil War battles. His pals had told him to shrug off the verbal digs, but he could not.

"My friends don't understand that every time I hear the word 'fag' it really hurts," he said. "It reminds me that I'm so far away from what kids see as normal."

Walking out of Sherman on that soggy Tuesday, buoyed by the hugs of several students and his principal, he said, "It was a good day. I only heard the word 'faggot' four times."

PERSONAL ACCOUNT

A White Male Rescued Me

There was one incident where a white male came to my rescue when I was being discriminated against for being a woman, a black woman, and a black-gay woman.

I was on the metro with my friends on the way to a club when two black men started making derogatory, disgusting statements about us. All of a sudden I heard this voice saying, "You need to leave those girls alone. They're college people and they're trying to experience life. This is the '90s. People have the right to express how they are no matter what you think about it." I turned around and it was a *white man.* I was shocked. Another gay person might have stood up for us, but I would never have expected a white, middle-aged man to do that. They all started to get in a fight, but when the train came to a stop the security guard got on and escorted the two harassers off. I thought it was very nice of the man to come to our rescue. I would like for people to stand up for those who are either in a minority status in society or just for those people who are in need of help. But I would also like to thank the man, regardless of his race, for coming to my rescue. Gay people are human beings too, and we also have rights. But a special thanks goes out to this gentleman for seeing me and my friends as people with feelings first, and gay women second. Thank you.

Meticia Watson

READING 34

All Souls' Night

Michael Patrick MacDonald

I was back in Southie, "the best place in the world," as Ma used to say before the kids died. That's what we call them now, "the kids." Even when we want to say their names, we sometimes get confused about who's dead and who's alive in my family. After so many deaths, Ma just started to call my four brothers "the kids" when we talked about going to see them at the cemetery. But I don't go anymore. They're not at the cemetery; I never could find them there. When I accepted the fact that I couldn't feel them at the graves, I figured it must be because they were in heaven, or the spirit world, or whatever you want to call it. The only things I kept from the funerals were the mass cards that said, "Do not stand at my grave and weep, I am not there, I do not sleep. I am the stars that shine through the night," and so on. I figured that was the best way to look at it. There are seven of us kids still alive, and sometimes I'm not even sure if that's true.

I came back to Southie in the summer of 1994, after everyone in my family had either died or moved to the mountains of Colorado. I'd moved to downtown Boston after Ma left in 1990, and was pulled one night to wander through Southie. I walked from Columbia Point Project, where I was born, to the Old Colony Project where I grew up, in the "Lower End," as we called it. On that August night, after four years of staying away, I walked the streets of my old neighborhood, and finally found the kids. In my memory of that night I can see them clear as day. *They're right here,* I thought, and it was an ecstatic feeling. I cried, and felt alive again myself. I passed by the outskirts of Old Colony, and it all came back to me—the kids were joined in my mind by so many others I'd last seen in caskets at Jackie O'Brien's Funeral Parlor. They were all here now, all of my neighbors and friends who had died young from violence, drugs, and from the other deadly things we'd been taught didn't happen in Southie.

We thought we were in the best place in the world in this neighborhood, in the all-Irish housing projects where everyone claimed to be Irish even if his name was Spinnoli. We were proud to be from here, as proud as we were to be Irish. We

---

Michael Patrick MacDonald helped launch Boston's successful gun-buyback program; he is the founder of the South Boston Vigil Group and works with survivor families and young people in the antiviolence movement.

didn't want to own the problems that took the lives of my brothers and of so many others like them: poverty, crime, drugs—those were black things that happen in the ghettos of Roxbury. Southie was Boston's proud Irish neighborhood.

On this night in Southie, the kids were all here once again—I could feel them. The only problem was no one else in the neighborhood could. My old neighbors were going on with their nightly business—wheeling and dealing on the corners, drinking on the stoops, yelling up to windows, looking for a way to get by, or something to fight for. Just like the old days in this small world within a world. It was like a family reunion to me. That's what we considered each other in Southie—family. There was always this feeling that we were protected, as if the whole neighborhood was watching our backs for threats, watching for all the enemies we could never really define. No "outsiders" could mess with us. So we had no reason to leave, and nothing ever to leave for. It was a good feeling to be back in Southie that night, surrounded by my family and neighbors; and I remember hating having to cross over the Broadway Bridge again, having to leave the peninsula neighborhood and go back to my apartment in downtown Boston.

Not long after, I got a call at Citizens for Safety, where I'd been working on antiviolence efforts across Boston since 1990. It was a reporter from *U.S. News & World Report* who was working on an article about what they were calling "the white underclass." The reporter had found through demographic studies that Southie showed three census tracts with the highest concentration of poor whites in America. The part of Southie he was referring to was the Lower End, my own neighborhood at the bottom of the steep hills of City Point, which was the more middle-class section with nicer views of the harbor. The magazine's findings were based on rates of joblessness and single-parent female-headed households. Nearly three-fourths of the families in the Lower End had no fathers. Eighty-five percent of Old Colony collected welfare. The reporter wasn't telling me anything new—I was just stunned that someone was taking notice. No one had ever seemed to believe me or to care when I told them about the amount of poverty and social problems where I grew up. Liberals were usually the ones working on social problems, and they never seemed to be able to fit urban poor whites into their world view, which tended to see blacks as the persistent dependent and their own white selves as provider. Whatever race guilt they were holding onto, Southie's poor couldn't do a thing for their consciences. After our violent response to court-ordered busing in the 1970s, Southie was labeled as the white racist oppressor. I saw how that label worked to take the blame away from those able to leave the city and drive back to all-white suburban towns at the end of the day.

Outsiders were also used to the image, put out by our own politicians, that we were a working-class and middle-class community with the lowest rates of social problems anywhere, and that we wanted to keep it that way by not letting blacks in with all their problems. Growing up, I felt alone in thinking this attitude was an injustice to all the Southie people I knew who'd been murdered. Then there were all the suicides that no one wanted to talk about. And all the bank robberies and truck hijackings, and the number of addicts walking down Broadway, and the people limping around or in wheelchairs, victims of violence.

The reporter asked me if I knew anyone in Southie he could talk to. He wanted to see if the socioeconomic conditions in the neighborhood had some of the same results evident in the highly concentrated black ghettos of America. I called some people, but most of them didn't want to talk. We were all used to the media writing about us only when something racial happened, ever since the neighborhood had erupted in antibusing riots during the seventies. Senator Billy Bulger, president of the Massachusetts Senate, had always reminded us of how unfair the media was with its attacks on South Boston. He told us never to trust them again. No news was good news. And his brother, neighborhood drug lord James "Whitey" Bulger, had liked it better that way. Whitey probably figured that all the shootings in the nearby black neighborhood of Roxbury, and all the activists willing to talk over there, would keep the media busy. They wouldn't meddle in Southie as long as we weren't as stupid and disorganized as Roxbury's drug dealers. And by the late eighties, murders in Southie had started to be less visible even to us in the community. Word around town was that Whitey didn't allow bodies to be left on the streets anymore; instead, people went missing, and sometimes were found hog-tied out in the suburbs, or washed up on the shores of Dorchester Bay. The ability of our clean-cut gangsters to keep up appearances complemented our own need to deny the truth. Bad guy stuff seemed to happen less often within the protected turf of South Boston. Maybe a few suicides here and there, or maybe an addict "scumbag," but that was the victim's own problem. Must have come from a bad family—nothing to do with "Our Beautiful World," as the *South Boston Tribune* was used to calling it, above pictures of church bazaars, bake sales, christenings, and weddings.

I agreed to take the reporter on a tour through Southie. We stayed in the car, because I was too nervous to walk around with an "outsider" in a suit. It was bad enough that I was driving his rented sports car. People in Southie usually drove big Chevys, or when they were in with "the boys," as we called our revered gangsters, they'd upgrade to an even bigger Caddy or Lincoln Continental. I wore sunglasses and a scally cap, the traditional local cap once favored by hard-working Irish immigrants and longshoremen, and more recently made popular by tough guys and wannabes. I disguised myself so I wouldn't be identified collaborating with an outsider. Everyone knew I was an activist working to reduce violence and crime. But when they saw me on the news, I was usually organizing things over in Roxbury or Dorchester, the black places that my neighbors thanked God they didn't live in. "That stuff would never happen in Southie," a mother in Old Colony once told me. Her own son had been run over by gangsters for selling cocaine on their turf without paying up.

When I rode around the Lower End with the reporter, I pointed to the landmarks of my childhood: St. Augustine's grammar school, where Ma struggled to keep up with tuition payments so we wouldn't be bused to black neighborhoods; the Boys and Girls Club, where I was on the swim team with my brother Kevin; Darius Court, where I played and watched the busing riots; the liquor store with a giant green shamrock painted on it, where Whitey Bulger ran the Southie drug trade; the sidewalk where my sister had crashed from a project rooftop after a fight over drugs; and St. Augustine's Church, down whose front steps I'd helped carry my brothers' heavy caskets. "I miss this place," I said to him. He looked horrified but kept scribbling notes as I went on about this being the best place in the world. "I always had a sense of security here, a sense of belonging that I've never felt anywhere else," I explained. "There was always a feeling that someone would watch your back. Sure, bad things happened to my family, and to so many of my neighbors and friends, but there was never a sense that we were victims. This place was ours, it was all we ever knew, and it was all ours."

Talking to this stranger, driving through the streets of Southie, and saying these things confused me. I thought about how much I'd hated this place when I'd learned that everything I'd just heard myself say about Southie loyalty and pride was a big myth, one that fit well into the schemes of career politicians and their gangster relatives. I thought about how I'd felt betrayed when my brothers ended up among all the other ghosts in our town who were looked up to when they were alive, and shrugged off when they were dead, as punks only asking for trouble.

I didn't know if I loved or hated this place. All those beautiful dreams and nightmares of my life were competing in the narrow littered streets of

Old Colony Project. Over there, on my old front stoop at 8 Patterson Way, were the eccentric mothers, throwing their arms around and telling wild stories. Standing on the corners were the natural-born comedians making everyone laugh. Then there were the teenagers wearing their flashy clothes, "pimp" gear, as we called it. And little kids running in packs, having the time of their lives in a world that was all theirs. But I also saw the junkies, the depressed and lonely mothers of people who'd died, the wounded, the drug dealers, and a known murderer accepted by everyone as warmly as they accepted anything else in the familiar landscape. "I'm thinking of moving back," I told the reporter.

I moved back to Southie after four years of working with activists and victims of violence, mostly in Roxbury, Dorchester, and Mattapan, Boston's largely black and Latino neighborhoods. In those neighborhoods I made some of the closest friends of my life, among people who too often knew the pain of losing their loved ones to the injustices of the streets. Families that had experienced the same things as many of my Southie neighbors. The only difference was in the black and Latino neighborhoods, people were saying the words: *poverty, drugs, guns, crime, race, class, corruption.*

Two weeks after I moved back home, every newsstand in town had copies of *U.S. News & World Report* with a picture of me, poster boy for the white underclass, leading the article, and demographic evidence telling just a few of Southie's dirty little secrets. South Boston's Lower End was called the white underclass capital of America, with a report showing all the obvious social problems that usually attend concentrated poverty in urban areas. The two daily papers in Boston wrote stories about the article's findings, with their own interviews of housing project residents, politicians, and a local priest, mostly refuting the findings. A group of women sitting on a stoop in the housing development laughed at the article. "We're not poor," one said. "We shop at Filene's and Jordan Marsh." I remember how I spent my teenage years, on welfare, making sure that I too had the best clothes from those department stores, whether stolen or bought with an entire check from the summer jobs program. I thought I looked rich, until I saw that all the rich kids in the suburbs were wearing tattered rags.

A local politician said that the article in *U.S. News* was a lie, that it was all about the liberal media attacking South Boston's tight-knit traditional community. A local right-wing community activist called the magazine a "liberal rag." And a *Boston Herald* columnist who'd grown up in one of the census tracts wrote that he was better off not knowing he was poor. But he grew up long before the gangsters started opening up shop in liquor stores on the edge of the housing projects, marketing a lucrative cocaine trade to the children of single women with few extended family support structures or men around.

Our priest said that it was terrible to stigmatize Southie children with such findings, labeling them "underclass." I didn't like the term either, but I thought at least now some of the liberal foundations might begin to offer real support for social service agencies struggling to keep up with the needs of Southie families in crisis. People from Southie nonprofits had told me that they were constantly denied funding because their population was not diverse, and probably also because the name "Southie" automatically brings "racists" to mind—the same kind of generalizing that makes all black children "gang bangers" in the minds of bigots. One thing growing up in Southie taught me is that the right wing has no monopoly on bigotry. Eventually, I saw, the priest and other local social service agencies started to refer to the article when they looked for funding or other support.

When I first moved back to Southie, I was always looking over my shoulder. I wasn't sure if anyone minded all the stuff I'd been saying to the press. Instead, people I didn't even know started coming up to me, telling me their own stories. It was as if they felt it was safe to come out, and they wanted to take the tape off their mouths. Before this, I would walk through the main streets of Southie and see so many people who had experienced drug- and crime-related catastrophes, but who didn't connect with others who'd suffered in similar ways, the way I'd been doing with people in Roxbury. It seemed that people wanted to talk after years of silence.

I knew we could do it in Southie once I'd seen how a group of families from Charlestown had banded together when their children were murdered, to break that neighborhood's own infamous code of silence. When I was organizing a citywide gun buyback, getting people in Boston to turn in their working firearms to be destroyed, I met Sandy King and Pam Enos. They had founded the Charlestown After Murder Program. Sandy's son Chris had been murdered in 1986 in front of a hundred people who remained silent. Then in 1991, her son Jay was murdered. Pam's son Adam was murdered in 1992 by the same person who'd murdered Jay. The women organized other mothers of the tight-knit one-square-mile Irish American neighborhood, which had experienced up to six public executions a year, to speak out against the gangsters who controlled the town. They assisted in their neighborhood's gun buyback, which brought in the most guns citywide in 1994 and 1995, and they built close bonds with mothers of murdered children in neighborhoods of color. They pressured law enforcement to pay attention to murder in Charlestown, put a media spotlight on "the town," exposed corruption, and organized an annual vigil to bring neighbors out of isolation and fear. When I went to Charlestown's vigil, I saw mothers' faces that looked so much like Southie faces, pictures of murdered children who looked so much like Southie kids, and I looked around at the symbols of a community so much like our own: shamrocks and claddaghs, symbolizing "friendship, loyalty, and love." Their vigil took place at St. Catherine's Church, just outside Charlestown's mostly Irish housing projects. By the time I moved back to Southie, I knew what we could do with all the people who at last seemed ready to tell their painful stories. . . .

READING 35

A Question of Class

Dorothy Allison

. . . My people were not remarkable. We were ordinary, but even so we were mythical. We were the *they* everyone talks about, the ungrateful poor. I grew up trying to run away from the fate that destroyed so many of the people I loved, and having learned the habit of hiding, I found that I also had learned to hide from myself. I did not know who I was, only that I did not want to be *they,* the ones who are destroyed or dismissed to make the real people, the important people, feel safer. By the time I understood that I was queer, that habit of hiding was deeply set in me, so deeply that it was not a choice but an instinct. Hide, hide to survive, I thought, knowing that if I told the truth about my life, my family, my sexual desire, my real history, then I would move over into that unknown territory, the land of *they,* would never have the chance to name my own life, to understand it or claim it.

Why are you so afraid? my lovers and friends have asked me the many times when I have suddenly seemed to become a stranger, someone who would not speak to them, would not do the things they believed I should do, simple things like applying for a job, or a grant, or some award they were sure I could acquire easily. Entitlement, I have told them, is a matter of feeling like *we,* not *they.* But it has been hard for me to explain, to make them understand. You think you

---

Dorothy Allison is an award-winning writer and author of *Bastard out of Carolina.*

have a right to things, a place in the world, I try to say. You have a sense of entitlement I don't have, a sense of your own importance. I have explained what I know over and over again, in every possible way I can, but I have never been able to make clear the degree of my fear, the extent to which I feel myself denied, not only that I am queer in a world that hates queers but that I was born poor into a world that despises the poor. The need to explain is part of why I write fiction. I know that some things must be felt to be understood, that despair can never be adequately analyzed; it must be lived. . . .

I have known I was a lesbian since I was a teenager, and I have spent a good twenty years making peace with the effects of incest and physical abuse. But what may be the central fact of my life is that I was born in 1949 in Greenville, South Carolina, the bastard daughter of a poor white woman from a desperately poor family, a girl who had left the seventh grade the year before, who worked as a waitress and was just a month past fifteen when she had me. That fact, the inescapable impact of being born in a condition of poverty that this society finds shameful, contemptible, and somehow deserved, has dominated me to such an extent that I have spent my life trying to overcome or deny it. I have learned with great difficulty that the vast majority of people pretend that poverty is a voluntary condition, that the poor are different, less than fully human, or at least less sensitive to hopelessness, despair, and suffering.

The first time I read Melanie Kaye Kantrowitz's poems, I experienced a frisson of recognition. It was not that my people had been "burned off the map" or murdered as hers had. No, we had been erased, encouraged to destroy ourselves, made invisible because we did not fit the myths of the middle class. Even now, past forty and stubbornly proud of my family, I feel the draw of that mythology, that romanticized, edited version of the poor. I find myself looking back and wondering what was real, what true. Within my family, so much was lied about, joked about, denied or told with deliberate indirection, an undercurrent of humiliation, or a brief pursed grimace that belies everything that has been said—everything, the very nature of truth and lies, reality and myth. What was real? The poverty depicted in books and movies was romantic, a kind of backdrop for the story of how it was escaped. The reality of self-hatred and violence was either absent or caricatured. The poverty I knew was dreary, deadening, shameful. My family was ashamed of being poor, of feeling hopeless. What was there to work for, to save money for, to fight for or struggle against? We had generations before us to teach us that nothing ever changed, and that those who did try to escape failed.

My mama had eleven brothers and sisters, of whom I can name only six. No one is left alive to tell me the names of the others. It was my grandmother who told me about my real daddy, a shiftless pretty man who was supposed to have married, had six children, and sold cut-rate life insurance to colored people out in the country. My mama married when I was a year old, but her husband died just after my little sister was born a year later. When I was five, Mama married the man she lived with until she died. Within the first year of their marriage Mama miscarried, and while we waited out in the hospital parking lot, my stepfather molested me for the first time, something he continued to do until I was past thirteen. When I was eight or so, Mama took us away to a motel after my stepfather beat me so badly it caused a family scandal, but we returned after two weeks. Mama told me that she really had no choice; she could not support us alone. When I was eleven I told one of my cousins that my stepfather was molesting me. Mama packed up my sisters and me and took us away for a few days, but again, my stepfather swore he would stop, and again we went back after a few weeks. I stopped talking for a while, and I have only vague memories of the next two years.

My stepfather worked as a route salesman, my mama as a waitress, laundry worker, cook, or fruit packer. I could never understand how, since they both worked so hard and such long hours, we never had enough money, but it was a fact that was true also of my mama's brothers and sisters, who worked in the mills or the furnace industry. In fact, my parents did better than anyone else in the family, but eventually my stepfather was fired and we hit bottom—nightmarish months of marshals at the door, repossessed furniture, and rubber checks. My parents worked out a scheme so that it appeared my stepfather had abandoned us, but instead he went down to Florida, got a new job, and rented us a house. In the dead of night, he returned with a U-Haul trailer, packed us up, and moved us south.

The night we left South Carolina for Florida, my mama leaned over the back seat of her old Pontiac and promised us girls, "It'll be better there." I don't know if we believed her, but I remember crossing Georgia in the early morning, watching the red clay hills and swaying gray blankets of moss recede through the back window. I kept looking back at the trailer behind us, ridiculously small to contain everything we owned. Mama had, after all, packed nothing that wasn't fully paid off, which meant she had only two things of worth, her washing and sewing machines, both of them tied securely to the trailer walls. Through the whole trip, I fantasized an accident that would burst that trailer, scattering old clothes and cracked dishes on the tarmac.

I was only thirteen. I wanted us to start over completely, to begin again as new people with nothing of the past left over. I wanted to run away completely from who we had been seen to be, who we had been. That desire is one I have seen in other members of my family, to run away. It is the first thing I think of when trouble comes, the geographic solution. Change your name, leave town, disappear, and make yourself over. What hides behind that solution is the conviction that the life you have lived, the person you are, are valueless, better off abandoned, that running away is easier than trying to change anything, that change itself is not possible, that death is easier than this life. Sometimes I think it is that conviction—more seductive than alcoholism or violence and more subtle than sexual hatred or gender injustice—that has dominated my life, and made real change so painful and difficult.

Moving to central Florida did not fix our lives. It did not stop my stepfather's violence, heal my shame, or make my mother happy. Once there our lives became dominated by my mother's illness and medical bills. She had a hysterectomy when I was about eight and endured a series of hospitalizations for ulcers and a chronic back problem. Through most of my adolescence she superstitiously refused to allow anyone to mention the word cancer. (Years later when she called me to tell me that she was recovering from an emergency mastectomy, there was bitter fatalism in her voice. The second mastectomy followed five years after the first, and five years after that there was a brief bout with cancer of the lymph system which went into remission after prolonged chemotherapy. She died at the age of fifty-six with liver, lung, and brain cancer.) When she was not sick, Mama, and my stepfather, went on working, struggling to pay off what seemed an insurmountable load of debts.

By the time I was fourteen, my sisters and I had found ways to discourage most of our stepfather's sexual advances. We were not close but we united against our stepfather. Our efforts were helped along when he was referred to a psychotherapist after losing his temper at work, and was prescribed psychotropic drugs that made him sullen but less violent. We were growing up quickly, my sisters moving toward dropping out of school, while I got good grades and took every scholarship exam I could find. I was the first person in my family to graduate from high school, and the fact that I went on to college was nothing short of astonishing.

Everyone imagines her life is normal, and I did not know my life was not everyone's. It was not until I was an adolescent in central Florida that I began to realize just how different we were. The people we met there had not been shaped by the rigid class structure that dominated the South Carolina Piedmont. The first time I looked around my junior high classroom and realized that I did not know who those people were—not only as individuals but as categories, who their people were and how they saw themselves—I realized also that they did not know me. In Greenville, everyone knew my family, knew we were trash, and that meant we were supposed to be poor, supposed to have grim low-paid jobs, have babies in our teens, and never finish school. But central Florida in the 1960s was full of runaways and immigrants, and our mostly white working-class suburban school sorted us out, not by income and family background, but by intelligence and aptitude tests. Suddenly I was boosted into the college-bound track, and while there was plenty of contempt for my inept social skills, pitiful wardrobe, and slow drawling accent, there was also something I had never experienced before, a protective anonymity, and a kind of grudging respect and curiosity about who I might become. Because they did not see poverty and hopelessness as a foregone conclusion for my life, I could begin to imagine other futures for myself.

Moving into that new world and meeting those new people meant that I began to see my family from a new vantage point. I also experienced a new level of fear, a fear of losing what before had never been imaginable. My family's lives were not on television, not in books, not even comic books. There was a myth of the poor in this country, but it did not include us, no matter how hard I tried to squeeze us in. There was an idea of the good poor—hardworking, ragged but clean, and intrinsically noble. I understood that we were the bad poor, the ungrateful: men who drank and couldn't keep a job; women, invariably pregnant before marriage, who quickly became worn, fat, and old from working too many hours and bearing too many children; and children with runny noses, watery eyes, and bad attitudes. My cousins quit school, stole cars, used drugs, and took dead-end jobs pumping gas or waiting tables. We were not noble, not grateful, not even hopeful. We knew ourselves despised.

But in that new country, we were unknown. The myth settled over us and glamorized us. I saw it in the eyes of my teachers, the Lions' Club representative who paid for my new glasses, and the lady from the Junior League who told me about the scholarship I had won. Better, far better, to be one of the mythical poor than to be part of the *they* I had known before. *Don't let me lose this chance,* I prayed, and lived in fear that I might suddenly be seen again as what I knew I really was.

As an adolescent, I thought that the way my family escaped South Carolina was like a bad movie. We fled like runaway serfs and the sheriff who would have arrested my stepfather seemed like a border guard. Even now, I am certain that if we had remained in South Carolina, I would have been trapped by my family's heritage of poverty, jail, and illegitimate children—that even being smart, stubborn, and a lesbian would have made no difference. My grandmother died when I was twenty and after Mama went home for the funeral, I had a series of dreams in which we still lived up in Greenville, just down the road from where Granny had died. In the dreams I had two children and only one eye, lived in a trailer, and worked at the textile mill. Most of my time was taken up with deciding when I would finally kill my children and myself. The dreams were so vivid, I became convinced they were about the life I was meant to have had, and I began to work even harder to put as much distance as I could between my family and me. I copied the dress, mannerisms, attitudes, and ambitions of the girls I met in college, changing or hiding my own tastes, interests, and desires. I kept my lesbianism a secret, forming a relationship with an effeminate male friend that served to shelter and disguise us both. I explained to friends that I went home so rarely because my stepfather and I fought too much for me to be comfortable in his house. But that was only part of the reason I avoided home, the easiest reason. The truth was that I feared the person I might become in my mama's house.

It is hard to explain how deliberately and thoroughly I ran away from my own life. I did not forget where I came from, but I gritted my teeth and hid it. When I could not get enough scholarship money to pay for graduate school, I spent a year of blind rage working as a salad girl, substitute teacher, and maid. I finally managed to get a job by agreeing to take any city assignment where the Social Security Administration needed a clerk. Once I had a job and my own place far away from anyone in my family, I became sexually and politically active, joining the Women's Center support staff and falling in love with a series of middle-class women who thought my accent and stories thoroughly charming. The stories I told about my family, about South Carolina, about being poor itself, were all lies, carefully edited to seem droll or funny. I knew damn well that no one would want to hear the truth about poverty, the hopelessness and fear, the feeling that nothing you do will make any difference, and the raging resentment that burns beneath the jokes. Even when my lovers and I formed an alternative lesbian family, sharing all our resources, I kept the truth about my background and who I knew myself to be a carefully obscured mystery. I worked as hard as I could to make myself a new person, an emotionally healthy radical lesbian activist, and I believed completely that by remaking myself I was helping to remake the world.

For a decade, I did not go home for more than a few days at a time.

It is sometimes hard to make clear how much I have loved my family, that every impulse to hold them in contempt has sparked in me a counter-surge of stubborn pride. (What is equally hard to make clear is how much that impulse toward love and pride is complicated by an urge to fit us into the acceptable myths and theories of both mainstream society—Steven Spielberg movies or Taylor Caldwell novels, the one valorizing and the other caricaturing—and a lesbian feminist reinterpretation—the patriarchy as the villain and the trivialization of the choices the men and women of my family have made.) I have had to fight broad generalizations from every possible theoretical viewpoint. Traditional feminist theory has had a limited understanding of class differences or of how sexuality and self are shaped by both desire and denial. The ideology implies that we are all sisters who should turn our anger and suspicion only on the world outside the lesbian community. It is so simple to say the patriarchy did it, that poverty and social contempt are products of the world of the fathers. How often I felt a need to collapse my sexual history into what I was willing to share of my class background, to pretend that both my life as a lesbian and my life as a working-class escapee were constructed by the patriarchy. The difficulty is that I can't ascribe everything that has been problematic or difficult about my life simply and easily to the patriarchy, or even to the invisible and much-denied class structure of our society. . . .

One of the things I am trying to understand is how we internalize the myths of our society even as we hate and resist them. Perhaps this will be more understandable if I discuss specifically how some of these myths have shaped my life and how I have been able to talk about and change my own understanding of my family. I have felt a powerful temptation to write about my family as a kind of moral tale with us as the heroes and the middle and upper classes as the villains. It would be within the romantic myth, for example, to pretend that we were the kind of noble Southern whites portrayed in the movies, mill workers for generations until driven out of the mills by alcoholism and a family propensity to rebellion and union talk. But that would be a lie. The truth is that no one in my family ever joined a union. Taken as far as it can go, the myth of the poor would make my family over into union organizers or people broken by the failure of the unions. The reality of my family is far more complicated and lacks the cardboard nobility of the myth.

As far as my family was concerned, union organizers, like preachers, were of a different class, suspect and hated as much as they might be admired for what they were supposed to be trying to achieve. Serious belief in anything—any political ideology, any religious system, or any theory of life's meaning and purpose—was seen as unrealistic. It was an attitude that bothered me a lot when I started reading the socially conscious novels I found in the paperback racks when I was eleven or so. I particularly loved Sinclair Lewis's novels and wanted to imagine my own family as part of the working man's struggle. But it didn't seem to be that simple.

"We were not joiners," my Aunt Dot told me with a grin when I asked her about the union. My cousin Butch laughed at that, told me the union charged dues and said, "Hell, we can't even be persuaded to toss money in the collection plate. Ain't gonna give it to no fat union man." It shamed me that the only thing my family wholeheartedly believed in was luck, and the waywardness of fate. They held the dogged conviction that the admirable and wise thing to do was to try and keep a sense of humor, not to whine or cower, and to trust that luck might someday turn as good as it had been bad—and with just as much reason. Becoming a political activist with an almost religious fervor was the thing I did that most outraged my family and the Southern working-class community they were part of.

Similarly, it was not my sexuality, my lesbianism, that was seen by my family as most rebellious; for most of my life, no one but my mama took my sexual preference very seriously. It was the way I thought about work, ambition, and self-respect that seemed incomprehensible to my aunts and cousins. They were waitresses, laundry workers, and counter girls. I was the one who went to work as a maid, something I never told any of them. They would have been angry if they had known, though the fact that some work was contemptible was itself a difficult notion. They believed that work was just work, necessary, that you did what you had to do to survive. They did not believe so much in taking pride in doing your job as they did in stubbornly enduring hard work and hard times when you really didn't have much choice about what work you did. But at the same time they did believe that there were some forms of work, including maid's work, that were only for black people, not white, and while I did not share that belief, I knew how intrinsic it was to how my family saw the world. Sometimes I felt as if I straddled cultures and belonged on neither side. I would grind my teeth at what I knew was my family's unquestioning racism but still take pride in their pragmatic endurance, but more and more as I grew older what I truly felt was a deep estrangement from the way they saw the world, and gradually a sense of shame that would have been completely incomprehensible to them.

"Long as there's lunch counters, you can always find work," I was told by both my mother and my aunts, and they'd add, "I can always get me a little extra with a smile." It was obvious that there was supposed to be nothing shameful about it, that needy smile across a lunch counter, that rueful grin when you didn't have rent, or the half-provocative, half-begging way my mama could cajole the man at the store to give her a little credit. But I hated it, hated the need for it and the shame that would follow every time I did it myself. It was begging as far as I was concerned, a quasi-prostitution that I despised even while I continued to use it (after all, I needed the money). But my mother, aunts, and cousins had not been ashamed, and my shame and resentment pushed me even further away from them.

"Just use that smile," my girl cousins used to joke, and I hated what I knew they meant. After college, when I began to support myself and study feminist theory, I did not become more understanding of the women of my family but more contemptuous. I told myself that prostitution is a skilled profession and my cousins were never more than amateurs. There was a certain truth in this, though like all cruel judgments made from the outside, it ignored the conditions that made it true. The women in my family, my mother included, had sugar daddies, not johns, men who slipped them money because they needed it so badly. From their point of view they were nice to those men because the men were nice to them, and it was never so direct or crass an arrangement that they would set a price on their favors. They would never have described what they did as prostitution, and nothing made them angrier than the suggestion that the men who helped them out did it just for their favors. They worked for a living, they swore, but this was different.

I always wondered if my mother had hated her sugar daddy, or if not *him* then her need for what he offered her, but it did not seem to me in memory that she had. Her sugar daddy had been an old man, half-crippled, hesitant and needy, and he treated my mama with enormous consideration and, yes, respect. The relationship between them was painful because it was based on the fact that she and my stepfather could not make enough money to support the family. Mama could not refuse her sugar daddy's money, but at the same time he made no assumptions about that money buying anything she was not already offering. The truth was, I think, that she genuinely liked him, and only partly because he treated her so well.

Even now, I am not sure whether or not there was a sexual exchange between them. Mama was a pretty woman and she was kind to him, a kindness he obviously did not get from anyone else in his life, and he took extreme care not to cause her any problems with my stepfather. As a teenager with an adolescent's contempt for moral failings and sexual complexity of any kind, I had been convinced that Mama's relationship with that old man was contemptible and also that I would never do such a thing. The first time a lover of mine gave me money, and I took it, everything in my head shifted. The amount she gave me was not much to her but it was a lot to me and I needed it. I could not refuse it, but I hated myself for taking it and I hated her for giving it to me. Worse, she had much less grace about my need than my mama's sugar daddy had displayed toward her. All that bitter contempt I had felt for my needy cousins and aunts raged through me and burned out the love I had felt. I ended the relationship quickly, unable to forgive myself for *selling* what I believed should only be offered freely—not sex but love itself.

When the women in my family talked about how hard they worked, the men would spit to the side and shake their heads. Men took real jobs—hard, dangerous, physically daunting work. They went to jail, not just the hard-eyed, careless boys who scared me with their brutal hands and cold eyes, but their gentler, softer brothers. It was another family thing, what people expected of my mama's family, my people. "His daddy's that one was sent off to jail in Georgia, and his uncle's another. Like as not, he's just the same," you'd hear people say of boys so young they still had their milk teeth. We were always driving down to the county farm to see somebody, some uncle, cousin, or nameless male relation. Shaven-headed, sullen and stunned, they wept on Mama's shoulder or begged my aunts to help. "I didn't do nothing, Mama," they'd say and it might have been true, but if even we didn't believe them, who would? No one told the truth, not even about how their lives were destroyed.

When I was eight years old, Butch, one of my favorite cousins, went to jail for breaking into pay phones with another boy. The other boy was returned to the custody of his parents. Butch was sent to the boys' facility at the county farm and after three months, my mama took us down there to visit, carrying a big basket of fried chicken, cold cornbread, and potato salad. Along with a hundred others we sat out on the lawn with Butch and watched him eat like he hadn't had a full meal in the whole three months. I stared at his head, which had been shaved near bald, and his ears, which were newly marked with fine blue scars from the carelessly handled razor. People were laughing, music was playing, and a tall lazy man in uniform walked past us chewing on toothpicks and watching us all closely. Butch kept his head down, his face hard with hatred, only looking back at the guard when he turned away.

"Sons-a-bitches," he whispered, and my mama shushed him. We all sat still when the guard turned back to us. There was a long moment of quiet and then that man let his face relax into a big wide grin.

"Uh-huh," he said. That was all he said. Then he turned and walked away. None of us spoke. None of us ate any more. Butch went back inside soon after and we left. When we got back to the car, my mama sat there for a while crying quietly. The next week Butch was reported for fighting and had his stay extended by six months.

Butch was fifteen. He never went back to school and after jail he couldn't join the army. When he finally did come home we never talked, never had to talk. I knew without asking that the guard had had his little revenge, knew too that my cousin would break into another phone booth as soon as he could, but do it sober and not get caught. I knew without asking the source of his rage, the way he felt about clean, well-dressed, contemptuous people who looked at him like his life wasn't as important as a dog's. I knew because I felt it too. That guard had looked at me and Mama with the same expression he used on my cousin. We were trash. We were the ones they built the county farm to house and break. The boy who had been sent home had been the son of a deacon in the church, the man who managed the hardware store.

As much as I hated that man, and his boy, there was a way in which I also hated my cousin. He should have known better, I told myself, should have known the risk he ran. He should have been more careful. As I became older and started living on my own, it was a litany that I used against myself even more angrily than I used it against my cousin. I knew who I was, knew that the most important thing I had to do was protect myself and hide my despised identity, blend into the myth of both the "good" poor and the reasonable lesbian. Even when I became a feminist activist, that litany went on reverberating in my head, but by then it had become a groundnote, something so deep and omnipresent, I no longer heard it even when everything I did was set to the cadence that it established.

By 1975, I was earning a meager living as a photographer's assistant in Tallahassee, Florida, but the real work of my life was my lesbian feminist activism, the work I did with the local Women's Center and the committee to found a Feminist Studies Department at Florida State University. Part of my role as I saw it was to be a kind of evangelical lesbian feminist, and to help develop a political analysis of this woman-hating society. I did not talk about class, more than by giving lip service to how we all needed to think about it, the same way I thought we all needed to think about racism. I was a serious and determined person, living in a lesbian collective, studying each new book that purported to address feminist issues and completely driven by what I saw as a need to revolutionize the world. . . .

The idea of writing fiction or essays seemed frivolous when there was so much work to be done, but everything changed when I found myself confronting emotions and ideas that could not be explained away or postponed for a feminist holiday. The way it happened was simple and completely unexpected. One week I was asked to speak to two completely divergent groups: an Episcopalian Sunday School class and a juvenile detention center. The Episcopalians were all white, well-dressed, highly articulate, nominally polite, and obsessed with getting me to tell them (without their having to ask directly) just what it was that two women did together in bed. The delinquents were all women, eighty percent black and Hispanic, dressed in green uniform dresses or blue jeans and workshirts, profane, rude, fearless, witty, and just as determined to get me to talk about what it was that two women did together in bed.

I tried to have fun with the Episcopalians, teasing them about their fears and insecurities, and being as bluntly honest as I could about my sexual practices. The Sunday School teacher, a man who had assured me of his liberal inclinations, kept blushing and stammering as the questions about my growing up and coming out became more detailed. When the meeting was over, I stepped out into the sunshine angry at the contemptuous attitude implied by all their questions, and though I did not know why, also so deeply depressed that I couldn't even cry. The delinquents were different. Shameless, they had me blushing within the first few minutes, yelling out questions that were partly curious and partly a way of boasting about what they already knew.

"You butch or femme?" "You ever fuck boys?" "You ever want to?" "You want to have children?" "What's your girlfriend like?" I finally broke up when one very tall confident girl leaned way over and called out, "Hey girlfriend! I'm getting out of here next weekend. What you doing that night?" I laughed so hard I almost choked. I laughed until we were all howling and giggling together. Even getting frisked as I left didn't ruin my mood. I was still grinning when I climbed into the waterbed with my lover that night, grinning right up to the moment when she wrapped her arms around me and I burst into tears.

It is hard to describe the way I felt that night, the shock of recognition and the painful way my thoughts turned. That night I understood suddenly everything that happened to my cousins and me, understood it from a wholly new and agonizing perspective, one that made clear how brutal I had been to both my family and myself. I understood all over again how we had been robbed and dismissed, and why I had worked so hard not to think about it. I had learned as a child that what could not be changed had to go unspoken, and worse, that those who cannot change their own lives have every reason to be ashamed of that fact and to hide it. I had accepted that shame and believed in it, but why? What had I or my cousins really done to deserve the contempt directed at us? Why had I always believed us contemptible by nature? I wanted to talk to someone about all the things I was thinking that night, but I could not. Among the women I knew there was no one who would have understood what I was thinking, no other working-class women in the women's collective where I was living. I began to suspect that we shared no common language to speak those bitter truths.

In the days after that I found myself remembering that afternoon long ago at the county farm, that feeling of being the animal in the zoo, the thing looked at and laughed at and used by the real people who watched us. For all his liberal convictions, that Sunday School teacher had looked at me with eyes that reminded me of Butch's long-ago guard. Suddenly I felt thrown back into my childhood, into all the fears and convictions I had tried to escape. Once again I felt myself at the mercy of the important people who knew how to dress and talk, and would always be given the benefit of the doubt while I and my family would not.

I felt as if I was at the mercy of an outrage so old I could not have traced all the ways it shaped my life. I understood again that some are given no quarter, no chance, that all their courage, humor, and love for each other is just a joke to the ones who make the rules, and I hated the rule makers. Finally I also realized that part of my grief came from the fact that I no longer knew who I was or where I belonged. I had run away from my family, refused to go home to visit, and tried in every way to make myself a new person. How could I be working-class with a college degree? As a lesbian activist? I thought about the guards at the detention center, and the way they had looked at me. They had not stared at me with the same picture-window emptiness they turned on the girls who came to hear me, girls who were closer to the life I had been meant to live than I could bear to examine. The contempt in their eyes was contempt for me as a lesbian, different and the same, but still contempt. . . .

In the late 1970s, the compartmentalized life I had created burst open. It began when I started to

PERSONAL ACCOUNT

That Moment of Visibility

I never realized how much my working-class background and beliefs played a role in my education. My family, friends, and neighbors never placed much importance on college. Instead, we were strongly encouraged to find work immediately after high school so we could support ourselves financially. My sisters and I were encouraged to do secretarial work until we married. There was no particular positive status attached to obtaining a degree except maybe the chance of making a lot of money. In fact, friends who went to college were looked at somewhat suspiciously. Among my reference group, college was often seen as a way to get out of having to work.

No one in my family had ever gone to college. It was not financially feasible and a college environment was equal to the unknown. It really was scary terrain. When I decided to go to a local community college after having worked for five years in a secretarial position, family and friends could not understand my decision. Why would I choose college when I already had a job? I could pay bills, buy what I needed, and I had a savings account. So I started by taking a course a semester—and I barely got through the first course. Although I received a good grade, I felt incredibly isolated, like I was an impostor who did not belong in a classroom. I had no idea how someone in college was supposed to act. I stayed silent, scared, and consciously invisible most of the time. I was not even close to making a commitment to a college education when I signed up for a second course—but because my job payed for it (one of the benefits), I felt I had nothing to lose. I signed up for Introduction to Juvenile Delinquency and midway through, our class received an assignment to do a fifteen-page self-analysis applying some of the theories we were learning. The thought of consciously revealing myself when I was trying so hard not to look, act, or be different was not something I was willing (or, I think, able at the time) to do. When I discussed the assignment with the people close to me, they agreed that the assignment was too personal and revealing. I decided not to do it and I also decided that college was probably not for me.

I went to see my professor (who was the only woman in her department) to let her know that I was refusing to do the assignment and would not complete the course. We had spoken two or three times outside of class and she knew a little about me. I knew that she was also from a working-class background and had returned to school after working some years. I felt the least I could do was tell her I was quitting the class. When I said that I was unwilling to do the assignment, she stared at me for some time, and then asked me what I would prefer to write about. I was stunned that I was noticed and was being asked what I would like to do. When I had no reply, she asked if I would write a paper on the importance of dissent. All I could think to say was yes. I completed the course successfully and found an ally in my department. I can't overstate the importance of that moment of acknowledgement. It was the first time I felt listened to. It was the moment when you feel safe enough to reveal who you are, the deep breath you can finally take when you figure out that the person you're talking to understands, appreciates, and may even share your identity.

I think of this experience as a turning point for me—when I realized that despite all my conscious efforts to be invisible and to "pass," it was that moment of visibility and acknowledgement that kept me in school.

Rose B. Pascarell

write and work out what I really thought about my family. . . . I went home again. I went home to my mother and my sisters, to visit, talk, argue, and begin to understand.

Once home I saw that, as far as my family was concerned, lesbians were lesbians whether they wore suitcoats or leather jackets. Moreover, in all that time when I had not made peace with myself, my family had managed to make a kind of peace with me. My girlfriends were treated like slightly odd versions of my sisters' husbands, while I was simply the daughter who had always been difficult but was still a part of their lives. The result was that I started trying to confront what had made me unable to really talk to my sisters for so many years. I discovered that they no longer knew who I was either, and it took time and lots of listening to each other to rediscover my sense of family, and my love for them.

It is only as the child of my class and my unique family background that I have been able to put together what is for me a meaningful politics, gained a sense of why I believe in activism, why self-revelation is so important for lesbians, reexamining the way we are seen and the way we see ourselves. There is no all-purpose feminist analysis that explains away all the complicated ways our sexuality and core identity are shaped, the way we see ourselves as parts of both our birth families and the extended family of friends and lovers we invariably create within the lesbian community. For me the bottom line has simply become the need to resist that omnipresent fear, that urge to hide and disappear, to disguise my life, my desires, and the truth about how little any of us understand—even as we try to make the world a more just and human place for us all. Most of all I have tried to understand the politics of *they,* why human beings fear and stigmatize the different while secretly dreading that they might be one of the different themselves. Class, race, sexuality, gender, all the categories by which we categorize and dismiss each other need to be examined from the inside.

The horror of class stratification, racism, and prejudice is that some people begin to believe that the security of their families and community depends on the oppression of others, that for some to have good lives others must have lives that are mean and horrible. It is a belief that dominates this culture; it is what made the poor whites of the South so determinedly racist and the middle class so contemptuous of the poor. It is a myth that allows some to imagine that they build their lives on the ruin of others, a secret core of shame for the middle class, a goad and a spur to the marginal working class, and cause enough for the homeless and poor to feel no constraints on hatred or violence. The power of the myth is made even more apparent when we examine how within the lesbian and feminist communities, where so much attention has been paid to the politics of marginalization, there is still so much exclusion and fear, so many of us who do not feel safe even within our chosen communities.

I grew up poor, hated, the victim of physical, emotional, and sexual violence, and I know that suffering does not ennoble. It destroys. To resist destruction, self-hatred, or lifelong hopelessness, we have to throw off the conditioning of being despised, the fear of becoming that *they* that is talked about so dismissively, to refuse lying myths and easy moralities, to see ourselves as human, flawed and extraordinary. All of us—extraordinary.

READING 36

At a Slaughterhouse, Some Things Never Die

Charlie LeDuff

Tar Heel, N.C.—It must have been 1 o'clock. That's when the white man usually comes out of his glass office and stands on the scaffolding above the factory floor. He stood with his palms on the rails, his elbows out. He looked like a tower guard up there or a border patrol agent. He stood with his head cocked.

One o'clock means it is getting near the end of the workday. Quota has to be met and the workload doubles. The conveyor belt always overflows with meat around 1 o'clock. So the workers double their pace, hacking pork from shoulder bones with a driven single-mindedness. They stare blankly, like mules in wooden blinders, as the butchered slabs pass by.

It is called the picnic line: 18 workers lined up on both sides of a belt, carving meat from bone. Up to 16 million shoulders a year come down that line here at the Smithfield Packing Co., the

---

Charlie LeDuff is a reporter for *The New York Times.*

largest pork production plant in the world. That works out to about 32,000 a shift, 63 a minute, one every 17 seconds for each worker for eight and a half hours a day. The first time you stare down at that belt you know your body is going to give in way before the machine ever will.

On this day the boss saw something he didn't like. He climbed down and approached the picnic line from behind. He leaned into the ear of a broad-shouldered black man. He had been riding him all day, and the day before. The boss bawled him out good this time, but no one heard what was said. The roar of the machinery was too ferocious for that. Still, everyone knew what was expected. They worked harder.

The white man stood and watched for the next two hours as the blacks worked in their groups and the Mexicans in theirs. He stood there with his head cocked.

At shift change the black man walked away, hosed himself down and turned in his knives. Then he let go. He threatened to murder the boss. He promised to quit. He said he was losing his mind, which made for good comedy since he was standing near a conveyor chain of severed hogs' heads, their mouths yoked open.

"Who that cracker think he is?" the black man wanted to know. There were enough hogs, he said, "not to worry about no fleck of meat being left on the bone. Keep treating me like a Mexican and I'll beat him."

The boss walked by just then and the black man lowered his head.

WHO GETS THE DIRTY JOBS

The first thing you learn in the hog plant is the value of a sharp knife. The second thing you learn is that you don't want to work with a knife. Finally you learn that not everyone has to work with a knife. Whites, blacks, American Indians and Mexicans, they all have their separate stations.

The few whites on the payroll tend to be mechanics or supervisors. As for the Indians, a handful are supervisors; others tend to get clean menial jobs like warehouse work. With few exceptions, that leaves the blacks and Mexicans with the dirty jobs at the factory, one of the only places within a 50-mile radius in this muddy corner of North Carolina where a person might make more than $8 an hour.

While Smithfield's profits nearly doubled in the past year, wages have remained flat. So a lot of Americans here have quit and a lot of Mexicans have been hired to take their places. But more than management, the workers see one another as the problem, and they see the competition in skin tones.

The locker rooms are self-segregated and so is the cafeteria. The enmity spills out into the towns. The races generally keep to themselves. Along Interstate 95 there are four tumbledown bars, one for each color: white, black, red and brown.

Language is also a divider. There are English and Spanish lines at the Social Security office and in the waiting rooms of the county health clinics. This means different groups don't really understand one another and tend to be suspicious of what they do know.

You begin to understand these things the minute you apply for the job.

BLOOD AND BURNOUT

"Treat the meat like you going to eat it yourself," the hiring manager told the 30 applicants, most of them down on their luck and hungry for work. The Smithfield plant will take just about any man or woman with a pulse and a sparkling urine sample, with few questions asked. This reporter was hired using his own name and acknowledged that he was currently employed, but was not asked where and did not say.

Slaughtering swine is repetitive, brutish work, so grueling that three weeks on the factory floor leave no doubt in your mind about why the turnover is 100 percent. Five thousand quit and five thousand are hired every year. You hear people say, "They don't kill pigs in the plant, they kill people." So desperate is the company for workers, its recruiters comb the streets of New York's immigrant communities, personnel staff members say, and word of mouth has reached Mexico and beyond.

The company even procures criminals. Several at the morning orientation were inmates on work release in green uniforms, bused in from the county prison.

The new workers were given a safety speech and tax papers, shown a promotional video and informed that there was enough methane, ammonia and chlorine at the plant to kill every living thing here in Bladen County. Of the 30 new employees, the black women were assigned to the chitterlings room, where they would scrape feces and worms from intestines. The black men were sent to the butchering floor. Two free white men and the Indian were given jobs making boxes. This reporter declined a box job and ended up with most of the Mexicans, doing knife work, cutting sides of pork into smaller and smaller products.

Standing in the hiring hall that morning, two women chatted in Spanish about their pregnancies. A young black man had heard enough. His small town the next county over was crowded with Mexicans. They just started showing up three years ago—drawn to rural Robeson County by the plant—and never left. They stood in groups on the street corners, and the young black man never knew what they were saying. They took the jobs and did them for less. Some had houses in Mexico, while he lived in a trailer with his mother.

Now here he was, trying for the only job around, and he had to listen to Spanish, had to compete with peasants. The world was going to hell.

"This is America and I want to start hearing some English, now!" he screamed.

One of the women told him where to stick his head and listen for the echo. "Then you'll hear some English," she said.

An old white man with a face as pinched and lined as a pot roast complained, "The tacos are worse than the niggers," and the Indian leaned against the wall and laughed. In the doorway, the prisoners shifted from foot to foot, watching the spectacle unfold from behind a cloud of cigarette smoke.

The hiring manager came out of his office and broke it up just before things degenerated into a brawl. Then he handed out the employment stubs. "I don't want no problems," he warned. He told them to report to the plant on Monday morning to collect their carving knives.

$7.70 AN HOUR, PAIN ALL DAY

Monday. The mist rose from the swamps and by 4:45 a.m. thousands of headlamps snaked along the old country roads. Cars carried people from the backwoods, from the single and double-wide trailers, from the cinder-block houses and wooden shacks: whites from Lumberton and Elizabethtown; blacks from Fairmont and Fayetteville; Indians from Pembroke; the Mexicans from Red Springs and St. Pauls.

They converge at the Smithfield plant, a 973,000-square-foot leviathan of pipe and steel near the Cape Fear River. The factory towers over the tobacco and cotton fields, surrounded by pine trees and a few of the old whitewashed plantation houses. Built seven years ago, it is by far the biggest employer in this region, 75 miles west of the Atlantic and 90 miles south of the booming Research Triangle around Chapel Hill.

The workers filed in, their faces stiffened by sleep and the cold, like saucers of milk gone hard. They punched the clock at 5 a.m., waiting for the knives to be handed out, the chlorine freshly applied by the cleaning crew burning their eyes and throats. Nobody spoke.

The hallway was a river of brown-skinned Mexicans. The six prisoners who were starting that day looked confused.

"What the hell's going on?" the only white inmate, Billy Harwood, asked an older black worker named Wade Baker.

"Oh," Mr. Baker said, seeing that the prisoner was talking about the Mexicans. "I see you been away for a while."

Billy Harwood had been away—nearly seven years, for writing phony payroll checks from the family pizza business to buy crack. He was Rip Van Winkle standing there. Everywhere he looked there were Mexicans. What he didn't know was that one out of three newborns at the nearby Robeson County health clinic was a Latino; that the county's Roman Catholic church had a special Sunday Mass for Mexicans said by a Honduran priest; that the schools needed Spanish speakers to teach English.

With less than a month to go on his sentence, Mr. Harwood took the pork job to save a few dollars. The word in jail was that the job was a cakewalk for a white man.

But this wasn't looking like any cakewalk. He wasn't going to get a boxing job like a lot of other whites. Apparently inmates were on the bottom rung, just like Mexicans.

Billy Harwood and the other prisoners were put on the picnic line. Knife work pays $7.70 an hour to start. It is money unimaginable in Mexico, where the average wage is $4 a day. But the American money comes at a price. The work burns your muscles and dulls your mind. Staring down into the meat for hours strains your neck. After thousands of cuts a day your fingers no longer open freely. Standing in the damp 42-degree air causes your knees to lock, your nose to run, your teeth to throb.

The whistle blows at 3, you get home by 4, pour peroxide on your nicks by 5. You take pills for your pains and stand in a hot shower trying to wash it all away. You hurt. And by 8 o'clock you're in bed, exhausted, thinking of work.

The convict said he felt cheated. He wasn't supposed to be doing Mexican work. After his second day he was already talking of quitting. "Man, this can't be for real," he said, rubbing his wrists as if they'd been in handcuffs. "This job's for an ass. They treat you like an animal."

He just might have quit after the third day had it not been for Mercedes Fernández, a Mexican. He took a place next to her by the conveyor belt. She smiled at him, showed him how to make incisions. That was the extent of his on-the-job training. He was peep-eyed, missing a tooth and squat from the starchy prison food, but he acted as if this tiny woman had taken a fancy to him. In truth, she was more fascinated than infatuated, she later confided. In her year at the plant, he was the first white person she had ever worked with.

The other workers noticed her helping the white man, so unusual was it for a Mexican and a white to work shoulder to shoulder, to try to talk or even to make eye contact.

As for blacks, she avoided them. She was scared of them. "Blacks don't want to work," Mrs. Fernández said when the new batch of prisoners came to work on the line. "They're lazy."

Everything about the factory cuts people off from one another. If it's not the language barrier, it's the noise—the hammering of compressors, the screeching of pulleys, the grinding of the lines. You can hardly make your voice heard. To get another's attention on the cut line, you bang the butt of your knife on the steel railings, or you lob a chunk of meat. Mrs. Fernández would sometimes throw a piece of shoulder at a friend across the conveyor and wave good morning.

THE KILL FLOOR

The kill floor sets the pace of the work, and for those jobs they pick strong men and pay a top wage, as high as $12 an hour. If the men fail to make quota, plenty of others are willing to try. It is mostly the blacks who work the kill floor, the stone-hearted jobs that pay more and appear out of bounds for all but a few Mexicans.

Plant workers gave various reasons for this: The Mexicans are too small; they don't like blood; they don't like heavy lifting; or just plain

"We built this country and we ain't going to hand them everything," as one black man put it.

Kill-floor work is hot, quick and bloody. The hog is herded in from the stockyard, then stunned with an electric gun. It is lifted onto a conveyor belt, dazed but not dead, and passed to a waiting group of men wearing bloodstained smocks and blank faces. They slit the neck, shackle the hind legs and watch a machine lift the carcass into the air, letting its life flow out in a purple gush, into a steaming collection trough.

The carcass is run through a scalding bath, trolleyed over the factory floor and then dumped onto a table with all the force of a quarter-ton water balloon. In the misty-red room, men slit along its hind tendons and skewer the beast with hooks. It is again lifted and shot across the room on a pulley and bar, where it hangs with hundreds of others as if in some kind of horrific dry-cleaning shop. It is then pulled through a wall of flames and met on the other side by more black men who, stripped to the waist beneath their smocks, scrape away any straggling bristles.

The place reeks of sweat and scared animal, steam and blood. Nothing is wasted from these beasts, not the plasma, not the glands, not the bones. Everything is used, and the kill men, repeating slaughterhouse lore, say that even the squeal is sold.

The carcasses sit in the freezer overnight and are then rolled out to the cut floor. The cut floor is opposite to the kill floor in nearly every way. The workers are mostly brown—Mexicans—not black; the lighting yellow, not red. The vapor comes from cold breath, not hot water. It is here that the hog is quartered. The pieces are parceled out and sent along the disassembly lines to be cut into ribs, hams, bellies, loins and chops.

People on the cut lines work with a mindless fury. There is tremendous pressure to keep the conveyor belts moving, to pack orders, to put bacon and ham and sausage on the public's breakfast table. There is no clock, no window, no fragment of the world outside. Everything is pork. If the line fails to keep pace, the kill men must slow down, backing up the slaughter. The boxing line will have little to do, costing the company payroll hours. The blacks who kill will become angry with the Mexicans who cut, who in turn will become angry with the white superintendents who push them.

10,000 UNWELCOME MEXICANS

The Mexicans never push back. They cannot. Some have legitimate work papers, but more, like Mercedes Fernández, do not.

Even worse, Mrs. Fernández was several thousand dollars in debt to the smugglers who had sneaked her and her family into the United States and owed a thousand more for the authentic-looking birth certificate and Social Security card that are needed to get hired. She and her husband, Armando, expected to be in debt for years. They had mouths to feed back home.

The Mexicans are so frightened about being singled out that they do not even tell one another their real names. They have their given names, their work-paper names and "Hey you," as their American supervisors call them. In the telling of their stories, Mercedes and Armando Fernández insisted that their real names be used, to protect their identities. It was their work names they did not want used, names bought in a back alley in Barstow, Texas.

Rarely are the newcomers welcomed with open arms. Long before the Mexicans arrived, Robeson County, one of the poorest in North Carolina, was an uneasy racial mix. In the 1990 census, of the 100,000 people living in Robeson, nearly 40 percent were Lumbee Indian, 35 percent white and 25 percent black. Until a dozen years ago the county schools were de facto segregated, and no person of color held any meaningful county job from sheriff to court clerk to judge.

At one point in 1988, two armed Indian men occupied the local newspaper office, taking hostages and demanding that the sheriff's department be investigated for corruption and its treatment of minorities. A prominent Indian lawyer, Julian Pierce, was killed that same year, and the suspect turned up dead in a broom closet before he could be charged. The hierarchy of power was summed up on a plaque that hangs in the courthouse commemorating the dead of World War I. It lists the veterans by color: "white" on top, "Indian" in the middle and "colored" on the bottom.

That hierarchy mirrors the pecking order at the hog plant. The Lumbees—who have fought their way up in the county apparatus and have built their own construction businesses—are fond of saying they are too smart to work in the factory. And the few who do work there seem to end up with the cleaner jobs.

But as reds and blacks began to make progress in the 1990s—for the first time an Indian sheriff was elected, and a black man is now the public defender—the Latinos began arriving. The United States Census Bureau estimated that 1,000 Latinos were living in Robeson County last year. People only laugh at that number.

"A thousand? Hell, there's more than that in the Wal-Mart on a Saturday afternoon," said Bill Smith, director of county health services. He and other officials guess that there are at least 10,000 Latinos in Robeson, most having arrived in the past three years.

"When they built that factory in Bladen, they promised a trickledown effect," Mr. Smith said. "But the money ain't trickling down this way. Bladen got the money and Robeson got the social problems."

In Robeson there is the strain on public resources. There is the substandard housing. There is the violence. Last year 27 killings were committed in Robeson, mostly in the countryside, giving it a higher murder rate than Detroit or Newark. Three Mexicans were robbed and killed last fall. Latinos have also been the victims of highway stickups.

In the yellow-walled break room at the plant, Mexicans talked among themselves about their three slain men, about the midnight visitors with obscured faces and guns, men who knew that the illegal workers used mattresses rather than banks. Mercedes Fernández, like many Mexicans, would not venture out at night. "Blacks have a problem," she said. "They live in the past. They are angry about slavery, so instead of working, they steal from us."

She and her husband never lingered in the parking lot at shift change. That is when the anger of a long day comes seeping out. Cars get kicked and faces slapped over parking spots or fender benders. The traffic is a serpent. Cars jockey for a spot in line to make the quarter-mile crawl along the plant's one-lane exit road to the highway. Usually no one will let you in. A lot of the scuffling is between black and Mexican.

BLACK AND BLEAK

The meat was backing up on the conveyor and spilling onto the floor. The supervisor climbed down off the scaffolding and chewed out a group of black women. Something about skin being left on the meat. There was a new skinner on the job, and the cutting line was expected to take up his slack. The whole line groaned. First looks flew, then people began hurling slurs at one another in Spanish and English, words they could hardly hear over the factory's roar. The black women started waving their knives at the Mexicans. The Mexicans waved theirs back. The blades got close. One Mexican spit at the blacks and was fired.

After watching the knife scene, Wade Baker went home and sagged in his recliner. CNN played. Good news on Wall Street, the television said. Wages remained stable. "Since when is the fact that a man doesn't get paid good news?" he asked the TV. The TV told him that money was everywhere—everywhere but here.

Still lean at 51, Mr. Baker has seen life improve since his youth in the Jim Crow South. You can say things. You can ride in a car with a white woman. You can stay in the motels, eat in the restaurants. The black man got off the white man's field.

"Socially, things are much better," Mr. Baker said wearily over the droning television. "But we're going backwards as black people economically. For every one of us doing better, there's two of us doing worse."

His town, Chad Bourne, is a dreary strip of peeling paint and warped porches and houses as run-down as rotting teeth. Young men drift from the cinder-block pool hall to the empty streets and back. In the center of town is a bank, a gas station, a chicken shack and a motel. As you drive out, the lights get dimmer and the homes older until eventually you're in a flat void of tobacco fields.

Mr. Baker was standing on the main street with his grandson Monte watching the Christmas parade march by when a scruffy man approached. It was Mr. Baker's cousin, and he smelled of kerosene and had dust in his hair as if he lived in a vacant building and warmed himself with a portable heater. He asked for $2.

"It's ironic isn't it?" Mr. Baker said as his cousin walked away only eight bits richer. "He was asking me the same thing 10 years ago."

A group of Mexicans stood across the street hanging around the gas station watching them.

"People around here always want to blame the system," he said. "And it is true that the system is antiblack and antipoor. It's true that things are run by the whites. But being angry only means you failed in life. Instead of complaining, you got to work twice as hard and make do."

He stood quietly with his hands in his pockets watching the parade go by. He watched the Mexicans across the street, laughing in their new clothes. Then he said, almost as an afterthought, "There's a day coming soon where the Mexicans are going to catch hell from the blacks, the way the blacks caught it from the whites."

Wade Baker used to work in the post office, until he lost his job over drugs. When he came out of his haze a few years ago, there wasn't much else for him but the plant. He took the job, he said, "because I don't have a 401K." He took it because he had learned from his mother that you don't stand around with your head down and your hand out waiting for another man to drop you a dime.

Evelyn Baker, bent and gray now, grew up a sharecropper, the granddaughter of slaves. She was raised up in a tarpaper shack, picked cotton and hoed tobacco for a white family. She supported her three boys alone by cleaning white people's homes.

In the late 60s something good started happening. There was a labor shortage, just as there is now. The managers at the textile plants started giving machine jobs to black people.

Mrs. Baker was 40 then. "I started at a dollar and 60 cents an hour, and honey, that was a lot of money then," she said.

The work was plentiful through the 70s and 80s, and she was able to save money and add on to her home. By the early 90s the textile factories started moving away, to Mexico. Robeson County has lost about a quarter of its jobs since that time.

Unemployment in Robeson hovers around 8 percent, twice the national average. In neighboring Columbus County it is 10.8 percent. In Bladen County it is 5 percent, and Bladen has the pork factory.

Still, Mr. Baker believes that people who want to work can find work. As far as he's concerned, there are too many shiftless young men who ought to be working, even if it's in the pork plant. His son-in-law once worked there, quit and now hangs around the gas station where other young men sell dope.

The son-in-law came over one day last fall and threatened to cause trouble if the Bakers didn't let him borrow the car. This could have turned messy; the 71-year-old Mrs. Baker keeps a .38 tucked in her bosom.

When Wade Baker got home from the plant and heard from his mother what had happened, he took up his pistol and went down to the corner, looking for his son-in-law. He chased a couple of the young men around the dark dusty lot, waving the gun. "Hold still so I can shoot one of you!" he recalled having bellowed. "That would make the world a better place!"

He scattered the men without firing. Later, sitting in his car with his pistol on the seat and his hands between his knees, he said, staring into the night: "There's got to be more than this. White people drive by and look at this and laugh."

LIVING IT, HATING IT

Billy Harwood had been working at the plant 10 days when he was released from the Robeson County Correctional Facility. He stood at the prison gates in his work clothes with his belongings in a plastic bag, waiting. A friend dropped him at the Salvation Army shelter, but he decided it was too much like prison. Full of black people. No leaving after 10 p.m. No smoking indoors. "What you doing here, white boy?" they asked him.

He fumbled with a cigarette outside the shelter. He wanted to quit the plant. The work stinks, he said, "but at least I ain't a nigger. I'll find other work soon. I'm a white man." He had hopes of landing a roofing job through a friend. The way he saw it, white society looks out for itself.

On the cut line he worked slowly and allowed Mercedes Fernández and the others to pick up his slack. He would cut only the left shoulders; it was easier on his hands. Sometimes it would be three minutes before a left shoulder came down the line. When he did cut, he didn't clean the bone; he left chunks of meat on it.

Mrs. Fernández was disappointed by her first experience with a white person. After a week she tried to avoid standing by Billy Harwood. She decided it wasn't just the blacks who were lazy, she said.

Even so, the supervisor came by one morning, took a look at one of Mr. Harwood's badly cut shoulders and threw it at Mrs. Fernández, blaming her. He said obscene things about her family. She didn't understand exactly what he said, but it scared her. She couldn't wipe the tears from her eyes because her gloves were covered with greasy shreds of swine. The other cutters kept their heads down, embarrassed.

Her life was falling apart. She and her husband both worked the cut floor. They never saw their daughter. They were 26 but rarely made love anymore. All they wanted was to save enough money to put plumbing in their house in Mexico and start a business there. They come from the town of Tehuacán, in a rural area about 150 miles southeast of Mexico City. His mother owns a bar there and a home but gives nothing to them. Mother must look out for her old age.

"We came here to work so we have a chance to grow old in Mexico," Mrs. Fernández said one evening while cooking pork and potatoes. Now they were into a smuggler for thousands. Her hands swelled into claws in the evenings and stung while she worked. She felt trapped. But she kept at it for the money, for the $9.60 an hour. The smuggler still had to be paid.

They explained their story this way: The coyote drove her and her family from Barstow a year ago and left them in Robeson. They knew no one. They did not even know they were in the state of North Carolina. They found shelter in a trailer park that had once been exclusively black but was rapidly filling with Mexicans. There was a lot of drug dealing there and a lot of tension. One evening, Mr. Fernández said, he asked a black neighbor to move his business inside and the man pulled a pistol on him.

"I hate the blacks," Mr. Fernández said in Spanish, sitting in the break room not 10 feet from Mr. Baker and his black friends. Mr. Harwood was sitting two tables away with the whites and Indians.

After the gun incident, Mr. Fernández packed up his family and moved out into the country, to a prefabricated number sitting on a brick foundation off in the woods alone. Their only contact with people is through the satellite dish. Except for the coyote. The coyote knows where they live and comes for his money every other month.

Their 5-year-old daughter has no playmates in the back country and few at school. That is the way her parents want it. "We don't want her to be American," her mother said.

"WE NEED A UNION"

The steel bars holding a row of hogs gave way as a woman stood below them. Hog after hog fell around her with a sickening thud, knocking her senseless, the connecting bars barely missing her face. As co-workers rushed to help the woman, the supervisor spun his hands in the air, a signal to keep working. Wade Baker saw this and shook his head in disgust. Nothing stops the disassembly lines.

"We need a union," he said later in the break room. It was payday and he stared at his check: $288. He spoke softly to the black workers sitting near him. Everyone is convinced that talk of a union will get you fired. After two years at the factory, Mr. Baker makes slightly more than $9 an hour toting meat away from the cut line, slightly less than $20,000 a year, 45 cents an hour less than Mrs. Fernández.

"I don't want to get racial about the Mexicans," he whispered to the black workers. "But they're dragging down the pay. It's pure economics. They say Americans don't want to do the job. That ain't exactly true. We don't want to do it for $8. Pay $15 and we'll do it."

These men knew that in the late 70s when the meatpacking industry was centered in northern cities like Chicago and Omaha, people had a union getting them $18 an hour. But by the mid-80s, to cut costs, many of the packing houses had moved to small towns where they could pay a lower, nonunion wage.

The black men sitting around the table also felt sure that the Mexicans pay almost nothing in income tax, claiming 8, 9, even 10 exemptions. The men believed that the illegal workers should be rooted out of the factory. "It's all about money," Mr. Baker said.

His co-workers shook their heads. "A plantation with a roof on it," one said.

For their part, many of the Mexicans in Tar Heel fear that a union would place their illegal status under scrutiny and force them out. The United Food and Commercial Workers Union last tried organizing the plant in 1997, but the idea was voted down nearly two to one.

One reason Americans refused to vote for the union was because it refuses to take a stand on illegal laborers. Another reason was the intimidation. When workers arrived at the plant the morning of the vote, they were met by Bladen County deputy sheriffs in riot gear. "Nigger Lover" had been scrawled on the union trailer.

Five years ago the work force at the plant was 50 percent black, 20 percent white and Indian, and 30 percent Latino, according to union statistics. Company officials say those numbers are about the same today. But from inside the plant, the breakdown appears to be more like 60 percent Latino, 30 percent black, 10 percent white and red.

Sherri Buffkin, a white woman and the former director of purchasing who testified before the National Labor Relations Board in an unfair-labor-practice suit brought by the union in 1998, said in an interview that the company assigns workers by race. She also said that management had kept lists of union sympathizers during the '97 election, firing blacks and replacing them with Latinos. "I know because I fired at least 15 of them myself," she said.

The company denies those accusations. Michael H. Cole, a lawyer for Smithfield who would respond to questions about the company's labor practices only in writing, said that jobs at the Tar Heel plant were awarded through a bidding process and not assigned by race. The company also denies ever having kept lists of union sympathizers or singled out blacks to be fired.

The hog business is important to North Carolina. It is a multibillion-dollar-a-year industry in the state, with nearly two pigs for every one of its 7.5 million people. And Smithfield Foods, a publicly traded company based in Smithfield, Va., has become the No. 1 producer and processor of pork in the world. It slaughters more than 20 percent of the nation's swine, more than 19 million animals a year.

The company, which has acquired a network of factory farms and slaughterhouses, worries federal agriculture officials and legislators, who see it siphoning business from smaller farmers. And environmentalists contend that Smithfield's operations contaminate local water supplies. (The Environmental Protection Agency fined the company $12.6 million in 1996 after its processing plants in Virginia discharged pollutants into the Pagan River.) The chairman and chief executive, Joseph W. Luter III, declined to be interviewed.

Smithfield's employment practices have not been so closely scrutinized. And so every year, more Mexicans get hired. "An illegal alien isn't going to complain all that much," said Ed Tomlinson, acting supervisor of the Immigration and Naturalization Service bureau in Charlotte.

But the company says it does not knowingly hire illegal aliens. Smithfield's lawyer, Mr. Cole, said all new employees must present papers showing that they can legally work in the United States. "If any employee's documentation appears to be genuine and to belong to the person presenting it," he said in his written response, "Smithfield is required by law to take it at face value."

The naturalization service—which has only 18 agents in North Carolina—has not investigated Smithfield because no one has filed a complaint, Mr. Tomlinson said. "There are more jobs than people," he said, "and a lot of Americans will do the dirty work for a while and then return to their couches and eat bonbons and watch Oprah."

NOT FIT FOR A CONVICT

When Billy Harwood was in solitary confinement, he liked a book to get him through. A guard would come around with a cartful. But when the prisoner asked for a new book, the guard, before handing it to him, liked to tear out the last 50 pages. The guard was a real funny guy.

"I got good at making up my own endings," Billy Harwood said during a break. "And *my* book don't end standing here. I ought to be on that roof any day now."

But a few days later, he found out that the white contractor he was counting on already had a full roofing crew. They were Mexicans who were working for less than he was making at the plant.

During his third week cutting hogs, he got a new supervisor—a black woman. Right away she didn't like his work ethic. He went too slow. He cut out to the bathroom too much.

"Got a bladder infection?" she asked, standing in his spot when he returned. She forbade him to use the toilet.

He boiled. Mercedes Fernández kept her head down. She was certain of it, she said: he was the laziest man she had ever met. She stood next to a black man now, a prisoner from the north. They called him K. T. and he was nice to her. He tried Spanish, and he worked hard.

When the paychecks were brought around at lunch time on Friday, Billy Harwood got paid for five hours less than everyone else, even though everyone punched out on the same clock. The supervisor had docked him.

The prisoners mocked him. "You might be white," K. T. said, "but you came in wearing prison greens and that makes you good as a nigger."

The ending wasn't turning out the way Billy Harwood had written it: no place to live and a job not fit for a donkey. He quit and took the Greyhound back to his parents' trailer in the hills.

When Mrs. Fernández came to work the next day, a Mexican guy going by the name of Alfredo was standing in Billy Harwood's spot.

READING 37

Why Are Droves of Unqualified, Unprepared Kids Getting into Our Top Colleges? Because Their Dads Are Alumni

John Larew

Growing up, she heard a hundred Harvard stories. In high school, she put the college squarely in her sights. But when judgment day came in the winter of 1988, the Harvard admissions guys were frankly unimpressed. Her academic record was solid—not special. Extracurriculars, interview, recommendations? Above average, but not by much. "Nothing really stands out" one admissions officer scribbled on her application folder. Wrote another, "Harvard not really the right place."

At the hyperselective Harvard, where high school valedictorians, National Merit Scholar-finalists, musical prodigies—11,000 ambitious kids in all—are rejected annually, this young woman didn't seem to have much of a chance. Thanks to Harvard's largest affirmative action program, she got in anyway. No, she wasn't poor, black, disabled, Hispanic, native American, or even Aleutian. She got in because her mom went to Harvard.

Folk wisdom at Harvard holds that "Mother Harvard does not coddle her young." She sure treats her grandkids right, though. For more than 40 years, an astounding one-fifth of Harvard's students have received admissions preference because parents attended the school. Today, these overwhelming affluent, white children of alumni—"legacies"—are three times more likely to be accepted to Harvard than high school kids who lack that handsome lineage.

Yalies, don't feel smug: Offspring of the Old Blue are two-and-a-half times more likely to be accepted than their unconnected peers. Dartmouth this year admitted 57 percent of its legacy applicants, compared to 27 percent of nonlegacies. At the University of Pennsylvania, 66 percent of legacies were admitted last year—thanks in part to an autonomous "office of alumni admissions" that actively lobbies for alumni children before the admissions committee. "One can argue that it's an accident, but it sure doesn't look like an accident," admits Yale Dean of Admissions Worth David.

If the legacies' big edge seems unfair to the tens of thousands who get turned away every year, Ivy League administrators have long defended the innocence of the legacy stat. Children of alumni are just smarter; they come from privileged backgrounds and tend to grow up in homes where parents encourage learning. That's what Harvard Dean of Admissions William Fitzsimmons told the campus newspaper, the *Harvard Crimson,* when it first reported on the legacy preference last year. Departing Harvard President Derek Bok patiently explained that the legacy preference worked only as a "tie-breaking factor" between otherwise equally qualified candidates.

Since Ivy League admissions data is a notoriously classified commodity, when Harvard officials said in previous years that alumni kids were just better, you had to take them at their word. But then federal investigators came along and pried open those top-secret files. The Harvard guys were lying.

This past fall, after two years of study, the U.S. Department of Education's Office for Civil Rights (OCR) found that, far from being more qualified or even equally qualified, the average admitted legacy at Harvard between 1981 and

---

No biographical information available.

1988 was significantly *less* qualified than the average admitted nonlegacy. Examining admissions office ratings on academics, extracurriculars, personal qualities, recommendations, and other categories, the OCR concluded that "with the exception of the athletic rating, [admitted] nonlegacies scored better than legacies in *all* areas of comparison."

Exceptionally high admit rates, lowered academic standards, preferential treatment . . . hmmm. These sound like the cries heard in the growing fury over affirmative action for racial minorities in America's elite universities. Only no one is outraged about legacies.

- In his recent book, *Preferential Policies,* Thomas Sowell argues that doling out special treatment encourages lackluster performance by the favored and resentment from the spurned. His far-ranging study flits from Malaysia to South Africa to American college campuses. Legacies don't merit a word.
- Dinesh D'Souza, in his celebrated jeremiad *Illiberal Education,* blames affirmative action in college admissions for declining academic standards and increasing racial tensions. Lowered standards for minority applicants, he hints, may soon destroy the university as we know it. Lowered standards for legacies? The subject doesn't come up.
- For all his polysyllabic complaints against preferential admissions, William F. Buckley Jr. (Yale '50) has never bothered to note that son Chris (Yale '75) got the benefit of a policy that more than doubled his chance of admission.

With so much silence on the subject, you'd be excused for thinking that in these enlightened times hereditary preferences are few and far between. But you'd be wrong. At most elite universities during the eighties, the legacy was by far the biggest piece of the preferential pie. At Harvard, a legacy is about twice as likely to be admitted as a black or Hispanic student. As sociologists Jerome Karabel and David Karen point out, if alumni children were admitted to Harvard at the same rate as other applicants. Their numbers in the class of 1992 would have been reduced by about 200. Instead, those 200 marginally qualified legacies outnumbered all black, Mexican-American, native American, and Puerto Rican enrollees put together. If a few marginally qualified minorities are undermining Harvard's academic standards as much as conservatives charge, think about the damage all those legacies must be doing.

Mind you, colleges have the right to give the occasional preference—to bend the rules for the brilliant oboist or the world-class curler or the guy whose remarkable decency can't be measured by the SAT. (I happened to benefit from a geographical edge: It's easier to get into Harvard from West Virginia than from New England.) And until standardized tests and grade point average perfectly reflect the character, judgment, and drive of a student, tips like these aren't just nice, they're fair. Unfortunately, the extent of the legacy privilege in elite American colleges suggests something more than the occasional tie-breaking tip. Forget meritocracy. When 20 percent of Harvard's student body gets a legacy preference, aristocracy is the word that comes to mind.

A CASTE OF THOUSANDS

If complaining about minority preferences is fashionable in the world of competitive colleges, bitching about legacies is just plain gauche, suggesting an unhealthy resentment of the privileged. But the effects of the legacy trickle down. For every legacy that wins, someone—usually someone less privileged—loses. And higher education is a high-stakes game.

High school graduates earn 59 percent of the income of four-year college graduates. Between high school graduates and alumni of prestigious colleges, the disparity is far greater. A *Fortune* study of American CEOs shows the usual suspects—graduates of Yale, Princeton, and Harvard—leading the list. A recent survey of the Harvard Class of 1940 found that 43 percent were worth more than $1 million. With some understatement, the report concludes, "A picture of highly advantageous circumstances emerges here, does it not, compared with American society as a whole?"

An Ivy League diploma doesn't necessarily mean a fine education. Nor does it guarantee future success. What it *does* represent is a big head start in the rat race—a fact Harvard will be the first to tell you. When I was a freshman, a counselor at the Office of Career Services instructed a group of us to make the Harvard name stand out on our resumes: "Underline it, boldface it, put it in capital letters."

Of course, the existence of the legacy preference in this fierce career competition isn't exactly news. According to historians, it was a direct result of the influx of Jews into the Ivy League during the twenties. Until then, Harvard, Princeton, and Yale had admitted anyone who could pass their entrance exams, but suddenly Jewish kids were outscoring the WASPs. So the schools began to use nonacademic criteria—"character," "solidity," and, eventually, lineage—to justify accepting low-scoring blue bloods over their peers. Yale implemented its legacy preference first, in 1925—spelling it out in a memo four years later: The school would admit "Yale sons of good character and reasonably good record . . . regardless of the number of applicants and the superiority of outside competitors." Harvard and Princeton followed shortly thereafter.

Despite its ignoble origins, the legacy preference has only sporadically come under fire, most notably in 1978's affirmative action decision, *University of California Board of Regents v. Bakke.* In his concurrence, Justice Harris Blackmun observed, "It is somewhat ironic to have us so deeply disturbed over a program where race is an element of consciousness, and yet to be aware of the fact, as we are, that institutions of higher learning . . . have given conceded preferences to the children of alumni."

If people are, in fact, aware of the legacy preference, why has it been spared the scrutiny given other preferential policies? One reason is public ignorance of the scope and scale of those preferences—an ignorance carefully cultivated by America's elite institutions. It's easy to maintain the fiction that your legacies get in strictly on merit as long as your admissions bureaucracy controls all access to student data. Information on Harvard's legacies became publicly available not because of any fit of disclosure by the university, but because a few civil rights types noted that the school had a suspiciously low rate of admission for Asian-Americans, who are statistically stronger than other racial groups in academics.

While the ensuing OCR inquiry found no evidence of illegal racial discrimination by Harvard, it did turn up some embarrassing information about how much weight the "legacy" label gives an otherwise flimsy file. Take these comments scrawled by admissions officers on applicant folders:

- "Double lineage who chose the right parents."
- "Dad's [deleted] connections signify lineage of more than usual weight. That counted into the equation makes this a case which (assuming positive TRs [teacher recommendations] and Alum IV [alumnus interview]) is well worth doing."
- "Lineage is main thing."
- "Not quite strong enough to get the clean tip."
- "Classical case that would be hard to explain to dad."
- "Double lineage but lots of problems."
- "Not a great profile, but just strong enough #'s and grades to get the tip from lineage."
- "Without lineage, there would be little case. With it, we'll keep looking."

In every one of these cases, the applicant was admitted.

Of course, Harvard's not doing anything other schools aren't. The practice of playing favorites with alumni children is nearly universal among private colleges and isn't unheard of at public institutions, either. The rate of admission for Stanford's alumni children is "almost twice the general population," according to a spokesman for the admissions office. Notre Dame reserves 25 percent of each freshman class for legacies. At the University of Virginia, where native Virginians make up two-thirds of each class, alumni children are automatically treated as Virginians even if they live out of state—giving them a whopping competitive edge. The same is true of the University of California at Berkeley. At many schools, Harvard included, all legacy applications are guaranteed a read by the dean of admissions himself—a privilege nonlegacies don't get.

LITTLE WHITE ELIS

Like the Harvard deans, officials at other universities dismiss the statistical disparities by pointing to the superior environmental influences found in the homes of their alums. "I bet that, statistically, [legacy qualifications are] a little above average, but not by much," says Paul Killebrew, associate director of admissions at Dartmouth. "The admitted group [of legacies] would look exactly like the profile of the class."

James Wickenden, a former dean of admissions at Princeton who now runs a college consulting firm, suspects otherwise. Wickenden wrote of "one Ivy League university" where the average combined SAT score of the freshman class was 1,350 out of a possible 1,600, compared to 1,280 for legacies. "At most selective schools, [legacy status] doubles, even trebles the chances of admission," he says. Many colleges even place admitted legacies in a special "Not in Profile" file (along with recruited athletes and some minority students), so that when the school's SAT scores are published, alumni kids won't pull down the average.

How do those kids fare once they're enrolled? No one's telling. Harvard, for one, refuses to keep any records of how alumni children stack up academically against their nonlegacy classmates—perhaps because the last such study, in 1956, showed Harvard sons hogging the bottom of the grade curve.

If the test scores of admitted legacies are a mystery, the reason colleges accept so many is not. They're afraid the alumni parents of rejected children will stop giving to the colleges' unending fundraising campaigns. "Our survival as an institution depends on having support form alumni," says Richard Steele, director of undergraduate admissions at Duke University, "so according advantages to alumni kids is just a given."

In fact, the OCR exonerated Harvard's legacy preference precisely because legacies bring in money. (OCR cited a federal district court ruling that a state university could favor the children of out-of-state alumni because "defendants showed that the alumni provide monetary support for the university.") And there's no question that alumni provide significant support to Harvard: Last year, they raised $20 million for the scholarship fund alone.

In a letter to OCR defending his legacies, Harvard's Fitzsimmons painted a grim picture of a school where the preference did not exist—a place peeved alumni turned their backs on when their kids failed to make the cut. "Without the fundraising activities of alumni," Fitzsimmons warned darkly, "Harvard could not maintain many of its programs, including needs-blind admissions."

Ignoring, for the moment, the question of how "needs-blind" a system is that admits one-fifth of each class on the assumption that, hey, their parents might give us money, Fitzsimmons's defense doesn't quite ring true. The "Save the Scholarship Fund" line is a variation on the principle of "Firemen First," whereby bureaucrats threatened with a budget cut insist that essential programs rather than executive perks and junkets will be the first to be slashed. Truth be told, there is just about nothing that Harvard, the richest university in the world, could do to jeopardize needs-blind admissions, provided that it placed a high enough priority on them.

But even more unclear is how closely alumni giving is related to the acceptance of alumni kids. "People whose children are denied admission are initially upset," says Wickenden, "and maybe for a year or two their interest in the university wanes. But typically they come back around when they see that what happened was best for the kids." Wickenden has put his money where his mouth is: He rejected two sons of a Princeton trustee involved in a $420 million fundraising project, not to mention the child of a board member who managed the school's $2 billion endowment, all with no apparent ill effect.

Most university administrators would be loath to take such a chance, despite a surprising lack of evidence of the legacy/largess connection. Fitzsimmons admits Harvard knows of no empirical research to support the claim that diminishing legacies would decrease alumni contributions, relying instead on "hundreds, perhaps thousands of conversations with alumni whose sons and daughters applied."

No doubt some of Fitzsimmons's anxiety is founded: It's only natural for alumni to want their kids to have the same privileges they did. But the historical record suggests that alumni are far more tolerant than administrators realize. Admit women and blacks? *Well, we would,* said administrators earlier this century—*but the alumni just won't have it.* Fortunately for American universities, the bulk of those alumni turned out to be less craven than administrators thought they'd be. As more blacks and women enrolled over the past two decades, the funds kept pouring in, reaching an all-time high in the eighties.

Another significant historical lesson can be drawn from the late fifties, when Harvard's selectiveness increased dramatically. As the number of applications soared, the rate of admission for legacies began declining from about 90 percent to its current 43 percent. Administration anxiety rose inversely, but Harvard's fundraising machine has somehow survived. That doesn't mean there's *no* correlation between alumni giving and the legacy preference, obviously; rather, it means that the people who would withhold their money at the loss of the legacy privilege were far outnumbered by other givers. "It takes time to get the message out," explains Fitzsimmons, "but eventually people start responding. We've had to make the case [for democratization] to alumni, and I think that they generally feel good about that."

HEIR CUT

When justice dictates that ordinary kids should have as fair a shot as the children of America's elite, couldn't Harvard and its sister institutions trouble themselves to "get the message out" again? Of course they could. But virtually no one—liberal or conservative—is pushing them to do so.

"There must be no goals or quotas for any special group or category of applicants," reads an advertisement in the right-wing *Dartmouth Review.* "Equal opportunity must be the guiding policy. Males, females, blacks, whites, Native Americans, Hispanics . . . can all be given equal chance to matriculate, survive, and prosper based solely on individual performance."

Noble sentiments from the Ernest Martin Hopkins Institute, an organization of conservative Dartmouth alumni. Reading on, though, we find these "concerned alumni" aren't sacrificing *their* young to the cause. "Alumni sons and daughters," notes the ad further down, "should receive some special consideration."

Similarly, Harvard's conservative *Salient* has twice in recent years decried the treatment of Asian-Americans in admissions, but it attributes their misfortune to favoritism for blacks and Hispanics. What about legacy university favoritism—a much bigger factor? *Salient* writers have twice endorsed it.

What's most surprising is the indifference of minority activists. With the notable exception of a few vocal Asian-Americans, most have made peace with the preference for well-off whites.

Mecca Nelson, the president of Harvard's Black Students Association, leads rallies for the hiring of more minority faculty. She participated in an illegal sit-in at an administration building in support of Afro-American studies. But when it comes to the policy that Asian-American activist Arthur Hu calls "a 20-percent-white quota," Nelson says, "I don't have any really strong opinions about it. I'm not very clear on the whole legacy issue at all."

Joshua Li, former co-chair of Harvard's Asian-American Association, explains his complacency differently: "We understand that in the future Asian-American students will receive these tips as well."

At America's elite universities, you'd expect a somewhat higher standard of fairness than that—especially when money is the driving force behind the concept. And many Ivy League types *do* advocate for more just and lofty ideals. One of them, as it happens, is Derek Bok. In one of Harvard's annual reports, he warned that the modern university is slowly turning from a truth-seeking enterprise into a money-grubbing corporation—at the expense of the loyalty of its alums. "Such an institution may still evoke pride and respect because of its intellectual achievements," he said rightly. "But the feelings it engenders will not be quite the same as those produced by an institution that is prepared to forgo income, if need be, to preserve values of a nobler kind."

Forgo income to preserve values of a nobler kind—it's an excellent idea. Embrace the preferences for the poor and disadvantaged. Wean alumni from the idea of the legacy edge. And above all, stop the hypocrisy that begrudges the great unwashed a place at Harvard while happily making room for the less qualified sons and daughters of alums.

After 70 years, it won't be easy to wrest the legacy preference away from the alums. But the long-term payoff is as much a matter of message as money. When the sons and daughters of today's college kids fill out *their* applications, the legacy preference should seem not a birthright, but a long-gone relic from the Ivy League's inequitable past.

SECTION III

THE MEANING OF DIFFERENCE

FRAMEWORK ESSAY

The first framework essay in this text considered how contemporary American master statuses are named, dichotomized, and stigmatized. The second essay focused on the experience of privilege and stigma that accompanies those master statuses. In this final section, we will look at the *meaning* that is attributed to difference. What significance are differences of race, sex, class, disability, and sexual orientation presumed to have? What difference does difference make? The concept of ideology is critical to understanding the specific meanings that are attributed to differences, and so we will focus on ideology in this essay.

Ideology

The concept of *ideology* originated in the work of Marx and Engels, particularly *The German Ideology* (1846). It is now a concept used throughout the social sciences and humanities. In general, an ideology can be defined as a widely shared belief or idea that has been constructed and disseminated by the powerful, primarily reflects their experiences, and functions for their benefit.

Ideologies are anchored in the experiences of their creators; thus, they offer only a partial view of the world. "Ideologies are not simply false, they can be 'partly true,' and yet also incomplete [or] distorted. . . . [They are not] consciously crafted by the ruling class and then injected into the minds of the majority; [they are] instead *produced* by specifiable, complex, social conditions" (Brantlinger, 1990:80). Because those who control the means of disseminating ideas have a better chance of having *their* ideas become the ones that prevail, Marx and Engels concluded that "the ideas of the ruling class are in every epoch the ruling ideas." Ideologies have the power to supplant, distort, or silence the experiences of those outside their production.

The idea that people are rewarded on the basis of their merit is an example of an ideology. It is an idea promoted by those with power—for example, teachers and supervisors—and many opportunities are created for the expression of the belief. Report cards, award banquets, and merit raises are all occasions for the expression of the belief that people are rewarded on the basis of their merit.

But certainly, most know this idea is not really true: People are not rewarded only or even primarily on the basis of their merit. The idea that merit is rewarded is only partly true and reflects only *some* people's experiences. The frequent repetition of the idea, however, has the potential to overwhelm contrary experience. Even those whose experience has not generally been that people are rewarded based on merit are likely to subscribe to this philosophy, because they hear it reproduced so often. In any event, there are few safe opportunities to describe beliefs to the contrary or have those beliefs widely disseminated.

Thus, the idea that people are rewarded on the basis of merit is an ideology. It is a belief that reflects primarily the experiences of those with power, but is presented as universally valid. The idea overwhelms and silences the voices of those who are outside its production. In effect, ideologies ask us to discount our own experience.

This conflict between one's own experience and the ideas conveyed by an ideology is implied in W. E. B. Du Bois's description of the "double consciousness" experienced by African Americans discussed in Framework Essay II (page 191). It is also what many feminists refer to as the double or fractured consciousness experienced by women. In both cases, the dominant ideas fail to reflect the real-life experiences of people in these categories. For example, the *actual* experience of poverty, discrimination, motherhood, disability, sexual assault, life in a black neighborhood, or in a gay relationship rarely coincides with the public discussion on these topics. Because those in stigmatized categories do not control the production or distribution of the prevailing ideas, *their* experience is not likely to be reflected in them. The ideology not only silences their experience; it may invalidate it even in their own minds: "I must be the one who's crazy!" In this way, the dominant discourse can invade and overwhelm our own experience, since what we know doesn't fit with it (Kasper, 1986; Smith, 1978, 1990).

An ideology that so dominates a culture as to become the prevailing and unquestioned belief was described in the 1920s by Italian political theorist Antonio Gramsci as the *hegemonic*, or ruling, ideology. Gramsci argued that social control was primarily accomplished by the control of ideas, and that whatever was considered to be "common sense" was especially effective as a mechanism of social control (Omi and Winant, 1994:67). Commonsense beliefs are likely to embody widely shared ideas primarily reflecting the interests and experience of those who are powerful. We are all encouraged to adhere to "common sense" even when that requires discounting our own experience. The discussion of natural-law language that follows especially shows how this operates.

Conveying Ideologies: Natural-Law Language and Stereotypes

Hegemonic, or ruling, ideologies often take the form of commonsense beliefs and are especially embodied in stereotypes and what is called *natural-law language.*

Natural-Law Language When people use the word *natural,* they usually mean that something is inevitable, predetermined, or outside human control (Pierce, 1971). *Human nature* and *instinct* are often used in the same way. For example, "It's only natural to care about what others think," "It's human nature to want to get ahead," or "It's just instinctive to be afraid of someone different" all convey the sense that something is inevitable, automatic, and independent of one's will.

Thus, it is not surprising when, in discussions about discrimination, someone says, "It's only natural for people to be prejudiced" or "It's human nature to want to be with your own kind." Each of these "common-sense" ideas conveys a belief in the inevitability of discrimination and prejudice, as if such processes emerged independently of anyone's will.

Even for issues of which we disapprove, the word *natural* can convey this sense of inevitability. For example, "I am against racism, but it's only natural" puts nature on the side of prejudice. Arguing that something is natural because it happens frequently has the same consequence. "All societies have discriminated against women, so there is little we can do about it" implies that something that happens frequently is therefore inevitable. But in truth, something that happens frequently could just as likely mean there is an extensive set of social controls ensuring the outcome.

At least three consequences follow from using natural-law language. First, it ends discussion, as if having described something as natural makes any further exploration of the topic unnecessary. This makes sense given that the word *natural* is equated with inevitability: If something is inevitable, there is little sense in questioning it.

Second, because natural-law language treats behavior as predetermined, it overlooks the actual cultural and historical variation of human societies. If something is natural, it should always happen. Yet there is virtually no human behavior that emerges everywhere and always; all social life is susceptible to change. Thus, natural-law language ignores the variability of social life.

Third, natural-law language treats individuals as passive, lacking an interest in or control over social life. If it is "natural" to dislike those who are different, then there is really nothing we can do about that feeling. It is no one's responsibility; it is just natural. If there is nothing I can do about my own behavior, there is little I could expect to do about the behavior of others. Human nature thus is depicted as a limitation beyond which people cannot expect to move (Gould, 1981). Describing certain behavior as "only natural" implies that personal and social change are impossible.

In all these ways—by closing off discussion, masking variation and change, and treating humans as passive—natural-law language tells us not to question the world that surrounds us. Natural-law language has this effect no matter what context it emerges in: "It's only natural to discriminate," "It's only natural to want to have children," "It's only natural to marry and settle down," "Inequality is only natural; the poor will always be with us," "Aggression and war are just human nature," "Greed is instinctive." In each case, natural-law language not only discourages questions, it carries a covert recommendation about what one *ought* to do. If something is "just natural," you cannot prevent others from doing it, and you are well advised to do it yourself. Thus, natural-law language serves as a forceful mechanism of social control (Pierce, 1971).

Natural-law language is used to convey hegemonic ideologies. It reduces the complexity and historic variability of the social world to a claim for universal processes, offering a partial and distorted truth that silences those with contrary experience. Natural-law language can make discrimination appear to be natural, normal, and inevitable. Thus, natural-law language itself creates and maintains ideas about difference.

Stereotypes A *stereotype* is a prediction that "members of a group will behave in certain ways" (Andre, 1988:259)—that black men will have athletic ability or that Asian American students will excel in the sciences. Stereotypes assume that all the individuals in a category possess the same characteristics. Stereotypes persist despite evidence to the contrary because they are not formulated in a way that is testable or falsifiable (Andre, 1988). In this way stereotypes differ from descriptions. Descriptions offer no prediction; they can be tested for accuracy and rejected when they are wrong; they encourage explanation and a consideration of historical variability.

For example, "Most great American athletes are African American" is a description. First, there is no prediction that a particular African American can be expected to be a good athlete, or that someone who is white will be a poor one. Second, the claim is falsifiable; that is, it can be tested for accuracy and proven wrong (e.g., by asking what proportion of the last two decades' Olympic medal winners were African American). Third, the statement turns our attention to explanation and historical variation: Why might this be the case? Has this always been the case?

In contrast, "African Americans are good athletes" is a stereotype. It attempts to characterize a whole population, thus denying the inevitable differences among the people in the category. It predicts that members of a group will behave in a particular way. It cannot be falsified since there is no direct way to test the claim. Further, the stereotype denies the reality of historical and cultural variation by suggesting that this has always been the case. Thus, stereotypes essentialize: they assume that if you know something about the physical package someone comes in, you can predict that person's behavior.

Both stereotypes and natural-law language offer broad-based predictions about behavior. Stereotypes predict that members of a particular category will possess particular attributes; natural-law language predicts that certain behavior is inevitable. Neither stereotypes nor natural-law language is anchored in any social or historical context and, for that reason, both are frequently wrong. Basketball great Bill Russell's reaction when asked if he thought African Americans were "natural" athletes makes clear the similarity of natural-law language and stereotyping. As Russell said, this was a stereotypic image of African American athletes that deprecated the skill and effort he brought to his craft—as if he were great because he was black rather than because of the talent he cultivated in hours of work.

Stereotyping and Asian Americans As we have said, stereotypes explain life outcomes by attributing some essential, shared quality to all those in a particular category. The current depiction of Asian Americans as a "model minority" is a good example of this. This stereotype masks the considerable economic, educational, and occupational heterogeneity among Asian Americans. For example, the college degree attainment rate of Vietnamese Americans is only one-quarter the rate for Asian Americans overall. The model-minority stereotype is itself a fairly recent invention. Its origin is described by Robert B. Lee in Reading 49. Among those now called "model minority" are categories of people previously barred as unworthy to immigrate, denied citizenship through naturalization, and placed in internment camps as potential traitors.

In American culture, stereotypes are often driven by the necessity to explain why some categories of people succeed more than others (Steinberg, 1989). Thus, the model-minority stereotype is often used to claim that if racism has not hurt Asian Americans' success, it could not have hurt African Americans'.

> The myth of the Asian-American "model minority" has been challenged, yet it continues to be widely believed. One reason for this is its instructional value. For whom are Asian Americans supposed to be a "model"? Shortly after the Civil War, southern planters recruited Chinese immigrants in order to pit them against the newly freed blacks as "examples" of laborers willing to work hard for low wages. Today, Asian Americans are again being used to discipline blacks. . . . Our society needs an Asian-American "model minority" in an era anxious about a growing black underclass. (Takaki, 1993:416)

A brief review of American immigration policy explains the misguided nature of the comparison between African and Asian Americans. From 1921 until 1965, U.S. immigration was restricted by quotas that set limits on the number of immigrants from each nation based on the percentage of people from that country residing in the United States at the time of the 1920 census. This had the obvious and intended effect of severely restricting immigration from Asia, as well as from Southern and Eastern Europe and Africa. The civil rights movement of the 1960s raised such national embarrassment about this quota system that in 1965 Congress replaced national-origin quotas with an annual 20,000-person limit for every nation regardless of its size. Within that quota, preference went first to those who were relatives of American citizens and then to those with occupational skills needed in America.

The result was a total increase in immigration and a change in its composition. Because few individuals from non-European countries could immigrate on the grounds of having family in America—previous restrictions would have made that almost impossible—the quotas were filled with people meeting designated *occupational* needs. Thus, those immigrating to the United States since 1965 have had high educational and occupational profiles. The middle- and upper-class professionals and entrepreneurs who have immigrated to the United States did not suddenly become successful here; rather, they continued their home-country success here. These high occupational and educational profiles have characterized immigrants from African as well as Asian countries.

The high Asian American educational and occupational profile has yielded the country's highest median *household* income, but not its highest *individual* income. The chart below compares family and individual income by race and shows the degree to which family size affects household income.

Race/ethnicity	Median family income	Median household size	Median per capita Income
White (non-Hispanic)	$45,904	2.45	$25,278
Black	$30,439	2.67	$15,159
Latino	$33,447	3.49	$12,306
Asian American	$55,521	3.10	$22,352

Source: U.S. Census Bureau, 2001.

Thus, despite a higher educational profile, Asian Americans' per capita income lags behind that of non-Hispanic whites. The following 1999 data compare college graduation with unemployment and poverty rates.

Race/ethnicity	Percent with college degree	Unemployment rate	Percent of families in poverty
Whites	25.9%	3.7%	8.0%
Blacks	15.4	8.0	23.4
Latinos	10.9	6.4	22.7
Asian Americans	42.4	4.2	11.0

Source: U.S. Census Bureau, 2000; in Le, 2001.

> A more telling statistic is how much more money a person earns with each additional year of schooling completed, or what sociologists call "returns on education." Using this measure, research consistently shows that for each additional year of education attained, Whites earn another $522 [a year.] That is, beyond a high school degree, a White [worker] with four more years of education (equivalent to a college degree) can expect to earn $2,088 [more] per year in salary.
>
> In contrast, return on each additional year of education for a Japanese American is only $438 a [year.] For a Chinese American, it's $320. For Blacks, it's even worse at only $284. What this means is that, basically, a typical Asian American has to get more years of education just to make the same amount of money that a typical White [worker] makes with less education. (Le, 2001)

While selective immigration goes a long way toward explaining the success of some recent immigrants from Asian countries, it's important to distinguish between people who are immigrants and those who are refugees. The circumstances of arrival and resettlement for those who have fled their home countries make the refugee population exceedingly heterogeneous and quite different from those who have immigrated to the United States (Haines, 1989). Thus, Vietnamese, Laotian, Cambodian, and Hmong refugees are unlikely to have the high occupational or educational profiles of other Asian immigrants.

The misguided contemporary formulation—if Asian Americans can make it, why can't African Americans?—echoes an earlier question: If European immigrants can make it, why can't African Americans? The answer to that question is summarized as follows:

> Conditions within the cities to which they had migrated [beginning in the 1920s], not slavery, strained blacks' ability to retain two-parent families. Within those cities, blacks faced circumstances that differed fundamentally from those found earlier by European immigrants. They entered cities in large numbers as unskilled and semiskilled manufacturing jobs were leaving, not growing. The discrimination they encountered kept them out

> of the manufacturing jobs into which earlier immigrants had been recruited. One important goal of public schools had been the assimilation and "Americanization" of immigrant children; by contrast, they excluded and segregated blacks. Racism enforced housing segregation, and residential concentration among blacks increased at the same time it lessened among immigrants and their children. Political machines had embraced earlier immigrants and incorporated them into the system of "city trenches" by which American cities were governed; they excluded blacks from effective political power until cities had been so abandoned by industry and deserted by whites that resistance to black political participation no longer mattered. All the processes that had opened opportunities for immigrants and their children broke down for blacks. . . . (Katz, 1989:51)

Stereotyping and African Americans Despite the significance of prejudice against blacks in American history, large-scale survey research on racial prejudice has been pursued only since the beginning of the 1990s (Sniderman and Carmines, 1997). That research shows a mixed picture.

While prejudice has decreased significantly over the last decades, negative stereotypes about African Americans still prevail among whites across all educational levels. "With the exception of citizens who are uncommonly well educated and uncommonly liberal, what is striking is the sheer pervasiveness throughout contemporary American society of negative characterizations of blacks" (Sniderman and Piazza, 1993:50). When whites are asked to select adjectives that describe "most blacks," few pick positive ones. Seventy-five percent are willing to describe African Americans as "friendly," but only "50–60 percent are prepared to describe blacks as 'smart at everyday things,' 'good neighbors,' 'hard-working,' 'intelligent at school,' 'dependable,' 'law-abiding,' or 'determined to succeed'" (Sniderman and Carmines, 1997:62–63). For negative characterizations, 20 percent of whites describe blacks as "irresponsible" and 50 percent say blacks are "aggressive or violent" (Sniderman and Carmines, 1997).

Still, when presented with real-life scenarios containing hidden tests of racial attitudes, whites who *said* they felt positively about African Americans appear to have actually *meant* it (Sniderman and Carmines, 1997). In addition, whites were less discriminatory when responding to scenarios about *individual* African Americans than they were when considering African Americans as a group.

> Claims for government assistance made on behalf of blacks as *individuals* are treated [by white survey respondents] as those made on behalf of individual whites, and indeed, insofar as race makes a difference, a black who has lost his or her job meets with a more sympathetic and generous response [in the survey] than a white who has lost his or her job. On the other hand, when it comes to judgments about what blacks as a group are entitled to, a racial double standard manifestly persists. . . .
>
> The evenhandedness characteristic of reactions to blacks as individuals is not characteristic of reactions to blacks as a group. We found significantly more support for government guarantees of equal opportunity for women than for blacks. (Sniderman and Piazza, 1993:13 and 169)

Well-educated whites did not operate from this double standard, but other whites—irrespective of their political orientation—did. "Thus, conservatives with a high school education or less are almost three times as likely to approve of government assurances of equal opportunity for women as for blacks—plainly a double standard. But the same is true on the left" (Sniderman and Piazza, 1993:83). (Sniderman and Piazza argue that education lessens this double standard because it encourages consistency in thinking.) "Given this duality of response, it is easier to understand why whites see themselves as living in a world where the meaning of race has changed, while blacks see themselves as living in a world where its meaning has remained much the same" (Sniderman and Piazza, 1993:68).

Social Institutions and the Support of Ideologies

The specific messages carried by natural-law language and stereotypes are often echoed by social institutions. The term *social institution* refers to the established mechanisms by which societies meet their predictable needs. For example, the need to socialize new members of the society is met by the institutions of the family and education. In addition to these, social institutions include science, law, religion, politics, the economy, military, medicine, and mass media or popular culture. Ideologies—in our case ideologies about the meaning of difference—naturally play a significant role in the operation of social institutions. Thus, the readings in this section are organized around the social institutions of law, politics, economy, science, and popular culture. We have also included a section on language, but that is not generally considered a social institution *per se.*

In the discussion that follows, we will consider how late-19th- and early-20th-century science and popular culture constructed the meaning of race, class, sex, and sexual orientation differences. Throughout, there is a striking congruence among scientific pronouncements, popular culture messages, and the prejudices of the day.

Science The need to explain the meaning of human difference forcefully emerged when 15th century Europeans' encountered previously unknown regions and peoples. "Three centuries of exploration brought home as never before the tremendous diversity of human behavior and life patterns within environments and under circumstances dramatically different from those of Europe. . . . Out of that large laboratory of human experience was born the [idea of the] conflict between nature and nurture" (Degler, 1991:4–5).

The "nature-nurture" conflict offered two ways to explain human variation. Explanations from the nature side stressed that the diversity of human societies—and the ability of some to conquer and dominate others—reflected significant biological differences among populations. Explanations from the nurture side argued that human diversity resulted from historical, environmental, and cultural difference. From the nature side, humans were understood to act out behaviors that are biologically driven. From the nurture side, humans were something of a *tabula rasa,* a blank slate, on which particular cultural expectations were inscribed.

Whether nature or nurture was understood to dominate, however, the discussion of the meaning of human difference always assumed that people could be ranked as to their worth (Gould, 1981). Thus, the real question was whether the rankings reflected in social hierarchies were the result of nature, and thus inevitable and fixed, or could be affected by human action and were thus subject to change.

The question was not merely theoretical. The 1800s in America witnessed appropriation of Native American territories and the forced relocation of vast numbers of people under the Indian Removal Act of 1830; the 1848 signing of the Treaty of Guadalupe Hidalgo ending the Mexican-American War and ceding what is now Texas, New Mexico, California, Utah, Nevada, and Arizona to the United States with the 75,000 Mexican nationals residing in those territories becoming U.S. citizens; passage of the Chinese Exclusion Act; a prolonged national debate about slavery and women's suffrage; and the unprecedented flow of poor and working-class immigrants from Southern and Eastern Europe. The century closed with the internationally publicized trial of English playwright Oscar Wilde, who was sentenced to two years' hard labor for homosexuality.

Thus, whether social hierarchy reflected natural, permanent, and inherent differences in capability (the nature side) or was the product of specific social and historical circumstances and therefore susceptible to change (the nurture side) raised a profound question. Because Africans were held by whites in slavery, did that mean Africans were by their nature inferior to whites? Were Native Americans literally "savages" occupying some middle ground between animals and civilized humans, and did they therefore benefit from domination by those who supposedly were more advanced? Did the dissimilarity of Chinese immigrants from American whites mean they were not "human" in the way whites were? If homosexuality was congenital, did that mean homosexuals were profoundly different from heterosexuals? Were women closer to plants and animals than to civilized men? Were the poor and working classes composed of those who not only lacked the talents by which to rise in society but also passed their defects on to their children? In all, were individuals and categories of people located in the statuses for which they were best suited? This was the question driving public debate (Degler, 1991). If one believed that the social order simply reflected immutable biological differences, the answer to the question would likely be affirmative. That would not have been the case, however, for those who believed these differences were the outcome of specific social and historical processes overlaying a shared humanity. In all, the question behind the nature-nurture debate was about the *meaning* of what appeared to be *natural* difference. The answer to that question was shaped by the hegemonic ideologies of the time—especially those informed by science.

Charles Darwin's publication of *The Origin of the Species* (1859) and *The Descent of Man* (1871) shifted the weight of popular and scholarly opinion toward the nature side of the equation (Degler, 1991). In its broadest terms, Darwin's conclusions challenged head on the two central beliefs of the time (Darwin himself was quite distressed to have arrived at these conclusions [Shipman, 1994]). First, the idea of evolutionary change challenged "traditional, Christian belief in a single episode of creation of a static, perfect, and unchanging world." The significance of evolutionary change was clear: "If the world were not created perfect, then there was no implicit justification for the way things were . . ." (Shipman, 1994:18).

Second, Darwin's work implied that all humans share a common ancestry. If differences among birds were the result of their adaptation to distinctive environments, then their differences existed within an overall framework of similarity and common ancestry. By analogy, the distinctiveness of human populations might also be understood as "variability within overall similarity" (Shipman, 1994:22)—a shocking possibility at the time. "It was the age of imperialism and most non-Europeans were regarded, even by Darwin, as 'barbarians'; he was astonished and taken aback by their wildness and animality. The differences among humans seemed so extreme that the humanity . . . of some living groups was scarcely credible" (Shipman, 1994:19).

The idea that change in the physical environment resulted in the success of some species and demise of others (the idea of natural selection) bolstered the pre-existent concept of "survival of the fittest." This phrase had been authored by English sociologist Herbert Spencer, who had been applying evolutionary principles to human societies several years before Darwin published *The Origin of the Species.*

Spencer's position, eventually called *social Darwinism,* was extremely popular in America. Spencer strongly believed that modern societies are inevitably improvements over earlier forms of social organization and that progress would necessarily follow from unimpeded competition for social resources. In all, social Darwinism argued that those who are more advanced naturally rise to the top of any stratification ladder.

Through social Darwinism, the prevailing hierarchies—slave owner over people held in slavery, white over Mexican and Native American, native-born over immigrant, upper-class over poor, male over female—could be attributed to natural processes and justified as a reflection of inherent differences among categories of people. As one sociologist at the turn of the century framed it, "under the tutelage of Darwinism the world returns again to the idea that *might* as evidence of fitness has something to do with *right*" (Degler, 1991:13).

Social Darwinism has since been discredited, since it attributes the supremacy of certain groups to biology and evolution rather than to the exercise of power within specific historical and economic contexts. Social Darwinism lacked a socially or historically grounded explanation for social stratification. Instead, it treated those hierarchies as a reflection of the biological merit of categories of people. Thus, the ideology of social Darwinism was used to justify slavery, colonialism, immigration quotas, the criminalization of homosexuality, the forced relocation of Native Americans, and the legal subordination of women.

Spencer argued that the specialization of tasks, also called the *division of labor,* was the outcome of a biologically mandated evolution. The sexual division of labor "was a product of the organic law of progress," thus making equal treatment of men and women impossible and even potentially dangerous.

The social Darwinist position was used by those opposed to providing equal education for women. Just when American institutions of higher education were opening to women—Vassar College was founded in 1865, Smith and Wellesley 10 years later, and by 1870 many state universities had become coeducational—biologist Edward Clarke published a book (1873) that argued that the physical energy education required would endanger women's reproductive abilities (an idea first put forward by Spencer). Clarke's case was based on meager and questionable empirical evidence, seven clinical cases, only one of which actually supported his position (Sayers, 1982:14). His work was a response to *social* rather than scientific developments, since it was prompted by no new discoveries in biology. Nonetheless, the book was an immediate and enduring success. For the next 30 years it was used in the argument against equal education despite the accumulation of evidence refuting its claims. While Clarke's research should have been suspect, it instead became influential in policymaking. In part, "the reason why Clarke's argument seemed so serviceable to those opposed to women's higher education was that it was couched in biological terms and thus appeared to offer a legitimate scientific basis for conservative opposition to equal education" (Sayers, 1982:11).

In a similar fashion, science shaped ideas about the meaning of same-sex relationships. By the turn of the century in Europe, a gay rights movement had arisen in Germany and gay themes had emerged in French literature (Adam, 1987). At the same time, however, an international move to criminalize sexual relations between men gathered momentum: a revision of the German criminal code increased the penalties for male homosexuality, the British imprisoned Oscar Wilde, and Europe and the United States experienced a social reform movement directed against prostitution and male homosexuality. (The possibility of sexual relations between women was not considered until later.)

The move to criminalize homosexuality was countered by physicians arguing, from a social Darwinist position, that homosexuality is the product of "hereditary weakness" and is thus beyond individual control. Though their hope was for increased tolerance, scientists who took this position offered the idea of "homosexuality as a medical entity and the homosexual as a distinctive kind of person" (Conrad and Schneider, 1980:184). Thus, they contributed to the idea that heterosexual and homosexual people were profoundly different from each other.

Science also supported the argument that people of different skin colors are different in significant, immutable ways. Certainly Spencer's idea of the survival of the fittest was understood to support the ideology that whites are superior to all people of color: "The most prevalent form of social Darwinism at the turn of the century was actually racism, that is, the idea that one people might be superior to another because of differences in their biological nature" (Degler, 1991:15).

The scientific defense of American slavery first emerged with the work of two eminent scientists, Swiss naturalist Louis Agassiz and Philadelphia physician Samuel Morton. Agassiz immigrated to America in 1840 and became a professor at Harvard. There he garnered immense popularity by countering the biblically based theory of the unity of all people (which attributed racial differences to "degeneration" from a shared origin) with a "scientific" theory that different races had descended from different moments of creation—"different Adams" as it was called (Gould, 1981:39).

Samuel Morton tested Agassiz's theories by assessing the skull capacity of people of different races. His idea was that the size of the skull would correlate with the intelligence of the race. His results "matched every good Yankee's prejudices—whites on top, Indians in the middle, and blacks on the bottom; and among whites, Teutons and Anglo-Saxons on top, Jews in the middle, and Hindus on the bottom" (Gould, 1981:53).

As we now know, Morton's findings were simply wrong. Others who replicated his measurements did not arrive at the same conclusions about skull capacity: There were "*no* significant differences among races for Morton's own data" (Gould, 1981:67). Morton's research was inadequate even by the scientific standards of his time. There is no evidence that Morton intended to deceive. Rather, his assumptions of white superiority were so firm that he was oblivious to his own errors and illogic, errors that yielded the conclusion of white superiority only because of his miscalculations.

The use of questionable research to support prevailing beliefs (Gould, 1981) was also evident in the development of intelligence testing. In 1904, Alfred Binet, director of the psychology lab at the Sorbonne, was commissioned by the French minister of public education to develop a test to identify children whose poor performance in school might indicate a need for special education. Binet developed a test with a series of tasks that children of "normal" intelligence were expected to have mastered. Binet's own claims for the test were fairly limited. He did not equate intelligence with the score produced by his test, arguing that intelligence was too complex a factor to be reduced to a simple number. Nor did he construe his test as measuring inborn, permanent, or inherited limitations (Gould, 1981).

Binet's hesitations regarding the significance of the test, however, were ignored by the emerging field of American psychology, which used intelligence as a way to explain social hierarchies. "The people who are doing the drudgery are, as a rule, in their proper places," wrote H. H. Goddard, who introduced the Binet test to America. Stanford psychologist Lewis M. Termin (author of the Stanford-Binet IQ test) argued that "the children of successful and cultured parents test higher than children from wretched and ignorant homes for the simple reason that their heredity is better" (Degler, 1991:50). Indeed, "Terman believed that class boundaries had been set by innate intelligence" (Gould, 1981:183).

Such conclusions were used to shape decisions about the distribution of social resources. For example, intelligence was described as a capacity like the capacity of a jug for a certain amount of milk. A pint jug could not be expected to hold a quart of milk; similarly, it was pointless to waste "too much" education on someone whose capacity was supposedly limited. The findings of intelligence testers were thus used to advocate particular social policies such as restrictions on immigration. While it is not clear that the work of intelligence testers *directly* affected the Immigration Restriction Act of 1924 (Degler, 1991), the ultimate shape of the legislation limited immigration from Southern and Eastern Europe, which was consistent with intelligence testers' claims about the relative intelligence of the "races" in Europe. These quotas barred the admission of European Jews fleeing the impending holocaust (Gould, 1981).

Still, by about 1930 a considerable body of research showed that social environment more than biology accounts for differing IQ scores and that the tests themselves measured not innate intelligence but familiarity with the culture of those who wrote the tests. In the end, the psychologists who had promoted intelligence testing were forced to repudiate the idea that intelligence is inherited or that it can be separated from cultural knowledge.[1]

Whether measuring cranial capacity, developing paper-and-pencil intelligence tests, positing the effect of education on women, or arguing for hereditary weakness as an explanation of homosexuality, the work of these scientists supported the prevailing ideologies about the merit and appropriate social position of people of different sexes, races, ethnic groups, sexual orientations, and social classes. Most of these scientists do not appear to have been ideologically motivated; indeed they were sometimes troubled by their own findings. Still, their research was riddled with technical errors and questionable findings. Their research proved "the surprising malleability of 'objective,' quantitative data in the interest of a preconceived idea" (Gould, 1981:147). Precisely because their research confirmed prevailing beliefs, it was more likely to be celebrated than scrutinized.

Why were these findings eventually repudiated? Since they offered a defense of the status quo and confirmed the prevailing ideology, who would have criticized them?

First, the scientific defense of immutable hierarchy was eroded by the steady accumulation of evidence about the "intellectual equality and therefore the equal cultural capacity of all peoples" (Degler, 1991:61). A good deal of the research that made that point was produced by the many "prominent or soon to be prominent" scholars of African American, Chinese, and European immigrant ancestry who, after finally being admitted to institutions of higher education, were pursuing scientific research. Black scholars such as W. E. B. Du Bois and E. Franklin Frazier, and scholars of recent European immigrant ancestry such as anthropologists Franz Boas, Alfred Kroeber, and Edward Sapir, trenchantly criticized the social science of the day and by their very presence challenged the prevailing expectations about the "inherent inferiority" of people like themselves (Degler, 1991).

The presumptions about the meaning of race were also challenged by increased interracial contact. The 1920s began the Great Migration, in which hundreds of thousands of African Americans from the rural South moved to northern cities. This movement continued through two world wars as black, Latino, Asian, and Native American men joined the armed forces and women followed wartime employment

[1]". . . There is also a lot of evidence for the whole American population, for American ethnic groups, and for populations wherever tests are given that IQ is changing in ways that can't possibly be genetic because they happen too fast. It is widely recognized that average IQs are increasing fairly rapidly. These changes in IQ clearly must have more to say about relationships between testing and real performance, or about social patterns of learning, than about biologically rooted 'intelligence.' The genes of a large population don't change that fast unless there is a very dramatic episode of natural selection such as an epidemic. It is also widely recognized that African Americans are slowly but steadily gaining on white Americans in IQ" (Cohen, 1998:210).

opportunities. The 1920s also brought the Harlem Renaissance, an outpouring of creativity from black writers, scholars, and artists in celebration of African and African American culture. Overall, white social scientists "gained an unprecedented opportunity to observe blacks in a fresh and often transforming way" (Degler, 1991:197). Their attitudes and expectations changed as a result of this increased contact.

In sum, the scientific argument for the inherent inferiority of some groups of people was advanced by upper-class, native-born, white male faculty of prestigious universities. Few others would have had the means with which to disseminate their ideas or the prestige to make those ideas influential. These theories of essential difference were not written by Native Americans, Mexicans, women, gays, African Americans, or immigrants from Asia or Southern and Eastern Europe. Most of these people lacked access to the public forums to present their experiences until the rise of the antislavery, suffrage, labor, and gay rights movements. Insofar as the people in these categories could be silenced, it was easier to depict them as essentially and profoundly different.

Popular Culture Like the sciences, popular culture (the forms of entertainment available for mass consumption such as popular music, theater, film, literature, and television) may convey ideologies about difference and social stratification. At virtually the same time that social Darwinism gained popularity in America—indeed within two years of Louis Agassiz's arrival in the States—America's first minstrel show was organized. Like social Darwinism, minstrel shows offered a defense of slavery.

Minstrel shows, which became an enormously popular form of entertainment, were musical variety shows in which white males in "blackface" ridiculed blacks, abolitionism, and women's suffrage. Their impact can be seen in the movies and cartoons of the 1930s and 1940s and in current American stereotypes. The shows built on strongly negative stereotypes about blacks. As the shows traveled the country, their images were impressed on whites who often had no direct contact with blacks and thus no information to contradict the minstrel images.

The three primary characters of the minstrel show were the happy slave, Zip Coon, and the mammy (Riggs, 1987). The image of the happy slave—singing and dancing, naive and childlike, taken care of through old age by the master, a virtual member of the family—asserted that blacks held in slavery were both content and cared for. Zip Coon was a northern, free black man characterized by a ridiculous use of language and laughable attempts to emulate whites; the caricature was used to show that blacks lacked the intelligence to handle freedom. The mammy was depicted as a large and presumably unattractive black woman fully devoted to the white family she served. Like the happy slave, the mammy was unthreatening and content—no sexual competition to the white mistress of the house, no children of her own needing attention, committed to and fulfilled by her work with her white family. Thus, the characters of the minstrel show hid the reality of slavery. The happy slave and mammy denied the brutality of the slave system. Zip Coon denied the reality of blacks' organization of the underground railroad, their production of slave narratives in books and lectures, and their undertaking of slave rebellions and escapes.

In all, minstrel shows offered an ideology about slavery constructed by and in the interests of those with power. They ridiculed antislavery activists and legitimatized the status quo. Minstrel shows asserted that blacks did not mind being held as slaves and that they did not suffer loss and pain in the same way whites did. The minstrel show was not the only source of this ideology, but as a form of popular entertainment it was a very effective means of disseminating such beliefs. The shows traveled to all parts of the country, with a message masked as mere entertainment. The fact that they were part of popular culture made it easier to ignore their serious message—after all, they were "just" entertainment.

But within popular culture, an effective counter to the ideology of the minstrel show emerged through the speakers of the antislavery lecture circuit and the publication of numerous slave narratives. Appearing as early as 1760, these narratives achieved an enormous and enduring popularity among northern white readers. Frederick Douglass, former slave and the renowned antislavery activist, was the most famous public lecturer in the history of the movement and wrote its best-selling slave narrative. Whether as book or lecture, slave narratives provided an image of blacks as human beings. Access to these life histories provided the first opportunity for most whites to see a shared humanity between themselves and those held in slavery (Bodziock, 1990). Thus, slave narratives directly countered the images of the minstrel show. While popular culture may offer a variety of messages, all parties do not meet equally on its terrain. Those with power have better access and more legitimacy, but popular culture cannot be so tightly controlled as to entirely exclude the voice of the less powerful.

Conclusion

As Karl Marx first considered it, ideology was "the mechanism whereby there can occur a difference between how things really are in the economy and the wider society and how people think they are" (Marshall, 1994:234). In this framework essay, we have examined how science and popular culture sometimes support the pervasive ideologies about the meanings of color, class, sexual orientation, and sex. The readings that follow focus on law and politics, the economy, science, and popular culture as social institutions that construct what difference is understood to mean. For example, in Reading 48, Michael Oliver describes how scientific research structures the meaning that is attributed to differences in human abilities. Similarly, in Reading 40, William Bowen and Derek Bok consider the meaning that is made of differences in test scores, grades, and race in admission to elite institutions of higher education; in Reading 41, Cheryl Zarlenga Kerchis and Iris Marion Young explore whether, in the context of social change movements, difference between groups is understood to be something valued or something to transcend; and in Reading 54, Ronald Schmidt, Sr., describes the politically volatile meanings attributed to language choice. Indeed, each of the Supreme Court decisions described in Reading 38 is ultimately about the *meaning* of difference—for example, in the determination of citizenship or access to higher education, what meaning are we going to attribute to race differences, or to sex differences? At the level of social institutions, the meaning that is made of difference has the potential for far-reaching impact.

KEY CONCEPTS

hegemonic Dominating or ruling. A **hegemonic ideology** is a belief that is pervasive in a culture. (page 309)

ideology A widely shared belief that primarily reflects the experiences of those with power, but is presented as universally valid. (pages 308–09)

natural-law language Language that treats human behavior as bound by natural law. (pages 309–10)

social Darwinism The belief that those who dominate a society are necessarily the fittest. (page 317)

social institution Established system for meeting societal needs; for example, the family. (page 315)

stereotype A characterization of a category of people as all alike, as possessing the same set of characteristics and likely to behave in the same ways. (pages 310–15)

REFERENCES

Adam, Barry D. 1987. *The Rise of a Gay and Lesbian Movement*. Boston: G. K. Hall & Co.

Andre, Judith. 1988. Stereotypes: Conceptual and Normative Considerations. Racism and Sexism: An Integrated Study. Ed. Paula S. Rothenberg, 257–62. New York: St. Martin's Press.

Bodziock, Joseph. 1990. The Weight of Sambo's Woes. *Perspectives on Black Popular Culture*. Ed. Harry B. Shaw, 166–79. Bowling Green, OH: Bowling Green State University Popular Press.

Brantlinger, Patrick. 1990. *Crusoe's Footprints: Cultural Studies in Britain and America*. New York: Routledge.

Cherry, Robert. 1989. *Discrimination: Its Economic Impact on Blacks, Women, and Jews*. Lexington, MA: Lexington Books.

Cohen, Mark Nathan. 1998. *Culture of Intolerance: Chauvinism, Class, and Race in the United States*. New Haven, CT: Yale University Press.

Conrad, Peter, and Joseph W. Schneider. 1980. *Deviance and Medicalization*. Philadelphia: Temple University Press.

Degler, Carl N. 1991. *In Search of Human Nature: The Decline and Revival of Darwinism in American Social Thought*. New York: Oxford University Press.

Garber, Marjorie. 1992. *Vested Interests: Cross Dressing and Cultural Anxiety*. New York: Harper.

Gould, Stephen Jay. 1981. *The Mismeasure of Man*. New York: W. W. Norton.

Haines, David W. 1989. *Refugees as Immigrants*. Totowa, NJ: Rowman and Littlefield.

Kasper, Anne. 1986. Consciousness Re-evaluated: Interpretive Theory and Feminist Scholarship. *Sociological Inquiry* 56(1).

Katz, Michael B. 1989. *The Undeserving Poor*. New York: Pantheon Books.

Le, C. N. 2001. The Model Minority Image. *Asian-Nation*. http://www.asian-nation.org/issues2.html.

Marshall, Gordon. 1994. *The Concise Oxford Dictionary of Sociology*. Oxford, UK: Oxford University Press.

Omi, Michael, and Howard Winant. 1994. *Racial Formation in the United States*. New York: Routledge.

Pierce, Christine. 1971. Natural Law Language and Women. *Woman in Sexist Society*. Ed. Vivian Gornick and Barbara K. Moran, 242–58. New York: New American Library.

Riggs, Marlon. 1987. *Ethnic Notions*. California Newsreel (video).

Sayers, Janet. 1982. *Biological Politics: Feminist and Anti-feminist Perspectives*. London: Tavistock Publications.

Shipman, Pat. 1994. *The Evolution of Racism: Human Differences and the Use and Abuse of Science*. New York: Simon and Schuster.

Smith, Dorothy. 1978. A Peculiar Eclipsing: Women's Exclusion from Men's Culture. *Women's Studies International Quarterly* 1:281–95.

——. 1990. *The Conceptual Practices of Power: A Feminist Sociology of Knowledge.* Boston: Northeastern University Press.

Sniderman, Paul M., and Thomas Piazza. 1993. *The Scar of Race.* Cambridge, MA: Harvard University Press.

——, and Edward G. Carmines. 1997. *Reaching Beyond Race.* Cambridge, MA: Harvard University Press.

Steinberg, Steven. 1989. *The Ethnic Myth: Race, Ethnicity, and Class in America.* Boston: Beacon Press.

Takaki, Ronald. 1993. *A Different Mirror: A History of Multicultural America.* Boston: Little, Brown.

U.S. Census Bureau. 2000. *Statistical Abstract of the United States: 2000* (120th ed.). Washington DC: United States Department of Commerce.

U.S. Census Bureau. 2001. *Money Income in the United States: 2000.* Current Population Reports. P60-213. September.

Law, Politics, and Policy

READING 38

Twelve Key Supreme Court Cases

Individuals' lives are affected not only by social practices but also by law as interpreted in the courts. Under U.S. federalism Congress makes laws, the president swears to uphold the law, and the Supreme Court interprets the law. When state laws appear to be in conflict with the United States Constitution or when the terminology of the Constitution is vague, the Supreme Court interprets such laws. We will focus here on Supreme Court rulings that have defined the roles individuals are allowed to assume in American society.

As the supreme law above laws enacted by Congress, the U.S. Constitution determines individual and group status. A brief document, the Constitution describes the division of power between the federal and state governments, as well as the rights of individuals. Only 16 amendments to the Constitution have been added since the ratification of the Bill of Rights (the first ten amendments). Although the Constitution appears to be sweeping in scope—relying on the principle that all men are created equal—in reality the Constitution is an exclusionary document. It omitted women, Native Americans, and African Americans except for the purpose of determining a population count. In instances where the Constitution was vague on the rights of each of these groups, clarification was later sought through court cases.

Federalism provides four primary methods by which citizens may influence the political process. First, the Constitution grants citizens the right to petition the government, that is, the right to lobby. Second, as a civic duty, citizens are expected to vote and seek office. Once in office citizens can change conditions by writing new legislation, known as *statutory law.* Third, changes can be achieved through the lengthy procedure of passing constitutional amendments, which affect all citizens. Controversial amendments have often become law after social movement activists advocated passage for several years or after a major national upheaval, such as the Civil War.

Last, the Constitution provides that citizens can sue to settle disputes. Through this method, sweeping social changes can take place when Supreme Court decisions affect all the individuals in a class. Thus, the assertion of individual rights has become a key tool of those who were not privileged by the Constitution to clarify their status in American society.

An examination of landmark cases reveals the continuous difficulties some groups have had in securing their rights through legal remedy. The Court has often taken a narrow perspective on what classes of people were to receive equal protection of the law, or were covered under the privileges and immunities clause.[1] Each group had to bring suit in every area where barriers existed. For example, white women who were citizens had to sue to establish that they had the right to inherit property, to serve on juries, to enter various professions, and in general to be treated as a class apart from their husband and family. Blacks sued to attend southern state universities and law schools, to participate in the all-white Democratic Party primary election,[2] to attend public schools which had been ordered to desegregate by the Supreme Court, and to vote without having to pay a poll tax. When these landmark cases were decided, they were perceived to herald sweeping changes in policy. Yet they proved to be only a guide to determining the rights of individuals.

I. *DRED SCOTT V. SANFORD* (1857)

Prior to the Civil War the Constitution was not precise on whether one was simultaneously a citizen of a given state and of the entire United

States. Slavery further complicated the matter because the status of slaves and free persons of color was not specified in the Constitution, nor were members of either group considered citizens. Each state had the option of determining the status and rights of these nonwhites.

A federal form of government permitted flexibility by allowing states to differ on matters such as rights for its citizens. Yet as a newly invented form of government, a number of issues that were clear under British law were not settled until the Thirteenth, Fourteenth, and Fifteenth Amendments were added to the United States Constitution. Federalism raised questions about rights and privileges because a citizen was simultaneously living under the laws of a state and of the United States. Who had rights and privileges guaranteed by the Constitution? Did all citizens have all rights and privileges?

For example, what was the status of women? The Constitution provided for citizenship, but did not specify which rights and privileges were granted to female citizens. State laws considered white men and white women citizens, yet white women were often not allowed to own property, sue in court, or vote. Under federalism, each state enacted laws determining the rights and status of free blacks, slaves, white men, and white women so long as the laws did not conflict with the United States Constitution.

The *Dred Scott* case of 1846 considered the issues of slavery, property, citizenship, and the supremacy of the United States over individual states when a slave was taken to a free territory. The Court's holding primarily affected blacks, now called African Americans,[3] who sought the benefits of citizenship. Broadly, the case addressed American citizenship, a matter not clearly defined until passage of the Fourteenth Amendment in 1868.

Dred Scott was an enslaved man owned by Dr. John Emerson, a U.S. Army surgeon stationed in Missouri. When Emerson was transferred to Rock Island, Illinois, where slavery was forbidden, he took Dred Scott with him. Emerson was subsequently transferred to Fort Snelling, a territory (now Minnesota) where slavery was forbidden by the Missouri Compromise of 1820. In 1838, he returned to Missouri with Dred Scott.

In 1846 Scott brought suit in a Missouri circuit court to obtain his freedom on the grounds he had resided in free territory for periods of time. Scott won the case and his freedom. However, the judgment was reversed by the Missouri Supreme Court. Later, when John Sanford, a citizen of New York and the brother of Mrs. Emerson, arranged for the sale of Scott, the grounds were established for Scott to take his case to the federal circuit court in Missouri. The federal court ruled that Scott and his family were slaves and therefore the "lawful property" of Sanford. With the financial assistance of abolitionists, Scott appealed his case to the Supreme Court.

The Court's decision addressed these key questions:

1. Are blacks citizens?
2. Are blacks entitled to sue in court?
3. Can one have all the privileges and immunities of citizenship in a state, but not the United States?
4. Can one be a citizen of the United States and not be qualified to vote or hold office?

Excerpts from the Supreme Court Decision in *Dred Scott v. Sanford*[4]

Mr. Chief Justice Taney delivered the opinion of the Court:

. . . The question is simply this: Can a Negro, whose ancestors were imported into this country and sold as slaves, become a member of the political community formed and brought into existence by the Constitution of the United States, and as such become entitled to all the rights, and privileges and immunities, guaranteed by that instrument to the citizen? One of which rights is the privilege of suing in a court of the United States. . . .

The question before us is whether the class of persons described are constituent members of this sovereignty? We think they are not, and that they are not included, and were not intended to be included, under the word "citizens" in the Constitution, and can therefore claim none of the rights and privileges which that instrument provides for and secures to citizens of the United States.

In discussing this question, we must not confound the rights of citizenship which a State may confer within its own limits and the rights of citizenship as a member of the Union. It does not by any means follow, because he has all the rights and privileges of a citizen of a State, that he must be a citizen of the United States. He may have all of the rights and privileges of a citizen of a State, and yet not be entitled to the rights and privileges of a citizen in any other State. . . .

Undoubtedly a person may be a citizen . . . although he exercises no share of the political power, and is incapacitated from holding particular office. Those who have not the necessary qualifications cannot vote or hold the office, yet they are citizens.

The court is of the opinion, that . . . Dred Scott was not a citizen of Missouri within the meaning of the Constitution of the United States, and not entitled as such to sue in its courts: and, consequently, that the Circuit Court had no jurisdiction. . . .

II. THE CIVIL WAR AMENDMENTS

The Civil War (1861–1865) was fought over slavery, as well as the issue of supremacy of the national government over the individual states.

After the Civil War, members of Congress known as the Radical Republicans sought to protect the freedom of the former slaves by passing the Thirteenth, Fourteenth, and Fifteenth Amendments. These amendments, especially the Fourteenth, have provided the foundation for African Americans, as well as women, gays, Native Americans, immigrants, and those who are disabled to bring suit for equal treatment under the law.

Amendment XIII, 1865

(Slavery)

This amendment prohibited slavery and involuntary servitude in the United States. The entire amendment follows:

Section 1. Neither slavery nor involuntary servitude, except as a punishment whereof the party shall have been duly convicted, shall exist within the United States, or any place subject to their jurisdiction.

Section 2. Congress shall have power to enforce this article by appropriate legislation.

Amendment XIV, 1868

(Citizenship, Due Process, and Equal Protection of the Laws)

This amendment defined citizenship; prohibited the states from making or enforcing laws that abridged the privileges or immunities of citizenship; forbade states to deprive persons of life, liberty, or property without due process of law; and forbade states to deny equal protection of the law to any person. Over time the Fourteenth Amendment became the most important of the Reconstruction amendments. Key phrases such as "privileges and immunities," "deprive any person of life, liberty, or the pursuit of justice," and "deny to any person within its jurisdiction equal protection of the law" have caused this amendment to be the subject of more Supreme Court cases than any other provision of the Constitution. The entire amendment follows:

Section 1. All persons born or naturalized in the United States, and subject to the jurisdiction thereof, are citizens of the United States and of the State wherein they reside. No State shall make or enforce any law which shall abridge the privileges or immunities of citizens of the United States; nor shall any State deprive any person of life, liberty, or property, without due process of law; nor deny to any person within its jurisdiction the equal protection of the laws.

Section 2. Representatives shall be apportioned among the several States according to their respective numbers, counting the whole number of persons in each State, excluding Indians not taxed. But when the right to vote at any election for the choice of electors for President and Vice President of the United States, Representatives in Congress, the Executive and Judicial officers of a State, or the members of the Legislature thereof, is denied to any of the male inhabitants of such State, being twenty-one years of age, and citizens of the United States, or in any way abridged, except for participation in rebellion, or other crime, the basis of representation therein shall be reduced in proportion which the number of such male citizens shall bear to the whole number of male citizens twenty-one years of age in such State.

Section 3. No person shall be a Senator or Representative in Congress, or elector or President and Vice President, or hold any office, civil or military, under the United States, or under any State, who, having previously taken an oath, as a member of Congress, or as an officer of the United States, or as a member of any State legislature, or as an executive or judicial officer of any State, to support the Constitution of the United States, shall have engaged in insurrection or rebellion against the same, or given aid or comfort to the enemies thereof. But Congress may by a vote of two-thirds of each House, remove such disability.

Section 4. The validity of the public debt of the United States, authorized by law, including debts incurred for payments of pensions and bounties for services in suppressing insurrection or rebellion, shall not be questioned. But neither the United States nor any State shall assume or pay any debt or obligation incurred in aid of insurrection or rebellion against the United States, or any claim for the loss or emancipation of any slave, but all such debts, obligations and claims shall be held illegal and void.

Section 5. The Congress shall have power to enforce, by appropriate legislation, the provisions of this article.

Amendment XV, 1870

(The Right to Vote)

The entire amendment follows:

Section 1. The right of citizens of the United States to vote shall not be denied or abridged by the United States or by any State on account of race, color, or previous condition of servitude.

Section 2. The Congress shall have power to enforce this article by appropriate legislation.

As we have seen, the Thirteenth, Fourteenth, and Fifteenth Amendments were added to the Constitution expressly with former slaves in mind. In Section 1 of the Fourteenth Amendment, the definition of *citizenship* was clarified and granted to blacks. In the Fifteenth Amendment black males, former slaves, were granted the right to vote. For women, however, the situation was different.

During the 19th century there was no doubt that white females were U.S. citizens, but their rights as citizens were unclear. For example, although they were citizens, women were not automatically enfranchised. Depending on state laws, they were barred from owning property, holding office, or voting. The 1872 case of *Bradwell v. The State of Illinois* specifically tested whether women as United States citizens had the right to become members of the bar. More generally, it addressed whether the rights of female citizens included the right to pursue any employment.

III. *MINOR V. HAPPERSETT* (1875)

The Fifteenth Amendment was not viewed as a triumph for women because it specifically denied them the vote. Section 2 of the Fourteenth Amendment for the first time made reference to males as citizens. Since black men were included but women of all races were omitted, women were left to continue to seek changes through the courts. This was a difficult route because in subsequent cases, judges often held a narrow view that the legislators wrote the amendment only with black males in mind. Thus, a pattern was soon established in which white women followed black men and women in asserting their rights as citizens as seen in the 1875 case of *Minor v. Happersett.* In *Dred Scott* the question was whether Scott was a citizen; in *Minor* the question was whether *Minor* as a citizen had the right to vote. In both cases the Supreme Court said no.

Virginia Minor, a native-born, free, white citizen of the United States and the state of Missouri, and over the age of 21 wished to vote for president, vice president, and members of

Congress in the election of November 1872. She applied to the registrar of voters but was not allowed to vote because she was not a "male citizen of the United States." As a citizen of the United States, Minor sued under the privileges and immunities clause of the Fourteenth Amendment.

The Court's decision addressed these key questions:

1. Who is covered under the term *citizen?*
2. Is suffrage one of the privileges and immunities of citizenship?
3. Did the Constitution, as originally written, make all citizens voters?
4. Did the Fifteenth Amendment make all citizens voters?
5. Can a state confine voting to only male citizens without violating the Constitution?

While women were citizens of the United States and the state where they resided, they did not automatically possess all the privileges granted to male citizens, such as suffrage. This landmark case was not overturned until the passage of the Nineteenth Amendment, which enfranchised women, in 1920.[5]

Excerpts from the Supreme Court Decision in *Minor v. Happersett*[6]

Mr. Chief Justice Waite delivered the opinion of the Court:

> . . . It is contended [by Minor's counsel] that the provisions of the Constitution and laws of the State of Missouri which confine the right of suffrage and registration therefore to men, are in violation of the Constitution of the United States, and therefore void. The argument is, that as a woman, born or naturalized in the United States is a citizen of the United States and of the State in which she resides, she has the right of suffrage as one of the privileges and immunities of her citizenship, which the State cannot by its laws or Constitution abridge.
>
> There is no doubt that women may be citizens. . . .
>
> . . . From this it is apparent that from the commencement of the legislation upon this subject alien women and alien minors could be made citizens by naturalization, and we think it will not be contended that native women and native minors were already citizens by birth.
>
> . . . More cannot be necessary to establish the fact that sex has never been made one of the elements of citizenship in the United States. In this respect men have never had an advantage over women. The same laws precisely apply to both. The Fourteenth amendment did not affect the citizenship of women any more than it did of men . . . therefore, the rights of Mrs. Minor do not depend upon the amendment. She has always been a citizen from her birth, and entitled to all the privileges and immunities of citizenship. The amendment prohibited the State, of which she is a citizen, from abridging any of her privileges and immunities as a citizen of the United States.
>
> . . . The direct question is, therefore, presented whether all citizens are necessarily voters.
>
> The Constitution does not define the privileges and immunities of citizens. For that definition we must look elsewhere.
>
> . . . The [Fourteenth] amendment did not add to the privileges and immunities of a citizen. It simply furnished an additional guarantee for the protection of such as he already had. No new voters were necessarily made by it.
>
> . . . No new State has ever been admitted to the Union which has conferred the right of suffrage upon women, and this has never been considered a valid objection to her admission.
>
> . . . Certainly, if the courts can consider any question settled, this is one. For nearly ninety years the people have acted upon the idea that the Constitution, when it conferred citizenship, did not necessarily confer the right of suffrage. . . . Our province is to decide what the law is, not to declare what it should be.

The *Dred Scott, Bradwell,* and *Minor* cases point to the similarity in the status of black men and women of all races in 19th-century America. As one judicial scholar noted, race and sex were comparable classes, distinct from all others. Historically, these "natural classes" were considered permanent and unchangeable.[7] Thus, both slavery and the subjugation of women have been described as a caste system where one's status is fixed from birth and not alterable based on wealth or talent.[8]

Indeed, the connection between the enslavement of black people and the legal and social standing of women was often traced to the Old Testament. Historically slavery was justified on the grounds that one should look to Abraham; the Bible refers to Abraham's wives, children, men servants, maid servants, camels, and cattle as his property. A man's wife and children were considered his slaves. By the logic of the 19th century, if women were slaves, why shouldn't blacks be also?

Thus, the concepts of race and sex have been historically linked. Since "the doctrines were developed by the same people for the same purpose it is not surprising to find anti-feminism to be an echo of racism, and vice versa."[9]

Additional constitutional amendments were necessary for women and African Americans to exercise the privileges of citizenship that were automatically granted to white males. Nonetheless, even after amendments were enacted, African Americans still had to fight for enforcement of the law.

IV. *PLESSY V. FERGUSON* (1896)

After the Civil War the northern victors imposed military rule on the South.[10] White landowners and former slave holders often found themselves with unproductive farmland and no free laborers. Aside from the economic loss of power, white males were in a totally new political environment: Black men had been elevated to citizens; former slaves were now eligible to vote, run for office, and hold seats in the state or national legislature. To ensure the rights of former slaves, the U.S. Congress passed the Civil War Amendments and provided federal troops to oversee federal elections.

However, when federal troops were withdrawn from the southern states in 1877, enfranchised black men became vulnerable to former masters who immediately seized political control of the state legislatures. In order to solidify political power, whites rewrote state constitutions to disenfranchise black men. To ensure that all blacks were restricted to a subordinate status, southern states systematically enacted "Jim Crow" laws, rigidly segregating society into black and white communities. These laws barred blacks from using the same public facilities as whites, including schools, hospitals, restaurants, hotels, and recreation areas. With the cooperation of southern elected officials, the Ku Klux Klan, a white supremacist, terrorist organization, grew in membership. The return of political power to whites without any federal presence to protect the black community set the stage for "separate but equal" legislation to become a constitutionally valid racial doctrine.

Under slavery, interracial sexual contact was forbidden but white masters nonetheless had the power to sexually exploit the black women who worked for them. The children of these relationships, especially if they looked white, posed potential inheritance problems because whites feared that such children might seek to exercise the privileges accorded to their white fathers. In order to keep all children of such relationships subordinate in the two-tiered racial system, descent was based on the race of the mother. Consequently, regardless of color, all the children of black women were defined as black.

This resulted in a rigid biracial structure where all persons with "one drop" of black blood were labeled black. Consequently, the "black" community consisted of a wide range of skin color based on this one-drop rule. Therefore, at times individuals with known black ancestry might look phenotypically white. This situation created a group of African Americans who had one-eighth or less African ancestry.

Louisiana was one of the few states to modify the one-drop rule of racial categorization because it considered mulattoes a valid racial category. A term derived from Spanish, *mulatto* refers to the offspring of a "pure African Negro" and a "pure white." Over time, *mulatto* came to encompass children of whites and "mixed Negroes."

These were the social conditions in 1896, when Homer Adolph Plessy, a mulatto, sought to test Louisiana laws that imposed racial segregation. Plessy and other mulattoes decided to test the applicability of the law requiring racial separation on railroad cars traveling in interstate transportation.

In 1890, Louisiana had followed other southern states in enacting Jim Crow laws that were written in compliance with the Equal Protection Clause of Section 1 of the Fourteenth Amendment. These laws required separate accommodations for white and black railroad passengers. In this case, Plessy, a U.S. citizen and a resident of Louisiana who was one-eighth black, paid for a first-class ticket on the East Louisiana Railway traveling from New Orleans to Covington, Louisiana. When he entered the passenger train, Plessy took a vacant seat in a coach designated for white passengers. He claimed that he was entitled to every "recognition, right, privilege, and immunity" granted to white citizens of the United States by the Constitution. Under Louisiana law, the conductor, who knew Plessy, was required to ask him to sit in a coach specifically assigned to nonwhite persons. By law, passengers who sat in the inappropriate coach were fined or imprisoned. When Plessy refused to comply with the order, he was removed from the train and imprisoned.

Plessy v. Ferguson is the one case that solidified the power of whites over blacks in southern states. Through state laws, and with the additional federal weight in the *Plessy* decision, whites began to enforce rigid separation of the races in every aspect of life.

In *Plessy,* Justice John Marshall Harlan wrote the only dissenting opinion. Usually in Supreme Court cases, attention is focused on the majority, rather than the dissenting opinion. However, in this case Justice Harlan's dissent is noteworthy because his views on race and citizenship pointed out a line of reasoning that eventually broke down segregation and second-class citizenship for blacks.

Justice Harlan's background as a Kentucky slaveholder who later joined the Union side during the Civil War is cited as an explanation of his views. Some scholars speculate that his shift from slaveholder to a defender of the rights of blacks was caused by his observation of beatings, lynchings, and the use of intimidation tactics against blacks in Kentucky after the Civil War. In a quirk of history, when *Plessy v. Ferguson* was overturned in 1954 by a unanimous opinion in *Brown v. Board of Education,* Justice Harlan's grandson was a member of the Supreme Court.

The Court's decision addressed these key questions:

1. How is a black person defined?
2. Who determines when an individual is black or white?
3. Does providing separate but equal facilities violate the Thirteenth Amendment?
4. Does providing separate but equal facilities violate the Fourteenth Amendment?
5. Does a separate but equal doctrine imply inferiority of either race?
6. Can state laws require the separation of the two races in schools, theaters, and railway cars?
7. Does the separation of the races when applied to commerce within the state of Louisiana abridge the privileges and immunities of the "colored man,"[11] deprive him of equal protection of the law, or deprive him of his property without due process of law under the Fourteenth Amendment?

Excerpts from the Supreme Court Decision in *Plessy v. Ferguson*[12]

Mr. Justice Brown delivered the opinion of the Court:

. . . An [1890] act of the General Assembly of the State of Louisiana, provid[ed] for separate railway carriages for the white and colored races.

. . . No person or persons, shall be admitted to occupy seats in coaches, other than the ones assigned to them on account of the race they belong to.

. . . The constitutionality of this act is attacked upon the ground that it conflicts both with the Thirteenth Amendment of the Constitution, abolishing slavery, and the Fourteenth Amendment, which prohibits certain restrictive legislation.

. . . A statute which implied merely a legal distinction between the white and colored races . . . has no tendency to destroy the legal equality of the two races, or reestablish a state of servitude.

. . . The object of the amendment [the Fourteenth Amendment] was undoubtedly to enforce the absolute equality of the two races before the law, but in the nature of things it could not have been intended to abolish distinctions based upon color, or a commingling of the two races upon terms unsatisfactory to either.

Laws permitting and even requiring their separation in places where they are liable to be brought into contact do not necessarily imply the inferiority of either race to the other, and have been generally, if not universally recognized as within the competency of the state legislatures in the exercise of their police power. The most common instance of this is connected with the establishment of separate schools for white and colored children, which has been held to be a valid exercise of the legislative power even by courts of States where the political rights of the colored race have been longest and most earnestly enforced. One of the earliest of these cases is that of *Roberts v. City of Boston,* 5 Cush. 198, in which the Supreme Judicial Court of Massachusetts held that the general school committee of Boston had power to make provision for the instruction of colored children in separate schools established exclusively for them, and to prohibit their attendance upon the other schools.

. . . We are not prepared to say that the conductor, in assigning passengers to the coaches according to their race, does not act at his peril. . . . The power to assign to a particular coach obviously implies the power to determine to which race the passenger belongs, as well as the power to determine who, under the laws of the particular State, is to be deemed a white, and who is a colored person.

. . . We consider the underlying fallacy of the plaintiff's argument to consist in the assumption that the enforced separation of the two races stamps the colored race with a badge of inferiority. If this be so, it is not by reason of anything found in the act, but solely because the colored race chooses to put that construction upon it. . . . The argument also assumes that social prejudices may be overcome by legislation, and that equal rights cannot be secured to the negro except by an enforced commingling of the two races. We cannot accept this proposition. If the two races are to meet upon terms of social equality, it must be the result of natural affinities, a mutual appreciation of each other's merits and a voluntary consent of individuals.

. . . If the civil and political rights of both races be equal one cannot be inferior to the other civilly or politically. If one race be inferior to the other socially, the Constitution of the United States cannot put them upon the same plane.

It is true that the question for the proportion of colored blood necessary to constitute a colored person, as distinguished from a white person, is one upon which there is a difference of opinion in the different States, some holding that any visible admixture of black blood stamps the persons as belonging to the colored races, others that it depends upon the preponderance of blood . . . still others that the predominance of white blood must only be in the proportion of three fourths. . . . But these are questions to be determined under the laws of each State. . . .

Mr. Justice Harlan in the dissenting opinion:

. . . It was said in argument that the statute of Louisiana does not discriminate against either race, but prescribes a rule applicable alike to white and colored citizens. . . . [But] everyone knows that the statute in question had its origin in the purpose, not so much to exclude white persons from railroad cars occupied by blacks, as to exclude colored people from coaches occupied by or assigned to white persons.

. . . It is one thing for railroad carriers to furnish, or to be required by law to furnish, equal accommodations for all whom they are under a legal duty to carry. It is quite another thing for government to forbid citizens of the white and black races from traveling in the same public conveyance, and to punish officers of railroad companies for permitting persons of the two races to occupy the same passenger coach. If a State can prescribe, as a rule of civil conduct, that whites and blacks shall not travel as passengers in the same railroad coach, why may it not so regulate the use of the streets of its cities and towns as to compel white citizens to keep on one side of a street and black citizens to keep on the other? Why may it not, upon like grounds, punish whites and blacks who ride together in street cars or in open vehicles on a public road or street? Why may it not require sheriffs to assign whites to one side of a court-room and blacks to the other? And why may it not also prohibit the commingling of the two races in the galleries of legislative halls or in public assemblages convened for the consideration of the political questions of the day? Further, if this statute of Louisiana is consistent with the personal liberty of citizens, why may not the State require the separation in railroad coaches of native and naturalized citizens of the United States, or of Protestants and Roman Catholics?

. . . In my opinion, the judgment this day rendered will, in time, prove to be quite pernicious as the decision made by this tribunal in the Dred Scott case.

. . . The thin disguise of "equal" accommodations for passengers in railroad coaches will not mislead anyone, nor atone for the wrong this day done.

Thus, the *Plessy v. Ferguson* decision firmly established the separate but equal doctrine in the South until the National Association for the Advancement of Colored Persons (NAACP) began to systematically attack Jim Crow laws. It is ironic that in *Plessy* the systematic social, political, and economic suppression of blacks in the South through Jim Crow laws was justified in terms of a case decided in the northern city of Boston, where the segregation of schools occurred in practice (*de facto*), but not by force of law (*de jure*). In that 1849 case (*Roberts v. City of Boston,* 5 Cush. 198), a parent had unsuccessfully sued on behalf of his daughter to attend a public school. Thus, educational access became both the first and last chapter—in the 1954 case of *Brown v. Board of Education*—of the doctrine of separate but equal.

V. *BROWN V. BOARD OF EDUCATION* (1954)

Unlike many of the earlier cases brought by individual women, blacks, or Native Americans, *Brown v. Board of Education* was the result of a concerted campaign against racial segregation led by Howard University School of Law graduates and the NAACP. In the 1930s, the NAACP Legal Defense Fund began to systematically fight for fair employment, fair housing, and desegregation of public education. Key lawyers in the campaign against segregation were Charles Houston, Thurgood Marshall, James Nabrit, and William Hastie. Marshall later became a Supreme Court justice, Nabrit became president of Howard University, and Hastie became a federal judge.

By using the Fourteenth Amendment, *Brown* became the key case in an attempt to topple the 1896 separate but equal doctrine. Legal strategists knew that educational opportunity and better housing conditions were essential if black Americans were to achieve upward mobility. While one group of lawyers focused on restrictive covenant cases,[13] which prevented blacks from buying housing in white neighborhoods, another spearheaded the drive for blacks to enter state-run professional schools.

In 1954, suits were brought in Kansas, South Carolina, Virginia, and Delaware on behalf of black Americans seeking to attend nonsegregated public schools. However, the case is commonly referred to as *Brown v. Board of Education.* The plaintiffs in the suit contended that segregation in the public schools denied them equal protection of the laws under the Fourteenth Amendment. The contention was that since segregated public schools were not and could not be made equal, black American children were deprived of equal protection of the laws.

The Court's unanimous decision addressed these key questions:

1. Are public schools segregated by race detrimental to black children?
2. Does segregation result in an inferior education for black children?
3. Does the maintenance of segregated public schools violate the Equal Protection Clause of the Fourteenth Amendment?
4. Is the maintenance of segregated public school facilities *inherently* unequal?
5. What was the intent of the framers of the Fourteenth Amendment regarding distinctions between whites and blacks?
6. Is the holding in *Plessy v. Ferguson* applicable to public education?
7. Does segregation of children in public schools *solely on the basis of race,* even though the physical facilities and other "tangible" factors may be equal, deprive the children of the minority group of equal educational opportunities?

Excerpts from the Supreme Court Decision in *Brown v. Board of Education*[14]

Mr. Chief Justice Warren delivered the opinion of the Court:

> . . . In each of these cases [NAACP suits in Kansas, South Carolina, Virginia, and Delaware] minors of the Negro race, through their legal representatives, seek the aid of the courts in obtaining admission to the public schools of their community on a nonsegregated basis. . . . This segregation was alleged to deprive the plaintiffs of the equal protection of the laws under the Fourteenth Amendment. In each of the cases other than the Delaware case, a three-judge federal district court denied relief to the plaintiffs on the so-called "separate but equal" doctrine announced by this Court in *Plessy v. Ferguson,* 163 U.S. 537. Under that doctrine, equality of treatment is accorded when the races are provided substantially equal facilities, even though these facilities be separated. . . .
>
> The plaintiffs contend that segregated schools are not "equal" and cannot be made "equal," and that hence they are deprived of the equal protection of the laws.
>
> . . . The most avid proponents of the post–[Civil] War amendments undoubtedly intended them to remove all legal distinctions among "all persons born or naturalized in the United States."
>
> In the first cases in this Court construing the Fourteenth Amendment, decided shortly after its adoption, the Court interpreted it as prescribing all state imposed discriminations against the Negro race. The doctrine of "separate but equal" did not make its appearance in this Court until 1896 in the *Plessy v. Ferguson, supra,* involving not education but transportation.
>
> In these days, it is doubtful that any child may reasonably be expected to succeed in life if he is denied the opportunity of an education. Such an opportunity where the state has undertaken to provide it, is a right which must be made available to all on equal terms.
>
> We come then to the question presented: Does segregation of children in public schools solely on the basis of race, even though the physical facilities and other "tangible" factors may be equal, deprive the children of the minority group of equal educational opportunities? We believe that it does.
>
> To separate them [the children] from others of similar age and qualifications solely because of their race generates a feeling of inferiority as to their status in the community that may affect their hearts and minds in a way unlikely ever to be undone.
>
> We conclude that in the field of public education the doctrine of "separate but equal" has no place. Separate educational facilities are inherently unequal. Therefore, we hold that the plaintiffs and others similarly situated for whom the actions have been brought are, by reason of the segregation complained of, deprived of the equal protection of the laws guaranteed by the Fourteenth Amendment.
>
> . . . We have now announced that such segregation is a denial of the equal protection of the laws.

VI. *YICK WO V. HOPKINS* (1886)

In the 1880s, the questions of citizenship and the rights of citizens were raised again by Native

Americans and Asian immigrants. While the status of citizenship for African Americans was settled by the Thirteenth and Fourteenth Amendments, the extent of the privileges and immunities clause still needed clarification. Yick Wo, a Chinese immigrant living in San Francisco, brought suit under the Fourteenth Amendment to see if it covered all persons in the territorial United States regardless of race, color, or nationality.

The Chinese were different than European immigrants because they came to the United States under contract to work as laborers building the transcontinental railroad. When Chinese workers remained, primarily in California, after the completion of the railroad in 1869, Congress became anxious about this "foreign element" that was non-Christian and non-European. Chinese immigrants were seen as an economic threat because they would work for less than white males. To address the issue of economic competition, the Chinese Exclusion Act was passed in 1882 to prohibit further immigration to the United States. This gave the Chinese the unique status among immigrants of being the only group barred from entry into the United States and barred from becoming naturalized U.S. citizens.

Yick Wo, a subject of the Emperor of China, went to San Francisco in 1861, where he operated a laundry at the same premise for 22 years with consent from the Board of Fire Wardens. When the consent decree expired on October 1, 1885, Yick Wo routinely reapplied to continue to operate a laundry. He was, however, denied a license. Of the over 300 laundries in the city and county of San Francisco, about 240 were owned by Chinese immigrants. Most of these laundries were wooden, the most common construction material used at that time, although it posed a fire hazard. Yick Wo and more than 150 of his countrymen were arrested and charged with carrying on business without having special consent, while those who were not subjects of China and were operating some 80 laundries under similar conditions, were allowed to conduct business.

Yick Wo stated that he and 200 of his countrymen with similar situations petitioned the Board of Supervisors for permission to continue to conduct business in the same buildings they had occupied for more than 20 years. The petitions of all the Chinese were denied, while all petitions of those who were not Chinese were granted (with one exception).

Did this prohibition of the occupation and destruction of the business and property of the Chinese laundrymen in San Francisco constitute the proper regulation of business, or was it discrimination and a violation of important rights secured by the Fourteenth Amendment?

The Court's decision addressed these key questions:

1. Does this municipal ordinance regulating public laundries within the municipality of San Francisco violate the United States Constitution?
2. Does carrying out this municipal ordinance violate the Fourteenth Amendment?
3. Does the guarantee of protection of the Fourteenth Amendment extend to all persons within the territorial jurisdiction of the United States regardless of race, color, or nationality?
4. Are the subjects of the Emperor of China who, temporarily or permanently, reside in the United States entitled to enjoy the protection guaranteed by the Fourteenth Amendment?

Excerpts from the Supreme Court Decision in *Yick Wo v. Hopkins*[15]

Mr. Justice Matthews delivered the opinion of the Court:

> . . . In both of these cases [*Yick Wo v. Hopkins* and *Wo Lee v. Hopkins*] the ordinance involved was simply a prohibition to carry on the washing and ironing of clothes in public laundries and washhouses, within the city and county of San Francisco, from ten o'clock p.m. until six o'clock a.m. of the following day. This provision was held to be purely a police regulation, within the competency of any municipality.

> . . . The rights of the petitioners are not less because they are aliens and subjects of the Emperor of China.
>
> The Fourteenth amendment to the Constitution is not confined to the protection of citizens. It says: "Nor shall any State deprive any person of life, liberty, or property without due process of law; nor deny to any person within its jurisdiction the equal protection of the laws." These provisions are universal in their application, to all persons within the territorial jurisdiction, without regard to any differences of race, or color, or of nationality; and the equal protection from the laws is a pledge of the protection of equal laws. . . .
>
> Though the law itself be fair on its face and impartial in appearance, yet, it is applied and administered by public authority with an evil eye and unequal hand, so as practically to make unjust and illegal discriminations between persons in similar circumstances. . . .
>
> . . . No reason whatever, except the will of the supervisors, is assigned why they should not be permitted to carry on, in the accustomed manner, their harmless and useful occupation, on which they depend for a livelihood. And while this consent of the supervisors is withheld from them and from two hundred others who have also petitioned, all of whom happened to be Chinese subjects, eighty others, not Chinese subjects, are permitted to carry on similar business under similar conditions. The fact of this discrimination is admitted. No reason for it is shown, . . . no reason for it exists except hostility to the race and nationality to which the petitioners belong, and which in the eye of the law is not justified. The discrimination is, therefore, illegal, and the public administration which enforces it is a denial of the equal protection of the laws and a violation of the Fourteenth amendment of the Constitution. The imprisonment of the petitioners is, therefore illegal, and they must be discharged.

The decision in *Yick Wo* demonstrated the Court's perspective that the Fourteenth Amendment applied to all persons, citizens and noncitizens.

VII. *ELK V. WILKINS* (1884)

In the late 19th century, Native Americans constituted a problematic class when the Supreme Court considered citizenship. Although Native Americans were the original inhabitants of the territory that became the United States, they were considered outside the concept of citizenship. They were viewed as a separate nation, and described as uncivilized, alien people who were not worthy of citizenship in the political community. As Native Americans were driven from their homeland and pushed farther west, the United States government developed a policy of containment by establishing reservations. Native Americans who lived with their tribes on such reservations were presumed to be members of "not strictly speaking, foreign states, but alien nations." The Constitution made no provisions for naturalizing Native Americans or defining the status of those who chose to live in the territorial United States rather than be assigned to reservations. It was presumed that Native Americans would remain on the reservations. The framers of the Constitution had not given any thought as to when or how a Native American might become a U.S. citizen. When the Naturalization Law of 1790 was written, only Europeans were anticipated as future citizens. The citizenship of Native Americans was not settled until 1924, when a statutory law, not a constitutional amendment, granted citizenship.

Elk v. Wilkins raised the question of citizenship and voting behavior as a privilege of citizenship. In 1857, the Court had easily dismissed Dred Scott's suit on the grounds that he was not a citizen. Since he did not hold citizenship, he could not sue. *Minor v. Happersett* in 1872 considered the citizenship and voting issue with a female plaintiff. In that case, citizenship was not in doubt but the court stated that citizenship did not automatically confer the right to suffrage. In *Elk,* a Native American claimed citizenship and the right to vote. Before considering the right to vote, the Court first examined whether Elk was a citizen and the process by which one becomes a citizen.

As midwestern cities emerged from westward expansion in the 1880s, a few Native Americans left their reservations to live and work in those cities. John Elk left his tribe and moved to Omaha, Nebraska, under the jurisdiction of the United States. In April 1880, he attempted to vote for members of the city council. Elk met the residency requirements in Nebraska and Douglas County for voting. Claiming that he complied with all of the statutory provisions, Elk asserted that under the Fourteenth and Fifteenth Amendments, he was a citizen of the United States who was entitled to exercise the franchise, regardless of race or color. He further claimed that Wilkins, the voter registrar, "designedly, corruptly, willfully, and maliciously" refused to register him for the sole reason that he was a Native American.

The Court's decision addressed these key questions:

1. Is a Native American still a member of an Indian tribe when he voluntarily separates himself from his tribe and seeks residence among the white citizens of the state?
2. What was the intent of the Fourteenth Amendment regarding who could become a citizen?
3. Can Native Americans become naturalized citizens?
4. Can Native Americans become citizens of the United States without the consent of the U.S. government?
5. Must Native Americans adopt the habits of a "civilized" life before they become U.S. citizens?
6. Is a Native American who is taxed a citizen?

Excerpts from the Supreme Court Decision in *Elk v. Wilkins*[16]

Mr. Justice Gray delivered the opinion of the Court.

> . . . The plaintiff . . . relies on the first clause of the first section of the Fourteenth amendment of the Constitution of the United States, by which "all persons born or naturalized in the United States, and subject to the jurisdiction thereof, are citizens of the United States and of the State wherein they reside"; and on the Fifteenth amendment, which provides that "the right of citizens of the United States to vote shall not be denied or abridged by the United States or by any State on account of race, color, or previous condition of servitude."
>
> . . . The question then is, whether an Indian, born a member of the Indian tribes within the United States, is, merely by reason of his birth within the United States, and of his afterwards voluntarily separating himself from his tribe and taking up his residence among white citizens, a citizen of the United States, within the meaning of the first section of the Fourteenth amendment of the Constitution.
>
> . . . The Indian tribes, being within the territorial limits of the United States, were not, strictly speaking, foreign States; but they were alien nations, distinct political communities, with whom the United States might and habitually did deal, as they thought fit, either through treaties made by the President and Senate, or through acts of Congress in the ordinary forms of legislation. The members of those tribes owed immediate allegiance to their several tribes, and were not a part of the United States. They were in a dependent condition, a state of pupilage, resembling that of a ward to his guardian.
>
> . . . They were never deemed citizens of the United States, except under explicit provisions of treaty or statute to that effect, either declaring a certain tribe, or such members of it as chose to remain behind on the removal of the tribe westward, to be citizens, or authorizing individuals of particular tribes to become citizens. . . .
>
> This [opening] section of the Fourteenth amendment contemplates two sources of citizenship, and two sources only: birth and naturalization.
>
> . . . Slavery having been abolished, and the persons formerly held as slaves made citizens. . . . But Indians not taxed are still excluded from the count [U.S. Census count for apportioning seats in the U.S. House of Representatives],[17] for the reason that they are not citizens. Their absolute exclusion from the basis of representation, in which all other persons are now included, is wholly inconsistent with their being considered citizens.
>
> . . . Such Indians, then, not being citizens by birth, can only become so in the second way mentioned in the Fourteenth amendment, by being "naturalized in the United States," by or under some treaty or statute.
>
> . . . The treaty of 1867 with the Kansas Indians strikingly illustrates the principle that no one can

become a citizen of a nation without its consent, and directly contradicts the supposition that a member of an Indian tribe can at will be alternately a citizen of the United States and a member of the tribe.

. . . But the question whether any Indian tribes, or any members thereof, have become so far advanced in civilization, that they should be let out of the state of pupilage, and admitted to the privileges and responsibilities of citizenship, is a question to be decided by the nation whose wards they are and whose citizens they seek to become, and not by each Indian for himself.

. . . And in a later case [Judge Deady in the District Court of the United States for the District of Oregon] said: "But an Indian cannot make himself a citizen of the United States without the consent and co-operation of the government. The fact that he has abandoned his nomadic life or tribal relations, and adopted the habits and manners of civilized people, may be a good reason why he should be made a citizen of the United States, but does not of itself make him one. To be a citizen of the United States is a political privilege which no one, not born to, can assume without its consent in some form.

Mr. Justice Harlan in the dissenting opinion:

. . . We submit that the petition does sufficiently show that the plaintiff is taxed, that is, belongs to the class which, by the laws of Nebraska, are subject to taxation.

. . . The plaintiff is a citizen and *bona fide* resident of Nebraska. . . . He is subject to taxation, and is taxed, in that State. Further: The plaintiff has become so far incorporated with the mass of the people of Nebraska that . . . he constitutes a part of her militia.

By the act of April 9, 1866, entitled "An Act to protect all persons in the United States in their civil rights, and furnish means for their vindication" (14 Stat. 27), it is provided that "all persons born in the United States and not subject to any foreign power, excluding Indians not taxed, are hereby declared to be citizens of the United States." . . . Beyond question, by that act, national citizenship was conferred directly upon all persons in this country, of whatever race (excluding only "Indians not taxed"), who were born within the territorial limits of the United States, and were not subject to any foreign power. Surely every one must admit that an Indian, residing in one of the States, and subject to taxation there, became by force alone of the act of 1866, a citizen of the United States, although he may have been, when born, a member of a tribe.

. . . If he did not acquire national citizenship on abandoning his tribe [moving from the reservation] and . . . by residence in one of the States, subject to the complete jurisdiction of the United States, then the Fourteenth amendment has wholly failed to accomplish, in respect of the Indian race, what, we think, was intended by it, and there is still in this country a despised and rejected class of persons, with no nationality; who born in our territory, owing no allegiance to foreign power, and subject, as residents of the States, to all the burdens of government, are yet not members of any political community nor entitled to any of the rights, privileges, or immunities of citizens of the United States.

In all, the Court never addressed Elk's right to vote because the primary question involved Elk's citizenship. By excluding him from citizenship because he had not been naturalized and because there was no provision for naturalization, John Elk was left outside of the political community as was Dred Scott.

VIII. *LAU V. NICHOLS* (1974)

In the 19th century, Native Americans and Asian immigrants sought to exercise rights under the Fourteenth Amendment although it had been designed explicitly to protect blacks. In the 20th century, issues first raised by African Americans, such as equality in public education, again presented other minority groups with an opportunity to test their rights under the Constitution.

Brown v. Board of Education forced the Court to consider the narrow question of the distribution of resources between black and white school systems. The *Brown* decision addressed only education. It did not extend to the other areas of segregation in American society, such as the segregation of public transportation (e.g., buses) or public accommodations (e.g., restaurants and hotels). Indeed, *Brown* had not even specified how the integration of the school system was to take place. All of these questions were taken up by the Civil Rights movement that followed the *Brown* decision.

Once the separate but equal doctrine was nullified in education, immigrants raised other issues of equality. In the 1970s, suits were brought on behalf of the children of illegal immigrants, non-English-speaking children of Chinese ancestry, and children of low-income parents.

In *Lau v. Nichols,* a non-English-speaking minority group questioned equality in public education. The case was similar to *Brown* because it concerned public education, the Equal Protection Clause of the Fourteenth Amendment, and the suit was brought on behalf of minors; but the two cases also differed in many respects. The 1954 decision in *Brown* was part of a series of court cases attacking segregated facilities primarily in southern states. It addressed only the issues of black/white interaction.

In *Lau v. Nichols,* a suit was brought on behalf of children of Chinese ancestry who attended public schools in San Francisco. Although the children did not speak English, their classes in school were taught entirely in that language. (Some of the children received special instruction in the English language; others did not.) The suit did not specifically ask for bilingual education, nor did the Court require it, but *Lau* led to the development of such programs. In bilingual education, the curriculum is taught in children's native language, but they are also given separate instruction in the English language, and over time they are moved into English throughout their courses.

The *Lau* decision hinged in part on Department of Health, Education, and Welfare guidelines that prohibited discrimination in federally assisted programs. The decision was narrow because it instructed only the lower court to provide appropriate relief. The Court's ruling did not guarantee minority language rights, nor did it require bilingual education.

The Court's decision addressed these key questions:

1. Does a public school system that provides for instruction only in English violate the equal protection clause of the Fourteenth Amendment?
2. Does a public school system that provides for instruction only in English violate section 601 of the Civil Rights Act of 1964?
3. Do Chinese-speaking students who are in the minority receive fewer benefits from the school system than the English-speaking majority?
4. Must a school system that has a minority of students who do not speak English provide bilingual instruction?

Excerpts from the Supreme Court Decision in *Lau v. Nichols*[18]

Mr. Justice Douglas delivered the opinion of the Court:

> The San Francisco, California, school system was integrated in 1971 as a result of a federal court decree. The District Court found that there are 2,856 students of Chinese ancestry in the school system who do not speak English. Of those who have that language deficiency, about 1,000 are given supplemental courses in the English language. About 1,800 however, do not receive that instruction.
>
> This class suit brought by non-English-speaking Chinese students against officials responsible for the operation of the San Francisco Unified School District seeks relief against the unequal educational opportunities, which are alleged to violate, *inter alia,* the Fourteenth Amendment. No specific remedy is urged upon us. . . .
>
> The Court of Appeals [holding that there was no violation of the Equal Protection Clause of the Fourteenth Amendment or of section 601 of the Civil Rights Act of 1964] reasoned that "[e]very student brings to the starting line of his educational career different advantages and disadvantages caused in part by social, economic and cultural background, created and continued completely apart from any contribution by the school system." . . . Section 71 of the California Education Code

states that "English shall be the basic language of instruction in all schools." That section permits a school district to determine "when and under what circumstances instruction may be given bilingually." . . .

Under these state-imposed standards there is no equality of treatment merely by providing students with the same facilities, textbooks, teachers, and curriculum; for students who do not understand English are effectively foreclosed from any meaningful education.

. . . We know that those who do not understand English are certain to find their classroom experiences wholly incomprehensible and in no way meaningful.

We do not reach the Equal Protection Clause argument which has been advanced but rely solely on section 601 of the Civil Rights Act of 1964, 42 U.S.C. section 2000d. to reverse the Court of Appeals.

That section bans discrimination based "on the ground of race, color, or national origin, in any program or activity receiving Federal financial assistance." The school district involved in this litigation receives large amounts of federal financial assistance. The Department of Health, Education, and Welfare (HEW), which has authority to promulgate regulations prohibiting discrimination in federally assisted school systems, in 1968 issued one guideline that "[s]chool systems are responsible for assuring that students of a particular race, color, or national origin are not denied the opportunity to obtain the education generally obtained by other students in the system." In 1970 HEW made the guidelines more specific, requiring school districts that were federally funded "to rectify the language deficiency in order to open" the instruction to students who had "linguistic deficiencies." . . .

It seems obvious that the Chinese-speaking minority receive fewer benefits than the English-speaking majority from respondents' school system which denies them a meaningful opportunity to participate in the educational program—all earmarks of the discrimination banned by the regulations. . . .

Lau differed from *Brown* because it was decided not on the basis of the Fourteenth Amendment but on the Civil Rights Act of 1964. In reference to *Brown*, the justices noted that equality of treatment was not achieved by providing students with the same facilities, textbooks, teachers, or curriculum. *Lau* underscores the idea that equality may not be achieved by treating different categories of people in the same way.

IX. *SAN ANTONIO SCHOOL DISTRICT V. RODRIGUEZ* (1973)

The 1973 case of *San Antonio School District v. Rodriguez* raised the question of equality in public education from another perspective. As was the case in *Brown* and *Lau,* the Fourteenth Amendment required interpretation. However, unlike the earlier cases, the issue was the financing of local public schools.

Education is not a right specified in the Constitution. Under a federal system, education is a local matter in each state. This allows for the possibility of vast differences among states and even within states on the quality of instruction, methods of financing, and treatment of nonwhite students. Whereas the *Brown* decision examined inequality between races, *San Antonio* considered inequality based on financial resources through local property taxes. *San Antonio* raised the question of the consequence of the unequal distribution of wealth among Texas school districts. As with *Brown* and *Lau,* minors were involved; however, the issue was not race or language instruction but social class. Did the Texas school system discriminate against the poor?

Traditionally, the states have financed schools based on property tax assessments. Since wealth is not evenly distributed, some communities are able to spend more on education and provide greater resources to children. This is the basis of the *San Antonio* case, where the charge was that children in less affluent communities necessarily received an inferior education because those communities had fewer resources to draw on. The Rodriguez family contended that the Texas school system of financing public schools through local property taxes denied them equal protection of the laws in violation of the Fourteenth Amendment.

Financing public schools in Texas entailed state and local contributions. About half of the revenues were derived from a state-funded program that provided a minimal educational base; each district then supplemented state aid with a property tax. The Rodriguez family brought a class action suit on behalf of school children who claimed to be members of poor families who resided in school districts with a low property tax base. The contention was that the Texas system's reliance on local property taxation favored the more affluent and violated equal protection requirements because of disparities between districts in per-pupil expenditures.

The Court's decision addressed these key questions:

1. Does Texas's system of financing public school education by use of a property tax violate the Equal Protection Clause (Section 1) of the Fourteenth Amendment?
2. Does the Equal Protection Clause apply to wealth?
3. Is education a fundamental right?
4. Does this state law impinge on a fundamental right?
5. Is a state system for financing public education by a property tax that results in interdistrict disparities in per-pupil expenditures unconstitutionally arbitrary under the Equal Protection Clause?

Excerpts from the Supreme Court Decision in *San Antonio School District v. Rodriguez*[19]

Mr. Justice Powell delivered the opinion of the Court:

> . . . The District Court held that the Texas system [of financing public education] discriminates on the basis of wealth in the manner in which education is provided for its people. Finding that wealth is a "suspect" classification and that education is a "fundamental" interest, the District Court held that the Texas system could be sustained only if the State could show that it was premised upon some compelling state interest.
>
> . . . We must decide, first, whether the Texas system of financing public education operates to the disadvantage of some suspect class or impinges upon a fundamental right explicitly or implicitly protected by the Constitution, thereby requiring strict judicial scrutiny. If so, the Texas scheme must still be examined to determine whether it rationally furthers some legitimate, articulated state purpose and therefore does not constitute an invidious discrimination in violation of the Equal Protection Clause of the Fourteenth Amendment.
>
> . . . In concluding that strict judicial scrutiny was required, the [District] court relied on decisions dealing with the rights of indigents to equal treatment in the criminal trial and appellate processes, and on cases disapproving wealth restrictions on the right to vote. Those cases, the District Court concluded, established wealth as a suspect classification. Finding that a local property tax system discriminated on the basis of wealth, it regarded those precedents as controlling. It then reasoned, based on decisions of this Court affirming the undeniable importance of education, that there is a fundamental right to education and that, absent some compelling state justification, the Texas system could not stand.
>
> We are unable to agree that this case, which in significant aspects is *sui generis,* may be so neatly fitted under the Equal Protection Clause. Indeed, we find neither the suspect-classification nor the fundamental-interest analysis persuasive.
>
> The wealth discrimination discovered by the District Court in this case, and by several other courts that have recently struck down school financing in other States, is quite unlike any of the forms of wealth discrimination heretofore reviewed by this Court.
>
> . . . First, in support of their charge that the system discriminates against the "poor," appellees have made no effort to demonstrate that it operates to the peculiar disadvantage of any class fairly definable as indigent, or as composed of persons whose incomes are beneath any designated poverty level. Indeed, there is reason to believe that the poorest families are not necessarily clustered in the poorest property districts. . . .

Second, neither appellees nor the District Court addressed the fact that . . . lack of personal resources has not occasioned an absolute deprivation of the desired benefit. The argument here is not that the children in districts having relatively low assessable property values are receiving no public education; rather, it is that they are receiving a poorer quality education than that available to children in districts having more assessable wealth. Apart from the unsettled and disputed question whether the quality of education may be determined by the amount of money expended for it, a sufficient answer to appellee's argument is that, at least where wealth is involved, the Equal Protection Clause does not require absolute equality or precisely equal advantages. . . .

For these two reasons . . . the disadvantaged class is not susceptible of identification in traditional terms. . . .

. . . [I]t is clear that appellee's suit asks this Court to extend its most exacting scrutiny to review a system that allegedly discriminates against a large, diverse, and amorphous class, unified only by the common factor of residence in districts that happen to have less taxable wealth than other districts. The system of alleged discrimination and the class it defines have none of the traditional indicia of suspectness: the class is not saddled with such disabilities, or subjected to such a history of purposeful unequal treatment, or relegated to such a position of political powerlessness as to command extraordinary protection from the majoritarian political process.

We thus conclude that the Texas system does not operate to the peculiar disadvantage of any suspect class. . . .

Education, of course, is not among the rights afforded explicit protection under our Federal Constitution. Nor do we find any basis for saying it is implicitly so protected. . . .

In sum, to the extent that the Texas system of school financing results in unequal expenditures between children who happen to reside in different districts, we cannot say that such disparities are the product of a system that is so irrational as to be invidiously discriminatory. . . .

Mr. Justice White, with whom Mr. Justice Douglas and Mr. Justice Brennan join, dissenting:

. . . In my view, the parents and children in Edgewood, and in like districts, suffer from an invidious discrimination violative of the Equal Protection Clause. . . .

There is no difficulty in identifying the class that is subject to the alleged discrimination and that is entitled to the benefits of the Equal Protection Clause. I need go no further than the parents and children in the Edgewood district, who are plaintiffs here and who assert that they are entitled to the same choice as Alamo Heights to augment local expenditures for schools but are denied that choice by state law. This group constitutes a class sufficiently definite to invoke the protection of the Constitution. . . .

In *San Antonio v. Rodriguez,* the Court did not find that the differences between school districts constituted invidious discrimination. A majority of the justices felt that Texas satisfied constitutional standards under the Equal Protection Clause. On the other hand, four justices in dissenting opinions saw a class (the poor) that was subject to discrimination and that lacked the protection of the Constitution.

X. *BOWERS V. HARDWICK* (1986)

In most of the cases we have considered, plaintiffs have sued on the basis that their rights under the Fourteenth Amendment were violated. However, cases can reach the Supreme Court by several routes, one of which is a *writ of certiorari,* which is directed at an inferior court to bring the record of a case into a superior court for reexamination and review. This was the case in *Bowers v. Hardwick,* in which the constitutionality of a Georgia sodomy statute was challenged. This became a key case in the battle for constitutional rights for gay women and men.

The case of *Bowers v. Hardwick* began on the issue of privacy because the behavior in question took place in Michael Hardwick's home. In deciding the case, however, the justices shifted from the issue of privacy to question whether gays have a fundamental right to engage in consensual sex.

Michael Hardwick's suit was based on the following facts. On August 3, 1982, a police officer went to Hardwick's home to serve Hardwick a warrant for failure to pay a fine. Hardwick's roommate answered the door, but was not sure if Hardwick was at home. The roommate allowed the officer to enter and approach Hardwick's bedroom. The officer found the bedroom door partly open and observed Hardwick engaged in oral sex with another man. The officer arrested both men, charged them with sodomy, and held them in the local jail for 10 hours.

The Georgia sodomy statute under which the men were charged made "any sexual act involving the sex organs of one person and the mouth or anus of another" a felony punishable by imprisonment for up to 20 years. When the district attorney decided not to submit the case to a grand jury, Hardwick brought suit attacking the constitutionality of the Georgia statute. Later, a divided court of appeals held that the Georgia statute violated Hardwick's fundamental rights. The attorney general of Georgia appealed that judgment to the Supreme Court.

The Court's decision on the case was split. Five justices ruled that the constitutional right of privacy did not apply to Hardwick's case; four argued that it did. While the Georgia statute did not specify that only homosexual sodomy was prohibited, the Court's majority opinion was framed in those terms. (Most legal prohibitions are directed at nonprocreative acts irrespective of the sex of the participants.) The majority opinion also equated consensual sex within the home to criminal conduct within the home, an equation criticized by both gay rights activists and the dissenting justices.

> [The majority opinion] emphasized that the home does not confer immunity for criminal conduct, comparing gay sex first to drugs, firearms, and stolen goods and then to adultery, incest, and bigamy. In so doing, the Court evoked images of dissolution, fear, seizure, and instability. . . . [and] the stereotypical fear of gay men as predators and child molestors. . . . The majority [opinion] advances, mostly by implication, its view of gay sexuality as unrelated to recognized forms of sexual activity or intimate relationships, and as exploitative, predatory, threatening to personal and social stability. [Writing for the dissent] Justice Blackmun excoriates the majority's choice of analogies and its failure to explain why it did not use nonthreatening analogies such as private, consensual heterosexual activity or even sodomy within marriage for comparison[20]

While the majority argued that the past criminalization of sodomy argued for its continued criminalization, critics responded that "Whereas the task of the Court was to decide whether the criminalization of sodomy is consistent with the Constitution, the majority treated the fact of past criminalization as determinative. . . . It had no answer to Justice Blackmun's contention 'that by such lights, the Court should have no authority to invalidate miscegenation laws.' "[21]

The Court's decision addressed these key questions:

1. Does Georgia's sodomy law violate the fundamental rights of gays?
2. Does the Constitution confer the fundamental right to engage in homosexual sodomy?
3. Is Georgia's sodomy law selectively being enforced against gays?

Excerpts from the Supreme Court Decision in *Bowers v. Hardwick*[22]

Mr. Justice White delivered the opinion of the Court:

> This case does not require a judgment on whether laws against sodomy between consenting adults in general, or between homosexuals in particular, are wise or desirable. . . . The issue presented is whether the Federal Constitution confers a fundamental right upon homosexuals to engage in sodomy and hence invalidates the laws of the many States that still makes such contact illegal and have done so for a very long time.
>
> We first register our disagreement with the Court of Appeals and with respondent that the Court's prior cases have construed the Constitution

to confer a right of privacy that extends to homosexual sodomy. . . .

Precedent aside, however, respondent would have us announce, as the Court of Appeals did, a fundamental right to engage in homosexual sodomy. This we are quite unwilling to do. . . .

It is obvious to us that neither of these formulations [*Palko v. Connecticut,* 302 U.S. 319 (1937) and *Moore v. East Cleveland,* 431 U.S. 494 (1977)] would extend a fundamental right to homosexuals to engage in acts of consensual sodomy. Proscriptions against that conduct have ancient roots. . . . Sodomy was a criminal offense at common law and was forbidden by the laws of the original thirteen States when they ratified the Bill of Rights. In 1868, when the Fourteenth Amendment was ratified, all but 5 of the 37 States in the Union had criminal sodomy laws. In fact, until 1961, all 50 States outlawed sodomy, and today 24 States and the District of Columbia continue to provide criminal penalties for sodomy performed in private and between consenting adults. . . . Against this background, to claim that a right to engage in such conduct is "deeply rooted in this Nation's history and tradition" or "implicit in the concept of ordered liberty" is, at best, facetious. . . .

Respondent . . . asserts that the result should be different where the homosexual conduct occurs in the privacy of the home. He relies on *Stanley v. Georgia,* 394 U.S. 557, (1969) . . . where the Court held that the First Amendment prevents conviction for possessing and reading obscene material in the privacy of one's home: "If the First Amendment means anything, it means that a State has no business telling a man, sitting alone in his house, what books he may read or what films he may watch . . .".

Stanley did protect conduct that would not have been protected outside the home, and it partially prevented the enforcement of state obscenity laws; but the decision was firmly grounded in the First Amendment. The right pressed upon us here has no similar support in the text of the Constitution, and it does not qualify for recognition under the prevailing principles for construing the Fourteenth Amendment. Its limits are also difficult to discern. Plainly enough, otherwise illegal conduct is not always immunized whenever it occurs in the home. Victimless crimes, such as the possession and use of illegal drugs, do not escape the law where they are committed at home. *Stanley* itself recognized that its holding offered no protection for the possession in the home of drugs, firearms, or stolen goods. . . . And if respondent's submission is limited to the voluntary sexual conduct between consenting adults, it would be difficult, except by fiat, to limit the claimed right to homosexual conduct while leaving exposed to prosecution adultery, incest, and other sexual crimes even though they are committed in the home. We are unwilling to start down that road. . . .

Justice Blackmun, with whom Justice Brennan, Justice Marshall, and Justice Stevens join, dissenting:

This case is no more about "a fundamental right to engage in homosexual sodomy," as the Court purports to declare, . . . than *Stanley v. Georgia,* 394 U.S. 557 (1969), . . . was about a fundamental right to watch obscene movies. . . . Rather, this case is about "the most comprehensive of rights and the right most valued by civilized men," namely, "the right to be let alone." *Olmstead v. United States,* 277 U.S. 438, (1928) (Brandeis, J., dissenting).

The statute at issue, Ga. Code Ann. section 16-6-2 (1984), denies individuals the right to decide for themselves whether to engage in particular forms of private, consensual sexual activity. The Court concludes that section 16-6-2 is valid essentially because "the laws of . . . many States . . . still make such conduct illegal and have done so for a very long time . . ." (Holmes, J., dissenting). Like Justice Holmes [dissenting in *Lochner v. New York,* 198 U.S. 45 (1905)], I believe that "[i]t is revolting to have no better reason for a rule of law than that it was laid down in the time of Henry IV. It is still more revolting if the grounds upon which it was laid down have vanished long since, and the rule simply persists from blind imitation of the past." Holmes, The Path of Law, 10 *Harvard Law Review* 457, 469 (1897). I believe we must analyze Hardwick's claim in the light of the values that underlie the constitutional right to privacy. If that right means anything, it means that, before Georgia can prosecute its citizens for making choices about the most intimate aspects of their lives, it must do more than assert that the choice they have made is

> an "'abominable crime not fit to be named among Christians.'"
>
> Like the statute that is challenged in this case, the rationale of the Court's opinion applies equally to the prohibited conduct regardless of whether the parties who engage in it are married or unmarried, or are of the same or different sexes. Sodomy was condemned as an odious and sinful type of behavior during the formative period of the common law. That condemnation was equally damning for heterosexual and homosexual sodomy. Moreover, it provided no special exemption for married couples. The license to cohabit and to produce legitimate offspring simply did not include any permission to engage in sexual conduct that was considered a "crime against nature."

The Court's decision did not uphold Michael Hardwick's contention that his sexual conduct in the privacy of his own home was constitutionally protected. While the decision was seen as a blow to the assertion of gay rights, the majority's narrow one-vote margin also indicated the Court's shifting opinion on this issue.

XI. *REGENTS OF THE UNIVERSITY OF CALIFORNIA V. BAKKE* (1978)

The Supreme Court has reviewed several cases concerning equitable treatment in public education. Key cases include racially separate public schools (*Brown v. Board of Education,* 1954); the practice of English-only instruction for Chinese students in public schools (*Lau v. Nichols,* 1974); and the practice of operating public schools based solely on revenue from local property taxes (*San Antonio School District v. Rodriguez,* 1973).

African Americans not only had to fight for equity in public schools but also had to sue to gain admission to law and medical schools in state universities. See *Sipuel v. Oklahoma,* 1948; *Missouri ex rel Gaines,* 1938; and *Sweatt v. Painter,* 1950.

In 1978, race-based admissions became an issue again when a *white* person sued for admission to the medical school at the University of California at Davis. The case of *The Regents of the University of California v. Bakke,* however, must be seen in light of the policy of affirmative action, which sought to redress historic injustices against racial minorities and other specified groups by providing educational and employment opportunities to members of these groups.

In 1968, the University of California at Davis opened a medical school with a track admission policy for a 100-seat class. In 1974, applicants who identified themselves as economically and/or educationally disadvantaged or a member of a minority group (blacks, Chicanos, Asians, American Indians) were reviewed by a special committee. They could also compete for the remaining 84 seats. However, no disadvantaged white was ever admitted to the school through the special admissions program, although some applied. Bakke, a white male, applied to the medical school in 1973 and 1974 under the general admissions program. He was rejected both times because he did not meet the requisite cutoff score. In both years, special applicants with significantly lower scores than Bakke were admitted. After his second rejection Bakke sued for admission to the medical school, alleging that the special admissions program excluded him on the basis of his race in violation of the Equal Protection Clause of the Fourteenth Amendment, a provision of the California Constitution, and section 601 of Title VI of the Civil Rights Act of 1964, which provides that no person shall, on the ground of race or color, be excluded from participating in any program receiving federal financial assistance. The California Supreme Court applied a strict-scrutiny standard. It concluded that the special admissions program was not the least intrusive means of achieving the goals of the admittedly compelling state interests of integrating the medical profession and increasing the number of doctors willing to serve minority patients. The California court held that Davis's special admissions program violated the Equal Protection Clause of the U.S. Constitution. The

Davis Medical School was ordered to admit Bakke.

The Court's divided opinion addressed these key questions:

1. Does the University of California, Davis Medical School's admission policy violate the Fourteenth Amendment?
2. Does giving preference to a group of non-white applicants constitute discrimination?
3. Does the University of California, Davis Medical School use a racial classification that is suspect?
4. Was Bakke denied admission to the University of California, Davis Medical School on the basis of race?
5. Can race be used as a criterion for admission to a university?

Excerpts from the Supreme Court Decision in *The Regents of the University of California v. Bakke*[23]

Mr. Justice Powell delivered the opinion of the Court:

> The guarantees of the Fourteenth Amendment extend to all persons. Its language is explicit: "No State shall . . . deny to any person within its jurisdiction the equal protection of the laws." . . . The guarantee of equal protection cannot mean one thing when applied to one individual and something else when applied to a person of another color. . . .
>
> . . . the [Fourteenth] Amendment itself was framed in universal terms, without reference to color, ethnic origin, or condition of prior servitude.
>
> Petitioner [University of California, Davis] urges us to adopt for the first time a more restrictive view of the Equal Protection Clause and hold that discrimination against members of the white "majority" cannot be suspect if its purpose can be characterized as "benign."
>
> . . . Moreover, there are serious problems of justice connected with the idea of preference itself. First, it may not always be clear that a so-called preference is in fact benign. . . . Second, preferential programs may only reinforce common stereotypes holding that certain groups are unable to achieve success without special protection based on a factor having no relationship to individual worth. Third, there is a measure of inequity in forcing innocent persons in respondent's position to bear the burdens of redressing grievances not of their making.
>
> . . . When a classification denies an individual opportunities or benefits enjoyed by others solely because of his race or ethnic background, it must be regarded as suspect.
>
> If petitioner's purpose is to assure within its student body some specified percentage of a particular group merely because of its race or ethnic origin, such a preferential purpose must be rejected. . . . Preferring members of any one group for no reason other than race or ethnic origin is discrimination for its own sake. This the Constitution forbids.
>
> . . . [A] goal asserted by petitioner is the attainment of a diverse student body. This clearly is a constitutionally permissible goal for an institution of higher education. Academic freedom, though not a specifically enumerated constitutional right, long has been viewed as a special concern of the First Amendment. . . .
>
> Ethnic diversity, however, is only one element in a range of factors a university properly may consider in attaining the goal of a heterogeneous student body.
>
> It may be assumed that the reservation of a specified number of seats in each class for individuals from the preferred ethnic groups would contribute to the attainment of considerable ethnic diversity in the student body. But petitioner's argument that this is the only effective means of serving the interest of diversity is seriously flawed. . . . Petitioner's special admissions program, focused solely on ethnic diversity, would hinder rather than further attainment of genuine diversity.
>
> . . . In summary, it is evident that the Davis special admissions program involves the use of an explicit racial classification never before countenanced by this Court. It tells applicants who are not Negro, Asian, or Chicano that they are totally excluded from a specific percentage of the seats in the class.
>
> The fatal flaw in petitioner's preferential program is its disregard of individual rights as guaranteed by the Fourteenth Amendment. Such rights are not absolute.

Mr. Justice Brennan, Mr. Justice White, Mr. Justice Marshall, and Mr. Justice Blackmun, concurring in part and dissenting in part:

> We conclude . . . that racial classifications are not *per se* invalid under the Fourteenth Amendment.
>
> Unquestionably we have held that a government practice or statute which restricts "fundamental rights" or which contains "suspect classifications" is to be subjected to "strict scrutiny" and can be justified only if it furthers a compelling government purpose. . . . But no fundamental right is involved here. Nor do whites as a class have any of the "traditional indicia of suspectness; the class is not saddled with such disabilities, or subjected to such a history of purposeful unequal treatment, or relegated to such a history of purposeful unequal treatment, or relegated to such position of political powerlessness as to command extraordinary protection from the majoritarian political process.". . .
>
> Certainly . . . Davis had a sound basis for believing that the problem of under-representation of minorities was substantial and chronic. . . . Until at least 1973, the practice of medicine in this country was, in fact, if not in law, largely the prerogative of whites. In 1950, for example, while Negroes constituted 10% of the total population, Negro physicians constituted only 2.2% of the total number of physicians. The overwhelming majority of these . . . were educated in two predominantly Negro medical schools, Howard and Meharry. By 1970, the gap between the proportion of Negroes in medicine and their proportion in the population had widened: The number of Negroes employed in medicine remained frozen at 2.2% while the Negro population had increased to 11.1%. The number of Negro admittees to predominantly white medical schools, moreover, had declined in absolute numbers during the years 1955 to 1964.
>
> Moreover, Davis had very good reason to believe that the national pattern of under-representation of minorities in medicine would be perpetuated if it retained a single admissions standard. . . .
>
> Davis clearly could conclude that the serious and persistent under-representation of minorities in medicine depicted by these statistics is the result of handicaps under which minority applicants labor as a consequence of . . . deliberate, purposeful discrimination against minorities in education and in society generally, as well as in the medical profession. . . .
>
> It is not even claimed that Davis' program in any way operates to stigmatize or single out any discrete . . . or even any identifiable, nonminority group. Nor will harm comparable to that imposed upon racial minorities by exclusion or separation on grounds of race be the likely result of the program. . . .
>
> Nor was Bakke in any sense stamped as inferior by the Medical School's rejection of him. Indeed, it is conceded by all that he satisfied those criteria regarded by the school as generally relevant to academic performance better than most of the minority members who were admitted. Moreover, there is absolutely no basis for concluding that Bakke's rejection that was a result of Davis' use of racial preference will affect him throughout his life in the same way as the segregation of the Negro schoolchildren in *Brown I* would have affected them. Unlike discrimination against racial minorities, the use of racial preferences for remedial purposes does not inflict a pervasive injury upon individual whites in the sense that wherever they go or whatever they do there is a significant likelihood that they will be treated as second-class citizens because of their color. . . .
>
> In addition, there is simply no evidence that the Davis program discriminated intentionally or unintentionally against any minority group which it purports to benefit. The program does not establish a quota in the invidious sense of a ceiling on the number of minority applicants to be admitted. . . .
>
> Finally, Davis' special admissions program cannot be said to violate the Constitution. . . .
>
> . . . we would reverse the judgment of the Supreme Court of California holding the Medical School's special admissions program unconstitutional and directing respondent's admission.

Justices Stevens and Stewart, along with Chief Justice Rehnquist, concurred and dissented in part. They found that the university's special admissions program violated Title VI of the Civil Rights Act of 1964, which prohibits discrimination under any program or activity receiving federal funding assistance. This dissent found that Bakke was not admitted to the Davis Medical School because of his race.

Race-based admissions were again considered in *Hopwood v. Texas,* a 1994 case in the Western District of Texas. The suit, brought by four white Texas residents, claimed that the affirmative action admissions program of the University of Texas School of Law violated the Equal Protection Clause of the Fourteenth Amendment and Title VI of the Civil Rights Act of 1964. The district court agreed that the plaintiffs' equal protection rights had been violated, but refused to direct the school to cease making admission decisions based on race. The case was subsequently appealed in the Court of Appeals for the Fifth Circuit, which held that the University of Texas School of Law could not use race as an admissions factor in order to achieve a diverse student body. The holding of the circuit court stands because the Supreme Court refused to hear the case.

This decision in effect overruled Justice Powell's opinion in *Bakke,* which held that universities can take account of an applicant's race in some circumstances. He asserted that the goal of achieving a diverse student body was permissible under the Constitution.

XII. *PGA TOUR V. CASEY MARTIN* (2001)

Historically, disabled people have been thought of as possessed or wicked. Often they were scorned and shut off from society in mental institutions. Today, however, the medical model is the dominant perspective that "those with disabilities have some kind of physical, mental, or emotional defect that not surprisingly limits their performance." Essentially, we don't expect those who are "flawed" to function as well as other people.[24]

Disabled people constantly face discrimination resulting in exclusion from housing, public buildings, and public transportation. This has prevented them from attending school, visiting museums, shopping, or living without assistance.

Only recently have disabled people used group pressure to achieve their rights. A turning point came in 1962 when Edward V. Roberts, a quadriplegic, won his suit to be admitted to the University of California. After graduating, Roberts established the Center for Independent Living.

In 1990, Congress passed the landmark Americans with Disabilities Act, which prohibited discrimination against people with physical or mental disability in employment, public accommodations, and transportation.

Casey Martin, a professional golfer, suffers from Klippel-Trenaunay-Weber Syndrome, a degenerative circulatory disorder that causes severe pain in his lower leg, which keeps him from being able to walk for long periods of time.

The PGA, a nonprofit association of professional golfers, sponsors three professional tours. Entry to the PGA tour is by competition in a qualifying school, which is conducted in three stages. During the first two stages, players are allowed to use golf carts. In the third stage, players are required to walk the course. After qualifying for the third and final stage of the 1997 qualifying school, Martin requested permission to use a golf cart. When the PGA denied this request, Martin sued.

The Court's decision addressed these key questions:

1. By participating in the PGA tour does Casey Martin seek to use a place of public accommodations?
2. Is refusing to waive the walking rule in the PGA a violation of making reasonable modifications to its policies to afford such accommodations to individuals with disabilities?
3. Does making such modifications "fundamentally alter the nature" of the accommodations?
4. Have Casey Martin's rights been violated under the Americans with Disabilities Act?

Excerpts from the Supreme Court Decision in *PGA Tour v. Casey Martin*

Mr. Justice Stevens delivered the opinion of the Court:

The case raises two questions concerning the application of the Americans with Disabilities Act of 1990, to a gifted athlete: first, whether the Act protects access to professional golf tournaments by a qualified entrant with a disability, and second, whether a disabled contestant may be denied the use of a golf cart because it would "fundamentally alter the nature" of the tournaments, to allow him to ride when all other contestants must walk.

There are various ways of gaining entry into particular tours. . . . Most participants, however, earn playing privileges in the PGA TOUR . . . by way of a three-stage qualifying tournament known as the "Q-School."

. . . Three sets of rules govern competition in tour events. . . . Those rules do not prohibit the use of golf carts at any time.

. . . The "Conditions of Competition and Local Rules," often described as the "hard card," apply specifically to petitioner's (PGA) professional tours.

The hard card for the PGA TOUR . . . requires players to walk the golf course during tournaments, but not during open qualifying rounds. The PGA TOUR hard card provides: "Players shall walk at all times during a stipulated round unless permitted to ride by the PGA TOUR Rules Committee." Additionally, . . . golf carts have not been permitted during the third stage of the Q-School since 1997. [The PGA] added this recent prohibition in order to "approximate a PGA TOUR event as closely as possible."

The basic Rules of Golf, the hard cards, . . . apply equally to all players in tour competitions. . . . The key is to have everyone tee off on the first hole under exactly the same conditions and all of them be tested over that 72-hole event under the conditions that exist during those four days of the event.

Casey Martin is a talented golfer. As an amateur he won 17 Oregon Golf Association junior events before he was 15, and won the state championship as a high school senior. He played on the Stanford University golf team that won the 1994 National Collegiate Athletic Association (NCAA) championship. As a professional, Martin qualified for the NIKE TOUR in 1998 and 1999, and based on his 1999 performance, qualified for the PGA TOUR in 2000. In the 1999 season, he entered 24 events, made the cut 13 times, and had 6 top-10 finishes, coming in second twice and third once.

Martin is also individual with a disability as defined in the Americans with Disabilities Act of 1990 (ADA). Since birth he has been afflicted with Klippel-Trenaunay-Weber Syndrome, a degenerative circulatory disorder. The disease is progressive; it causes severe pain and has atrophied his right leg. During the latter part of his college career, because of the progress of the disease, Martin could no longer walk an 18-hole golf course. Walking not only caused him pain, fatigue, and anxiety, but also created a significant risk of hemorrhaging. . . . For these reasons, Stanford made a written request to the Pacific 10 Conference and the NCAA to waive for Martin their rules requiring players to walk and carry their own clubs. The requests were granted.

When Martin turned pro and entered petitioner's Q-School, the hard card permitted him to use a cart during his successful progress through the first two stages. He made a request, supported by detailed medical records, for permission to use a golf cart during the third stage. Petitioner refused to review those records or to waive its walking rule for the third stage. Martin therefore filed this action.

Congress enacted the ADA in 1990 to remedy widespread discrimination against disabled individuals . . . Congress concluded that there was a "compelling need" for a "clear and comprehensive national mandate" to eliminate discrimination against disabled individuals, and to integrate them "into the economic and social mainstream of American life."

In the ADA, Congress provided that broad mandate. In fact, one of the Act's "most impressive strengths" has been identified as its "comprehensive character." . . . accordingly the Act has been described as " a milestone on the path to a more decent, tolerant, progressive society," . . . the ADA forbids discrimination against disabled individuals in major areas of public life, among them employment, public services, and public accommodations.

Title III of the ADA prescribes, as a "general rule":

"No individual shall be discriminated against on the basis of disability in the full and equal enjoyment of the goods, services, facilities, privileges, advantage or accommodations of any place of public accommodation by any person who . . . operates a place of public accommodation.

. . . It seems apparent, from both the general rule and the comprehensive definition of "public accommodation," that petitioner's golf tours and their qualifying rounds fit comfortably within the coverage of Title III, and Martin within its protection. The events occur on "golf courses," a type of place specifically identified by the Act as a public accommodation.

. . . Our conclusion is consistent with case law in the analogous context of Title II of the Civil Rights Act of 1964. . . . Title II prohibits public accommodations from discriminating on the basis of race, color, religion, or national origin.

. . . Martin's claim thus differs from one that might be asserted by players with less serious afflictions that make walking the course uncomfortable or difficult, but not beyond their capacity. In such cases, an accommodation might be reasonable but not necessary. In this case, however, the narrow dispute is whether allowing Martin to use a golf cart, despite the walking requirement that applies to the PGA TOUR, the NIKE TOUR, and the third stage of the Q-School, is a modification that would "fundamentally alter the nature" of those events.

In theory, a modification of petitioner's golf tournaments might constitute a fundamental alteration in two different ways. It might alter such an essential aspect of the game of golf that it would be unacceptable even if it affected all competitors, equally; changing the diameter of the hole from three to six inches might be such a modification. . . . We are not persuaded that a waiver of the walking rule for Martin would work a fundamental alteration in either sense.

. . . we observe that the use of carts is not itself inconsistent with the fundamental character of the game of golf. From early on, the essence of the game has been shot-making—using clubs to cause a ball to progress from the teeing ground to a hole some distance away with as few strokes as possible. . . . Originally, so few clubs were used that each player could carry them without a bag. Then came golf bags, caddies, carts that were pulled by hand, and eventually motorized carts that carried players as well as clubs. . . . There is nothing in the Rules of Golf that either forbids the use of carts, or penalizes a player for using a cart. That set of rules, as we have observed, is widely accepted in both the amateur and professional golf world as the rules of the game. The walking rule that is contained in petitioner's hard cards is not an essential attribute of the game itself.

Indeed, the walking rule is not an indispensable feature of tournament golf either. . . . petitioner permits golf carts to be used in the SENIOR PGA TOUR, the open qualifying events for tournaments, the first two stages of the Q-School, and, until 1997, the third stage of the Q-School as well.

The PGA argument is, first of all, mitigated by the fact that golf is a game in which it is impossible to guarantee that all competitors will play under exactly the same conditions or that an individual's ability will be the sole determinant of the outcome. For example, changes in the weather may produce harder greens and more head winds for the tournament leader than for his closest pursuers.

. . . the purpose of the walking rule is to subject players to fatigue, which in turn may influence the outcome of the tournaments. Even if the rule does not serve that purpose, it is an uncontested finding of the District Court that Martin "easily endures greater fatigue even with a cart than his able-bodied competitors do by walking." . . . The purpose of the walking rule is therefore not compromised in the slightest by allowing Martin to use a cart.

The provisions of the ADA are subject to reinterpretation in every Supreme Court case. In January 2002 the Supreme Court decided in *Toyoto Motor Manufacturing, Kentucky Inc. v. Williams* that Williams, an employee who was suffering from carpal tunnel syndrome, was not disabled. Although she requested exemptions from certain tasks at the plant, she was not considered disabled under the ADA because her condition did not limit major life activities such as walking, seeing, and hearing.

NOTES

1. *Privileges and immunities* refer to the ability of one state to discriminate against the citizens of

another state. A resident of one state cannot be denied legal protection, access to the courts, or property rights in another state.

2. In *Smith v. Allwright,* 321 U.S. 649 (1944), the Supreme Court held that a 1927 Texas law that authorized political parties to establish criteria for membership in the state Democratic party violated the Fifteenth Amendment. In effect, the criteria excluded nonwhites from the Democratic party. Since only party members could vote in the primary election, the result was a whites-only primary. The Democratic party so dominated politics in the southern states after the Civil War that winning the primary was equivalent to winning the general election.
3. Americans of African descent have been called *blacks, Negroes, colored,* or *African Americans,* depending on the historical period.
4. 19 Howard 393 (1857).
5. The Nineteenth Amendment that was ratified on August 18, 1920, stated, "The right of citizens of the United States to vote shall not be denied or abridged by the United States or by any state on account of sex. Congress shall have the power to enforce this article by appropriate legislation."
6. 21 Wallace 162 (1875).
7. Crozier, "Constitutionality of Discrimination Based on Sex," 15 *B.U.L. Review,* 723, 727–28 (1935) as quoted in William Hodes, "Women and the Constitution: Some Legal History and a New Approach to the Nineteenth Amendment" *Rutgers Law Review,* Vol. 25, 1970, p. 27.
8. Hodes, p. 45.
9. Gunnar Myrdal, *An American Dilemma: The Negro Problem and Modern Democracy.* New York: Harper and Row (2nd ed. 1962 [1944]), pp. 1073–74, as quoted in Hodes, p. 29. This same biblical ground has yielded the idea that a woman is an extension of her husband and his status.
10. The states under military rule were Virginia, North Carolina, South Carolina, Georgia, Florida, Tennessee, Alabama, Mississippi, Texas, Louisiana, and Arkansas.
11. The term *colored* was used in Louisiana to describe persons of mixed race who had some African ancestry.
12. 163 U.S. 537 (1896).
13. Restrictive covenants were written in deeds restricting the use of the land. Covenants could prohibit the sale of land to nonwhites or non-Christians.
14. 347 U.S. 483 (1954).
15. 118 U.S. 356 (1886).
16. 112 U.S. 94 (1884).
17. Native Americans and slaves posed a problem when taking the census count, which was the basis for apportioning seats in the U.S. House of Representatives. Some states stood to lose representation if some of their slave or Native American population was not counted. Blacks were counted as three-fifths of a white man, and only those Native Americans who were taxed were counted.
18. 414 U.S. 563 (1974).
19. 411 U.S. 1 (1973).
20. Rhonda Copelon, "A Crime Not Fit to Be Named: Sex, Lies, and the Constitution," p. 182. In David Kairys (ed.), *The Politics of Law,* pp. 177–94, New York: Pantheon.
21. Copelon, p. 184.
22. 478 U.S. 186 (1986).
23. 438 U.S. 265 (1978).
24. Paul C. Higgins, *Making Disability.* Springfield, IL: Charles C. Thomas (1992), pp. 26–27.

READING 39

Group Rights

Reconciling Equality and Difference

David Ingram

In the heat of the race riots that burned the nation's cities during the spring of 1967, President Lyndon Johnson appointed a commission headed by Governor Otto Kerner of Illinois to examine the causes and potential remedies for the violence. The opening line of the commission's report issued what has since become the rallying

David Ingram is professor of philosophy at Loyola University of Chicago.

cry for a generation of reformers: absent aggressive government intervention, the United States will continue moving "toward two societies one black, one white—separate and unequal."[1]

But how accurately do these symptoms describe the . . . country? Despite some recent gains in their quality of life,[2] a third of all black families live in poverty as compared with 11.6 percent of white families. Currently, only a third of all black families earn middle-class incomes of $20,000 or more.[3] Data provided by the U.S. Census Bureau show that the median income for black families *fell* from $18,378 in 1970 to $18,098 in 1987, while during that same period the median income for white families *increased* from $29,960 to $32,274. Today, the average white household commands more than *ten times* the financial assets of the average black household. The rate of unemployment among blacks (10 percent in 1995) is more than twice that among whites, with black youths currently registering a whopping 34 percent unemployment rate.

In 1995 the Glass Ceiling Commission reported that, although blacks currently constitute about 13 percent of the U.S. population, they occupy less than 1 percent of senior management positions (defined as vice presidents and above), while white men, who constitute 43 percent of the population, occupy 95 percent of such positions. White women, who have benefited most from affirmative action, now hold 40 percent of middle management jobs, but black women and men hold only about 9 percent. In general, whites comprise a disproportionately higher proportion (between 87 and 95 percent) of professionals, technicians, managers, sales personnel, and craftspeople, while a third of all employed blacks occupy minimum or low-paying jobs as laborers or service workers.

Inequalities in economic power are reflected in political inequalities. Despite the fact that more blacks and Latinos have been elected and appointed to political offices than ever before, they remain (as do women) grossly underrepresented in legislative, executive, and judicial bodies. For example, only 2 percent of elected officials in the United States are black.

Disparities in educational opportunity and achievement no doubt account for many of the economic and political inequalities dividing whites and blacks. Although the high school completion rate for blacks between the ages of eighteen and twenty-four had gradually climbed to 77 percent by 1994 (as compared with 83 percent for whites and only 57 percent for Hispanics), the total percentage of blacks attending college—about 59 percent—still remained relatively low compared with the percentage of whites (68 percent). Furthermore, test scores show that most black children are not receiving nearly the same quality of education as their white peers and so are less well prepared to compete with them at the college level.[4] Equally distressing is a recent study by the Commerce Department's National Telecommunications and Information Administration showing that as of 1998 only 12 percent of black households and 13 percent of Hispanic households had home Internet access (as compared with 33 percent of white households). Interestingly, the disparities in personal computer ownership between whites and Asians, on one side, and blacks and Latinos, on the other, narrows as income rises.

These facts must be interpreted against the background of educational and residential segregation patterns that have remained virtually constant for the past thirty years. Although it is true that the percentage of blacks living in neighborhoods that are 90 to 100 percent black has declined from 35 percent to 31 percent, fully 80 percent of blacks in most cities would have to relocate in nonblack neighborhoods in order to achieve racial balance.[5] The inability to relocate is partly caused by economic hardship, which has steadily worsened during the twenty-year decline of manufacturing and heavy industry experienced by U.S. cities. But even well-educated middle-class blacks who have moved to the suburbs tend to locate in predominantly black enclaves.

Discrimination in securing mortgages, real estate redlining, and racial hostility have conspired to render patterns of residential segregation all but intractable. One need only look at the results of scientifically designed studies, polls, and surveys showing the prevalence of persistent patterns of discriminatory treatment favoring whites over equally qualified blacks in securing jobs,[6] loans,[7] salaries,[8] houses,[9] fair prices on selected merchandise,[10] decent health care, affordable insurance, and fair treatment from law enforcement agencies. Apposite here is a recent study showing that 15–19 percent of all eligible white voters would not vote for a qualified black candidate for governor or president under any circumstances.[11]

As for education, a 1992 Harvard survey found that public schools across the nation were more segregated than they were in 1967. In the public school systems of larger northern cities, the percentage of white students enrolled ranges from 9–11 percent in Chicago, Detroit, Newark, and New York, 16–17 percent in Baltimore and Philadelphia, and 32–35 percent in Boston, Cincinnati, and Milwaukee.[12]

These gloomy statistics confirm William Julius Wilson's negative diagnosis of urban ghettos as socially isolated concentrations of poverty that are pathologically bereft of social support networks, responsible collective supervision, and formal and informal organizations (churches and political parties as well as block clubs and parent-teacher associations). Even if, as some critics have argued, this diagnosis reflects mainstream middle-class biases, there can be no disputing the fact that poverty, unemployment, segregation, powerlessness, and lack of education have together transformed what were once stable working-class neighborhoods into war zones contested by fractious drug lords.[13] Blacks are incarcerated at a rate seven times that of whites—and in a country that incarcerates a higher percentage of its population (373 per 100,000) than any other nation, excepting the former Soviet Union. In 1991 it was estimated that 42 percent of all black men between the ages of eighteen and thirty-five living in Washington, D.C., were either in prison, on probation, awaiting trial, or being sought by police. In Baltimore, the comparable figure for this period was 56 percent. According to a 1993 Justice Department report, 22 percent of male students attending inner-city schools reported owning a gun, and nearly 70 percent of all students stated that guns were present in their homes. Not surprisingly, homicide is now the leading cause of death among young black men.[14] Even more startling, two-thirds of black male teenagers can expect to die before reaching the age of 65 (and they are less likely to reach the age of 45 than their white counterparts are of reaching 65) because of cardiovascular disease, cancer, and other chronic illnesses that medical researchers attribute to the daily stress of having to cope with poverty, discrimination, and the threat of violence.[15]

DIVIDED BY COLOR

Who (or what) is to blame for this tragic state of affairs? A recent study by Donald Kinder and Lynn Sanders shows just how divided blacks and whites are on this question. Although most whites concede that blacks as a group have faced and continue to face discrimination and hardship—there is a considerable discrepancy between whites and blacks in assessing the extent of that discrimination and hardship—a substantial majority of them say that government should no longer try to remedy these harms. As might be expected, blacks disagree quite strongly with whites on this score.[16]

On the positive side, Kinder and Sanders note that the incidence of *biological* racism—the view that blacks are genetically inferior to whites in intelligence and moral character—has dramatically declined since the thirties. On the negative side, they observe that biological racism has been replaced by a more subtle, *symbolic* form of racism: a majority of whites think that blacks are solely responsible for their problems. They resent blacks for being pushy and lazy—in short, for wanting a free government handout without having to work hard for a living (as they have done). The belief that blacks *as a group* are less morally responsible than other groups varies somewhat in relation to class and income, but even affluent suburban whites whose schools, neighborhoods, jobs, and incomes are not "threatened" by blacks subscribe to this negative stereotype.[17]

Is such a stereotypical view of black moral failing tantamount to a racist prejudice? It would seem so, at least insofar as whites remain unwilling to give up their racial resentment in light of disconfirming sociological data, including knowledge of the social causes underlying welfare dependency, teen pregnancy, and crime. As things currently stand, conservative political leaders have been only too willing to play upon the largely unfounded fears of resentful whites, while the mass media have done little to dispel—and much to reinforce—current racial stereotypes.

Unfortunately, the available evidence indicates that most resentful whites will hold on to their stereotypes no matter what social scientists say. First, the pervasive belief in the Protestant work ethic among resentful whites inclines them to the view that individuals, not social institutions, are responsible for what happens to them.[18] The widespread presence of crime, ignorance, and poverty among a substantial segment of the black urban "underclass" will therefore be perceived by resentful whites as a tendency toward moral and intellectual failing among blacks generally, which distinguishes them as a class from whites.[19] Second, the need to come up with a nonsocial scientific explanation for the black underclass that goes beyond mass individual moral failing (or absence of willpower) predictably leads some sociobiologists to posit natural inheritance as the reason why blacks score lower than whites on IQ tests. Richard Herrnstein and Charles Murray's recent best-seller, *The Bell Curve,* shows just how alarmingly fashionable this scientifically unsustainable racism has become once again among some conservatives.[20]

Finally, the treatment of blacks in the criminal justice system indicates that discrepancies in criminalizing behavior, processing cases, and sentencing are explicable only on the basis of white racial resentment. Although young blacks compose only 15 percent of the U.S. population, they constitute 26 percent of arrests, 32 percent of court referrals, 36 percent of those formally charged, 41 percent of those detained pending trial, 46 percent of those incarcerated, and 52 percent of those who are transferred to adult court (meanwhile, young Latinos are 60 percent more likely to be in jail than their white counterparts).[21] Contrasted with the incarceration of "predatory" urban blacks and Latinos, middle-class white youths who commit crimes are regarded as merely "troubled" and "in need of therapy." The long-term effects of this dual justice system also merit observation: over 500,000 black ex-felons have permanently lost their right to vote, thereby further weakening the political power base of black communities. Significantly, despite the fact that in 1992 Congress passed the so-called "disproportionate minority confinement" mandate requiring states to analyze "minority overrepresentation" in juvenile prisons and take steps to reduce it on pain of losing millions of dollars of federal delinquency prevention funds, the Senate is today debating a bill (S. 254) that would eliminate the mandate and allow children over thirteen years of age to be tried and incarcerated as adults. Even the criminal code reflects racial bias. For example, 88.3 percent of federal defendants convicted of selling crack (cocaine that has been cooked with baking soda) are black, while 73 percent of those convicted of selling pure cocaine are white. Could one plausibly argue that the one hundred times more severe, federally mandated penalties assessed for possession of crack (five years for a first-time offender possessing just five grams) in comparison to those assessed for trafficking in cocaine (five years for possession of five hundred grams) stem from the gang violence typically associated with the former drug and have nothing to do with race? Perhaps. But then one can only hope that recent research showing the roughly comparable behavioral effects of crack and pure cocaine will induce Congress to reduce the existing discrepancy in sentencing guidelines.[22] Unfortunately, Congress, with President Clinton's approval, recently rejected a 1995 recommendation by the U.S. Sentencing Commission to eliminate that gap, despite the commission's warning that the guidelines reflected a most serious form of racial discrimination (incidentally, this gap was upheld as constitutional by the Supreme Court in its ruling in May 1996, which argued that the discrepancy did not sufficiently prove evidence of racial discrimination).

Skeptics of the federal government's selective prosecution of blacks, however, must still confront the by now well-documented evidence of racial profiling used by state law enforcement agencies in stopping vehicles driven by blacks and Latinos and in issuing citations.[23] The savage beating meted out to Rodney King by the Los Angeles Police Department and the damning testimony in the O. J. Simpson trial concerning Detective Mark Fuhrman's planting of evidence in order to convict blacks only confirm that harassment for "driving while black" often is a prelude for much worse treatment. One need only mention the much praised study of Georgia's sentencing procedures by University of Iowa professor David Baldus, which showed that between 1973 and 1979, blacks who killed whites were seven times more likely to be sentenced to death than whites who killed blacks, while white-victim cases were eleven times more likely to result in a death sentence than black-victim cases.

RACE AND CASTE: THE UNIQUENESS OF THE AFRICAN-AMERICAN DILEMMA

Conservatives often blame the black underclass for its plight, arguing that immigrants of ethnic stock, who also were discriminated against, managed to raise themselves up from poverty and powerlessness through dint of hard work and without the aid of government preferences.

Rebutting this claim requires showing that the kind of discrimination meted out to African Americans is qualitatively distinct from that visited upon ethnic immigrants. It is unique in that no ethnic group experienced a form of oppression remotely as vicious as the slavery, Jim Crow segregation, and widespread prejudice to which African Americans were subjected. Although Native Americans experienced the incomparable horrors of government-sanctioned genocide, they were never subjected to the same degree of systematic dehumanization to which African slaves and their descendants were subjected.

Nothing comparable to this catastrophe ever befell any other ethnic group. True, racism runs deep in the American psyche. Many ethnic groups—Irish, Jewish, Polish, Italian, Mexican, Chinese, and Japanese—have experienced virulent forms of racial discrimination. But the discrimination meted out to these groups has been of a lesser degree and duration. Their lighter skin enabled them (or their children) to shed their ethnic racial identity. More important, many Jewish, Irish, Italian, and German immigrants benefited from racism; they were awarded good jobs previously held by blacks and, in some instances, formed ethnic trade unions, such as the Greek furriers' local, the Italian dressmakers' union, and the Jewish waiters' organization, that were explicitly closed to blacks.

Many recent immigrants today continue to enjoy a competitive advantage over urban blacks. In particular, many enter under INS guidelines that give preference to persons already possessing capital assets or desirable skills. Modestly affluent families in Korea and India, for example, provide substantial financial support to family members who immigrate to the United States and set up businesses.

Conservative critics of affirmative action like Nicholas Capaldi cite Thomas Sowell's[24] controversial sociological study of African Americans who emigrated from the West Indies: "African Americans who immigrated to the United States voluntarily from the West Indies have been remarkably successful despite facing the same obstacles as those who were descendants of slaves."[25] Although subsequent studies have shown that West Indians face racial discrimination in housing, employment, and other areas of life comparable to that experienced by the descendants of American slaves, they hardly confirm Capaldi's claim that these immigrants have been "remarkably successful."[26] The census data for 1980 show that West Indian household incomes and the earnings of West Indian males remain significantly lower that similar statistics for comparably situated whites.[27] The extent to which West Indians have been more successful than American blacks in advancing along the path toward upward mobility may be accounted for by significant disanalogies in their situation. (Haitians, for example, overthrew their white slave masters two hundred years ago and so managed to avoid much of the oppression endured by American blacks.) To cite Gertrude Ezorsky,

> The virtual absence of a white working class in the West Indian homeland, where blacks held majority status, facilitated their acquisition of skilled trades. According to immigration records in the 1920's, West Indians had advantages in literacy and skills, advantages that are conducive to an achievement orientation and that would tend to be replicated in their children.[28]

Despite the persistence of overt discrimination, the real key to understanding America's racial caste system is the prevalence of *unintended* institutionalized racism. Institutionalized racism occurs whenever procedures for admissions, hiring, promoting, and contracting that are racially neutral in wording and intent work to exclude a disproportionate percentage of minorities. For instance, a high percentage of job openings (possibly as high as 86 percent) are advertised through word of mouth rather than through classified ads, so personal acquaintance with the employer, or living in close proximity to his or her business, becomes a necessary condition for obtaining employment.[29] Given the undeniable reality of residential segregation—exacerbated by "white flight" to the suburbs—and the large concentration of businesses of all sizes in the hands of white employers, word-of-mouth hiring alone serves to exclude a sizable percentage of inner-city blacks from even being considered for employment.

Referral unions that recommend candidates for good-paying jobs in construction, printing, and transportation also rely heavily on personal contacts, but these, too, have been controlled by whites. Patronage remains an important feature of government life, and most elected officials, who are predominantly white, will fill government posts with persons whom they trust: acquaintances, family members, and associates. Finally, studies have shown that, because blacks and whites rarely interact outside the workplace, blacks are systematically excluded from personal connections.[30] This exclusion continues to handicap well-educated blacks looking for good jobs even after they have relocated to job-rich suburbs.

Another form of institutionalized racism is the seniority system. It has only been in the past twenty years or so that blacks have gained admission to occupations controlled by formerly all-white labor unions. Unfortunately, blacks' lack of seniority has made them especially vulnerable to layoffs during times of recession. Given the cyclical frequency of recessions, being "last hired and first fired" means that many blacks will always find themselves at the bottom rung of the economic ladder.

Institutionalized racism has a profoundly crippling impact on the capacity African Americans to succeed economically—hence, the great disparities between income levels and total family assets that exist between whites and blacks. Market mechanisms magnify these inequalities further by generating a cumulative effect over time. As noted economist Lester Thurow has remarked, 66 percent of the improved fortune of succeeding generations is explained by the intergenerational transfer of assets, and "approximately half of all great wealth is inherited."[31]

Fully one-third of all black families have only cash on hand, and only those few who possess enough assets to invest in high-yield CD accounts, stocks and bonds, and other capital-generating ventures will manage to accumulate significant savings once inflation is factored in.

The castelike nature of oppression facing most blacks—the combination of race and economic deprivation—would not be complete without factoring in a third element: political powerlessness. Political powerlessness is endemic to poverty generally. It is not simply that the wealthy have the resources to curry favor with candidates, and that governments must appease them with favorable tax policies in order to ensure that they continue to invest in the domestic economy. It is rather that the poor lack the education and the time to inform themselves about public policy debates, and in some instances are even discouraged from voter registration by municipal and state government.[32]

This powerlessness applies to wealthier blacks who occupy positions of authority. Despite the fact that blacks as a whole have increased their political involvement overall in comparison to whites and have seen a fourfold increase in the number of black elected officeholders since 1970, the money-driven nature of American democracy and the economic and racial demographics of American political life place severe limits on the capacity of blacks to acquire meaningful power: Blacks constitute only 12 percent of the population; whites are disinclined to vote for black candidates unless they are running for lower office or are otherwise perceived as nonthreatening to their interests; and most black candidates sympathetic to the needs of the black community who do succeed in being elected typically serve in districts mainly inhabited by poor black populations. Unable to amass the war chests available to white candidates serving wealthier constituents, the most successful of these black officeholders are elected to marginalized congressional seats or the mayoral offices of financially strapped, impoverished cities. Beholden to white governors and state representatives who control the cities' purse strings, their power to effect policy reforms on behalf of their constituents is severely limited.

Power is also a scarce commodity even for "successful" blacks. A significant number of black executives feel that their "token" positions give them symbolic but not real power over company policy. The same can be said of black principals of inner-city schools, who—ironically—often lose their positions to white school administrators when school districts are *de*segregated.[33]

We may conclude, following Jennifer Hochschild, that "inequalities of race, class, and power accumulate, that cumulative inequalities worsen the inequalities of each dimension alone, and that blacks are more constrained than whites in translating achievement in one dimension into further achievements in that or other dimensions."[34] What all this means is that blacks in the United States have suffered—and continue to suffer—the cumulative disadvantages of a unique form of overt and institutionlized racism that no other ethnic minority in the United States has had to bear.

THE CURRENT STATUS OF AFFIRMATIVE ACTION

Despite suffering from the cumulative disadvantages of racism, some African Americans have managed to improve their lot over the last thirty years. Since 1970 the percentage of African-American households recording yearly earnings of more than $50,000 in constant dollars has grown from 11.6 percent to 21.2 percent.[35] During this period, blacks more than doubled their representation among telephone operators (from 2.6 percent to 21 percent), firefighters (from 2.5 percent to 7.5 percent), accountants (from 1.6 percent to 7.0 percent), secretaries (from 2.0 percent to 7.7 percent), retail salespersons (from 2.4 percent to 9.7 percent), electricians (from 2.2 percent to 6.1 percent), and lawyers (from 1.3 percent to 2.7 percent).[36] As for women, they now constitute 54 percent of all persons receiving bachelor's degrees (up from 43 percent in 1970 and 35 percent in 1960), and their share of managerial, executive, and administrative positions has climbed from 16 percent in 1970 to 43 percent today. Meanwhile, white men—who now make up less than half of the entire workforce—have ceded much of their dominance to Asians and women except in two blue-collar occupations: electricians and sheet metal workers.[37]

What explains this monumental shift in the composition of the workforce? From the few data that we have, Asians have increased their representation among engineers, computer analysts, physicians, and college faculty largely owing to their possession of skills that are in great demand. Asians who immigrate to the United States are among the most highly motivated and well-educated members of their native country; excelling in school and willing to relocate in less desirable areas of the country, they have not had to rely on affirmative action to accomplish their gains.

The case of women is more complicated. On the lower end of the earnings scale, many women (single or married, with or without children) have been forced by recent changes in welfare law or by sheer economic necessity to accept minimum wage jobs. On the upper end of the scale, women are outperforming men in school, and this fact, combined with their willingness to work for less pay than men, may well explain why they have made such impressive inroads into the business world. Aside from these factors, affirmative action undoubtedly provided a vital catalyst for initially boosting the representation of women in the professions, even if their advances have been restricted by a "glass ceiling."

Only African Americans and Latinos seem to have relied heavily on affirmative action for their gains, although they now comprise less than 50 percent of its beneficiaries. A recent study published in the *Chronicle of Higher Education* explains why. The percentage of blacks and Latinos admitted to the University of California at Los Angeles in 1994 was 7.1 percent and 20 percent respectively; without affirmative action—basing admissions solely on academic criteria—that figure becomes 1.2 percent and 5 percent.[38] A recent national study of law school admissions found that basing admissions solely on test scores and grades would return law schools to their former, overwhelmingly white status (currently 26 percent of black applicants and 32 percent of Latino applicants are admitted; without affirmative action that figure reduces to 3 percent and 9 percent respectively).[39]

In light of the reduced number of blacks and Latinos among the applicants and admissions to the University of Texas Law School and the University of California system following the abolition of affirmative action programs at those institutions in 1995, it is sobering to recall that in 1968, using only test scores, grades, and interviews, the School of Medicine at the University of California at Davis admitted no blacks or Latinos. Thanks to the abolition of affirmative action, this remarkable feat of exclusion is being reduplicated: out of 268 first-year students currently enrolled at the law school of the University of California at Berkeley for 1997, only one is black—in stark contrast to the period from 1970 to 1992, when 5 percent of the first-year enrollment was black and 10 percent was Latino.[40] (To appreciate the enormity of this statistic, consider that over 40 percent of the prison population consists of black males.) The full impact of affirmative action in higher education becomes most apparent when one realizes that even black and Latino students whose families earn between $60,000 and $70,000 still achieve only average scores of 800 and 887 respectively on the SAT test in contrast to scores of 1,011 and 959 recorded for Asian Americans and whites.[41]

My point in citing these depressing statistics is not to reinforce racial prejudices regarding the cognitive deficiencies of blacks and Latinos, since whatever cognitive deficiencies they possess are likely attributable to the innumerable effects of chronic discrimination. Rather, my point is that affirmative action is the principal reason why blacks and Latinos have increased their representation in the professions and trades; without it they would likely be excluded to a degree not witnessed since the early sixties.

All of this is but a prelude to our present concern. Affirmative action may not be the most useful litmus test for gauging the legitimacy of group preferences, but it certainly has become the lightning rod around which Americans have debated this issue. As we approach the millennium, the declining popularity of affirmative action among jurists and laypersons seems part and parcel of a general conservative reaction against government intervention on behalf of persons who find themselves economically and politically marginalized. Kinder and Sanders report that 85 percent of white respondents oppose "preferential hiring and promotion of blacks"; fewer than half of them think that government ought to redress unfair treatment of blacks in the job market. Significantly, opposition to affirmative action diminishes to as little as 31 percent when women and minorities—rather than blacks—are mentioned as the beneficiaries of preferential treatment.[42] This discrepancy testifies to a widespread sentiment among whites that blacks as a group, or at least poor blacks, are morally undeserving of governmental assistance of any kind. The discrepancy also underscores the confusing complexity of affirmative action itself.

AFFIRMATIVE ACTION AND MULTICULTURAL PREFERENCE

Affirmative action was originally designed to compensate African Americans for the peculiar disadvantages of past and present oppression by granting them preferential treatment in education and employment. The preferences bestowed on them, however, were eventually extended to a substantial majority of the population, encompassing women, Native Americans, Aleuts, Eskimos, South Sea Islanders, and persons of ethnic immigrant stock, a situation that sometimes pits one preferred group against another in competing for scarce positions.[43] Certainly, many in this majority who were singled out for preferential treatment could justifiably claim that they had suffered discrimination. Others in this group—for instance, immigrants from Sri Lanka—might have received preferential treatment simply for the sake of increasing diversity.

To compound the confusion, groups that have benefited from affirmative action in certain situations have been harmed by it in others. Some colleges and universities extend preferential treatment to persons of Asian background in order to increase their representation among the faculty and student body; others, such as the University of California, do not, ostensibly on the grounds that such persons are already adequately represented among the faculty and student body.[44]

The confusion over affirmative action stems not only from its multiple rationales and beneficiaries but also from its multiple applications, which range from weak preferential treatment, the voluntary recruitment of women and minorities for placement in schools and businesses, to strong preferential treatment, such as setting aside a fixed percentage of government contracts earmarked for women- and minority-owned businesses. Despite this confusion, I think it is legitimate to distinguish between the primary and secondary aims of affirmative action, especially as regards the aim of diversification, which it shares with multicultural reform.

Proponents of multiculturalism view diversification as an end in itself. Ensuring the representation of different cultures and groups in education, for instance, ostensibly enriches our understanding of ourselves and others while at the same time recognizing the positive value of distinct lifestyles and belief systems. By contrast, proponents of affirmative action see integration, rather than diversification, as the chief aim. Affirmative action preferences are not aimed at preserving group differences; instead, they function to eliminate differences (i.e., racial and class distinctions that hinder individuals from achieving the basic and universal qualifications of citizenship). Because affirmative action has its roots in the civil rights movement that sought to end discrimination against racial minorities and women, its aim has always been to bring about a society in which differences in gender and race no longer matter.

For this reason, it is misleading to think of affirmative action as a policy of diversification. Unfortunately, educators and policy-makers frequently make just this mistake. They fail to notice that admitting and hiring African Americans in higher education is mainly intended to procure them equal opportunity citizenship, while admitting and hiring [Asian Americans] is mainly intended to enrich the cultural and experiential diversity of the whole student body while also showing respect to [Asian American] students.

Of course, the aims of inclusion and diversification are by no means exclusive. Admitting and hiring [African Americans] in higher education also serves the secondary function of exposing the student body to different perspectives and experiences, even if these perspectives and experiences, largely born out of the legacy of racial oppression, are ones that we hope will disappear some day along with the passing of racism. Conversely, admitting [Asian Americans] in higher education also serves the secondary function of ensuring that [Asian Americans] in general are guaranteed the same degree of access to doctors, lawyers, and teachers enjoyed by the rest of the community.[45]

THE LIMITS OF AFFIRMATIVE ACTION IN REMEDYING AFRICAN-AMERICAN OPPRESSION

Leaving aside for now the role of affirmative action in promoting diversity, I would like to focus instead on its original aim: compensating African Americans for past oppression and counteracting present discrimination. The question frequently asked these days is: Is affirmative action really necessary for compensating African Americans and counteracting discrimination? Underlying this question is the suspicion that white Americans owe African Americans nothing and that whatever oppression African Americans endure today is largely of their own making.

This suspicion is well confirmed by numerous studies that show that the fate of affirmative action, especially as it applies to blacks, is closely tied to that of welfare. Many whites erroneously believe that recipients of welfare are overwhelmingly black. They also believe that welfare recipients are largely responsible for their own condition due to moral failing. This stereotypical impression finds parallel expression in the negative impression many whites have about beneficiaries of affirmative action. Not only do they mistakenly believe that most beneficiaries are black, but they also believe that beneficiaries are morally less deserving than the white men whose positions and contracts they have supposedly robbed.[46] Thus, one often hears (from white men, especially) that affirmative action simply discriminates in reverse by awarding positions on the basis of race rather than qualifications—despite findings by the Department of Labor that only six of the more than three thousand discrimination cases filed in federal district courts from 1990 to 1994 ruled in favor of white plaintiffs claiming "reverse discrimination."

Be that as it may, the common consensus today seems to agree that blacks' failure to be economically integrated into mainstream American society is not a function of past and present discrimination but of a simple lack of willpower to do what every other ethnic group who "immigrated" to this country has managed to do: internalize the work ethic of self-discipline and individual achievement. Defenders of affirmative action must counter this diagnosis with an alternative one, which must first show that the possibility for exercising willpower—and therewith the possibility for internalizing a work ethic of self-discipline and individual achievement—is not a metaphysical given, internally planted in the soul of each individual from birth. It must show, in other words, that these possibilities are dependent for their cultivation on economic, political, and educational opportunities, both legally mandated and federally implemented. Without decent jobs, schools, housing, child and health care services, *and* opportunities for advancement, "working" families—especially those living in gang- and drug-infested slums—will have a hard time raising their kids to be self-disciplined individual achievers.

Second, the alternative must show that the continuing presence of family breakdown in the black urban ghetto and the failure of blacks to be fully integrated into all strata of economic life (from middle management on up) are not caused by individual moral deficiency or (as some critics claim) by welfare and affirmative action programs that breed passive dependence and disincentives to achieve. Even allowing for the disincentive effects of welfare programs, the defense of affirmative action must show that the main reason for the failure of black families to be fully integrated into American life is the continuing effects of past and present discrimination.

I think the case for both assumptions is strongly supported by social scientific data, some of which I have already noted. Conservative critics of affirmative action, of course, disagree. They argue, correctly, that statistical data are subject to interpretation and that strong statistical correlations linking racial discrimination, economic deprivation, and social and political subordination do not conclusively demonstrate a simple and exclusive causal relationship between these factors. Still, among mainstream social scientists there is much less disagreement regarding the correct interpretation of these data than conservatives care to admit. In any case, the standard of proof demanded by conservatives would be impossible to meet even among biologists.[47] Confronted with this truth, conservatives sometimes resort to slinging ad hominem arguments criticizing mainstream social scientists as ideologically motivated radicals and dismissing social science as pseudoscience.[48] More often than not they cite a small minority of ideologically conservative social scientists whose causal explanations for the failure of black integration—ranging from the dysfunctional tribalism of Afrocentric culture to the genetic inferiority of blacks generally—are a great deal more speculative than any adduced by their so-called "radical" counterparts.[49]

But defenders of affirmative action must not only show the presence of institutionalized racism; they also must show that affirmative action efficiently and fairly counteracts it. Indeed, given the perception that affirmative action violates our ideal of a just society—wherein, as the Reverend Martin Luther King Jr. once put it, one is judged by "the content of one's character" and not by "the color of one's skin"—one must show that it is the *only* viable remedy.

First of all, defenders of affirmative action must concede that as currently implemented it remedies only part of the underrepresentation of blacks in the economy. Affirmative action mainly benefits blacks who already possess sufficient skills and education to own their own businesses or apply to professional and trade schools (or positions requiring degrees and licenses testifying to advanced secondary education). However, it also benefits unemployed or unskilled blacks by providing them with a preferential advantage in job training programs and the like.[50] Although affirmative action could (and perhaps should) be extended to enhance minority job placement in all occupations, its current implementation was never intended to rectify the so-called injustices of the marketplace.

Second, defenders of affirmative action must concede that it might not be the most direct method for remedying the underrepresentation of blacks in skilled vocations. A more direct approach would ensure that black children living in inner-city ghettos receive the same quality of education (*and* educational support) as children living in affluent white suburbs. Unfortunately, most Americans would find this approach to be either too costly or too egalitarian (because the values of properties are directly linked to the quality of school districts). In any case, no one contemplating educational reform can plausibly expect it to work without the equalization of educational support systems—decent employment, housing, education, safety, health, food, clothing, and the like. Such an all-out assault on urban and rural poverty would be very costly, indeed so costly that it might have a recessionary effect on the economy. Given the structural limits that capitalism imposes on the taxing and spending capacity of the welfare state,[51] the general disinclination of Americans to sacrifice their incomes for the sake of rectifying social injustice, and the persistence of overt and institutionalized racism in the occupational sphere, educational reform seems a very distant hope on which to pin one's resistance to affirmative action.

SOME STANDARD CRITICISMS OF AFFIRMATIVE ACTION

Critics of affirmative action argue that it

- produces inefficiency by promoting the unqualified ahead of the qualified;
- increases racial tension;
- unjustly deprives white males of positions they have earned;
- stigmatizes its beneficiaries as inferior and undeserving; and
- reinforces the very dependency and laziness that is the principal cause of a failure to achieve on one's own.

NOTES

1. *Report of the U.S. National Advisory Commission on Civil Disorders* (New York: Bantam Books, 1968), p. 1.
2. The 1996 report issued by the Joint Center for Political and Economic Studies, a Washington group that tracks trends among African Americans, indicates that in 1995 the black teenage birth rate fell by 9 percent (17 percent since 1991), the average life expectancy for black men rose to 65.4 years (thanks in part to a 17 percent decline in the murder rate), and the median income for black households rose by 3.6 percent (higher than the 2.2 percent registered by white households), with black married couples now earning 87 percent as much as their white counterparts. The proportion of black adults, age twenty-five to twenty-nine, who have completed high school has equaled that of white adults in the same age bracket, and black students are showing more improvement than white students on the SAT verbal examination and other national tests. Although these statistics are encouraging, William Julius Wilson, a professor of social policy at the John F. Kennedy School of Government at Harvard University, notes that they largely reflect improvements in the overall economic prosperity of the country and—most important—do not count the 800,000 black men in prisons when computing unemployment and high school completion rates. Furthermore, the apparent success of blacks in comparison with whites is somewhat misleading, since Latinos—who earn and achieve considerably less than whites on average—were counted among the white population in the statistics cited. See "Quality of Life Is Up for Many Blacks, Data Show," *New York Times,* November 18, 1996, p. A13.
3. It should he noted that the poverty rate among Latinos (28 percent) is also high.
4. Cf. "Education Gap between Races Closes," *New York Times,* September 6, 1996, p. A8.
5. See Tom Wicker, *Tragic Failure: Racial Integration in America* (New York: William Morrow, 1996), p. 131; Donald Kinder and Lynn Sanders, *Divided by Color: Racial Politics and Democratic Ideals* (Chicago: University of Chicago Press, 1996), p. 286.
6. A recent controlled study shows that whites are three times more likely to receive job offers than equally qualified blacks—and this despite affirmative action. The study, involving matched pairs of white and black job applicants, showed that 20 percent of the former group advanced beyond initial interviews, while only 7 percent of the latter did. Among those who advanced, whites received 15 percent more job offers than blacks, who bested their white competitors in only 5 percent

of the audits. Cf. Margery Turner, Michael Fix, and Raymond Struyk, *Opportunities Denied, Opportunities Diminished: Racial Discrimination in Hiring* (Washington, DC: Urban Institute Press, 1991); also cited by Albert G. Mosley in A. G. Mosley and Nicholas Capaldi, *Affirmative Action: Social Justice or Unfair Preference* (Lanham, MD: Rowman and Littlefield, 1996), p. 41. Job discrimination results in some surprising racial imbalances in occupations such as athletics in which minorities actually predominate. Although the percentage of minority coaches in *professional* baseball (14 percent), basketball (24 percent), and football (10 percent) pales in comparison with the percentage of minority athletes represented in these occupations (well over 55 percent), the percentage is even lower in the *college* ranks. The Center for the Study of Sport in Society at Northeastern University recently reported that college teams lag far behind their pro counterparts in hiring minorities. Although blacks constitute a majority of college football players (52 percent) and basketball players (61 percent), only 7 percent of all football coaches and 17 percent of all basketball coaches in Division 1-A are black (more disturbing still, only 2.4 percent of all Division 1 baseball coaches are Latino or black).

7. The practice of increasing qualifications for mortgage loans in specified (redlined) minority districts continues to be a chronic problem. A 1996 study of 561 Chicago lending institutions conducted by the nonprofit Association of Community Organizations for Reform Now (ACORN) showed that upper-income blacks were seventeen times more likely to be rejected than whites with similar incomes and were one and one-half times more likely to be denied loans than whites who earned half as much. In general, it showed that blacks were three times as likely to be turned down for loans as whites. One of the worst offenders, Marquette National Bank, has its main and branch offices located in minority and median-income white areas. It rejected loan applications from minorities ten times more frequently than those from whites. Indeed, only 1.5 percent of its loans went to minority neighborhoods (10 percent of its loans went to poor white and minority tracts, while nearly half went to affluent white suburban and city neighborhoods). These shocking results are confirmed by other studies. A 1989 study by the Federal Reserve Board of loaning practices in the Boston area showed that banks extended loans to black applicants half as often as they did to white applicants. Other studies in New York and Ohio replicated this result for less qualified whites and minorities (blacks and Latinos), while showing greater parity between well-qualified applicants of all racial backgrounds. Cf. "Bank Given Poor Mark on Lending," *Chicago Tribune,* January 23, 1998; *New York Times,* July 13, 1995, p. D1; and *Columbus Dispatch,* February 14, 1995, p. 4C, which included a report by Ohio Commerce Director Nancy Chiles (the *Times* and *Dispatch* items are cited in Mosley and Capaldi, *Affirmative Action,* p. 41).
8. Studies show, for example, that black athletes are consistently paid less than similarly skilled and experienced white athletes. See Lawrence Kahn and Peter Sherer, "Racial Differences in Professional Basketball Players' Compensation," *Journal of Labor Economics* 6 1988: 40–61; also cited in Mosley and Capaldi, *Affirmative Action,* p. 40.
9. In 1987, the Department of Housing and Urban Development estimated that every year there were two million instances of housing discrimination against minorities. Cf. "Stepping Up the War on Discrimination," *New York Times,* November 1, 1987.
10. Ian Ayres, "Fair Driving: Gender and Race Discrimination in Retail Car Negotiations," *Harvard Law Review* 104, no. 4 (February 1991): 817–72.
11. Howard Schuman, Charlotte Steh, and Lawrence Bobo, *Racial Attitudes in America* (Cambridge, MA: Harvard University Press, 1985), pp. 73–82; also cited by Gertrude Ezorsky. *Racism and Justice: The Case for Affirmative Action* (Ithaca, NY: Cornell University Press, 1991), p. 13.
12. Wicker, *Tragic Failure,* p. 95.
13. For a more balanced view of poor urban communities than that given by Wilson, *The Truly Disadvantaged* (Chicago: University of Chicago Press, 1990), and one in particular that positively stresses their unique organizational strengths, see Larry Bennett and Adolph Reed Jr., "The New Face of Urban Renewal: The Near North Redevelopment Initiative and the Cabrini-Green Neighborhood," in *Without Justice for All: The New*

Liberalism and Our Retreat from Racial Equality, ed. Adolph Reed (Boulder, CO: Westview Press, 1999), pp. 175–211. According to Bennett and Reed, Wilson's traditional view that physically concentrated poverty produces "deviant" behavior has led to the adoption of scattered housing urban renewal projects that seek to integrate low-income and middle-income households (e.g., in accordance with a 30/70 percent ratio, as in the Chicago Housing Authority's plan for Cabrini-Green). The problem with many of these plans is that they presume that physical design (low-rise and single-family low-income units scattered throughout middle-income neighborhoods) will automatically generate community esprit de corps across races and income levels, thereby altering the "deviant" behavior of poor blacks and Latinos—a presumption that has yet to be borne out.

14. Wicker, *Tragic Failure,* pp. 141–51.
15. These findings were reported in a 1996 University of Michigan School of Public Health study of Harlem, published in the *New England Journal of Medicine* (cited by Bob Herbert in the editorial section of the *New York Times,* December 2, 1996, p. A13).
16. Kinder and Sanders, *Divided by Color,* pp. 12–34.
17. Ibid., pp. 92–127.
18. Ibid., pp. 136–37.
19. Cf. Andrew Hacker, "Black Crime, White Racism," *New York Review of Books* (March 3, 1988): 36–41. Of course, the fears and suspicions that many whites direct toward blacks are recounted by nearly all blacks as almost constant parts of their daily experience of never feeling, to quote Toni Morrison, "as though I were an American" (p. 41).
20. For a thorough documentation of the overtly racist and white supremicist research sources on which Murray and Herrnstein based their conclusions, see Charles Lane, "The Tainted Sources of 'the Bell Curve,'" *New York Review of Books* (December 1, 1994): 14–19. For criticisms of their selective use and interpretation of data, cf. Russell Jacoby and Naomi Glauberman, eds., *The Bell Curve Debate: History, Documents, Opinions* (New York: Random House, 1995).
21. Steven A. Drizin, "Race Does Matter in Juvenile Justice System," *Chicago Tribune,* May 13, 1999, sec. 1, p. 23.
22. The study, by Dorothy Hatsukami and Marian Fischman, appeared in the fall 1996 issue of the *Journal of the American Medical Association.* Both researchers—psychologists who specialize in drug addiction—suggest sharply reducing the disparities in cocaine sentencing from a 100 to 1 to a 2 to 1 ratio. See "Study Poses a Medical Challenge to Disparity in Cocaine Sentences," *New York Times,* November 20, 1996, pp. A1 and A11.
23. New Jersey recently attempted to forestall a federal civil rights lawsuit by negotiating a consent decree to settle allegations that state police had deployed racial profiling in pulling over an overwhelmingly disproportionate percentage of black and Latino drivers (similar consent decrees have been negotiated by police departments in Pittsburgh and Steubenville, Ohio). The ACLU has filed a civil rights lawsuit against the Illinois State Police, arguing that their policy of stopping rental vehicles and cars with license plates from six states (New York, Arizona, California, Florida, New Mexico, and Texas) is a thinly veiled justification for racial profiling (although Latinos make up just 2.7 percent of Illinois drivers, they constitute nearly one-third of all drug inspection stops). See "Report on Police Stops Adds to Fire," *Chicago Tribune,* June 9, 1999, sec. 2, p. 1.
24. See Thomas Sowell, *The Economics and Politics of Race* (New York: William Morrow, 1983), and *Civil Rights: Rhetoric or Reality?* (New York: William Morrow, 1984), especially pp. 77 and 130–31.
25. Nicholas Capaldi, "Affirmative Action: Con," in Mosley and Capaldi, *Affirmative Action,* p. 99.
26. Nancy Foner, "New Immigrants and Changing Patterns in New York City," in *New Immigrants in New York,* ed. N. Foner (New York: Columbia University Press, 1987), p. 11.
27. Ezorsky, *Racism and Justice,* p. 60, cites an unpublished manuscript by Reynolds Farley ("West Indian Success: Myth or Fact?" Population Studies Center, University of Michigan, 1987) which states that in New York City a native white male college graduate can expect to earn 50 percent more than an equally educated black male of West Indian ancestry.
28. Ezorsky, *Racism and Justice,* pp. 59–60.
29. This report comes from Kathleen Parker of the National Center for Career Strategies, cited in *Executive Edge* (August 1990).

30. "Study Finds Segregation in Cities Worse Than Scientists Imagined," *New York Times,* August 5, 1989.
31. Lester Thurow, *Generating Inequality* (New York: Basic Books, 1975), p. 197.
32. For a discussion of class-based differences in voter participation and class biases in voter registration, see Sidney Verba and Norman H. Nie, *Participation in America, Political Democracy, and Social Equality* (New York: Harper and Row, 1972), and Richard A. Cloward and Francis Fox Piven, *Why Americans Don't Vote* (New York: Pantheon, 1987).
33. During the height of desegregation efforts (between 1963 and 1971) the number of black high school principals in ten southern and border states decreased by two-thirds. Cf. John W. Smith and Bette M. Smith, "Desegregation in the South and the Demise of the Black Educator," *Journal of Social and Behavioral Sciences* 20, no. 1 (Winter 1974): pp. 33–40.
34. Jennifer L. Hochschild, "Race, Class, Power and the American Welfare State," in *Democracy and the Welfare State,* ed. Amy Gutmann (Princeton, NJ: Princeton University Press, 1989), p. 169.
35. Andrew Hacker, "Goodbye to Affirmative Action," *New York Review of Books* (July 11, 1996): 29.
36. Andrew Hacker, *Two Nations: Black and White, Separate, Hostile, Unequal* (New York: Ballantine Books, 1995), p. 118.
37. Hacker, "Goodbye to Affirmative Action," p. 27.
38. Ibid., p. 21.
39. Linda F. Wightman, "The Threat to Diversity in Legal Education: An Empirical Analysis of the Consequences of Abandoning Race as a Factor in Law School Admission Decisions," *New York University Law Review* 72 (April 1997): 1–53.
40. "Minority College Applications Rise," *Chicago Tribune,* January 29, 1998, sec. 1, p. 12. Although select minority applications to the University of California system for 1998 increased by 3 percent for blacks and about 10 percent for Native Americans and Mexican Americans after recording a two-year decline, applications from other Hispanic students continued to fall (by 3 percent), and the apparent decline in white and Asian-American applicants by about 10 percent and 2 percent respectively could not be confirmed owing to a 200 percent increase in the number of students who declined to state their ethnicity.
41. Hacker, "Goodbye to Affirmative Action," p. 25.
42. Ibid., p. 24.
43. As for the problem of competition, Hacker, "Goodbye to Affirmative Action," p. 26, mentions the suit, brought by some black-owned companies seeking a share of government contracts, against the state of Ohio for its decision to include companies owned by immigrants from India on its eligibility list for state contracts expressly set aside for beneficiaries of Ohio's affirmative action mandate. The judge ruled in favor of the state on the grounds that the affirmative action mandate indirectly included immigrants from India among its beneficiaries since it expressly targeted "Orientals" as well as blacks.
44. Using academic criteria alone, Asians would have constituted 51.1 percent of all students admitted to UCLA in 1994; with affirmative action, they in fact constituted only 42.2 percent—a large percentage when one considers that Asians make up only about 7 percent of California's population. Despite their overrepresentation in the University of California's student body, many believe that Asians have been discriminated against by the admissions officers of that institution and its Ivy League counterparts. Statistics for 1984 showed that Asians were admitted to these campuses at a rate of only 82 percent of that of comparably qualified whites. Noting that both whites and Asians experienced somewhat lower admission rates due to affirmative action policies, administrators at these schools nonetheless denied that such policies were to blame for the discrepancy between white and Asian admission rates. Instead, they pointed out that admissions are contingent on other nonacademic factors—such as ensuring that students are drawn from geographically diverse regions and are evenly distributed across major disciplines—that favor whites and work against Asians, who tend to be disproportionately concentrated in certain geographic regions and academic fields (most notably the natural sciences). For a discussion of this issue, see Don Toshiaki Nakanshi, "A Quota on Excellence? The Asian American Admissions Debate," *Change* (November/December 1989): 39–47.
45. I am assuming here that providing decent services to some Asians will sometimes require possessing

a deep familiarity with Asian languages and customs that only a person of Asian background might possess.

46. According to the Green Book, a compilation of data by the House Ways and Means Committee, the percentages of whites, blacks, and Hispanics receiving welfare are 38.9, 37.2, and 17.8, respectively.
47. The statistical correlation between racial discrimination, economic deprivation, and political powerlessness testifies to a "causal" connection at least as strongly confirmable as that between cigarette smoking and lung cancer. In both cases, exceptions to the rule do not disprove causal links between hazardous lifestyles and increased risk of mortality. For a more detailed discussion of causation in science, see chapter 2 of David Ingram, *Reason, History, and Politics: The Communitarian Grounds of Legitimacy in the Modern Age* (Albany: State University of New York Press, 1995).
48. For example, Nicholas Capaldi argues that it is dangerous to substitute "sociological principles that are extraneous to the law and highly controversial if not downright false" for "certain moral principles and traditional practices" (Mosley and Capaldi, *Affirmative Action,* p. 129). His belief in the falsehood of social science stems from its supposed resistance to "empirical confirmation" and its proliferation of competing theories and languages. Capaldi does not try to defend this (in my opinion) erroneous view of social science (as contrasted with natural science). Nor does he seem bothered by his own highly speculative and problematic moral principles (derived from Lockean natural law theory), whose divine cosmology sanctifies individualism and free will while denigrating communalism and environmental conditioning (pp. 96ff.). For a refutation of the naive view of science espoused by Capaldi, see my *Reason, History, and Politics,* chapter 2.
49. For a sampling of the literature espousing the "dysfunctional culture" and "cognitive inferiority" hypotheses respectively, see Sowell, *The Economics and Politics of Race,* and Richard J. Herrnstein and Charles Murray, *The Bell Curve: Intelligence and Class Structure in American Life* (New York: Free Press, 1994).
50. Increased representation of blacks in the skilled professions, however, may benefit unemployed or underemployed blacks by providing them with the services of professionals who live and work in their communities.
51. By its very nature, capitalism exacerbates economic inequalities and limits the capacity of the welfare state to increase employment, raise minimum wages, and siphon off investment capital (through borrowing and taxing) for purposes of eliminating systemic poverty.

READING 40

The Shape of the River

Long-Term Consequences of Considering Race in College and University Admissions

William G. Bowen and Derek Bok

"You've got to know the shape of the river perfectly. It is all there is left to steer by on a very dark night. . . ."

"Do you mean to say that I've got to know all the million trifling variations of shape in the banks of this interminable river as well as I know the shape of the front hall at home?"

"On my honor, you've got to know them better."

—*Mark Twain,* Life on the Mississippi

The "river" that is the subject of this [study] can never be "learned" once and for all. The larger society changes, graduates of colleges and universities move from one stage of life to another, and educational institutions themselves evolve. Similarly, there is much yet to be learned about the future lives of those who have attended selective colleges and professional schools over the last thirty years. This study, then, does not purport to provide final answers to questions about

---

William G. Bowen is president of the Andrew W. Mellon Foundation and former president of Princeton University. Derek Bok is a university professor at Harvard University. He is a former president of Harvard University and former dean of the Harvard Law School.

race-sensitive admissions in higher education. No piece of this river can ever be considered to be "all down" in anyone's book. But we are persuaded of the value of examining each piece "*both* ways"—when "coming upstream," as students enroll in college, and "when it was behind me," as graduates go on to pursue their careers and live their lives.

So much of the current debate relies on anecdotes, assumptions about "facts," and conjectures that it is easy for those who have worked hard to increase minority enrollments to become defensive or disillusioned. It is easy, too, for black and Hispanic graduates, as well as current minority students, to be offended by what they could well regard as unjustified assaults on their competence and even their character. Some of the critics of affirmative action may also feel aggrieved, sensing that they are unjustly dismissed as Neanderthals or regarded as heartless. In short, the nature of the debate has imposed real costs on both individuals and institutions just as it has raised profound questions of educational and social policy that deserve the most careful consideration. In the face of what seems like a veritable torrent of claims and counterclaims, there is much to be said for stepping back and thinking carefully about the implications of the record to date before coming to settled conclusions.

On inspection, many of the arguments against considering race in admissions—such as allegations of unintended harm to the intended beneficiaries and enhanced racial tensions on campus—seem to us to lack substance. More generally, our data show that the overall record of accomplishment by black students after graduation has been impressive. But what more does this detailed examination of one sizable stretch of the river suggest about its future course? What wide-angle view emerges?

THE MEANING OF "MERIT"

One conclusion we have reached is that the meaning of "merit" in the admissions process must be articulated more clearly. "Merit," like "preference" and "discrimination," is a word that has taken on so much baggage we may have to re-invent it or find a substitute.

Still, it is an important and potentially valuable concept because it reminds us that we certainly do not want institutions to admit candidates who *lack* merit, however the term is defined. Most people would agree that rank favoritism (admitting a personal friend of the admissions officer, say) is inconsistent with admission "on the merits," that no one should be admitted who cannot take advantage of the educational opportunities being offered, and that using a lottery or some similar random numbers scheme to choose among applicants who are over the academic threshold is too crude an approach.

One reason why we care so much about who gets admitted "on the merits" is because, as this study confirms, admission to the kinds of selective schools included in the College and Beyond [C&B]* universe pays off handsomely for individuals of all races, from all backgrounds. But it is not individuals alone who gain. Substantial additional benefits accrue to society at large through the leadership and civic participation of the graduates and through the broad contributions that the schools themselves make to the goals of a democratic society. These societal benefits are a major justification for the favored tax treatment that colleges and universities enjoy and for the subsidies provided by public and private donors. The presence of these benefits also explains why these institutions do not allocate scarce places in their entering classes by the simple expedient of auctioning them off to the highest bidders. The limited number of places is an exceedingly valuable resource—valuable both to the students admitted and to the society at large—which is why admissions need to be based "on the merits."

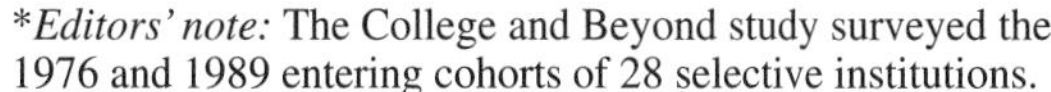

**Editors' note:* The College and Beyond study surveyed the 1976 and 1989 entering cohorts of 28 selective institutions.

Unfortunately, however, to say that considerations of merit should drive the admissions process is to pose questions, not answer them. There are no magical ways of automatically identifying those who merit admission on the basis of intrinsic qualities that distinguish them from all others. Test scores and grades are useful measures of the ability to do good work, but they are no more than that. They are far from infallible indicators of other qualities some might regard as intrinsic, such as a deep love of learning or a capacity for high academic achievement. Taken together, grades and scores predict only 15–20 percent of the variance among all students in academic performance and a smaller percentage among black students. . . . Moreover, such quantitative measures are even less useful in answering other questions relevant to the admissions process, such as predicting which applicants will contribute most in later life to their professions and their communities.[1]

Some critics believe, nevertheless, that applicants with higher grades and test scores are more deserving of admission because they presumably worked harder than those with less auspicious academic records. According to this argument, it is only "fair" to admit the students who have displayed the greatest effort. We disagree on several grounds.

To begin with, it is not clear that students who receive higher grades and test scores have necessarily worked harder in school. Grades and test scores are a reflection not only of effort but of intelligence, which in turn derives from a number of factors, such as inherited ability, family circumstances, and early upbringing, that have nothing to do with how many hours students have labored over their homework. Test scores may also be affected by the quality of teaching that applicants have received or even by knowing the best strategies for taking standardized tests, as coaching schools regularly remind students and their parents. For these reasons, it is quite likely that many applicants with good but not outstanding scores and B+ averages in high school will have worked more diligently than many other applicants with superior academic records.

More generally, selecting a class has much broader purposes than simply rewarding students who are thought to have worked especially hard. The job of the admissions staff is not, in any case, to decide who has earned a "right" to a place in the class, since we do not think that admission to a selective university is a right possessed by anyone. What admissions officers must decide is which set of applicants, *considered individually and collectively,* will take fullest advantage of what the college has to offer, contribute most to the educational process in college, and be most successful in using what they have learned for the benefit of the larger society. Admissions processes should, of course, be "fair," but "fairness" has to be understood to mean only that each individual is to be judged according to a consistent set of criteria that reflect the objectives of the college or university. Fairness should not be misinterpreted to mean that a particular criterion has to apply—that, for example, grades and test scores must always be considered more important than other qualities and characteristics so that no student with a B average can be accepted as long as some students with As are being turned down.

Nor does fairness imply that each candidate should be judged in isolation from all others. It may be perfectly "fair" to reject an applicant because the college has already enrolled many other students very much like him or her. There are numerous analogies. When making a stew, adding an extra carrot rather than one more potato may make excellent sense—and be eminently "fair"—if there are already lots of potatoes in the pot. Similarly, good basketball teams include both excellent shooters and sturdy defenders, both point guards and centers. Diversified investment portfolios usually include some mix of stocks and bonds, and so on.

To admit "on the merits," then, is to admit by following complex rules derived from the institution's own mission and based on its own experiences educating students with different talents and backgrounds. These "rules" should not be thought of as abstract propositions to be deduced through contemplation in a Platonic cave. Nor are they rigid formulas that can be applied in a mechanical fashion. Rather, they should have the status of rough guidelines established in large part through empirical examination of the actual results achieved as a result of long experience. How many students with characteristic "x" have done well in college, contributed to the education of their fellow students, and gone on to make major contributions to society? Since different institutions operate at very different places along our metaphorical river (some placing more emphasis on research, some with deeper pools of applicants than others), the specifics of these rules should be expected to differ from one institution to another. They should also be expected to change over time as circumstances change and as institutions learn from their mistakes.

Above all, merit must be defined in light of what educational institutions are trying to accomplish. In our view, race is relevant in determining which candidates "merit" admission because taking account of race helps institutions achieve three objectives central to their mission—identifying individuals of high potential, permitting students to benefit educationally from diversity on campus, and addressing long-term societal needs.

Identifying Individuals of High Potential

An individual's race may reveal something about how that person arrived at where he or she is today—what barriers were overcome, and what the individual's prospects are for further growth. Not every member of a minority group will have had to surmount substantial obstacles. Moreover, other circumstances besides race can cause "disadvantage." Thus colleges and universities should and do give special consideration to the hard-working son of a family in Appalachia or the daughter of a recent immigrant from Russia who, while obviously bright, is still struggling with the English language. But race is an important factor in its own right, given this nation's history and the evidence presented in many studies of the continuing effects of discrimination and prejudice.[2] Wishing it were otherwise does not make it otherwise. It would seem to us to be ironic indeed—and wrong—if admissions officers were permitted to consider all other factors that help them identify individuals of high potential who have had to overcome obstacles, but were proscribed from looking at an applicant's race.

Benefiting Educationally from Diversity on the Campus

Race almost always affects an individual's life experiences and perspectives, and thus the person's capacity to contribute to the kinds of learning through diversity that occur on campuses. This form of learning will be even more important going forward than it has been in the past. Both the growing diversity of American society and the increasing interaction with other cultures worldwide make it evident that going to school only with "the likes of oneself" will be increasingly anachronistic. The advantages of being able to understand how others think and function, to cope across racial divides, and to lead groups composed of diverse individuals are certain to increase.

To be sure, not all members of a minority group may succeed in expanding the racial understanding of other students, any more than all those who grew up on a farm or came from a remote region of the United States can be expected to convey a special rural perspective. What does seem clear, however, is that a student body containing many different backgrounds, talents, and experiences will be a richer environment in which to develop. In this respect, minority students of all kinds can have something to offer their classmates. The black student with high grades from Andover may challenge the stereotypes of many classmates just as much as the black student from the South Bronx.

Until now, there has been little hard evidence to confirm the belief of educators in the value of diversity. Our survey data throw new light on the extent of interaction occurring on campuses today and of how positively the great majority of students regard opportunities to learn from those with different points of view, backgrounds, and experiences. Admission "on the merits" would be short-sighted if admissions officers were precluded from crediting this potential contribution to the education of all students.

Imposition of a race-neutral standard would produce very troubling results from this perspective: such a policy would reduce dramatically the proportion of black students on campus—probably shrinking their number to less than 2 percent of all matriculants at the most selective colleges and professional schools. Moreover, our examination of the application and admissions files indicates that such substantial reductions in the number of black matriculants, with attendant losses in educational opportunity for all students, would occur without leading to any appreciable improvement in the academic credentials of the remaining black students and would lead to only a modest change in the overall academic profile of the institutions.[3]. . .

HOW FAST ARE WE HEADING DOWNSTREAM?

Final questions to ponder concern a longer sweep of the river. What is our ultimate objective? How much progress has been made? How far do we still have to go? Along with many others, we look forward to a day when arguments in favor of race-sensitive admissions policies will have become unnecessary. Almost everyone, on all sides of this debate, would agree that in an ideal world race would be an irrelevant consideration. As a black friend said almost thirty years ago: "Our ultimate objective should be a situation in which every individual, from every background, feels *unselfconsciously included.*"

Many who agree with Justice Blackmun's aphorism, "To get beyond racism, we must first take account of race," would be comforted if it were possible to predict, with some confidence, when that will no longer be necessary. But we do not know how to make such a prediction, and we would caution against adopting arbitrary timetables that fail to take into account how deep-rooted are the problems associated with race in America.

At the same time, it is reassuring to see, even within the C&B set of institutions, the changes that have occurred between the admission of the '76 and '89 cohorts. Over that short span of time, the average SAT scores of black matriculants at the C&B schools went up 68 points—a larger gain than that of white matriculants. The overall black graduation rate, which was already more than respectable in the '76 cohort (71 percent), rose to 79 percent. Enrollment in the most highly regarded graduate and professional schools has continued to increase. The '89 black matriculants are even more active in civic affairs (relative to their white classmates) than were the '76 black matriculants. Appreciation for the education they received and for what they learned from diversity is voiced even more strongly by the '89 cohort than by their '76 predecessors.

Whatever weight one attaches to such indicators, and to others drawn from national data, the trajectory is clear. To be sure, there have been mistakes and disappointments. There is certainly much work for colleges and universities to do in finding more effective ways to improve the academic performance of minority students. But, overall, we conclude that academically selective colleges and universities have been highly successful in using race-sensitive admissions policies to advance educational goals important to them and societal goals important to everyone. Indeed, we regard these admissions policies as an impressive example of how venerable institutions with established ways of operating can adapt to serve newly perceived needs. Progress has been made and continues to be made. We are headed downstream, even though there may still be miles to go before the river empties, finally, into the sea.

NOTES

1. Martin Luther King, Jr., now regarded as one of the great orators of this century, scored in the bottom half of all test-takers on the verbal GRE (Cross and Slater, 1997, p. 12).
2. One of the most compelling findings of this study is that racial gaps of all kinds remain after we have tried to control for the influences of other variables that might be expected to account for "surface" differences associated with race. We have described and discussed black-white gaps in SAT scores, socioeconomic status, high school grades, college graduation rates, college rank in class, attainment of graduate and professional degrees, labor force participation, average earnings, job satisfaction, marital status, household income, civic participation, life satisfaction, and attitudes toward the importance of diversity itself. In short, on an "other things equal" basis, race is a statistically significant predictor of a wide variety of attributes, attitudes, and outcomes. People will debate long and hard, as they should, whether particular gaps reflect unmeasured differences in preparation and previous opportunity, patterns of continuing discrimination, failures of one kind or another in the educational system itself, aspects of the culture of campuses and universities, individual strengths and weaknesses, and so on. But no one can deny that race continues to matter.
3. While it is, of course, possible for an institution to be so committed to enrolling a diverse student population that it enrolls unprepared candidates who can be predicted to do poorly, we do not believe that this is a consequential problem today in most academically selective institutions. Three pieces of evidence are relevant: (1) the close correspondence between the academic credentials of those students who would be retrospectively rejected under a race-neutral standard and those who would be retained; (2) the modest associations (within this carefully selected population) of the test scores and high school grades of black matriculants at the C&B schools with their in-college and after-college performance; and (3) the remarkably high graduation rates of black C&B students—judged by any national standard.

REFERENCE

Cross, Theodore, and Robert Bruce Slater. 1997. "Why the End of Affirmative Action Would Exclude All but a Very Few Blacks from America's Leading Universities and Graduate Schools." *Journal of Blacks in Higher Education* 17 (Autumn): 8–17.

READING 41

Social Movements and the Politics of Difference

Cheryl Zarlenga Kerchis and Iris Marion Young

There was once a time of caste and class when tradition held that each group had its place in the social hierarchy—that some were born to rule and others to be ruled. In this time of darkness, rights, privileges, and obligations were different for people of different sexes, races, religions, classes, and occupations. Inequality between groups was justified by both the state and the church on the grounds that some kinds of people were better than others.

Then one day, a period in the history of ideas known as the Enlightenment dawned, and revolutionary ideas about the equality of people emerged. During the Enlightenment, which reached its zenith in Europe in the eighteenth century, philosophers called into question traditional ideas and values that justified political inequality between groups. They declared that all people are created equal because all people are able to reason and to think about morality. They also argued that because all people are created equal, all people should have equal political and civil rights.

Cheryl Zarlenga Kerchis is a doctoral student in public policy at the university of Pittsburgh. Iris Marion Young is a professor of political science at the University of Chicago.

The ideas of Enlightenment thinkers have marked the battle lines of political struggle in the United States for the past two hundred years. The Revolutionary War was fought on Enlightenment principles, and our Constitution was based on the principles of liberty and equality. In the beginning, however, the vision of liberty and equality of our founders (as well as most Enlightenment philosophers) excluded certain groups. Women did not have equal political and civil rights, and African Americans were enslaved. Inspired by the ideals of liberty and equality, women and African Americans engaged in a long and bitter struggle for political equality. By the 1960s, the battle for legal equal political and civil rights was won, though the struggle for equality in all walks of life continues.

Today in our society, prejudice and discrimination remain, but in many respects we have realized the vision that the Enlightenment thinkers set out. Our laws express rights in universal terms, that is, applied equally to everyone. We strive for a society in which differences of race, sex, religion, and ethnicity do not affect people's opportunities to participate in all aspects of social life. We believe that people should be treated as individuals, not as members of groups, and that their rewards in life should be based on their individual achievement—not on their race, sex, or any other purely accidental characteristic.

Though there is much to admire in this vision of a society that eliminates group differences, it has its own limitations, which contemporary social movements have called into question. Just as Enlightenment social movements challenged widely held traditional ideas and values that justified oppression in their time, today's social movements are challenging widely held ideas about justice that justify oppression in our time. These social movements criticize the idea that a just society is one that eliminates group differences under the law and guarantees equal treatment for all individuals. The central question they wish to ask is this: is it possible that the ideal of equal treatment of all persons under the law and the attempt to eliminate group differences under the law in fact perpetuates oppression of certain groups?

. . . We will argue that the answer to this question is yes. In our argument we will first discuss the ideal of justice that defines liberation as the transcendence of group difference. We call this the *ideal of assimilation.* This ideal usually promotes the equal treatment of all groups as the primary way to achieve justice. In this discussion, we will show how recent social movements of oppressed groups in the United States have challenged this ideal of assimilation. These movements believe that by organizing themselves and defining their own positive group cultural identity they will be more likely to achieve power and increase their participation in public institutions. We call this positive recognition of difference the politics of difference, and explain how it is more likely to aid in the liberation of oppressed groups.

. . . We will [also] discuss the need to change the way we think about group differences in order to have a politics of difference that leads to the liberation of oppressed groups. We will explore the risks associated with a politics of difference, in particular, the risk of recreating the harmful stigma that group difference has had in the past. To avoid this restigmatizing of groups, we will argue for a new and positive understanding of difference that rejects past exclusionary understandings of difference.

. . . [Finally,] we will consider practical issues of policy and representation in relation to a politics of difference. First, we will discuss the issue of group-neutral versus group-conscious policies. By this we mean policies that treat all groups in the same way (group-neutral) versus policies that treat different groups differently (group-conscious). We will discuss two specific cases in which group-conscious policies are needed to ensure fairness to disadvantaged groups. Lastly, we will argue for group representation in American social institutions including governmental and non-governmental institutions.

We will explain how group representation promotes justice, suggest the kinds of groups that should be represented, and give some examples of group representation within some already-existing organizations and movements in the United States.

LIBERATION FOR OPPRESSED GROUPS THROUGH THE IDEAL OF ASSIMILATION

The Ideal of Assimilation and Equal Treatment of Social Groups

What strategy of reform is most effective for achieving the liberation of oppressed groups? If we desire a non-racist, non-sexist society, how can we get there? One strategy for achieving this society is to pursue what we call an ideal of assimilation. The ideal of assimilation as a strategy for the liberation of oppressed groups involves the elimination of group-based differences under the law. Thus, in a truly non-racist, non-sexist society, a person's race or sex would be no more significant in the eyes of the law than eye color or any other accidental characteristic. People would have different physical characteristics (such as skin color), but these would play no part in determining how people treated each other or how they were treated under the law. Over time, people would see no reason to consider race or sex in policies or in everyday activities, and group-based differences by and large would no longer matter.

Many contemporary thinkers argue for this ideal of assimilation and against the ideal of diversity that we will argue for later in this chapter. And there are many convincing reasons to support such an ideal. Perhaps the most convincing reason is that the principle of equal treatment of groups provides a clear and easily applied standard of equality and justice for use by courts and government institutions that deal with issues of race and sex discrimination. Under a standard of equal treatment, any discrimination whatsoever on the basis of group differences is considered illegal. Any law, regulation, employment practice, or government policy that treats persons differently on the basis of the race or sex is labeled unjust. The simplicity of this principle of equal treatment makes it a very attractive standard of justice.

There are two other convincing reasons to support the ideal of assimilation and the principle of justice as equal treatment. First, the ideal of assimilation may help to change the way people think about group differences. It treats classifications of people according to accidental characteristics like skin color or gender as arbitrary, not natural or necessary. Some people happen to be Black. Some are female or Hispanic or Jewish or Italian. But these differences do not mean that these people have different moral worth or that they necessarily aspire to anything different than anyone else in political life, in the workplace, or in the family. By suggesting that these categories are not important, the ideal of assimilation helps us realize how often we limit people's opportunities in society (because they are Black, female, and so on) for arbitrary reasons. Second, the ideal of assimilation gives individuals a great deal of choice in their lives. When group differences have no social importance, people are free to develop themselves as individuals, without feeling the pressures of group expectations. If I am a woman, I can aspire to anything I wish to and not feel any special pressure to pursue or settle for, for instance, one occupation versus another.

The ideal of assimilation, which calls for equal treatment of groups and the elimination of group difference in social life, has been extremely important in the history of oppressed groups. Its assertion of the equal moral worth of all persons (regardless of their group characteristics) and the right of all to participate in the institutions of society inspired many movements against discrimination. There is no question that it continues to have considerable value in our nation today, where many forms of discrimination against groups persist.

Contemporary Challenges to the Ideal of Assimilation

Since the 1960s, a number of groups have questioned the value of this ideal of assimilation and equal treatment. Is it possible, they have asked, that this ideal is not truly liberating for some oppressed groups? Instead of seeking to eliminate group difference, they wonder, would it not be more liberating for groups to organize themselves and assert their own positive group cultural identity? These groups see a politics of difference as opposed to a politics without difference as a better strategy for achieving power and participation in the institutions of social and political life. In the next section, we will discuss the efforts of four contemporary social movements to redefine the importance of group difference and cultural identity in social and political life in a way that they find more liberating.

The African American Movement In the 1960s, with the enactment of the Civil Rights Act of 1964, the Voting Rights Act of 1965, and numerous lawsuits spawned by these new laws, African Americans won major victories that declared racial discrimination in politics and the workplace illegal. Despite these successes, however, criticisms of the civil rights strategy emerged from within the African American community in the form of the Black Power movement. Black Power leaders criticized the civil rights movement for three reasons: they were unhappy with the civil rights movement's goal of integration of African Americans into a society dominated by whites; they criticized the movement's alliance with white liberals and instead called upon African Americans to confidently affirm their cultural identity; and they criticized the movement for not encouraging African Americans to organize themselves on their own terms and to determine their political goals within their own organizations.

Instead of supporting integration with whites, Black Power leaders called on African Americans to strengthen their own separate and culturally distinct neighborhoods as a better means of obtaining economic and political power. In sum, they rejected the ideal of assimilation and the suppression of group difference in political and economic life. In its place, they advocated self-organization and a strengthening of cultural identity as a better strategy for achieving power and participation in dominant institutions.

In recent years, many of the ideas of the Black Power movement have resurfaced among African Americans. Despite the legal protections won during the civil rights era, African American economic and political oppression persists. In economic life today, African Americans experience unemployment rates more than twice those of whites and poverty rates more than three times those of whites. And they still face substantial discrimination in educational opportunities, business opportunities, and the housing market.

What has happened since the 1960s? Why the persistence of inequalities almost forty years after *Brown v. Board of Education,* and almost thirty years after the Civil Rights and Voting Rights acts? Many African Americans argue that the push toward integration by the civil rights movement had unintended negative effects on the African American community. While civil rights protections opened the doors of opportunity for some African Americans, those left behind were made worse off. Many African Americans have been assimilated into the middle class and no longer associate as closely with poor and working class African Americans. As a consequence, African American solidarity has been weakened, and in many neighborhoods African American businesses, schools, and churches have been hurt by the exodus of middle-class African American families. Hence, once again, many African American leaders are calling for a rejection of the goal of integration and assimilation and are calling upon African Americans to organize themselves and seek economic and political empowerment within their own neighborhoods.

Another legacy of the Black Power movement that lives on today is the assertion of a positive Black cultural identity. The "Black is beautiful" movement that emerged in the 1960s celebrated a distinct African American culture and struggled against the assimilation of that culture into the dominant culture of American society. In their clothing and hairstyles, members confidently asserted their own cultural styles and rejected the narrow definition of style and beauty of the predominantly white culture. Since that time, African American historians and educators have sought to recover the rich history of African America and have retold the stories of African American writers, artists, musicians, inventors, and political figures, who received little attention in the history textbooks of white America. And they have subsequently fought with school boards across the nation to ensure that respect for African American history and culture is integral to the history curricula under which every student in this country is educated.

All of these examples reflect a rejection of the idea that assimilation of African Americans into the dominant culture of America is a desirable goal. They instead reflect a desire for an alternative politics of difference through which African Americans can gain their fair share of power and increase their participation in social, political, and economic life in America without shedding their own self-determined group cultural identity.

The American Indian Movement Not long after the Black Power movement emerged in the 1960s, a movement with similar ideals arose among Native Americans. American Indian Movement leaders called for Red Power, which, like Black Power, rejected the assimilation of Native American peoples that had been the goal of government policies toward Indians throughout the nineteenth and twentieth centuries. In many ways, their rejection of the dominant culture and its values was even stronger than that of Black Power.

The American Indian Movement claimed a right to self-government on Indian lands and struggled to gain a powerful Indian voice in the federal government branch responsible for policy making toward Native American peoples—the Bureau of Indian Affairs. They went to the courts to fight for land taken away from them. They also used the court system to fight for Indian control of natural resources on reservations that were being exploited by mining companies and other corporations.

Like Black Power, Red Power also extended its struggle beyond political and economic issues. Red Power advocates wanted to restore and strengthen cultural pride among Native Americans. In the last twenty years, Native Americans have struggled to recover and preserve elements of their traditional culture such as religious rituals, crafts, and languages that have been ravaged by the government's policy of Indian assimilation.

The Gay and Lesbian Movement The gay and lesbian movement that emerged in the 1960s began, much like the African American movement of that period, as a struggle for equality and civil rights. Gay-rights advocates wanted to protect gay men and lesbians from discrimination in government institutions and in employment. The movement strived for the ideal of assimilation and equal treatment that we have talked about throughout this [article]. They asked society to recognize that gay people are no different from anyone else in their aspirations or moral worth, and that they too deserve the same protections under the law extended to all other U.S. citizens.

Over time, however, many members of the gay and lesbian movement came to believe that the achievement of civil rights alone would not liberate gay men and lesbians from the discrimination they faced in society. Though they had achieved some legal victories, gay men and lesbians were still often harassed, beaten up, and intimidated by heterosexuals who disapproved of their gay "lifestyle." It seemed the dominant culture could tolerate gays and even extend limited legal protection to gay people as long as they kept their sexuality a *private* matter. But *public* displays of gay lifestyles were (and still are) often met with hostility and violence. For many gay men and lesbians, concealing their sexuality and lifestyles in a private world is just as oppressive as the public and explicit discrimination they often face in institutions.

Today, most gay and lesbian liberation groups seek not only equal protection under the law but also group solidarity and a positive affirmation of gay men and lesbians as social groups with shared experiences and cultures. They reject the ideal of assimilation that suppresses group differences in political and social life and makes these differences a purely private matter. They refuse to accept the dominant heterosexual culture's definition of healthy sexuality and respectable family life, and instead have insisted on the right to proudly display their gay or lesbian identity. Like the other groups mentioned above, they have engaged in a politics of difference that they find more liberating than the politics of assimilation.

The Women's Movement Until the late 1970s, the aims of the contemporary women's movement were for the most part those of the ideal of assimilation. Women's movement members fought for women's civil rights and the equal treatment of and equal opportunity for women in political institutions and the workplace. The movement strived to eliminate the significance of gender differences in social life. Women and men were to be measured by the same standards and treated in the same way in social institutions. Women's rights advocates saw any attempt to define men and women as fundamentally different in their aspirations for successful careers outside the home as just another means of oppressing women and limiting their opportunity to participate in the male-dominated spheres of government and business. This strategy of assimilation was extremely successful in undermining traditional ways of thinking about sex differences and women's roles. The idea that women naturally aspired to less in terms of participation in politics and the workplace was finally overturned.

Despite these successes, however, many in the women's movement grew uncomfortable with this strategy of assimilation, which defined equality as the elimination of sex differences in social life. Since the late seventies, a politics of difference has emerged from within the women's movement that rejects the goals of gender assimilation. The first signs of this rejection were seen among women who advocated feminist separatism.

Feminist separatists believed that women should aspire to more than formal equality in a male-dominated world. They argued that entering the male-dominated world meant playing according to rules and standards that men had set up and had used against women for centuries and across cultures. Instead of trying to measure up to male-defined standards, they called for the empowerment of women through self-organization and the creation of separate and safe places where women could share their experiences and devise their own rules of the game. In such separate and safe places, women could decide for themselves what was socially valuable activity instead of uncritically accepting the values and activities of a male-dominated society. One of the outcomes of this separatism was the creation of women's organizations and services to address the needs of women that have historically received little attention from male-dominated society. The organizations formed in this period include women's health clinics, battered women's shelters, and rape crisis centers, all of which today continue to improve the lives of many women.

Some of the ideas of this separatist movement are reflected in the recent work of feminist philosophers and political thinkers. Unlike earlier feminist thinkers, these women question the idea that women's liberation means equal participation of women in male-dominated political institutions and workplaces. While they do not suggest that women withdraw from such institutions, they suggest that society ought to rethink the value of femininity and women's ways of approaching human relations. These theorists suggest that women tend to be socialized in a way that, in comparison with men, makes them more sensitive to others' feelings, more empathetic, more nurturing of others and the world, and better at smoothing over tensions between people.

They argue that this more caring, nurturing, and cooperative approach to relations with other people should not be rejected out of hand by feminists as limiting women's human potential or their ability to contribute to the world. They suggest that women's attitudes toward others and toward nature constitute a healthier way to think about the world than the competitive and individualistic attitudes that characterize male-dominated culture in the Western world. By holding on to these values, women can help to transform institutions, human relations, and the interaction of people with nature in ways that may better promote people's self-development within institutions and better protect the environment.

Thus, a political strategy that asks women to give up the values of caring or nurturing in order to succeed in the workplace or in politics not only undervalues what women have to contribute to those spheres, but undermines the possibility of transforming male-dominated institutions in a way that will result in a healthier society as a whole. To resolve this dilemma, then, the politics of assimilation needs to be replaced by a politics of difference that makes it possible for women to participate fully in social and political institutions without suppressing or undervaluing gender differences.

WHY IS THE POLITICS OF DIFFERENCE LIBERATING?

The Importance of Group Difference in Social Life

All of the social movements discussed above have offered an alternative view of liberation that rejects the ideal of assimilation. In their assertion of a positive sense of group difference, these social movements have put forth an ideal of liberation that we will call the politics of difference. In their view, a just society does not try to eliminate or ignore the importance of group differences. Rather, society seeks equality among social groups, requiring each to recognize and respect the value of the experiences and perspectives of all other groups. No group asks another to give up or hide its distinct experiences and perspectives as a condition of participation in social institutions.

Is a politics of difference really necessary? Are group differences really that important? Many political philosophers deny the importance of social groups. To them, the notion of group difference was created and kept alive by people who sought to justify their own privilege and the oppression of specific groups. Some theorists agree that there are important differences among groups that affect the way people see themselves and others, but they see these differences as undesirable. The ideal of assimilation either denies the importance of social groups or sees them as undesirable.

In contrast, we doubt that a society without social groups is possible *or* desirable. Today, whether we like it or not, our society is structured by social groups that have important consequences for people's lives. Social groups do affect the way people see themselves and others in both positive and negative ways. People form their identities—their sense of who they are—in part through their membership in social or cultural groups. There is nothing inherently bad about people identifying with certain groups. Attachment to an ethnic tradition, language, culture, or set of common experiences has always been a feature of social life. The problem for a democratic nation occurs when group membership affects people's capacities to participate fully in our social institutions. In the United States today, some groups are privileged while others are oppressed. The politics of difference offers a way of retaining the positive, identity-affirming aspect of group difference while eliminating the negative aspect—the privileging of some groups over others.

The Oppressive Consequences of Ignoring Group Difference

None of the social movements that we have discussed deny the claim that the strategy of eliminating group difference and treating all groups the same has helped improve the situation of oppressed social groups. On the contrary, each of these social movements at one time pursued such a strategy. But why did they eventually begin to question its effectiveness in eliminating group oppression? Why was assimilation called into question?

Many of these social movements of oppressed groups found that the achievement of formal equality under the law did not put an end to their disadvantaged position. Even though in many respects the law is now blind to group differences like sex and race, certain groups continue to be oppressed while other groups are privileged. Many forms of oppression, such as racial slurs, are more subtle, yet they are just as corrosive than the more easily identifiable forms of overt and intentional discrimination. They persist in the structure of institutions that make it difficult for members of disadvantaged groups to develop their capacities. Oppression also exists in forms of everyday interaction and decision making in which people make assumptions about the aspirations and needs of women, African Americans, Hispanics, gay men and lesbians, and other groups that continue to be oppressed. The idea that equality and liberation can only be achieved by ignoring group differences has three oppressive consequences for disadvantaged social groups.

First, ignoring group difference disadvantages groups whose experience and culture differ from those of privileged groups. The strategy of assimilation aims to bring excluded groups into the mainstream of social life. But assimilation always implies coming into the game after it has already begun, after the rules and standards have already been set. Therefore, disadvantaged groups play no part in making up the rules and standards that they must prove themselves by—those rules and standards are defined by privileged groups. The rules and standards may appear to be neutral since they are applied equally to all groups. In actuality though, their formation was based only upon the experiences of privileged groups—oppressed groups being excluded from the rule-making process.

If such standards are applied equally to all groups, why do they then place some groups at a disadvantage? The real differences between oppressed groups and dominant groups often make it difficult for oppressed groups to measure up to the standards of the privileged. These real differences may have to do with cultural styles and values or with certain distinct capacities (for example, women's capacity to bear children). But quite often these differences are themselves the result of group oppression. For example, the long history of exclusion and marginalization of African American people from the economic and educational systems of this country has made it very difficult for many of them to gain the levels of educational attainment and technical skills that whites have. Yet, despite this history of oppression, they must compete for jobs on the basis of qualifications that are the same for all groups, including historically privileged groups.

The second oppressive consequence of ignoring group difference is that it allows privileged groups in society to see their own culture, values, norms, and experiences as universal (shared by all groups) rather than group specific. In other words, ignoring group differences allows the norms and values that express the point of view and experience of privileged groups to appear neutral and uncontroversial. When the norms and values of particular privileged groups are held as normal, neutral, and universal, those groups that do not adhere to those norms and values are viewed by society as deviant or abnormal. . . .

When groups that do not share the supposedly neutral values and norms of privileged groups are viewed as deviant or abnormal, a third oppressive consequence of ignoring difference is produced. Members of those groups that are viewed as deviant often internalize society's view of them as abnormal or deviant. The internalization of the negative attitudes of others by members of oppressed groups often produces feelings of self-hatred and ambivalence toward their own culture. The ideal of assimilation asks members of oppressed groups to fit in and be like everyone else, yet society continues to see them as different, making it impossible for them to fit in comfortably. Thus, members of groups marked as different or deviant in comparison to privileged groups are caught in a dilemma they cannot resolve. On one hand, participating in mainstream society means accepting and adopting an identity that is not their own. And on the other, when they do try to participate, they are reminded by society and by themselves that they do not fit in.

The Liberating Consequences of the Politics of Difference

We have given three reasons why a strategy of assimilation that attempts to ignore, transcend, or devalue group differences is oppressive. We would now like to turn to the politics of difference and to explain the ways in which it is liberating and empowering for members of oppressed groups. The key difference between the politics of difference and the politics of assimilation lies in the definition of group difference itself. The politics of assimilation defines group difference in a negative way, as a liability or disadvantage to be overcome in the process of assimilating into mainstream society. In contrast, the politics of difference defines group difference in a positive way, as a social and cultural condition that can be liberating and empowering for oppressed groups. There are four ways in which this positive view of difference is liberating for oppressed groups.

First, a politics of difference that defines group difference in a positive way makes it easier for members of oppressed groups to celebrate and be proud of their identity, which the dominant culture has taught them to despise. In a politics of difference, members of oppressed groups are not asked to assimilate, to try to be something they are not. They are not asked to reject or hide their own culture as a condition of full participation in the social life of the nation. Instead, the politics of difference recognizes that oppressed groups have their own cultures, experiences, and points of view that have positive value for themselves *and* society as a whole. Some of their values and norms may even be superior to those of more privileged groups in society.

Second, by recognizing the value of the cultures and experiences of oppressed groups, the politics of difference exposes the values and norms of privileged groups as group specific, not neutral or universal. The politics of difference recognizes that the values and norms of privileged groups are expressions of their own experience and may conflict with those of other groups. In the politics of difference, oppressed groups insist on the positive value of their own cultures and experiences. When they insist on this, it becomes more and more difficult for dominant groups to parade their norms and values as neutral, universal, or uncontroversial. It also becomes more difficult for dominant groups to point to oppressed groups as deviant, abnormal, or inferior.

Thus, for example, when feminists assert the positive value of a caring and nurturing approach to the world, they call into question the competitive and individualistic norms of white male society. When African Americans proudly affirm the culture and history of Afro-America, they expose the culture and history of white society as expressing a particular experience—only *one* part of America's story. When Native Americans assert the value of a culture tied to and respectful of the land, they call into question the dominant culture's materialism, which promotes pollution and environmental destruction. All of these questions posed by oppressed groups suggest that the values and norms of dominant groups comprise one perspective, one way of looking at the world, that is neither neutral, shared, nor necessarily superior to the ways of oppressed groups.

When we realize that the norms and values of privileged groups are not universal, it becomes possible to think about the relation between groups in a more liberating way. Oppressed groups are not deviant with respect to privileged groups. They simply differ from privileged groups in their values, norms, and experiences, just as privileged groups are different from them. Difference is a two-way street; each group differs from the other; each earns the label "different." When the relations among groups are defined this way, we eliminate the assumption of the inferiority of oppressed groups and the superiority of privileged groups and replace it with a recognition and respect for the value of the particular experiences and perspectives of all groups.

Third, by asserting the positive value of different groups' experiences, the politics of difference makes it possible to look critically at dominant institutions and values from the perspective of oppressed groups. In other words, the experiences and perspectives of oppressed groups provide critical insights into mainstream social institutions and values that can serve as a starting point for reform of those institutions and values. For example, by referring to their members as "brother" or "sister," African Americans engender in their traditional neighborhoods a sense of community and solidarity not found in the highly individualistic mainstream society. As mentioned earlier, feminists find in the human values of nurturing and caring a more superior way of approaching social and ecological relations than the competitive, militarist, and environmentally destructive approach of male-dominated society. The politics of difference takes these critiques by oppressed groups seriously, as a basis for reform of dominant institutions. Such critiques shed light on the ways that dominant institutions should be changed so that they no longer reinforce patterns of privilege and oppression.

Fourth, the politics of difference promotes the value of group solidarity amidst the pervasive individualism of contemporary social life and the politics of assimilation. Assimilationist politics treats each person as an individual, ignoring differences of race, sex, religion, and ethnicity; everyone should be treated equally and evaluated according to his or her individual effort and achievement. It is true that under this politics of assimilation many members of oppressed groups have achieved individual success, even by the standards of privileged groups. However, as we have already learned, many groups continue to be oppressed despite the individual success of some group members. For example, over the last thirty years, Blacks have increased their representation in well-paying occupations such as law, medicine, and engineering. Yet they are still very much underrepresented in these fields and overrepresented in less well-paying occupations like orderlies, taxicab drivers, and janitors. That is why oppressed groups refuse to see these individual successes as evidence that group oppression has been eliminated. Instead of celebrating the success of some of their members, they insist that the celebration wait until their whole group is liberated. In the politics of difference, oppressed groups, in solidarity, struggle for the fundamental institutional changes that will make this liberation possible.

By now, the distinctions between the politics of assimilation and the politics of difference should be clear. Some people might object to the way we have made these distinctions. We anticipate that the strongest objection will be that we have not presented fairly the advantages of a politics of assimilation that strives to transcend or get beyond group differences. Many who support the politics of assimilation do recognize the value of a pluralistic society in which a variety of lifestyles, cultures, and associations can flourish. We do not, however, take issue with this vision of a pluralistic society. What we emphasize is that this vision does not deal with fundamental issues that suggest the need for the politics of difference.

As we have repeated throughout this [article], we think it is counterproductive and dishonest to try to eliminate the public and political significance of group difference in a society in which some groups are more privileged than others. The danger in this approach is that group differences get pushed out of the sphere of public discussion and action and come to be seen as a purely private or non-political matter. When this happens, the problem of oppression of some groups tends to go unaddressed in our public institutions, and patterns of privilege and oppression among groups are reinforced. The politics of difference that we advocate recognizes and takes seriously the public and political importance of group differences, and takes the experiences of oppressed groups as a starting point for reform of our public institutions. The goal of this politics of difference is to change our institutions so that no group is disadvantaged or advantaged due to its distinct culture or capacities, thus ensuring that all groups have the opportunity to participate fully in the nation's social and political institutions.

REDEFINING THE MEANING OF DIFFERENCE IN CONTEMPORARY LIFE

The Risk of Restigmatizing Oppressed Groups

Many people inside and outside the liberation movements we have discussed in this chapter are fearful of the politics of difference and its rejection of the politics of assimilation. The fear of many is that any public admission of the fact that groups are different will be used to justify once again the exclusion and separation of certain kinds of people from mainstream society. Feminists fear that the affirmation of values of caring and nurturing that are associated with motherhood will lead to a call for women to return to the kitchen and the home, places where it is claimed those values can best be utilized.

African Americans fear that an affirmation of their different values and experiences will lead again to a call for separate schools and communities, "where they can be with their own kind." Many in these groups are willing to accept the fact that formal equality (treating everyone the same under the law) reinforces current patterns of advantage. This, they say, is preferable to a politics of difference that risks the restigmatization of certain groups and the reestablishment of separate and unequal spheres for such groups.

We are sympathetic to these fears. It certainly is not unusual in political life for one's ideas, actions, or policies to have unintended negative effects because others have used them to justify ends different from those intended. Nevertheless, we believe that this risk is warranted since the strategy of ignoring group differences in public policy has failed to eliminate the problem of group oppression; the same patterns of privilege and oppression continue to be reproduced. All of which begs the question, Is there a way to avoid this risk of restigmatizing groups and rejustifying their exclusion? We believe there is a solution and it depends on redefining the meaning of difference itself.

Rejecting the Oppressive Meaning of Difference

In order to avoid the risk of recreating the stigma that oppressed groups have faced in the past, the meaning of difference itself must be redefined. In other words, we must change the way people think about differences among groups. In the politics of difference, the meaning of difference itself becomes an issue for political struggle.

There is an oppressive way of understanding difference that has dominated Western thinking about social groups for many centuries. This meaning of difference, which we will call the essentialist meaning, defines social groups in opposition to a normative group—typically the dominant social group. The culture, values, and standards of one social group provide the standards against which all other groups are measured.

The attempt to measure all groups against some universal standard or norm generates a meaning of difference as dichotomy, a relation of two opposites. Thus we have paired categories of groups—men/women, white/Black, healthy/disabled, rich/poor, young/old, civilized/uncivilized, to name a few. Very often, the second term in the pair is defined negatively in relation to the first. Those in the second category are defined as lacking valued qualities of those in the first. There are rational men, and there are irrational women. There are productive, active young people, and there are feeble old people. There is a superior standard of humanity, and there is an inferior one.

This way of thinking about difference as a good/bad opposition in which groups are defined in relation to a supposedly universal norm has oppressive consequences. Some groups are marked out as having different natures, which leads quickly to the assumption that they therefore must have different aspirations and dispositions that fit them for some activities and not others. It also leads to the argument that because nature is static, change is impossible. Women are defined as lacking men's rationality, which justifies their exclusion from high-ranking positions in business and government. People with disabilities are seen as unhealthy or helpless, which justifies isolating them in institutions.

The essentialist meaning of difference just described lies at the heart of racism, sexism, anti-Semitism, homophobia, and other negative attitudes toward specific groups. In these ideologies only the oppressed groups are defined as different. When oppressed groups are thought of as having fundamentally different natures from the "normal" group, it becomes easier for the "normal" group to justify excluding those groups from mainstream institutions and communities. On the other hand, once it is admitted that all groups have some things in common and that no group represents a universal or "normal" standard, it becomes more difficult to justify any group's exclusion from political and social life.

Redefining Difference as Variation

The politics of difference rejects the essentialist definition of difference, which defines it as deviance from a neutral norm and holds that some groups have essentially different natures and aspirations. In the politics of difference, however, group difference is seen as ambiguous and shifting, without clear categories of opposites that narrowly define people. Difference represents variation among groups that have similarities and dissimilarities. Groups are neither completely the same nor complete opposites. In the politics of difference, the meaning of group difference encompasses six key principles:

1. *Group difference is relational.* We can only understand groups in relation to each other. Group differences can be identified when we compare different groups, but no group can be held up as the standard of comparison. Thus, whites are just as specific a group as African Americans or Hispanics, men just as specific as women, able-bodied people just as specific as people with disabilities. Difference does not mean a clear and specific set of attributes that a group shares, but means variation and heterogeneity. It appears as a relationship between groups and the interaction of groups with social institutions.
2. *Group difference is contextual.* That difference is contextual simply means that group differences may be more or less relevant depending on the context or situation in which they come up. In any context, the importance of group difference will depend on the groups being compared and the reasons for the comparison. For example, in the context of athletics, health care, or social service support, wheel chair–bound people are different from

others in terms of the special needs they might have. But in many other contexts, these differences would be unimportant. In the past, people with disabilities were often excluded and segregated in institutions because their physical difference was seen as extending to all their capacities and all facets of their lives. Understanding difference as contextual eliminates this oppressive way of thinking about difference as all-encompassing.

3. *Group difference does not mean exclusion.* An understanding of difference as relational and contextual rejects the possibility of exclusion. No two groups lie exclusively outside each other in their experiences, perspectives, or goals. All groups have overlapping experiences and therefore are always similar in some respects.
4. *Members within a group share affinity for each other, not a fixed set of attributes.* Groups are not defined by a fixed set of characteristics or attributes that all group members share. What makes a group a group is the fact that they have a particular affinity for each other. The people I have an affinity for are simply those who are familiar to me and with whom I feel the most comfortable. Feelings of affinity develop through a social process of interaction and shared experience. People in an affinity group often share common values, norms, and meanings that express their shared experience. No person's affinities are fixed: a person's affinities may shift with changes in his or her life. Likewise, group identities may shift over time with changes in social realities. . . .
5. *Groups define themselves.* Once we reject the idea that groups are defined by a set of common, essential attributes, groups are left to define for themselves what makes their particular group a group. This process of *self*-definition is emancipating in that it allows groups to reclaim a positive meaning for their difference and to decide collectively what they wish to affirm as their culture. Thus, the culture of oppressed groups is no longer defined by dominant groups in negative relation to mainstream culture. Many social movements of oppressed groups have begun this process of redefining their group identity for themselves. Both African American and Native American social movements have sought to redefine and reaffirm their cultural distinctiveness, often reclaiming from the past traditional values and norms that have meaning for them today. Some gays and lesbians are reappropriating the term "queer" and redefining it themselves.
6. *All groups have differences within them.* Our society is highly complex and differentiated, and no group is free of intragroup difference. For instance, a woman who is African American and a lesbian might identify with a variety of social groups—women, African Americans, lesbians. A woman who is Hispanic and heterosexual might have different affinities. Within the context of a social movement such as the women's movement, these differences between women are potential sources of wisdom and enrichment as well as conflict and misunderstanding. Because there is a potential for conflict within groups among persons who identify with more than one group, groups, like society as a whole, must also be attentive to difference. . . .

CONCLUSION

This [article] relies on a handful of clear principles, which we will summarize here. Social justice requires democracy. People should be involved in collective discussion and decision making in all the settings that ask for their obedience to rules—workplaces, schools, neighborhoods, and so on. Unfortunately, these social and political institutions privilege some groups over others. When some groups are more disadvantaged than others, ensuring democracy requires group representation for the disadvantaged. Group representation gives oppressed groups a

PERSONAL ACCOUNT

Memories of Summer Camp

I first set foot on Camp Sunrise as a timid eight-year-old camper along the beautiful shores of a New England lake. Summers at Sunrise became a tradition for the next eight years. Following my sophomore year in high school, I was overjoyed to learn I had been accepted as a counselor in training (CIT). What could be better? I considered the camp, along the shore of a New England lake, my home away from home. Eight weeks at the place I loved most, a place where I could be myself—or so I thought. Camp Sunrise is a Lutheran camp. And my religion? Well, I am a Catholic. I had never encountered a problem because of my religion. As I recall, there were always several nonpracticing Lutheran campers. However, when you are paying hundreds of dollars a week to attend, the camp makes sure every child feels welcome.

Every Sunday the camp held a church service. My Irish Catholic parents, however, had asked that I not receive communion. It was their only request of their Catholic daughter, so I agreed to obey their wishes. The majority of my CIT group was Lutheran, although there were a few Catholics whose parents allowed them to receive communion. On the first Sunday service, I was the only one from my CIT group not to receive communion. I thought nothing of it.

As the CITs were walking back to their tents, however, a bunkmate asked, "How come you didn't take communion?" "Well, my parents asked that I not receive because I am a baptized Catholic," I replied. "Well, do you want to?" she asked. "I don't really know. I just feel that this is the least I can do for them after all they have done for me," I answered, while thinking that the only time the camp focused on Lutheranism was during the Sunday services. At other times Christianity was discussed in general, and I certainly joined the discussion. Her response cut through my stomach like a knife. "Then why do you come here?" she asked before walking away.

I could not believe what I had just heard. I was in shock. It didn't make sense. How could this be happening? I could never imagine being treated this way. Why did she think she belonged here more than I did? This camp was like my second home. I was just as good a counselor as she was whether or not I received communion. I had never been looked down on because of my religious beliefs. I wanted to go home then and there, but I knew better.

I told my CIT trainer about this confrontation. She helped me to understand that no matter where you go in life, if you are not part of the majority, you may be resented for your differences. This, unfortunately, also held true at Sunrise. Nevertheless, I went on to have one of the best summers of my life. I have continued as a counselor, while following my religious beliefs, which do not interfere with my counseling abilities. My peers now understand that my Catholicism is as important to me as Lutheranism is to them, and respect me for my beliefs. However, I will never forget that Sunday of my CIT summer. It still hurts. But I have learned that you can't please everyone and you must hold strong to what is important to you.

Patricia Kelley

voice in setting the public agenda and discussing matters on it. It also helps to ensure just outcomes of the democratic process by making sure that the needs and interests of all groups are expressed.

. . . We have asserted that the ideal of a society that eliminates, transcends, or ignores group difference is both unrealistic and undesirable. Justice in a society with groups requires the social equality of all groups, and mutual and explicit recognition and affirmation of the value of group differences. The politics of difference promotes social equality and undermines group oppression by affirming the value of group difference, attending to group-specific needs, and providing for group representation in social institutions.

The challenges faced by such a politics are formidable. While many public and private institutions have begun to recognize the value of diversity, demands for a real voice for oppressed groups in decision-making processes are often met with fear and hostility. Still, we are hopeful that a politics of difference may be on the horizon. The United States is becoming more diverse, not less. Women and minorities comprise increasing proportions of the labor force and their needs are more and more difficult for employers and public officials to ignore.

However, demographic changes alone are unlikely to induce substantive policy change. Politics matters. While oppressed groups are increasing their representation in political institutions, social movements of oppressed groups will continue to play a critical role in shaping attitudes and dialogues about change and mobilizing the public to act. It is our hope that the ideas [presented here] provide a source of inspiration to social movements. The politics of difference is an alternative vision of politics that challenges the assumption that the present system is the only or best system. It is not meant as a blueprint for change, but as a starting point for dialogue. It provides a standpoint from which we can identify forms of injustice in our current institutions and explore different strategies to remedy them.

READING 42

Facing History, Facing Ourselves

Interracial Justice

Eric K. Yamamoto

If I am not for myself, who will be for me?
If I am not for others, what am I?
And if not now, when?
—*Rabbi Hillel, first-century poem*

Interracial justice entails a hard acknowledgment of ways in which racial groups harm one another, along with affirmative efforts to redress grievances with present-day effects. Set in a larger context of the "wages of whiteness," it encompasses messy, shifting, continual, and often localized efforts at interracial reconciliation. Indeed, for racialized communities in post–civil rights America, interracial justice means "facing history, facing ourselves." And in so doing, it means looking at self-interest ("if I am not for myself, who will be") and then looking beyond ("if I am not for others, what am I").

Framed in this manner, interracial justice is an integral, although often overlooked, component of peaceable relations and coalition building among communities of color. For groups seeking to live together peaceably and work together politically, interracial justice serves in many instances as a bridge between currently felt racial wounds and workable intergroup relations.[1]

To assist in bridging, I connect the conceptual to the practical. Empirical studies reveal that in addition to ideas and ideals, justice is something experienced.[2] It is grounded in gritty racial realities; it is something racial communities struggle with viscerally and intellectually. . . .

FOUR DIMENSIONS OF INTERRACIAL JUSTICE

This [discussion] endeavors to translate theoretical insights into concepts, language, and methods that are useful to both scholars and frontline justice practitioners. That translation takes the form of four dimensions of interracial justice inquiry. These dimensions are not a formula for justice. How justice is conceived and experienced in a relationship is determined by the interactions of the participants and the justice setting in which they interact—by racial realities. These culturally influenced interactions vary from relationship to relationship. What follows, therefore, is neither a list of elements of justice nor a catalog of specific techniques for cross-cultural conflict resolution.

Rather, what follows are the dimensions of an approach for inquiring into and acting on intergroup tensions marked both by conflict and

Eric K. Yamamoto is a professor of law at the William S. Richardson School of Law, University of Hawaii at Manoa.

distrust and by a desire for peaceable and productive relations. These dimensions of interracial justice inquiry are characterized by the four "Rs." The first dimension is *recognition.* It asks racial group members to recognize, and empathize with, the anger and hope of those wounded; to acknowledge the disabling constraints imposed by one group on another and the resulting group wounds; to identify related justice grievances often underlying current group conflict; and to critically examine stock stories of racial group attributes and interracial relations ostensibly legitimating those disabling constraints and justice grievances. The second is *responsibility.* It suggests that amid struggles over identity and power, racial groups can be simultaneously subordinated in some relationships and subordinating in others. In some situations, a group's power is both enlivened and limited by social and economic conditions and political alignments. Responsibility therefore asks racial groups to assess carefully the dynamics of racial group agency in imposing disabling constraints on others and, when appropriate, accepting group responsibility for healing resulting wounds.

The third dimension is *reconstruction.* It entails active steps (performance) toward healing the social and psychological wounds resulting from disabling group constraints. Those performative acts might include apologies by aggressors and, when appropriate, forgiveness by those injured and a joint reframing of stories of group identities and intergroup relations. The fourth dimension, closely related to the third, is *reparation.* It seeks to repair the damage to the material conditions of racial group life in order to attenuate one group's power over another. This means material changes in the structure of the relationship (social, economic, political) to guard against "cheap reconciliation," in which healing efforts are "just talk."...

Recognition

Recognition is akin to the first step in healing a lingering physical wound: a person's suffering must be recognized and the wound carefully assessed.[3] That assessment must include social and psychological inquiry. Long-term pain reflects not only physical feeling but also one's relationships and perceptions of societal norms.[4] ...

One task of recognition is empathy. Members of each group work to understand the woundedness of the other groups' members. The specific goal is for groups to look beneath surface appearances to gain an appreciation for the struggles and hopes of the "other," to understand the other's experiences of oppression and resulting pain and anger, hope and resilience. The larger goal is to begin humanizing the other and transforming the other from object (out there) to subject (in here).[5]

Empathizing with those harmed means recognizing at least two kinds of wounds. One kind of wound is the immediate harm. This harm is the anger, hurt, and material loss resulting from disabling group constraints, such as the denial of a job, the refusal of hotel accommodations, the physical assault over a customer-store owner dispute. A second, more pervasive kind of wound varies for all racialized groups in the United States. It is the pain buried in collective memories of group exclusion from or subjugation within a primarily white-dominated social structure, a deep wound for many now exacerbated by a nonwhite racial group's apparent deployment of oppressive structures.

Empathizing also with those inflicting harm is difficult but necessary. First, those racial groups, too, carry wounds of historical (and, more subtly, current) exclusion and subjugation. Second, particularly in borderland locales, where power flows simultaneously in multiple directions, those groups can be oppressed in some relationships (perhaps even in the relationship with the harmed group in other realms) and oppressive in others. Third, these groups self-inflict psychic or moral wounds by harming, and dividing themselves from, other struggling racial communities while they themselves are struggling for social and economic survival.

How are groups to empathize in this fashion? Mutual storytelling and listening are one means of empathic communication—"perhaps the only basis for gaining an understanding of both ourselves and the hopes and fears of others."[6] Theologian James Cone suggests that sharing stories helps groups transcend day-to-day obstacles to peaceable relations.

> Every people has a story to tell, something to say to themselves, their children, and to the world about how they think and live, as they determine their reason for being. . . . When people can no longer listen to the other people's stories, they become enclosed. . . . And then they feel they must destroy other people's stories.[7]

. . . Think about the stories of Latinas/os after the passage of California's anti-immigrant Proposition 187 initiative. Legal resident immigrants and even citizens were subjected to the vilest epithets, job harassment, and violence. What was the pain of the family of the elderly Latina who suffered a fatal stroke on a public street while under verbal and physical siege by white youths whose anger was unleashed by the California electorate?

Recall also the death of single mother Cynthia Wiggins in Cheektowaga, New York. Think about the story's resonance with many African Americans and the resulting frustration: owners of a suburban shopping mall for eight years vigorously refused the city's requests to allow buses from largely black, inner-city Buffalo to stop on the mall premises (as buses from predominantly white suburban areas were allowed to do). While attempting to get from an inconvenient off-site bus stop to her clerk's job at the mall, Wiggins was killed by a truck as she tried to cross a snow-bordered six-lane freeway without a traffic light. One African American damned the mall owners' eight-year campaign to keep inner-city buses off the mall as "sanitized, guiltless racism."

Think also about a Japanese American's struggles upon his release from a U.S. World War II internment camp. His family had lost everything during their incarceration—home, business, belongings, freedom. His imprisonment with 120,000 others on account of race, without charges or trial, was later recognized by a congressional commission and the courts to have resulted from political agitation, mass hysteria, and racism. After his release, he boarded a public bus. Continuing racial apartheid in America meant that whites sat in the front of the bus, blacks in the back. Where should he sit? In the front as if he were white (or at least free to sit with whites)? Or in the back as if he were black (acknowledging African Americans in their suffering but also accepting their inferior social status)?[8]

Understandably, African Americans might not sympathize with his dilemma, since the Japanese American appeared to have a choice (front or back of the bus), and either choice for him still meant the continuing legalized subordination of African Americans. When faced with this story, African Americans nevertheless might empathize with the difficulty of his choice in light of his historical situation, wonder whether Asian Americans face similar choices today, ponder what African Americans might do under similar circumstances, and contemplate whether all communities of color at least sometimes face related dilemmas (whether some middle-class African Americans, for instance, experience an affiliational dilemma concerning poor blacks).

In short, the first recognition task is for groups to empathize, not sympathize; to listen, not analyze; to acknowledge, not blame. The result of "entering into the pain of the other," the exchange of pain, is the kind of "deepened understanding of the other and of oneself" that makes reconciliation possible.[9] . . .

Interrogating Present-Day Intergroup Tensions and Underlying Justice Grievances A second recognition task complements empathy with critical sociolegal inquiry. It asks racial groups to interrogate critically both the particular/contextual and structural/discursive aspects of a relationship in controversy. This is the critical analysis of intergroup histories underlying present-day conflicts.

Interrogation begins with sometimes straightforward, sometimes complicated assessments of the particulars of a controversy. The assessments are basic journalism. Who, for example, are the principals, and who are the aligned interests in an African American–organized boycott of an inner-city store owned by a Korean American woman? What is the specific dispute about? How did it arise? In what locale? What legal claims might be asserted? How are the principals dealing with the initial dispute, and how and why is it escalating? How might it be resolved, according to what principles and with what intervention?

This inquiry also examines the agendas and reactions of those with power—politicians, bureaucrats, police, business, clergy, community organizations, and media. In related fashion, it scrutinizes the interests, histories, and methods of individuals (community leaders, mediators, social workers, lawyers) and institutions (mediation centers, courts, schools, community organizations, churches) engaged in dispute resolution.

The interrogation of these particulars then broadens to sketch the controversy's socioeconomic setting. How do the racial demographics and political economy of the area and the class and gender of the principals shape the conflict? How does the conflict relate to others in the local area, the region, the country? . . .

The examination of the controversy's particulars and context then shifts to the stock stories that groups themselves tell to explain the conflict and justify the groups' responses. Stock stories are narratives shaped, told, and embraced by groups about themselves and others. They are usually a conglomeration of group members' selective historical recollections, partial information about events and socioeconomic conditions, and speculations about the future. Some of these narratives are tied to time and place; some transcend temporal and physical boundaries. As forms of cultural representation, the narratives create social identities for the group members. They also influence the dynamics of interracial relations by providing the lens through which group members see and understand other groups.[10]

For instance, African Americans and Korean American grocery store owners tell stock stories about their interactions. One story told by some African Americans is that immigrant Korean grocers receive government and bank financial support unavailable to African Americans and that this support enables "foreigners" to displace black entrepreneurs and exploit and disrespect black customers.[11] It is through this story's lens that some African Americans view Korean American merchants and, with limited investigation or negotiation, justify short-term store boycotts and long-term takeover strategies. A competing story told by some Korean American merchants is that young, urban blacks are not interested in getting a job, belong to gangs, steal, and threaten violence to get their way and that adult African Americans lack the business values to be successful entrepreneurs.[12] It is through this story's lens that some Korean Americans see young African American store patrons, like Latasha Harlins, and justify their suspicious and sometimes violent treatment of African Americans.

These stock stories and others like them are constructed from a melange of direct experiences, ancestral memory, rumor, the written word, and media images. In simplified yet important ways, the stories shape how groups comprehend their and others' justice grievances, inform perpetrator-victim identities, and legitimate occasionally harsh actions toward one another—witness African Americans' apparent targeting of Korean American stores for burning after the first Rodney King police trial as well as store owner Soon Ja Du's fear of young African Americans and her shooting of Harlins. . . .

The decoding of stock stories informing specific interracial conflicts sometimes reveals shaky or even illusory factual bases. Inner-city

Korean American store owners do not receive private bank or government financial support unavailable to African American entrepreneurs. African Americans are willing to work, and exceedingly few in inner cities are gang members intent on ripping off neighborhood stores; many, despite economic discrimination, are capable entrepreneurs. In light of the shaky and misleading factual foundations of many stock stories, Harlon Dalton asks African Americans and Asian Americans to carefully analyze each other's racial conditions and not "ignore the true circumstances in which [the groups] find themselves." His accounts are worth repeating at length. Concerning Asian Americans:

> One can, of course, point to Asian-American success stories. But there are also Asian-American immigrants, including males from Korea, Vietnam, and the Philippines, who are economically no better off on average than African-Americans . . . [N]early half of Southeast Asian immigrants live in poverty with annual income below ten thousand dollars. Moreover, many of the success stories rely on incomplete or misleading data. For example, comparisons of median family income do not take account of the fact that immigrants from Japan, China, and Korea have more workers per family than do African-Americans (or Whites. . .). . . .
>
> Moreover, it is a mistake to assume that Asian-Americans who have succeeded economically have thereby been exempted from racism. Ask anyone who has been shunted into a particular job category or denied admission to an elite school based solely on her Asian appearance and name. . . .
>
> Not only does the bandying about of the "model-minority myth" work to keep African-Americans in their place and to sow dissension between them and Asian-Americans. It tends to keep Asian-Americans in their place as well. After all, if they are being held out as a model, how can they complain? . . .

In addition to revealing shaky factual accounts and often differing historical grievances and claims, the interrogation of stock stories sometimes also illuminates purposeful distortions of history by political leaders in order to legitimate continuing oppression. For example, critical inquiry revealed a tortuous remaking of history integral to postcommunism ethnic and religious violence in the Balkan states. The International Commission on the Balkans found that Balkan leaders—Serbian president Slobodan Milosevic, Croatian president Fanjo Tudjman, and Bosnia Serb leader Radovan Karadzic—identified ancestral and religious strife as the main sources of recent atrocities. The commission also found that the political leaders' specific characterizations of ancestral strife were unsupported by historical circumstances. The postcommunist politicians deployed falsely constructed ancient enmities to "justify the unjustifiable." According to the commission, the politicians "have invoked 'ancient hatreds' to pursue their respective nationalist agendas and deliberately used their propaganda machines to justify the unjustifiable: the use of violence for territorial conquest, the expulsion of the 'other peoples,' and the perpetuation of authoritarian systems of power."[13]

Perhaps most important, the critical interrogation of stock stories often reveals the political and cultural shaping of those stories and the complexity and malleability of the group memories sustaining them. Groups often recall events, relationships, and institutional practices in widely divergent ways. Social-psychological study of collective memory suggests that groups in conflict filter and twist, recall and forget "information," both in reframing shameful past acts to lessen perpetrator responsibility and in intensifying continued suffering to enhance victim status. As implied by Dalton's deconstructed stories of Asian Americans and African Americans, collective memory not only vivifies a group's past; it also remakes group narratives and thereby situates a group's current relationships with others along a power hierarchy. It contributes to shaping the meanings of group, community, and nation[14] and attendant understandings of culpability and harm. How groups shape these meanings is integral to how groups understand disabling constraints and resulting intergroup grievances. The unraveling of stock stories, including collective memories, thus in part aims to unpack these understandings.

Empathizing with others, critically interrogating particulars and context, and unraveling stock stories advance the recognition process of interracial justice. They open fresh possibilities for exploring racial group agency in the generation of intergroup grievances and responsibility for racial wounds and for healing.

Responsibility

. . . Sometimes the line between perpetrators and victims is brightly marked, with the group's responsibility for racial harms easily attributable and confession clearly called for. In 1997 Texaco Company's white treasurer was caught on tape making derogatory comments about African Americans while planning to destroy smoking-gun corporate documents sought by African American employees for their class action race discrimination lawsuit.[15] Texaco's president immediately apologized to African American employees and customers (later partially recanted) and settled the suit. In the 1990s Native Hawaiians called for and received "a clear acknowledgement of the United States' responsibility for the overthrow of the Hawaiian native government in 1893" and the harmful effects of the annexation of Hawaii and the confiscation of Hawaiian government and crown lands in 1900.[16]

At other times, this line blurs with changing circumstances. Since power often flows in multiple directions in a relationship, along varying social and political axes, a racial group can be both subordinated in some respects and an agent of subordination in others. Especially in these situations, critical analysis of group agency and responsibility is in order. . . .

The Western ethic of individualism, supported by the law's emphasis on individual rights, militates against the acceptance of group responsibility. Even more important, the sincere acceptance of responsibility, or confession, reallocates group power. Laying "oneself open is nothing less than an act of disarmament. You put down the weapons you employed to dominate others; you renounce the power you gained" over others.[17] Aggressor groups, including national governments, concerned about power loss, employ the psychological device of denial to avoid moral consequences. In addition, according to Raphael Moses's account of a healing workshop attended by Palestinians and Israelis, even when group members desire some form of healing, "each side comes to a fear . . . that if they were to 'admit' mistakes and wrongdoing, this would weaken [the] position" of their group or "likely be misused for propaganda or political purpose."[18]

It is therefore predictable that for political reasons members of aggressor groups often resist responsibility for hurts inflicted on members of other groups. Cognitive psychology suggests an additional reason. Group members sometimes lack conscious knowledge of wrongdoing: "the human mind defends itself against the discomfort of guilt by denying or refusing to recognize those ideas, wishes, and beliefs that conflict with what the individual has learned is good or right." This idea is reinforced by a "strain theory" of unconscious racism—in which the recognition of one's racism collides with one's sanguine self-perception of egalitarianism, and the resulting strain causes one to deny the racism. In this view, those meanings and values that are most deeply ingrained in the culture are transmitted through tacit understandings.[19]

A final impediment to a group acceptance of responsibility of another's justice grievances is the pull of legal culture. . . . American law focuses on individual, not group, rights and duties. Equally important, the assignment of fault, rather than the acknowledgment of responsibility, drives the formal legal system. Legal remedies flow from assessments of liability that turn on judicial findings of fault. Wrongdoer acknowledgment of fault is superfluous. When legal claims are tried to judgment, juries or judges evaluate evidence and "find" culpability. When claims are settled through negotiation, the settlement agreement almost always states that the charged wrongdoer "admits no liability." When it finds fault, the legal system imposes the acknowledgment of wrongdoing, often in the face of continuing refutation. Voluntary wrongdoer acknowledgment thus lies beyond the legal conception of justice. Law, enforced by state authority, makes no claim on parties jointly to analyze historical roots of conflict, recognize injustice, or accept responsibility. This cultural predilection, or resistance, usually unspoken, presents another formidable obstacle to group acceptance of responsibility for justice grievances.

In light of these difficulties, a group's acceptance of responsibility for addressing justice grievances might, in some instances, be broadened to include responsibility for helping heal racial wounds impeding peaceable and productive intergroup interactions, regardless of their source. In this sense, responsibility is broader than a group's obligation to remedy the harms its members inflict on others. It means a commitment to assist in healing another group's wounds, even wounds inflicted principally by groups outside the immediate relationship, not necessarily for purposes of redress but for purposes of community building. It reflects the recognition of a dual reality in which racial wounds are inflicted by multiple sources (particularly in settings with a history of white dominance) and in which racial healing begins in the immediate relationship (regardless of the sources of conflict).

The Asian American churches' apology resolution, for example, apologized for Asian American complicity in the cultural and economic subordination of Native Hawaiians following the United States–aided overthrow of the Hawaiian nation. The clergy authors of the resolution committed the churches to helping heal Hawaiian wounds in and beyond the church, immense social wounds for which Asian American responsibility was proportionately small (compared with the responsibility of the U.S. government and the former ruling white oligarchy).

In other settings, acceptance of broader healing responsibility by Asian Americans might mean empathizing with and a commitment to assisting African Americans in their efforts to heal the continuing wounds of slavery and Jim Crow segregation—possibly including support for African American reparations, for affirmative action for black students and contractors or for African American city council candidates. For African Americans and Latinas/os, accepting some responsibility for healing Asian American wounds inflicted by historical and continuing anti-Asian sentiment in America might include a commitment to oppose efforts to tar all Asian Americans with the brush of suspicious foreignness—efforts such as the vituperative Republican-controlled and Democrat-supported investigation into illegal "Asian" campaign contributions. For African Americans and Asian Americans, acceptance of broader responsibility might mean a greater commitment to resist English Only initiatives excluding Latina/o immigrants from full participation in social and economic life. For all three groups, acceptance of this responsibility might mean supporting indigenous peoples' intensifying struggles against states and the United States over various forms of economic and political sovereignty.

Reconstruction

. . . Reconstructive action proceeds in two parts. The first is mutuality of performance, often in the form of apology by those responsible and corresponding forgiveness by those harmed.[20] The second part, frequently overlooked, is efforts to remake and retell stories about the self, the other, and the relationship.

Apology and Forgiveness

Apology In his sophisticated sociological study of apologies, Nicholas Tavuchis describes the main function of an apology in terms of restoring group membership. Membership in a community depends on validation by other community members. Immediate conflicts and underlying grievances present obstacles to validation. They generate perpetrator and victim identities and fuel long-term enmities, thereby dismembering community relationships. An apology means re-membering the community, a "painful re-membering, literally of being mindful again, of what we were and had as members and, at the same time, what we have jeopardized or lost by virtue of our offensive . . . action."[21] Part of that re-membering is recalling; part of it is seeking forgiveness for harmful acts threatening community belonging.[22] . . .

A group apology and responsive forgiveness are a kind of social contract, securing common moral ground and committing to group harmony over individual desires.[23] That commitment requires participants to give up something personal to secure a larger collective good. Aggressors must give up self-righteousness and dominating power; those harmed must relinquish resentment and victim status. Group harmony (forward looking, relationally directed) is deemed more important than individual rights (backward looking, individually oriented).

The Southern Baptist apology to African Americans, for example, encouraged group reconciliation. By apologizing for past historical wrongs, the leaders of the church spoke not only on behalf of themselves but also for others and their ancestors. Although not all Southern Baptists felt remorse or even agreed that an apology for support of slavery was appropriate, the denomination's apology allowed group members to express collective remorse for oppressive actions to begin healing historic wounds.

In a local setting, a letter by a Japanese American minister and former immigrant that recounted his apology to Chinese immigrant congregants in Los Angeles illustrates the potency of these intergroup apology dynamics.

> My Personal Background
>
> I was born in Osaka, Japan. My family immigrated to the United States in 1956. 1 have lived in the Los Angeles area ever since.
>
> My Experience
>
> I was asked to minister at a Chinese church in Westminster last November. This congregation was primarily composed of first and second generation Chinese, so that the majority spoke in Chinese and I had to speak with the aid of a translator.
>
> Before the meeting, the Lord impressed on my heart the need to ask forgiveness on behalf of the Japanese for the atrocities committed against the Chinese people before and during World War II. After this word came from the Lord I sensed that this might be very significant, as my father served in Manchuria with the Japanese during World War II.
>
> Thus, I asked the people at the beginning of my ministry to forgive me on behalf of the Japanese for the acts they committed. As I spoke, the Lord seemed to give me the words to speak: "You must have been hurt deeply, losing friends and family, losing property, seeing destruction and terror." As I continued, the majority of the congregation began to weep; then, I found myself welling up and deep emotions and I, too, began to weep.
>
> I don't quite understand the dynamics of what transpired that evening, but the Lord, indeed, gave us great release.
>
> R. Shin Asami[24]

While potentially transformative in these kinds of situations in which no formal claims are asserted, the promise of intergroup apologies is undermined by Western legal culture. In the United States, a genuine apology is neither recognized as a legitimate legal remedy nor perceived as a component of justice. Instead, Western law views an apology as an "admission of liability that complicates the process of settlement—a process in which the denial of liability serves as a lever to negotiate an acceptable level of damages." An individual may risk personal liability by electing to apologize and focus on restoring the broken relationship; hence the tentativeness of many American race apologies—"I apologize for comments you may have perceived as insensitive."[25]

In light of these difficulties, Hiroshi Wagatsuma and Arthur Rosett explore the promise and limitations of apologies in legal disputes. In their cross-cultural social-psychological study, they recognize that apologies alone for some kinds of harms are clearly inadequate. They also recognize, however, that traditional common law remedies are sometimes unsatisfactory and that an apology may help rebuild human relationships.

To explain this point, Wagatsuma and Rosett describe the differing cultural perceptions of apologies in the American and Japanese legal systems. Americans tend to view apologies as simply self-expression. They rely on adversarial adjudication and court pronouncements to determine a person's rights and duties. Paying damages or accepting punishment ends their personal responsibility. Expression of contrition is unnecessary. In addition, the absence of apology in the American legal system may be tied to the legal system's translation of psychic hurts into losses compensable by monetary awards. As a result, if "any legal authority—perhaps a judge or the police—[were] to seek an apology from an American as part of the settlement of a serious dispute, such an apology would probably be perceived as either insincere, personally degrading or obsequious."[26]

By contrast, the Japanese legal system attaches great significance to the act of apologizing as an acknowledgement of group harmony. The Japanese are less concerned about compensation than reparation—repairing harm to both the relationship and the social order. In the Japanese legal system, an offer to compensate or accept punishment without an apology is considered insincere.[27]

The American and Japanese legal systems are embedded in differing cultural systems with differing ideas about legal wrongs, injuries, and remedies. Suggestions about cross-system borrowing are fraught with the risk of incoherence. Indeed, a suggestion that the American legal system immediately and fully embrace remedial apologies is meaningless in light of the system's focus on individual rights, monetary remedies, and adversarial dispute resolution. Nevertheless, America's justice systems—including its legal system—can begin to rethink intergroup justice by scrutinizing other disciplines' recognition of selective apologies as viable means for at least partially redressing past wrongs. As described earlier, social psychology finds that when genuine, the act of apologizing has significant therapeutic value. Christian theology recognizes that the path to reconciliation begins with the act of expressing contrition. The indigenous Hawaiian practice of ho'oponopono similarly prescribes "mihi, . . . [the] sincere confession of wrongdoing and the seeking of forgiveness," as a key step toward reconciliation. Peace studies stresses the importance of group apologies for redressing human rights abuses and restoring breaches in the polity. For these disciplines, the performative "words 'I'm sorry' and 'we were wrong' can, if sincere, be profoundly therapeutic—even if made years after the offense by people who didn't do it."[28] . . .

Forgiveness Three choices face a person who has suffered serious harm. The first is revenge. Often driven by bitterness, this option creates formidable obstacles to healing. The second choice is martyrdom or the passive embrace of victimhood. This option creates an initial feeling of power and entitlement but ultimately is self-defeating.

The third choice is forgiveness. Indeed, whether acts of apology and reparation help rebuild a relationship depends in part on their capacity to elicit some form of forgiveness. Forgiveness is "not an arbitrary, free act of pardon given out of the unilateral generosity of the forgiver—forgiveness is an interpersonal transaction between two parties."[29] This transactional understanding of forgiveness highlights the relational nature of intergroup grievance and reconciliation. It underscores the notion that restoration of a relationship is a struggle for all involved and that the responsive act of forgiveness furthers a difficult process of mutual transformation. . . .

This process of mutual liberation transforms the relationship by altering the balance of power.

The perpetrator and the victim undertake "acts of disarmament" in front of the other, a painful process that requires vulnerability and internal strength. For the perpetrator, it means relinquishing power and accepting responsibility for participation in the oppression of another group. For the victim, it means reopening and cleansing old wounds and returning to the source of painful memories to release them. Forgiveness is "more than an encounter; it is an exchange of pain. The result is a deepened understanding of the other and of oneself. By entering into the pain of the other an overwhelming liberation takes place."[30] It is the process of looking into the heart of one's pain and the willingness to release oneself from the constraints of the past in order to heal. . . .

Reparation

Reparation is the fourth dimension of interracial justice. In its singular form, reparation means "repair." It encompasses both acts of repairing damage to the material conditions of racial group life—transferring money and land, building schools and medical clinics, allowing unfettered voting—and of restoring injured human psyches—enabling those harmed to live with, but not in, history.

So viewed, reparation means transformation. It avoids "the traps of individualism, neutrality and indeterminacy that plague many mainstream concepts of rights or legal principles."[31] Reparation is grounded in group, rather than individual, rights and responsibilities and provides tangible benefits to those wronged by those in power. Properly cast, reparation targets substantive barriers to liberty—education, housing, medical care, employment, cultural preservation, political participation. In addition, coupled with acknowledgment and apology, reparation can be transformative because of what it symbolizes: reparation "condemns exploitation and adopts a vision of a more just world."

For these reasons, some scholars argue that reparation is an essential part of redress for justice grievances. Manning Marable contends that the post–Civil War Reconstruction eventually failed because the federal government refused to support broad land grant reparations to African Americans. Without large-scale land redistribution (forty acres and a mule), the Emancipation, the Fourteenth Amendment, and civil rights statutes failed to uplift blacks socially and economically. Marable observes that because economic power was held by whites, equality in political and social relations was an illusion. Without change in the material conditions of racial life, "reconciliation [had] meaning only for the privileged in society."[32]. . .

[But] symbolic compensation without accompanying efforts to repair damaged conditions of racial group life is likely to be labeled insincere. For instance, despite modest monetary restitution, the Japanese government's refusal to acknowledge responsibility for World War II crimes or to take active measures to rehabilitate surviving victims has generated charges of insincerity and foot-dragging. For many, the government's refusal to express regret undermines the possibility of forgiveness and prospects for healing.[33] By contrast, Germany's efforts to heal the wounds of Jewish Holocaust survivors extends beyond monetary reparations. The German government has also opened its war archives, passed legislation barring race hatred, overhauled Holocaust educational materials, and commemorated war victims.

Reparation, as repair, therefore aims for more than a monetary salve for those hurting. Multifaceted reparations are a vehicle, along with an apology, for groups in conflict to rebuild their relationship through attitudinal changes and institutional restructuring.[34] In terms of changed attitudes, making apologies part of a group's public history—as the Southern Baptists did through their formal apology to African Americans—is one means of reparation. Committing to end derogatory stereotyping of racial others—as the Asian American churches' proposed apology resolution did—is another.

In terms of dismantling disabling social structures or supporting empowering ones, reparation might mean, as it does in South Africa, the government's new struggling but active Reconstruction and Development Programme aimed at redistributing land; changing education, health, and housing policies; and establishing public and private affirmative action programs.[35] In the United States, it might mean supporting rather than challenging affirmative action programs in education and employment whose primary beneficiaries are from other communities of color. It might mean politicians appointing and local businesses hiring members of other racial groups. Or it might also mean the formation of inner-city business and political coalitions to expand entrepreneurial opportunities. . . .

Joe Singer identifies a dilemma of reparation that bears directly on [one] concern about reconciliation. He asks, "Will reparation right a wrong" and aid healing, or "will it create further victimization of the oppressed group," exacerbating the wound?[36] Seeing those dual possibilities in all reparation efforts, Singer explores the potential for further victimization in two contemporary situations.

Singer describes Jews' highly publicized demands in 1997 that Swiss banks account for and restore Jewish money and gold held by the banks for Nazis during World War II. Acknowledgment and restitution by the banks would treat Jews as worthy human beings with rights, including the right to own property. Restitution counters the anti-Semitic myth of Jews misappropriating the property of others. Jewish "victimhood is acknowledged, but Jews are not treated as mere victims, but as agents in calling Swiss banks to account." One problem, however, is that Jews' claims for monetary restitution resurrect for some the harsh historical stereotypes of them "as money-grubbing, as having both accumulated secret bank accounts in the past and as caring now about nothing more than money." Another, and broader, problem is that continuing Jewish reparations claims spark reparations claims by other groups (such as the Hungarian gypsies who were exterminated by the Nazis), breeding resentment toward the Jews when their claims are not satisfied.[37]

Singer also examines the reparation demands by African Americans. Some understand those demands as a call for redress of past injustice, whereas others see them as a "refusal to grow up." The result, evident in the volatile affirmative action debates, is that "calls to repair the current effects of past injustice are met with derisory denials that continuing injustice exists and that the problems of African Americans are now purely of their own making." As Singer observes about the mixed healing potential in both situations, the "very thing that restoration is intended to combat may be the result of the demand for restoration."[38]

In addition, even when individuals' psychic wounds are salved and there is no further victimization, reparation can mask lurking dangers. When reparation is little more than a monetary buy-off of protest, an assuaging of dominant group guilt without attitudinal and institutional restructuring, reparation can ultimately help perpetuate the institutional power structures and public attitudes that suppress freedom for those whom society views as different and vulnerable. Concerning these hidden risks of monetary reparations for Japanese American internees,

> the "danger lies in the possibility of enabling people to 'feel good' about each other" for the moment, "while leaving undisturbed the attendant social realities" creating the underlying conflict. . . . redress and reparations could in the long term "unwittingly be seduced into becoming one more means of social control that attempts to neutralize the need to strive for justice."[39]

Notwithstanding legal and political objections and larger social concerns, reparation has been attempted with increasing frequency in recent years. Reparatory efforts include the United Church of Christ's monetary and land reparations to indigenous Hawaiians (nongovernmental reparations), the Florida legislature's monetary reparations for African American survivors of the Rosewood massacre (state and local government), the United States' reparations to Japanese Americans wrongfully interned during World War II (federal government), and the British government's monetary payments to New Zealand's

Maoris (former colonial government). Pending reparation claims in the United States can be characterized as societal (including African Americans' claims for the continuing harms of slavery and Native Hawaiians' claims for the overthrow of the sovereign Hawaiian nation) and community based (including Korean American merchants' claims for burned stores and African Americans' claims of economic exploitation).

Studies of the sociopsychological effects of reparation for Japanese American internees and initial reports of other reparation efforts indicate significant benefits accruing to the beneficiaries.[40] One woman expressed how redress had at last "freed her soul." Other beneficiaries responded with a collective sigh of relief. Ben Takeshita, for instance, expressed the sentiments of many when he said that although monetary payment "could not begin to compensate. . . for his . . . lost freedom, property, livelihood or the stigma of disloyalty," it demonstrated the sincerity of the government's apology.[41]

Because of both the dangers and the transformative potential, the reparation dimension of interracial justice offers two insights into specific reparation efforts. One is normative: that acts of reparation by government or groups must result over time in a restructuring of the institutions and relationships that gave rise to the underlying justice grievance. Otherwise, as a philosophical and practical matter, reparations cannot be effective in addressing root problems of misuse of power, particularly in the maintenance of oppressive systemic structures, or integrated symbolically into a group's (or government's) moral foundation for responding to intergroup conflicts or for urging others to restructure oppressive relationships.

A second insight is descriptive: Restructuring those institutions and changing societal attitudes will not flow naturally and inevitably from the reparations themselves. Dominant interests, whether government or private, will cast reparation in ways that tend to perpetuate existing power structures and relationships. Therefore, those benefiting from specific reparations need to draw on the material benefits of reparations and the political insights and commitments derived from their particular reparations process and join with others to push for bureaucratic, legal, and attitudinal restructuring—to push for material change. And their efforts must extend beyond their own repair.

This brings to mind a popular phrase, which I suggest inverting. Reparation can bridge the recognition and reconstruction dimensions of interracial justice if recipients "think locally and act globally": thinking locally to grasp the experiential lessons of power and value learned throughout the hands-on process of the reparation drive and acting globally to link with others different in culture or race but similar in efforts to restructure attitudes and institutions.

For racial communities, the four dimensions of interracial justice inquiry just described mean facing history, facing ourselves. And in the words of Rabbi Hillel, "If not now, when?"

NOTES

1. Harlon Dalton, *Racial Healing: Confronting the Fear between Blacks and Whites* (1995), p. 65. See also Sally Engle Merry and Neal Milner, *The Possibility of Popular Justice* (1995), p. 361; John Paul Ledarach and Ron Kraybill, *The Paradox of Popular Justice: A Practitioner's View* (1995), pp. 357–78.
2. E. Allen Lind and Tom Tyler, *The Social Psychology of Procedural Justice* (1988).
3. See generally Dalton, *Racial Healing* (using healing metaphor in discussing racial conflict); Rhonda V. Magee, "The Master's Tools, From the Bottom Up: Response to African American Reparations Theory in Mainstream and Outsider Remedies Discourse," 79 *Va. L. Rev.* 863, 879 (1993) ("Opening old wounds [is] necessary to cure current ills").
4. Arthur Kleinman, *The Illness Narratives: Suffering, Healing, and the Human Condition* (1989).
5. See generally Toni Massaro, "Empathy, Legal Storytelling, and the Rule of Law: New Words, Old Wounds?" 87 *Mich. L. Rev.* 2099 (1989) (describing empathy, legal justice and the "call to context").

6. Charles Villa-Vicencio, "Telling One Another Stories: Toward a Theology of Reconciliation," in Greg Baum and Harold Wells, eds., *The Reconciliation of Peoples: Challenge to the Churches* (1997), p. 31.
7. James Cone, *God of the Oppressed* (1995), pp. 102–3.
8. David Mura, *Where the Body Meets the Memory* (1995) (describing his father's difficult choice, while on a pass from the internment camp, to sit in the front of the bus).
9. Mueller-Fahrenholz, *The Art of Forgiveness,* p. 26.
10. Richard Delgado, "Legal Storytelling: Storytelling for Oppositionists and Others: A Plea for Narrative," 87 *Mich. L. Rev.* 2411 (1989); Eric K. Yamamoto, Moses Haia, and Donna Kalama, "Courts and the Cultural Performance: Native Hawaiians' Uncertain Federal and State Law Rights to Sue," 16 *U. Haw. L. Rev.* 1 (1994).
11. Reginald Leamon Robinson, "'The Other Against Itself': Deconstructing the Violent Discourse between Korean and African-Americans," 67 *S. Cal. L. Rev.* 15 (1993).
12. *People v. Superior Court of Los Angeles County* (Soon Ja Du), 5 Cal. App. 4th 822 (1993).
13. Carnegie Endowment for International Peace, *Unfinished Peace: Report of the International Commission on the Balkans* (1996).
14. See Iwona Irwin-Zarecka, *Frames of Remembrance: The Dynamics of Collective Memory* (1994).
15. Jack E. White, "Texaco's High-Octane Racism Problems," *Time,* November 25, 1996, p. 33.
16. Ramon Lopez-Reyes, "The Demise of the Hawaiian Kingdom: A Psycho-Cultural Analysis and Moral Legacy (Something Lost, Something Owed)," 18 *Haw. Bar J.* 3, 19 (1983).
17. Mueller-Fahrenholz, *The Art of Forgiveness*, p. 26.
18. Rafael Moses, "Acknowledgment: The Balm of Narcissistic Hurts," *Austin Riggs Center Review* 3 (1990): 5–6.
19. See Charles R. Lawrence III, "The Id, the Ego, and Equal Protection: Reckoning with Unconscious Racism," 39 *Stan. L. Rev.* 317, 322 (citing S. Freud, *The Ego and the Id*, in vol. 3 of *The Standard Edition of the Complete Psychological Works of Sigmund Freud*, ed. J. Strachey [1951], p. 19).
20. Different cultures shape performative steps differently. See, for example, Hiroshi Wagatsuma and Arthur Rosett, "The Implications of Apology: Law and Culture in Japan and the United States," 20 *Law & Soc. Rev*. 461 (1986) (describing Japanese and American cultural differences and the effect of those differences on approaches to dispute resolution).
21. Nicholas Tavuchis, *Mea Culpa: A Sociology of Apology and Reconciliation* (1991), p. 8.
22. Ibid. p. 18.
23. Mark O'Keefe and Tom Bates, "Sorry about That," *Portland Oregonian,* July 23, 1995, p. F01.
24. Letter by Rev. Shin Asami, quoted in Dawson, *Healing America's Wounds,* pp. 261–62.
25. Wagatsuma and Rosett, "The Implications of Apology," pp. 248, 496.
26. Ibid. pp. 462, 464, 492.
27. Ibid. pp. 462, 473, 492.
28. O'Keefe and Bates, "Sorry about That," p. F01. Elazar Barkan also suggests that even in cases without the redistribution of resources, the injured group that receives a public apology or open admission of guilt at a minimum "benefits from the . . . recognition of its victimization and of its previously ignored history, which consequently becomes part of global history" (Elazar Barkan, "Payback Time: Restitution and the Moral Economy of Nations," *Tikkun,* September 19, 1996, p. 52).
29. David W. Augsburger, *Conflict Mediation across Cultures: Pathways and Patterns* (1992), p. 283. See also Donald W. Shriver Jr., *An Ethic for Enemies: Forgiveness in Politics* (1995), p. 178.
30. Mueller-Fahrenholz, *The Art of Forgiveness,* p. 26.
31. Mari Matsuda, "Looking to the Bottom: Critical Legal Studies and Reparations," 22 *Harv. C.R.–C.L. L. Rev.* 323, 391, 393–94 (1987). See also Magee, "The Master's Tools," p. 913 ("Reparations would be powerful symbols of white group responsibility for the continued degradation of African American life and culture").
32. Manning Marable, *Race, Reform and Rebellion: The Second Reconstruction in Black America—1945–1990,* 2d ed. (1991), pp. 6, 24.
33. See Tong Yu, "Reparations for Former Comfort Women of World War II," 36 *Harv. Int'l L. J.* 528, 539 (1995).
34. John Stevens Keali'iwahamana Hoag, "The Moral, Historical and Theoretical Framework for

Restitution and Reparation for Native Hawaiians," April 28, 1995 (unpublished paper), p. 19. Elazar Barkan observes that injured groups often seek to achieve a more moderate goal than full retroactive justice, such as lessening conflict or improving their economic condition (Barkan, "Payback Time," p. 52).
35. John de Gruchy, "The Dialectic of Reconciliation: Church and the Transition to Democracy in South Africa," in Baum and Wells, *Reconciliation of Peoples,* p. 26.
36. Joseph Singer, "Reparation," April 10, 1997 (unpublished manuscript), pp. 2–3.
37. Alex Bundy, "Gypsies Demand Compensation for Suffering during Holocaust," *Honolulu Advertiser,* August 4, 1997, p. A10.
38. Singer, "Reparation," pp. 3, 4.
39. Eric K. Yamamoto, "Friend, Foe or Something Else: Social Meanings of Redress and Reparations," 20 *Denv. J. Int'l. Law. & Pol.* 223–24, 232 (1992).
40. Ibid. pp. 224, 227.
41. Tavuchis, *Mea Culpa,* p. 107 (quoting Ben Takeshita).

The Economy

READING 43

The Possessive Investment in Whiteness

How White People Profit from Identity Politics

George Lipsitz

Whiteness is everywhere in U.S. culture, but it is very hard to see. As Richard Dyer suggests, "[W]hite power secures its dominance by seeming not to be anything in particular."[1] As the unmarked category against which difference is constructed, whiteness never has to speak its name, never has to acknowledge its role as an organizing principle in social and cultural relations.[2] To identify, analyze, and oppose the destructive consequences of whiteness, we need what Walter Benjamin called "presence of mind." Benjamin wrote that people visit fortunetellers less out of a desire to know the future than out of a fear of not noticing some important aspect of the present. "Presence of mind," he suggested, "is an abstract of the future, and precise awareness of the present moment more decisive than foreknowledge of the most distant events."[3] In U.S. society at this time, precise awareness of the present moment requires an understanding of the existence and the destructive consequences of the possessive investment in whiteness that surreptitiously shapes so much of our public and private lives." . . .

. . . The possessive investment is not simply the residue of conquest and colonialism, of slavery and segregation, of immigrant exclusion and "Indian" extermination. Contemporary whiteness and its rewards have been created and re-created by policies adopted long after the emancipation of slaves in the 1860s and even after the outlawing of *de jure* segregation in the 1960s. There has always been racism in the United States, but it has not always been the same racism. Political and cultural struggles over power have shaped the contours and dimensions of racism differently in different eras. Antiracist mobilizations during the Civil War and civil rights eras meaningfully curtailed the reach and scope of white supremacy, but in each case reactionary forces engineered a renewal of racism, albeit in new forms, during succeeding decades. Racism has changed over time, taking on different forms and serving different social purposes in each time period.

George Lipsitz is a professor of ethnic studies at the University of California, San Diego.

Contemporary racism has been created anew in many ways over the past five decades, but most dramatically by the putatively race-neutral, liberal, social democratic reforms of the New Deal Era and by the more overtly race-conscious neoconservative reactions against liberalism since the Nixon years. It is a mistake to posit a gradual and inevitable trajectory of evolutionary progress in race relations; on the contrary, our history shows that battles won at one moment can later be lost. Despite hard-fought battles for change that secured important concessions during the 1960s in the form of civil rights legislation, the racialized nature of social policy in the United States since the Great Depression has actually increased the possessive investment in whiteness among European Americans over the past half century.

During the New Deal Era of the 1930s and 1940s, both the Wagner Act and the Social Security Act excluded farm workers and domestics from coverage, effectively denying those disproportionately minority sectors of the work force protections and benefits routinely afforded whites. The Federal Housing Act of 1934 brought home ownership within reach of millions of citizens by placing the credit of the federal government behind private lending to home buyers, but overtly racist categories in the Federal Housing Agency's (FHA) "confidential" city surveys and appraisers' manuals channeled almost all of the loan money toward whites and away from communities of color.[4] In the post–World War II era, trade unions negotiated contract provisions giving private medical insurance, pensions, and job security largely to the white workers who formed the overwhelming majority of the unionized work force in mass production industries, rather than fighting for full employment, medical care, and old-age pensions for all, or even for an end to discriminatory hiring and promotion practices by employers in those industries.[5]

Each of these policies widened the gap between the resources available to whites and those available to aggrieved racial communities. Federal housing policy offers an important illustration of the broader principles at work in the possessive investment in whiteness. By channeling loans away from older inner-city neighborhoods and toward white home buyers moving into segregated suburbs, the FHA and private lenders after World War II aided and abetted segregation in U.S. residential neighborhoods. FHA appraisers denied federally supported loans to prospective home buyers in the racially mixed Boyle Heights neighborhood of Los Angeles in 1939, for example, because the area struck them as a "'melting pot' area literally honeycombed with diverse and subversive racial elements."[6] Similarly, mostly white St. Louis County secured five times as many FHA mortgages as the more racially mixed city of St. Louis between 1943 and 1960. Home buyers in the county received six times as much loan money and enjoyed per capita mortgage spending 6.3 times greater than those in the city.[7]

The federal government has played a major role in augmenting the possessive investment in whiteness. For years, the General Services Administration routinely channeled the government's own rental and leasing business to realtors who engaged in racial discrimination, while federally subsidized urban renewal plans reduced the already limited supply of housing for communities of color through "slum clearance" programs. In concert with FHA support for segregation in the suburbs, federal and state tax monies routinely funded the construction of water supplies and sewage facilities for racially exclusive suburban communities in the 1940s and 1950s. By the 1960s, these areas often incorporated themselves as independent municipalities in order to gain greater access to federal funds allocated for "urban aid."[8]

At the same time that FHA loans and federal highway building projects subsidized the growth of segregated suburbs, urban renewal programs in cities throughout the country devastated minority neighborhoods. During the 1950s and 1960s, federally assisted urban renewal projects destroyed 20 percent of the central-city housing units occupied by blacks, as opposed to only

10 percent of those inhabited by whites.[9] More than 60 percent of those displaced by urban renewal were African Americans, Puerto Ricans, Mexican Americans, or members of other minority racial groups.[10] The Federal Housing Administration and the Veterans Administration financed more than $120 billion worth of new housing between 1934 and 1962, but less than 2 percent of this real estate was available to non-white families—and most of that small amount was located in segregated areas.[11]

Even in the 1970s, after most major urban renewal programs had been completed, black central-city residents continued to lose housing units at a rate equal to 80 percent of what had been lost in the 1960s. Yet white displacement declined to the relatively low levels of the 1950s.[12] In addition, the refusal first to pass, then to enforce, fair housing laws has enabled realtors, buyers, and sellers to profit from racist collusion against minorities largely without fear of legal retribution. During the decades following World War II, urban renewal helped construct a new "white" identity in the suburbs by helping to destroy ethnically specific European American urban inner-city neighborhoods. Wrecking balls and bulldozers eliminated some of these sites, while others were transformed by an influx of minority residents desperately competing for a declining supply of affordable housing units. As increasing numbers of racial minorities moved into cities, increasing numbers of European American ethnics moved out. Consequently, ethnic differences among whites became a less important dividing line in U.S. culture, while race became more important. The suburbs helped turn Euro-Americans into "whites" who could live near each other and intermarry with relatively little difficulty. But this "white" unity rested on residential segregation, on shared access to housing and life chances largely unavailable to communities of color.[13]

During the 1950s and 1960s, local "pro-growth" coalitions led by liberal mayors often justified urban renewal as a program designed to build more housing for poor people, but it actually destroyed more housing than it created. Ninety percent of the low-income units removed for urban renewal during the entire history of the program were never replaced. Commercial, industrial, and municipal projects occupied more than 80 percent of the land cleared for these projects, with less than 20 percent allocated for replacement housing. In addition, the loss of taxable properties and the tax abatements granted to new enterprises in urban renewal zones often meant serious tax increases for poor, working-class, and middle-class home owners and renters.[14] Although the percentage of black suburban dwellers also increased during this period, no significant desegregation of the suburbs took place. From 1960 to 1977, 4 million whites moved out of central cities, while the number of whites living in suburbs increased by 22 million; during the same years, the inner-city black population grew by 6 million, but the number of blacks living in suburbs increased by only 500,000.[15] By 1993, 86 percent of suburban whites still lived in places with a black population below 1 percent. At the same time, cities with large numbers of minority residents found themselves cut off from loans by the FHA. For example, because of their growing black and Puerto Rican populations, neither Camden nor Paterson, New Jersey, in 1966 received one FHA-sponsored mortgage.[16]

In 1968, lobbyists for the banking industry helped draft the Housing and Urban Development Act, which allowed private lenders to shift the risks of financing low-income housing to the government, creating a lucrative and thoroughly unregulated market for themselves. One section of the 1968 bill authorized FHA mortgages for inner-city areas that did not meet the usual eligibility criteria, and another section subsidized interest payments by low-income families. If administered wisely, these provisions might have promoted fair housing goals, but FHA administrators deployed them in ways that actually promoted segregation in order to provide banks, brokers, lenders, developers, realtors, and speculators with windfall profits. As a U.S. Commission on Civil Rights investigation later revealed, FHA officials collaborated with blockbusters in financing the flight of low-income whites out of inner city neighborhoods, and then aided unscrupulous realtors and speculators by arranging purchases of substandard housing by minorities desperate to own their own homes. The resulting sales and mortgage foreclosures brought great profits to lenders (almost all of them white), but their actions led to price fixing and a subsequent inflation of housing costs in the inner city by more than 200 percent between 1968 and 1972. Bankers then foreclosed on the mortgages of thousands of these uninspected and substandard homes, ruining many inner-city neighborhoods. In response, the Department of Housing and Urban Development essentially red-lined inner cities, making them ineligible for future loans, a decision that destroyed the value of inner-city housing for generations to come.[17]

Federally funded highways designed to connect suburban commuters with downtown places of employment also destroyed already scarce housing in minority communities and often disrupted neighborhood life as well. Construction of the Harbor Freeway in Los Angeles, the Gulf Freeway in Houston, and the Mark Twain Freeway in St. Louis displaced thousands of residents and bisected neighborhoods, shopping districts, and political precincts. The processes of urban renewal and highway construction set in motion a vicious cycle: population loss led to decreased political power, which made minority neighborhoods more vulnerable to further urban renewal and freeway construction, not to mention more susceptible to the placement of prisons, incinerators, toxic waste dumps, and other projects that further depopulated these areas.

In Houston, Texas—where blacks make up slightly more than one quarter of the local population—more than 75 percent of municipal garbage incinerators and 100 percent of the city-owned garbage dumps are located in black neighborhoods.[18] A 1992 study by staff writers for the *National Law Journal* examined the Environmental Protection Agency's response to 1,177 toxic waste cases and found that polluters of sites near the greatest white population received penalties 500 percent higher than penalties imposed on polluters in minority areas—an average of $335,566 for white areas contrasted with $55,318 for minority areas. Income did not account for these differences—penalties for low-income areas on average actually exceeded those for areas with the highest median incomes by about 3 percent. The penalties for violating all federal environmental laws regulating air, water, and waste pollution were 46 percent lower in minority communities than in white communities. In addition, superfund remedies left minority communities waiting longer than white communities to be placed on the national priority list, cleanups that began from 12 to 42 percent later than at white sites, and with a 7 percent greater likelihood of "containment" (walling off a hazardous site) than cleanup, while white sites experienced treatment and cleanup 22 percent more often than containment.[19]

The federal Agency for Toxic Substances and Disease Registry's 1988 survey of children suffering from lead poisoning showed that among families with incomes under $6,000 per year, 36 percent of white children but 68 percent of black children suffered from excess lead in their bloodstreams. Among families with incomes above $15,000 per year, only 12 percent of white children but 38 percent of black children suffered from toxic levels of lead.[20] In the Los Angeles area, only 34 percent of whites inhabit areas with the most polluted air, but 71 percent of African Americans and 50 percent of Latinos live in neighborhoods with the highest levels of air pollution.[21] Nationwide, 60 percent of African Americans and Latinos live in communities with uncontrolled toxic waste sites.[22]

Scholarly studies reveal that even when adjusted for income, education, and occupational status, aggrieved racial minorities encounter higher levels of exposure to toxic substances than white people experience.[23] In 1987, the Commission for Racial Justice of the United Church of Christ found race to be the most significant variable in determining the location of commercial hazard facilities.[24] In a review of sixty-four studies examining environmental disparities, the National Wildlife Federation found that racial disparities outnumbered disparities by income, and in cases where disparities in race and income were both present, race proved to be more important in twenty-two out of thirty tests.[25] As Robert D. Bullard demonstrates, "race has been found to be an independent factor, not reducible to class" in predicting exposure to a broad range of environmental hazards, including polluted air, contaminated fish, lead poisoning, municipal landfills, incinerators, and toxic waste dumps.[26] The combination of exposure to environmental hazards and employment discrimination establishes a sinister correlation between race and health. One recent government study revealed that the likelihood of dying from nutritional deficiencies was two and a half times greater among African Americans than among European Americans.[27] Another demonstrated that Asian and Pacific Islander recipients of aid for at-risk families exhibited alarming rates of stunted growth and underweight among children under the age of five.[28] Corporations systematically target Native American reservations when looking for locations for hazardous waste incinerators, solid waste landfills, and nuclear waste storage facilities; Navajo teenagers develop reproductive organ cancer at seventeen times the national average because of their exposure to radiation from uranium mines.[29] Latinos in East Los Angeles encounter some of the worst smog and the highest concentrations of air toxins in southern California because of prevailing wind patterns and the concentration of polluting industries, freeways, and toxic waste dumps.[30] Environmental racism makes the possessive investment in whiteness literally a matter of life and death; if African Americans had access to the nutrition, wealth, health care, and protection against environmental hazards offered routinely to whites, seventy-five thousand fewer of them would die each year.[31]

Minorities are less likely than whites to receive preventive medical care or costly operations from Medicare. Eligible members of minority communities are also less likely than European Americans to apply for food stamps.[32] The labor of migrant farm workers from aggrieved racialized groups plays a vital role in providing adequate nutrition for others, but the farm workers and their children suffer disproportionately from health disorders caused by malnutrition.[33] In her important research on health policy and ethnic diversity, Linda Wray concludes that "the lower life expectancies for many ethnic minority groups and subgroups stem largely from their disproportionately higher rates of poverty, malnutrition, and poor health care."[34]

Just as residential segregation and urban renewal make minority communities disproportionately susceptible to health hazards, their physical and social location gives these communities a different relationship to the criminal justice system. A 1990 study by the National Institute on Drug Abuse revealed that while only 15 percent of the thirteen million habitual drug users in the United States were black and 77 percent were white, African Americans were four times more likely to be arrested on drug charges than whites in the nation as a whole, and seven to nine times more likely in Pennsylvania, Michigan, Illinois, Florida, Massachusetts, and New Jersey. A 1989 study by the Parents' Resource Institute for Drug Education discovered that African American high school students consistently showed lower levels of drug and alcohol use than their European American counterparts, even in high schools populated by residents of low-income housing projects. Yet, while comprising about 12 percent of the U.S. population, blacks accounted for 10 percent of drug arrests in 1984, 40 percent in 1988, and 42 percent in 1990. In addition, white drug defendants receive considerably shorter average prison terms than African Americans convicted of comparable crimes. A

U.S. Sentencing Commission study found in 1992 that half of the federal court districts that handled cases involving crack cocaine prosecuted minority defendants *exclusively.* A *Los Angeles Times* article in 1995 revealed that "black and Latino crack dealers are hammered with 10-year mandatory federal sentences while whites prosecuted in state court face a minimum of five years and often receive no more than a year in jail." Alexander Lichtenstein and Michael A. Kroll point out that sentences for African Americans in the federal prison system are 20 percent longer than those given to whites who commit the same crimes. They observe that if blacks received the same sentences as whites for these offenses, the federal prison system would require three thousand fewer prison cells, enough to close completely six of the new five-hundred bed institutions.[35]

Racial animus on the part of police officers, prosecutors, and judges accounts for only a small portion of the distinctive experience that racial minorities have with the criminal justice system. Economic devastation makes the drug trade appealing to some people in the inner city, while the dearth of capital in minority neighborhoods curtails opportunities for other kinds of employment. Deindustrialization, unemployment, and lack of intergenerational transfers of wealth undermine parental and adult authority in many neighborhoods. The complex factors that cause people to turn to drugs are no more prevalent in minority communities than elsewhere, but these communities and their inhabitants face more stress while having fewer opportunities to receive private counseling and treatment for their problems.

The structural weaknesses of minority neighborhoods caused by discrimination in housing, education, and hiring also play a crucial role in relations between inner-city residents and the criminal justice system. Cocaine dealing, which initially skyrocketed among white suburban residents, was driven into the inner city by escalating enforcement pressures in wealthy white communities. Ghettos and barrios became distribution centers for the sale of drugs to white suburbanites. Former New York and Houston police commissioner Lee Brown, head of the federal government's antidrug efforts during the early years of the Clinton presidency and later mayor of Houston, noted, "There are those who bring drugs into the country. That's not the black community. Then you have wholesalers, those who distribute them once they get here, and as a rule that's not the black community. Where you find the blacks is in the street dealing."[36]

You also find blacks and other minorities in prison. Police officers in large cities, pressured to show results in the drive against drugs, lack the resources to effectively enforce the law everywhere (in part because of the social costs of deindustrialization and the tax limitation initiatives designed to shrink the size of government). These officers know that it is easier to make arrests and to secure convictions by confronting drug users in areas that have conspicuous street corner sales, that have more people out on the street with no place to go, and that have residents more likely to plead guilty and less likely to secure the services of attorneys who can get the charges against them dropped, reduced, or wiped off the books with subsequent successful counseling and rehabilitation. In addition, politicians supported by the public relations efforts of neoconservative foundations often portray themselves to suburban voters as opponents of the "dangerous classes" in the inner cities.

Minority disadvantages craft advantages for others. Urban renewal failed to provide new housing for the poor, but it played an important role in transforming the U.S. urban economy from one that relied on factory production to one driven by producer services. Urban renewal projects subsidized the development of downtown office centers on previously residential land, and they frequently created buffer zones of empty blocks dividing poor neighborhoods from new shopping centers designed for affluent commuters. To help cities compete for corporate investment by making them appealing to high-level executives, federal urban aid favored construction of luxury housing units and cultural centers like symphony halls and art museums over affordable housing for workers. Tax abatements granted to these producer services centers further aggravated the fiscal crisis that cities faced, leading to tax increases on existing industries, businesses, and residences.

Workers from aggrieved racial minorities bore the brunt of this transformation. Because the 1964 Civil Rights Act came so late, minority workers who received jobs because of it found themselves more vulnerable to seniority-based layoffs when businesses automated or transferred operations overseas. Although the act initially made real progress in reducing employment discrimination, lessened the gaps between rich and poor and between black and white workers, and helped bring minority poverty to its lowest level in history in 1973, that year's recession, initiated a reversal of minority progress and a reassertion of white privilege.[37] In 1977, the U.S. Civil Rights Commission reported on the disproportionate impact of layoffs on minority workers. In cases where minority workers made up only 10 to 12 percent of the work force in their area, they accounted for from 60 to 70 percent of those laid off in 1974. The principle of seniority, a trade union triumph designed to protect workers from age discrimination, in this case guaranteed that minority workers would suffer most from technological changes, because the legacy of past discrimination by their employers left them with less seniority than white workers.[38]

When housing prices increased dramatically during the 1970s, white home owners who had been able to take advantage of discriminatory FHA financing policies in the past realized increased equity in their homes, while those excluded from the housing market by earlier policies found themselves facing even higher costs of entry into the market in addition to the traditional obstacles presented by the discriminatory practices of sellers, realtors, and lenders. The contrast between European Americans and African Americans is instructive in this regard. Because whites have access to broader housing choices than blacks, whites pay 15 percent less than blacks for similar housing in the same neighborhood. White neighborhoods typically experience housing costs 25 percent lower than would be the case if the residents were black.[39]

A recent Federal Reserve Bank of Boston study revealed that Boston bankers made 2.9 times as many mortgage loans per 1,000 housing units in neighborhoods inhabited by low-income whites than in neighborhoods populated by low-income blacks.[40] In addition, loan officers were far more likely to overlook flaws in the credit records of white applicants or to arrange creative financing for them than they were with black applicants.[41] A Los Angeles study found that loan officers more frequently used dividend income and underlying assets as criteria for judging black applicants than for whites.[42] In Houston, the NCNB Bank of Texas disqualified 13 percent of middle-income white loan applicants but 36 percent of middle-income black applicants.[43] Atlanta's home loan institutions gave five times as many home loans to whites as to blacks in the late 1980s. An analysis of sixteen Atlanta neighborhoods found that home buyers in white neighborhoods received conventional financing four times as often as those in black sections of the city.[44] Nationwide, financial institutions receive more money in deposits from black neighborhoods than they invest in them in the form of home mortgage loans, making home lending a vehicle for the transfer of capital away from black savers toward white investors.[45] In many locations high-income blacks were denied loans more often than low-income whites.[46]

When confronted with evidence of systematic racial bias in home lending, defenders of the possessive investment in whiteness argue that the disproportionate share of loan denials to members of minority groups stems not from discrimination, but from the low net worth of minority applicants, even those who have high incomes. This might seem a reasonable position, but net worth is almost totally determined by past opportunities for asset accumulation, and therefore is the one figure most likely to reflect the history of discrimination. Minorities are told, in essence, "We can't give you a loan today because we've discriminated against members of your race so effectively in the past that you have not been able to accumulate any equity from housing and to pass it down through the generations."

Most white families have acquired their net worth from the appreciation of property that they secured under conditions of special privilege in a discriminatory housing market. In their prize-winning book *Black Wealth/White Wealth,* Melvin Oliver and Thomas Shapiro demonstrate how the history of housing discrimination makes white parents more able to borrow funds for their children's college education or to loan money to their children to enter the housing market. In addition, much discrimination in home lending is not based on considerations of net worth; it stems from decisions made by white banking officials based on their stereotypes about minority communities. The Federal Reserve Bank of Boston study showed that black and Latino mortgage applicants are 60 percent more likely to be turned down for loans than whites, even after controlling for employment, financial, and neighborhood characteristics.[47] Ellis Cose reports on a white bank official confronted with evidence at a board of directors' meeting that his bank denied loans to blacks who had credit histories and earnings equal to those of white applicants who received loans. The banker replied that the information indicated that the bank needed to do a better job of "affirmative action," but one of his colleagues pointed out that the problem had nothing to do with affirmative action—the bank was simply letting prejudice stand in the way of its own best interests by rejecting loans that should be approved.[48]

Yet bankers also make money from the ways in which discrimination creates artificial scarcities in the market. Minorities have to pay more for housing because much of the market is off limits to them. Blockbusters profit from exploiting white fears and provoking them into panic selling. Minority home owners denied loans in mainstream banks often turn to exploitative lenders who make "low end" loans at enormously high interest rates. If they fail to pay back these loans, regular banks can acquire the property cheaply and charge someone else exorbitant interest for a loan on the same property.

Federal home loan policies have put the power of the federal government at the service of private discrimination. Urban renewal and highway construction programs have enhanced the possessive investment in whiteness directly through government initiatives. In addition, decisions about where to locate federal jobs have also systematically subsidized whiteness. Federal civilian employment dropped by 41,419 in central cities between 1966 and 1973, but total federal employment in metropolitan areas grew by 26,558.[49] While one might naturally expect the location of government buildings that serve the public to follow population trends, the federal government's policy of locating offices and records centers in suburbs aggravated the flight of jobs to suburban locations less accessible to inner-city residents. Because racial discrimination in the private sector forces minority workers to seek government positions disproportionate to their numbers, these moves exact particular hardships on them. In addition, minorities who follow their jobs to the suburbs must generally allocate more for commuter costs, because housing discrimination makes it harder and more expensive for them than for whites to relocate. . . .

. . . Even seemingly race-neutral policies supported by both neoconservatives and liberals in the 1980s and 1990s have increased the absolute value of being white. In the 1980s, changes in federal tax laws decreased the value of wage income and increased the value of investment income—a move harmful to minorities, who suffer from a gap between their total wealth and that of whites even greater than the disparity between their income and white income. The failure to raise the minimum wage between 1981 and 1989 and the decline of more than one-third in the value of Aid to Families with Dependent Children (AFDC) payments injured all poor people, but they exacted special costs on nonwhites, who faced even more constricted markets for employment, housing, and education than poor whites.[50]

Similarly, the "tax reforms" of the 1980s made the effective rate of taxation higher on investment in actual goods and services than on profits from speculative enterprises. This change encouraged the flight of capital from industrial production with its many employment opportunities toward investments that can be turned over quickly to allow the greatest possible tax write-offs. Government policies thus discouraged investments that might produce high-paying jobs and encouraged investors to strip companies of their assets to make rapid short-term profits. These policies hurt almost all workers, but they fell particularly heavily on minority workers, who because of employment discrimination in the retail and small business sectors were over-represented in blue-collar industrial jobs.

On the other hand, while neoconservative tax policies created incentives for employers to move their enterprises elsewhere, they created disincentives for home owners to move. Measures like California's Proposition 13 (passed in 1978) granting tax relief to property owners badly misallocate housing resources, because they make it financially unwise for the elderly to move out of large houses, further reducing the supply of housing available to young families. While one can well understand the necessity for protecting senior citizens on fixed incomes from tax increases that would make them lose their homes, the rewards and punishments provided by Proposition 13 are so extreme that they prevent the kinds of generational succession that have routinely opened up housing to young families in the past. This reduction works particular hardships on those who also face discrimination by sellers, realtors, and lending institutions. . . .

Because they are ignorant of even the recent history of the possessive investment in whiteness—generated by slavery and segregation, immigrant exclusion and Native American policy, conquest and colonialism, but augmented by liberal and conservative social policies as well—Americans produce largely cultural explanations for structural social problems. The increased possessive investment in whiteness generated by disinvestment in U.S. cities, factories, and schools since the 1970s disguises as *racial* problems the general social problems posed by deindustrialization, economic restructuring, and neoconservative attacks on the welfare state. It fuels a discourse that demonizes people of color for being victimized by these changes, while hiding the privileges of whiteness by attributing the economic advantages enjoyed by whites to their family values, faith in fatherhood, and foresight—rather than to the favoritism they enjoy through their possessive investment in whiteness.

The demonization of black families in public discourse since the 1970s is particularly instructive in this regard. During the 1970s, the share of low-income households headed by blacks increased by one-third, while black family income fell from 60 percent of white family income in 1971 to 58 percent in 1980. Even adjusting for unemployment and for African American disadvantages in life-cycle employment (more injuries, more frequently interrupted work histories, confinement to jobs most susceptible to layoffs), the wages of full-time year-round black workers fell from 77 percent of white workers' income to 73 percent by 1986. In 1986, white workers with high school diplomas earned $3,000 per year more than African Americans with the same education.[51] Even when they had the same family structure as white workers, blacks found themselves more likely to be poor.

Recent economic gains by blacks brighten the picture somewhat, but the deindustrialization and economic restructuring of the 1970s and 1980s imposes yet another racial penalty on wage earners from minority communities, who suffered setbacks while members of other groups accumulated equity-producing assets. And even when some minority groups show improvement, others do not. In 1995, for example, every U.S. ethnic and racial group experienced an increase in income except the twenty-seven million Hispanics, who experienced a 5.1 percent drop in income during that year alone.[52]

Forty-six percent of black workers between the ages of twenty and twenty-four held blue-collar jobs in 1976, but only 20 percent by 1984. Earnings by young black families that had reached 60 percent of white families' income in 1973, fell to 46 percent by 1986. Younger African American families experienced a 50 percent drop in real earnings between 1973 and 1986, with the decline in black male wages particularly steep.[53] . . .

Group interests are not monolithic, and aggregate figures can obscure serious differences within racial groups. All whites do not benefit from the possessive investment in whiteness in precisely the same ways; the experiences of members of minority groups are not interchangeable. But the possessive investment in whiteness always affects individual and group life chances and opportunities. Even in cases where minority groups secure political and economic power through collective mobilization, the terms and conditions of their collectivity and the logic of group solidarity are always influenced and intensified by the absolute value of whiteness in U.S. politics, economics, and culture.[54] . . .

Walter Benjamin's praise for "presence of mind" came from his understanding of how difficult it may be to see the present. But more important, he called for presence of mind as the means for implementing what he named "the only true telepathic miracle"—turning the forbidding future into the fulfilled present.[55] Failure to acknowledge our society's possessive investment in whiteness prevents us from facing the present openly and honestly. It hides from us the devastating costs of disinvestment in America's infrastructure over the past two decades and keeps us from facing our responsibility to reinvest in human resources by channeling resources toward education, health, and housing—and away from subsidies for speculation and luxury. After two decades of disinvestment, the only further disinvestment we need is from the ruinous pathology of whiteness, which has always undermined our own best instincts and interests. In a society suffering so badly from an absence of mutuality, an absence of responsibility and an absence of justice, presence of mind might be just what we need.

NOTES

1. Richard Dyer, "White," *Screen* 29, 4 (Fall 1998): 44.
2. I thank Michael Schudson for pointing out to me that since the passage of civil rights legislation in the 1960s whiteness dares not speak its name, cannot speak in its own behalf, but rather advances through a color-blind language radically at odds with the distinctly racialized distribution of resources and life chances in U.S. society.
3. Walter Benjamin, "Madame Ariane: Second Courtyard on the Left," in *One-Way Street* (London: New Left Books, 1969), 98–99.
4. See Kenneth Jackson, *Crabgrass Frontier: The Suburbanization of the United States* (New York: Oxford University Press, 1985), and Douglas S. Massey and Nancy A. Denton, *American Apartheid: Segregation and the Making of the Underclass* (Cambridge, MA: Harvard University Press, 1993).
5. I thank Phil Ethington for pointing out to me that these aspects of New Deal policies emerged out of political negotiations between the segregationist Dixiecrats and liberals from the North and West. My perspective is that white supremacy was not a gnawing aberration within the New Deal coalition but rather an essential point of unity between southern whites and northern white ethnics.
6. Records of the Federal Home Loan Bank Board of the Home Owners Loan Corporation, City Survey File, Los Angeles, 1939, Neighborhood D-53, National Archives, Box 74, RG 195.
7. Massey and Denton, *American Apartheid,* 54.

8. John R. Logan and Harvey Molotch, *Urban Fortunes: The Political Economy of Place* (Berkeley and Los Angeles: University of California Press, 1987), 182.
9. Ibid., 114.
10. Arlene Zarembka, *The Urban Housing Crisis: Social, Economic, and Legal Issues and Proposals* (Westport, CT: Greenwood, 1990), 104.
11. Jill Quadagno, *The Color of Welfare: How Racism Undermined the War on Poverty* (New York: Oxford University Press, 1994), 92, 91.
12. Logan and Molotch, *Urban Fortunes,* 130.
13. See Gary Gerstle, "Working-Class Racism: Broaden the Focus," *International Labor and Working Class History* 44 (Fall 1993): 36.
14. Logan and Molotch, *Urban Fortunes,* 168–69.
15. Troy Duster, "Crime, Youth Unemployment, and the Underclass," *Crime and Delinquency* 33, 2 (April 1987): 308, 309.
16. Massey and Denton, *American Apartheid,* 55.
17. Quadagno, *The Color of Welfare,* 105, 113; Massey and Denton, *American Apartheid,* 204–5.
18. Logan and Molotch, *Urban Fortunes,* 113.
19. Robert D. Bullard, "Environmental Justice for All," in *Unequal Protection: Environmental Justice and Communities of Color,* ed. Robert Bullard (San Francisco: Sierra Club, 1994), 9–10.
20. Robert D. Bullard, "Anatomy of Environmental Racism and the Environmental Justice Movement," in *Confronting Environmental Racism: Voices from the Grass Roots,* ed. Robert D. Bullard (Boston: South End, 1993), 21.
21. Bullard, "Environmental Justice for All," 13.
22. Charles Lee, "Beyond Toxic Wastes and Race," in *Confronting Environmental Racism,* 49. Two corporate-sponsored research institutes challenged claims of racial bias in the location and operation of toxic and hazardous waste systems. Andy B. Anderson, Douglas L. Anderton, and John Michael Oakes made the corporate case in "Environmental Equity: Evaluating TSDF Siting over the Past Two Decades," *Waste Age,* July 1994. These results were trumpeted in a report by the Washington University Center for the Study of American Business, funded by the John M. Olin Foundation. But the study by Anderson, Anderton, and Oakes was sponsored by the Institute of Chemical Waste Management, an industry trade group. The researchers claimed that their results were not influenced by corporate sponsorship, but they limited their inquiry to urban areas with toxic storage, disposal, and treatment facilities, conveniently excluding seventy facilities, 15 percent of TSDFs, and 20 percent of the population. The world's largest waste company, WMX Company, contributed $250,000 to the study, and the study's research plan excluded from scrutiny two landfills owned by WMX: the nation's largest commercial landfill, located in the predominately African American city of Emelle, Alabama, and the nation's fifth largest landfill, in Kettelman City Hills, California, a predominately Latino community.
23. Bunyan Bryant and Paul Mohai, *Race and the Incidence of Environmental Hazards* (Boulder, CO: Westview, 1992).
24. Lee, "Beyond Toxic Wastes and Race," 48.
25. Robert D. Bullard, "Decision Making," in Laura Westra and Peter S. Wenz, eds., *Faces of Environmental Racism: Confronting Issues of Global Justice* (Lanham, MD: Rowman and Littlefield, 1995), 4.
26. Bullard, "Anatomy of Environmental Racism," 21.
27. David L. L. Shields, "What Color is Hunger?" in David L. L. Shields, ed., *The Color of Hunger: Race and Hunger in National and International Perspective* (Lanham, MD: Rowman and Littlefield, 1996), 4.
28. Centers for Disease Control, "Nutritional Status of Minority Children: United States, 1986," *Morbidity and Mortality Weekly Reports (MMWR)* 36, 23 (June 19, 1987): 366–69.
29. Peter S. Wenz, "Just Garbage," in *Faces of Environmental Racism,* 66; Robert D. Bullard, "Decision Making," in *Faces of Environmental Racism,* 8.
30. Laura Pulido, "Multiracial Organizing among Environmental Justice Activists in Los Angeles," in Michael J. Dear, H. Eric Shockman, and Greg Hise, eds., *Rethinking Los Angeles* (Thousand Oaks, CA, London, New Delhi: Sage, 1996): 175.
31. Charles Trueheart, "The Bias Most Deadly," *Washington Post,* October 30, 1990, sec. 7, cited in Shields, *The Color of Hunger,* 3.
32. George Anders, "Disparities in Medicare Access Found among Poor, Black or Disabled Patients,"

Wall Street Journal, November 2, 1994; Lina R. Godfrey, "Institutional Discrimination and Satisfaction with Specific Government Services by Heads of Households in Ten Southern States," paper presented at the Rural Sociological Society annual meeting, 1984, cited in Shields, *The Color of Hunger,* 6, 13.

33. Jeffrey Shotland, *Full Fields, Empty Cupboards: The Nutritional Status of Migrant Farmworkers in America* (Washington, DC: Public Voice for Food and Health: 1989), cited in Shields, *The Color of Hunger,* 3.
34. Linda A. Wray, "Health Policy and Ethnic Diversity in Older Americans: Dissonance or Harmony," *Western Journal of Medicine* 157, 3 (September 1992): 357–61.
35. Eva Bertram, Morris Blachman, Kenneth Sharpe, and Peter Andreas, *Drug War Politics: The Price of Denial* (Berkeley and Los Angeles: University of California Press, 1996), 38–42; Alexander C. Lichtenstein and Michael A. Kroll, "The Fortress Economy: The Economic Role of the U.S. Prison System," in Elihu Rosenblatt, ed., *Criminal Injustice: Confronting the Prison Crisis* (Boston: South End, 1996), 21, 25–26.
36. Ibid., 41.
37. Massey and Denton, *American Apartheid,* 61.
38. Gertrude Ezorsky, *Racism and Justice: The Case for Affirmative Action* (Ithaca, NY: Cornell University Press, 1991), 25.
39. Logan and Molotch, *Urban Fortunes,* 116.
40. Jim Campen, "Lending Insights: Hard Proof that Banks Discriminate," *Dollars and Sense,* January–February 1991, 17.
41. Mitchell Zuckoff, "Study Shows Racial Bias in Lending," *Boston Globe,* October 9, 1992.
42. Paul Ong and J. Eugene Grigsby III, "Race and Life-Cycle Effects on Home Ownership in Los Angeles, 1970 to 1980," *Urban Affairs Quarterly* 23, 4 (June 1988): 605.
43. Massey and Denton, *American Apartheid,* 108.
44. Gary Orfield and Carol Ashkinaze, *The Closing Door: Conservative Policy and Black Opportunity* (Chicago: University of Chicago Press, 1991), 58, 78.
45. Logan and Molotch, *Urban Fortunes,* 129.
46. Campen, "Lending Insights," 18.
47. Alicia H. Munnell, Lyn E. Browne, James McEneany, and Geoffrey M. B. Tootel, "Mortgage Lending in Boston: Interpreting HMDA Data" (Boston: Federal Reserve Bank of Boston, 1993); Kimberly Blanton, "Fed Blocks Shawmut's Bid to Gain N.H. Bank," *Boston Globe,* November 16, 1993.
48. Ellis Cose, *Rage of a Privileged Class* (New York: HarperCollins, 1993), 191.
49. Gregory Squires, "'Runaway Plants,' Capital Mobility, and Black Economic Rights," in *Community and Capital in Conflict: Plant Closings and Job Loss,* ed. John C. Raines, Lenora E. Berson, and David McI. Gracie (Philadelphia: Temple University Press, 1983), 70.
50. Orfield and Ashkinaze, *The Closing Door,* 225–26.
51. William Chafe, *The Unfinished Journey* (New York: Oxford University Press, 1986), 442; Noel J. Kent, "A Stacked Deck: Racial Minorities and the New American Political Economy," *Explorations in Ethnic Studies* 14, 1 (January 1991): 11.
52. Carey Goldberg, "Hispanic Households Struggle as Poorest of the Poor in the U.S.," *New York Times,* January 30, 1997, sec. A.
53. Kent, "A Stacked Deck," 13.
54. The rise of a black middle class and the setbacks suffered by white workers during deindustrialization may seem to subvert the analysis presented here. Yet the black middle class remains fragile, far less able than other middle-class groups to translate advances in income into advances in wealth and power. Similarly, the success of neoconservatism since the 1970s has rested on securing support from white workers for economic policies that do them objective harm by mobilizing countersubversive electoral coalitions against busing and affirmative action, while carrying out attacks on public institutions and resources by representing "public" space as black space. See Oliver and Shapiro, "Wealth of a Nation." See also Logan and Molotch, *Urban Fortunes.*
55. Benjamin, "Madame Ariane," 98, 99.

READING 44

Strangers Among Us

How Latino Immigration Is Transforming America

Roberto Suro

On Imelda's fifteenth birthday,[1] her parents were celebrating everything they had accomplished by coming north to make a new life in the United States. Two short people in brand-new clothes, they stood in the driveway of their home in Houston and greeted relatives, friends, and neighbors, among them a few people who had come from the same village in central Mexico and who would surely carry gossip of the party back home. A disc jockey with a portable stereo presided over the backyard as if it were a cabaret instead of a patch of grass behind an overcrowded bungalow where five people shared two bedrooms. A folding table sagged with platters of tacos and fajitas. An aluminum keg of beer sat in a wheelbarrow atop a bed of half-melted ice cubes. For Imelda's parents, the festivities that night served as a triumphant display of everything they had earned by working two jobs each. Like most of the other adults at the party, they had come north to labor in restaurants, factories, warehouses, or construction sites by day and to clean offices at night. They had come to work and to raise children in the United States.

Imelda, who had been smuggled across the Rio Grande as a toddler, wore a frilly dress ordered by catalog from Guadalajara, as befits a proper Mexican celebrating her *quinceañera,* which is the traditional coming-out party for fifteen-year-old Latin girls. Her two younger sisters and a little brother, all U.S. citizens by birth, wore new white shirts from a discount store. Their hair had been combed down with sharp, straight parts and dabs of pomade.

When it came time for Imelda to dance her first dance, her father took her in his arms for one of the old-fashioned polkas that had been his favorite when a band played in the town square back home. By tradition, boys could begin courting her after that dance. Imelda's parents went to bed that night content they had raised their children according to proper Mexican custom.

The next morning at breakfast, Imelda announced that she was pregnant, that she was dropping out of school, and that she was moving in with her boyfriend, a Mexican-American who did not speak Spanish and who did not know his father. That night, she ate a meal purchased with food stamps and cooked on a hot plate by her boyfriend's mother. She remembers the dinner well. "That night, man, I felt like an American. I was free."

This is the promise and the peril of Latino immigration. Imelda's parents had traveled to Texas on a wave of expectations that carried them from the diminishing life of peasant farmers on a dusty *rancho* to quiet contentment as low-wage workers in an American city. These two industrious immigrants had produced a teenage welfare mother, who in turn was to have an American baby. In the United States, Imelda had learned the language and the ways. In the end, what she learned best was how to be poor in an American inner city.

Latino immigration delivers short-term gains and has long-term costs. For decades now, the United States has engaged in a form of deficit spending that can be measured in human lives. Through their hard work at low wages, Latinos have produced immediate benefits for their families, employers, and consumers, but American society has never defined a permanent place for these immigrants or their children and it has repeatedly put off considering their future. That future, however, is now arriving, and it will produce a reckoning. The United States will need new immigration policies to decide who gets into the country. More importantly, the nation will need new means of assuring political equality and freedom of economic opportunity. Soon

Roberto Suro, the American-born son of a Puerto Rican father and an Ecuadorean mother, is a staff writer for *The Washington Post.*

Americans will learn once again that in an era of immigration, the newcomers not only demand change; they create change.[2]

When I last met Imelda, she was just a few weeks short of her due date, but she didn't have anything very nice to say about her baby or her boyfriend. Growing up in Houston as the child of Mexican immigrants had filled her with resentment, especially toward her parents, and that was what she wanted to talk about.

"We'd get into a lot of yelling and stuff at home because my parents, they'd say, 'You're Mexican. Speak Spanish. Act like a Mexican girl,' and I'd say, 'I'm here now and I'm going to be like the other kids.' They didn't care."

Imelda is short and plump, with wide brown eyes and badly dyed yellow hair. She wore a denim shirt with the sleeves ripped off, and her expression was a studied pout. Getting pregnant was just one more way of expressing anger and disdain. She is a dime-store Madonna.

Imelda is also a child of the Latino migration. She is a product of that great movement of people from Latin America into the United States that is older than any borders but took on a startling new meaning when it gradually gained momentum after the 1960s and then turned into something huge in the 1980s. Latino immigrants were drawn north when America needed their services, and they built communities known as barrios in every major city. But then in the 1990s, as these newcomers began to define their permanent place here, the ground shifted on them. They and their children—many of them native-born Americans—found themselves struggling with an economy that offered few opportunities to people trying to get off the bottom. They also faced a populace sometimes disconcerted by the growing number of foreigners in its midst. Immigration is a transaction between the newcomers and the hosts. It will be decades before there is a final tally for this great wave of immigration, but the terms of the deal have now become apparent.

Imelda's story does not represent the best or the worst of the Latino migration, but it does suggest some of the challenges posed by the influx. Those challenges are defined first of all by demography. No other democracy has ever experienced an uninterrupted wave of migration that has lasted as long and that has involved as many people as the recent movement of Spanish-speaking people to the United States. Twelve million foreign-born Latinos live here. If immigration and birth rates remain at current levels, the total Hispanic population will grow at least three times faster than the population as a whole for several decades, and Latinos will become the nation's largest minority group, surpassing the size of the black population [in just] a few years. . . . after the turn of the [twenty-first] century. Despite some differences among them, Latinos constitute a distinctive linguistic and cultural group, and no single group has ever dominated a prolonged wave of immigration the way Latinos have for thirty years. By contrast, Asians, the other large category of immigrants, come from nations as diverse as India and Korea, and although the Latino migration is hardly monolithic, the Asian influx represents a much greater variety of cultures, languages, and economic experiences. Moreover, not since the Irish potato famine migration of the 1840s has any single nationality accounted for such a large share of an immigrant wave as the Mexicans have in recent decades. The 6.7 million Mexican immigrants living in the United States in 1996 made up 27 percent of the entire foreign-born population, and they outnumbered the entire Asian immigrant population by more than 2 million people. Latinos are hardly the only immigrants coming to the United States in the 1990s, but they will define this era of immigration, and this country's response to them will shape its response to all immigrants.

Latinos, like most other immigrants, tend to cluster together. Their enclaves are the barrios, a Spanish word for neighborhoods that has become part of English usage because barrios have become such a common part of every American city. Most barrios, however, remain a place apart, where Latinos live separated from others by custom, language, and preference. They are surrounded by a city but are not part of it. Imelda lived in a barrio named Magnolia Park, after the trees that once grew along the banks of the bayou there. Like other barrios, Magnolia is populated primarily by poor and working-class Latinos, and many newly arrived immigrants start out there. Magnolia was first settled nearly a hundred years ago by Mexicans who fled revolution in their homeland and found jobs dredging the ship channel and port that allowed Houston to become a great city. Latinos continued to arrive off and on, especially when Houston was growing. Since the 1980s, when the great wave of new arrivals began pouring into Magnolia, it hasn't mattered whether the oil city was in boom or bust—Latinos always find jobs, even when they lack skills and education. Most of Magnolia is poor, but it is also a neighborhood where people go to work before dawn and work into the night.

Like other barrios, Magnolia serves as an efficient port of entry for Latino immigrants because it is an easy place to find cheap housing, learn about jobs, and keep connected to home. Some newcomers and their children pass through Magnolia and find a way out to more prosperous neighborhoods where they can leave the barrio life behind. But for millions like Imelda who came of age in the 1990s, the barrios have become a dead end of unfulfilled expectations.

"We could never get stuff like pizza at home," Imelda went on, "just Mexican foods. My mother would give me these silly dresses to wear to school. No jeans. No jewelry. No makeup. And they'd always say, 'Stick with the Mexican kids. Don't talk to the Anglos; they'll boss you. Don't run around with the Chicanos [Mexican-Americans]; they take drugs. And just don't go near the *morenos* [blacks] for any reason.'"

Imelda's parents live in a world circumscribed by the barrio. Except for the places where they work, the rest of the city, the rest of America, seems to them as remote as the downtown skyline visible off in the distance on clear days. After more than a dozen years, they speak all the English they need, which isn't much. What they know best is how to find and keep work.

Imelda learned English from the television that was her constant childhood companion. Outside, as Magnolia became a venue for gangs and drug sales, she learned to be streetwise and sassy. Growing up fast in Magnolia, Imelda learned how to want things but not how to get them. . . .

Latinos are different from all other immigrants past and present because they come from close by and because many come illegally. No industrialized nation has ever faced such a vast migration across a land border with the virtual certainty that it will continue to challenge the government's ability to control that border for years to come. No immigrant group has carried the stigma of illegality that now attaches itself to many Latinos. Unlike most immigrants, Latinos arrive already deeply connected to the United States. Latinos come as relations, distant relations perhaps, but familiar and connected nonetheless. They seem to know us. We seem to know them, and almost as soon as they are in the house, they become part of our bedroom arguments. They are newcomers, and yet they find their culture imbedded in the landscape of cities that have always had Spanish names, such as Los Angeles and San Antonio, or that have become largely Spanish-speaking, such as Miami and New York. They do not consider themselves strangers here because they arrive to something familiar.

They come from many different nations, many different races, yet once here they are treated like a pack of blood brothers. In the United States, they live among folk who share their names but have forgotten their language, ethnic kinsmen who are Latinos by ancestry but U.S. citizens by generations of birthright. The newcomers and the natives may share little else, but for the most part they share neighborhoods, the Magnolias, where their fates become intertwined. Mexican-Americans and Puerto Ricans account for most of the native-born Latino population. They are the U.S.-made vessel into which the new immigration flows. They have been Americans long enough to have histories, and these are sad histories of exploitation and segregation abetted by public authorities. As a result, a unique designation was born. "Hispanics" became a minority group. This identity is an inescapable aspect of the Latino immigrant experience because newcomers are automatically counted as members of the group for purposes of public policy and because the discrimination that shaped that identity persists in some segments of the American public. However, it is an awkward fit for several reasons. The historical grievances that led to minority group designation for Latinos are significant, but compared to slavery or Jim Crow segregation they are neither as well known nor as horrible. As a result, many Americans simply do not accept the idea that Latinos have special standing, and not every native Latino embraces this history as an inescapable element of self-concept. Moreover, Latinos do not carry a single immutable marker, like skin color, that reinforces group identity. Minority group status can be an important element of a Latino's identity in the United States, but it is not such a clear and powerful element of American life that it automatically carries over to Latino immigrants.

"Hispanic" has always been a sweeping designation attached to people of diverse cultures and economic conditions, different races and nationalities, and the sweep has vastly increased by the arrival of immigrants who now make up about 40 percent of the group. The designation applies equally to a Mexican-American whose family has been in Texas since before the Alamo and a Mexican who just crossed the Rio Grande for the first time. Minority group status was meant to be as expansive as the discrimination it had to confront. But now for the first time, this concept is being stretched to embrace both a large native Latino population with a long undeniable history of discrimination and immigrants who are just starting out here. The same is occurring with some Asian groups, but the Latino phenomenon has a far greater impact because of the numbers involved. Latino immigrants are players in the old and unresolved dilemma of race in America, and because they do not fit any of the available roles, they are a force of change.

Like all other newcomers, Latino immigrants arrive as blank slates on which their future course has yet to be written. They are moving toward that future in many directions at once, not en masse as a single cohesive group. Some remain very Latino; others become very American. Their skin comes in many different colors and shades. Some are black, and some of them can pass very readily as white. Most Latinos arrive poor, but they bring new energy to the labor force even as they multiply the ranks of the chronically poor. Latino immigrants challenge the whole structure of social science, politics, and jurisprudence that categorizes people in terms of lifetime membership in racial or ethnic groups. The barrios do not fit into an urban landscape segregated between rich and poor, between the dependent and the taxed.

Latino immigrants come in large numbers. They come from nearby. They join fellow Latinos who are a native minority group. Many arrive poor, illegally, and with little education. Those are the major ingredients of a challenge unlike any other. . . .

More than a third of all Latinos are younger than eighteen years old. This vast generation is growing faster than any other segment of the population. It is also failing faster. While dropout rates among Anglos and African-Americans steadily decline, they continue to rise among Latino immigrants, and mounting evidence suggests that many who arrive in their teens simply never enter American schools at all. A 1996 Rand study of census data found that high school participation rates were similarly high—better than 90 percent—for whites, blacks, and Asians, native and immigrant alike, and for native Latinos, as well. Latino immigrants, especially from Mexico, were the only group lagging far behind, with less than 75 percent of the school-age teens getting any education. Only 62 percent of the Mexican immigrant seventeen-year-olds were in school, and these young people are the fuel of U.S. population growth into the twenty-first century.[3]

Dropout rates are only one symptom. This massive generation of young people is adapting to an America characterized by the interaction of plagues. Their new identities are being shaped by the social epidemics of youth homicides, pregnancy, and drug use, the medical epidemic of AIDS, and a political epidemic of disinvestment in social services. These young Latinos need knowledge to survive in the workforce, but the only education available to them comes from public school systems that are on the brink of collapse. They are learning to become Americans in urban neighborhoods that most Americans see only in their nightmares. Imelda and a vast generation of Latino young people like her are the victims of a vicious bait and switch. The United States offered their parents opportunities. So many of the children get the plagues.

For the parents, movement to the United States almost always brings tangible success. They may be poor by U.S. standards, but they measure their accomplishments in terms of what they have left behind. By coming north, they overcome barriers of race and class that have been insuperable for centuries in Latin America. Meanwhile, the children are left on the wrong side of the barriers of race and class that are becoming ever more insuperable in the United States. With no memory of the *rancho,* they have no reason to be thankful for escaping it. They look at their parents and all they see is toil and poverty. They watch American TV, and all they see is affluence. Immigrant children learning to live in this dark new world face painful challenges but get little help. Now, on top of everything else, they are cursed by people who want to close the nation's doors against them. The effects are visible on their faces.

"I can tell by looking in their eyes how long they've been here," said the Reverend Virgil Elizondo, rector of San Fernando Cathedral in San Antonio, Texas. "They come sparkling with hope, and the first generation finds that hope rewarded. Their children's eyes no longer sparkle. They have learned only to want jobs and money they can't have and thus to be frustrated."

The United States may not have much use now for Imelda's son, but he will be eighteen and ready to join the labor force in the second decade of the next century, just as the bulk of the baby-boom generation hits retirement age. Then, when the proportion of elderly to young workers is going out of whack, this country will have a great need for him and the other children born in the barrios, who will contribute financial sustenance in the form of their payroll deductions and other taxes. This is already an inescapable fact because of the relatively low birth rates among U.S.'s whites and African-Americans for the past several decades. Women of Mexican ancestry had fertility rates three times higher than non-Hispanic women in the 1990s (and they were the least educated mothers of any group). Mexican immigrant women account for more than a quarter of all the births in California and nearly a third of the births to teenage mothers. The United States may not care about the children of the barrios, but it must start to address their problems now. If it lets them fail, there will be a great price to pay.

Not all immigrants are in such straits. Social scientists have taken to describing an "hourglass effect" in the distribution of income, education, and skills among recent immigrants because they are bunched at the extremes. At the top, an extraordinary two-thirds of all immigrants from India arrive with at least four years of college. Newcomers from Korea, the Philippines, China, and several other Asian nations also arrive with more education than the average native-born American. At the bottom of the hourglass are most of the Latino nationalities that have recently produced large inflows. Less than 8 percent of the immigrants from the Dominican Republic or El Salvador and less than 4 percent of the Mexicans have four years of college. Many Latino immigrants lack not only the credentials to prosper but also the minimum education necessary to survive in the U.S. economy. Less than a quarter of all Mexican immigrants have a high school degree.[4]

The immigrants at the top—mostly Asians—generate a few policy controversies that generally fall under the heading "embarrassment of riches," such as when they contribute to a glut of medical specialists. A considerable number of Latino immigrants have achieved middle-class stability and are unlikely to cause much concern. However, the real social, political, and economic challenges arising from immigration today are posed by those at the bottom, and they are overwhelmingly Latinos. Again demography defines the challenge because the top and the bottom of the hourglass are not the same size. At the top, 760,000 Indian immigrants contribute exceptional skills. At the bottom, 6.7 million Mexicans represent extraordinary needs.

About a third of all recent Latino immigrants live below the official poverty line. More than a million and a half Mexicans who entered the country legally and illegally since 1980—43 percent of the total—were officially designated as poor in 1994. With little education and few skills, they have nowhere to start but low on the economic ladder, and in America today, people who start low tend to stay low and their children stay low as well unless they get an education. For two decades now, immigration has quietly added to the size of that perennially poor population and it has changed the nature of poverty in the United States. Twenty years ago there were nearly three times more poor African-Americans in this country than poor Latinos, but those numbers have been converging during the economic expansion of the 1990s with the African-American poverty figures trending down and the Latino numbers rising so that they are now nearly equal. However, they represent strikingly different forms of poverty.[5] In 1996 the workforce participation rate for Latinos was higher than for blacks, indeed it was even higher than for whites, but Latinos also had the highest poverty rate of any group. Latinos suffer the poverty of the working poor. While that is not unusual in the immigrant experience, it marks a historic departure from the kind of poverty that has plagued American cities for the past several decades. William Julius Wilson, the Harvard sociologist who invented the concept of the underclass, argues that "the disappearance of work and the consequences of that disappearance for both social and cultural life are the central problems in the inner-city ghetto." That diagnosis from Wilson's 1996 book, *When Work Disappears,* applies to urban African-American communities, but not to the barrios. As Wilson himself notes, nearly a decade of detailed research in Chicago showed that poor Mexican immigrants can share the same kind of dilapidated neighborhoods as poor blacks, but the Mexicans will be surrounded by small businesses owned by fellow immigrants and will benefit from tightly knit social networks that help them find jobs.[6]

Latino poverty will not be remedied by the welfare-to-work programs that are now virtually the sole focus of U.S. social policy, and it will not be fixed by trying to close the nation to further immigration. The Latino poor are here and they are not going to go away. Unless new avenues of upward mobility open up for Latino immigrants and their children, the size of America's underclass will quickly double and in the course of a generation it will double again. That second generation will be different than the first. It will not only suffer the economic and political disenfranchisement that plagues poor blacks today but it will also be cut off from the American mainstream in even more profound and dangerous ways. . . .

Latino immigrants present more of a mixed picture than their native coethnics. Historically, immigrants start out earning less than native-born workers of a similar age and similar skills because the newcomer usually is facing a language barrier and lacks familiarity with the labor market, but over time that wage gap shrinks. The conventional benchmark is that immigrants who arrive when they are twenty-five or younger will close the gap and earn wages equivalent to those of a native worker after twenty years in the labor force. It is a long pull, but for many millions of people it has proved fruitful. Considerable evidence now shows that Latino immigrants, especially Mexicans, are not closing the gap. In the most extensive nationwide study of immigration's economic, fiscal, and demographic impacts on the United States, the National Research Council concluded in 1997 that Mexicans start out with the lowest wage levels of any immigrant nationality and that their wage gap actually widens substantially over time.[7] Meanwhile, European and Asian immigrants are closing the wage gap at something like the traditional pace. A 1997 UCLA study found that Mexicans who had been in the United States for thirty years had achieved modest economic gains, while recent arrivals suffered actual declines in their earnings.[8] Nearly three-quarters of the recent arrivals went to work in "low-skill occupations out of which there are few avenues of escape," writes the study's author, Vilma Ortiz, a UCLA sociologist. "Clearly, the traditional ethnic saga of hard labor followed by rewards does not apply to Latino immigrants."

The latest wave of immigrants has come to the United States only to find the ladder broken. Their arrival has coincided with changes in the structure of the U.S. economy that make the old three-generation formula obsolete. The middle rungs of the ladder, which allowed for a gradual transition into American life, are more precarious because so many jobs disappeared along with the industrial economy of smokestacks and assembly lines. In addition, the wages paid at the bottom of the labor force have declined in value steadily since the early 1980s.

The old blue-collar jobs are not the only rungs of the ladder that are now wobbly. The United States greatly expanded its system of public education in order to prepare the children and the grandchildren of the European immigrants for the workforce, extending it first to high schools and then to universities. Latino immigrants have arrived, only to find this education system dangerously in disrepair. As with the demise of the industrial economy, this reflects a fundamental change in the structure of American society. Government's priorities have shifted in ways that alter the nature of opportunity. The results have quickly become apparent. The State of California now pays better salaries to experienced prison guards than to tenured Cal State professors. The guards are more in demand. Labor unions, big-city political machines, and other institutions that helped the European immigrants are also less vigorous and far less interested in the immigrants' cause than in the early decades of this century. The Roman Catholic church gave vital help to the Europeans in establishing enclaves, gaining education, and developing ethnic solidarity, but it moved to the suburbs with the second and third generations and has played a minor institutional role—primarily as a lobbyist for liberal immigration policies—in helping the new Latinos gain a foothold in the United States.

Starting at the bottom has usually been an immigrant's fate, but this takes on a new meaning in an increasingly immobile and stratified society. Skills and education have come to mark a great divide in the U.S. workforce, and the gap is growing ever broader. The entire population is being divided into a two-tier workforce, with a college education as the price of admission to the upper tier. In the new knowledge-based economy, people with knowledge prosper. People without it remain poor. These divisions have the makings of a new class system because this kind of economic status is virtually hereditary. Very few Latino immigrants arrive with enough education to make it into the upper tier of the workforce. Their children, like the children of all poor people, face the greatest economic pressures to drop out and find work. When they do stay in school, the education they receive is, for the most part, poor.

Like Latinos today, the European ethnics built enclaves, and some were places of exceptional misery and rejection. But the Europeans' enclaves became places to make a gradual transition into American life. As they built their communities, they could nurture ethnic identity and cohesion until it evolved into a source of political strength. The Europeans established their economic claims over long periods of time, slowly moving into the mainstream as they did so.

Blacks also built enclaves when they moved north, although their separation was forced on them. A blue-collar class developed and in another generation a middle class and a professional class of blacks emerged. This upward mobility resulted from employment in the industrial economy, antipoverty programs, and a concerted effort to grant African-Americans at least minimal access to good schools and universities. Even with these vehicles of upward mobility, it took a long time to achieve limited success.

Today, Latinos do not have the luxury of time. Immigrants and their children are no longer allowed missteps or setbacks. And there are fewer programs to ensure that at least a few of the worthy move up. Newcomers today either make it or they don't. Instead of a gradual evolution, the process of finding a place in America has become a sudden-death game.

The United States sits atop the Western Hemisphere like a beacon atop a lighthouse, a sole source, powerfully distorting everything it illuminates even as it points the way. For a hundred years, it has exercised a powerful influence over Latin America, and whether the medium was the Marine Corps or the Peace Corps, the message has always been that Americans knew better, did better, lived better. Whenever the United States became scared of Nazis or Communists, it expended huge resources to portray itself as the paragon of civic virtue and a land of boundless economic opportunity. Meanwhile, the American consumer culture penetrated deep into the Latin psyche, informing every appetite and defining new desires. With TV shows, soldiers, and political ideals, the United States has reached out and touched people across an entire hemisphere. It has gotten back immigrants in return.

America beckons, but massive human flows occur only after migrant channels have evolved into highly efficient conduits for human aspirations. In Mexico's case, emigration to the United States developed out of proximity, shared history, and encouraging U.S. business practices and government policies. When the Mexican revolution displaced millions of peasants after 1910, railroad foremen greeted them at the border and recruited them into track gangs. Dispersed by the Southern Pacific and the Santa Fe railroads, they remained in hundreds of farm towns and built the first urban barrios. Aside from these permanent settlements, a kind of circular traffic developed. Many thousands of Mexicans came to the United States for sojourns of work often lasting no more than a harvesting season but sometimes stretching to years. This migration was expanded and legalized by an agricultural guest-worker program launched in 1942 to help with wartime labor shortages. American farmers liked the cheap, disposable labor so much that that program survived until 1964. By that time, 4.5 million *braceros,* as the workers were known, had learned the way north. The *bracero* program ended, but the traffic continued even as the United States started trying to control the flow. Many Mexicans had acquired some kind of legal status here, including those born in the United States to migrant-worker parents. Others came illegally and found shelter in such barrios as Magnolia and East L.A., which had become permanent Spanish-speaking enclaves. Major changes in U.S. immigration law enacted in 1965 raised the overall ceilings for legal immigration and removed biases that favored Northern and Western Europeans. The most important change in the long run, however, gave preference to immigrants who were reuniting with kin. Having a relative here became the key qualification for a visa, rather than a prospective employer or marketable skills, and immigrant flows became self-duplicating as every new legal immigrant eventually became a potential sponsor for others. . . .

Once efficient linkages had developed, a variety of economic circumstances in the United States generated the demand for immigrant labor, which encouraged the continuation of migrant flows. Just as the rise of the industrial era created jobs for the great wave of European immigrants, the end of that era created opportunities for Latinos. Some manufacturers in old industries such as garments, furniture, and auto parts turned to low-cost immigrant labor as a way of remaining competitive with foreign producers. As the U.S. population shifted south to the Sun Belt, Latinos arrived to build the new cities. Immigrants filled hundreds of new job niches as the United States developed a postindustrial service economy that saw booms in light manufacturing and all manner of consumer and financial services.

In addition to economic demand, changes in U.S. immigration law have also promoted continued movement from Latin America. The Immigration Reform and Control Act of 1986 was meant to halt illegal immigration, but it actually encouraged its growth. It created amnesties that allowed nearly 3 million former illegal aliens—nearly 90 percent of them Latinos—to acquire legal residence and eventually become eligible for citizenship. They, in turn, have become hosts to about a million relatives, who have lived in the United States illegally while applying for legal status, and to uncounted others who have no claim on residency. The 1986 reform also imposed sanctions for the first time—mostly civil fines—on employers who hire illegal aliens. No mechanism was ever created to enforce the law, and so it eventually became a meaningless prohibition. Then in 1990, Congress raised the limits on several forms of legal immigration, thus ensuring a protracted influx.

. . . The Irish came across the Atlantic as early as the seventeenth century and kept coming steadily for nearly two hundred years in response to demand for low-wage workers. This well-established linkage allowed for a massive, explosive migration during the potato famine in the middle of the nineteenth century and another huge wave in the 1880s during a period of rapid industrialization. Although the U.S. government now tries to regulate immigration, Mexico resembles the Irish case. As with the Irish in the nineteenth century, the migrant channels are abundant and efficient—there are large receiving communities here and the native-born descendants of immigrants have begun to penetrate the mainstream of American society. When Mexico suffered a devastating economic crisis in the 1980s and the U.S. economy boomed, the number of Mexican immigrants living in the United States doubled in a decade. That explosion continues so forcefully that the numbers might nearly double again in the 1990s. And the explosion does not involve just Mexicans now. The flows from the Dominican Republic and El Salvador are also running at a rate headed for a doubling by the end of the decade.

Americans are only just waking up to the size of this immigrant wave, and yet the foreign-born already account for 9 percent of the total population—the highest proportion since World War II. For fifty years after the end of the European wave in the 1920s, there was no steady immigration, and then the long lull was followed by a demographic storm. Some 7 million more immigrants, counting the estimates of the illegal flow, came to the United States between 1975 and 1995 than during the preceding half-century hiatus. Now, like Rip van Winkle aroused from his slumber, the United States is trying to understand something that is at once familiar but changed. The nation's reference points for large-scale immigration are set in an era of steamships and telegraphs, yet the United States needs to manage a massive influx at a time of jet travel and global television. Moreover, the Latino immigration is not just unexpected and unfamiliar; many Americans consider it unwanted. No national policy debate and no clear process of decision making led to formal action opening the doors to a level of immigration unfamiliar in living memory.

When the counterreaction hit, it hit hard. In the early 1990s an extraordinary variety of events combined to present immigration as a menacing force. It began quietly during the recession at the start of the decade and grabbed the public's attention with the nanny problems of Zoë Baird, President Clinton's first nominee for attorney general. Then came the World Trade Center bombing, perpetrated by evildoers who slipped through the immigration system. Chinese smuggling ships, Haitian boat people, Cuban rafters, and swarms of Tijuana border jumpers all fueled anxieties about a chaotic world infringing on America. Even though the United States remained more open to foreigners than any other nation, immigrants had come to represent mysterious and uncontrollable dangers. . . .

NOTES

1. Imelda's story: Author's account of his first encounters with Imelda appeared in the *New York Times,* January 20, 1992.
2. Twelve million foreign-born Latinos: U.S. Census Bureau, *The Foreign Born Population: 1994* (Current Population Reports P20-486, 1995), Current Population Survey, March 1996, FB96CPS.

   Latinos will become the nation's largest minority group: U.S. Census Bureau, *Population Projections of the United States by Age, Sex, Race and Hispanic Origin: 1995 to 2050* (Current Population Reports P25-1130, 1996).

   No single group has ever dominated a prolonged wave of immigration: In the 1890s, for example, Italy, Russia, Austria-Hungary, and Germany had almost equal shares of the influx (around 15 percent each), with Scandinavia, Ireland, and Great Britain not far behind (around 10 percent each).

   The 6.7 million Mexican immigrants: U.S. Census Bureau, *The Foreign Born Population: 1994.*
3. More than a third of all Latinos are younger than eighteen years old: Georges Vernez, Allan Abrahamse, *How Immigrants Fare in U.S. Education* (Rand, 1996).
4. Fertility rates: U.S. Census Bureau, *Fertility of American Women: June 1994* (Current Population Reports P20 482, 1995). B. Meredith Burke, "Mexican Immigrants Shape California's Future," *Population Today,* September 1995 (Population Reference Bureau Inc., Washington, DC).

   The hourglass effect: Philip L. Martin, "The United States: Benign Neglect towards Immigration," in *Controlling Immigration: A Global Perspective,* eds. Wayne A. Cornelius, Philip L. Martin, and James F. Hollifeld (Stanford University Press, 1995). And for statistics on the distribution of education among immigrants: Alejandro Portes and Rubén G. Rumbaut, *Immigrant America: A Portrait,* 2d ed. (University of California Press, 1996).

   About a third of all recent Latino immigrants live below the official poverty line: U.S. Census Bureau, *The Foreign Born Population: 1994.*
5. Twenty years ago there were: U.S. Census Bureau, *Poverty Income in the United States: 1996* (Current Population Reports P60-198, 1996).
6. In 1996 the workforce participation: U.S. Census Bureau, *Money Income in the United States: 1996* (Current Population Reports P60-197, 1996).

   William Julius Wilson: William Julius Wilson, *When Work Disappears* (Knopf, 1996), pp. 52, 65.
7. In the most extensive nationwide study: James P. Smith and Barry Edmonston, eds., *The New Americans: Economic, Demographic and Fiscal Effects of Immigration* (National Academy Press, 1997), chapter 5.
8. Mexicans who had been in the United States for thirty years had achieved modest economic gains: Vilma Ortiz, "The Mexican Origin Population: Permanent Working Class or Emerging Middle Class?" in *Ethnic L.A.,* eds. Roger Waldinger and Mehdi Bozogrmehr (Russell Sage Foundation, 1996).

   Prison guards and professors: Barry Munitz, "Never Make Predictions, Particularly about the Future" (American Association of State Colleges and Universities, 1995).

PERSONAL ACCOUNT

Just Like My Mama Said

I remember when I was just a little boy, my mother used to tell me, "Anthony you have to work twice as hard in life as everyone else, because being black means that you already have one strike against you." When I was growing up in a predominately black area, I did not know what she meant by this. Then we moved to an area that was filled with white people. I found myself constantly lagging behind, and I couldn't figure out why.

When I was 19 years old, I hit rock bottom and had nothing. I then remembered what my mama had said, and I began to work twice as hard as everyone else. I managed to afford my own apartment and eventually get married.

My wife is white, but her parents dislike me because of my color. They told her all the stereotypes about "the black male" and swore to her that I would follow suit. Soon after we moved in together, I was laid off from my job. I began to worry that she would think her parents were correct, so I tried to teach her about the black experience. I began to worry that her parents would negatively influence her and I would lose her. I was ready to give in and let her parents win, when I remembered something that my mama had said: "Sometimes you can't teach people; they have to learn on their own." Little did I know an appropriate lesson would soon follow.

As I was going through the want ads, I saw an advertisement for a job delivering pianos. The job paid nine dollars an hour, more money than I had ever earned. I set up an interview for that evening. When my then-fiancée arrived home, I put on a shirt and a tie, grabbed my resumé, and headed for the interview. When I asked her if she thought I would get the job, she said, "I don't see why not. You work hard, you have good references, and you are enrolled in school." Needless to say I felt pretty good about my chances. I interviewed with a middle-aged white lady. The interview went very well. She nearly assured me that I had the job, but said that she just needed to run it by the storeowner. She left and returned with the owner minutes later. He was a middle-aged man of apparently white and Asian descent. He looked at me for a few seconds, and our eyes met. Then he shook his head and said, "No this is not who I want for the job" and walked out. The lady and I dejectedly looked at each other. She attempted to make an excuse for him, but I told her "Don't worry, it's not your fault." I walked out and told my fiancée what had happened. We rode home in silence. She had just gotten her first taste of what it is like to be black in America.

Anthony McNeill

READING 45

Sex, Race, and Ethnic Inequality in United States Workplaces

Barbara F. Reskin

Irene Padavic

The last third of [the] twentieth century witnessed revolutionary reductions in sex and race inequality in the workplace. At the beginning of the 1960s, employers legally could refuse to hire people, assign them to jobs, and set their pay on the basis of their sex and race. The first signs of change were already present: married women had begun to catch up with their single sisters in their participation in the labor force, and African-Americans with their migration North were also pursuing different kinds of work from when they were in the South, especially women who were abandoning domestic work as other opportunities opened to them. But it took the Civil Rights Movement of the early 1960s, the Women's Liberation Movement of the late 1960s, and a series of federal and state laws to challenge the race

Barbara F. Reskin is professor of sociology at Harvard University. Irene Padavic is associate professor of sociology at Florida State University.

and sex discrimination that were customary in the United States.

As we will see in this [discussion], sex, race, and ethnic inequality persist in the kinds of paid work that people do, their advancement opportunities, and their earnings. We shall also see, however, indications of the erosion of these forms of inequality since 1970. We focus on two forms of employment inequality: the differential distribution of workers across occupations and jobs based on their sex, race, and ethnicity, and pay disparities associated with these characteristics. In a departure from most research, we consider three important bases of inequality: sex, race, and ethnicity. Although workers' sex, race, and ethnicity jointly affect their work experiences, few quantitative studies have simultaneously considered both sex and race, and only a handful of studies have examined the joint effects of sex, race, and ethnicity (see Reskin & Charles, 1997).[1] Within the constraints of the available research, we discuss the extent and causes of sex, race, and ethnic inequality in the workplace.

JOB SEGREGATION BY SEX, RACE, AND ETHNICITY

Workers are not distributed across jobs based solely on their qualifications and interests; their sex, race, and ethnicity exert strong effects on the industries and occupations in which they work and thus the jobs they hold.[2] Job segregation is the linchpin in workplace inequality because the relegation of different groups to different kinds of work both facilitates and legitimates unequal treatment. Segregation facilitates unequal treatment in part because the jobs to which women and people of color are assigned are inherently less desirable than those open to white Anglo men. In addition, jobs that are filled predominantly by women and perhaps by minorities are devalued because society devalues women and minorities. Segregation legitimates unequal treatment because both U.S. values and the law permit unequal pay for different work. For these reasons, segregation generates pay and status disparities between persons of different sexes and races.

At the beginning of the twentieth century, Asians, African-Americans, and white women were confined to a limited number of occupations. A straightforward indicator of the degree to which workers are segregated based on some characteristic is the index of segregation (Duncan & Duncan, 1955). The value of this index, which ranges from 0 to 100, indicates the proportion of one of two groups that would have to change to an occupation in which that group is underrepresented for the two groups to be identically distributed across occupations. Between 1900 and 1970, the index of occupational segregation hovered around 70 for women and men (Gross, 1968). In fact, the sexes and races were so segregated that until 1940 the U.S. Census Bureau treated census returns with atypical worker–occupation combinations, such as female train engineer, as errors (Conk, 1981, p. 69).[3] Sex and race discrimination gave white men a semimonopoly over most technical, managerial, and professional jobs until the middle 1960s.[4] Race discrimination confined most blacks to menial agricultural and service jobs, and custom and law closed all but a handful of occupations to women.[5]

After 1940, however, the occupational race segregation index declined among both sexes, from 44 to 24 for men and from 65 to 22 for women. Race segregation began declining at this time because the labor shortage brought on by World War II forced factories to hire blacks. The effect of these new opportunities was revolutionary for black women who formerly had few options apart from working in white people's homes.[6] In the 1970s, sex segregation also began declining. About one quarter of the drop in the segregation index was due to the shrinking proportion of the labor force working in occupations that were heavily sex segregated, such as heavy manufacturing, and the increasing proportion in occupations that were moderately integrated; the other three quarters resulted as women began integrating customarily male occupations, such as manager (Spain & Bianchi, 1996, Table 4.6). As a result, between 1970 and 1990 the index of occupational sex segregation fell from 67 to 53 (50.5 for blacks, 53.6 for whites, and 52.7 for Hispanics; Jacobs, 1989a; Reskin, 1994; additional computations from U.S. Bureau of the Census, 1992a). In 1990, to fully sex-integrate occupations would have required that 53% of all female workers—more than 32 million persons—shift to mostly male occupations. Eliminating segregation among whites would have required that 25% of Asians (29% of men and 21% of women), 26.5% of African-American (28% of men and 25% of women), and 27% of Hispanics (29% of men and 24% of women) change occupations (Reskin, 1994; additional computations from U.S. Bureau of the Census, 1992a). To eliminate both sex and race segregation across occupations in 1990 would have required 60% of black women, 58% of Hispanic women, 53% of white women, and 30% of black and Hispanic men to shift to occupations in which white men predominated. Asians tend to be less segregated from same-sex whites than are blacks (Reskin, 1994).

Interpreting segregation indices as the proportion of members of a sex/race group that would have to change occupations is a convenient way of summarizing the extent of occupational segregation, but in reality such shifts would take generations under the best of conditions. In 1990, for example, almost 14 million black and white women—about one fifth of these women—held administrative-support occupations (in other words, they did clerical work) compared to 8% of black men and 5% of white men, while almost 19% of white men and 14% of black men held skilled blue-collar jobs, compared to 2% of both white and black women (U.S. Bureau of Labor Statistics, 1997, Table 10). To bring women's representation in administrative-support and skilled blue-collar occupations in line with that of white men would have meant the transfer of more than 10 million female clerical workers to skilled blue-collar occupations.

Regardless of their race, most women work in predominantly female occupations. Of the 57 million women in the labor force in 1990, one third worked in just 10 of the 503 detailed occupations (U.S. Bureau of Labor Statistics, 1996a),[7] and only one woman in nine pursued an occupation that was at least 75% male (Kraut & Luna, 1992, p. 3). Men likewise remain concentrated in predominately male occupations: one quarter of the 69 million men in the labor force worked in just 10 occupations in 1990. Only two occupations appeared on both sex's top 10 list; "manager or administrator, not elsewhere classified" and "sales supervisor or proprietor" (U.S. Bureau of Labor Statistics, 1996a), and these two heterogeneous categories conceal substantial job-level sex segregation. The large number of women working as managers, administrators, sales supervisors, and proprietors are disproportionately white. Neither manager or administrator (not elsewhere classified), nor sales supervisor or proprietor was among the five largest occupations for black women or Latinas (or Latinos) in 1995 (see Table 1). Except for black female nurses, none of the occupations that employed large numbers of Hispanic or black women or men were professional or managerial.[8] Black women were overrepresented in just a few professional occupations—dietitian, educational or vocational counselor, and social worker in 1995 (computed from U.S. Bureau of Labor Statistics, 1996a). Hispanic men and women were underrepresented in all professions (U.S. Bureau of Labor Statistics, 1996b, Table 637). Most of the top five occupations for black and Hispanic women and men involved cleaning or personal service (maid, private household servant, janitor, cook, gardner, nursing aide); a few involved unskilled labor (farm worker, laborer; see Table 1).

Ethnicity also affects workers' occupational outcomes. For example, Filipina, American Indian, and Puerto Rican women resembled black women in that nursing aide was among their top

TABLE 1

TOP OCCUPATIONS FOR BLACK, HISPANIC, AND WHITE WOMEN AND MEN, 1995

White women	Number	%	White men	Number	%
Secretary	2942	6.1	Manager, n.e.c*	4503	7.7
Manager, n.e.c.*	1741	3.6	Sales, supervisor, proprietor	2483	4.3
Cashier	1709	3.5	Truck driver	2301	4.0
Registered nurse	1600	3.3	Engineer	1593	2.7
Sales, supervisor, proprietor	1566	3.2	Vehicle mechanic	1516	2.6
Total labor force	48344	100.0	Total labor force	58146	100.0
Black women	**Number**	**%**	**Black men**	**Number**	**%**
Nursing aide, orderly	482	7.0	Truck driver	352	5.5
Cashier	349	5.1	Janitor	267	4.2
Cook	166	2.4	Manager, n.e.c.*	198	3.1
Maid	151	2.2	Cook	187	2.9
Registered nurse	150	2.2	Laborer, except construction	159	2.5
Total labor force	6857	100.0	Total labor force	6422	100.0
Hispanic women	**Number**	**%**	**Hispanic men**	**Number**	**%**
Secretary	210	4.8	Truck driver	285	4.2
Cashier	205	4.7	Farm worker	279	4.1
Private household servant	130	3.0	Janitor	267	4.0
Janitor	128	2.9	Cook	263	3.9
Nursing aid, orderly	126	2.9	Gardener	196	2.9
Total labor force	4403	100.0	Total labor force	6725	100.0

Note: Blacks and whites include people of Hispanic origin.
*The abbreviation "n.e.c." refers to occupations that are not elsewhere classified.
Source: Unpublished tabulations of 1995 Current Population Survey data by the U.S. Bureau of Labor Statistics (1997).

three occupations in 1995. Among the top three occupations for Central American, Chinese, Cuban, Korean, and Southeast Asian women was textile operative. The top three occupations for Mexican and Central American women and for Puerto Rican, Mexican, and Southeast Asian men included janitor (the second largest occupation for black men). Cook was among the top three occupations for Japanese, Chinese, Filipino, Southeast Asian, and Central American men, as it was for black women (computed from the U.S. Bureau of Labor Statistics, 1996a).[9] All recent data on race and sex workplace segregation are for occupations—a category that combines jobs involving similar activities in the same and in different establishments (Bielby & Baron, 1986, p. 764). Thus, most nominally sex or racially integrated occupations include predominantly female and male specialties (Bielby & Baron, 1984). For example, although the occupation of real estate sales has become sex integrated, women are concentrated in residential sales, while men dominate the more lucrative commercial sales (Reskin & Roos, 1990). Occupational specialties may be differentiated as well by workers' race and ethnicity. For example, black workers tend to hold jobs in which they are more intensely supervised than are white workers in the same occupation (Tomaskovic-Devey, 1993, p. 148). Often members of different race/sex groups perform the same occupation in different establishments or even different parts of the country (Reskin, 1997b). Although declining occupational sex and race segregation signals some job-level integration, the extent of job segregation far exceeds measured levels of occupational segregation (Peterson & Morgan, 1995). In general, women and people of color—regardless of their sex—are underrepresented in desirable and lucrative jobs and disproportionately concentrated in low-status, low-paying service jobs.

Hierarchical Segregation

Because the desirability of the jobs in which group members are concentrated is positively correlated with the social status of the race/sex group, job segregation is often expressed hierarchically, with women and people of color concentrated in the lower ranks within occupations and organizations and white men dominating the top positions. Hierarchical segregation—by which we mean the segregation of workers across different ranks in the same job (e.g., assistant manager versus manager)—consigns members of favored groups to jobs that are higher in occupational or organizational hierarchies and hence confer more status, authority, and pay. Thus, hierarchical segregation further exacerbates the earnings and authority gaps (McGuire & Reskin, 1993; Reskin & Ross, 1992).[10] Hierarchical segregation—as expressed in the differential distribution of the races and sexes across vertical levels within organizations or occupations—includes both "glass ceilings" that exclude minorities and women from the top jobs in organizations and "sticky floors" that confine women and minorities—especially women of color—to low-ranking jobs (Berheide, 1992). A mere handful of minorities and women have reached the top of corporate hierarchies. In 1990, only five of the 1000 CEOs listed in the *Business Week* 1000 were nonwhite, and only 2.6% of senior managers in nine Fortune 500 companies that the U.S. Department of Labor studied were not white (Bell & Nkomo, 1994). In 1995, only 57 (2.4%) of the 2430 top officers in Fortune 500 companies were women (Catalyst, 1996). Other work settings show variations on this theme. In 1990, one in 11 partners in large law firms was female, compared to one in three associates (Epstein, 1993). Although corporate sales offer a fast track to management, only one in seven saleswomen get beyond the level of district manager (Catalyst, 1996). While women held half of all federal government jobs in 1992, only one quarter of supervisors and only 10% of senior executives were women, and fewer than 2% of senior executives were minority women (U.S. Merit Systems Protection Board, 1992, p. 33). Even in traditionally female occupations such as librarian or social worker, men advance more rapidly than women (Williams, 1995).

Minorities' and women's representation in managerial jobs offers a summary indicator of hierarchical segregation. Women and people of color remain underrepresented in management compared to white men, although the disparities have been shrinking since 1970. In 1990, almost 13.1% of non-Hispanic white workers held managerial jobs (14.1% of men, 11.8% of women), compared to 12.3 percent of Asians and Pacific Islanders (13.4% of men, 11.1% of women), 7.9% of Native American groups (7.2% of men, 8.7% of women), 7.3% of African-American workers (6.6% of men, 7.4% of women), and 6.5% of Hispanics (6.2% of men, 7.0% of women; U.S. Bureau of the Census, 1992b, Table 2). Although the representation of African Americans has been increasing, . . . African-American men's progress stalled during the 1980s, and by 1990 African-American women were more likely to work in managerial occupations than African-American men.

While the trends . . . show marked progress, we must remember that women and minorities tend to be low- rather than high-level managers. It is white male managers who usually have the final say in important decisions such as hiring, firing, promotions, raises, and issues that affect other units. A study comparing the sexes' roles in decision-making found that female managers' input was more often to provide information or make recommendations while male managers more often made final decisions (Reskin & Ross, 1992). Indeed, other evidence indicates that women and minorities are ghettoized into less desirable managerial jobs that white men eschew (Collins, 1989, p. 329; Reskin & McBrier, 1998). In addition, these and other findings suggest that some of women's and minorities' gains in managerial occupations represent "job-title inflation"—managerial titles without managerial authority—in response to increased federal scrutiny (Smith & Welch, 1984).

The patterns by sex and race . . . depart from the tendency for the effect of sex to exceed that of race that holds for occupational segregation and therefore for earnings. This departure probably reflects employers' practice of selecting managers of the same or a more highly esteemed sex and race than the workers who will be their subordinates.

Group differences in promotion rates also indicate hierarchical segregation. In the early 1990s, whites were twice as likely as blacks to have been promoted and men were almost twice as likely as women to have been promoted, after taking into account education, training, experience, and type of firm (Baldi & McBrier, 1997; see also Kalleberg & Reskin, 1995). In eight New York law firms, male associates were three times as likely as female associates to be promoted to partner (American Bar Association, 1996). In 1995, minority women were less likely to be promoted than white women with equivalent experience, although minority men in the federal government were promoted at the same rate as white men (U.S. Merit Systems Protection Board, 1996).

Explaining Sex and Race Segregation

Workers' sex and race are linked to the kinds of jobs they do because of employers' and workers' characteristics, preferences, and actions. However, some explanations for the relationship between workers' ascriptive characteristics and their jobs differ for race and sex. Explanations for segregation in general, and hierarchical segregation in particular, emphasize workers' characteristics and preferences—"supply-side" explanations—by assuming a two-step process: (1) people decide the kind of work they want to do, and (2) they obtain the necessary credentials. These explanations treat getting a job in one's preferred line of work as nonproblematic. Supply-side explanations for sex segregation tend to stress the first step in this process—work preferences, whereas supply-side explanations for race segregation emphasize the second step—obtaining qualifications. . . .

Workers' Characteristics and Preferences

The sexes are concentrated in different kinds of work, according to supply-side approaches, because women and men prefer different kinds of jobs. Social scientists have proposed two reasons the sexes' preferences differ. According to a socialization perspective, men and women pursue different kinds of jobs because gender-role socialization induces in them different life goals; instills in them different values regarding the importance of occupational success, autonomy, or high earnings; teaches them different skills; fosters different personality traits; and induces a distaste for sex-atypical activities and for working with members of the other sex (Marini & Brinton, 1984; see Chafetz, 1999). To the extent that gender-role socialization has these effects, the kinds of jobs that attract men should disinterest women and vice versa.

Although gender-role socialization may incline young people toward jobs that society labels as appropriate for their sex (Subich, Barrett, Doverspike, & Alexander, 1989), young people's occupational aspirations are both quite unstable and unrelated to the occupations they hold as adults (Jacobs, 1989b). Moreover, adults—especially women—move between predominantly female and predominantly male occupations (Jacobs, 1989b). Despite gender-role socialization—and readers must bear in mind that no systematic data compare the socialization of contemporary women and men—the sexes tend to value the same job rewards: good pay, autonomy, and prestige (Jencks, Perman, & Rainwater, 1988; Marini, Fan, Finley, & Beutel, 1996). With respect to vertical segregation, women are as likely as men to value promotions (Markham, Harlan, & Hackett, 1987, p. 227). These and other findings suggest that early gender-role socialization is not an important cause of job segregation. Far more influential are the opportunities, social pressures, and social rewards workers face as adults (Reskin & Hartmann, 1986).

The neoclassical economic perspective, another supply-side approach, assumes that occupational preferences are sex differentiated as a result of women's and men's conscious decisions to maximize household well-being. Hypothetically, in response to their different roles in the sexual division of labor, men and women pursue different employment strategies. Men's role as primary breadwinner induces them to maximize their earnings by pursuing jobs that pay well and reward experience and by maximizing the amount of time they spend doing paid work. Women's primary responsibility for homemaking and child-rearing and their recognition that their husbands will earn enough to adequately support the family hypothetically lead women to select jobs that are compatible with domestic duties, both in scheduling and ease of reentry after time out of the labor force (see, e.g., Polachek, 1981). If women can rely on economic support by their husbands, they can eschew lucrative jobs that require overtime, continuous labor force participation, and the exertion of considerable effort, thereby reducing conflict between paid and family work. In anticipation of their differential involvement in labor-market and family work, this approach also assumes that men invest in more education and training than women, making them more qualified for jobs that require skills.

Most research evidence is inconsistent with the neoclassical explanation of sex segregation. First, researchers have found that single women are as likely as married women to work in predominantly female occupations (Reskin & Hartmann, 1986, pp. 71–72). In any event, women who plan to leave the labor force to have children earn more in customarily male than female jobs. Second, predominantly male and female occupations require similar levels of education and skills (England, Chassie, & McCormack, 1982), and most workers acquire their skills on the job. Contrary to the neoclassical theory, women are more likely than men to obtain training before employment (Amirault, 1992). Thus, there is little evidence that men's and women's concentration in different jobs results from their responses to their anticipated or actual family roles. The human-capital account of occupational sex segregation is problematic on other counts as well. If women place family responsibilities ahead of their careers, they should evidence less job commitment than men; yet women's commitment does not differ from men's (Marsden, Kalleberg, & Cook, 1993). Women also expend as much energy on their jobs as men do (in fact, net of family responsibilities, women expend more effort on the job than men; Bielby & Bielby, 1988). Both sexes aspire to advance at work and will work hard for a promotion (Markham et al., 1987; Reskin & Cassirer, 1996). Compared to 74% of male federal employees, 78% of women (and 86% of minority women) were willing to devote as much time as necessary to advance in their career (U.S. Merit Systems Protection Board, 1992).[11] Finally, the characteristics of predominantly female jobs are not especially compatible with stereotypical female domestic roles: jobs in predominantly female occupations are no more flexible, easier, or cleaner than those in predominantly male occupations (Glass, 1990, p. 791; Jacobs & Steinberg, 1990). Two types of evidence are consistent with the neoclassical explanation of sex segregation. First, women are more likely than men to work part-time (in 1990, 22.4% of women and 7.6% of men worked part-time; computed from U.S. Bureau of the Census, 1992a), and part-time employment is associated with higher levels of occupational sex segregation. Second, sex differences in college majors are consistent with the neoclassical explanation (Jacobs, 1995). For example, women earned 47% of the bachelor's degrees in business administration in 1992, but only 34% of the master's degrees. Also, the greater workers' education, the less segregated the sexes are. In 1990, the index of sex segregation was considerably lower for college graduates than for high school graduates: 16.5 points lower for blacks and 18.5 points lower for whites (computed from U.S. Bureau of the Census, 1992a; see also Jacobsen, 1997, p. 235). Nonetheless, we must be careful not to overstate the effect of education on sex segregation. Even among college graduates, the sex segregation index is 38 for blacks and 44 for whites.

The occupational preferences of men and women might differ for a reason unrelated to their domestic roles: people pursue jobs that they believe are available to them (Reskin & Hartmann, 1986; Schultz, 1991, p. 141). Prospective workers do not apply for jobs unless they have reason to expect that they might be hired. Just as the sex-segregated help-wanted ads, common before the enactment of Title VII of the 1964 Civil Rights Act, steered workers into sex-typical lines of work, the sex and race composition of jobs signal would-be employees whether they have a reasonable chance of being hired and being accepted by co-workers. Minorities and women who are pioneers in occupations typically reserved for white men often encounter resistance—heckling, sabotage, and worse—by supervisors, co-workers, or customers (Bergmann & Darity, 1981; Padavic, 1991a; Schroedel, 1985; Swerdlow, 1989; U.S. Department of Labor, 1996), contributing to the "revolving door" that returns women to sex-typical occupations (Jacobs, 1989b). When employers make customarily male jobs genuinely accessible to women and mostly white occupations accessible to minorities, the attractiveness of these jobs draws plenty of women and minorities (Reskin & Hartmann, 1986; Reskin & Roos, 1990).

The neoclassical approach to race segregation emphasizes workers' qualifications rather than their preferences. Blacks and Latinos/as have less education and job experience than whites (England, Christopher, & Reid, 1997; Kilbourne, England, & Beron, 1994a, Table 1). Increasing parity in educational quality and quantity appear to have contributed to the occupational integration of black and white women between 1940 and 1990 (King, 1992). For example, in 1990 the segregation index for black and white women was 10 points lower for college graduates than for high school graduates (King, 1992; additional computations from U.S. Bureau of the Census, 1992a). However, men's educational attainment had little effect on the extent of race segregation—the index of race segregation for male high school graduates was 28.2; for college graduates it was 25.4 (computed from U.S. Bureau of the Census, 1992a). Also, 1990 census data indicate that race and ethnic differences in educational attainment—as well as nativity and English fluency—played only minor roles in occupational segregation by race and ethnicity (Reskin, 1997a).

In sum, the neoclassical approach is consistent with white males' concentration in customarily male occupations and their underrepresentation in predominantly female occupations: white men—whose options are not limited by discrimination—pursue the most desirable jobs and eschew predominantly female jobs because they pay less and offer fewer opportunities for advancement. However, the value of neoclassical approach for explaining women's and minorities' concentration in some occupations and underrepresentation in others is limited and largely inconsistent with our understanding of how workers get jobs.[12]

Employers' Preferences and Practices A major reason women and minorities are concentrated in different jobs than white men is because employers prefer persons of different sexes and races for different jobs. They do so because of their stereotypes and biases and out of deference to their customers' or employees' biases. Employers also segregate workers as a result of superficially neutral employment practices.

One reason employers consider sex and race in filling jobs is out of loyalty to their own group—usually white men. Although little research has focused explicitly on the segregative effects of in-group preference, several studies suggest its importance for the degree of segregation in organizations. First, the sex and race of decision-makers affect their responses to members of their own group and other groups. For example, having a female agency head was associated with progress toward sex integration in California state agencies (Baron, Mittman, & Newman, 1991). In addition, a review of more than 70 studies found that evaluators rated same-race persons higher than other-race persons (Kraiger & Ford, 1985). Second, the nepotism characteristic of small firms and some industries such as construction is, of course, for one's own group (Waldinger & Bailey, 1991), and its effect is segregative. Third, a shortage of white male workers is a major reason firms employ female and minority workers in customarily white-male occupations (Padavic & Reskin, 1990; Reskin & Roos, 1990). Fourth, by restricting cronyism—that is, in-group favoritism—formalized personnel practices appear to have reduced job segregation (Dobbin, Sutton, Meyer, & Scott, 1993).

According to several recent studies, race and sex stereotyping and bias contribute to sex segregation. For example, comparisons of the job-search outcomes of white-minority pairs in "audit" studies in four cities revealed that white men were substantially more likely to receive job offers than their minority matches (Fix & Struyk, 1992).[13] Qualitative studies in several cities reveal the reasons for the patterns from the audit studies. Employers, most of whom are white men, frankly admit their reluctance to hire black workers based on their stereotypes of blacks as lazy, unintelligent, insubordinate, and prone to criminal acts (Bobo, 1996; Holzer, 1996; Kasinitz & Rosenberg, 1996; Moss & Tilly, 1996; Neckerman & Kirschenman, 1991; Smith, 1990; Wilson, 1996, Chapter 5). The refusal of some employers to hire minorities or their willingness to hire them for only menial jobs inevitably segregates the races. Stereotypes also restrict women's employment opportunities. Stereotyped as unable to do physically demanding jobs, lacking career commitment, and disinterested in advancement (Bielby & Baron, 1986; Fiske, Bersoff, Bogida, Deaux, & Heilman, 1991; Reskin & Padavic, 1988; Segura, 1992, p. 173; Williams & Best, 1986), women are excluded from rewarding white-collar and blue-collar jobs. . . .

Regardless of their source—in-group preference, out-group antipathy, stereotypes, or biases—race and sex discrimination significantly restrict workers' options. The large number of formal complaints to antidiscrimination agencies, in combination with employers' candid reports of their stereotypes, suggest that discrimination is widespread: The federal government received more than 91,000 such complaints in 1994 (Leonard, 1994, p. 24; U.S. Department of Labor, 1996).[14] When enforced, antidiscrimination laws, such as Title VII of the 1964 Civil Rights Act (which banned employment discrimination based on race, national origin, or sex) and affirmative action requirements for federal contractors, opened thousands of semiskilled and skilled blue- and white-collar jobs to black men and women (Burstein, 1979, 1985; Donohue & Heckman, 1991; Heckman & Payner, 1989; for a review, see Badgett & Hartmann, 1995). Federal scrutiny helps to reduce sex and race segregation. The requirement by the Equal Employment Opportunity Commission (EEOC; the agency charged with enforcing Title VII) that firms with at least 50 employees annually report employees' distribution across broad occupational categories by race and sex has been an incentive for employers to place more women and minorities in managerial and administrative jobs. Thus, in 1960, 2% of black women, 4% of black men, and 5.5% of white women worked in the broad occupation of managers; by 1996, 9.6% of black women, 8.3% of black men, and 14% of white women were managers (U.S. Bureau of Labor Statistics, 1961, 1997, Table 10).

Recent history shows that when the government enforces antidiscrimination and affirmative-action regulations, minorities' and women's representation in sex- and race-atypical occupations increases (Ashenfelter & Heckman, 1976; Leonard, 1984a, b). More generally, sanctioning discriminating employers reduces job segregation (Badgett & Hartmann, 1995; Martin, 1991; Leonard, 1994, p. 21; Reskin & Roos, 1990). The uneven enforcement of the affirmative action required of federal contractors by Presidential Executive Order 11246 (11374) provided a natural experiment. During the 1980s, when there was no presidential mandate to enforce the executive order, minorities were more poorly represented at federal contractors than at noncontractors (Leonard, 1994), suggesting that federal contractors had reverted to the discriminatory practices that had prompted President Nixon to issue the executive order in the first place. Without the threat of governmental intervention, most employers do business as usual, which means making hiring and promotion decisions that are influenced by sex and race biases (Kern, 1996; Leonard, 1994).

Structural Discrimination Employers' personnel practices—even those that seem to be race and gender neutral—nonetheless affect race and sex segregation in firms. The clearest example is filling jobs through referrals by current workers. This common recruiting practice perpetuates segregation because workers' social networks tend to be sex and race segregated (Marsden, 1994, p. 983). In contrast, open-recruitment techniques, such as posting all job openings, can reduce segregation by allowing everyone to learn of sex- and race-atypical jobs.

Requiring credentials that are more common among white men than women and minorities also contributes to segregation. Sometimes segregation itself prevents women and minorities from acquiring qualifications. For example, the military's past exclusion of women from combat positions has blocked their advancement in military careers (Williams, 1989, p. 51). Analogously, blacks' exclusion from apprenticeship programs has kept them out of well-paying unionized craft jobs. Required credentials also can disproportionately affect women and minorities because employers more frequently exempt white men than others from formal requirements (Baron & Bielby, 1985, p. 243).

Pervasive sex segregation has prompted employers to organize work schedules and the labor process on the assumption that men will do some jobs and women will do others. The result can be barriers to women performing some customarily male jobs. For example, most machinery is designed to accommodate white, Anglo men. As a result, people who are shorter than the average white, Anglo man—including many women and some Latino and Asian men—cannot operate it safely or efficiently. Some companies design plant jobs so that workers rotate across different shifts—day, evening, and graveyard—which can discourage women from these jobs by making childcare arrangements difficult (Padavic, 1991b).

Segregated entry-level jobs maintain hierarchical segregation by disproportionately concentrating women and minorities in jobs with limited opportunity for mobility because they are on short ladders, restrict workers' opportunity to acquire skills, and lack visibility (Marsden, 1994, p. 983).[15] Firms tend to employ female and minority managers in staff positions, such as personnel or public relations, while male managers are concentrated in organizationally central line positions, such as sales, finance, and production, from which senior managers are selected. Employers often assign African-Americans to positions that deal with other minorities, such as community relations or affirmative action, regardless of their areas of expertise (Collins, 1989, p. 329, 1997). While staff positions provide few opportunities for workers to display their abilities, complex and challenging line jobs give incumbents a chance to develop and display their skills, such as exercising authority, supervising subordinates, or dealing with difficult situations (Bell & Nkomo, 1994, p. 39; Tomaskovic-Devey, 1994). Thus the segregation of minorities and women into nonchallenging jobs reduces their chances of being promoted by restricting their chances to acquire or demonstrate skills (Erdreich, Slavet, & Amador, 1996, p. xiii).

Minorities' and women's relegation to dead-end or short-ladder jobs is critical for hierarchical segregation (Bell & Nkomo, 1994, pp. 32, 39; Collins, 1989, 1997). To improve advancement opportunities for clerical and service workers, some companies have created "bridge" positions that help workers to switch job ladders—for example, move from a clerical job ladder to a production or administrative one—without risk or penalty (Kanter, 1976; Northrup & Larson, 1979; Roos & Reskin, 1984). Seniority systems can also affect the amount of hierarchical segregation in an organization (Kelley, 1984). For instance, USX (formerly U.S. Steel) helped to integrate customarily male production jobs by altering its seniority rules to allow workers to transfer to plant jobs without losing their seniority (Reskin & Hartmann, 1986, p. 93; Ullman & Deaux, 1981). Other case studies also demonstrate that organizations can eliminate structural barriers that exclude women and minorities from jobs (Badgett, 1995; Deaux & Ullman, 1983; DiTomaso, 1993; Northrup & Larson, 1979).

The segregation of women and men into different kinds of establishments also contributes to hierarchical segregation. The sheer size of large organizations lets them create more opportunities to promote workers, and they are more likely to have job ladders (Kalleberg, Marsden, Knoke, & Spaeth, 1996). Therefore, women's concentration in small, entrepreneurial firms and nonprofit organizations and men's concentration in large corporations and for-profit companies reduce women's odds of promotion relative to men (Kalleberg & Reskin, 1995). Some industries are better than others in promoting women. In female-intensive industries such as apparel, banking, retail trade, and insurance, women are more likely to be high-level managers (Shaeffer & Lynton, 1979). For instance, in 1990 women were only 2.2% of the officers in the chemicals industry, but 10% of the officers in the apparel industry. Although only five percent of the directors in the electronics industry were women in the late 1980s, almost 17% of the directors in the cosmetics and soap industries were (Von Glinow, 1988). Why do women have greater access to high-level jobs in female-dominated industries? Jobs in female-intensive industries pay less and are thus less desirable to men. Furthermore, firms' experience with female workers makes them less likely to stereotype women.

In sum, workplace segregation is largely due to employers' use of workers' sex, race, and ethnicity in assigning workers to jobs because of stereotypes and outright bias. Pressure from regulatory agencies, internal constituencies, and the public has prompted some employers to reduce stereotyping and bias by replacing informal personnel practices, such as word-of-mouth hiring, with formal ones, such as advertising and posting all openings, reassessing the qualifications jobs require, and using objective criteria for hiring and promotion (Roos & Reskin, 1984; Szafran, 1982). . . .

ACKNOWLEDGMENTS

We are grateful to Kathryn A. Barry for her help with the references, Naomi R. Cassirer for her help with data analysis, and Debra B. McBrier for preparing the table and figures.

NOTES

1. Space limitations and limitations in available research preclude our considering other factors that influence workplace outcomes, such as social class, sexual orientation, or disability.
2. An occupation is a collection of jobs involving similar activities within or across establishments (Bielby & Baron, 1986, p. 764). The 1990 census distinguished 503 detailed occupations. In contrast, a job is a specified position in an establishment in which workers perform particular activities (Bielby & Baron, 1986, p. 764). *The Dictionary of Occupational Titles* (U.S. Department of Labor, 1977) distinguishes more than 20,000 jobs.
3. The Census Bureau instructed its coders in 1930, for example, to "look up any occupations which involve responsibility and high standing in the community, if the person is colored, Chinese, Japanese, or other" (quoted in Conk, 1981, p. 68).
4. Exceptions were teaching, nursing, and social work for white women, and professional jobs serving black clientele for blacks.
5. Among the occupations that some state laws closed to women were bartending and street car conductor.
6. Despite the existence of better opportunities, some southern white women were able to hold on to their black cleaning women through the passage of local Work or Fight ordinances (Rollins, 1995, p. 163).
7. The most common lines of work for women in 1990 are all but identical to those that employed the most women in 1940. The only recent addition to women's top 10 occupations is the census category "miscellaneous salaried managers."
8. African-American female professionals were concentrated in two customarily female professions—nursing and elementary school teaching (computed from U.S. Bureau of Labor Statistics, 1995). Asian-American women were concentrated in only one profession—accounting.
9. It was the fourth largest occupation for black and Hispanic men.
10. Even women in high-level positions seldom have as much authority as men at the same level (Reskin & Ross, 1992). For example, McGuire and Reskin (1993) found that if black and female workers had received the same authority returns to their experience and other credentials as white men, the authority gap with white men would have shrunk by 62% for white women, 71% for black women, and 93% for black men.
11. The publication did not report the proportion of minority men who were willing to work hard for a promotion.
12. Few job seekers have their choice of jobs; most receive only one or two offers and accept the first offer that meets their minimum acceptable pay (Gera & Hasan, 1982; Kahn, 1978).
13. An audit of sex discrimination found that more expensive restaurants favored males as server, whereas cheaper ones favored women (Newmark, Bank, & Van Nort, 1995).
14. Approximately 3% charged "reverse discrimination" (Bendick, 1996; Blumrosen, 1995).
15. Many employers adhere to what Bergmann (1986, pp. 114–116) called an "informal segregation code" that prohibits women from supervising men and reserves the training slots leading to higher-level jobs for men. Men rule over women and junior men, women rule over women, but women rarely if ever rule over men. This code applies to minorities as well: minorities may give orders to other minorities, but not to whites.

REFERENCES

American Bar Association Commission on Opportunities for Women in the Profession. (1996). *Unfinished business.* Chicago: The American Bar Association.

Amirault, T. (1992). Training to qualify for jobs and improve skills, 1991. *Monthly Labor Review, 115,* 31–36.

Ashenfelter, O., & Heckman, J. (1976). Measuring the effect of an anti-discrimination program. In O. Ashenfelter & J. Blum (Eds.), *Evaluating the labor market effects of social programs* (pp. 46–84). Princeton, NJ: Princeton University Press.

Badgett, M. V. L. (1995). Affirmative action in a changing legal and economic environment. *Industrial Labor Relations, 34,* 489–506.

Badgett, M.V. L., & Hartmann, H. I. (1995). The effectiveness of equal employment opportunity policies.

In M. C. Simms (Ed.), *Economic perspectives on affirmative action* (pp. 55–97). Washington, DC: Joint Center for Political and Economic Studies.

Baldi, S., & McBrier, D. B. (1997). Do the determinants of promotion differ for blacks and whites? Evidence from the U.S. labor market. *Work and Occupations, 24,* 470–497.

Baron, J. N., & Bielby, W. T. (1985). Organizational barriers to gender equality: Sex segregation of jobs and opportunities. In A. S. Rossi (Ed.), *Gender and the life course* (pp. 233–251). New York: Aldine.

Baron, J. N., Mittman, B. S., & Newman, A. E. (1991). Targets of opportunity: Organizational and environmental determinants of gender integration within the California Civil Service, 1979–1985. *American Journal of Sociology, 96,* 1362–1401.

Bell, E. L. J., & Nkomo, S. (1994). Barriers to workplace advancement experienced by African-Americans. *Report to the Glass Ceiling Commission.* U.S. Department of Labor, April.

Bendick, M., Jr. (1996). *Declaration.* (Brief challenging California Civil Rights Initiative.) Submitted to the California State Court of Appeals.

Bergmann, B. R. (1986). *The economic emergence of women.* New York: Basic Books.

Bergmann, B. R., & Darity, W., Jr. (1981). Social relations, productivity, and employer discrimination. *Monthly Labor Review, 104,* 47–49.

Berheide, C. W. (1992). Women still 'stuck' in low-level jobs. *Women in public services: A bulletin for the Center for Women in Government* 3 (Fall).

Bielby, W. T., & Baron, J. N. (1984). A woman's place is with other women: Sex segregation within organizations. In B. F. Reskin (Ed.), *Sex segregation in the workplace* (pp. 27–55). Washington, DC: National Academy Press.

Bielby, W. T., & Baron, J. N. (1986). Men and women at work: Sex segregation and statistical discrimination. *American Journal of Sociology, 91,* 759–799.

Bielby, D. D., & Bielby, W. T. (1988). She works hard for the money: Household responsibilities and the allocation of work effort. *American Journal of Sociology, 93,* 1031–1059.

Blumrosen, A. W. (1995). Draft report on reverse discrimination, commissioned by U.S. Department of Labor: How courts are handling reverse discrimination cases. *Daily Labor Report,* March 23. Washington, DC: The Bureau of National Affairs.

Bobo, L. (1996). *Declaration.* Submitted to the California State Court of Appeals. November 1.

Burstein, P. (1979). Equal employment opportunity legislation and the income of women and nonwhites. *American Sociological Review, 44,* 367–391.

Burstein, P. (1985). *Discrimination, politics, and jobs.* Chicago: University of Chicago Press.

Catalyst. (1996). *Women in corporate leadership.* New York: Catalyst.

Chafetz, Janet Saltzman. (1999). *Handbook of the sociology of gender.* New York: Kluwer Academic/Plenum Publishers.

Collins, S. M. (1989). The marginalization of black executives. *Social Problems, 36,* 317–331.

Collins, S. M. (1997). *Black corporate executives: The making and breaking of a black middle class.* Philadelphia: Temple University Press.

Conk, M. (1981). Accuracy, efficiency and bias: The interpretation of women's work in the U.S. Census of Occupations, 1890–1940. *Historical Methods, 14,* 65–72.

Deaux, K., & Ullman, J. P. (1983). *Women of steel: Female blue-collar workers in the basic steel industry.* New York: Praeger.

DiTomaso, N. (1993). *Notes on Xerox case: Balanced workforce at Xerox.* Unpublished.

Dobbin, F., Sutton, J., Meyer, J., & Scott, W. R. (1993). Equal opportunity law and the construction of internal labor markets. *American Journal of Sociology, 99,* 396–427.

Donohue, J. J., & Heckman, J. (1991). Re-evaluating federal civil rights policy. *Georgetown Law Review, 79,* 1713–1735.

Duncan, O. D., & Duncan, B. (1955). A methodological analysis of segregation indices. *American Sociological Review, 20,* 200–217.

England, P., Chassie, M., & McCormack, L. (1982). Skill demands and earnings in female and male occupations. *Sociology and Social Research, 66,* 47–68.

England, P., Christopher, K., & Reid, L. L. (1997). How do intersections of race-ethnicity and gender affect pay among young cohorts of African Americans, European Americans, and Latinos/as? In I. Browne (Ed.), *Race, gender and economic inequality: African American and Latina women in the labor market.* New York: Russell Sage.

Erdreich, B., Slavet, B., & Amador, A. (1996). *Fair and equitable treatment: A progress report on minority employment in the federal government.* Washington, DC: U.S. Merit Systems Protection Board.

Fiske, S. T., Bersoff, D. N., Borgida, E., Deaux, K., & Heilman, M. E. (1991). Social science research on trial: Use of sex stereotyping research in Price Waterhouse v. Hopkins. *American Psychologist, 46,* 1049–1060.

Fix, M., & Struyk, R. J. (Eds.). (1992). *Clear and convincing evidence. Measurement of discrimination in America.* Washington, DC: The Urban Institute.

Gera, S., & Hasan, A. (1982). More on returns to job search: A test of two models. *Review of Economics and Statistics, 64,* 151–156.

Glass, J. (1990). The impact of occupational segregation on working conditions. *Social Forces, 68,* 779–796.

Gross, E. (1968). Plus ca change: The sexual segregation of occupations over time. *Social Problems, 16,* 198–208.

Heckman, J. J., & Payner, B. S. (1989). Determining the impact of anti-discrimination policy on the economic status of blacks: A study of South Carolina. *American Economic Review, 79,* 138–177.

Holzer, H. J. (1996). *What employers want.* New York: Russell Sage Foundation.

Jacobs, J. A. (1989a). Long-term trends in occupational segregation by sex. *American Journal of Sociology, 95,* 160–173.

Jacobs, J. A. (1989b). *Revolving doors.* Stanford, CA: Stanford University Press.

Jacobs, J. A. (1995). Gender and academic specialties: Trends among degree recipients during the 1980s. *Sociology of Education, 68,* 81–98.

Jacobs, J. A., & Steinberg, R. J. (1990). Compensating differentials and the male-female wage gap: Evidence from the New York State Comparable Worth Study. *Social Forces, 69,* 439–468.

Jacobsen, J. P. (1997). Trends in workforce segregation: 1980 and 1990 Census figures. *Social Science Quarterly, 78,* 234–235.

Jencks, C., Perman, L., & Rainwater, L. (1988). What is a good job? A new measure of labor-market success. *American Journal of Sociology, 93,* 1322–1357.

Kahn, L. M. (1978). The returns to job search: A test of two models. *Review of Economics and Statistics, 15,* 496–503.

Kalleberg, A. & Reskin, B. F. (1995). Gender differences in promotion in the U.S. and Norway. *Research in Social Stratification and Mobility, 13,* 237–264.

Kalleberg, A., Marsden, P. V., Knoke. D., & Spaeth, J. L. (1996). Formalizing the employment relationship: Internal labor markets and dispute resolution procedures. In A. L. Kalleberg. D. Knoke, P. V. Marsden, & J. L. Spaeth (Eds), *Organizations in America* (pp. 87–112). Newbury Park, CA: Sage.

Kanter, R. M. (1976). The policy issues: Presentation VI. In M. Blaxall & B. Reagan (Eds.), *Women and the workplace* (pp. 282–291). Chicago: University of Chicago Press.

Kasinitz, P., & Rosenberg, J. (1996). Missing the connection: Social isolation and employment on the Brooklyn waterfront. *Social Problems, 43,* 180–196.

Kelley, M. R. (1984). Commentary: The need to study the transformation of job structures. In B. F. Reskin (Ed.), *Sex segregation in the workplace: Trends, explanations, remedies* (pp. 261–264). Washington, DC: National Academy Press.

Kern, L. (1996). Hiring and seniority: Issues in policing in the post-judicial intervention period. Unpublished paper. Columbus, OH: Ohio State University.

Kilbourne, B., England, P., & Beron, K. (1994a). Effects of individual, occupational, and industrial characteristics on earnings: Intersections of race and gender. *Social Forces, 72,* 1149–1176.

King, M. C. (1992). Occupational segregation by race and sex, 1940–88. *Monthly Labor Review, 115,* 30–36.

Kraiger, K., & Ford, J. K. (1985). A meta-analysis of ratee race effects in performance ratings. *Journal of Applied Psychology, 70,* 56–65.

Kraut, K., & Luna, M. (1992). *Work and wages: Facts on women and people of color in the workforce.* Washington, DC: National Committee on Pay Equity.

Leonard, J. S. (1984a). The impact of affirmative action on employment. *Journal of Labor Economics, 2,* 439–463.

Leonard, J. S. (1984b). Employment and occupational advance under affirmative action. *The Review of Economics and Statistics, 66,* 377–385.

Leonard, J. S. (1994). Use of enforcement techniques in eliminating glass ceiling barriers. Report to the Glass Ceiling Commission, U.S. Department of Labor, April.

Marini, M. M., & Brinton, M. C. (1984). Sex typing in occupational socialization. In B. F. Reskin (Ed.), *Sex segregation in the workplace: Trends, explanations, remedies* (pp. 192–232). Washington, DC: National Academy Press.

Marini, M. M., Fan, P., Finley, E., & Beutel, A. (1996). Gender and job values. *Sociology of Education, 69,* 49–64.

Markham, W. T., Harlan, S., & Hackett, E .J. (1987). Promotion opportunity in organizations. *Research in Personnel and Human Resource Management, 5,* 223–287.

Marsden, P. V. (1994). The hiring process: Recruitment methods. *American Behavioral Scientist, 7,* 979–991.

Marsden, P. V., Kalleberg, A. L., & Cook, C. R. (1993). Gender differences in organizational commitment: Influences of work positions and family roles. *Work and Occupations, 20,* 368–390.

Martin, S. E. (1991). The effectiveness of affirmative action: The case of women in policing. *Justice Quarterly, 8,* 489–504.

McGuire, G. M., & Reskin, B. F. (1993). Authority hierarchies at work: The impact of race and sex. *Gender & Society, 7,* 487–506.

Moss, P., & Tilly, C. (1996). 'Soft' skills and race. *Work and Occupations, 23,* 252–276.

Neckerman, K. M., & Kirschenman, J. (1991). Hiring strategies, racial bias, and inner-city workers: An investigation of employers' hiring decisions. *Social Problems, 38,* 433–447.

Neumark, D., Bank, R., & Van Nort, K. (1995). Sex discrimination in the restaurant industry: An audit study. Working Paper No. 5024. Washington, DC: National Bureau of Economic Research.

Northrup, H. R., & Larson, S. A. (1979). The impact of the AT&T-EEO consent decrees. *Labor Relations and Public Policy Series,* No. 20. Philadelphia: Industrial Research Unit, University of Pennsylvania.

Padavic, I. (1991a). The re-creation of gender in a male workplace. *Symbolic Interaction, 14,* 279–294.

Padavic, I. (1991b). Attractions of male blue-collar jobs for black and white women: Economic need, exposure, and attitudes. *Social Science Quarterly, 72,* 33–49.

Padavic, I., & Reskin, B. F. (1990). Men's behavior and women's interest in blue-collar jobs. *Social Problems, 37,* 613–628.

Peterson, T. & Morgan, L. (1995). Separate and unequal: Occupation-establishment sex segregation and the gender wage gap. *American Journal of Sociology, 101,* 329–365.

Polachek, S. (1981). A supply side approach to occupational segregation. Presented at the American Sociological Association meeting, Toronto.

Reskin, B. F. (1994). Segregating workers: Occupational differences by ethnicity, race, and sex. *Annual Proceedings of the Industrial Relations Research Association, 46,* 247–255.

Reskin, B. F. (1997a). Dimensions of segregation: An MDS analysis of occupational segregation by race, ethnicity, and sex. Paper presented at the University of Pennsylvania, March.

Reskin, B. F. (1997b). Occupational segregation by race and ethnicity among female workers. In I. Browne (Ed.), *Race, gender, and economic inequality: African American and Latina women in the labor market.* New York: Russell Sage Foundation.

Reskin, B. F., & Cassirer, N. (1996). The effect of organizational arrangements on men's and women's promotion expectations and experiences. Unpublished manuscript. Columbus: Ohio State University.

Reskin, B. F., & Charles, C. Z. (1997). Now you see 'em, now you don't: Theoretical approaches to race and gender in labor markets. In I. Browne (Ed.), *Race, gender and economic inequality: African American and Latina women in the labor market.* New York: Russell Sage Foundation.

Reskin, B. F., & Hartmann, H. I. (1986). *Women's work, men's work: Sex segregation on the job.* Washington, DC: National Academy Press.

Reskin, B. F., & McBrier, D. B. (1998). Organizational determinants of the sexual division of managerial labor. Unpublished manuscript.

Reskin, B. F., & Padavic, I. (1988). Supervisors as gatekeepers: Male supervisors' response to women's integration in plant jobs. *Social Problems, 35,* 401–415.

Reskin, B. F., & Roos, P. (1990). *Job queues, gender queues.* Philadelphia: Temple University Press.

Reskin, B. F., & Ross, C. E. (1992). Jobs, authority, and earnings among managers: The continuing significance of sex. *Work and Occupations, 19,* 342–365.

Rollins, J. (1995). *All is never said: The narrative of Odette Harper Hines.* Philadelphia: Temple University Press.

Roos, P. A., & Reskin, B. F. (1984). Institutionalized barriers to sex integration in the workplace. In B. F. Reskin (Ed.), *Sex segregation in the workplace* (pp. 235–260). Washington, DC: National Academy Press.

Schroedel, J. (1985). *Alone in a crowd.* Philadelphia: Temple University Press.

Schultz, V. (1991). Telling stories about women and work: Judicial interpretation of sex segregation in the workplace in Title VII cases raising the lack of interest argument. In K. Bartlett & R. Kennedy (Eds.), *Feminist legal theory* (pp. 124–43). Boulder, CO: Westview.

Segura, D. (1992). Chicanas in white-collar jobs: "You have to prove yourself." *Sociological Perspectives, 35,* 163–182.

Shaeffer, R. G., & Lynton, E. F. (1979). Corporate experience in improving women's job opportunities. Report no. 755. New York: The Conference Board.

Smith, J. P., & Welch, F. (1984). Affirmative action and labor markets. *Journal of Labor Economics, 2,* 269–301.

Smith, T. W. (1990). Ethnic images. *General Social Survey Report.* Chicago: National Opinion Research Center.

Spain, D., & Bianchi, S. M. (1996) *Balancing act: Motherhood, marriage, and employment among American women.* New York: Russell Sage Foundation.

Subich, L. M., Barrett, G. V., Doverspike, D., & Alexander, R. A. (1989). The effects of sex-role related factors on occupational choice and salary. In R. T. Michael, H. I. Hartmann, & B. O'Farrell (Eds.), *Pay equity: Empirical inquiries* (pp. 91–104). Washington, DC: National Academy Press.

Swerdlow, M. (1989). Men's accommodations to women entering a nontraditional occupation: A case of rapid transit operatives. *Gender & Society, 3,* 373–387.

Szafran, R. F. (1982). What kinds of firms hire and promote women and blacks? A review of the literature. *Sociological Quarterly, 23,* 171–190.

Tomaskovic-Devey, D. (1993). *Gender and racial inequality at work: The sources and consequences of job segregation.* Ithaca, NY: ILR Press.

Tomaskovic-Devey, D. (1994). Race, ethnicity, and gender earnings inequality: The sources and consequences of employment segregation. Report to the Glass Ceiling Commission, U.S. Department of Labor.

Ullman, J. P., & Deaux, K. (1981). Recent efforts to increase female participation in apprenticeship in the basic steel industry in the Midwest. In V. M. Briggs, Jr. & F. Foltman (Eds.), *Apprenticeship research: Emerging findings and future trends* (pp. 133–149). Ithaca: NY State School of Industrial and Labor Relations, Cornell University.

U.S. Bureau of the Census. (1992a). *Census of population and housing, 1990: public use microdata samples U.S.* [machine-readable data files, prepared by the Bureau of the Census]. Washington, DC: Census Bureau.

U.S. Bureau of the Census. (1992b). *Detailed occupation and other characteristics from the EEO file for the United States. 1990 CP-S-1-1.* Washington, DC: U.S. Department of Commerce.

U.S. Bureau of Labor Statistics. (1961). *Employment and earnings 8 (January).* Washington, DC: U.S. Government Printing Office.

U.S. Bureau of Labor Statistics. (1995). *Employment and earnings 42 (January).* Washington, DC: U.S. Government Printing Office.

U.S. Bureau of Labor Statistics. (1996a). *Current population survey, February 1995: Contingent work supplement* [machine-readable data file]. Conducted by the Bureau of the Census for the Bureau of Labor Statistics. Washington, DC: Bureau of the Census [producer and distribution].

U.S. Bureau of Labor Statistics. (1996b). *Employment and earnings 43 (January).* Washington, DC: U.S. Government Printing Office.

U.S. Bureau of Labor Statistics. (1997). *Employment and earnings 44 (January).* Washington, DC: U.S. Government Printing Office.

U.S. Department of Labor. (1977). *Dictionary of occupational titles* (4th ed.). Washington, DC: U.S. Government Printing Office.

U.S. Department of Labor. (1996). Employment standards administration, Office for Federal Contract Compliance Programs. OFCCP egregious discrimination cases. Nov. 19. Washington, DC: U.S. Department of Labor.

U.S. Merit Systems Protection Board. (1992). *A question of equity: Women and the glass ceiling in the federal government.* A Report to the President and Congress by the U.S. Merit Systems Protection Board. Washington DC: U.S. Merit Systems Protection Board.

U.S. Merit Systems Protection Board. (1996). *Fair and equitable treatment: A progress report on minority employment in the federal government.* Washington, DC: U.S. Merit Systems Protection Board.

Von Glinow, M. A. (1988). Women in corporate America: A caste of thousands. *New Management, 6,* 36–42.

Waldinger, R., & Bailey, T. (1991). The continuing significance of race: Racial conflict and racial discrimination in construction. *Politics and Society, 19,* 291–323.

Williams, C. L. (1989). *Gender differences at work: Women and men in nontraditional occupations.* Berkeley: University of California Press.

Williams, C. L. (1995). *Still a man's world: Men who do "women's work."* Berkeley: University of California Press.

Williams, J. B., & Best, D. (1986). Sex stereotypes and intergroup relations. In S. Worchel & W. G. Austin (Eds.), *Psychology of intergroup relations* (pp. 244–259). Chicago: Nelson-Hall.

Wilson, W. J. (1996). *When work disappears: The world of the new urban poor.* New York: Knopf.

Science

READING 46

The Health of Black Folk: Disease, Class, and Ideology in Science

Nancy Krieger and Mary Bassett

Since the first crude tabulations of vital statistics in colonial America, one stark fact has stood out: black Americans are sicker and die younger than whites. As the epidemic infectious diseases of the nineteenth century were vanquished, the black burden of ill health shifted to the modern killers: heart disease, stroke, and cancer. Today black men under age 45 are ten times more likely to die from the effects of high blood pressure than white men. Black women suffer twice as many heart attacks as white women. A variety of common cancers are more frequent among blacks—and of cancer victims, blacks succumb sooner after diagnosis than whites. Black infant mortality is twice that of whites. All told, if the mortality rates for blacks and other minorities today were the same in the United States as for whites, more than 60,000 deaths in minority communities could be avoided each year.

What is it about being black that causes such miserable odds? One answer is the patently racist view that blacks are inherently more susceptible to disease—the genetic model. In contrast, environmental models depict blacks as victims of factors ranging from poor nutrition and germs to lack of education and crowded housing. Initially formulated as an alternative to the genetic model by liberals and much of the left, the environmental view has now gained new support from the right. . . . Instead of blaming the victims' genes, these conservatives blame black lifestyle choices as the source of the racial gap in health.

We will argue that these analytic models are seriously flawed, in essence as well as application. They are not the product of a racist use of allegedly "neutral" science, but reflect the ways in which ideology and politics penetrate scientific theory and research. Typically, they deny or

Nancy Krieger is associate professor of health and social behavior in the Department of Health and Social Behavior at the Harvard School of Public Health. Mary Bassett is the Associate Director of Health Equity with the Rockefeller Foundation. She is based in the Southern African Regional Office in Zimbabwe.

obscure that the primary source of black/white health disparities is the social production of disease under conditions of capitalism and racial oppression. The "facts of being black" are not, as these models suggest, a genetically determined shade of skin color, or individual deprived living conditions, or ill-informed lifestyle choices. The facts of being black derive from the joint social relations of race and class: racism disproportionately concentrates blacks into the lower strata of the working class and further causes blacks in all class strata to be racially oppressed. It is the left's challenge to incorporate this political reality into how we approach racial differences in health.

THE GENETIC MODEL

Despite overwhelming evidence to the contrary, the theory that "race" is primarily a biological category and that black-white differences in health are genetically determined continues to exert profound influence on both medical thinking and popular ideology. For example, an editorial on racial differences in birth weight (an important determinant of infant mortality) in the January 1986 *Journal of the American Medical Association* concluded: "Finally, what are the biologic or genetic differences among racial or ethnic groups? Should we shrink from the possibility of a biologic/genetic influence?" Similarly, a 1983 handbook prepared by the International Epidemiologic Association defined "race" as "persons who are relatively homogeneous with respect to biological inheritance." Public health texts continue to enshrine "race" in the demographic triad of "age, race, and sex," implying that "race" is as biologically fundamental a predictor of health as aging or sex, while the medical literature remains replete with studies that examine racial differences in health without regard to class.

The genetic model rests on three basic assumptions, all of which are flawed: that "race" is a valid biological category; that the genes which determine "race" are linked to the genes which affect health; and that the health of any community is mainly the consequence of the genetic constitution of the individuals of which it is composed. In contrast, we will argue that the health of the black community is not simply the sum of the health of individuals who are "genetically black" but instead chiefly reflects the social forces which create racially oppressed communities in the first place.

It is of course true that skin color, hair texture, and other visible features used to identify "race" are genetically encoded—there *is* a biologic aspect to "race." The importance of these particular physical traits in the spectrum of human variation, however, has been determined historically and politically. People also differ in terms of stature and eye color, but these attributes are rarely accorded significance. Categories based primarily on skin color correlate with health because race is a powerful determinant of the location and life-destinies of individuals within the class structure of U.S. society. Ever since plantation owners realized that differences in skin color could serve as a readily identifiable and permanent marker for socially determined divisions of labor (black runaway slaves were easier to identify than escaped white indentured servants and convicts, the initial workforce of colonial America), race and class have been inextricably intertwined. "Race" is not a neutral descriptive category, but a social category born of the antagonistic relation of white supremacy and black oppression. The basis of the relative health advantage of whites is not to be found in their genes but in the relative material advantage whites enjoy as a consequence of political prerogative and state power. As Richard Lewontin has pointed out, "If, after a great cataclysm, only Africans were left alive, the human species would have retained 93 percent of its total genetic variation, although the species as a whole would be darker skinned." The fact that we all know which race we belong to says more about our society than about our biology.

Nevertheless, the paradigm of a genetic basis for black ill health remains strong. In its defense, researchers repeatedly trot out the few diseases for which a clear-cut link of race is established: sickle cell anemia, G&PD deficiency, and lactose intolerance. These diseases, however, have a tiny impact on the health of the black population as a whole—if anything, even less than those few diseases linked to "whiteness," such as some forms of skin cancer. Richard Cooper has shown that of the tens of thousands of excess black deaths in 1977, only 277 (0.3 percent) could be attributed to diseases such as sickle cell anemia. Such uncommon genetic maladies have become important strictly because of their metaphorical value: they are used to support genetic explanations of racial differences in the "big diseases" of the twentieth century—heart disease, stroke, and cancer. Yet no current evidence exists to justify such an extrapolation.

Determined nonetheless to demonstrate the genetic basis of racial health differences, investigators today—like their peers in the past—use the latest techniques. Where once physicians compared cranial capacity to explain black/white inequalities, now they scrutinize surface markers of cells. The case of hypertension is particularly illustrative. High blood pressure is an important cause of strokes and heart attacks, contributing to about 30 percent of all deaths in the United States. At present, the black rate of hypertension in the United States is about twice that of whites. Of over five hundred recent medical journal articles on the topic, fewer than a dozen studies explored social factors. The rest instead unsuccessfully sought biochemical/genetic explanations—and of these, virtually none even attempted to "define" genetically who was "white" and who was "black," despite the alleged genetic nature of their enquiry. As a consequence of the wrong questions being asked, the causes of hypertension remain unknown. Nonetheless, numerous clues point to social factors. Hypertension does not exist in several undisrupted hunter/gatherer tribes of different "races" but rapidly emerges in these tribes after contact with industrial society; in the United States, lower social class begets higher blood pressure.

Turning to cancer, the authors of a recent major government report surmised that blacks have poorer survival rates than whites because they do not "exhibit the same immunologic reactions to cancerous processes." It is noteworthy, however, that the comparably poor survival rates of British breast cancer patients have never elicited such speculation. In our own work on breast cancer in Washington state, we found that the striking "racial" difference in survival evaporated when we took class into account: working-class women, whether black or white, die sooner than women of higher social class standing.

To account for the persistence of the genetic model, we must look to its political significance rather than its scientific content. First used to buttress biblical arguments for slavery in a period when science was beginning to replace religion as sanction for the status quo, the genetic model of racial differences in health emerged toward the end of the eighteenth century, long before any precise theory of heredity existed. In well-respected medical journals, doctors debated whether blacks and whites were even the same species (let alone race), and proclaimed that blacks were intrinsically suited to slavery, thrived in hot climates, succumbed less to the epidemic fevers which ravaged the South, and suffered extraordinary rates of insanity if allowed to live free. After the Civil War effectively settled the argument about whether blacks belonged to the human species, physicians and scientists began elaborating hereditarian theories to explain the disparate health profiles not only of blacks and whites, but of the different white "races"—as defined by national origin and immigrant status. Virtually every scourge, from TB to rickets, was postulated to be inherited. Rheumatic fever, now known to be due to strep bacteria combined with the poverty which permits its expression in immunocompromised malnourished people, was long believed to be linked with the red hair and pale complexions of its Irish working-class victims. Overall, genetic explanations of differences in disease rates have politically served to justify existing class relations and excuse socially created afflictions as a result of immutable biology.

Nowadays the genetic model—newly dressed in the language of molecular genetics—continues to divert attention from the class origin of disease. Genetic explanations absolve the state of responsibility for the health profile of black America by declaring racial disparities (regrettably) inevitable and normal. Intervention efforts based on this model founder for obvious reasons: short of recombinant DNA therapies, genetic screening and selective reproduction stand as supposed tools to reduce the racial gap in health.

Unfortunately, the genetic model wields influence even within the progressive health movement, as illustrated by the surge of interest in sickle cell anemia in the early 1970s. For decades after its initial description in 1925, sickle cell anemia was relegated to clinical obscurity. It occurs as often in blacks as does cystic fibrosis in whites. By linking genetic uniqueness to racial pride, such groups as the Black Panther Party championed sickle cell anemia as the number one health issue among blacks, despite the fact that other health problems—such as infant mortality—took a much greater toll. Because the sickle cell gene provides some protection against malaria, sickle cell seemed to link blacks to their African past, now three centuries removed. It raised the issue of racist neglect of black health in a setting where the victims were truly blameless: the fault lay in their genes. From the point of view of the federal government, sickle cell anemia was a uniquely black disease which did not raise the troubling issues of the ongoing oppression of the black population. In a period of political turmoil, what more could the government ask for? Small wonder that President Nixon jumped on the bandwagon and called for a national crusade.

THE ENVIRONMENTAL MODEL

The genetic model's long history and foundations in the joint race and class divisions of our society assure its continued prominence in discussions on the racial gap in health. To rebut this model, many liberals and progressives have relied upon environmental models of disease causation—only to encounter the right on this turf as well.

Whereas the rise of slavery called forth genetic models of diseases, environmental models were born of the antagonistic social relations of industrial capitalism. In the appalling filth of nineteenth-century cities, tuberculosis, typhus, and infant diarrhea were endemic in the newly forming working class; periodically, epidemics of yellow fever and cholera would attack the entire populace. A sanitary reform movement arose, advocating cleaner cities (with sewer systems and pure water) to protect the well-being of the wealthy as well as the poor, and also to engender a healthier, more productive workforce.

In the United States, most of the reformers were highly moralistic and staunchly procapitalist, seeing poverty and squalor as consequences of individual intemperance and ignorance rather than as necessary correlates of capital accumulation. In Europe, where the working-class movement was stronger, a class-conscious wing of the sanitary reform movement emerged. Radicals such as Frederick Engels and Rudolph Virchow (later the founder of modern pathology) argued that poverty and ill health could only be eliminated by resolving the antagonistic class relations of capitalism.

The early sanitary reform movement in the United States rarely addressed the question of racial differences in health per se. In fact, environmental models to explain black/white disparities emerged only during the mid-twentieth century, a consequence of the urban migration of blacks from the rural South to the industrial North and the rise of the civil-rights movement.

Today's liberal version of the environmental model blames poverty for black ill health. The noxious features of the "poverty environment" are catalogued and decried—lead paint from tenement walls, toxins from work, even social features like discrimination. But as in most liberal analyses, the unifying cause of this litany of woes remains unstated. We are left with an apparently unconnected laundry list of problems and no explanation of why blacks as a group encounter similar sickening conditions.

The liberal view fetishizes the environment: individuals are harmed by inanimate objects, physical forces, or unfortunate social conditions (like poverty)—by *things* rather than by people. That these objects or social circumstances are the *creations* of society is hidden by the veil of "natural science." Consequently, the "environment" is viewed as a natural and neutral category, defined as all that is external to individuals. What is not seen is the ways in which the underlying structure of racial oppression and class exploitation—which are relationships among people, not between people and things—shape the "environments" of the groups created by these relations.

The debilitating disease pellagra serves as a concrete example. Once a major health problem of poor southern farm and mill laborers in the United States, pellagra was believed to be a genetic disease. By the early 1920s, however, Joseph Goldberger had proved that the disease stemmed from a dietary deficiency in niacin and had also demonstrated that pellagra's familial nature existed because of the inheritance of nutritional options, not genes. Beyond this, Goldberger argued that pellagra, in essence, was a *social* disease caused by the single cash-crop economy of the South: reliance on cotton ensured seasonal starvation as food ran out between harvests, as well as periodic epidemics when the cotton market collapsed. Southern workers contracted pellagra because they had limited diets—and they had limited diets *because* they were southern workers. Yet governmental response was simply to supplement food with niacin: according to this view, vitamin deficiency—not socially determined malnutrition—was the chief cause of pellagra.

The liberal version of the environmental model also fails to see the causes of disease and the environment in which they exist as a historical product, a nature filtered through, even constructed by, society. What organisms and chemicals people are exposed to is determined by both the social relations and types of production which characterize their society. The same virus may cause pneumonia in blacks and whites alike, just as lead may cause the same physiologic damage—but *why* the death rate for flu and pneumonia and *why* blood lead levels are consistently higher in black as compared to white communities is not addressed. While the liberal conception of the environment can generate an exhaustive list of its components, it cannot *comprehend* the all-important assemblage of features of black life. What explains why a greater proportion of black mothers are single, young, malnourished, high-school dropouts, and so on?

Here the right is ready with a "lifestyle" response as a unifying theme: blacks, not racism, are the source of their own health woes. . . . The Reagan administration [was a] chief promoter of this view—made evident by the 1985 publication of the Report of the Secretary's Task Force on Black and Minority Health. Just one weapon among many in the government's vicious ideological war to justify its savage gutting of health and social service programs, the report shifts responsibility for the burden of disease to the minority communities themselves. Promoting "health education" as a panacea, the government hopes to counsel minorities to eat better, exercise more, smoke and drink less, be less violent, seek health care earlier for symptoms, and in general be better health-care consumers. This "lifestyle" version of the environmental model accordingly is fully compatible with the genetic model (i.e., genetic disadvantage can be exaggerated by lifestyle choices) and echoes its ideological messages that individual shortcomings are at the root of ill health.

In focusing on individual health habits, the task force report ironically echoes the language of many "health radicals," ranging from iconoclasts such as Ivan Illich to counterculture advocates of individually oriented self-help strategies. United in practice, if not in spirit, these apparently disparate camps all take a "holistic" view, arguing that disease comes not just from germs or chemicals but from lifestyle choices about food, exercise, smoking, and stress. Their conflation of lifestyle choices and life circumstance can reach absurd proportions. Editorializing on the task force report, the *New York Times* agreed that: "Disparities may be due to cultural or lifestyle differences. For example, a higher proportion of blacks and hispanics live in cities, with greater exposure to hazards like pollution, poor housing, and crime." But what kind of "lifestyle" causes pollution, and who chooses to live in high-crime neighborhoods? Both the conservative and alternative "lifestyle" versions of the environmental model deliberately ignore or distort the fact that economic coercion and political disenfranchisement, not free choice, locate minority communities in the most hazardous regions of cities. What qualitatively constrains the option of blacks to "live right" is the reality of being black and poor in the United States.

But liberals have had little response when the right points out that even the most oppressed and impoverished people make choices affecting their health: it may be hard to eat right if the neighborhood grocer doesn't sell fresh vegetables, but teenage girls do not have to become pregnant. For liberals, it has been easier to portray blacks as passive, blameless victims and in this way avoid the highly charged issue of health behaviors altogether. The end result is usually just proposals for more health services *for* blacks, bandaids for the gaping wounds of oppression. Yet while adequate health services certainly are needed, they can do little to stem the social forces which cause disease.

Too often the left has been content merely to trail behind the liberals in campaigns for health services, or to call only for social control of environmental and occupational exposures. The right, however, has shifted the terrain of battle to the issue of individual behavior, and we must respond. It is for the left to point out that society does not consist of abstract individuals, but rather of people whose life options are shaped by their intrinsic membership in groups defined by the social relations of their society. Race and class broadly determine not only the conditions under which blacks and whites live, but also the ways in which they can respond to these conditions and the political power they have to alter them. The material limits produced by oppression create and constrain not only the type of housing you live in, but even the most intimate choices about what you do inside your home. . . .

READING 47

Media, Science, and Sexual Ideology: The Promotion of Sexual Stability

Gilbert Zicklin

In March 1994, the Gay and Lesbian Association of the Cornell University Medical College organized a conference boldly called "The Biological Nature of Homosexuality." Among the guest speakers were Laura Allen, Dean Hamer, and Simon LeVay, all of whom have published research reports contributing to the proposition that homosexuality has a biological basis. No one on the panel argued that there is no biological basis to homosexuality, or that whatever biological factors are associated with homosexuality, they are of minimal significance in the material development of homosexual desire. No one on the panel commented critically on the biological position or on the research that has been deemed to support it.

I begin by mentioning this conference, which followed upon wide media dissemination of the

---

Gilbert Zicklin is on the faculty at Montclair State University, where he teaches the sociology of sexuality.

reports of biologically oriented research into the origins of homosexuality, because its bias is illustrative of the currency recently gained for discussing homosexuality as a biological phenomenon. I intend to argue the following:

1. that the relationship between the data and the conclusions about a biological basis to homosexuality that some researchers assert, and the media have highlighted, is largely without scientific merit;
2. that the media's treatment of the research as "discoveries" offers the public a distorted view of the state of scientific knowledge on this subject;
3. that the narrative about sexuality underlying both the media's and the scientific community's interest in biological explanations for erotic attraction ignores the socially constructed, highly symbolic codes that make sexual desire and desirability meaningful.

To show this I will first describe a sample of studies published since 1990 that assume a biological perspective on sexual desire. I will present a critical analysis of the methodological problems of each of these studies, contrasting my critique with the print media's portrayal of the research findings. I will then focus on an exemplary journalist's coverage of the issue for the *New York Times.* I conclude with an analysis of what lies behind both the researchers' and the media's tendency to see homosexuality as a fixed condition that is set at birth or very shortly thereafter, rather than viewing it more sociologically, the way we do kinship or religious ties.

The biologically oriented research I will examine flows from two streams: (1) neuroanatomical studies of the structural similarities and differences in the brains of male and female laboratory animals, and in humans, among samples that differ by gender and by sexual orientation; and (2) studies that purport to show a chromosomal basis for homosexual desire, or from whose data such a chromosomal basis can logically be inferred. In the interests of space, I will not consider the line of study looking at brain-mediated neuroendocrine effects on sexual behavior, though I believe the logic works the same.

I will sample this research by considering the reports of Simon LeVay, Michael Bailey and Richard Pillard, Roger Gorski and Laura Allen, and Dean Hamer et al.[1] First, a snapshot of these studies.

Simon LeVay, a biologist formerly at the Salk Institute in La Jolla, reported that he found a difference in the size of the INAH-3 region of the hypothalamus in brains identified as belonging to gay males compared with those of nongay males. The size of the gay males' region was similar to that of the females in the study (who were not identified with respect to sexual orientation).

Michael Bailey, a psychologist at Northwestern University, and Richard Pillard, a professor of psychiatry at Boston University School of Medicine, compared concordance rates for homosexuality in a sample of male identical co-twins, nonidentical co-twins, and adoptive brothers. They found that about half of the identical, or monozygotic, twins in their sample shared the trait of homosexuality, while for the dizygotic twins the concordance figure was between one-fourth and one-fifth. This translates into the highest concordance rates for the closest genetic relationship, that of monozygotic twins. Bailey and Pillard carried out a comparable study of females and reported similar results.[2]

Roger Gorski and Laura Allen, researchers at UCLA, reported a difference between homosexually and heterosexually identified males, and between males and females, in the size of the anterior commissure, an area that binds the two hemispheres of the brain. They reported that homosexual males had the largest commissures, heterosexual males the smallest.

Dean Hamer et al., of the National Cancer Institute, studied the distribution of homosexual relatives among a sample of homosexual subjects, and examined DNA samples of forty pairs of self-identified gay brothers. Subjects reported more homosexuals among their maternal relatives, and the researchers found similar DNA sequences in thirty-three out of the forty pairs of gay brothers in a region of the X chromosome known as Xq25. These findings led Hamer et al. to hypothesize the genetic transmission of homosexuality through the maternal line.

In the LeVay study, three problems stand out.[3] First, and most important, LeVay relies on hospital records for the measure of a key variable, the sexual orientation of the subjects whose brains he is dissecting. The [study of] record keeping tells us that these official designations are liable to be off the mark. What one decides to reveal to a record keeper, what the record keeper surmises one does not want to reveal but thinks should be included, what the record keeper decides is meant by certain signs the person exhibits—all these may go into the act of fixing a label on a person. The designation of a sexual orientation that is made in a hospital setting in situations of extremis may bear only a tangential relationship to the truth of a person's sexual life. LeVay relied *solely* on such hospital designations for the determination of a principal variable in his study. It is therefore unclear that sexual orientation differentiated LeVay's subjects, whatever other factors may have been involved.

The second problem with the LeVay study involves a likely confounding of independent variables. There was a disproportionate number of deaths from HIV infection among his homosexual subjects. HIV infection is known to damage brain cells directly, as well as through the lowering of testosterone levels in males, which in turn affects brain tissue. This, in itself, may account for an observed correlation between homosexual orientation and the smaller size of the INAH-3 region. . . .

LeVay engaged in the unusual practice of measuring the size of the INAH-3 area himself; scientists more commonly use additional or other researchers for this task. The absence of blind raters, coupled with his well-known desire to find a biological basis for homosexuality, leaves his work open to the charge of experimenter bias.[4] Since his findings have not been replicated, and given the methodological problems with his research, the reliability of his data as well as his interpretation of them can be questioned.

The other anatomical study, that of Gorski and Allen, also suffers from the designation of research subjects' brains as belonging to "homosexuals" or "heterosexuals," without clear operational definitions for these terms. But even if this were not so, there is a larger problem with the research. Gorski and Allen found a larger anterior commissure in the brains of "gay" males than in those of "straight" males, those of the former being comparable to that found in females' brains. But the anterior commissure has not been shown to have any relationship to sexuality; rather, it is thought to aid communication between the two brain hemispheres. Why compare this particular structure among samples with different sexual orientations, if you have no theoretical reason for looking for this difference? It is on a par with recent research reporting that the finger whorls, testicular laterality, and so forth of gay males differ in direction from those of straight males. Since we are given no theoretical basis for these associations, they have little meaning for a study of sexual orientation. In fact, this pig-in-a-poke way of searching for neuroanatomical correlates of behavior increases the risk of false positives, since five times out of one hundred, observed correlations will occur by chance and mean nothing.

Bailey and Pillard's research method included asking male monozygotic (MZ) and dizygotic (DZ) twins and biological and nonbiological nontwin siblings about their sexual orientation. They acquired their subjects through advertisements placed in gay publications in several cities in the Midwest and Southwest. The authors conclude from their data that there is a genetic basis to sexual orientation. They base their claim on the significantly higher percentage of MZ twins concordant for sexual orientation than the other, less genetically connected siblings.

But the method of subject selection undermines the study's validity. Self-selection of subjects, that is, using volunteers, introduces the possibility of a very particular bias in the case of a disapproved behavior: if more homosexual monozygotic twins with homosexual co-twins volunteered for the study than a random sample would find, or as Bailey and Pillard recognize, "if discordant MZ twins were less likely to participate than discordant DZ twins," then the difference in concordance rates for these two types of relatives could not be attributed to genetic differences but rather to the peculiarity of the sample. The overrepresentation of concordant MZ twins is quite possible, since gay MZ twins are likely to be more interested in studies that highlight the special meaning of close biological connections, and they might also have less trepidation about participating since there is a greater likelihood that they would be "out" with one another than would any other pair of male siblings. Conversely, some twins who perceive themselves as discordant on sexual orientation may be motivated to avoid studies wherein this difference may be revealed. Thus, Bailey and Pillard have a double problem: they attract the kind of twins who fit their hypothesis and deter the ones who might weaken it. . . .

The authors do not take into account the possibility that MZ twin relationships create a unique psychosocial environment that in itself can account for higher rates of concordance. The intensely shared life of identical twins including the phenomena of identification, mirroring, and imitation, might plausibly constitute fertile ground for the development of same-sex erotics.

Parenthetically, while there has been no report of a reliable replication of the Bailey and Pillard study, it is worth noting that King and McDonald recently reported far less concordance for identical twin pairs than did Bailey and Pillard.[5]

The study reported by Hamer et al. has been presented as making the most convincing case for the role of heredity. Its problems of methodology are different, but quite serious. Hamer and his colleagues recruited seventy-six homosexual men for a pedigree study to determine which other members of the families of these men were also homosexual. They reported homosexuality to be significantly more common among the maternal relatives and concluded that a putative gene for homosexuality is passed through female family members. Yet the sociology of family life in the United States suggests that women are more likely than men to keep in touch with relatives, so a son might well know more about his mother's side of the family than his father's. Moreover, in this culture as a function of gender politics, a homosexual son might be closer to his mother than to his father and might therefore be more identified with and knowledgeable about his mother's relatives, including the question of their sexual preferences. American gender and family patterns, not genes, may account for the data.

Postulating genetic transmission of homosexuality through the maternal line, Hamer et al. examined the X chromosome in forty pairs of gay brothers recruited through advertisements in homophile publications. They report finding a region of the X chromosome that was shared in thirty-three of the forty pairs. They took this to mean that a linkage was established between a region of the X chromosome and homosexuality, that is, that the gay concordant brothers received the same X chromosome from the mother significantly more often than by chance. But we do not know whether it was more often than their straight siblings, for they did not examine the X chromosome of any heterosexual brothers of the homosexual sib-pair subjects. . . .

Why didn't Hamer et al. look at these brothers' DNA? Hamer says it was because of a supposed difficulty in being sure that a heterosexually identified brother was not a secret homosexual, since if such "faux heterosexuals" were in the sample it would distort—that is, weaken—the anticipated results of the study. He suggests that since homosexual desire is morally questionable in our culture, a heterosexual would be loath to confess his homosexual desires, while someone who already experiences the opprobrium of being known as a homosexual would be unlikely to be hiding significant heterosexual desires. This *may* be true, but surely skilled researchers could have elicited the existence of homosexual desire and practice from heterosexually identified brothers with appropriate open-ended interviews. Eliminating these brothers from the study did more to undermine its validity than including them would have, even with the possible concealment of their homosexual desires. . . .

Finally, and most tellingly for the direct genetic transmission hypothesis, Hamer et al. cannot . . . state that the presence of a certain DNA pattern or gene in the Xq28 region of the X chromosome actually influences sexual desire. (This is the same logical problem encountered in the work of Bailey and Pillard.) . . .

Research that appears to accept the direct biological basis of sexual orientation has drawn criticism from many quarters in the biological and social sciences. R. Hubbard, D. Nelkin, E. Balaban, W. Byne, T. McGuire, R. Lewontin, H. Fingarette, and J. N. Katz, among others, have expressed serious reservations about the claims of biological causation of what are seen as complex social behaviors. Yet when the research of LeVay, Gorski and Allen, Bailey and Pillard, and Hamer et al. has been reported in the popular press, it is almost always represented as contributing to *"mounting evidence"* that homosexuality is biologically based.

These scientific reports have generated a great deal of attention from the popular media. From front-page stories in the *New York Times* to feature articles in *Time, Newsweek,* and *U.S. News and World Report,* from a lead article in the *Atlantic Monthly* to pieces in the *Chronicle of Higher Education, Mother Jones, Discover, National Review,* and the *Nation,* the coverage of purported anatomical and genetic findings with respect to homosexuality has been robust. I searched a select group of newspapers, news magazines, journals of opinion, and monthlies for the years 1990–93 and found dozens of articles, feature stories, personal essays, and editorial page commentaries about this work. The periodicals I searched included only the most prestigious newspapers such as the *New York Times,* the *Washington Post,* the *Los Angeles Times,* the *Houston Post,* and so on; they did not include the thousands of local newspapers, unindexed in library catalogues, that may have carried stories about this research as well.

Overwhelmingly, the articles reporting on this research tend to stress the likely validity of asserted biological bases to sexual orientation. The titles of some of these newspaper and magazine articles suggest the tilt: "Brain Differences Linked to Sexual Preferences," "Are Some Men Born to Be Gay?" "Brain Feature Linked to Sexual Orientation," "Are Some Men Born to Be Homosexual?" "Are Gay Men Born That Way?" "Study Ties Part of Brain to Men's Sexual Orientation," "Exploring the Brain for Secrets of Sexuality," "Study Shows Homosexuality Is Innate," "Report Suggests Homosexuality Is Linked to Genes," "X Marks the Spot: Male Homosexuality May Be Linked to a Gene," "Study of Gay Men and Their Brothers Links Homosexuality to Genetics," "Study Suggests Genes Sway Lesbians' Sexual Orientation," "Genes Tied to Sexual Orientation," "The Search for Sexual Identity: Genes vs. Hormones," "Study Links Genes to Homosexuality," "Research Points toward a 'Gay' Gene," "Born or Bred: The Origins of Homosexuality," "Born Gay? Studies of Family Trees and DNA Make the Case that Male Homosexuality Is in the Genes," "Opening a Window: Genes May Play a Role in Homosexuality," "The Gay Science of Genes and Brains," "Evidence for Homosexuality Gene," and finally, "Genetic Clue to Male Homosexuality Emerges." For these journalists, the mystery of homosexuality is thus solved.

While one reads the occasional dubious headline, such as "Media Hype about the 'Gay Gene,'" and "The Search for Sexual Identity: False Genetic Markers," the media tend mainly to follow a pattern in reporting on this subject. The pattern is (1) repeat claims made by the researchers about the findings; (2) quote them or a couple of friendly experts about the *import* of their findings; (3) quote one or two sources who issue a caveat about the validity of the study; and (4) imply that, caveats notwithstanding, a biological basis for sexual orientation is likely, if not yet proved. This sequence, lacking as it does any developed critical viewpoint, is seen often. While there appear to be systematic differences between the newsmagazines and newspapers, with the former even less likely to pay serious attention to any critique of these studies, on the whole, media representation of this research depicts it as a cumulative body of scientific work. It accepts the assumption of a fixed, unchanging "sexual orientation" that is biologically rooted.

Let us move beyond the headlines for a moment and see how the reporting of a *New York Times* journalist uses this structure in her reportage. The *Times* reporter, Natalie Angier, is . . . one of the most sophisticated covering this story. Her work is untypically inclusive of criticism from expert sources about both the methods and the claims of the biological research. Yet her work still illustrates the distorting media paradigm described above.

An article that illustrates her approach comes from the July 16, 1993, edition of the *Times*. It begins with an attempt to characterize the significance of the Hamer study: "Ushering the politically explosive study of the origins of sexual orientation into a new and *perhaps* more scientifically rigorous phase, researchers report that they have linked male homosexuality to a small region of one human chromosome" (my italics). Then the caveat: this is "just a single chapter in the intricate story of sexual orientation and behavior," followed by a repeat of the "importance" of the findings. The "findings" are then further elaborated, followed by another caveat: "But researchers warn against overinterpreting the work, or in taking it to mean anything as simplistic as that the 'gay gene' had been found" (Angier's quotation marks around *gay gene*). Are we then to think that the idea of a "gay gene" is a function of simplistic thinking? Or is it that believing a *single* gene could control sexual orientation is simplistic? Or is it rather that concluding from the Hamer study, alone, that the gay gene has already been found is simplistic? In her very *next* sentence Angier writes, "The researchers emphasized that they do not yet have a gene isolated, but merely know the rough location of where the gene or genes may sit." The air is cleared: there *are* gay genes. Only where they are is a mystery.

Angier continues in a cautionary style, reporting that even if they do pinpoint this gene there are probably other genes on other chromosomes involved in sexual orientation. She then speculates about how "the gene" could work, using that term now without any quotation marks that might convey doubt. It could work either by directly influencing "sexual proclivity" or by doing so indirectly, through affecting temperament. Thus, Angier has now fully envisioned the existence and operation of a "gay gene," when only some paragraphs before she had signaled the wrongheadedness of such a concept.

When toward the very end of the article Angier turns to some of the methodological problems of the study, for example the lack of a control, she says, "So far the study has been limited to men who said they were gay, eliminating the ambiguity that would come from considering the genes of men who called themselves heterosexual." Instead of actually clarifying why the heterosexual brothers were not part of the DNA study—a very serious problem, as I indicated—Angier has merely restated the researchers' unconvincing explanation, which she now treats as self-explanatory. She concludes her article with the prospect of the work ahead for these scientists, who must sort out "which gene or genes is relevant." Her apparent caveat about the complex nature of sexual desire and whether it could be accounted for by a "gay gene" has now vanished; she has adopted the researchers' account of their work and their perspective on sexual orientation, namely, that it is biologically given.

Though I focus on Angier, her method is an instance of what is actually a widespread tendency in the reportage on this research. It is the use of a rhetoric that subtly inserts the belief that sexual orientation is caused by a biological condition, in gradual steps, amid all-too-stillable doubts. Despite the ambiguous, often equivocal findings that result from the studies' methodologically faulty designs, we have seen dozens of news articles proclaiming supposedly valid, reliable findings.

Questions naturally arise: (1) How is it that this bandwagon has gotten rolling, in the media and even in the lesbian/gay community, for a biological explanation of sexual desire, with so little evidence? (2) What in the scientists' perspective accounts for their persistence in pursuing the biological basis of homosexuality, despite both the experimental impossibility of showing that it is *directly* biologically caused, and the pile of equivocal findings? and (3) What are the ramifications of promoting such a perspective?

To amplify the first question, especially for this audience, we might ask why no such media attention has been showered on scholarly work in the *social sciences* that conceptualizes in a sociocultural framework: the sociological analyses of Bell and Weinberg, of Klassen, Williams, and Levitt, or of Ira Reiss; the work in history of Trumbach, Bray, or Faderman; in social psychology, Herek; in anthropology, Herdt and Williams—just to name a few of the scholars doing notable research bearing on issues related to the nature of homosexuality. Among many other things, this research has examined what sociological factors, if any, a homosexual preference is related to; what are the prevalent beliefs of the U.S. population about what causes homosexuality, what should be done about it, what is its current moral status, how prevalent is it; historically, when did our current ideas and practices first appear and why; what factors are associated with homophobic attitudes; how do other cultures organize sexual practices, and how do they explain these arrangements; how does gender intersect with homosexual preference, both in this culture and in non-Western cultures; and so forth.

An answer to why the media play up the biological studies as opposed to the sociocultural is that the former are appealing because they present themselves as having solved "the riddle of sexual desire," that is, they offer something akin to certainty. Moreover, researchers themselves have encouraged this attitude toward their studies by making grandiose claims for their findings. For example, in a *New York Times* article of December 17, 1991, one scientist, asked to comment on the first Bailey and Pillard study, asserted that "Some of the earlier evidence suggested there was a genetic effect, but the studies were not well done. This is something that really sort of clinches it." Bailey and Pillard themselves write in a *New York Times* op-ed piece, "Our own research *has shown* [my italics] that male sexual orientation is substantially genetic."[6] A reporter for the *Chronicle of Higher Education,* referring to an unnamed scientist, writes, "He found the results [of the Bailey and Pillard study] so compelling that he has decided to start a search for the gene or genes that may cause homosexuality."[7] Natalie Angier reports that Gorski and Allen "believe the[ir] finding supports the idea that brains of homosexuals differ in many subtle ways from those of heterosexuals, and that sexual orientation has a *deep biological basis*" (my italics).[8] Reporters are able to hype these studies in good conscience, since in this enterprise they apparently have the assistance of some scientists.

Interestingly, some of the researchers themselves quite consciously want the public to subscribe to a biological model of sexual orientation. LeVay talks of how he hoped to get the results he did because he thought it would be good for the gay population, both in terms of legal outcomes in civil rights cases and with respect to reducing prejudice should biological explanations come to replace moral ones in the public's understanding of homosexuality. Like LeVay, Bailey and Pillard also believe that if sexual orientation is innate, "it is," in their words "good news for homosexuals and their advocates."[9] Richard Green, another sex researcher with a biological model of homosexuality, commented to a *New York Times* reporter that "if sexual orientation were demonstrated to be essentially inborn, most laws that discriminate against gays and lesbians, including sodomy laws, housing and employment discrimination laws, all would fall."[10] Thus, there is a politics at play in this scientific quest. It is a *liberal* politics, based on the impulse to normalize and include. . . .

I will make that argument by offering another answer to the question of why the media have given this story so much play. I suggest that the assumptions behind the biological research are part of a particular politico/cultural framework for understanding erotic life. It is a framework that seeks to allay the fear of the "normals" by allowing them to believe that one is given an essential sexual orientation at birth. This can reduce some of a heterosexually identified person's fears about whether he or she is sufficiently masculine or feminine, with which fear the modern erotic is so bound up. For if sexuality is in one's genetic makeup, then in a heterosexually identified person, any erotic interest in one's *own* sex can be dismissed as small potatoes, clearly not adding up to the main thing, the *real* thing, biological homosexuality. Dichotomizing the erotic into two biologically based identities reduces the anxiety of those who might worry about being "possibly homosexual" because they experience some sexual interest in and desire for the same sex: "After all," they can reason, "to be a homosexual you've got to be born one, and if I were born one, I probably wouldn't have any heterosexual desire; I would only be attracted to my own sex, and I'm not." Klassen, Williams, and Levitt found that a fairly large minority of Americans (about 40 percent in their sample) agree "strongly" or "somewhat" with the statement that "there is some homosexuality in everyone." At the same time, large majorities believe homosexuality is morally wrong. A sizable group, then, is precariously positioned with respect to the meaning of whatever homosexual desire they experience.[11]

As such, the situation represents a classic instance of cognitive dissonance. The dissonance may be reducible if we accept the model of erotic life that says that if you are strongly disposed, in your brain, to the same sex and not much, if at all, disposed to the opposite sex, are you *really,* that is, *bodily* queer. By advancing the cut-and-dried biological model of sexual orientation, the media fulfill the hidden wishes of the public (and here I would include some of the gay public) to be free from the taint of possible perversity with respect to their sexual desires and, *within each group,* free from the deviant status to which these desires might consign them. Gays are always and only erotically interested in their own gender; the same goes in reverse for straights. In this way, identities are formed that anchor individuals in subcommunities of like-desiring persons, and a culture and politics are built around those identities that function as part of their reification. This, in turn, protects those who hold to the reified identity from the uncomfortable oscillation of erotic interest and desire. For hitherto scorned, isolated, and therefore individually often defenseless persons, the opportunity to now identify with a large and significant community that claims normal social and psychological status has strong appeal, an appeal understood early on by sociologists.

Thus genetic explanations of the gender we are sexually attracted to appeal to us and make prima facie sense in part because they do provide certain and unchanging identities (gay, straight, even bisexual) on which a supportive community can be built. We learn not to pay attention to discrepant feelings that might jeopardize our hard-won identities. And we feel under attack by those who would destabilize sexual orientations, who would see them as a complex but socially learned praxis rather than a biologically given destiny.

But our sexuality is not genetically coded. Human sexual desire long ago became unloosed from the reproductive cycle. For us, sexual contact is a richly textured experience suffused, as are all signifying acts, with culturally created meanings. We see this clearly when we look at the cross-cultural and historical studies of sexuality, but it is equally the case with the mundane heterosexual and homosexual practice of our own day. It is elementary sociology to state that far more is at stake in sexual interplay than the accomplishment of a genetically coded act, though it may be more comfortable for people to think of themselves as infra-human sexual animals, and unsociologically place responsibility for their sexual attractions on their genes, than to imagine and claim the freedom humans actually enjoy in the sexual realm.

In this sense, the biological approach to sexual orientation is a conservative one. By imagining sexual desire as akin to a biological trait like eye color or left-handedness, we neutralize the spontaneous and inventive in sexual relations, and create an essential grid of strictly coded sexual identities. Handedness is a genetically coded trait, and while it can be modified by sociocultural prescription, the underlying organization of right and left hemispheres will not be rearranged, nor will it shift apparently without warning, the way desire does. This is the framework imagined by the biologist model. It is an approach grounded in the view that "gays" are biologically, in effect categorically, different from "straights," a difference sealed by nature in hormone and brain, and ultimately, in DNA. . . .

The choice scientists make in looking for *the biological causes* of homosexuality reflects both sociopolitical and epistemological pressures. Historically, it is associated with a number of sociologically relevant conditions: the decline of the psychoanalytic model of homosexuality as an illness; the chance for medically oriented researchers to obtain research funds; the initiative and momentum created by massive spending of money and human capital on the Human Genome Project; a significant weakening of older sexual values and norms, and the consequent anxiety attendant on normlessness. Epistemologically, the conviction that the best understanding of numerous human behavioral and experiential phenomena is one that reduces them to biological, physiological, tissue-bound, and cellular etiologies is obviously pre-sociological. Such a reductionist and anti-sociological tack accounts for the persistent pursuit of biological causes for many behaviors that are politically and interpersonally quite complex—madness of various sorts, repeated violations of law, heavy drinking, individual and group differences on IQ and achievement tests, all sorts of gender-coded behaviors, and now, sexual attraction.

The biological model functions conservatively to restore stability in sexual life: it fixes sex in an ahistorical order, resolves certain tensions and ambiguities of desire, and reinforces the gender system (males do not desire other males; females do not desire other females, unless they are born that way [in which case they are forgivable]: heterosexuals have no homosexual desire; homosexuals have no heterosexual interests). It makes for a neater view of the erotic universe. But it is a retrograde choice from the point of view of a sociological model of sexuality and gender. It would be far more consonant with a sociological view of self and identity for the gay community to proclaim the message of the early gay liberation movement, that "we must free the homosexual (and the heterosexual) in all of us." . . .

NOTES

I thank David Schwartz for his inestimable help in the preparation of this essay. I would also like to thank Bill Byne for starting me thinking about the shortcomings of the new biological research into sexuality. Of course, neither one bears responsibility for the final product.

1. S. LeVay, A difference in hypothalamic structure between heterosexual and homosexual men, *Science* 253 (1991): 1034–37; M. J. Bailey and R. C. Pillard, A genetic study of male sexual orientation, *Archives of General Psychiatry* 48 (1991): 1089–96; L. S. Allen and R. Gorski, Sexual orientation and the size of the anterior commissure in the human brain, *Proceedings of the National*

Academy of Science 89 (1992): 7199–7202; D. H. Hamer, S. Hu, V. L. Magnuson, N. Hu, and A. M. L. Pattatucci, A linkage between DNA markers on the X chromosome and male sexual orientation, *Science* 261 (1993): 321–27.

2. J. M. Bailey and D. S. Benishay, Familial aggregation of female sexual orientation, *American Journal of Psychiatry* 150 (1993): 272; J. M. Bailey, R. C. Pillard, M. C. Nealem, and Y. Agyei, Heritable factors influence sexual orientation in women, *Archives of General Psychiatry* 50 (1993): 217.
3. Others have noted some of these as well. See W. Byne and B. Parsons, Human sexual orientation: The biologic theories reappraised, *Archives of General Psychiatry* 50 (1993): 228–39, for an excellent review article.
4. See E. Marshall, *Science* 257 (1992): 620–21. It makes LeVay's rejection of an offer from a reputable neuroanatomist to undertake a reexamination of his brain samples, as reported by Marshall, somewhat questionable.
5. M. King and E. McDonald, Homosexuals who are twins: A study of 46 probands, *British Journal of Psychiatry* 160 (1992): 407–9.
6. *New York Times,* December 17, 1991.
7. *Chronicle of Higher Education,* December 18, 1991.
8. *New York Times,* August 1, 1992.
9. *New York Times,* December 17, 1991.
10. *New York Times,* July 18, 1993.
11. A. D. Klassen, C. J. Williams, and E. E. Levitt, *Sex and Morality in the U.S.* (Middletown: Wesleyan University Press, 1989).

PERSONAL ACCOUNT

You Can't Forget Humiliation

People who are considered minorities hardly ever forget times when they encounter a bigot. You can't forget being humiliated by the look in their eyes. Instead, you grow long, bitter memories and a defensive stance spurred by anger and fear that someone, someday, will say or do something, and you won't be able to protect yourself. So you are always on guard.

I'll never forget when I was fourteen and my mother shook and screamed at me in a 7–11 parking lot for giving a flower to my best friend because everyone would think I was a lesbian. Or the time that I watched my baby niece, Katie, one afternoon weeks after I told her mom that I was gay.

I had accidently dropped my car keys on the bed when I laid the baby down for a nap. When she woke up, it was time to take her back to my sister. My roommate (who is also gay) and I searched furiously for my keys with no luck. We were locked out of the car, so my sister had to come to our apartment to pick up the baby. My roommate found the keys on the bed when he went to make a phone call, and said "Oh! Here they are. They were on the bed. They must have dropped when you put Katie down for her nap." And my sister said, "What were you doing in bed with my child!" At first, I was stunned that she would say that, but then I started to protest and so did my roommate. She told me she was "just kidding." I told her she was gross. After she left with Katie I cried.

I guess I'm angry now because I'm no longer ashamed to be gay. And when things happen to you, you just get angry because it is not fair. And anger stems from something else—something I never had my entire life until now. And that's pride. I didn't grow up with the same pride as an African American or Jewish kid does, hearing stories of how their ancestors survived. My pride was given to me. I got it much later in life than those kids because I didn't have proud parents who had the same "blood" as me or any role models to emulate. I was raised straight, and worse than that, I was raised with hate for the people I now call family. I earned my pride slowly and gently after I came out to myself. I paid for it with many years of self-denial, and many tears, until I found decent and wonderful gay friends that I could love and know that they went through the same trials I did. Now that pride I can share with my "family" and pass it on to some kid who needs it right now as much as I did when I didn't even know it existed.

Amy L. Helm

READING 48

Disability Definitions: The Politics of Meaning

Michael Oliver

THE IMPORTANCE OF DEFINITIONS

The social world differs from the natural world in (at least) one fundamental respect; that is, human beings give meanings to objects in the social world and subsequently orientate their behaviour towards these objects in terms of the meanings given to them. W. I. Thomas (1966) succinctly puts it thus: "if men define situations as real, they are real in their consequences." As far as disability is concerned, if it is seen as a tragedy, then disabled people will be treated as if they are the victims of some tragic happening or circumstance. This treatment will occur not just in everyday interactions but will also be translated into social policies which will attempt to compensate these victims for the tragedies that have befallen them.

Alternatively, it logically follows that if disability is defined as social oppression, then disabled people will be seen as the collective victims of an uncaring or unknowing society rather than as individual victims of circumstance. Such a view will be translated into social policies geared towards alleviating oppression rather than compensating individuals. It almost goes without saying that at present, the individual and tragic view of disability dominates both social interactions and social policies.

A second reason why definitions are important historically centres on the need to identify and classify the growing numbers of the urban poor in modern industrial societies. In this process of identification and classification, disability has always been an important category, in that it offers a legitimate social status to those who can be defined as unable to work as opposed to those who may be classified as unwilling to do so (Stone, 1985). Throughout the twentieth century this process has become ever more sophisticated, requiring access to expert knowledge, usually residing in the ever-burgeoning medical and paramedical professions. Hence the simple dichotomy of the nineteenth century has given way to a whole new range of definitions based upon clinical criteria or functional limitation.

A third reason why definitions are important stems from what might be called "the politics of minority groups." From the 1950s onwards, though earlier in the case of alcoholics, there was a growing realisation that if particular social problems were to be resolved, or at least ameliorated, then nothing more or less than a fundamental redefinition of the problem was necessary. Thus a number of groups including women, black people and homosexuals, set about challenging the prevailing definitions of what constituted these problems by attacking the sexist and racist biases in the language used to underpin these dominant definitions. They did this by creating, substituting or taking over terminology to provide more positive imagery (e.g., gay is good, black is beautiful, etc.). Disabled people too have realised that dominant definitions of disability pose problems for individual and group identity and have begun to challenge the use of disablist language. Whether it be offensive (cripple, spastic, mongol, etc.) or merely depersonalising (the handicapped, the blind, the deaf, and so on), such terminology has been attacked, and organisations of disabled people have fostered a growing group consciousness and identity.

There is one final reason why this issue of definitions is important. From the late fifties onwards there was an upswing in the economy and an increasing concern to provide more services for disabled people out of an ever-growing

---

Michael Oliver is professor of disability studies at the University of Greenwich in the United Kingdom.

national cake. But clearly, no government (of whatever persuasion) was going to commit itself to a whole range of services without some idea of what the financial consequences of such a commitment might be. Thus, after some pilot work, the Office of Population Censuses and Surveys (OPCS) was commissioned in the late sixties to carry out a national survey in Britain which was published in 1971 (Harris, 1971). Subsequent work in the international context (Wood, 1981) and more recently a further survey in this country, which has recently been published (Martin, Meltzer and Elliot, 1988), built on and extended this work. However, this work has proceeded isolated from the direct experience of disability as experienced by disabled people themselves, and this has led to a number of wide-ranging and fundamental criticisms of it. . . .

TABLE 1

SURVEY OF DISABLED ADULTS—OPCS, 1986

Can you tell me what is wrong with you?
What complaint causes your difficulty in holding, gripping or turning things?
Are your difficulties in understanding people mainly due to a hearing problem?
Do you have a scar, blemish or deformity which limits your daily activities?
Have you attended a special school because of a long-term health problem or disability?
Does your health problem/disability mean that you need to live with relatives or someone else who can help look after you?
Did you move here because of your health problem/disability?
How difficult is it for you to get about your immediate neighbourhood on your own?
Does your health problem/disability prevent you from going out as often or as far as you would like?
Does your health problem/disability make it difficult for you to travel by bus?
Does your health problem/disability affect your work in any way at present?

THE POLITICS OF MEANING

It could be argued that in polarising the tragic and oppressive views of disability, a conflict is being created where none necessarily exists. Disability has both individual and social dimensions and that is what official definitions from Harris (1971) through to WHO [World Health Organization] (Wood, 1981) have sought to recognise and to operationalise. The problem with this, is that these schemes, while acknowledging that there are social dimensions to disability, do not see disability as arising from social causes. . . .

This view of disability can and does have oppressive consequences for disabled people and can be quite clearly shown in the methodology adopted by the OPCS survey in Britain (Martin et al., 1988). [Table 1 presents] a list of questions drawn from the face-to-face interview schedule of this survey.

These questions clearly ultimately reduce the problems that disabled people face to their own personal inadequacies or functional limitations. It would have been perfectly possible to reformulate these questions to locate the ultimate causes of disability as within the physical and social environments [as they are in Table 2].

This reformulation is not only about methodology or semantics, it is also about oppression. In order to understand this, it is necessary to understand that, according to OPCS's own figures, 2231 disabled people were given face-to-face interviews (Martin et al., 1988, Table 5.2). In these interviews, the interviewer visits the disabled person at home and asks many structured questions in a structured way. It is in the nature of the interview process that the interviewer presents as expert and the disabled person as an isolated individual inexperienced in research, and thus unable to reformulate the questions in a more appropriate way. It is hardly surprising that, given the nature of the questions and their direction that, by the end of the interview, the disabled person has come to believe that his or her problems are caused by their own health/disability problems rather than by the organisation of

TABLE 2

ALTERNATIVE QUESTIONS

Can you tell me what is wrong with society?
What defects in the design of everyday equipment like jars, bottles and tins causes you difficulty in holding, gripping or turning them?
Are your difficulties in understanding people mainly due to their inabilities to communicate with you?
Do other people's reactions to any scar, blemish or deformity you may have, limit your daily activities?
Have you attended a special school because of your education authority's policy of sending people with your health problem or disability to such places?
Are community services so poor that you need to rely on relatives or someone else to provide you with the right level of personal assistance?
What inadequacies in your housing caused you to move here?
What are the environmental constraints which make it difficult for you to get about in your immediate neighbourhood?
Are there any transport or financial problems which prevent you from going out as often or as far as you would like?
Do poorly designed buses make it difficult for someone with your health problem/disability to use them?
Do you have problems at work because of the physical environment or the attitudes of others?

society. It is in this sense that the process of the interview is oppressive, reinforcing on to isolated, individual disabled people the idea that the problems they experience in everyday living are a direct result of their own personal inadequacies or functional limitations. . . .

IMPAIRMENT: A STRUCTURED ACCOUNT

Recently it has been estimated that there are some 500 million severely impaired people in the world today, approximately one in ten of the population (Shirley, 1983). These impairments are not randomly distributed throughout the world but are culturally produced.

> The societies men live in determine their chances of health, sickness and death. To the extent that they have the means to master their economic and social environments, they have the means to determine their life chances. (Susser and Watson, 1971, p. 45)

Hence in some countries impairments are likely to stem from infectious diseases, poverty, ignorance and the failure to ensure that existing medical treatments reach the population at risk (Shirley, 1983). In others, impairments resulting from infectious diseases are declining, only to be replaced by those stemming from the ageing of the population, accidents at work, on the road or in the home, the very success of some medical technologies in ensuring the survival of some severely impaired children and adults and so on (Taylor, 1977). To put the matter simply, impairments such as blindness and deafness are likely to be more common in the Third World, whereas heart conditions, spina bifida, spinal injuries and so on, are likely to be more common in industrial societies.

Again, the distribution of these impairments is not a matter of chance, either across different societies or within a single society, for

> Social and economic forces cause disorder directly; they redistribute the proportion of people at high or low risk of being affected; and they create new pathways for the transmission of disorders of all kinds through travel, migration and the rapid diffusion of information and behaviour by the mass communication media. Finally, social forces affect the conceptualisation, recognition and visibility of disorders. A disorder in one place and at one time is not seen as such in another; these social perceptions and definitions influence both the provision of care, the demands of those being cared for, and the size of any count of health needs. (Susser and Watson, 1971, p. 35)

Social class is an important factor here both in terms of the causes of impairments or what Doyal (1979) calls degenerative diseases, and in terms of outcomes, what Le Grand (1978) refers to as longstanding illnesses.

Just as we know that poverty is not randomly distributed internationally or nationally (Cole and Miles, 1984; Townsend, 1979), neither is impairment, for in the Third World at least

> Not only does disability usually guarantee the poverty of the victim but, most importantly, poverty is itself a major cause of disability. (Doyal, 1983, p. 7)

There is a similar relation in the industrial countries. . . . Hence, if poverty is not randomly distributed and there is an intrinsic link between poverty and impairment, then neither is impairment randomly distributed.

Even a structured account of impairment cannot, however, be reduced to counting the numbers of impaired people in any one country, locality, class or social group, for

> Beliefs about sickness, the behaviours exhibited by sick persons, and the ways in which sick persons are responded to by family and practitioners are all aspects of social reality. They, like the health care system itself, are cultural constructions, shaped distinctly in different societies and in different social structural settings within those societies. (Kleinman, 1980, p. 38)

The discovery of an isolated tribe in West Africa where many of the population were born with only two toes illustrates this point, for this made no difference to those with only two toes or indeed the rest of the population (Barrett and McCann, 1979). Such differences would be regarded as pathological in our society, and the people so afflicted subjected to medical intervention.

In discussing impairment, it was not intended to provide a comprehensive discussion of the nature of impairment but to show that it occurs in a structured way. However

> such a view does not deny the significance of germs, genes and trauma, but rather points out that their effects are only ever apparent in a real social and historical context, whose nature is determined by a complex interaction of material and non-material factors. (Abberley, 1987, p. 12)

This account of impairment challenges the notion underpinning personal tragedy theory, that impairments are events happening to unfortunate individuals. . . .

REFERENCES

Abberley, P. (1987). "The Concept of Oppression and the Development of a Social Theory of Disability," *Disability, Handicap and Society,* Vol. 2, no. 1, 5–19.

Barrett, D., and McCann, E. (1979). "Discovered: Two Toed Man," *Sunday Times Colour Supplement,* n.d.

Cole, S., and Miles, I. (1984). *Worlds Apart* (Brighton: Wheatsheaf).

Doyal, L. (1979). *The Political Economy of Health* (London: Pluto Press).

Doyal L. (1983). "The Crippling Effects of Underdevelopment" in Shirley, O. (ed.).

Harris, A. (1971). *Handicapped and Impaired in Great Britain* (London: HMSO).

Le Grand, J. (1978). "The Distribution of Public Expenditure: the Case of Health Care," *Economica,* Vol. 45.

Le Grand, J., and Robinson, R. (ed.) (1984). *Privatisation and the Welfare State* (London: Allen & Unwin).

Martin, J., Meltzer, H., and Elliot, D. (1988). *The Prevalence of Disability Amongst Adults* (London: HMSO).

Shirley, O. (ed.) (1983). *A Cry for Health: Poverty and Disability in the Third World* (Frome: Third World Group and ARHTAG).

Stone, D. (1985). *The Disabled State* (London: Macmillan).

Susser, M., and Watson, W. (2nd ed.) (1971). *Sociology in Medicine* (London: Oxford University Press).

Taylor, D. (1977). *Physical Impairment—Social Handicap* (London: Office of Health Economics).

Thomas, W. I. (1966). In Janowitz, M. (ed.), *Organization and Social Personality: Selected Papers* (Chicago: University of Chicago Press).

Townsend, P. (1979). *Poverty in the United Kingdom* (Harmondsworth: Penguin).

Wood, P. (1981). *International Classification of Impairments, Disabilities and Handicaps* (Geneva: World Health Organization).

PERSONAL ACCOUNT

Seeing Race, Seeing Disability

I am an international student who hails from Guyana, a country located on the coast of South America. Although called South American by a few, I am identified by most others as a West Indian (native of the Caribbean) because our culture and way of life is so similar to that of the little islands that comprise the West Indies.

I have experienced culture shock in America, from aspects of food and clothing to language and weather, but my most complex adjustment pertained to the issue of race. It is still less than one year since I have taken up residence in the "Land of the Free," but I have already begun to lose the gift of being colorblind.

America and Guyana have many cultural differences; yet, at the same time, there are many noteworthy similarities. One of these similarities would be the ethnic/racial diversity evident in both societies. Guyana is a blend of six races—Indian, Portuguese, Chinese, Caucasian, Amerindian (the indigenous people), and African. In Guyana, the color of one's skin or the texture of one's hair does not generally serve as a means of dichotomization, as seems to be common in America.

I was given the opportunity to work with a disabled student in a particular course. This young man's disability had been the result of an accident as a child. I had neither seen nor met him when I decided to peruse his web page, which was conveniently divided into areas that gave helpful information about his experience, hobbies, achievements, disability history, and career goals. It also provided a section with photographs. Without a moment's thought, I opened this photographic collection and later realized that I had done so only to satisfy my curiosity as to his race. In retrospect, I found this frightening because this behavior is foreign to me. I knew that it would have made no difference what race he represented because I would still have been enthusiastic about working with him.

Being as diverse as we are in Guyana, I would not have been immediately interested in his phenotypic identity, but possibly more concerned with (the extent of) his disability because there is a greater stigma attached to disabled persons in the Third World than there is in America. In comparison, diversity in my country is generally looked upon like the colors of a rainbow . . . all different but creating a thing of beauty when combined. In this part of the world, it seems as though diversity has created division.

R. B.

Popular Culture

READING 49

Orientals

Robert G. Lee

MAKING THE MODEL MINORITY MYTH

In January 1966, the *New York Times Magazine* published an article with the title "Success Story: Japanese-American Style," and in December *U.S. News and World Report* published an article focusing on Chinese Americans, "Success Story of One Minority in the US."[1] As their titles suggest, both articles told the story of Asians in America as a narrative of triumphant ethnic assimilation.

This new popular representation of Asian Americans as the model of successful "ethnic assimilation" was created in the crisis of racial policy that had surfaced at the highest levels of the federal government the previous year. The policy debate that emerged in 1965 reflected deep ideological division over responses to the demands for racial equality that had developed in the two decades since the end of the Second World War.

The Watts riot in the summer of 1964 and the growing demands of African Americans for economic equity as well as formal political rights,

Robert G. Lee is associate professor of American Civilization, Brown University.

along with the gradual dismantling of Jim Crow segregation in the South, plunged racial policy into crisis. The contours of the crisis can be seen in the conflicting responses of the Johnson Administration to black demands for racial equality. In March 1965, Lyndon Johnson's assistant secretary of Labor, Daniel Patrick Moynihan, published a *Report on the Black Family* which laid much of the blame for black poverty on the "tangle of pathology" of the black family. He admonished African Americans to rehabilitate their dysfunctional families in order to achieve economic and social assimilation. In June, at commencement exercises at all-black Howard University in Washington, D.C., the president articulated a vision of racial equality through sweeping social reconstruction in a massive War on Poverty. Both men genuinely claimed to support racial equality and civil rights, but their two documents could not have been further apart in their analysis and proposed solutions. The conflict between Johnson's response and Moynihan's response forms the ideological context in which the Asian Americans emerged as the model minority.

Johnson's speech emphasized the historical reality of race in America as compelling logic for extending civil rights into the economic sphere. Referring to the disadvantaged position of many blacks in the American economic structure, Johnson declared, "You do not take a person who for years has been hobbled by chains and liberate him, bring him up to the starting line of a race and then say, 'You are free to compete with all the others,' and still justly believe that you have been completely fair."[2] The president went on to lay the principal responsibility for black poverty on white racism, both historical and present, and he outlined an agenda of government-sponsored social change to ameliorate discrimination and poverty.

Moynihan took a radically different political tack. Quoting his former Harvard colleague, sociologist Nathan Glazer, Moynihan complained that "the demand for economic equality is now not the demand for equal opportunities for the equally qualified; it is now the demand for equality of economic results. . . . The demand for equality in education . . . has also become a demand for equality of results, of outcomes."[3]

Moynihan left implicit Glazer's ominous threat that American society, despite a commitment toward the former, would he "ruthless" in suppressing the latter. Moynihan went on to describe a black culture of poverty as a "tangle of pathology" born in slavery but "capable of perpetuating itself without assistance from the white world."[4] In particular, Moynihan identified the prevalence of female-headed households as a barrier to economic success. For Moynihan, the key to both racial integration and economic mobility was not in structural changes or social reorganization that might correct past injustice, but in the rehabilitation of "culturally deprived" black families.

The *U.S. News* article was quite explicit about the political context of its report when it asserted, "At a time when it is being proposed that hundreds of billions be spent on uplifting Negroes and other minorities, the nation's 300,000 Chinese Americans are moving ahead on their own with no help from anyone else." Foreshadowing an obsession that was to shape Richard Nixon's campaign rhetoric a year later, the writer of the *U.S. News* article described America's Chinatowns as "havens for law and order" and made no fewer than six references to low rates of delinquency among Chinese American youth.[5]

Making the Silent Minority

The construction of the model minority was based on the political silence of Asian America. An often cited example of Asian American self-reliance was the underutilization of welfare programs in 1970. Despite the fact that 15 percent of Chinese families in New York city had incomes below the federal poverty level, only 3.4 percent had enrolled to receive public assistance. This statistic has often been used as an example of a cultural trait of self-reliance and family cohesion. An alternative explanation, grounded in recent Asian American history, would stress apprehension and mistrust of the state's intentions toward them.

[World War II] incarceration had left deep wounds in the Japanese American communities. The removal to fairgrounds and racetracks, the relocation to remote, barbed-wired camps, the uncertainty of loyalty oaths, the separation of family members, all traumatized the Japanese American community. The Japanese American Citizens League's policy of accommodation with the War Relocation Authority and its role in suppressing dissent within the camps had left bitter divisions among many Japanese Americans. Japanese Americans, for the most part, were anxious to rebuild their lives and livelihoods and reluctant to relive their experience. In particular, the American-born Nisei generation remained remarkably silent about its camp experience until the emergence of the Asian American movement in the 1970s and the Redress Movement of the 1980s. Social psychologists have likened the response of Japanese Americans who had been unjustly incarcerated to that of victims of rape or other physical violation. They demonstrated anger, resentment, self-doubt, and guilt, all symptoms of post-traumatic stress syndrome.[6]

While postwar Japan became America's junior partner, the People's Republic of China became its principal enemy. After the Korean War broke out in 1950, and especially after China entered the war in 1951, the United States made every effort to isolate communist China, economically and diplomatically, and embarked on a military policy of confrontation aimed at "containing" the expansion of Chinese influence throughout Asia and the Third World.

The fear of Red China extended to the Chinese American community. In 1949, Chinese communities in the United States were divided in their attitudes toward the communist revolution. Although the number of communists in Chinese American communities was tiny, many who were not communist or even leftist nonetheless found some satisfaction in the fact that a genuinely nationalist, reputedly honest, and apparently more democratic government had finally united China after a century of political chaos, weakness, and humiliation. On the other hand, Chiang Kai-shek's Kuomintang Party had long enjoyed the support of the traditional elites in the larger Chinatowns.[7]

When the Korean War broke out in 1950, Congress passed the Emergency Detention Act, which vested the U.S. Attorney General with the authority to establish concentration camps for any who might be deemed a domestic threat in a national emergency. The mere authorization of such sweeping powers of detention served as a stark warning to Chinese Americans that what had been done to Japanese Americans a decade earlier could also be done to them without effort.

The pro–Chiang Kai-shek Chinatown elite, working with the FBI, launched a systematic attempt to suppress any expression of support for the new communist regime in China. The Trading with the Enemy Act, which prohibited any currency transfers to the Peoples Republic of China, including remittances to family, was used as a tool to attempt to deport suspected communist sympathizers. Although only a few leftists and labor leaders were actually deported, the threat of deportation had a deeply chilling effect, since many hundreds of Chinese had come to the United States as "paper sons" during the long decades of exclusion and were in the United States under false pretenses.

In 1952 Congress passed the McCarran-Walter Immigration and Nationality Act, which dismantled racial prohibitions on immigration and established an Asian-Pacific Triangle with an immigration quota cap of two thousand visas. Even though McCarran-Walter still strictly limited Asian immigration, the red scare that was its impetus was contagious. In 1955, Everett F. Drumwright, the U.S. consul in Hong Kong, issued a report warning that communist China was making use of "massive" fraud and deception to infiltrate agents into the United States under cover as immigrants. Drumwright's hysterical and largely unsubstantiated report provided the rationale for massive FBI and INS raids into Chinatowns around the country to search out pro-China subversives. Chinatowns were flooded with public notices and street flyers warning of potential spies and subversives, while "innocent residents" were encouraged to report suspected subversives to the FBI.

In 1957 Congress authorized the Chinese Confession Program. Chinese Americans who had come as paper sons were encouraged to confess their illegal entry. In return for consideration for an appropriate (but not guaranteed) adjustment of their status, the applicant had also to make a full disclosure on every relative and friend. The information gathered in the Chinese Confession Program was used to try to deport those who were identified by the FBI's informants as supporters of China or as domestic troublemakers. Membership in leftist support organizations, in labor unions, in "pro-China" organizations melted away in the face of the sustained harassment and attack from the conservative elite within Chinatowns, and the FBI and INS from without.[8] . . .

THE MODEL MINORITY AND THE NEOCONSERVATIVE RACIAL PROJECT

. . . Moynihan's early characterization of the matriarchal black family as "a tangle of pathology" able to reproduce itself "without help from white racism" suggested that the "culture of poverty" could be understood without reference to poverty itself. Increasingly the discussion of poverty focused on the multigenerational and self-reproducing. The metaphor of black pathology displaced analysis of social crisis, the effects of massive unemployment, poverty, and the collapse of family life. Since it was the dysfunctionality of the black family, and not genetics, that determined black behavior (not, of course poverty or discrimination), race could be encoded as cultural difference into public debates over social policy.

In the 1980s, African Americans were constantly identified with social chaos and violence: witness Ronald Reagan's invocation of the infamous unnamed "welfare queen," George Bush's use of black rapist Willie Horton in ads during his first presidential campaign, tales of "wilding" black teenagers, even the sexual harassment charges against Clarence Thomas, President Bush's black conservative nominee to the Supreme Court. Although race was made to disappear as a category of analysis, dressed up as cultural difference it became ubiquitous as a coded trope in the discussion of social policy; it is nowhere and yet everywhere. Although the appeal to culture appears to be non-biological, hence non-racist, in fact it has become a mode of perpetuating race as a category of immutable cultural difference.

The model minority representation of Asian Americans that had originated in the Cold War and gained visibility in the mid-1960s has been expanded and transformed to fit the current crisis. Asian cultural difference is held to be a source of social capital. A mythic Asian American family, the imagined product of an ahistorical and reified Asian "traditional" culture, is a central image, expanded to fit a wider target. Increasingly, the imagined Asian American family has been upheld as a model not only to blacks and Latinos but to working-class and middle-class whites as well. In the updated model minority story fitted to ideological demands . . . not only social conservatism but also productivity is emphasized. Recent articles in the national press on Asian Americans emphasize their persistence in overcoming language barriers, their superior disciplinary and motivational roles as parents, and their "intact" families' success at savings.[9]

Twenty years after Asian Americans were first heralded as a potential model for the upward mobility of nonwhites in American society, David Bell theorized Asian American success in a 1985 essay in the *New Republic,* "The Triumph of Asian Americans." Bell summarized Asian American virtues as "self-sufficiency" and proclaimed this the secret to Asian American success. At the center of such self-sufficiency he placed the traditional Asian American family, an "intact" family, significant in three ways: It provides a secure environment for children; it pushes those children to work harder; and it fosters savings.[10]

The *New Republic* did not hesitate to make an invidious comparison between Asian and African Americans. Bell's article characterizing Asian Americans as a self-sufficient racial minority that made no demands for institutional change followed an article in the same issue titled "Brown's Blacks." This article excoriated black students at Brown University for protesting a recent spate of assaults on minority students on campus and demanding greater representation among the faculty and in the curriculum. While the student protesters at Brown had been a broad coalition of Asian, Latino, and black students and had gained substantial support among white students at the liberal campus, the *New Republic* article ignored the multiracial aspect of the protest and chose to characterize the movement as solely a black protest, the black students as malcontents, and the troubles on campus as yet another negative result of misguided affirmative action. When read back to back, the comparison between the "good," self-disciplined and submissive Asian Americans and the ungrateful and complaining blacks could not have been made more clear.

In 1988, a news report that ten of the twelve winners of the prestigious Westinghouse Prizes for achievement in science among high school students were Asian American prompted Stephen Graubard, a history professor at Brown University and the editor of *Daedalus,* the prestigious journal of the American Academy of Arts and Sciences, to publish an essay in the *New York Times* titled "Why Do Asian Pupils Win Those Prizes?" In a series of paradigmatic questions, Graubard laid out the implications of the traditional Asian American family model for all other Americans.

> Is the "stability" [of a dual parent family and a single family home] almost a prerequisite for school accomplishment? . . .
>
> If so, what is to be done for those hundreds of thousands of other New York children, many of illegitimate birth, who live with one parent often in public housing, knowing little outside their dilapidated housing and decaying neighborhoods?

Graubard does not answer his own questions, but the family to which his questions lead us is unmistakable. It is the traditional Asian American family, presumed to be intact and self-sufficient, and certain to be disciplinary and motivational.

> Do [non-Asian students] have teachers prepared to tell them that personal appearance matters, that a price is paid for spiked hair and blue lipstick? . . .
>
> Who, for the impoverished black or Puerto Rican student, advises something other than the conventional educational path?

In Graubard's view it is not only African American and Latino families who will do well to learn from Asian Americans. In a peculiar formulation of racial and ethnic difference, Graubard asks, "What would it take for Puerto Rican, black and *white children of certain ethnic origins* to become serious competitors for such honors, and what would such an academic 'revolution' mean?" [Emphasis added.]

In Graubard's view, it is not only racial and ethnic minorities (including those mysterious "white children of certain ethnic origins") who should learn from the disciplined and motivated traditional Asian American family; America's middle class can also improve its performance by taking a lesson from Asian America. After all, the glittering prizes now captured by Asian American students had once been the patrimony of middle-class white students. Graubard asks what has happened to those students: "What about the others [of the middle class]? . . . Are the children of such families reaching out and securing the great prizes? . . . The children of the middle class, who are much more privileged but appear both indolent and incompetent . . ."[11]

For both Bell and Graubard, Asian American "success" is a product of an unspecified and decontextualized traditional Asian culture. Tradition is reduced to the values of obedience, discipline, and motivation enacted by the family, those traditions most valued in the late capitalist economy. In contrast, at the heart of the economic and academic difficulties of black, Hispanic, working-class, and even middle-class America is the cultural pathology of family structures that tolerate spiked hair and blue lipstick.

What distinguishes the model minority myth as a hegemonic mode of racial representation is not primarily its distance from reality but rather its power to dominate or displace other social facts. Ideological hegemony operates through its power to absorb, co-opt, or displace oppositional views, to tie a diverse and sometimes contradictory set of images and representations into an explanatory whole. It is the location of specific images and representations within the hegemonic paradigm that endows those images with ideological power.

The hegemonic power of culture as the new defining category of difference can be seen in an August 1987 cover story of *Time* Magazine, "The New Whiz Kids." This article attempts to provide a more balanced and informed picture of the educational achievements of young Asian Americans. It showcases their scholastic triumphs but also discusses both the institutional barriers that still stand in the way of Asian American students and the cost in stress that many pay for such success.

The article quotes extensively from a variety of experts on education, including scholars who study Asian American communities. Nevertheless, both the structure of the inquiry and the outcome of the article's conclusions are built around the reified concept of the "traditional" Asian family. The *Time* writers cite Professor William Liu of the University of Illinois at Chicago who asserts that Japanese, Korean, Chinese, and Vietnamese students perform better because "the Confucian ethic drives people to work, excel and repay the debt they owe their parents." The article contrasts this information to the observation of Professor Ruben G. Rumbaut, a sociologist at San Diego State University, that "Laotians and Cambodians, who do somewhat less well, have a gentler Buddhist approach to life."[12]

Assigning the differences in achievement and social mobility of various Asian American ethnic groups to assumed differences between a disciplined Confucian tradition (supposedly shared by Japanese, Koreans, Chinese, and Vietnamese) and a "gentler" Buddhist tradition (shared by Laotians and Cambodians) is, at best, astoundingly simplistic. Whatever impact a millennium of Buddhism may have had on China, Japan, or Vietnam is gently ignored. The high proportion of ethnic Chinese among the Cambodian and Laotian immigrant communities is also ignored. The high proportion of second-, third-, and fourth-generation American-born and middle-class Japanese Americans is ignored. Perhaps the most important ignored factor is the higher educational and occupational skill levels, and greater capital, that Chinese, Korean, and first-wave Vietnamese brought with them to the United States. Indeed, the entire history of Asia, a region in which social and cultural change has been nothing less than revolutionary in the twentieth century, is ignored in this rush to reify traditional culture as the key to Asian American success.

In their rush to judgment on the cultural superiority of Asian Americans, these commentators almost completely ignore recent Asian American history. Indeed, although these articles draw heavily on the images of recent Asian immigrants, all but the most self-evident facts about the revolutionary changes in the demography of Asian America since 1965 are elided by the hegemonic status of culture as the determining variable of social mobility. Bell, Graubard, and *Time* Magazine fail to ask even the most basic questions about the American economy and the place of Asians, blacks, Latinos, or "whites of certain ethnic origins" within it.

Recent Asian American history offers a different interpretative paradigm for understanding patterns of Asian American economic success and hardship. Since 1970, the Asian/Pacific Islander population (to use the Census Bureau's designation) has been the fastest growing nonwhite minority in America. Between 1970 and 1994, the Asian American population grew from 1.4 million to 8.8 million people.[13] The huge growth through immigration of the Asian American population has not been evenly distributed across ethnic groups, class, or sex. While there has been considerable economic success among Asian Americans, they also experience undeniable poverty. Both phenomena can be explained more accurately by the realities of Asian immigration patterns than by the secrets of traditional Asian family values.[14]

The explosion of the Asian/Pacific Islander population was due primarily to massive immigration from Asia after the passage of Immigration Reform Act of 1965. In addition to dismantling the national quota system that had been designed to exclude Asian immigration, the Immigration Reform Act of 1965 contained two provisions that encouraged immigration from Asia. The new policy favored the entry of scientific, technical, and professional personnel, and it gave preference to family members of immigrants already resident in the United States.

The most significant factor in accounting for Asian American economic prosperity—and that undermines the notion of Asian American cultural superiority—is the fact that a large proportion of this new Asian immigration was already middle-class on arrival in the United States. The 1965 immigration act favoring technical and scientific personnel and those who met specific occupational needs (particularly medical personnel) not only encouraged immigration from Asia, where economic development policies had created a pool of well-educated technical personnel eager to emigrate, but it also made likely the successful economic integration of Asian immigrants in the 1970s. Between 1965 and the mid-1970s, the majority of immigrants from Asia were middle-class professionals.[15]

In addition to their immediate integration into the professional, technical, and managerial sectors of the work force, the large proportion of middle-class immigrants among Asian Americans resulted in a second generation of children who were academically advantaged. Thus the "brain drain" from Asia in the 1970s resulted in an Asian American population that was already highly educated. According to the Census Bureau's 1994 statistics, slightly more Asian Americans than non-Hispanic whites over the age of twenty-five had completed four years of high school, and almost twice as many had completed college.[16]

In some respects Asian immigration has matched the demand for capital and labor at both ends of the . . . economy. Since the late 1970s, the demand for semiskilled, unskilled, and entrepreneurial labor in the new low-wage manufacturing and service sectors of the . . . economy has been met in large part by Asian and Latin American immigrants. Although the absolute number of professionals among Asian immigrants has remained high, since the mid-1970s they no longer make up the majority of immigrants from Asia. Working-class immigrants and refugees now make up the majority of Asian immigrants. In particular, women now outnumber men among immigrants from Asian countries. Some come independently as workers; others come as spouses to American citizens and as permanent resident aliens. Many have had work experience in Asia—in the needle trades, electronic assembly work, institutional custodial or housekeeping work, or food service. Some come with semiprofessional skills, particularly in the health industry, as nurses and technicians.[17] In sum, Asian Americans, particularly immigrant Asian workers, have a highly visible position in both ends of the . . . economy, in what urban sociologist Saskia Sassen has called "global cities"—the command centers for serving the financial needs of the new transnational economy.

The suggestion of parity between Asian Americans and non-Hispanic white Americans is, therefore, deceptive. The figure cited most often to illustrate the Asian American success story is the median income of Asian American families ($42,250 in the 1980s and 90s), slightly higher than the median income for white families. When controlled for geography and the number of wage earners per family, however, the income of Asian Americans falls short of that for non-Hispanic white Americans.[18]

Despite the fact that a large number of Asian Americans are successful, a disproportionate number of Asian Americans are poor. In 1990, while 8 percent of non-Hispanic white families had incomes below the Federal poverty guidelines, 11 percent of Asian/Pacific Islander families had incomes below the poverty guidelines. In 1994, despite their higher educational attainment and similar family income, the poverty rate for Asian/Pacific Islander families was almost double that of non-Hispanic white families. Among families with high school educated householders, the poverty rate was almost twice that of non-Hispanic white families; among college-educated householders, the poverty rate of Asian/Pacific Islander families was almost three times that of non-Hispanic white families. The poverty rate for Asian/Pacific Islander married couples was more than twice that of white married couples.[19]

The Asian American as Gook

The model minority concept as theorized by Bell, Graubard and *Time* Magazine singles out for praise those values most closely identified with the Protestant work ethic. Obedience, self-control, individualism, and loyalty to the needs of the nuclear family, as opposed to either anarchic libertarianism (spiked hair and blue lipstick) or social consciousness (black radicalisms), are mobilized in an imagined Asian American tradition that is deployed in the attempt to restore American hegemony in the global marketplace.

The model minority has two faces. The myth presents Asian Americans as silent and disciplined; this is their secret to success. At the same time, this silence and discipline is used in constructing the Asian American as a new yellow peril. In contemporary dystopian narratives of . . . urban America, the Asian American is both identified with the enemy that defeated the United States in Vietnam and figured as the agent of the current collapse of the American empire. The Vietnam War story, told as the tragedy of America's lost innocence, works as a master narrative of national collapse while defining the . . . crisis as a product of invasion and betrayal.

The constant refrain in Vietnam War narratives is that the Americans are unable to see and know, and thereby to conquer, the Viet Cong—reason enough for My Lai, free fire zones, tiger cages, and, ultimately, defeat. The supposed invisibility of the Viet Cong led to the racialization of the Vietnam War. "Gook" became the most common racial epithet used by Americans to describe Vietnamese, enemy and ally alike. Indeed, the supposed invisibility of the communist enemy led American soldiers, who measured the war in body counts, to invoke the "mere gook rule," whereby any dead Vietnamese could be counted as a dead enemy.

The term "gook" has a long history in the American vocabulary of race and in the American imperial career in Asia and the Pacific. A bastardization of the Korean *hankuk* (Korean), or *mikuk* (American), it was used by Americans in the Korean War to refer to North and South Koreans and Chinese alike. The term also has links to "goo-goo," used by American soldiers to describe Filipino insurgents at the turn of the century.

Such broad ethnic inclusiveness makes this racial epithet emblematic in describing Asian Americans as the ubiquitous and invisible enemy. Asian Americans, figured as gooks, the flip side of the model minority, become the scapegoats onto which anxiety over economic decline and the psychic trauma of the Vietnam War can be transferred. They appear silently, like the Viet Cong, as an alien threat in these narratives of multicultural dystopia and besieged nationhood, at once ubiquitous and invisible, ersatz and inauthentic.

The myth that America lost the war in southeast Asia because it had been betrayed by the liberal elite mobilizes a populist working-class rejection of liberal economic and social policy and lays the foundation for an attempt to restore American hegemony by revitalizing an undivided American people. The theme of betrayal as the cause of America's fall from grace attributes the defeat of the United States in southeast Asia to the sapping of American strength as a result of radical divisiveness and liberal tolerance. This breakdown of American unity is reflected in the breakdown of the traditional American nuclear family. The embattled nuclear family becomes a trope for national unity beset by the divisiveness of feminism, multiculturalism, and class conflict. In this dystopian vision of post-Vietnam America, the Asian American model minority becomes the enemy within, economically productive but culturally inauthentic, and thus unsuitable as model for national restoration.

NOTES

1. William Peterson, "Success Story: Japanese-American Style," *New York Times Magazine* (January 9, 1966), 38; "Success Story of One Minority in the U.S.," *U.S. News and World Report* (December 26, 1966), 73.
2. Lee Rainwater and William Yancey, *The Moynihan Report and the Politics of Controversy* (Cambridge, MA: Massachusetts Institute of Technology Press, 1967), 79.
3. Ibid., 124.
4. Ibid., 49. The likelihood that Moynihan also drafted Johnson's speech does not negate the point that the speech and the report reflect two quite different ideological tendencies.
5. "Success Story of One Minority in the U.S.," 73–78.
6. Yasuko I. Takezawa, *Breaking the Silence: Redress and Japanese American Ethnicity* (Ithaca, NY: Cornell University Press, 1995).
7. See H. Mark Lai, "The Chinese Marxist Left in America to the 1960s," in *Chinese America: History and Perspectives* (San Francisco: Chinese Historical Association of America, 1992), 3–82.
8. See Bill Ong Hing, *Making and Remaking of Asian America through Immigration Policy, 1850–1990* (Stanford, CA: Stanford University Press, 1993); Robert G. Lee, "The Hidden World of Asian Immigrant Radicalism," in *The Immigrant Left in the United States,* ed. Paul Buhle and Dan Georgakas (Albany, NY: SUNY Press, 1996), 256–288.
9. See David A. Bell, "The Triumph of Asian Americans," *The New Republic,* July 15–22, 1985, 24–31.
10. Ibid., 30.
11. Stephen G. Graubard, "Why Do Asian Pupils Win Those Prizes?" *New York Times,* January 29, 1988, A35.
12. "The New Whiz Kids," *Time* Magazine, August 31, 1987, 47.
13. The U.S. Census Bureau estimates that by the turn of the century, twelve million Asian Americans will make up 4 percent of the national population, and by the middle of the next century Asian Americans will account for 10 percent of the U.S. population.
14. See Bill Hing, *Making* and *Remaking of Asian America;* Yen Espiritu, *Asian-American Pan-Ethnicity: Bridging Institutions and Identities* (Philadelphia: Temple University Press, 1992); and Paul Ong, Edna Bonacich, and Lucie Cheng, eds., *The New Asian Immigration in Los Angeles and Global Restructuring* (Philadelphia: Temple University Press, 1994), 14.
15. See Hing, *Making and Remaking of Asian America.*
16. U.S. Census Bureau Report, 1994.
17. See Lisa Lowe, *Immigrant Acts: On Asian American Cultural Politics* (Durham: Duke University Press, 1996).
18. 1994 U.S. Census Reports.
19. Ibid.

PERSONAL ACCOUNT

Let Me Work for It!

I remember once in a Sociology of Education class that I was asked to describe my educational experience. At first, I was quick to say that it was very positive. Although racial remarks and jokes were passed around school, teachers and administrators paid little or no attention to them. I always felt uneasy with such remarks, but because the teachers and administrators would play ignorant to what was being said, I felt that maybe I was being too sensitive. Therefore, I learned to suck it up and was taught to view such comments as harmless.

Still, at a very young age I was very aware of racism and sexism. Both of my Vietnamese parents came to the United States when they were 20 years old. They arrived right before the Vietnam War ended, which explains the stigmatization they experienced. "VC" was a common epithet addressed to my dad along with "Gook" and "Charlie." My mom, on the other hand, struggled with gender/racial stereotypes such as being labeled mindless, dependent, and subservient. I can recall many times watching people mentally battering my parents. Numerous looks of disgust and intolerance of my parents' accent or confusion with the English language were some unpleasant cases that I experienced. Yet, the snide remarks and mistreatment thrown at my parents remain the most hurtful. Many times my parents were told that their lack of proficiency in English would doom them from success and from any self-worth. They were also ostracized for holding on to their Vietnamese culture and were persuaded to assimilate to the American culture. The accumulation of these events reinforced the idea that being different, in this case Vietnamese, was negative. As far as I was concerned, my family was my only community. It was only within my family that I felt the sense of security, love, support, and, most importantly, connection. After all, I was just a "Gook" like my parents.

Yet, I experienced support and love at school. I can trace this feeling all the way back to third grade. I remember how I was constantly praised for being so bright, even before turning in my first assignment. This did not send alarms to my brain. As a student, I felt great. I felt validated. But looking back on it now, there *are* alarms going off for me. Why? Because now I wonder if I was being labeled as a model student, a positive stereotype. Many Americans have held positive stereotypes about Asians and their work/study ethic, and making these stereotypes prior to a person's performance can create the possibility of drowning in the pressure of high expectations. Teachers have always had unreasonably high expectations for me. Although I did not experience this as pressure, I do feel that I have been robbed of the equal chance to prove myself, to see my mistakes and grow. I feel that I have so much to give, but my audience is content with what they "know" of me (which is usually built upon assumptions). I was never given the chance to work for the standing ovation; nor was I given the privilege of criticism.

At the personal level, the model minority stereotype has denied me human dignity, individuality, and the acknowledgment of my own strengths and weaknesses. I feel that I have been prejudged in this fictitious view of Asian Americans. These positive portrayals depict Asians as so flawless that they are robbed of any humanity. Some may feel indifferent to my story or ask if I really reject the positive stereotype. My only reply is this: positive and negative stereotyping are different sides of the same coin. Both invalidate individuals as human beings and lead to negative consequences.

Isabelle Nguyen

READING 50

Women-Becoming-Men

Voices of Kickbutt Culture

Benjamin DeMott

Take a random walk through the culture, eyes on the trivial as well as the weighty, and new male and female images fill your gaze. Men and women looking and sounding roughly the same. Women mimicking male stereotypes, trying on "basically masculine" attitudes and feelings. Women represented as eager to appropriate the other sex's traditional roles, traits, styles of talk, body parts, illicit desires.

Item: A cover story in *Cosmopolitan* titled "Infidelity—It's Not Just For Men Any More."[1] Rejecting cliché-idealizations of women as morality bearers, this snippet of gender shift in course affirms women's rights to parity in perfidy. Let all have equal opportunity access henceforth, says *Cosmo*, to the fun or whatever of straying.

Item: The National Fluid Milk Processor Promotion Board decides mustaches aren't just for men anymore and paints white ones on exercycling women. A jokey gender shift. The promoters of a food product assert, with a wink, that fitness and a healthy diet erase differences between "the weaker sex" and the stronger.[2]

Item: Santa Claus drops down a chimney—in a Marshall's commercial—and emerges female. Another jokey gender shift. An equal opportunity employer curries seasonal favor with its predominantly female clientele by grinning at the silly patriarchal past. *I can be anything I want, including the voice of HoHoHo.*

Item: Joy Behar greets an all-female audience gathered for a Ms. Foundation fundraiser with these words: "Good evening, girls . . . No, it's 1998. Good evening, men."

The tone of such material is often sly, enigmatic, ironically self-protective, eager to undercut its own claims to seriousness. And none of the material is more amusing than *The New Yorker*'s continuing series of cartoons about the masculinization and feminization of the middle classes. William Hamilton draws four young women who, in the manner of yesteryear's frat boys anatomizing prom dates, sit at a table smoking cigars and exchanging crude notes on a list of eligible men. ("Great legs, good cook, not half bad in the sack," runs the caption, "but hopelessly tied to his mother's apron strings.")[3] Richard Cline draws junior law associates mockingly admiring each other's high-gloss unisex toughness. ("Thank you, Nathaniel," says a female suit&briefcase to a male suit&briefcase. "I think you, too, are a very scary young lawyer.")[4] Peter Steiner draws a briefcase-bearing lobbyist-mother explaining herself—the U.S. Capitol in the background—as she walks hand in hand with her kindergartner: "Mommy can be tough like Janet Reno. But she can also be vulnerable like Al Gore."[5] Ed Koren tweaks New Man inhibition. Five middle-aged urban cowboys—refugees, maybe, from the movie *City Slickers*—male-bond around a campfire, all but one drinking soda pop and making un-macho nice. The rascally fifth has a beer bottle and a beer glow, plus a question: "Would any of you guys be offended if I told a joke that is a touch prurient?"[6] Stuart Leeds kids macho militiapersons. Five middle-aged women armed with knives, automatic pistols, and rifles, and dressed in ammo bandoliers and berets, sit around a table planning mayhem. Says the leader, "We've gathered enough. Let's hunt."[7]

But it's not the wit or banality that warrants notice. It's the pervasiveness, the omnipresence of similar figures, concepts, and themes in every contemporary genre—sitcoms, road movies, first-person confessionals, wedding pages, consumer columns, tall stories, fables, porn flicks, lyric poetry, ballets, beer ads . . .

Benjamin DeMott is a journalist and freelance writer, and professor emeritus at Amherst College.

A pretty young woman on a bar stool gossips (for Miller Lite) about a mutual acquaintance to an aggressively inattentive friend; suddenly the pretty young woman begins speaking in an All-Pro lineman's voice, deep and gruff, whereupon the friend listens (*I can be anything I want, including bass-voiced.*)[8] A woman driver in a Chevy Camaro commercial passes a leering truck driver and —*almost* off camera—gives him the finger. A woman driver in a Dodge Avenger ad lets her mate, Tim, have the keys to the fun car "because he knows who really sits in the driver's seat." "Why Women Love Trucks," a column in *New Woman,* spends pages comparing compacts with half-tons, advancing at the end to a rhapsody power boost conferred by a pickup perch. "The appeal is one of control—even of intimidation. . . . When you're up higher . . . you're in charge. . . . There's a feeling of power you get from riding high in the cabin of a four-wheel drive truck that makes you think you could, if you really had to, drive up and over the problems around you."[9]

A "little old lady" golfer with a swing arc resembling Tiger Woods's strokes a 300-yard drive to the green (for O'Doul's pseudo-beer), cowing the wiseass males who are tailgating her and her partner, expecting an invitation to play through. Two ferocious deep-voiced old ladies, furious because the Stovetop Stuffing they've just tasted is so much better than their own homemade dressing, lash out viciously at the camera lens, trying to smash it. Trencherwomen party on at a single-sex barbecue for Baked Lay's; as the camera lingers over the gluttonizing—tight shots of women's hands wrist-deep in chow, women's faces sauce-smeared and sweaty—a relishing male voiceover intones, "Now girls can eat like guys."

And stand and sit like them as well, in a thousand Sunday supplement fashion layouts. A model with the familiar menacing look brushes back her scarlet Jones New York jacket, hands on her hips Texas Ranger style (thumbs behind, fingers forward); on the facing page a model in an Albert Nippon pegged pantsuit sits mannishly forward on her chair, hands and arms action-ready, no jewelry, legs way akimbo, feet planted so firmly they communicate booted ruggedness although she's wearing slingbacks. Fashion magazines push "bruiser chic"—brown eyeshadow for the black-eyed look, "biker gear for glamazons," "beefy leathers, brassy cuffs, big boots," kickboxer postures for models.[10] At Helmut Lang's New York show "the models march about in combat trousers, khaki anoraks [and] flight suits."[11] The magazine *Teen* promotes boys' clothes for girls in a cover story ("Steal His Look/Boy-Meets-Girl Style").[12]

Bruiser chic guy-talk resounds in ad copy. "When Was the Last Time You Got Screwed?"[13] asks the top line of an ad for EOT, "the new long distance company" (in the artwork three young women frown at a phone bill). "Testosterone Isn't Just a Guy Thing Anymore" announces a seven-page spread, in *Prevention,* on the "hormone of desire."[14] "Don't Ask Me to Be Faithful," warns a defiant sports heroine in Reebok's Monogamy/This is my Planet campaign.[15] Sandra Bernhard tells *Vanity Fair* her motto is "Kiss 'em, slap 'em, send 'em home."[16] Hydro Clara, journeyman technician for a big city daily, tells *Moxie* magazine she handles male co-workers with a series of fixed commands: "Don't call me dear, dear. Don't wait for me to leave to get out of the elevator so you can look at my ass. Quit staring at my tits while I try to explain something to you. No, I don't need your opinions on my hair."[17]

Celebrity magazines admiringly profile rich widows who terrorize male staffs. Courtney Ross, hard-driving widow of the late Warner chairman, has the professionals in her employ bowing and scraping, according to *Vanity Fair;* she's turned museum curators into "dusters and polishers" who tremble at her approach, and her young chef is a "a nervous wreck."[18] *Marie Claire* features "Women Who Sell Men's Bodies" model agency bigwigs who intimidate males aspiring to modeling careers. (The piece opens with a get-cracking order—"Take off your shirt. . . . Now your pants"—addressed to "a beautiful young man, 6′2″, blue eyes, short blond hair,"[19] by a bored young woman executive.)

Talk profiles a professional wrestler (six-three, two hundred pounds) who performs under the name Chyna and describes herself as "an empowered woman who kicks guys in the nuts for a living."[20] *People* reports that Christy Martin, lightweight boxing champ, woman's division, 35–2–2 with twenty-five KOs, could easily trash half the men who fight at her weight. (So says Martin's chief sparring partner, well ranked in his pro class.) Martin's trainer, who's also her husband, acknowledges that he never thought he'd be kissing one of his fighters, "but after one fight I was so proud of her I just gave her a hug and a kiss." ("If he didn't kiss me that night," she tells a girlfriend, "I was going to lay one on him.")[21] The award for best direction at the Sundance 2000 Film Festival goes to *Girlfight,* a movie about a high school senior who "lives to fight," hangs out in boxing gyms, and has a "snapping hook [that makes] her look like a natural." Muhammad Ali's daughter—Joe Frazier's as well—are embarked on ring careers.[22]

Fights grow more common at women's pro basketball games: "Suddenly, eight more players arrived, and the Liberty's backup center, Venus Lacy (six-four, two hundred and thirty-four pounds), leaned over to help. [Debbie] Black let go of [Teresa] Weatherspoon's neck to take a swing at Lacy, who retaliated by slapping Black," etc.[23] The cover story of the premier issue of *Jump,* a "magazine for girls who dare to be real," is called "Girls Who Kick Guys' Butts,"[24] and profiles girls who are teenage wrestlers, football and hockey players, and water poloists. Brandi Chastain kicks the winning goal in World Cup soccer, tears off her shirt guy-fashion, and is saluted for having "met the androgynous ideal of women as men who can have babies: muscular, irreverent, aggressive."[25]

The *New York Times* reports that female "Killer Instinct" players—they beat half the top-seeded males in a recent national electronic games tournament—are needling the industry about wimpy products. " 'Barbie Super Model' is stupid," declares Kate Crook, teenaged semifinalist in the Blockbuster World Game Championship. "Games should be made for both sexes [because girls] like fighting games and role-playing adventures."[26]

The industry's response was to create a new game called Sissy-fight 2000 in which the players are girls on a playground. ("It's not just that Sissyfight is fun," writes one young female player. "This game has stirred something inside of me I thought was dead: the urge to bludgeon someone. . . . It's a vicious pleasure that I never got to indulge as a child. . . . The object is to fight your opponents until [only] two of you remain.")[27] Levi's Jeans for Women derisively lists bygone noncombatant fantasies in its ads—"the princess dream . . . the pony dream . . . the pretty bride dream"—and then asks, "Ready for the kick-butt dream?"[28] (The art focuses on the jeans-clad behind of a woman in karate first posture.) Finlandia vodka ads pose young women on high diving boards and detail their inner thoughts: "In a past life I was an Amazon Queen. As for men . . . Well, as long as they had dinner on the table, we kept them around." Alone and underarmed, beach book heroines conquer teams of killer bad guys. In Joseph Finder's *Zero Hour* (1996), FBI agent Sarah Cahill not only whips mercenary terrorists and paranoid billionaires but also saves the nation's banking system.

TV for its part has warrior princesses (*Xena*), mobster matriarchs (*The Sopranos*), female Harley-riding cop killers (*Renegade*), and a heroine who takes a wrench to the private parts of a bearish male auto mechanic (*3rd Rock from the Sun*).[29] "Babes with Blades," an "all-woman's showcase of stage combat," runs at Chicago's Footsteps Theater ("these fightin' females kick ass," says the *Chicago Reader*'s reviewer).[30] At moviehouses adolescent heroines play outlaws, kidnappers, and thieves (*Foxfire, Manny and Lo, Girls Town*). ("As an actress," says Heather

Graham—Rollergirl in *Boogie Nights*—"it's fun to do rageful things.")[31] The heroine of Disney's animated epic *Mulan* dons "male military drag" and "bur[ies] a horde of enemy Huns under tons of snow."[32] In other highly promoted movies women are killers—trigger-happy cops, trigger-ready moms, kickboxer-avengers, hit "men," soldiers of fortune, and the like. Sony ads depict a downed woman flyer crawling intrepidly through deep brush, computer mouse grenade in hand. "I've Committed Murder," sings Macy Gray in the "gutsiest track" of her debut album. (Gray imagines herself killing her lover's oppressive female boss in an instance of "class revolt for which she refuses to apologize.")[33] "Goodbye Earl," a hit from the Dixie Chicks, tells how Maryanne and Wanda murder Wanda's abusive husband ("We'll pack a lunch, stuff you in a trunk, Earl/Is that alright?").

"I have a confession to make," says the producer Elizabeth Hurley to an interviewer. "I grew up dreaming of being a gangster."[34] "I pattern myself after Frank [Sinatra]," said Roseanne shortly before the singer died. "He beats people up, I beat people up."[35] "Quite often," says Lynne Russell of CNN's *Headline News,* "even the suggestion of a woman's ability to hit a guy so hard that when he stops rolling his clothes will be out of style is all you need to improve your day."[36] Geena Davis, a pirate in *Cutthroat Island* and a paid assassin in *The Long Kiss Goodnight,* taunts her enemies remorselessly: "You're gonna die screaming and I'm gonna watch."[37]

"Go Ahead, Be a Bitch," says a cover story plugging aggression in *Woman's Own.* The piece notes that bitches "don't settle," that "bitches have that my-girlfriend-can-beat-up-your-girlfriend sex appeal," and that bitches "will stiletto-kick [anybody] who gets in their way." Bitchery is obligatory, the magazine explains, because men nowadays "stay nice by having their worse halves do their dirty work."[38] Gina, young wife of John, observes that "I'm always the one to do battle. John is not good at confrontation. While I'm fighting the landlord, John's off getting a Coke."[39] Or else having himself a spa day. The actor Richard T. Jones recommends, in *Jane,* five-hour spa stints—a loofah glove scrub and deep massage plus a eucalyptus leaf beating. ("I think more men should do the spa thing. Men *need* this kind of thing.")[40]

Eyewitnesses tell the *New York Post* about a battle between O. J. Simpson and a woman named Christine Prody that took place recently in a Miami Airport hotel. (A hotel security guard said Prody, twenty-five, "was slapping and kicking the shit" out of Simpson.) Men's magazines fill up with first-person narratives by males physically abused by females. "It happened several years ago," writes Daniel Frankel in a representative *Men's Fitness* piece, "in an office where I used to work."

> A female colleague said something during a meeting that pushed my button. "You know, if this was grade school, I'd sock you for that," I replied, mostly in jest. "Well, we're not in grade school, and it's me who could kick your ass," she shot back, not in jest. (A martial artist, she regularly kept us apprised of her belt status.) . . . I found myself replaying the conversation over and over again in my head. You see, I've had my ass kicked by chicks before. . . . My career as a cross-gender punching bag goes back to when I was eight, hanging out with Jan, my next door neighbor.

Frankel's memoir climaxes with a bout in which a girlfriend kicks him three times in the face. ("It could have been worse; she held back a bit.")[41]

Males beaten by their mates are favorite talk show guests. Rick tells Oprah that his wife "liked to slap my face a lot, she enjoyed kicking me—going for the ribs—punching me in the face. A lot of kicking. A *lot* of kicking." Now dependent on Mace for protection, Rick feels "betrayed by the system." Patty, a Catholic schoolgirl, beats up a new boyfriend in *Downtown,* the MTV cartoon series. ("She's mean," says the narrator. "She put her last boy in the hospital.") A freshly shaven man in a Norelco shaver ad eyes a passing women and she pats his face approvingly; the woman seated beside the freshly shaven man hits him hard with a rubber bat. In the porn flick *Hardwood* (1999) Bobbi finds Dave, her man, packing a suitcase to leave her because she's too male in her behavior. ("You work like a guy. Hell, you even drink beer like a guy.")[42] Bobbi socks Dave hard in the jaw, whereupon he moans, "You even hit like a guy." . . .

What counts more than the question of origins is simply the astonishing ubiquity of images of women-becoming-men: the ceaseless weaving of the key themes of gender shift into the texture of dailiness, the saturation of the public air with sounds, gestures, and behavior that dumb down women's struggle into a campaign for universal masculinization—and declare its total victory. The ascendant discourse—attacks, salutes, "neutral" reports—dissolves the feminist analysis of forces underpinning sexism. It overwhelms the feminist challenge to market value dominance, silences the feminist call for models of humane interaction between the sexes and for institutions capable of nourishing its growth. The understandings and values that lent saliency to the ideal of gender flexibility itself begin to disappear: reverence for human potentiality and for openness and social and imaginative access; the sense of the irreducibility of the human creature however sexed; the belief that settling for thinned-out, role-constrained, culturally implanted versions of male or female "personality" or "character" amounts, for the individual, to an act of self-mutilation. . . .

NOTES

1. A 1996 *Newsweek* poll adds confirmation, reporting that "in the '90s . . . more of the cheaters are women." Jerry Adler, "Adultery/A New Furor over an Old Sin," *Newsweek,* September 30, 1996, p. 54.
2. "Hey, let's talk about the F-word," says the copy in one milk mustache ad. See *Vanity Fair,* November 1996, p. 149.
3. *The New Yorker,* October 7, 1996, p. 46.
4. *The New Yorker,* November 20, 1995, p. 44.
5. *The New Yorker,* January 19, 1998, p. 65.
6. *The New Yorker,* October 14, 1996, p. 74.
7. *The New Yorker,* December 8, 1997, p. 78.
8. A related voice prank comes from @rtwork, an artists' collective represented in the Whitney Biennial 2000. @rtwork switches the voice boxes of GI Joe and Barbie dolls on toy store shelves. See Janelle Brown, "The Net as Canvas," *Salon,* March 15, 2000, p. 3.
9. Jean Lindamond, "Truckin' It," *New Woman,* November 1995, p. 126.
10. See, e.g., *Harper's Bazaar*, September 1995, p. 335, and *Allure,* December 1996, pp. 134ff.
11. Michael Roberts, "Craving Private Ryan," *The New Yorker,* March 22, 1999, p. 82.
12. *Teen,* September 1997, cover and pp. 106ff.
13. EOT ad in *Village Voice,* September 24, 1996, p. 7.
14. Tobey Hanlon, "Do You Need the Hormone of Desire?" *Prevention,* August 1997, pp. 73ff.
15. Reebok ad, *Time,* May 6, 1966.
16. "Proust Questionnaire," *Vanity Fair,* August 1999, p. 100.
17. Hydro Clara, "On the Road to Becoming a Journeyman," *Moxie,* Fall 1999, pp. 31ff.
18. Michael Schnayerson, "Life After Steve," *Vanity Fair,* November 1996, p. 236.
19. Susannah Hunnewell, "The Women Who Make or Break Male Supermodels," *Marie Claire,* December 1995, p. 34.
20. Mark Kriegel, "Chyna Doll," *Talk,* June/July 2000, p. 92.
21. William Plummer and Meg Grant, "Woman Warrior," *People,* June 24, 1996, p. 103.
22. See Timothy W. Smith, "Frazier's Daughter Has Fast Debut," *New York Times,* February 7, 2000, p. B2.
23. Jean Strouse, "She Got Game," *The New Yorker,* August 16, 1999, p. 38.
24. Dana Silberger, "Playing with the Boys," *Jump,* October 1997, p. 62.
25. Fred Barnes, "Sometimes a Game Is Just a Game," *Weekly Standard,* July 26, 1999, pp. 22–24. Barnes's attitude to Chastain—and to her media adulators—is disapproving.
26. Nancy Malitz, "Invasion of the Girls Surprises Video-Game Makers," *New York Times,* December 21, 1995, p. C2.
27. Amy Silverman, "The Virtual Bitch Slag," *Salon,* April 27, 2000, p. 2.
28. Women who kick butt are now as conventional as women with balls. "Madam Secretary [admitted],"

PERSONAL ACCOUNT

Just Something You Did as a Man

In a class we had discussed the ways men stratify themselves in terms of masculinity. I decided I would put that discussion to the test at work.

As I sat at a table, one of my coworkers approached me with a copy of a popular men's magazine, which portrays nude women. He said, "Frank, there is this bitch in here with the most beautiful big tits I have ever seen in my life." I told him that I wasn't interested in looking at the magazine because I had decided I did not agree with the objectification of women. His reply was, "What's the matter, are you getting soft on us?" I joked that it was not a matter of getting soft, it was simply a decision I had made due to a "new and improved consciousness."

At, my job, talk about homosexuals, the women who walk by, and graphic (verbal) depictions of sexual aggression toward women abound, but on this occasion I either rejected the conversation or said nothing at all. By the end of the day I was being called, sometimes jokingly and sometimes not, every derogatory homosexual slur in the English language. I was no longer "one of the boys." I did not engage in the "manly" discourse of the day so therefore I was labeled (at best) a "sissy."

My coworkers assumed that I had had or was about to have a change of sexual orientation simply because I did not engage in their conversations about women and homosexuals. Since men decide how masculine another man is by how much he is willing to put down women and gays, I was no longer considered masculine.

This experience affected me as much as it did because it opened my eyes to a system of stratification in which I have been immersed but still had no idea existed. Demeaning women and homosexuals, to me, was just something you did as a man. But to tell you the truth, I don't think I could go back to talking like that. I am sure that my coworkers will get used to my new thinking, but even if they don't I believe that it is worth being rejected for a cause such as this. I had not thought about it, but I would not want men talking about my sisters and mother in such a demeaning way.

Francisco Hernandez

writes Nancy Franklin, "that she got a laugh out of the recent cartoon showing a woman trying on clothes in a store and being given this hard-line sales pitch: 'Madeleine Albright kicked butt in that suit.'" See "Talk of the Town," *The New Yorker,* December 15, 1997, p. 64.

29. Lucy Lawless, who plays, Xena, says, "Xena's agenda is just to get through the day without killing someone." See David Rensin, "The Woman Behind the Warrier," *TV Guide,* May 3, 1997, p. 22. On the movie and video history of tough women from *The Avenger* to *Thelma and Louise* and beyond, see Sherrie A. Inness, *Tough Girls: Women Warriors and Wonder Women in Popular Culture* (Philadelphia: University of Pennsylvania Press, 1998).
30. "Babes with Blades," *Chicago Reader,* February 27, 1998, p. 28.
31. See Margy Rochlin, "Beauty, Brains and a Knack for Giving the Censors Pause," *New York Times,* April 12, 1998, p. AR20.
32. Gina Belafonte, "Feminism/It's All About Me," *Time,* June 29, 1998, p. 61.
33. Ann Powers, "The New Conscience of Pop Music," *New York Times,* September 19, 1999, Section 2, p. 1.
34. "Wise Girl," *Jane,* September 1999, p. 172.
35. See "Frankly Admiring," *People,* December 14, 1995, p. 86.
36. Lynne Russell, *How to Win Friends, Kick Ass and Influence People* (New York: St. Martin's, 2000), p. 28.
37. As always the cartoonists chuckle. In *The New Yorker* drawing by V. Twohy (March 11, 1996), one woman to another, both enjoying a box of chocolates and gazing at a vase of roses: "They're from David. He's been so much more considerate since I shot him."
38. Elissa Schappell, "Why Bitches Get the Best Men," *Woman's Own,* August 1996, p. 11.
39. Ibid.
40. "He Spas/She Spas," *Jane,* September 1999, p. 116.
41. Daniel Frankel, "I've Had My Ass Kicked Before," *Men's Fitness,* December 1966, p. 107.

42. The dialogue in the key scene runs as follows:
    Dave: I'm leaving.
    Bobbi: You're leaving. Where? Why?
    Dave: You're why. Bobbi, you're never gonna change. It's just the way you are.
    Bobbi: What are you saying?
    Dave: I'm saying, look at yourself. You dress like a guy. You work like a guy. Hell, you even drink beer like a guy. I can't take it no more.
    Bobbi: You know what you can't take? You can't take me for who I am. You've never accepted me, Dave—and that really hurts.
    Dave: Accept? Lemme ask you a question. When we go out, what do you wear? Jeans and a blazer.
    Bobbi: Yeah, so what?
    Dave: So what? And then the waiter ends up bringing you the check. No, I don't think so. How can I accept it when people think you're more of a man in this fucking relationship than I am? . . .
    Bobbi: (Socks him on the jaw) You fucking bastard, you. (Stomping out) You make me sick.
    Dave: (Holding his chin) You even hit like a guy.

READING 51

Toward a Poetics of the Disabled Body

Rosemarie Garland-Thomson

My eighty-two-year-old mother told me about an unnerving experience she recently had at the beauty shop. Slow and unsure on her feet now, wobbly and often confused about her surroundings, this woman who has spent a lifetime being brisk, efficient, and unobtrusive rather suddenly is experiencing a new relationship with her aging body. But more than that, to her surprise, she is having to cope as well with her own sense of being conspicuous. "Everyone was staring at the crippled up old lady," she said accusingly and disparagingly of herself, distancing herself from the "old lady" others saw in place of the person she imagined herself to be. Her point was that being looked at as "crippled" was for her more dismaying than actually being "crippled."

This was an interesting moment for me, the daughter who has spent a lifetime deflecting the stares of strangers by cultivating a demeanor of dignity and authority that ranges from haughty to congenial, from gregarious to aloof. What my mother is learning too late, and with too little self-consciousness to help her, is something I have known my entire life. For me, this knowledge is best expressed in the language of critical theory: that difference is constructed relationally. In other words, my body, my "congenital disability," becomes different, abnormal, disabled, only in comparison to the socially established and enforced bodily standards and expectations that interpret it so within a social context. Being stared at is one of the social practices that creates my disability, my sense of myself as different from what I should be.

As anyone with a visible disability knows, enduring stares is one of the universal social experiences of being disabled. Staring is one of the definitive, unifying social practices that establishes disability identity and gives the disabled body meaning in the collective cultural imagination. We are marked not by our bodies themselves, but by responses to our bodies: by the stares that record our otherness, by the narratives that establish our inadequacy, by the barriers that keep us out, by the norms that render us abnormal. Even disabilities that are considered "hidden," thought of as internal functional impairments such as seizure disorders, HIV status, or chronic fatigue syndrome, always threaten to erupt as physical signifiers, no matter how

Rosemarie Garland-Thomson is associate professor of English at Howard University.

subtle, that will visually announce difference as surely as the wheelchair, the empty sleeve, the unfocused eye, or the unregulated tic.

My aim in this [discussion] is twofold: first, to outline how the stare creates disability identity; and, second, to analyze the performance art of two disabled women artists, Mary Duffy and Cheryl Marie Wade, in order to lay out what I call a poetics of the disabled body, one that is grounded in the staring dynamic. This poetics of the disabled body exemplified by Duffy and Wade directly engages staring both as an oppressive social mechanism and at the same time as a visual interaction that can be appropriated to protest and to redefine disabled female subjectivity.

Staring is a social relationship between the starer and the object of the stare that constitutes the starer as normal and the object of the stare as different. The exchange between starer and object registers both the anonymity that confers agency on the starer and the singularity that stigmatizes the one who is stared at. Staring is the ritual enactment of exclusion from an imagined community of the fully human. As such, it is one of the cultural practices that create disability as a state of absolute difference rather than as simply one more variation in human form. Many other cultural practices, of course, create disability as well. For example, medical discourse pathologizes certain bodies and deems others "healthy" or "fit." Architectural features such as stairs disable those with mobility impairments, while ramps do not. A print-reliant workplace turns the impairment of blindness into a disability, while Braille and voice software mitigate it. My blind friend, for example, became much more disabled—more "blind"—when she left an urban area with good public transportation and moved to a suburban area that required driving for mobility.

In this sense, disability is not simply the natural state of bodily inferiority and inadequacy that my mother took it to be that day in the beauty shop. Rather, disability is a culturally fabricated narrative of the body, similar to what we understand as the fictions of race and gender. Disability is a comparison of bodies that legitimates the distribution of resources, status, and power within a biased cultural and architectural environment. As such, disability has three aspects: first, it is a system for interpreting bodily variations; second, it is a relationship between bodies and their environments; and third, it is a way of describing the inherent instability of the embodied self. The category of disability exists as a way to exclude the kinds of bodily forms, functions, impairments, changes, or ambiguities that call into question our cultural fantasy of the body as a neutral, compliant instrument of a transcendent will.

Moreover, disability is a broad term within which cluster ideological categories as varied as sick, deformed, ugly, old, maimed, afflicted, abnormal, or debilitated—all of which disadvantage people by devaluing bodies that do not conform to cultural standards. Thus, disability functions to preserve and validate such privileged designations as beautiful, healthy, normal, fit, competent, intelligent—all of which provide cultural capital to those who can claim such status, who can reside within these subject positions. It is, then, the various interactions between bodies and world that make disability from the raw material of human variation and precariousness.

STARING

Staring, as I have suggested, is one of those interactions between body and world that disables people. Yet, the dynamic of staring remains understudied in the burst of critical analyses from academics and activists as disability has emerged over the last twenty years as a social identity, a critical category, a political cause, and a civil rights issue.[1] Whereas feminist scholars have elaborated theories of the gaze that confront the sexualized display of women, disability studies has not yet fully conceptualized the implications of the stare.[2] Although it is not possible to undertake so complex a project here, I will nevertheless sketch out briefly the centrality and operation of staring in the social construction of disability and then turn to the performances of Mary Duffy and Cheryl Marie Wade.

The history of disabled people in the Western world is in part the history of being on display, of being visually conspicuous while being politically and socially erased. For example, the earliest record of disabled people is of their exhibition as prodigies, as "monsters" taken as omens from the gods that were read as indexes of the natural or divine worlds. In religious discourse from the New Testament to miracles at Lourdes, the lame, the halt, and the blind provide the spectacle for the narrative of bodily rehabilitation as spiritual redemption that is so essential to Christianity.

From antiquity through modernity, the bodies of disabled people considered to be freaks and monsters have been displayed by the likes of medieval kings and P. T. Barnum for entertainment and profit in courts, street fairs, dime museums, and sideshows. Moreover, medicine has from its beginnings exhibited the disabled body as what Michel Foucault calls the "case," in medical theaters and other clinical settings in order to pathologize the exceptional and to normalize the ordinary.[3] Disabled people have variously been objects of awe, scorn, terror, delight, inspiration, pity, laughter, or fascination—but we have always been stared at.

Staring simultaneously centralizes and marginalizes the disabled person. As it confers the stigmata of difference, staring literally foregrounds the person viewed at the same time that it objectifies and challenges his or her position as an accepted member of the human community. Staring interrupts—if not precludes—the comfortable, yet highly conventionalized, interactions that make up social intercourse between anonymous fellow humans. The established, predictable social rituals that characterize exchanges among seeming equals dissolve into tense and confusing relations when one person's disability is introduced into the social dynamic. Staring often disrupts the assumption of commonality and enforces a difference that usually makes both parties uncomfortable and unsure of how to respond to one another in any way other than the staring relation.

Moreover, staring frequently incites an embarrassment in both people that engulfs the relationship. For example, one of my own worst staring experiences occurred when a particularly bold child followed me around the grocery store taunting me while his horrified mother stared not only at me but at the scene her child created by demanding that I show him my arm. As this incident suggests, staring starkly registers a breach of commonality that occurs when one of the majority confronts one of the minority, when the ordinary encounters the extraordinary. In short, staring produces an asymmetrical relation that imparts what Erving Goffman calls "a spoiled identity" to the disabled person at the same time that it verifies the normative status of the starer.[4]

Disabled people, however, must eventually learn to manipulate the stare, to use it as a forum for asserting our dignity and humanity. It is a matter of survival, for one cannot endure such constant visual stoning and remain psychically intact. For example, in the grocery store incident I just described, I tactfully refused the role of the monster and instead asserted my humanity by authoritatively diverting the child's attention, aligning myself sympathetically with the disconcerted mother, and reassuring her that her child had not really bothered me. Thus, my strategy was to control the encounter with firmness and grace, the only tools I believed I had to defend myself from being, as cultural critics awkwardly say, "othered" by the stare.

Repeatedly, other disabled people testify as well that the hardest adjustment to moving into the disabled subject position is becoming visually conspicuous, of losing the privilege of anonymity. A psychiatrist friend tells me, for example, of a man who cannot go into a restaurant ever since the end of his little finger was amputated. For the prominent anthropologist Robert Murphy, his wheelchair became a flagrant sign that exposed his literally lowered status.[5] The writer Lucy Grealy, who lost her jaw to cancer, found that Halloween masks allowed her each year to "walk among the blessed for a few brief, sweet hours." Masks became her only deliverance from the intrusive stares constituting the "ugliness" that defined her.[6] Each of us has our own strategies for dealing with the daily stares that enact our status as different and threaten to cast us out of the human circle.

STARING BACK

As performance artists, Mary Duffy and Cheryl Marie Wade make their manipulation of the stare into an art form. I will limit my analysis of this art form to these two women, although other fine disabled performance artists abound, both male and female, whose work engages on the staring dynamic. Bob Flanagan and Orlan are perhaps the best known. Duffy's and Wade's performances in particular fold together in suggestive ways critiques of both the gender system and what Lennard Davis suggests we call "the normalcy system"[7] that produces disabled identity.

In other words, these women's performances explore the intersections of femininity and disability, subject positions both constituted within patriarchal culture by visual appropriation. One might ask why these women, who have bodies that so disrupt the expectations of the complacently normal, would deliberately invite the stare in a public setting. Duffy, an Irishwoman, who presents herself nude in performance, is armless, with one delicate hand attached directly to her shoulder. Wade, an American, emphatically gesticulates from her wheelchair with hands that she describes as "gnarly." Both women would be characterized as "severely disabled" by the standards of what my colleague Paul Longmore calls with great irony the "severely able-bodied."[8]

The answer, of course, is that such performances are forums for profoundly liberating assertions and representations of the self in which the artist controls the terms of the encounter. In addition to allowing individual expression, their artistic engagement with self-display also provides a medium for positive identity politics, an opportunity to protest cultural images of disabled people, especially of disabled women. Simultaneously, these performances renarrate the scripts of disability and femininity.

The disabled performance artist faces a complex challenge by placing herself in the public view. In her performance, she must invite the staring that objectifies her body and then orchestrate that performance so as to create the image she wishes to project. It is the same task writ large that all disabled people encounter. Duffy's and Wade's performances make serious art from the quotidian stuff of my grocery store encounter with the curious and persistent youngster. Displaying the disabled body as a work of art involves, of course, more than just managing the stares we all face.

First, presenting the disabled body as art confounds aesthetic notions of beauty. Indeed, disability's departure from the ideal human form has been traditionally cast as an aesthetic violation. Second, regardless of how prevalent staring at disabled people may be, it is fugitive looking, considered variously impolite, disgusting, tasteless, insensitive, sensational, or kinky. In short, the disabled body is imagined as an inappropriate art object. Social norms endorse looking at art as a proper visual practice, whereas staring at disabled bodies is illicit looking. This is the paradox that Duffy and Wade exploit in their performances.

Simply by using her body as an art form, the female artist invokes a perdurable tradition of displaying the female body as a beautiful ornament, decorative object, or work of art. As John Berger has described so succinctly and as countless feminist critiques have affirmed, women are the ones looked at in Western culture.[9] In the highly visual culture of modernity, female display, from classical art to contemporary media, has been a way to establish the literal contours of female appearance and sexual norms. How women are looked at is determined by the ideology of feminine beauty.

Lynn S. Chancer asserts that this ideology produces what she calls—not without irony—"looks-ism." Looks-ism, according to Chancer, is "a discriminatory phenomenon [that] sets up categorical divisions, placing far greater importance for one sex than the other on the cultivation and maintenance of particular bodily appearances to gain love, status, and recognition." Moreover, she continues, these "beauty expectations are systemic," that is, they are a "social fact," to use Emile Durkheim's term for an aspect of culture that "exist[s] above and beyond the ability of individuals to control."[10] Beauty, then—not unlike disability—is a system of practices and meanings, a historically shifting ideology of the female body that is at once culturally determined and yet by no means unalterable.

Disability, like feminine beauty, involves a politics of appearance based on culturally established body norms. The emergence in modernity of the ideological concept of the norm, in both the statistical and scientific discourses, controls our interpretation of physical impairment. The rationalization of the body in modernity uses scientific measurement and medical diagnosis to create the abstract, culturally validated figure of the "normal person" against which bodies are measured and evaluated. With the normal as a standard of value, both impairment and anomaly are seen not as part of the continuum of human variation or the inevitable transformation of bodies over a lifetime, but rather as the pathological exception, as the abnormal.[11] So while bodies that are impaired and anomalous have always been interpretive occasions in history—often as sources of wonder and awe—modernity has made them visible as medically deviant, a theme that informs both Duffy's and Wade's performances.

MARY DUFFY

Duffy and Wade summon controversial questions as they braid together the several cultural traditions of looking at the body that I discussed above. First, their performances raise the issue of what is appropriate looking; second, they query what constitutes beauty; and third, they ask what the truth of the body is. These women's performances unsettle cultural assumptions about humanity, femaleness, disability, and self by invoking and juxtaposing all of these categories. By simultaneously using the traditional format of female display to present bodies with disabilities, Duffy and Wade turn their performances into critiques of the politics of appearance and an inquiry into what it means to be an embodied person. To do this, Duffy primarily uses her body, whereas Wade mainly uses words.

The dominant aspect of Duffy's performance is the allusion to the classical female nude that her body announces. Her performances begin with a totally darkened room that wipes away all ocular options, clearing the audience's visual palate. For an almost uncomfortable period of time, the viewers see nothing. Amid the darkness, a series of enigmatic black and white images seem to float up; they are piles of smooth stones that increase in number as each image changes to the next. During this critical introduction, the clusters of stones grow, and the sound of a chugging train that transforms into a beating heart begins to accompany the images. The suggestion of embryonic development and fetal heartbeat becomes clear.

Then, out of the darkness, the form of Mary Duffy suddenly appears spotlit from the front and against a black background. The scene dramatically obliterates all visual alternatives except Duffy's ultrawhite form, forcing the audience to look at her completely naked body, posed in the posture of the Venus de Milo, the quintessential icon of female beauty. Young, full-breasted, voluptuous, beautiful, and armless, this living Venus demands with her silent presence that the audience stare at her. This arresting choreography hyperbolically, almost parodically, stages the dynamic of two opposing modes of looking: staring at the freakish body and gazing at the female body as a beautiful work of art.

The observer has been trained by the discourses of modernity to see Duffy's body as a pathological lack, a deviation from the norm that either has been hidden away in the asylum or displayed in medical photographs with a black bar over the eyes to obliterate personhood. For modern viewers, hers is the sensationally abnormal body that has been glimpsed furtively in the tabloids and yet proscribed as an object of proper bourgeois looking. Like gawking at a fatal traffic accident or the primal scene, looking at Duffy is at once compelling and illicit. But while Duffy's body calls up these visual discourses of the disabled body, it also invokes the familiar contours of beauty.

Duffy's simultaneously starkly disabled and classically beautiful body elicits a confusing combination of the rapt gaze and the intrusive stare. The literally in-your-face white figure against the black background is at once the degraded and the exalted body of Western tradition of looking. The templates that culture has supplied her audience are inadequate to make sense of her body. Framed as a work of art, her body is paradox incarnate, leaving her viewers' sense of the order of things in ruins. Hers is the art that transforms consciousness, granting a new way of seeing the known world.

While the visual aspect of Duffy's performance is central, words nonetheless are fundamental to her performance as well. Shifting the classical allusion from Venus de Milo to Pygmalion, Duffy begins to speak:

> You have words to describe me that I find frightening. Every time I hear them they're whispered or screamed silently, wordlessly through front to middle page spreads of newspapers. Only you dare to speak them out loud. I look for them in my dictionary and I only find some. The words you use to describe me are: "congenital malformation." In my child's dictionary I learn that the first part means "born with." How many times have I answered that question, "Were you born like that or did your mother take them dreadful tablets?" How come I always felt ashamed when answering those big staring eyes and gaping mouths? "Did you have an accident or did your mother take them dreadful tablets?" Those big words those doctors used—they didn't have any that fitted me properly. I felt, even in the face of such opposition, that my body was the way it was supposed to be. It was right for me, as well as being whole, complete and functional.[12]

Unlike Pygmalion, however, in this performance Duffy does not affirm the perspective of her creator when she turns from silent object of the gaze/stare into a speaking subject. The words she cites are the verbal equivalents of the stare she sets up between herself and the audience. Yet here the words come from her own voice in performance rather than from the array of starers she has faced during her lifetime. By appropriating the words that have been used to describe her body, she upsets the dynamic of the stare, repeating in a kind of testimony the words of her starers while forcing the audience to look at a classic image of female beauty bearing witness to its own enfreakment by those words.[13]

Duffy flings the words, the questions, and the stares back at her lookers, rebuking the aggregate "you" who have tried to create her as a pathological specimen, freak of nature, or quintessential lack. She accuses them with their own accusing questions to her about being "born like that." She stares out at them, upbraiding them for their intrusive "staring eyes and gaping mouths" that made her feel "ashamed." Dismissing their perceptions of her body, she insists upon her own self-definition, asserting that "words" such as "congenital malformation" do not accurately describe her experience of herself. Her soliloquy moves from exorcizing the language her oppressors use to determine her to voicing her own version of herself as "being whole, complete and functional."

Another of Duffy's performances continues this critique of "the words you use to describe me" by redeploying them in the context of her own self-presentation. Highlighting her own agency, she affirms: "I'm winning battles every day against my own monster, my inner critic, who has internalized all my childhood oppressions: the oppression of constantly trying to be fixed, to be changed, to be made more whole, less visible, to hide and to be hidden."[14] Here Duffy appropriates the word "monster," which traditionally has been used to define her body. The words "congenital malformation" are a recent medical term for the older religious and early scientific designation "monster," which named the extraordinary body and gave rise to the nineteenth-century science of teratology, the study of monsters.

Duffy insists that the "monster" is not her body, as the dominant culture would have it, but rather the "monster" is the abstract, internalized version of herself that they have created and that she has absorbed from being stared at. "My monstrosity," she avows in another performance, "is in your imagination." Her perspective differentiates her body from the audience's interpretation of her body as monstrous, as a lack that needs to be "fixed." Her oppression, then, arises from the perceptual conflict between Duffy's sense of herself as "complete" and the dominant view of her as incomplete, as deficient rather than "whole."

The perception of the disabled body as lacking or excessive has consequences that go beyond staring, however. The power of the dominant culture to enforce this view by "fixing" our bodies is a constant threat for Duffy. In another variation of her performance, she succinctly protests the compulsory practice of medically normalizing the disabled body with procedures that are euphemistically known as "reconstructive surgery." Reaffirming that her perception of her body is "an essential part of [her] being," Duffy clarifies the "you" she addresses as the doctors who promote a medical model of disability. "You were always trying to change me in your image," she charges, "always trying to slice off my hand."[15]

This arresting image of mutilation, of having her hand sliced off, alludes to an experience common to people whose bodies are marked with what medicine terms "congenital malformations." For example, fashion model Aimee Mullins and performance artist Nomi Lamm both had their legs amputated when they were young in order that they could wear cosmetic prostheses. Intersexed children and conjoined twins are special targets of routine surgical normalization because they so challenge our cultural understanding of persons as unambiguously sexed and unambiguously separate. Such disciplinary practices maim disabled persons by standardizing their appearance and functioning, which is skin lightening and hair straightening with a vengeance.

It is part of the fantasy of the plastic body described by both Mike Featherstone and Susan Bordo as one of the hallmarks of consumer culture. The notion of what Bordo calls "postmodern plasticity" assumes that the body is infinitely sculptable into multiple variations of itself, into a range of simulacra that conform to the mandates of postmodernity.[16] Whereas cosmetic surgery has been critically analyzed by feminists as a violent and coercive practice that normalizes the female body so that it conforms to beauty standards, reconstructive surgery is excluded from these critiques, suggesting that such procedures are justified in the case of disability.

In the name of making these children more acceptable to other people, their bodies are surgically altered to assuage the anxieties of those who look at them. In the collective cultural consciousness, reconstructive surgery is imagined as an act of rescue, a medical miracle that redeems the disabled body from its suffering and delivers it from a state of deviance. To the child whose body is simply the given of her or his existence, however, the "reconstruction" we are often subjected to repeatedly at early ages is a violent trauma that brands into our flesh the message that our bodies are simply intolerable to the world we live in.

CHERYL MARIE WADE

Complementing Mary Duffy's display of her body as art form, Cheryl Marie Wade's performances provoke and manipulate the stare. Whereas Duffy is a soliloquist, Wade is a poet. Nevertheless, Wade's body is essential to her poetic project. Like Duffy, Wade also appropriates the dominant culture's words for her body and hurls them back at her starers in a new context of empowerment, agency, and sexuality—the three aspects of personhood that have been denied the disabled subject. In "My Hands," Wade parodically puts on the monster role she has been assigned, using its potency and taunting her starers with it:

Mine are the hands of your bad dreams.
Booga booga from behind the black curtain.
Claw hands.
The ivory girl's hands after a decade of
roughing it.
Crinkled, puckered, sweaty, scarred,
a young woman's dwarf knobby hands
that ache for moonlight—that tremble, that
struggle.
Hands that make your eyes tear.
My hands. My hands. My hands
that could grace your brow, your thigh.
My hands! Yeah![17]

With her invocation of "your bad dreams" and her truculent "booga booga," Wade mocks her position as monster by conjuring up popular culture's formidable anxiety-turned-fear response to bodies like hers that has thrilled and titillated normals. The hands that she invokes verbally are at the same time emphatically shoved in the audience's faces as she speaks, forcing her viewers to enact the stare they might try to suppress or furtively commit in some other social context. But here, Wade controls the terms of the encounter.

Like Duffy's shockingly naked body, Wade's shockingly naked hands breach the rules, both social and physiological. She acknowledges the normative ideal of "the ivory girl's hands," only to override that commercialized image of feminine beauty with a string of descriptors for her own hands that trounce its authority Hers are "claw hands" that are defiantly "crinkled, puckered, sweaty, scarred . . . dwarf knobby hands." Wade's hands do not look beautiful, indeed they are a sight so evocative as to "make your eyes tear," perhaps with shock, repugnance, or sympathy.

Rather than displaying the soft static beauty of the "ivory girl's," these hands are the agents of Wade's subjectivity: they "ache," "tremble," and "struggle," exhibiting not loveliness but the evidence of a life of "roughing it." Moreover, these hands are sexual, not in the normatively feminine way of attracting and pleasing the male gaze, but rather as sexual agents. Wade's hands "could grace your brow, your thigh." "Could" here functions ambiguously as a proposition both threatening and tender, at once an offer of gentle love and a menacing "booga, booga" to the squeamish who imagine that the only legitimate caress might come from hands like the "ivory girl's."

Wade avows this version of her hands as active rather than passive with her final line, "My hands! Yeah!" as she gazes admiringly and lovingly at her own hands with a sign of satisfaction reminiscent of sexual release. Here she reclaims the stare from her audience and transforms it into the look of love, a self-love here that is not narcissism but rather the affirmation of her own body as whole and right.

Wade's, like Duffy's, is a project of redefinition, of offering counternarratives to the prevailing cultural images of the disabled body. As I have suggested, theirs is a dual project both verbal and visual. Wade's best-known poem, "I am not one of the physically challenged," echoes her effort in "My Hands" to forge a self-description that captures the power and the pervasiveness of the disabled body:

I am not of the physically challenged—

I'm a sock in the eye with a gnarled fist
I'm a French kiss with a cleft tongue
I'm orthopedic shoes sewn on a last of your
 fears

I am not one of the differently abled—

I'm an epitaph for a million imperfect babies
 left untreated
I'm an ikon carved from bones in a mass grave
 at Tiergarten, Germany
I'm withered legs hidden with a blanket

I am not one of the able disabled—

I'm a black panther with green eyes and scars
 like a picket fence
I'm pink lace panties teasing a stub of milk
 white thigh
I'm the Evil Eye

I'm the first cell divided
I'm mud that talks
I'm Eve I'm Kali
I'm the Mountain That Never Moves
I've been forever I'll be here forever
I'm the Gimp
I'm the Cripple
I'm the Crazy Lady

I'm The Woman With Juice[18]

Wade dismisses the awkward terms for the disabled that attempt to flatten the power of the disabled body. Instead, she invokes the archetype of the monstrous, awful, wondrous, primal body that is everywhere and always. She is "not one of the physically challenged," the "differently abled," or the "able disabled." Wade instead aligns herself with "Eve" and "Kali," becoming "the Gimp," "the Cripple," "the Crazy Lady," whose difference is the potent stuff of myth and legend. In this performed poem, Wade's body operates very much like Whitman's poetic body in "Song of Myself." Her body here is a communal body that absorbs and represents the aggregate individual members of her group, which extends beyond the disabled community to incorporate all humanity throughout history.

Whitman announces in "Song of Myself" that he begins his poetic project in "perfect health," suggesting that his national body empties out all the diversity of his catalogs into a normative image.[19] In contrast, Wade becomes the universal body that registers singularity rather than typicality. She is "the Mountain That Never Moves," "the first cell divided," and the primal "mud" that has "been forever" and will "be here forever." The body that represents the human experience is disabled, not in "perfect health." As "a million imperfect babies left untreated," the "ikon" of a "mass grave," and "withered legs hidden with a blanket," her incarnations range across human existence from birth to death to old age.

Such a portrayal suggests that embodied differences are the rule rather than the exception and that bodily stability is a fantasy. What we call "disability" is simply particularity intensified, the quality that makes us most fully human. Moreover, in our singularity is power: our bodies become marked with life experience, making us into "black panther[s] with green eyes and scars like a picket fence." This is the power of the body that bears witness to its own history, a figure that Toni Morrison portrays, for example, in *Beloved*'s Sethe, whose scarred back bears the oppressive history of her enslavement.[20]

The marked body functions here as the transgressive body, overturning at once the cultural scripts of femininity and disability. Countering the stereotype of the disabled person as asexual, Wade creates a poetic persona whose difference is sexual: she is "a French kiss with a cleft tongue." She claims erotic agency in the tradition of the poet-warrior, Audre Lorde,[21] by asserting herself as "pink lace panties teasing a stub of milk white thigh." Wade rejects standard disability imagery as well. She is no sweet poster child, no victim displayed to elicit sympathy and contributions. Instead, her position in a wheelchair is one of agency, even aggression.

Manipulating the dynamic of the stare, she reimagines her role as the object of the stare not as a passive acceptance, but as an active visual assault, as "a sock in the eye with a gnarled fist." Her final self-proclamation, "I'm The Woman With Juice," invokes exuberance and sexuality, affirming—as was evident in "My Hands"—Wade's embodied self as fully human and vital. Her performance, then, is a kind of outlaw lyric that reimagines disabled female subjectivity by rejecting the limp and dry "physically challenged" label and embracing her self-description as "The Woman With Juice."

CONCLUSION

This chapter augments my larger scholarly aim, which is to introduce disability as a category of analysis in literary and cultural studies. My goal is to advance what Eve Sedgwick has called a "universalizing view" of disability that will cast disability as "an issue of continuing, determinative importance in the lives of people across the spectrum."[22] This process involves helping to define and launch the new field of disability studies in the humanities. The fundamental goal of disability studies, in my view, is to reimagine disability. The most important contribution that a literary studies approach brings to the subject of disability is a focus on the issue of representation. I mean here representation in its broadest sense, of course: as the saturating of the material world with meaning. In this sense, disability is a story we tell about bodies. The important point, of course, is that these stories shape the material world, inform human relations, and mold our senses of who we are.

The cultural work of Duffy's and Wade's performances is to challenge our collective stories about disability: in other words, to renarrate disability, to reimagine it as an integral part of all human experience and history, rather than an isolated misfortune that ruins bodies, evokes a patronizing pity, or prompts rejection. Duffy's and Wade's performances inaugurate a poetic genre of the disabled body that is necessarily visual; it is a poetics of the stare. Body and word signify together in an act of self-making. Unique to disability, this genre manipulates the stare in order to renarrate disability. The body is integral to the poetry operating as a material signifier that generates the stare. By appropriating the social practice that constitutes their oppression in order to reimagine their identities, Duffy and Wade enact a kind of communal exorcizing of the objectification that they so commandingly reject in these poetic performances. In creating such an art form, they boldly reimagine disability on behalf of their community: other disabled people for whom the daily business of life is managing, deflecting, resisting, or renouncing that stare.

NOTES

1. The emerging critical field of disability studies, which is most fully developed within sociology and the humanities, lays out in various forms a theoretical model of disability as a social construction. In doing so, it reframes disability according to a social or a minority model rather than the traditional medical model.
2. See Rosemarie Garland-Thomson, "Narratives of Deviance and Delight: Staring at Julia Pastrana, the 'Extraordinary Lady,'" in *Beyond the Binary: American Identity and Multiculturalism,* ed. Timothy Powell (New Brunswick, NJ: Rutgers University Press, 1999).
3. Michel Foucault, *Birth of the Clinic: An Archaeology of Medical Perception* (New York: Vintage Books, 1994).
4. Erving Goffman, *Stigma: Notes on the Management of a Spoiled Identity* (New York: Simon and Schuster, 1986).

5. Robert Murphy, *The Body Silent* (New York: W. W. Norton, 1990).
6. Lucy Grealy, *Autobiography of a Face* (New York: Harperperennial Library, 1995).
7. Conversation with the author.
8. Conversation with the author.
9. John Berger, *Ways of Seeing* (New York: Viking Press, 1995).
10. Lynn S. Chancer, *Reconcilable Differences: Confronting Beauty, Pornography, and the Future of Feminism* (Berkeley: University of California Press, 1998), 83.
11. Georges Canguilhem, *The Normal and the Pathological*, trans. Caroline R. Faucet (New York: Zone Books, 1989).
12. Mary Duffy, *Vital Signs, Crip Culture Talks Back,* directed and produced by David T. Mitchell and Sharon Snyder (Marquette, MI: Brace Yourself Productions, 1996).
13. "Enfreakment" is a term coined by David Hevey.
14. Duffy, *Vital Signs.*
15. Ibid.
16. Mike Featherstone, "The Body in Consumer Culture," in *The Body: Social Process and Cultural Theory,* ed. Mike Featherstone, Mike Hepworth, and Bryan S. Turner (London: Sage Publications, 1991), 170–196; Susan Bordo, *Unbearable Weight* (Berkeley: University of California Press, 1995).
17. Cheryl Marie Wade, *Vital Signs.*
18. Ibid.
19. Walt Whitman, *Leaves of Grass* (New York: Bantam Classics and Loveswept, 1983).
20. Toni Morrison, *Beloved* (New York: Plume, 1998).
21. Audre Lorde, "The Uses of the Erotic," in *Sister Outsider: Essays and Speeches* (Freedom, CA: Crossing Press, 1984).
22. Eve Kosofsky Sedgwick, *The Epistemology of the Closet* (Berkeley: University of California Press, 1992).

READING 52

Both Sides Come Out Fighting: The Argument Culture and the Press

Deborah Tannen

"TAKE A SIDE" the advertisement blares in big block letters. In smaller print, it continues:

> Join the battle as opinion leaders fire off their views about today's issues on two of the most dynamic shows on the air.[1]

Photographs of the hosts appear under the logos of the two shows—*Hardball* and *Equal Time*—arrayed as if they were at war with each other. Each show occupies one side of the page, and over each logo is a photograph of an army marching into battle, one side brandishing blue flags, the other waving red.

An ad for the popular political talk show *Crossfire* has a similar theme: Four people are featured, with arms crossed, looking grim. Over each one's head is a banner headline in block letters: "IT'S A LEFT," "AND A RIGHT," "AND ANOTHER LEFT," "AND ANOTHER RIGHT"—playing on the double entendre of punches in a boxing match and the political "left," represented by Geraldine Ferraro and Bill Press, glaring at the political "right," represented by John Sununu and Robert Novak. The two "lefts" (on the left-hand side of the page, of course) are separated from the "right" by a crack in concrete that opens to show a brick wall background against which appears the commentary "There's new fuel on the left. The old fire's back on the right."

These ads, like the shows they promote, tell Americans that issues can be understood as having two—and only two—diametrically opposed and warring sides, rather than having many sides that reflect complex interacting forces and

Deborah Tannen is professor of linguistics at Georgetown University.

interests. The two ads end: "Watch what happens" and "Now watch the sparks really fly," sending another message: Politics is a spectator sport. You may root for one side or the other, but nothing else is expected of you. This is as different from participatory democracy as watching a ball game on television is from going out and playing one.

Almost any news item can be described as a fight—and often is. For example, a newsmagazine article about the Guggenheim Museum Bilbao—a joint venture of the Guggenheim Museum in New York and the city of Bilbao, Spain—implies that the architect, Frank Gehry, was picking a fight with another architect when he designed the building:

> When you think "Guggenheim," you think Frank Lloyd Wright, and the towering central atrium in Bilbao—at 165 feet, half again the height of Wright's New York spiral—seems to say "Take that!" to the master.[2]

Yet Gehry himself says his work pays homage to a film, as the article goes on to quote:

> It is full of light, soaring spaces and is criss-crossed by catwalks, with three levels of galleries spinning off it. "The whole idea here was Fritz Lang's 'Metropolis,' to make a visionary city," says Gehry.

How different to think of the new museum as a visionary city inspired by another artist rather than an aggressive assault by an upstart who beats the master by building a higher atrium.

Business news also fits easily into the fighting frame. For example, the headline "A CLASSIC MATCHUP"[3] is aided by the subhead, "It's only the opening bell, but the merger battle between Hilton and ITT promises to be bloody." Alongside is a color photograph of two boxers in red gloves punching each other in a boxing ring identified as Caesar's Palace. The photograph is captioned, "Business brawl: Fighting over assets like ITT's Caesar's Palace." When I was flipping pages in search of this story, I missed it the first time through because, despite knowing what page it was on, when I saw the photograph, I drew the hasty conclusion that I had reached the sports section and kept dipping.

In a single issue of a national newsmagazine we find a Chinese political leader who is "well positioned to win this battle, which is why he's likely to fight it," traditional car dealers who are "about to become road kill," "telecommunications price wars," "cereal wars," the prediction that Alan Greenspan might "launch a preemptive strike against inflation" and that consumers, by shopping for the lowest prices, may be "the real anti-inflation fighters."[4]

All these accounts simply report events, but the way events are reported shapes our thinking about them—and can affect the events themselves. Writing in terms of opposition can actually create the opposition and all that goes with it. A magazine for college professors entitled *Lingua Franca* focuses on behind-the-scenes academic intrigue. By reporting on battles, the magazine also foments them. Someone who was party to such a "battle" commented, "There is a way in which certain *Lingua Franca* accounts of academic debates needlessly polarize academic communities and generate more division than exists."[5]

The most extreme battle imagery, as seen in the *Crossfire* ad, is associated with television and its desire to create lively programming—often defined as provocative programming. In this view, the more extreme a statement is, the more readers or viewers will be interested. As *Washington Post* media critic Howard Kurtz put it in *Hot Air,* "The middle ground, the sensible center, is dismissed as too squishy, too dull, too likely to send the audience channel surfing."[6] Getting a rise out of audiences is seen as good, regardless of what that rise consists of. Print journalists are not immune to this motivation. I once asked a magazine editor whether he and his colleagues regret publishing pieces that so anger and offend readers that a large number of them write to express disapproval. No, he replied. Anytime a piece triggers a flood of mail, the editors are happy. (An ironic result is that writing a letter to express outrage can have an effect opposite to the one intended: Rather than discouraging editors from presenting such material in the future, it may serve as encouragement.)

Democracy is not only a matter of giving everyone a right to vote. People need to understand what they're voting about. Framing news as a fight between two sides often results in needed information not getting out—and even in false information getting spread. In the worst cases, our situation is comparable in this respect to that of totalitarian countries whose governments deliberately mislead their people by spreading disinformation.

NO FIGHT, NO NEWS

Any day you open a newspaper or magazine, you can find evidence of the belief that controversy is interesting and the absence of controversy is dull. For example, a newspaper reports that at an annual meeting of the mutual fund industry "the hallway chatter focused all week on the possibility of fireworks at the final session, when two industry titans with no love lost between them would face off," but "the debate turned out to be disappointingly tame."[7]

Because the belief that fights—and only fights—are interesting, any news or informational item that is not adversarial is less likely to be reported. I have talked to many heads of organizations and institutions who are frustrated because they cannot get press coverage to inform the public of what they do unless someone is protesting it—and then coverage focuses on the protesters. James Billington, director of the Library of Congress, for example, was frustrated that few people knew about a major exhibition the library mounted in 1995, "Creating French Culture: Treasures from the Bibliothèque Nationale de France."[8] But everyone seemed to know about an exhibit on Freud that was not mounted that year. Billington maintains that the exhibition had to be postponed because of lack of funds—a message he was never able to communicate because news stories focused on protesters' belief that the library had cravenly caved in to political pressure from other protesters—critics of Freud. (In fact, the Freud exhibition was later rescheduled to open in fall 1998.)

I also heard from the head of a public institution who spent hours talking to a journalist preparing a story on one of their programs—a story that never ran because no one could be found who opposed the program: no fight, no story.

Few people who have experienced this are eager to talk on record because they fear offending journalists whose goodwill they need for future coverage. No one wants to step on the tail of a sleeping dragon. In order to tell a true story with all the details, I'll use my own experience, with the caveat that I have, over the years, received more than fair treatment from journalists, some of whom I count among—you should pardon the expression—my best friends. But I ran headlong into the no-fight-no-story principle when I appeared on a platform with Robert Bly, the poet, author, and leader of men's retreats.[9] Following the trail of media coverage of this event offers a glimpse into the conviction that only fights are news.

Bly invited me to engage in a public conversation with him at New York's Open Center. Our conversation was advertised in the Open Center bulletin under the title "Where Are Men and Women Now?" The bulletin referred to the event as a "dialogue," promised that we would discuss "the differing modes of language that men and women inhabit," and asked how understanding these differences could help "in working toward a reconciliation of men and women." Despite this decidedly peaceful description, notice of the dialogue appeared in the major New York newspaper under the heading of—what else?—"Battle of the Sexes." The column referred to our meeting as a "face-to-face, word-to-word confrontation" and "a debate"—the first time Bly and I would "face off publicly."

On the basis either of this notice or of their own curiosity, organizations that requested complimentary tickets included *The New York Times, The New York Post, The New Yorker, People* magazine, *USA Today Weekend, The Village Voice,* and *The Economist.* A *Newsweek* photographer photographed Bly and me as we sat down to dinner before the event, at which we went ahead with our plans to have a conversation rather than a fight. The media disappointment was resounding.

Most of those who had asked for complimentary tickets decided not to publish reports. *The New York Times* did cover the evening, contrasting our "unrelenting agreement" unfavorably with the 1971 Town Hall encounter between novelist Norman Mailer and feminist author Germaine Greer. *New York Newsday,* we learned, had prepared a favorable article but decided not to run it after the *Times* piece appeared; they did not want to appear "soft" by taking seriously an event at which the *Times* had scoffed. *The Economist* echoed the *Time*'s tone, running a one-page story under the ironic heading "GREAT DEBATES" with a subhead "Bill and Coo." The disappointed reporter blamed us for not fulfilling *The New York Times*'s promise: "It was advertised as a battle of the sexes," he began. "One that would revive memories of the bruising clashes between Norman Mailer, a self-confessed 'Prisoner of Sex,' and militant feminists in the early 1970s." He expressed his disapproval by calling our interchange "a throwback to the 1870s." Continuing to use the image of us fighting as a backdrop, he wrote, "Both contestants came out of their corners cooing."

Newsweek was perhaps the most inventive, devoting most of its article to describing the fight we did not have. The audience, readers were told, "spent the whole time wondering if he would hit her over the head with his mandolin," which was described as "a savage-looking instrument." Things looked "promising," the account went on, "when Bly asserted that 'both men and women want to fight in a healthy way'" but turned disappointing because "he didn't do any fighting with Tannen, healthy or otherwise." The writer opined that the hope that Bly and I would fight was the only thing that could explain the sellout crowd. But tickets were sold out within a week of the appearance of the Open Center catalogue, long before *The New York Times* mentioned the event and reported that "thousands of requests continue to flood the office." . . .

WHAT'S LEFT OUT

It was no great loss to the world that my public conversation with Robert Bly was less widely reported than it might have been, or that what we said was obscured by what we did not do. But the habitual preference for stories about fights often results in important news not being covered, either because it doesn't seem controversial enough to be interesting or simply because there is no space left. Airtime and column inches devoted to controversy and fights are not devoted to discussing the issues and problems that our nation faces. . . .

Several years ago I was on a local television talk show with a representative of the men's movement. I didn't foresee any problem, since there is nothing in my work that is anti-male. But in the room where guests wait to go on, I found a man with waist-length red hair wearing a shirt and tie and a floor length skirt. He politely introduced himself and told me that he'd read and liked my book. He also expressed surprise that we were waiting in the same room; usually, he said, producers keep fellow guests apart from him until airtime. I recalled that I had experienced this on shows that had ferreted out guests who would oppose me, like isolating boxers in their own corners. Then he added, "When I get out there, I'm going to attack you. But don't take it personally. That's why they invite me on, so that's what I'm going to do."

When the show began and I spoke for the first time, I got as far as a sentence or two before this man nearly jumped out of his chair, threw his arms before him in gestures of anger, and began shrieking—first attacking me, but soon moving on to rail against women. The strangest thing about his hysterical attack was what it sparked in the studio audience: They too turned vicious, attacking not me (I hadn't gotten a chance to say anything) and not him (who wants to tangle with someone who will scream at you?) but the innocent and helpless guests: unsuspecting women who had agreed to appear on the show to talk about problems they had communicating with their spouses. This is one of the most dangerous effects of the argument culture: It creates an atmosphere of animosity that spreads like a fever.

The screaming man had been invited on this show to be outrageous and pick a fight. It would be easy to dismiss this as an aberrant local show; certainly, it was an extreme, not a typical, example. But I have also been on a talk show that prides itself on offering light rather than heat and encountered a fellow panelist whose expertise was not related to this topic yet who made false statements with a great air of authority. When I later asked how the panel members had been chosen, I was told that this guest was highly opinionated and could be depended on to make the show lively. If you're looking for a fight, you will get heat, not light. . . .

THE MEDIA AND ME: "LET'S YOU AND HIM FIGHT"

Headlines are the most likely place to find war imagery. Because I write about communication between women and men, I have had plenty of opportunity to experience firsthand the impulse to frame gender relations as a fight—as well as the consequences. Here's just one example.

In 1996, I wrote an article for *The New York Times Magazine* about apologies.[10] I explored both the good that apologies can do and the reasons many people resist uttering them. There is a gender dimension to this issue: In our culture, men are more likely than women to avoid apologizing. But this does not mean that all men avoid apologizing, nor that all women are quick to apologize. Furthermore, saying "I'm sorry" is not always preferable. I gave examples showing that sometimes it's better to resist apologizing. And the gender pattern was not the main point. A large portion of my essay discussed cultural differences, such as the Japanese custom of uttering apologies more elaborately and more frequently than Americans.

When the article appeared, it was packaged to focus on the gender aspect alone, and it did so in a way that seemed designed to make men feel angry and attacked. I had called the piece "I'm Sorry, I'm Not Apologizing," referring to women's frequent use of "I'm sorry" to mean "I'm sorry that happened." The editors changed it to "I'm Sorry, I Won't Apologize," referring to men's refusal to say they're sorry. By itself, this difference is subtle and minor; when the change was suggested, its impact went right by me. But the cover of the issue announced my essay as "Why Men Don't Apologize," and the subhead read, "A simple statement of contrition can fix an honest mistake. So why can't men seem to do it?" The illustration also went for the stereotype: A man in the foreground is holding his head on a platter, offering it to a fuming woman standing with her arms crossed and smoke rising from her head. The illustration is more subtle than might at first appear: The man has his fingers crossed behind his back, a visual analogue to my observation that when people say "I'm sorry I hurt your feelings" (in private) or "I'm sorry if my words offended anyone" (in public), they may appear to apologize and yet stop short of admitting fault. In fairness, art often draws on stereotypes to achieve quick recognition. But choosing a stereotype that pits men against women aggravates the battle of the sexes at the same time that it attempts to draw on it for humor.

When I learned of the subhead, I pleaded with the editor to change it but was told it was too late and that, furthermore, the packaging of a story—headlines, subheads, and illustrations—has to attract attention. But I paid a price for this. A caller to a talk show I appeared on shortly after was typical. He said, "I've followed Dr. Tannen's work for years and always appreciated her fairness and even hand, but this article was the first time she offended me." Generously, *The New York Times Magazine* later ran an apology explaining that the headline treatment did not accurately represent the spirit of the article. I greatly appreciated this unusual gesture. But I doubt it did much to repair the animosity stirred up in men who took the article to be one more male-bashing attack by a woman. And women feel the repercussions of men's anger against women in public and individual women in private. The harm was done. And it is done daily when the battle of the sexes is used to stir up interest but at the same time stirs up the battle.

Editors, producers, and advertisers need to stir audience interest, which means arousing emotions. Anger is one of the easiest emotions to arouse. And I'm sure it is tempting to step into existing debate frameworks, like stepping into a ready-made suit rather than spending far more time getting one fitted to size. When polarized debate is sought, those with the greatest expertise are often rejected or refuse to take part because they resist slotting complex issues into a simplified debate format. Those who are willing or eager to cloak their moderate expertise—or lack of it—in fiery capes are given the platform instead. When this happens, the entire society loses. . . .

WHAT TO DO

The way television and radio present ideas and information does matter. Presenting everything in terms of two sides fighting may be intended simply to catch interest, but it helps shape the way people regard the world, events, and other people. Is it necessary to highlight opposition and conflict to interest audiences? There is evidence that it isn't. Oprah Winfrey, for example, made a unilateral decision to reshape her show as less sensationalist, more helpful—and is still top-rated. There is other evidence, as well.

The March 9, 1997, issue of *The New York Times Magazine,* devoted to "The Age Boom," offered a positive look at the subject of aging. Reader response was overwhelmingly favorable. Jack Rosenthal, the editor of the magazine, was invited to appear on *The Jim Lehrer News Hour* to talk about the topic. He also appeared on *The Diane Rehm Show,* a national radio talk show, for the same purpose.[11] Weeks after the issue came out, it was still being discussed. The themes developed in these discussions and in the special issue were in sharp contrast to the culture of critique. Rather than taking the generation-war approach that has dominated recent coverage (old folks who are draining the economy versus young folks who are sick of working to pay old folks' bills), Rosenthal claimed that the income transfer from old to young far outstrips the flow in the opposite direction. The special issue emphasized the positive aspects of aging. And according to Rosenthal, the public response to this special issue was an all-time record high, out of perhaps twenty that had been done in the three years the magazine had been putting out special issues at the rate of eight per year.

Changes are already taking place within journalism. There is a movement in the press to provide more "news you can use." But these changes must not be limited to features and items that run in addition to coverage of politics and current events. Changes need to be made in the way all material is presented. We need a general truce, so television and radio stations, newspapers and magazines, do not fear falling behind if they make a unilateral retreat from covering news as battle.

Sometimes it will be obviously appropriate to present a story as a two-sides fight. But not *all* stories fit naturally into this format. And framing everything as a fight may lose more readers and listeners in the end. When polls ask people why they dislike "the media," results always show the negativity of the press at the top of the list. Highlighting conflict to keep audiences may be a case of what anthropologist Gregory Bateson called "complementary schismogenesis,"[12] a situation in which each party's behavior eggs on the other to more and more exaggerated forms of an opposing behavior in a mutually aggravating spiral. Dwindling readership drives journalists to emphasize conflict in an effort to interest readers, but the rising level of opposition drives more readers away.

In an early draft of [*The Argument Culture*], I wrote, "I do not believe that journalists set out to polarize citizens, incite them to anger, and undermine our respect for each other." Someone who read that draft wrote in the margin, "You don't? The alternative is great naïveté." It is chilling that an educated consumer of news believes that the press is intentionally poisoning his informational food. The widespread mistrust, contempt, and even hatred that many citizens now feel against the press is as dangerous as—if less widely reported than—the mistrust, contempt, and even hatred that many citizens feel against the government.

I prefer to believe that the troubling effects I've described are the unintended result of the argument culture. If I'm right, then understanding the argument culture—and the related culture of critique—should be the first step in finding ways to communicate news that are less destructive to society and more enlightening to us all.

NOTES

1. The "TAKE A SIDE" ad appeared in *The Washington Post,* February 24, 1997. The *Crossfire* ad appeared in *Newsweek,* May 6, 1996.
2. *Newsweek,* January 13, 1997, pp. 68–70; the quote is from p. 69.
3. *Newsweek,* February 10, 1997, pp. 47, 49.
4. *Newsweek,* March 10, 1997. Quotations are from pp. 39, 48, and 45.
5. Janny Scott, "At Home with Jeffrey Kittay: Whipsawing the Groves of Academe," *The New York Times,* December 12, 1996, p. C1.
6. Howard Kurtz, *Hot Air,* p. 4.
7. Edward Wyatt, "Mutual Funds: Why Fidelity Doesn't Want You to Shop at Schwab," *The New York Times,* July 14, 1996, p. F7.
8. Personal communication with James Billington. For a news story, see Marc Fisher, "Under Attack, Library Shelves Freud Exhibit," *The Washington Post,* December 5, 1995, p. A1.
9. For reports of my appearance with Robert Bly, see: Esther B. Fein, "Book Notes," *The New York Times,* October 30, 1991, p. C20; Esther B. Fein, "Battle of the Sexes Gets Fuzzy as Authors Meet," *The New York Times,* November 3, 1991, p. L44; "Speaking Softly, Carrying No Stick," *Newsweek,* November 11, 1991, p. 66; "Great Debates: Bill and Coo," *The Economist,* November 9–15, 1991, pp. 107, 108.
10. My article on apologizing appeared in *The New York Times Magazine,* July 24, 1996, pp. 34–35.
11. The radio talk show on which Rosenthal appeared was *The Diane Rehm Show,* March 25, 1997.
12. See Gregory Bateson, *Steps to an Ecology of Mind.* I have shown how this works in personal relationships in several books; see *That's Not What I Meant!,* pp. 129–31, and *You Just Don't Understand,* p. 282.

READING 53

What Americans Don't Know about Indians

Jerry Mander

In 1981, when my sons Yari and Kai were attending San Francisco's Lowell High School, they complained to me that their American History class began with the arrival of whites on this continent and omitted any mention of the people who were already here. The class was taught that Columbus "discovered" America and that American "history" was what came afterward.

That same year, Ronald Reagan gave his first inaugural speech, in which he praised the "brave pioneers who tamed the empty wilderness." Still,

---

Jerry Mander is senior fellow at the Public Media Center, program director of deep ecology, and director of the International Forum on Globalization.

I was surprised to hear that the wilderness was also empty for the faculty at Lowell High, a school usually considered among the top public high schools in this country.

The American History teacher asked my kids why they were so keen on the subject of Indians, leading them to mention the book I was planning to write. This in turn led to an invitation for me to speak to the class. As a result, I got some insight about the level of Indian awareness among a group of high-school kids.

The youngsters I met had never been offered one course, or even an extended segment of a course, about the Indian nations of this continent, about Indian-Anglo interactions (except for references to the Pilgrims and the Indian wars), or about contemporary Indian problems in the U.S. or elsewhere. These teenagers knew as little as I did at their age, and as little as their teacher knew at their age—or now, as he regretfully acknowledged to me. The American educational curriculum is almost bereft of information about Indians, making it difficult for young non-Indian Americans to understand or care about present-day Indian issues. European schools actually teach more about American Indians. In Germany, for example, every child reads a set of books that sensitizes them to Indian values and causes. It is not surprising, therefore, that the European press carries many more stories about American Indians than does the American press. . . .

THE MEDIA: INDIANS ARE NON-NEWS

That the Lowell High students should know nothing about Indians is not their fault. It is one of many indicators that this country's institutions do not inform people about Indians of either present or past. Indians are non-history, which also makes them non-news. Not taught in schools, not part of American consciousness, their present-day activities and struggles are rarely reported in newspapers or on television.

On the rare occasions when the media do relate to Indians, the reports tend to follow very narrow guidelines based on pre-existing stereotypes of Indians; they become what is known in the trade as "formula stories."

My friend Dagmar Thorpe, a Sac-and-Fox Indian who, until 1990, was Executive Director of the Seventh Generation Fund, once asked a network producer known to be friendly to the Indian cause about the reasons for the lack of in-depth, accurate reporting on Indian stories. According to Dagmar, the producer gave three reasons. The first reason was guilt. It is not considered good programming to make your audience feel bad. Americans don't want to see shows that remind them of historical events that American institutions have systematically avoided discussing.

Secondly, there is the "what's-in-it-for-me?" factor. Americans in general do not see how anything to do with Indians has anything to do with them. As a culture, we are now so trained to "look out for number one" that there has been a near total loss of altruism. (Of course American life itself—so speedy and so removed from nature—makes identifying with the Indians terribly difficult; and we don't see that we might have something to learn from them.)

The third factor is that Indian demands seem preposterous to Americans. What most Indians want is simply that their land should be returned, and that treaties should be honored. Americans tend to view the treaties as "ancient," though many were made less than a century ago—more recently, for example, than many well-established laws and land deals among whites. Americans, like their government and the media, view treaties with Indian nations differently than treaties with anyone else.

In fairness to the media, there are some mitigating factors. Just like the rest of us, reporters and producers have been raised without knowledge of Indian history or Indian struggles. Perhaps most important, media people have had little personal contact with Indians, since Indians live mostly in parts of the country, and the world, where the media isn't. Indians live in non-urban regions, in the deserts and mountains and tundras that have been impacted least by Western society, at least until recently. They live in the places that we didn't want. They are not part of the mainstream and have not tried to become part.

When our society *does* extend its tentacles to make contact—usually when corporations are seeking land or minerals, or military forces are seeking control—there is little media present to observe and report on what transpires. Even in the United States, virtually all Indian struggles take place far away from media: in the central Arizona desert, in the rugged Black Hills, the mountains of the Northwest, or else on tiny Pacific islands, or in the icy vastness of the far north of Alaska. *The New York Times* has no bureau in those places; neither does CBS. Nor do they have bureaus in the Australian desert or the jungles of Brazil, Guatemala, or Borneo.

As a result, some of the most terrible assaults upon native peoples today never get reported. If reports do emerge, the sources are the corporate or military public relations arms of the Western intruders, which present biased perspectives.

When reporters are flown in to someplace where Indians are making news, they are usually ill prepared and unknowledgeable about the local situation. They do not speak the language and are hard pressed to grasp the Indian perception, even if they can find Indians to speak with. In addition, these reporters often grew up in that same bubble of no contact/no education/no news about Indians.

To make matters even more difficult, as I explained at length in my TV book, it is also in the nature of modern media to distort the Indian message, which is far too subtle, sensory, complex, spiritual, and ephemeral to fit the gross guidelines of mass-media reporting, which emphasizes conflict and easily grasped imagery. A reporter would have to spend a great deal of time with the Indians to understand why digging up the earth for minerals is a sacrilege, or why diverting a stream can destroy a culture, or why cutting a forest deprives people of their religious and human rights, or why moving Indians off desert land to a wonderful new community of private homes will effectively kill them. Even if the reporter does understand, to successfully translate that understanding through the medium, and through the editors and the commercial sponsor—all of whom are looking for action—is nearly impossible.

So most reporters have little alternative but to accept official handouts, or else to patch together, from scanty reports, stories that are designed for a world predisposed to view Indian struggles as anomalies in today's technological world: formula stories, using stereotyped imagery.

PREVALENT STEREOTYPES AND FORMULAS

The dominant image of Indians in the media used to be of savages, of John Wayne leading the U.S. Cavalry against the Indians. Today the stereotype has shifted to *noble savage,* which portrays Indians as part of a once-great but now-dying culture; a culture that could talk to the trees and the animals and that protected nature. But sadly, a losing culture, which has not kept up with our dynamic times.

We see this stereotype now in many commercials. The Indian is on a horse, gazing nobly over the land he protects. Then there's a quick cut to today: to oil company workers walking alongside the hot-oil pipeline in Alaska. The company workers are there to protect against leaks and to preserve the environment for the animals. We see quick cuts of caribou and wolves, which imply that the oil company accepts the responsibility that the Indians once had.

The problem here is that the corporate sponsor is lying. It does not feel much responsibility toward nature; if it did, it would not need expensive commercials to say so, because the truth would be apparent from its behavior. More important, however, is that treating Indians this way in commercials does terrible harm to their cause.

It makes Indians into conceptual relics; artifacts. Worse, they are confirmed as existing only in the past, which hurts their present efforts.

Another stereotype we see in commercials these days is the *Indian-as-guru.* A recent TV spot depicted a shaman making rain for his people. He is then hired by some corporate farmers to make rain for them. He is shown with his power objects, saying prayers, holding his hands toward the heavens. The rains come. Handshakes from the businessmen. Finally the wise old Indian is shown with a satisfied smile on his flight home via United Airlines.

Among the more insidious formula stories is the one about how Indians are always fighting each other over disputed lands. This formula fits the Western paradigm about non-industrial peoples' inability to govern themselves; that they live in some kind of despotism or anarchy. For example, in the Hopi-Navajo "dispute," . . . the truth of the matter is that U.S. intervention in the activities and governments of both tribes eventually led to American-style puppet governments battling each other for development rights that the traditional leadership of each tribe does not want. But the historical reality of that case, and most Indian cases, is unknown to the mass media and therefore left unreported.

Another very popular formula story is the one with the headline INDIANS STAND IN THE WAY OF DEVELOPMENT, as, for example, in New Guinea or Borneo or in the Amazon Basin. These stories concern Indian resistance to roads, or dams, or the cutting of forests, and their desire for their lands to be left inviolate.

The problem with these formula stories is not that they are inaccurate—Indian peoples around the world most certainly are resisting on hundreds of fronts and do indeed stand in the way of development—but that the style of reporting carries a sense of foregone conclusion. The reporters tend to emphasize the poignancy of the situation: "stone-age" peoples fighting in vain to forestall the inevitable march of progress. In their view, it is only a matter of time before the Indians lose, and the forests *are* cut down, and the land is settled by outsiders. However tragic the invasion, however righteous the cause of the Indians, however illegal the acts being perpetrated against them, however admirable the Indian ways, reporters will invariably adopt the stance that the cause is lost, and that no reversal is possible. This attitude surely harms the Indians more than if the story had not been reported at all.

Finally, and perhaps most outrageous, is the *rich Indian* formula story. Despite the fact that the average per-capita income of Indians is lower than any other racial or ethnic group in the United States, and that they suffer the highest disease rates in many categories, and have the least access to health care, the press loves to focus on the rare instance where some Indian hits it big. Sometimes the story is about an oil well found on some Indian's land, or someone getting rich on bingo, but often the stories emphasize someone's corruption, e.g., Peter MacDonald, the former chairman of the Navajo Nation. This formula story has a twofold purpose: it manages to confirm the greatness of America—where *anyone* can get rich, even an Indian—and at the same time manages to confirm Indian leaders as corrupt and despotic.

A corollary to this story is how certain Indian tribes have gotten wealthy through land claims cases, as, for example, the Alaska natives via the Alaska Native Claims Settlement Act. As we will see, a little digging into the story—if reporters only would—exposes that settlement as a fraud that actually deprived the Alaska natives of land *and* money.

The press's failure to pursue and report the full picture of American Indian poverty, while splashing occasional stories about how some are hitting it big, creates a public impression that is the opposite of the truth. The situation is exacerbated when national leaders repeat the misconceptions. Ronald Reagan told the Moscow press in 1987 that there was no discrimination against Indians in this country and the proof of that was that so many Indians, like those outside Palm Springs (oil wells), have become wealthy.

INDIANS AND THE NEW AGE

While most of our society manages to avoid Indians, there is one group that does not, though its interest is very measured.

I was reminded of this recently during my first visit to a dentist in Marin County, an affluent area north of San Francisco. The dentist, a friendly, trendy young man wearing a moustache, looked as if he'd stepped out of a Michelob ad. While poking my gums, he made pleasant conversation, inquiring about my work. When he pulled his tools from my mouth, I told him I was writing about Indians, which got him very excited. "Indians! Great! I love Indians. Indians are my hobby. I have Indian posters all over the house, and Indian rugs. And hey, I've lately been taking lessons in 'tracking' from this really neat Indian guide. I've learned how to read the tiniest changes in the terrain, details I'd never even noticed before."

In this expression of enthusiasm, this young man was like thousands of other people, particularly in places like Marin or Beverly Hills, or wherever there is sufficient leisure to engage in inner explorations. Among this group, which tends to identify with the "New Age," or the "human potential movement," there has been a renaissance of awareness about Indian practices that aid inner spiritual awakening.

A typical expression of this interest may be that a well-off young professional couple will invite friends to a lawn party to meet the couple's

PERSONAL ACCOUNT

Basketball

I frequently watch my boyfriend play basketball at an outdoor court with many other males in pick-up games. One time when I was there, there was a new face among the others waiting to play—a female face, and she was not sitting with the rest of the women who were watching. She was dressed and ready to play. I had never seen her in all the time I'd been there before, nor had I ever seen another woman there try to play.

For several games, she did not play. The guys formed teams and she was not asked to join. It was almost like there was a purposeful avoidance of her, with no one even acknowledging that she was there. Finally, she made a noticeable effort and with some reluctance she was included in the next team waiting to play the winner of the current game. There were whispers and snickers among the guys, and I think it had a lot to do with the perception that she was challenging their masculinity. A "girl" was intruding into their area. My guess is that they were also somewhat nervous about the fact that she really might be good and embarrass some of them.

Anyway, the first couple of times up and down the court she was not given the ball despite the fact that she was wide open. The other guys on the team forced bad shots and tried super hard in what seemed like an effort to prove that she was not needed. The guy who was supposed to guard her on defense really didn't pay her much attention and that same guy who she was guarding at the other end made sure he drove around her and scored on two occasions.

Finally, one time down the court she called for the ball and sank a shot from at least 16 feet. A huge feeling of relief and satisfaction came over me. Being a basketball player myself, I figured she was probably good or would not be there in the first place, but being a woman I was also happy to see her *first* shot go in. I found out later she had played basketball for a university and she had a great outside shot.

Even after she made one more shot off a rebound that ended up in her hands, she was not given the ball again. I suppose after some of the loud comments from some of the guys on the sidelines, that she was beating the male players out there, she wasn't going to get the ball again. I was kind of shocked that she wasn't *more* accepted even after she showed she was talented. I haven't seen her there since.

Andrea M. Busch

personal Indian medicine person. The shaman will lead the guests through a series of rituals designed to awaken aspects of themselves. These events may culminate in a sweat ceremony, or even a "firewalk." There was a period in the seventies when you could scarcely show up at a friend's house without having to decide whether or not to walk on hot coals, guided by a medicine man from the South Pacific.

Those who graduate from sweat ceremonies or firewalks, as my dentist had, might proceed to the now popular "vision quests." You may feel as you read this that I am ridiculing these "human potential" explorers. Actually, I find something admirable in them. Breaking out of the strictures of our contemporary lifestyles is clearly beneficial, in my opinion, but there is also a serious problem. For although the New Age gleans the ancient wisdoms and practices, it has assiduously avoided directly engaging in the actual lives and political struggles of the millions of descendants who carry on those ancient traditions, who are still alive on the planet today, and who want to continue living in a traditional manner. . . .

Language

READING 54

Language Policy and Identity Politics in the United States

Ronald Schmidt, Sr.

PRECONDITIONS: LANGUAGE DIVERSITY IN AN ACTIVIST STATE

How is it that language policy debate has erupted in many parts of the contemporary world, including the United States? The argument made here is that virtually everywhere language policy conflicts are fueled by a politics of identity in which competing rhetorical strategies are deployed on behalf of two competing public values: *national unity* and *equality.* These fuels can only ignite, however, in facilitative contexts, and this [discussion] argues that the most conducive settings exist in countries where significant political actors expect the state to play an active role in relation to *language diversity, language contact* and *language competition.*

Ronald Schmidt, Sr., is professor of political science at California State University, Long Beach.

One of the primary preconditions of contemporary language policy conflict is the sheer fact of language diversity. Before a state can experience conflict over language policy, it must have multiple language groups within its jurisdiction. This condition is widespread in the contemporary world. Linguists estimate that there are between four thousand and eight thousand different languages spoken in the world today (Wardhaugh, 1987: 1). While about a hundred of these languages are used by some 95 percent of the world's people, it is a rare country that incorporates a unilingual population within its boundaries.

Most states have at least several, significant linguistic groups, and many have populations speaking a wide range of written and unwritten languages. Indeed, it could hardly be otherwise. With only about 180 autonomous states in the world today, if we take the figure of 5,000 languages as a reasonable count, the result is about 28 active languages in the "average" state. An extreme case is represented by India, which recorded almost 800 languages and over 1,600 dialects in its 1961 and 1971 censuses. While many of these language groups are small, 33 had more than a million speakers each in 1971 (Apte, 1976: 141–42).

Another highly multilingual state is Nigeria, with nearly 400 recognized language groups (Akinnaso, 1989). The former Soviet Union's peoples speak over 130 different languages, and the USSR's 1989 census reported 22 nationality groups of more than a million people (Marshall, 1996: 9). Other well-known examples of multilingual states are Belgium, Canada, China, Malaysia, Paraguay, Peru, the Philippines, Spain, South Africa, Switzerland, and Uganda. In many cases even states that do not immediately come to mind when thinking about multilingual countries (e.g., Australia, Finland, France, Great Britain, Norway, and Sweden) contain varied language groups within their populations. Thus, the fact that the United States—a self-proclaimed "nation of immigrants"—is also a multilingual state should occasion no surprise. And, in fact, . . . the 1990 U.S. Census reported 18 different language groups with at least 200,000 members. Nearly 32 million people, or 15 percent of the U.S. population, reported in 1990 that they usually spoke a language other than English in their homes.

In addition to linguistic diversity, language contact and competition are also omnipresent facts of life in many countries of the world. Through human mobility and technological advances, the people who use the multiple languages of the world are in ever-increasing contact with each other, requiring some degree of mutual adaptation to linguistic difference. Through contacts with members of other language groups, people incorporate new words and language rules into their own tongues and/or adopt other peoples' languages (in part or sometimes in whole) as their own. These adaptations result in changes to what linguists refer to as the *corpus* and the *status* of the affected languages (Weinstein, 1983: chap. 1). The corpus of a language refers to its "body" (i.e., vocabulary, spelling, meanings, pronunciation, rules of grammar, etc.), while its status is related to the language's prestige and prevalence of use in the various linguistic domains of a given society (Fishman, 1972).

The notion of a language's status is derived from the fact that linguistic change includes the birth and death of languages as well as their spread, growth, and decline. Most often the spread of one language involves the decline of another. Thus, Francophones around the world have invested considerable resources in recent decades in an attempt to halt the decline of the French language in the face of the seemingly irresistible march of Anglophone domination. From this point of view, then, languages—like states and empires—may be seen as being in competition with each other (Wardhaugh, 1987).

Finally, a third important precondition for language policy conflict is the expectation among political actors that the state should play an active role in doing something about the social facts of linguistic diversity, contact, and competition. This may seem obvious, but until the significant expansion of the role of the state occurred during the last several centuries, it was common to find multilingual states and empires in which it was not expected that language corpus and status should be the subjects of public policy. . . .

FUELS FOR THE FIRE: NATIONAL UNITY, THE QUEST FOR EQUALITY, AND THE POLITICS OF IDENTITY

. . . What is it that generates the heat of political conflict over language? Or, put differently, what are the stakes in these conflicts? What is to be gained or lost, and by whom, in the politics of language?

A clue to answering these questions lies in the fact that throughout the world there is a consistent pattern in the rhetoric of language policy conflicts, a pattern that pits the proponents of national unity against advocates of greater equality for ethnic minorities.[1] In virtually every documented case of political conflict over language policy, partisans speaking on behalf of minority language groups argue that a proposed or existing national language policy is unjust because it diminishes or suppresses the equal rights, opportunities, and/or well-being of members of these subordinated ethnolinguistic groups. The only just remedy, minority activists assert, is increased recognition, status, and opportunity for the minority language and its speakers.

Equally ubiquitous are the claims of opponents of minority-language status enhancement that such an elevation is certain to undermine national unity, bringing the nation-state unnecessary and destructive social and political conflict. The remedy for linguistic discord, therefore, is the adoption of a national language policy that will bring peace and harmony to the state. Advocates for minority language equality thus speak in the language of justice, while proponents of national unity speak in terms of the national good. One of the complexities of language policy conflict, in consequence, is that its partisans often appear to be speaking past each other—participating in parallel discourses—rather than to each other, seemingly motivated by differing concerns. The aim of this [discussion] is to explicate the motivating forces behind each rhetorical strategy while seeking to uncover the common core that brings them into conflict with each other.

National Unity and Language Diversity

Proponents of language policies employing the rhetoric of national unity typically argue that the use of state policy to elevate the status of minority languages is dangerous because it is divisive, engenders political conflict, and threatens the stability of the national state. This line of reasoning derives from the modern project of nation-building, which is viewed here as continuous and ongoing rather than as a single, founding event. As used in this study, then, the nation-building concept refers not only to "new" states (such as those in Africa, Asia, and Eastern Europe released from formal imperial domination in the mid to late twentieth century), but to virtually all independent states. Beginning with the eighteenth century, the dominant ideal form of political association in the world has been the nation-state, and since such a structure does not exist in nature, it has had to be constructed and maintained through human agency. Almost everywhere in the modern world,[2] accordingly, state political elites have sought to bind their members into some form of consciousness of belonging to a "nation," membership in which is to be experienced as paramount in one's political identity.

What, then, is a nation? It is at minimum a collection of people who share a sense of collective identity—as belonging together in some deep political sense—in distinction to the members of other national collectivities. The perceived uniqueness of each national group, in turn, is marked by boundaries that distinguish it from other equally unique national groups. These boundaries take many forms, typically one or several of the following: belief in a common nationality expressed through narratives of formative collective experiences, perceived inherently distinctive characteristics (e.g., consanguinity or "race"), distinctive customs and traditions, rituals of collective commemoration, and other cultural traits including language. In the politics of modernity, in addition, national groups nearly always seek territorial boundaries, land of their own in which they can achieve self-determination (Ronen, 1979), usually through state sovereignty.

As Benedict Anderson (1983) depicted so well, every nation is an "imagined community" in the sense that it exists preeminently in the minds of its members. This is necessarily so, "because the members of even the smallest nation will never know most of their fellow members, meet them, or even hear of them, yet in the minds of each lives the image of their communion" (Anderson, 1983: 15). In the context of the present discussion, this serves to highlight the fact that all nations are constantly in the process of being built. Every nation is an ongoing and always unfinished project. Would-be political leaders must remember this fact, Rogers Smith (1997) has observed, because it confronts them with two constant challenges: "First, aspirants to power require a population to lead that imagines itself to be a 'people'; and, second, they need a people that imagines itself in ways that make leadership by those aspirants appropriate" (p. 6).

One of the always unfinished tasks of national political leaders, therefore, is to attend to the construction, repair, and renewal of the "image of their communion" in the minds of members of the nation. Furthermore, the process of nation-building must be attended to in the mind of every newcomer, whether that person enters the nation through birth or migration. To assist in this task, early in the modern era nationalist political elites discovered the potential power of nationalism as an ideology. . . .

Ethnic Equality and Language Diversity

This problematization of the process of nation-building directs our attention to the virtually worldwide phenomenon of *ethnic* revival. Contrary to the expectations of most modern intellectuals (e.g., liberals, Marxists, humanists, nationalists, and other Enlightenment universalists), one of the most striking developments of the second half of the twentieth century has been an upsurge of ethnic solidarity and political mobilization throughout the world (for overviews, see Horowitz, 1985; Smith, 1981; Young, 1976, 1993). On every settled continent of the globe, ethnic groups have made it clear that they do not intend to self-destruct by being absorbed into larger national or universalistic groupings, and that they will resist the subordination of their interests to those of other groups.

The distinction between *national* and *ethnic* groupings has been the subject of considerable intellectual discussion in recent decades (see, e.g., Connor, 1994: esp. chap. 4). As used in this study, however, the difference to be emphasized is that ethnic groups do not aspire to sovereign statehood for themselves. If an ethnic group develops a clear goal that it should achieve collective independence, with effective and separate control over its own territory, it becomes by virtue of that goal a nationalist group. Apart from this distinction, ethnic groups share many of the same sociological characteristics as national groups. That is, they are recognized—by their own members and by outsiders—through boundaries that may take one or more of a variety of forms very similar to the boundaries of national groups outlined above, including, of course, language. And ethnic groups, like nations, are "imagined communities" whose "images of communion" are constructed and maintained through human agency.

Twentieth-century ethnic mobilizations have been inspired in no small measure by the fact of systematic ethnic inequality. Nearly all societies are multiethnic, and multiethnic societies are usually stratified along ethnic lines; that is, membership in minority ethnic groups is systematically associated with lower-than-average amounts of many of the goods that people struggle for in those societies, such as income, wealth, status, education, political power, and recognition. Some scholars, indeed, believe that the primary function of ethnic identities is to create and perpetuate structures of social inequality (see, e.g., Wilmsen and McAllister, 1996). In any case, the rhetorical strategies of ethnic mobilizations in the twentieth century have usually been articulated in the language of equality (Horowitz, 1985). Since equality has been one of the central public values of the modern age,[3] leaders of subordinated ethnic communities have been able to mobilize their followers and to challenge state political elites by pointing to these systematic patterns of inequality as being derived from unjust oppression by dominant groups in violation of widely shared egalitarian norms.

As a key boundary of many ethnic groups, language sometimes plays a critical role in the struggle over ethnic inequality. Indeed, in multilingual societies prestige and power are typically stratified along ethnolinguistic lines (Wolfson and Manes, 1985). In such societies, the life chances of any given individual are deeply affected by that individual's membership in a given ethnolinguistic community. Members of powerful and affluent ethnolinguistic communities have a broad range of advantages over members of weak and subordinate groups.

In this context, the language policy of the state plainly affects the interest of members of differing language groups in different ways. Unlike the case of religion, the state cannot claim to be neutral in respect to language. There can be no wall of separation between the state and language because the state must employ language to function at all. As Hannah Arendt (1958) reminded us, the essential and central medium of political life is speech. Thus, if the state chooses to use not *my* language but some other group's language as the medium for its authority, my interests will have been negatively affected. The same is true of nonstate institutions and arenas in civil society (e.g., economic, religious, and cultural institutions). Given the normative power of egalitarianism in the modern world, it is easy to see how differential patterns of language use and policy may become key elements in the mobilization of ethnic identities and conflict in the political arena.

Identity Politics and Language: Another Take on the Stakes

By exploring these broad patterns of political rhetoric in language policy conflicts, it is possible to uncover some of what is at stake in these struggles. Still, the fundamental issue that pits partisans mobilized for national unity against those having a vital interest in ethnolinguistic equality is not yet in focus. I shall argue that language policy conflicts can be understood best in terms of the politics of identity. In other words, the dispute between nationalist and ethnic minority activists is essentially a disagreement over the meanings and uses of group identity in the public life of the nation-state, and not language as such.

Still an evolving concept in social scientific analysis, identity politics involves the increasing contention over several aspects of group membership in nation-states today. For example, should the state use identity group designations in making public policy? What are the consequences of the answer to this question for the group members themselves? For those who are not members of designated groups? For the society as a whole? A steadily increasing array of social groups have been connected to the politics of identity in relation to these issues (e.g., women and men, homosexuals and bisexuals, and the physically challenged), but among the most important politically are ethnic and nationalist groups.

How can we understand what is at stake in the politics of identity? Why should anyone care, for example, if ethnic identity seems centrally important to some people, while others argue for the preeminence of national identity? More specifically, how do we answer this question when the subject in dispute is language policy? In what follows, it is suggested that there are three key aspects to understanding the importance of group identity for individual human beings: group identity is central (1) to the constitution of the self and (2) to the self's relationships with other selves; and (3) group identity is of great significance in the structuring and allocation of goods through the decision-making processes of the society. Further, language can play a key role in each of these facets of identity.

Identity as Constitutive and Relational One of the deepest and most perplexing questions confronting any of us is, "Who am I?" As a beginning point, identity is the basis for meaning, coherence, and achievement in our lives. Building on the work of Erik Erikson, Kenneth Hoover (1997) argues that successful identity formation is the indispensable foundation for human competence, integrity, and mutuality. Without the formation of an identity, indeed, we cannot be "selves" at all. The price we pay for identity, however, is difference, for without boundaries between ourselves and others, there is no self and no identity (Connolly, 1991).

Despite, or perhaps because of, this need for boundaries, our identities are not constructed by ourselves alone, but in dialectically intertwined relationships with others. All personal identities are social constructions in which others play a part. The communitarian philosopher Alisdair MacIntyre (1984) captured this notion well in noting that our "story" as individuals is already partly told before we are born, and that while we are the "co-authors" of our lives, we must remember that we are *only* the co-authors: "We enter upon a stage which we did not design and we find ourselves part of an action that was not of our making. Each of us being a main character in his own drama plays subordinate parts in the dramas of others, and each drama constrains the others" (p. 213). . . .

. . . The constitutive and relational nature of personal identity is helpful in understanding how language becomes perceived as an important issue in the politics of identity. For while it is possible for me to change by language and my language loyalties, it is also possible—depending on the circumstances—that I will experience my language as a fundamental and constitutive part of who I am. Although I did not invent my own language, I may experience it as constitutive of my core identity, so that any attack on my language is experienced as an attack on my very being. This understanding of the constitutive nature of language has been given one of its most evocative articulations by the political scientist Harold R. Isaacs (1975) in his now-classic primordialist treatment of the ethnic revival:

> That first learned language is, to begin with, the *mother's* tongue, with all that conveys and contributes to the forming of the self and the development of the individual personality. It opens into every aspect of life. . . .
>
> "The world of communicable facts" is the world as it is seen by the family, the group, the culture in which the child enters. It is the world as named and described in the group's language, the tongue in which the child learns what the world is and how it came to be, the words and tones in which the group describes itself, spins its tales of the past, sings its songs of joy or sorrow, celebrates the beauties of its land, the greatness of its heroes, the power of its myths. It is the language in which he learns, absorbs, repeats, and passes on all the group's given truths, its system of beliefs, its answers to the mysteries of creation, life, and death, its ethics, aesthetics, and its conventional wisdom. The mother's tongue serves to connect the child to a whole universe of others now living or long dead. It thus extends to all who share or have shared this tongue, as Herbert Kelman has put it, "some of the emotional intensity and irreducible quality" attached to "those primordial bonds that tie the child to his mother and immediate kin." (pp. 94–95)

Although his formulation was perhaps hyperbolic, Isaacs's depiction may go a long way toward explaining the intense emotions often expressed in the political conflict over language policy. And if, through the social context of my life, my core identity is closely linked to what I see as a national language, while the core identity of another in my society has been linked by equally powerful circumstances with an ethnic group's language, the conditions have been set to motivate us toward deeply felt political conflict. . . .

Identity and the Quest for Goods Political conflict derives ultimately from the coexistence of human interdependence and difference. We need each other for certain goods, but we differ from each other in our interests in relation to these goods, and in our views of how these goods should be understood, structured, and allocated. As seen above, identities themselves are constituted out of both interdependence and difference, and hence are susceptible to being incorporated into political conflict. When people engage in political conflict over language, they are expressing the view (at least implicitly) that language is connected to some sort of good that they desire or believe they need. What sorts of goods are at stake in political conflicts over identity in which language is an important political terrain? How can political disputes over identity and language affect the well-being of individuals, groups, and societies?

A recent spate of political theorizing on identity politics (see, e.g., Benhabib, 1996; Connolly,

1991, 1995; Fraser, 1997; Kymlicka, 1989, 1995; Lash and Friedman, 1992; Norton, 1988; Taylor, 1994; Young, 1990) has produced several clarifying discussions that may prove useful in answering this question. In particular, I want to argue that two key forms of goods are helpful in understanding how language becomes an important terrain for the politics of identity. These go by various names, each of which contributes an understanding of what is at stake, but I will use the terms *symbolic recognition* and *material interests* to signify them.

Symbolic recognition refers to the acknowledgment, acceptance, and respect by others of the legitimacy and value of particular identity formations and communities. Because personal and group identities are constituted relationally, as we saw above, they cannot be constructed from the inside alone. We need others to recognize us, and the manner in which they do so has profound implications for our well-being as individuals and as groups. The two chief evils in relation to symbolic recognition, as Charles Taylor (1994) has pointed out, are *misrecognition* (in which we are represented in inaccurate, hurtful, and/or harmful ways) and *nonrecognition* (in which our identities are ignored, or rendered invisible for the deficiencies or maliciousness of others).[4] The central thrust of the contemporary movement for multiculturalism, accordingly, is described by Taylor (1994) as follows:

> The thesis is that our identity is partly shaped by recognition or its absence, often by the *mis*representation of others, and so a person or group of people can suffer real damage, real distortion, if the people or society around them mirror back to them a confining or demeaning or contemptible picture of themselves. Nonrecognition or misrecognition can inflict harm, can be a form of oppression, imprisoning someone in a false, distorted, and reduced mode of being. (p. 25, emphasis in original)

This misrecognition and/or nonrecognition has figured prominently in the mobilization of the ethnic revival of the late twentieth century. The struggle for ethnic equality has aimed, in part, at winning greater acknowledgment, acceptance, and respect for the boundary-marking characteristics and ways of life of subordinated or despised ethnic minorities. Therefore, if language, for example, becomes an important marker of ethnic identity, then language policy represents one avenue through which to gain greater public recognition and respect for a particular ethnic community. By gaining public recognition for my language, I enhance the status not only of my language, but of my ethnic community and myself. Insofar as my language infuses and represents my way of life,[5] the latter is given public validation and respect through a status-enhancing language policy. Conversely, language policy may be used by a state's political elites to demean or deny recognition to an ethnic community, thus contributing to its continuing subordination in the larger society (Weinstein, 1983).[6]

This explication of the role of symbolic recognition in identity politics emphasizes the significance of gaining appropriate and enhancing affirmation from those outside ourselves (individually or as a group). Another aspect of symbolic recognition that needs to be outlined, however, derives from the fact that our memberships in significant identity groups renders our personal identities vulnerable to the behaviors and characteristics of those within our group as well. That is, the need for mutual recognition of our identity's characteristics applies not only to outsiders but to insiders as well. Thus, for example, if I believe that my personal identity is centrally associated with being an American, and I further believe that being American entails speaking English as our national language, then my personal identity is vulnerable to the recognition that this is the case by others both within and outside my "imagined community." The same dynamic, of course, works for the recognition and maintenance of boundary markers for ethnic minority identities. If being Quebecois means speaking French, then seeing one of us conversing publically in English represents a threat to our (and therefore my) identity. It is easy to see, then, how symbolic recognition functions as a central dynamic and motivating force for the politics of identity, and how language can function as a key signifier in this process. Under these circumstances, it should be clear that two incompatible claims for symbolic recognition of language as identity signifier can serve to pit the holders of these claims in deep political conflict.

This discussion deepens and enriches our understanding of the rhetorical conflicts outlined above in relation to national unity and ethnic equality. Those who express strong concerns about the threat of multiple languages to national unity may be motivated, at least in part, by concerns for the unity of their own personal identities (on this point, see Connolly, 1991). Further, if my language has been successfully installed as a hegemonic[7] national language signifying a core part of a national identity, efforts to reimagine (re-cognize) that national identity as multilingual and multicultural will represent a direct threat to my personal identity. By the same token, the very existence of a hegemonic language in a multilingual society represents and expresses a subordination of the minority language(s) and language group(s) in that society.

Material interests constitute the second form of goods at stake in identity politics. The most common referents to material goods are wealth, income, property, and office or position, but the concept is also used to refer to other objective social indicators of status (e.g., educational attainment) and to access to services thought to promote people's material well-being (e.g., health care, electronic communications, and recreational opportunities).

Material interests become intertwined with identity politics when the distribution of material goods becomes systematically linked with group identities. And, as noted, every multiethnic society for which information is available has been characterized by the systematic inequality of material goods and, more generally, life chances, along ethnic lines. Thus, one's group identity is nearly always linked in important ways to one's material interest. This linkage has led some social scientists (usually described as instrumentalists or circumstantialists) to explain the attachment to ethnic identity in terms of the competition for material resources. . . . Group identities matter to people, in short, because they are usually directly connected to their material well-being.

Moreover, there is also an important link between the symbolic recognition aspect of identity politics and the distribution of material resources. That is, recognition is important not only because it has symbolic meaning, but also because it functions to facilitate or inhibit access to material goods. Due to the relational nature of identity, this operates—once again—both internally and externally. Externally, recognition of group identity is used as a cue for making the myriad qualitative judgments about others that either open or close doors to opportunity and material well-being. A familiar example is the social science research demonstrating that teachers' expectations about the capacities of students (filtered through the lenses of group identity) greatly influence the nature and quality of their work with those students and of the students' performance.

In addition, self-identity—formed in part through the internalization of external symbolic recognition—creates self-expectations and patterns of behavior that can greatly influence one's capacity for effective agency in the pursuit of material goods. Indeed, this is one of the ways in which misrecognition and nonrecogntion can operate as forms of oppression, as Taylor noted. If I am convinced that "my kind of people" have no chance of success in the dominant avenues leading to relative material abundance (e.g., professional education), that conviction will influence my capacity to pursue those directions. In this sense, negative forms of group recognition serve to create internal—in addition to external—obstacles to social mobility. . . .

Of course, these same policies that deny access to members of some language groups serve to advantage the members of other groups.

And language functions not only instrumentally, as a gatekeeping device, but also symbolically. Even those who are fluent in the dominant language of a society may be marked by an accent, which is then used as an ethnic identifier for purposes of invidious comparison and discrimination. This is the social dynamic underlying political conflict over corpus language planning.

This discussion of the material interests at stake in identity politics should once again facilitate understanding of the rhetorical competition in language policy conflicts between those motivated by considerations of national unity and those most concerned about ethnic equality. There are not only important symbolic goods at stake, but material interests as well.

It should no longer be a mystery that language policy has emerged as a point of political contention in the contemporary world. The preconditions of language diversity, contact, and competition are widespread throughout the world. Moreover, political conflicts in our era are preeminently managed by nation-states, which are increasingly activist but which also characteristically are troubled by the problematic character of the nation in a time of widespread identity politics. Because of its own characteristics and potential importance in the constitution of identities (individual, ethnic, national), language has the capacity to engage people's interests and political imaginations on a deeply emotional level. . . .

NOTES

1. It is acknowledged here that the term "minority" is problematic in contemporary scholarly discourse. As used here, "minority" is not a numerical signifier, but represents the descriptive perception that dominant ethnolinguistic groups have minoritized less powerful ethnic groups and their languages in multiple ways.
2. The most prominent exceptions, of course, were the leaders of Marxist-Leninist states during their heydays following the Soviet Revolution in Russia. Most scholars, however, believe that the ideology of Marxist internationalism never successfully overcame the political imperative to pursue the national interest as the top priority, even within what was known until the revolutions of 1989 as the "communist world." See, e.g., Connor, 1984.
3. Alexis de Tocqueville (1835 [1964]: 6) articulated the theme early in the nineteenth century:

   > In running over the pages of our history for seven hundred years, we shall scarcely find a single great event which has not promoted equality of condition. . . . The gradual development of the principle of equality is, therefore, a Providential fact. It has all the chief characteristics of such a fact: it is universal, it is durable, it constantly eludes all human interference, and all events as well as all men contribute to its progress.

4. One of the most powerful evocations of both misrecognition and nonrecognition I have read is that of Ralph Ellison in *The Invisible Man* (1952 [1995]).
5. Both Rachel F. Moran (1987) and Raymond Tatalovich (1995) describe U.S. language politics in terms of a conflict over values about ways of life.
6. Some scholars, in fact, argue that the primary function of both racial (Miles and Torres, 1996) and "ethnic" identities (Wilmsen and McAllister, 1996) is the creation and perpetutation of structures of social inequality.
7. I use this term in the sense of David D. Laitin's (1986) reformulation of Antonio Gramsci: Hegemony is "the political forging—whether through coercion or elite bargaining—and institutionalization of a pattern of group activity in a state and the concurrent idealization of that schema into a dominant symbolic framework that reigns as common sense" (p. 19).

REFERENCES

Akinnaso, F. Niyi. 1989. "One Nation, Four Hundred Languages: Unity and Diversity in Nigeria's Language Policy," *Language Problems and Language Planning* 13:2 (Summer), pp. 133–46.

Anderson, Benedict. 1983. *Imagined Communities: Reflections on the Origin and Spread of Nationalism* (London:Verso Press).

Apte, Mahadev L. 1976. "Multilingualism in India and Its Socio-Political Implications: An Overview," in William M. O'Barr and Jean F. O'Barr, eds., *Language and Politics* (The Hague: Mouten & Co.), pp. 141–64.

Arendt, Hannah. 1958. *The Human Condition* (Chicago: University of Chicago Press).

Benhabib, Seyla, ed. 1996. *Democracy and Difference: Contesting the Boundaries of the Political* (Princeton, NJ: Princeton University Press).

Connolly, William E. 1991. *Identity/Difference: Democratic Negotiations of Political Paradox* (Ithaca, NY: Cornell University Press).

Connolly, William E. 1995. *The Ethos of Pluralization* (Minneapolis: University of Minnesota Press).

Connor, Walker. 1994. *Ethnonationalism: The Quest for Understanding* (Princeton, NJ: Princeton University Press).

Fishman, Joshua. 1972. *The Sociology of Language* (Rowley, MA: Newbury House).

Fraser, Nancy. 1997. *Justice Interruptus: Critical Reflections on the "Postsocialist" Condition* (New York: Routlege).

Hoover, Kenneth. 1997. *The Power of Identity: Politics in a New Key,* with James Marcia and Kristen Parris (Chatham, NJ: Chatham House).

Horowitz, Donald L. 1985. *Ethnic Groups in Conflict* (Berkeley: University of California Press).

Isaacs, Harold R. 1975. *Idols of the Tribe: Group Identity and Political Change* (New York: Harper & Row).

Kymlicka, Will. 1989. *Liberalism, Community, and Culture* (New York: Oxford University Press).

Kymlicka, Will. 1995. *Multicultural Citizenship: A Liberal Theory of Minority Politics.* (New York: Oxford University Press).

Lash, Scott, and Jonathan Friedman, eds. 1992. *Modernity and Identity* (Cambridge: Blackwell).

MacIntyre, Alasdair. 1984. *After Virtue,* 2nd ed. (Notre Dame, IN: University of Notre Dame Press).

Marshall, David F. 1996. "The Role of Language in the Mobilization of Soviet Ethnic Nationalities," in Hans R. Duz, ed., "Language Planning and Political Theory," *International Journal of the Sociology of Language* 118, pp. 7–46.

Norton, Anne. 1988. *Reflections on Political Identity* (Baltimore, MD: Johns Hopkins University Press).

Smith, Rogers. 1997. *Civic Ideals: Conflicting Visions of Citizenship in U.S. History* (New Haven, CT: Yale University Press).

Taylor, Charles. 1994. *Multiculturalism: Examining the Politics of Recognition,* edited and introduced by Amy Gutmann, with responses by K. Anthony Appiah, Jurgen Habermas, Steven C. Rockefeller, Michael Walzer, and Susan Wolf (Princeton, NJ: Princeton University Press).

Wardhaugh, Ronald. 1987. *Languages in Competition: Dominance, Diversity, and Decline* (Oxford: Basil Blackwell).

Weinstein, Brian. 1983. *The Civic Tongue: Political Consequences of Language Choice* (New York: Longman).

Wilmsen, Edwin N., and Patrick McAllister, eds. 1996. *The Politics of Difference: Ethnic Premises in a World of Power* (Chicago: University of Chicago Press).

Wolfson, Nessa, and Joan Manes, eds. 1985. *Language of Inequality* (Berlin: Mouton).

Young, Crawford. 1976. *The Politics of Cultural Pluralism* (Madison: University of Wisconsin Press).

Young, Crawford. 1993. "The Dialectics of Cultural Pluralism: Concept and Reality," in Crawford Young, ed., *The Rising Tide of Cultural Pluralism: The Nation-State at Bay?* (Madison: University of Wisconsin Press), pp. 3–35.

Young, Iris Marion. 1990. *Justice and the Politics of Difference* (Princeton, NJ: Princeton University Press).

READING 55

Racism in the English Language

Robert B. Moore

LANGUAGE AND CULTURE

An integral part of any culture is its language. Language not only develops in conjunction with a society's historical, economic and political evolution; it also reflects that society's attitudes and thinking. Language not only *expresses* ideas and concepts but actually *shapes* thought.[1] If one accepts that our dominant white culture is racist, then one would expect our language—an indispensable transmitter of culture—to be racist as well. Whites, as the dominant group, are not subjected to the same abusive characterization by our language that people of color receive. Aspects of racism in the English language that will be discussed in this essay include terminology, symbolism, politics, ethnocentrism, and context.

Before beginning our analysis of racism in language we would like to quote part of a TV film review which shows the connection between language and culture.[2]

> Depending on one's culture, one interacts with time in a very distinct fashion. One example which gives some cross-cultural insights into the concept of time is language. In Spanish, a watch is said to "walk." In English, the watch "runs." In German, the watch "functions." And in French, the watch "marches." In the Indian culture of the Southwest, people do not refer to time in this way. The value of the watch is displaced with the value of "what time it's getting to be." Viewing these five cultural perspectives of time, one can see some definite emphasis and values that each culture places on time. For example, a cultural perspective may provide a clue to why the negative stereotype of the slow and lazy Mexican who lives in the "Land of Manana" exists in the Anglo value system, where time "flies," the watch "runs" and "time is money."

No biographical information available.

A SHORT PLAY ON "BLACK" AND "WHITE" WORDS

Some may blackly (angrily) accuse me of trying to blacken (defame) the English language, to give it a black eye (a mark of shame) by writing such black words (hostile). They may denigrate (to cast aspersions; to darken) me by accusing me of being blackhearted (malevolent), of having a black outlook (pessimistic, dismal) on life, of being a blackguard (scoundrel)—which would certainly be a black mark (detrimental fact) against me. Some may black-brow (scowl at) me and hope that a black cat crosses in front of me because of this black deed. I may become a black sheep (one who causes shame or embarrassment because of deviation from the accepted standards), who will be blackballed (ostracized) by being placed on a blacklist (list of undesirables) in an attempt to blackmail (to force or coerce into a particular action) me to retract my words. But attempts to blackjack (to compel by threat) me will have a Chinaman's chance of success, for I am not a yellow-bellied Indian-giver of words, who will whitewash (cover up or gloss over vices or crimes) a black lie (harmful, inexcusable). I challenge the purity and innocence (white) of the English language. I don't see things in black and white (entirely bad or entirely good) terms, for I am a white man (marked by upright firmness) if there ever was one. However, it would be a black day when I would not "call a spade a spade," even though some will suggest a white man calling the English language racist is like the pot calling the kettle black. While many may be niggardly (grudging, scanty) in their support, others will be honest and decent—and to them I say, that's very white of you (honest, decent).

The preceding is of course a white lie (not intended to cause harm), meant only to

illustrate some examples of racist terminology in the English language.

OBVIOUS BIGOTRY

Perhaps the most obvious aspect of racism in language would be terms like "nigger," "spook," "chink," "spic," etc. While these may be facing increasing social disdain, they certainly are not dead. Large numbers of white Americans continue to utilize these terms. "Chink," "gook," and "slant-eyes" were in common usage among U.S. troops in Vietnam. An NBC nightly news broadcast, in February 1972, reported that the basketball team in Pekin, Illinois, was called the "Pekin Chinks" and noted that even though this had been protested by Chinese Americans, the term continued to be used because it was easy, and meant no harm. Spiro Agnew's widely reported "fat Jap" remark and the "little Jap" comment of lawyer John Wilson during the Watergate hearings, are surface indicators of a deep-rooted Archie Bunkerism.

Many white people continue to refer to Black people as "colored," as for instance in a July 30, 1975 *Boston Globe* article on a racist attack by whites on a group of Black people using a public beach in Boston. One white person was quoted as follows:

> We've always welcomed good colored people in South Boston but we will not tolerate radical blacks or Communists. . . . Good colored people are welcome in South Boston, black militants are not.

Many white people may still be unaware of the disdain many African Americans have for the term "colored," but it often appears that whether used intentionally or unintentionally, "colored" people are "good" and "know their place," while "Black" people are perceived as "uppity" and "threatening" to many whites. Similarly, the term "boy" to refer to African American men is now acknowledged to be a demeaning term, though still in common use. Other terms such as "the pot calling the kettle black" and "calling a spade a spade" have negative racial connotations but are still frequently used, as for example when President Ford was quoted in February 1976 saying that even though Daniel Moynihan had left the U.N., the U.S. would continue "calling a spade a spade."

COLOR SYMBOLISM

The symbolism of white as positive and black as negative is pervasive in our culture, with the black/white words used in the beginning of this essay only one of many aspects. "Good guys" wear white hats and ride white horses, "bad guys" wear black hats and ride black horses. Angels are white, and devils are black. The definition of *black* includes "without any moral light or goodness, evil, wicked, indicating disgrace, sinful," while that of *white* includes "morally pure, spotless, innocent, free from evil intent."

A children's TV cartoon program, *Captain Scarlet,* is about an organization called Spectrum, whose purpose is to save the world from an evil extraterrestrial force called the Mysterons. Everyone in Spectrum has a color name—Captain Scarlet, Captain Blue, etc. The one Spectrum agent who has been mysteriously taken over by the Mysterons and works to advance their evil aims is Captain Black. The person who heads Spectrum, the good organization out to defend the world, is Colonel White.

Three of the dictionary definitions of white are "fairness of complexion, purity, innocence." These definitions affect the standards of beauty in our culture, in which whiteness represents the norm. "Blondes have more fun" and "Wouldn't you really rather be a blonde" are sexist in their attitudes toward women generally, but are racist white standards when applied to third world women. A 1971 *Mademoiselle* advertisement pictured a curly-headed, ivory-skinned woman over the caption, "When you go blonde go all the way," and asked: "Isn't this how, in the back of your mind, you always wanted to look? All wide-eyed and silky blonde down to there, and innocent?" Whatever the advertising people meant by this particular woman's innocence, one must remember that "innocent" is one of the definitions of the word white. This standard of beauty when preached to all women is racist. The statement "Isn't this how, in the back of your mind, you always wanted to look?" either ignores third world women or assumes they long to be white.

Time magazine in its coverage of the Wimbledon tennis competition between the black Australian Evonne Goolagong and the white American Chris Evert described Ms. Goolagong as "the dusky daughter of an Australian sheep-shearer," while Ms. Evert was "a fair young girl from the middle-class groves of Florida." *Dusky* is a synonym of "black" and is defined as "having dark skin; of a dark color; gloomy; dark; swarthy." Its antonyms are "fair" and "blonde." *Fair* is defined in part as "free from blemish, imperfection, or anything that impairs the appearance, quality, or character; pleasing in appearance, attractive; clean; pretty; comely." By defining Evonne Goolagong as "dusky," *Time* technically defined her as the opposite of "pleasing in appearance; attractive; clean; pretty; comely."

The studies of Kenneth B. Clark, Mary Ellen Goodman, Judith Porter and others indicate that this persuasive "rightness of whiteness" in U.S. culture affects children before the age of four, providing white youngsters with a false sense of superiority and encouraging self-hatred among third world youngsters.

ETHNOCENTRISM OR FROM A WHITE PERSPECTIVE

Some words and phrases that are commonly used represent particular perspectives and frames of reference, and these often distort the understanding of the reader or listener. David R. Burgest[3] has written about the effect of using the terms "slave" or "master." He argues that the psychological impact of the statement referring to "the master raped his slave" is different from the impact of the same statement substituting the words: "the white captor raped an African woman held in captivity."

> Implicit in the English usage of the "master-slave" concept is ownership of the "slave" by the "master," therefore, the "master" is merely abusing his property (slave). In reality, the captives (slave) were African individuals with human worth, right and dignity and the term "slave" denounces that human quality thereby making the mass rape of African women by white captors more acceptable in the minds of people and setting a mental frame of reference for legitimizing the atrocities perpetuated against African people.

The term "slave" connotes a less than human quality and turns the captive person into a thing. For example, two McGraw-Hill Far Eastern Publishers textbooks (1970) stated, "At first it was the slaves who worked the cane and they got only food for it. Now men work cane and get money." Next time you write about slavery or read about it, try transposing all "slaves" into "African people held in captivity," "Black people forced to work for no pay" or "African people stolen from their families and societies." While it is more cumbersome, such phrasing conveys a different meaning.

PASSIVE TENSE

Another means by which language shapes our perspective has been noted by Thomas Greenfield,[4] who writes that the achievements of Black people—and Black people themselves—have been hidden in

> the linguistic ghetto of the passive voice, the subordinate clause, and the "understood" subject. The seemingly innocuous distinction (between active/passive voice) holds enormous implications for writers and speakers. When it is effectively applied, the rhetorical impact of the passive voice—the art of making the creator or instigator of action

> totally disappear from a reader's perception—can be devastating.

For instance, some history texts will discuss how European immigrants came to the United States seeking a better life and expanded opportunities, but will note that "slaves *were brought* to America." Not only does this omit the destruction of African societies and families, but it ignores the role of northern merchants and southern slaveholders in the profitable trade in human beings. Other books will state that "the continental railroad *was built,*" conveniently omitting information about the Chinese laborers who built much of it or the oppression they suffered.

Another example. While touring Monticello, Greenfield noted that the tour guide

> made all the black people at Monticello disappear through her use of the passive voice. While speaking of the architectural achievements of Jefferson in the active voice, she unfailingly shifted to passive when speaking of the work performed by Negro slaves and skilled servants.

Noting a type of door that after 166 years continued to operate without need for repair, Greenfield remarks that the design aspect of the door was much simpler than the actual skill and work involved in building and installing it. Yet his guide stated: "Mr. Jefferson designed these doors . . ." while "the doors **were installed** in 1809." The workers who installed those doors were African people whom Jefferson held in bondage. The guide's use of the passive tense enabled her to dismiss the reality of Jefferson's slaveholding. It also meant that she did not have to make any mention of the skills of those people held in bondage.

POLITICS AND TERMINOLOGY

"Culturally deprived," "economically disadvantaged" and "underdeveloped" are other terms which mislead and distort our awareness of reality. The application of the term "culturally deprived" and third world children in this society reflects a value judgment. It assumes that the dominant whites are cultured and all others without culture. In fact, third world children generally are bicultural, and many are bilingual, having grown up in their own culture as well as absorbing the dominant culture. In many ways, they are equipped with skills and experiences which white youth have been deprived of, since most white youth develop in a monocultural, monolingual environment. Burgest[5] suggests that the term "culturally deprived" be replaced by "culturally dispossessed," and that the term "economically disadvantaged" be replaced by "economically exploited." Both these terms present a perspective and implication that provide an entirely different frame of reference as to the reality of the third world experience in U.S. society.

Similarly, many nations of the third world are described as "underdeveloped." These less wealthy nations are generally those that suffered under colonialism and neo-colonialism. The "developed" nations are those that exploited their resources and wealth. Therefore, rather than referring to these countries as "underdeveloped," a more appropriate and meaningful designation might be "over exploited." Again, transpose this term next time you read about "underdeveloped nations" and note the different meaning that results.

Terms such as "culturally deprived," "economically disadvantaged" and "underdeveloped" place the responsibility for their own conditions on those being so described. This is known as "Blaming the Victim."[6] It places responsibility for poverty on the victims of poverty. It removes the blame from those in power who benefit from, and continue to permit, poverty.

Still another example involves the use of "non-white," "minority" or "third world." While people of color are a minority in the U.S., they are part of the vast majority of the world's population, in which white people are a distinct minority. Thus, by utilizing the term minority to describe people of color in the U.S., we can lose sight of the global majority/minority reality—a fact of some importance in the increasing and interconnected struggles of people of color inside and outside the U.S.

To describe people of color as "non-white" is to use whiteness as the standard and norm against which to measure all others. Use of the term "third world" to describe all people of color overcomes the inherent bias of "minority" and "nonwhite." Moreover, it connects the struggles of third world people in the U.S. with the freedom struggles around the globe.

The term "third world" gained increasing usage after the 1955 Bandung Conference of "non-aligned" nations, which represented a third force outside of the two world superpowers. The "first world" represents the United States, Western Europe and their sphere of influence. The "second world" represents the Soviet Union and its sphere. The "third world" represents, for the most part, nations that were, or are, controlled by the "first world" or West. For the most part, these are nations of Africa, Asia and Latin America.

"LOADED" WORDS AND NATIVE AMERICANS

Many words lead to a demeaning characterization of groups of people. For instance, Columbus, it is said, "discovered" America. The word *discover* is defined as "to gain sight or knowledge of something previously unseen or unknown; to discover may be to find some existent thing that was previously unknown." Thus, a continent inhabited by millions of human beings cannot be "discovered." For history books to continue this usage represents a Eurocentric (white European) perspective on world history and ignores the existence of, and the perspective of, Native Americans. "Discovery," as used in the Euro-American context, implies the right to take what one finds, ignoring the rights of those who already inhabit or own the "discovered" thing.

Eurocentrism is also apparent in the usage of "victory" and "massacre" to describe the battles between Native Americans and whites. *Victory* is defined in the dictionary as "a success or triumph over an enemy in battle or war; the decisive defeat of an opponent." *Conquest* denotes the "taking over of control by the victor, and the obedience of the conquered." *Massacre* is defined as "the unnecessary, indiscriminate killing of a number of human beings, as in barbarous warfare or persecution, or for revenge or plunder." *Defend* is described as "to ward off attack from; guard against assault or injury; to strive to keep safe by resisting attack."

Eurocentrism turns these definitions around to serve the purpose of distorting history and justifying Euro-American conquest of the Native American homelands. Euro-Americans are not described in history books as invading Native American lands, but rather as defending *their* homes against "Indian" attacks. Since European communities were constantly encroaching on land already occupied, then a more honest interpretation would state that it was the Native Americans who were "warding off," "guarding" and "defending" their homelands.

Native American victories are invariably defined as "massacres," while the indiscriminate killing, extermination and plunder of Native American nations by Euro-Americans is defined as "victory." Distortion of history by the choice of "loaded" words used to describe historical events is a common racist practice. Rather than portraying Native Americans as human beings in highly defined and complex societies, cultures and civilizations, history books use such adjectives as "savages," "beasts," "primitive," and "backward." Native people are referred to as "squaw," "brave," or "papoose" instead of "woman," "man," or "baby."

Another term that has questionable connotations is *tribe*. The Oxford English Dictionary defines this noun as "a race of people; now applied especially to a primary aggregate of people in a primitive or barbarous condition, under a headman or chief." Morton Fried,[7] discussing "The Myth of Tribe," states that the word "did not become a general term of reference to American

Indian society until the nineteenth century. Previously, the words commonly used for Indian populations were 'nation' and 'people.'" Since "tribe" has assumed a connotation of primitiveness or backwardness, it is suggested that the use of "nation" or "people" replace the term whenever possible in referring to Native American peoples.

The term *tribe* invokes even more negative implications when used in reference to American peoples. As Evelyn Jones Rich[8] has noted, the term is "almost always used to refer to third world people and it implies a stage of development which is, in short, a put-down."

"LOADED" WORDS AND AFRICANS

Conflicts among diverse peoples within African nations are often referred to as "tribal warfare," while conflicts among the diverse peoples within European countries are never described in such terms. If the rivalries between the Ibo and the Hausa and Yoruba in Nigeria are described as "tribal," why not the rivalries between Serbs and Slavs in Yugoslavia, or Scots and English in Great Britain, Protestants and Catholics in Ireland, or the Basques and the Southern Spaniards in Spain? Conflicts among African peoples in a particular nation have religious, cultural, economic and/or political roots. If we can analyze the roots of conflicts among European peoples in terms other than "tribal warfare," certainly we can do the same with African peoples, including correct reference to the ethnic groups or nations involved. For example, the terms "Kaffirs," "Hottentot" or "Bushmen" are names imposed by white Europeans. The correct names are always those by which a people refer to themselves. (In these instances Xhosa, Khoi-Khoin and San are correct.[9])

The generalized application of "tribal" in reference to Africans—as well as the failure to acknowledge the religious, cultural and social diversity of African peoples—is a decidedly racist dynamic. It is part of the process whereby Euro-Americans justify, or avoid confronting, their oppression of third world peoples. Africa has been particularly insulted by this dynamic, as witness the pervasive "darkest Africa" image. This image, widespread in Western culture, evokes an Africa covered by jungles and inhibited by "uncivilized," "cannibalistic," "pagan," "savage" peoples. This "darkest Africa" image avoids the geographical reality. Less than 20 percent of the African continent is wooded savanna, for example. The image also ignores the history of African cultures and civilizations. Ample evidence suggests this distortion of reality was developed as a convenient rationale for the European and American slave trade. The Western powers, rather than exploiting, were civilizing and christianizing "uncivilized" and "pagan savages" (so the rationalization went). This dynamic also served to justify Western colonialism. From Tarzan movies to racist children's books like *Doctor Dolittle* and *Charlie and the Chocolate Factory,* the image of "savage" Africa and the myth of "the white man's burden" has been perpetuated in Western culture.

A 1972 *Time* magazine editorial lamenting the demise of *Life* magazine, stated that the "lavishness" of *Life*'s enterprises included "organizing safaris into darkest Africa." The same year, the *New York Times*' C. L. Sulzberger wrote that "Africa has a history as dark as the skins of many of its people." Terms such as "darkest Africa," "primitive," "tribe" ("tribal") or "jungle," in reference to Africa, perpetuate myths and are especially inexcusable in such large circulation publications.

Ethnocentrism is similarly reflected in the term "pagan" to describe traditional religions. A February 1973 *Time* magazine article on Uganda stated, "Moslems account for only 500,000 of Uganda's 10 million people. Of the remainder, 5,000,000 are Christians and the rest pagan." Pagan is defined as "Heathen, a follower of a polytheistic religion; one that has little or no religion and that is marked by a frank delight in and uninhibited seeking after sensual pleasures and material goods." *Heathen* is defined as "Unenlightened; an unconverted member of a people or nation that does not acknowledge the God of the Bible. A person whose culture or enlightenment is of an inferior grade, especially an irreligious person." Now, the people of Uganda, like almost all Africans, have serious religious beliefs and practices. As used by Westerners, "pagan" connotes something wild, primitive and inferior—another term to watch out for.

The variety of traditional structures that African people live in are their "houses," not "huts." A *hut* is "an often small and temporary dwelling of simple construction." And to describe Africans as "natives" (noun) is derogatory terminology—as in, "the natives are restless." The dictionary definition of *native* includes: "one of a people inhabiting a territorial area at the time of its discovery or becoming familiar to a foreigner; one belonging to a people having a less complex civilization." Therefore, use of "native," like use of "pagan" often implies a value judgment of white superiority.

QUALIFYING ADJECTIVES

Words that would normally have positive connotations can have entirely different meanings when used in a racial context. For example, C. L. Sulzberger, the columnist of the *New York Times,* wrote in January 1975, about conversations he had with two people in Namibia. One was the white South African administrator of the country and the other a member of SWAPO, the Namibian liberation movement. The first is described as "Dirk Mudge, who as senior elected member of the administration is a kind of acting Prime Minister. . . ." But the second person is introduced as "Daniel Tijongarero, an intelligent Herero tribesman who is a member of SWAPO. . . ." What need was there for Sulzberger to state that Daniel Tijongarero is "intelligent"? Why not also state that Dirk Mudge was "intelligent"—or do we assume he wasn't?

A similar example from a 1968 *New York Times* article reporting on an address by Lyndon Johnson stated, "The President spoke to the well-dressed Negro officials and their wives." In what similar circumstances can one imagine a reporter finding it necessary to note that an audience of white government officials was "well-dressed"?

Still another word often used in a racist context is "qualified." In the 1960s white Americans often questioned whether Black people were "qualified" to hold public office, a question that was never raised (until too late) about white officials like Wallace, Maddox, Nixon, Agnew, Mitchell, et al. The question of qualifications has been raised even more frequently in recent years as white people question whether Black people are "qualified" to be hired for positions in industry and educational institutions. "We're looking for a qualified Black" has been heard again and again as institutions are confronted with affirmative action goals. Why stipulate that Blacks must be "qualified," when for others it is taken for granted that applicants must be "qualified"?

SPEAKING ENGLISH

Finally, the depiction in movies and children's books of third world people speaking English is often itself racist. Children's books about Puerto Ricans or Chicanos often connect poverty with a failure to speak English or to speak it well, thus blaming the victim and ignoring the racism which affects third world people regardless of their proficiency in English. Asian characters speak a stilted English ("Honorable so and so" or "Confucius say") or have a speech impediment ("roots or ruck," "very solly," "flied lice"). Native American characters speak another variation of stilted English ("Boy not hide. Indian take boy"), repeat certain Hollywood-Indian phrases ("Heap big" and "Many moons") or simply grunt out "Ugh" or "How." The repeated use of these language characterizations functions to make third world people seem less intelligent and less capable than the English-speaking white characters.

WRAP-UP

A *Saturday Review* editorial[10] on "The Environment of Language" stated that language

> . . . has as much to do with the philosophical and political conditioning of a society as geography or climate. . . . people in Western cultures do not realize the extent to which their racial attitudes have been conditioned since early childhood by the power of words to ennoble or condemn, augment or detract, glorify or demean. Negative language infects the subconscious of most Western people from the time they first learn to speak. Prejudice is not merely imparted or superimposed. It is metabolized in the bloodstream of society. What is needed is not so much a change in language as an awareness of the power of words to condition attitudes. If we can at least recognize the underpinnings of prejudice, we may be in a position to deal with the effects.

To recognize the racism in language is an important first step. Consciousness of the influence of language on our perceptions can help to negate much of that influence. But it is not enough to simply become aware of the effects of racism in conditioning attitudes. While we may not be able to change the language, we can definitely change our usage of the language. We can avoid using words that degrade people. We can make a conscious effort to use terminology that reflects a progressive perspective, as opposed to a distorting perspective. It is important for educators to provide students with opportunities to explore racism in language and to increase their awareness of it, as well as learning terminology that is positive and does not perpetuate negative human values.

NOTES

1. Simon Podair, "How Bigotry Builds Through Language," *Negro Digest,* March 1967.
2. Jose Armas, "Antonio and the Mayor: A Cultural Review of the Film," *The Journal of Ethnic Studies,* Fall 1975.
3. David R. Burgest, "The Racist Use of the English Language," *Black Scholar,* September 1973.
4. Thomas Greenfield, "Race and Passive Voice at Monticello," *Crisis,* April 1975.
5. David R. Burgest, "Racism in Everyday Speech and Social Work Jargon," *Social Work,* July 1973.
6. William Ryan, *Blaming the Victim,* Pantheon Books, 1971.
7. Morton Fried, "The Myth of Tribe," *National History,* April 1975.
8. Evelyn Jones Rich, "Mind Your Language," *Africa Report,* September/October 1974.
9. Steve Wolf, "Catalogers in Revolt Against LC's Racist, Sexist Headings," *Bulletin of Interracial Books for Children,* Vol. 6, Nos. 3&4, 1975.
10. "The Environment of Language," *Saturday Review,* April 8, 1967.

Also see:

Roger Bastide, "Color, Racism and Christianity," *Daedalus,* Spring 1967.

Kenneth J. Gergen, "The Significance of Skin Color in Human Relations," *Daedalus,* Spring 1967.

Lloyd Yabura, "Towards a Language of Humanism," *Rhythm,* Summer 1971.

UNESCO, "Recommendations Concerning Terminology in Education on Race Questions," June 1968.

READING 56

Gender Stereotyping in the English Language

Laurel Richardson

Everyone in our society, regardless of class, ethnicity, sex, age, or race, is exposed to the same language, the language of the dominant culture. Analysis of verbal language can tell us a great deal about a people's fears, prejudices, anxieties, and interests. A rich vocabulary on a particular subject indicates societal interests or obsessions (e.g., the extensive vocabulary about cars in

---

Laurel Richardson is emeritus professor of sociology at The Ohio State University.

America). And different words for the same subject (such as *freedom fighter* and *terrorist, passed away* and *croaked, make love* and *ball*) show that there is a range of attitudes and feelings in the society toward that subject.

It should not be surprising, then, to find differential attitudes and feelings about men and women rooted in the English language. Although the English language has not been completely analyzed, six general propositions concerning these attitudes and feelings about males and females can be made.

First, in terms of grammatical and semantic structure, women do not have a fully autonomous, independent existence; they are part of man. The language is not divided into male and female with distinct conjugations and declensions, as many other languages are. Rather, *women* are included under the generic *man.* Grammar books specify that the pronoun *he* can be used generically to mean *he* or *she.* Further, *man,* when used as an indefinite pronoun, grammatically refers to both men and women. So, for example, when we read *man* in the following phrases we are to interpret it as applying to both men and women: "man the oars," "one small step for man, one giant step for mankind," "man, that's tough," "man overboard," "man the toolmaker," "alienated man," "garbageman." Our rules of etiquette complete the grammatical presumption of inclusivity. When two persons are pronounced "man and wife," Miss Susan Jones changes her entire name to Mrs. Robert Gordon (Vanderbilt, 1972). In each of these correct usages, women are a part of man; they do not exist autonomously. The exclusion of women is well expressed in Mary Daly's ear-jarring slogan "the sisterhood of man" (1973:7–21).

However, there is some question as to whether the theory that *man* means everybody is carried out in practice (see Bendix, 1979; Martyna, 1980). For example, an eight-year-old interrupts her reading of "The Story of the Cavemen" to ask how we got here without cavewomen. A ten-year-old thinks it is dumb to have a woman post*man.* A beginning anthropology student believes (incorrectly) that all shamans ("witch doctors") are males because her textbook and professor use the referential pronoun *he.*

But beginning language learners are not the only ones who visualize males when they see the word *man.* Research has consistently demonstrated that when the generic *man* is used, people visualize men, not women (Schneider & Hacker, 1973; DeStefano, 1976; Martyna, 1978; Hamilton & Henley, 1982). DeStafano, for example, reports that college students choose silhouettes of males for sentences with the word *man* or *men* in them. Similarly, the presumably generic *he* elicits images of men rather than women. The finding is so persistent that linguists doubt whether there actually is a semantic generic in English (MacKay, 1983).

Man, then, suggests not humanity but rather male images. Moreover, over one's lifetime, an educated American will be exposed to the prescriptive *he* more than a million times (MacKay, 1983). One consequence is the exclusion of women in the visualization, imagination, and thought of males and females. Most likely this linguistic practice perpetuates in men their feelings of dominance over and responsibility for women, feelings that interfere with the development of equality in relationships.

Second, in actual practice, our pronoun usage perpetuates different personality attributes and career aspirations for men and women. Nurses, secretaries, and elementary school teachers are almost invariably referred to as *she;* doctors, engineers, electricians, and presidents as *he.* In one classroom, students referred to an unidentified child as *he* but shifted to *she* when discussing the child's parent. In a faculty discussion of the problems of acquiring new staff, all architects, engineers, security officers, faculty, and computer programmers were referred to as *he;* secretaries and file clerks were referred to as *she.* Martyna (1978) has noted that speakers consistently use *he* when the referent has a high-status occupation (e.g., doctor, lawyer, judge) but shift to *she* when the occupations have lower status (e.g., nurse, secretary).

Even our choice of sex ascription to nonhuman objects subtly reinforces different personalities for males and females. It seems as though the small (e.g., kittens), the graceful (e.g., poetry), the unpredictable (e.g., the fates), the nurturant (e.g., the church, the school), and that which is owned and/or controlled by men (e.g., boats, cars, governments, nations) represent the feminine, whereas that which is a controlling forceful power in and of itself (e.g., God, Satan, tiger) primarily represents the masculine. Even athletic teams are not immune. In one college, the men's teams are called the Bearcats and the women's teams the Bearkittens.

Some of you may wonder whether it matters that the female is linguistically included in the male. The inclusion of women under the pseudogeneric *man* and the prescriptive *he,* however, is not a trivial issue. Language has tremendous power to shape attitudes and influence behavior. Indeed, MacKay (1983) argues that the prescriptive *he* "has all the characteristics of a highly effective propaganda technique": frequent repetition, early age of acquisition (before age 6), covertness (*he* is not thought of as propaganda), use by high-prestige sources (including university texts and professors), and indirectness (presented as though it were a matter of common knowledge). As a result, the prescriptive affects females' sense of life options and feelings of well-being. For example, Adamsky (1981) found that women's sense of power and importance was enhanced when the prescriptive *he* was replaced by *she.*

Awareness of the impact of the generic *man* and prescriptive *he* has generated considerable activity to change the language. One change, approved by the Modern Language Association, is to replace the prescriptive *he* with the plural *they*—as was accepted practice before the 18th century. Another is the use of *he or she.* Although it sounds awkward at first, the *he or she* designation is increasingly being used in the media and among people who have recognized the power of the pronoun to perpetuate sex stereotyping. When a professor, for example, talks about "the lawyer" as "he or she," a speech pattern that counteracts sex stereotyping is modeled. This drive to neutralize the impact of pronouns is evidenced further in the renaming of occupations: a policeman is now a police officer, a postman is a mail carrier, a stewardess is a flight attendant.

Third, linguistic practice defines females as immature, incompetent, and incapable and males as mature, complete, and competent. Because the words *man* and *woman* tend to connote sexual and human maturity, common speech, organizational titles, public addresses, and bathroom doors frequently designate the women in question as *ladies.* Simply contrast the different connotations of *lady* and *woman* in the following common phrases:

Luck, be a lady (woman) tonight.
Barbara's a little lady (woman).
Ladies' (Women's) Air Corps.

In the first two examples, the use of *lady* desexualizes the contextual meaning of *woman.* So trivializing is the use of *lady* in the last phrase that the second is wholly anomalous. The male equivalent, *lord,* is never used; and its synonym, *gentleman,* is used infrequently. When *gentleman* is used, the assumption seems to be that certain culturally condoned aspects of masculinity (e.g., aggressivity, activity, and strength) should be set aside in the interests of maturity and order, as in the following phrases:

A gentlemen's (men's) agreement.
A duel between gentlemen (men).
He's a real gentleman (man).

Rather than feeling constrained to set aside the stereotypes associated with *man,* males frequently find the opposite process occurring. The contextual connotation of *man* places a strain on males to be continuously sexually and socially potent, as the following examples reveal:

I was not a man (gentleman) with her tonight.
This is a man's (gentleman's) job.
Be a man (gentleman).

Whether males, therefore, feel competent or anxious, valuable or worthless in particular contexts is influenced by the demands placed on them by the expectations of the language.

Not only are men infrequently labeled *gentlemen,* but they are infrequently labeled *boys.* The term *boy* is reserved for young males, bellhops, car attendants, and as a putdown to those males judged inferior. *Boy* connotes immaturity and powerlessness. Only occasionally do males "have a night out with the boys." They do not talk "boy talk" at the office. Rarely does our language legitimize carefreeness in males. Rather, they are expected, linguistically, to adopt the responsibilities of manhood.

On the other hand, women of all ages may be called *girls.* Grown females "play bridge with the girls" and indulge in "girl talk." They are encouraged to remain childlike, and the implication is that they are basically immature and without power. Men can become men, linguistically, putting aside the immaturity of childhood; indeed, for them to retain the openness and playfulness of boyhood is linguistically difficult.

Further, the presumed incompetence and immaturity of women are evidenced by the linguistic company they keep. Women are categorized with children ("women and children first"), the infirm ("the blind, the lame, the women"), and the incompetent ("women, convicts, and idiots"). The use of these categorical designations is not accidental happenstance; "rather these selectional groupings are powerful forces behind the actual expressions of language and are based on distinctions which are not regarded as trivial by the speakers of the language" (Key, 1975:82). A total language analysis of categorical groupings is not available, yet it seems likely that women tend to be included in groupings that designate incompleteness, ineptitude, and immaturity. On the other hand, it is difficult for us to conceive of the word *man* in any categorical grouping other than one that extends beyond humanity, such as "Man, apes, and angels" or "Man and Superman." That is, men do exist as an independent category capable of autonomy; women are grouped with the stigmatized, the immature, and the foolish. Moreover, when men are in human groupings, males are invariably first on the list ("men and women," "he and she," "man and wife"). This order is not accidental but was prescribed in the 16th century to honor the worthier party.

Fourth, in practice women are defined in terms of their sexual desirability (to men); men are defined in terms of their sexual prowess (over women). Most slang words in reference to women refer to their sexual desirability to men (e.g., *dog, fox, broad, ass, chick*). Slang about men refers to their sexual prowess over women (e.g., *dude, stud, hunk*). The fewer examples given for men is not an oversight. An analysis of sexual slang, for example, listed more than 1,000 words and phrases that derogate women sexually but found "nowhere near this multitude for describing men" (Kramarae, 1975:72). Farmer and Henley (cited in Schulz, 1975) list 500 synonyms for *prostitute,* for example, and only 65 for *whoremonger.* Stanley (1977) reports 220 terms for a sexually promiscuous woman and only 22 for a sexually promiscuous man. Shuster (1973) reports that the passive verb form is used in reference to women's sexual experiences (e.g., *to be laid, to be had, to be taken*), whereas the active tense is used in reference to the male's sexual experience (e.g., *lay, take, have*). Being sexually attractive to males is culturally condoned for women and being sexually powerful is approved for males. In this regard, the slang of the street is certainly not countercultural; rather it perpetuates and reinforces different expectations in females and males as sexual objects and performers.

Further, we find sexual connotations associated with neutral words applied to women. A few examples should suffice. A male academician questioned the title of a new course, asserting it was "too suggestive." The title? "The Position of Women in the Social Order." A male tramp is simply a hobo, but a female tramp is a slut. And consider the difference in connotation of the following expressions:

It's easy.
He's easy.
She's easy.

In the first, we assume something is "easy to do"; in the second, we might assume a professor is an "easy grader" or a man is "easygoing." But when we read "she's easy," the connotation is "she's an easy lay."

In the world of slang, men are defined by their sexual prowess. In the world of slang and proper speech, women are defined as sexual objects. The rule in practice seems to be: If in doubt, assume that *any* reference to a women has a sexual connotation. For both genders, the constant bombardment of prescribed sexuality is bound to have real consequences.

Fifth, women are defined in terms of their relations to men; men are defined in terms of their relations to the world at large. A good example is seen in the words *master* and *mistress.* Originally these words had the same meaning—"a person who holds power over servants." With the demise of the feudal system, however, these words took on different meanings. The masculine variant metaphorically refers to power over something; as in "He is the master of his trade"; the feminine variant metaphorically (although probably not in actuality) refers to power over a man sexually, as in "She is Tom's mistress." Men are defined in terms of their power in the occupational world, women in terms of their sexual power over men.

The existence of two contractions for Mistress (*Miss* and *Mrs.*) and but one for Mister (*Mr.*) underscores the cultural concern and linguistic practice: women are defined in relation to men. Even a divorced woman is defined in terms of her no-longer-existing relation to a man (she is still *Mrs. Man's Name*). But apparently the divorced state is not relevant enough to the man or to the society to require a label. A divorced woman is a *divorcee*, but what do you call a divorced man? The recent preference of many women to be called *Ms.* is an attempt to provide for women an equivalency title that is not dependent on marital status.

Sixth, a historical pattern can be seen in the meanings that come to be attached to words that originally were neutral: those that apply to women acquire obscene and/or debased connotations but no such pattern of derogation holds for neutral words referring to men. The processes of *pejoration* (the acquiring of an obscene or debased connotation) and *amelioration* (the reacquiring of a neutral or positive connotation) in the English language in regard to terms for males and females have been studied extensively by Muriel Schulz (1975).

Leveling is the least derogative form of pejoration. Through leveling, titles that originally referred to an elite class of persons come to include a wider class of persons. Such democratic leveling is more common for female designates than for males. For example, contrast the following: *lord-lady (lady); baronet-dame (dame); governor-governess (governess).*

Most frequently what happens to words designating women as they become pejorated, however, is that they come to denote or connote sexual wantonness. *Sir* and *mister,* for example, remain titles of courtesy, but at some time *madam, miss,* and *mistress* have come to designate, respectively, a brothelkeeper, a prostitute, and an unmarried sexual partner of a male (Schulz, 1975:66).

Names for domestic helpers, if they are females, are frequently derogated. *Hussy,* for example, originally meant "housewife." *Laundress, needlewoman, spinster* ("tender of the spinning wheel"), and *nurse* all referred to domestic occupations within the home, and all at some point became slang expressions for prostitute or mistress.

Even kinship terms referring to women become denigrated. During the 17th century, *mother* was used to mean "a bawd"; more recently *mother (mothuh f——)* has become a common derogatory epithet (Cameron, 1974). Probably at some point in history every kinship term for females has been derogated (Schulz, 1975:66).

Terms of endearment for women also seem to follow a downward path. Such pet names as Tart, Dolly, Kitty, Polly, Mopsy, Biddy, and Jill all eventually became sexually derogatory (Schulz, 1975:67). *Whore* comes from the same Latin root as *care* and once meant "a lover of either sex."

Indeed, even the most neutral categorical designations—*girl, female, woman, lady*—at some point in their history have been used to connote sexual immorality. *Girl* originally meant "a child of either sex"; through the process of semantic degeneration it eventually meant "a prostitute." Although *girl* has lost this meaning, *girlie* still retains sexual connotations. *Woman* connoted "a mistress" in the early 19th century; *female* was a degrading epithet in the latter part of the 19th century; and when *lady* was introduced as a euphemism, it too became deprecatory. "Even so neutral a term as *person,* when it was used as substitute for *woman*, suffered [vulgarization]" (Mencken, 1963: 350, quoted in Schulz, 1975:71).

Whether one looks at elite titles, occupational roles, kinship relationships, endearments, or age-sex categorical designations, the pattern is clear. Terms referring to females are pejorated—"become negative in the middle instances and abusive in the extremes" (Schulz, 1975:69). Such semantic derogation, however, is not evidenced for male referents. *Lord, baronet, father, brother, nephew, footman, bowman, boy, lad, fellow, gentleman, man, male,* and so on "have failed to undergo the derogation found in the history of their corresponding feminine designations" (Schulz, 1975:67). Interestingly, the male word, rather than undergoing derogation, frequently is replaced by a female referent when the speaker wants to debase a male. A weak man, for example, is referred to as a *sissy* (diminutive of sister), and an army recruit during basic training is called a *pussy.* And when one is swearing at a male, he is referred to as a *bastard* or a *son-of-a-bitch*—both appellations that impugn the dignity of a man's mother.

In summary, these verbal practices are consistent with the gender stereotypes that we encounter in everyday life. Women are thought to be a part of man, nonautonomous, dependent, relegated to roles that require few skills, characteristically incompetent and immature, sexual objects, best defined in terms of their relations to men. Males are visible, autonomous and independent, responsible for the protection and containment of women, expected to occupy positions on the basis of their high achievement or physical power, assumed to be sexually potent, and defined primarily by their relations to the world of work. The use of the language perpetuates the stereotypes for both genders and limits the options available for self-definition.

REFERENCES

Adamsky, C. 1981. "Changes in pronominal usage in a classroom situation." *Psychology of Women Quarterly* 5:773–79.

Bendix, J. 1979. "Linguistic models as political symbols: Gender and the generic 'he' in English." In J. Orasanu, M. Slater, and L. L. Adler, eds., *Language, sex and gender; Does la différence make a difference?* pp. 23–42. New York: New Academy of Science Annuals.

Cameron, P. 1974. "Frequency and kinds of words in various social settings, or What the hell's going on?" In M. Truzzi, ed., *Sociology for pleasure*, pp. 31–37. Englewood Cliffs, NJ: Prentice-Hall.

Daly, M. 1973. *Beyond God the father.* Boston: Beacon Press.

DeStefano, J. S. 1976. Personal communication. Columbus: Ohio State University.

Hamilton, N., & Henley, N. 1982. "Detrimental consequences of the generic masculine usage." Paper presented to the Western Psychological Association meetings, Sacramento.

PERSONAL ACCOUNT

Becoming a Minority

"Sticks and stones may break my bones, but names will never hurt me." Names *will* hurt me, I thought to myself as the young girl across from me yelled, "I'm not like *them!* I'm normal, I don't have *their* problem!" Contrary to the childhood rhyme, her words did indeed hurt me. Those words created an emotional pain that exceeded any physical pain I had endured. They made me feel inferior and different from the rest of the world.

After a week at the hospital I had become accustomed to the daily group meetings, the morning weigh-ins, the scheduled meals, and the strict rules for all patients. I came to accept my problem: I was anorexic. The other patients had similar problems. They suffered the same loneliness and confusion that I suffered. They fought the same battle I fought every day. As we helped each other, we became a community. I was accepted in these walls.

This was shattered by a girl who was admitted to the hospital with a bingeing problem. We all had our own problems. Some were anorexic, bulimic, or bingers; others were suicidal, suffered from obsessive-compulsive disorders, or were addicted to alcohol or drugs. Therapy and support were there for everyone. Since we were understanding of each other, I never once thought of myself as a minority, different from anyone I had met. I figured that we were all people who were there for the same reason—until the day those words of criticism hit me.

All members of the eating disorder group had three meals to eat together every day. You had to eat everything on your tray in a half-hour. Any patient who failed to do so had to drink two "Ensures," which were loaded with fat and calories. The young girl sat across from me, ate half of the food on her plate, then exclaimed that she was done. I looked at her in horror because I was aware of what awaited her. I wondered if she had any idea what she was doing to herself by breaking the rules. She was told to eat the rest of her food but she refused, saying that she was full and had had enough. After a verbal exchange, she got up in exasperation and said that she wasn't like us. She didn't have our problem, she wasn't so crazy that she would deprive herself of food. She claimed that she was there because she ate too much and should be eating less, not more. After her offensive speech, she left the table. Her parents checked her out the next day.

Tears came to my eyes as her words hit me. I remembered the stares I got before coming into the hospital, the snickering and whispering I heard from behind me. Then I remembered the television talk shows I had seen about people suffering from eating disorders. I remembered my disgust and confusion and my belief that they were different from me. And now, without warning, I too was part of that minority. A rush of emotions came to me. I felt angry for ever looking at those people as different or with disgust; I felt lonely because I was now part of a minority. I felt angry because this girl was heartless and weak. I had allowed her actions to make me feel different, not good enough, not acceptable.

I suffer from an eating disorder, something most people are not able to understand. Something I myself don't quite understand. I may be different in the fact that I suffer this ongoing battle, but this disorder does not make me different from others because we are all people.

Elizabeth Lukos

Key, M. R. 1975. *Male/female language.* Metuchen, NJ: Scarecrow Press.

Kramarae, Cheris. 1975. "Woman's speech: Separate but unequal?" In Barrie Thorne and Nancy Henley, eds., *Language and sex: Difference and dominance,* pp. 43–56. Rowley, MA: Newbury House.

MacKay, D. G. 1983. "Prescriptive grammar and the pronoun problem." In B. Thorne, C. Kramarae, and N. Henley, eds., *Language, gender, and society,* pp. 38–53. Rowley, MA: Newbury House.

Martyna, W. 1978. "What does 'he' mean? Use of the generic masculine." *Journal of Communication* 28:131–38.

Martyna, W. 1980. "Beyond the 'he/man' approach: The case for nonsexist language." *Signs* 5:482–93.

Mencken, H. L. 1963. *The American language.* 4th ed. with supplements. Abr. and ed. R. I. McDavis. New York: Knopf.

Schneider, J., & Hacker, S. 1973. "Sex role imagery in the use of the generic 'man' in introductory texts:

A case in the sociology of sociology." *American Sociologist* 8:12–18.

Schulz, M. R. 1975. "The semantic derogation of women." In B. Thorne and N. Henley, eds., *Language and sex: Difference and dominance,* pp. 64–75. Rowley, MA: Newbury House.

Shuster, Janet. 1973. "Grammatical forms marked for male and female in English." Unpublished paper. Chicago: University of Chicago.

Stanley, J. P. 1977. "Paradigmatic woman: The prostitute." In D. L. Shores, ed., *Papers in language variation.* Birmingham: University of Alabama Press.

Vanderbilt, A. 1972. *Amy Vanderbilt's etiquette.* Garden City, NY: Doubleday.

READING 57

To Be and Be Seen: The Politics of Reality*

Marilyn Frye

. . . Reality is that which is.

The English word "real" stems from a word which meant *regal,* of or pertaining to the king.

"Real" in Spanish means *royal.*

Real property is that which is proper to the king.

Real estate is the estate of the king.

Reality is that which pertains to the one in power, is that over which he has power, is his domain, his estate, is proper to him.

The ideal king reigns over everything as far as the eye can see. His eye. What he cannot see is not royal, not real.

He sees what is proper to him.

To be real is to be visible to the king.

The king is in his counting house.

I say, "I am a lesbian. The king does not count lesbians. Lesbians are not real. There are no lesbians." To say this, I use the word "lesbian," and hence one might think that there is a word for this thing, and thus that the thing must have a place in the conceptual scheme. But this is not so. Let me take you on a guided tour of a few standard dictionaries, to display some reasons for saying that lesbians are not named in the lexicon of the King's English.

If you look up the word "lesbian" in *The Oxford English Dictionary,* you find an entry that says it is an adjective that means *of or pertaining to the island of Lesbos,* and an entry describing at length and favorably an implement called a lesbian rule, which is a flexible measuring device used by carpenters. Period.

Webster's Third International offers a more pertinent definition. It tells us that a lesbian is a homosexual female. And going on, one finds that "homosexual" means *of or pertaining to the same sex.* The elucidating example provided is the phrase "homosexual twins" which means *same-sex twins.* The alert scholar can conclude that a lesbian is a same-sex female.

A recent edition of *Webster's Collegiate Dictionary* tells us that a lesbian is a woman who has sex, or sexual relations, with other women. Such a definition would be accepted by many speakers of the language and at least seems to be coherent, even if too narrow. But the appearance is deceptive, for this account collapses into nonsense, too. The key word in this definition is "sex": having sex or having sexual relations. But what is having sex? It is worthwhile to follow this up because the pertinent dictionary entries obscure an important point about the logic of sex. Getting clear about that point helps one see that there is semantic closure against recognition of the existence of lesbians, and it also prepares the way for

---

*This is a very slightly revised version of the essay which appeared in *Sinister Wisdom* 17 with the title, "To Be and Be Seen: Metaphysical Misogyny."
Marilyn Frye is a professor of feminist philosophy at Michigan State University.

understanding the connection between the place of *woman* and the place of *lesbian* with respect to the phallocratic scheme of things.[1]

Dictionaries generally agree that "sexual" means something on the order of *pertaining to the genital union of a female and a male animal,* and that "having sex" is having intercourse—intercourse being defined as the penetration of a vagina by a penis, with ejaculation. My own observation of usage leads me to think these accounts are inadequate and misleading. Some uses of these terms do fit this dictionary account. For instance, parents and counselors standardly remind young women that if they are going to be sexually active they must deal responsibly with the possibility of becoming pregnant. In this context, the word "sexually" is pretty clearly being used in a way that accords with the given definition. But many activities and events fall under the rubric "sexual," apparently without semantic deviance, though they do not involve penile penetration of the vagina of a female human being. Penile penetration of almost anything, especially if it is accompanied by ejaculation, counts as having sex or being sexual. Moreover, events which cannot plausibly be seen as pertaining to penile erection, penetration and ejaculation will, in general, not be counted as sexual, and events that do not involve penile penetration or ejaculation will not be counted as having sex. For instance, if a girlchild is fondled and aroused by a man, and comes to orgasm, but the man refrains from penetration and ejaculation, the man can say, and speakers of English will generally agree, that he did not have sex with her. No matter what is going on, or (it must be mentioned) *not* going on, with respect to female arousal or orgasm, or in connection with the vagina, a pair can be said without semantic deviance to have had sex, or not to have had sex; the use of that term turns entirely on what was going on with respect to the penis.

When one first considers the dictionary definitions of "sex" and "sexual," it seems that all sexuality is heterosexuality, by definition, and that the term "homosexual" would be internally contradictory. There are uses of the term according to which this is exactly so. But in the usual and standard use, there is nothing semantically odd in describing two men as having sex with each other. According to that usage, any situation in which one or more penises are present is one in which something could happen which could be called having sex. But on this apparently "broader" definition there is nothing women could do in the absence of men that could, without semantic oddity, be called "having sex." Speaking of women who have sex with other women is like speaking of ducks who engage in arm wrestling.

When the dictionary defines lesbians as women who have sex or sexual relations with other women, it defines lesbians as logically impossible.

Looking for other words in the lexicon which might denote these beings which are non-named "lesbians," one thinks of terms in the vernacular, like "dyke," "bulldagger" and so on. Perhaps it is just as well that standard dictionaries do not pretend to provide relevant definitions of such terms. Generally, these two terms are used to denote women who are perceived as imitating, dressing up like, or trying to be men. Whatever the extent of the class of women who are perceived to do such things, it obviously is not coextensive with the class of lesbians. Nearly every feminist, and many other women as well, have been perceived as wishing to be men, and a great many lesbians are not so perceived. The term "dyke" has been appropriated by some lesbians as a term of pride and solidarity, but in that use it is unintelligible to most speakers of English.

One of the current definitions of "lesbianism" among lesbians is *woman-loving*—the polar opposite of misogyny. Several dictionaries I checked have entries for "misogyny" (hatred of women), but not for "philogyny" (love of women). I found one which defines "philogyny" as fondness for women, and another dictionary defines "philogyny" as *Don Juanism.* Obviously neither of these means *love of women* as it is intended by lesbians combing the vocabulary for ways to refer to themselves. According to the dictionaries, there is no term in English for the polar opposite of misogyny nor for persons whose characteristic orientation toward women is the polar opposite of misogyny.

Flinging the net wider, one can look up the more Victorian words, like sapphism and sapphist. In *Webster's Collegiate,* "sapphism" is defined just as *lesbianism.* But *The Oxford English Dictionary* introduces another twist. Under the heading of "sapphism" is an entry for "sapphist" according to which sapphists are those addicted to unnatural sexual relations between women. The fact that these relations are characterized as unnatural is revealing. For what is unnatural is contrary to the laws of nature, or contrary to the nature of the substance of entity in question. But what is contrary to the laws of nature cannot happen: that is what it means to call these laws the laws of nature. And I cannot do what is contrary to my nature, for if I could do it, it would be in my nature to do it. To call something "unnatural" is to say it cannot be. This definition defines sapphists, that is lesbians, as *naturally* impossible as well as *logically* impossible. . . .

Lesbian.

One of the people of the Isle of Lesbos.

It is bizarre that when I try to name myself and explain myself, my native tongue provides me with a word that is so foreign, so false, so hopelessly inappropriate. Why am I referred to by a term which means *one of the people of Lesbos?*

The use of the word "lesbian" to name us is a quadrifold evasion, a laminated euphemism. To name us, one goes by way of a reference to the island of Lesbos, which in turn is an indirect reference to the poet Sappho (who used to live there, they say), which in turn is itself an indirect reference to what fragments of her poetry have survived a few millennia of patriarchy, and this in turn (if we have not lost you by now) is a prophylactic avoidance of direct mention of the sort of creature who would write such poems or to whom such poems would be written . . . assuming you happen to know what is in those poems written in a dialect of Greek over two thousand five hundred years ago on some small island somewhere in the wine dark Aegean Sea.

This is a truly remarkable feat of silence.

. . . I think there is much truth in the claim that the phallocratic scheme does not include women. But while women are erased in history and in speculation, physically liquidated in gynocidal purges and banished from the community of those with perceptual and semantic authority, we are on the other hand regularly and systematically invited, seduced, cajoled, coerced and even paid to be in intimate and constant association with men and their projects. In this, the situation of women generally is radically different from the situation of lesbians. Lesbians are not invited to join—the family, the party, the project, the procession, the war effort. There is a place for a woman in every game. Wife, secretary, servant, prostitute, daughter, assistant, babysitter, mistress, seamstress, proofreader, nurse, confidante, masseusse, indexer, typist, mother. Any of these is a place for a woman, and women are much encouraged to fill them. None of these is a place for a lesbian.

The exclusion of women from the phallocratic scheme is impressive, frightening and often fatal, but it is not simple and absolute. Women's existence is both absolutely necessary to and irresolvably problematic for the dominant reality and those committed to it, for our existence is *presupposed* by phallocratic reality, but it is not and cannot be *encompassed* by or countenanced by that reality. Women's existence is a background against which phallocratic reality is a foreground.

A foreground scene is created by the motion of foreground figures against a static background. Foreground figures are perceptible, are defined, have identity, only in virtue of their movement against a background. The space in which the motion of foreground figures takes place is created and defined by their movement with respect to each other and against the background. But nothing of the background is *in* or is *part of* or is *encompassed* by the foreground scene and space. The background is unseen by the eye which is focused on foreground figures, and if anything somehow draws the eye to the background, the foreground dissolves. What would draw the eye to the background would be any sudden or well-defined motion in the background. Hence there must be either no motion at all in the background, or an unchanging buzz of small, regular and repetitive motions. The background must be utterly un*event*ful if the foreground is to continue to hang together, that is, if it is to endure as a *space* within which there are discrete *objects* in relation to each other.

I imagine phallocratic reality to be the space and figures and motion which constitute the foreground, and the constant repetitive uneventful activities of women to constitute and maintain the background against which this foreground plays. It is essential to the maintenance of the foreground reality that nothing within it refer in any way to anything in the background, and yet it depends absolutely upon the existence of the background. It is useful to carry this metaphor on in a more concrete mode—thinking of phallocratic reality as a dramatic production on a stage.

The motions of the actors against the stage settings and backdrop constitute and maintain the existence and identities of the characters in a play. The stage setting, props, lights and so forth are created, provided, maintained and occasionally rearranged (according to the script) by stagehands. The stagehands, their motions and the products of those motions, are neither in nor part of the play, are neither in nor part of the reality of the characters. The reality in the framework of which Hamlet's actions have their meaning would be rent or shattered if anything Hamlet did or thought referred in any way to the stagehands or their activities, or if that background blur of activity were in any other way to be resolved into attention-catching events.

The situation of the actors is desperately paradoxical. The actors are absolutely committed to the maintenance of the characters and the characters' reality: participation as characters in the ongoing creation of Reality is their *raison d'etre*. The reality of the character must be lived with fierce concentration. The actor must be immersed in the play and undistracted by any thought for the scenery, props or stagehands, lest the continuity of the characters and the integrity of their reality be dissolved or broken. But if the character must be lived so intently, who will supervise the stagehands to make sure they don't get rowdy, leave early, fall asleep or walk off the job? (Alas, there is no god nor heavenly host to serve as Director and Stage Managers.) Those with the most intense commitment to the maintenance of the reality of the play are precisely those most interested in the proper deportment of the stagehands, and this interest competes directly with that commitment. There is nothing the actor would like better than that there be no such thing as stagehands, posing as they do a constant threat to the very existence, the very life, of the character and hence to the meaning of the life of the actor; and yet the actor is irrevocably tied to the stagehands by his commitment to the play. Hamlet, of course, has no such problems; there are no stagehands in the play.

To escape his dilemma, the actor may throw caution to the wind and lose himself in the character, whereupon stagehands are unthinkable, hence unproblematic. Or he may construct and embrace the belief that the stagehands share exactly his own perceptions and interests and that they are as committed to the play as he—that they are like robots. On such a hypothesis he can assume them to be absolutely dependable and go on about his business single-mindedly and without existential anxiety. A third strategy, which is in a macabre way more sane, is that of trying to solve the problem technologically by constructing actual robots to serve as stagehands.[2] Given the primacy of his commitment to the play, all solutions must involve one form or another of annihilation of the stagehands. Yet all three require the existence of stagehands; the third, he would hope, requiring it only for a while longer.

The solution to the actor's problem which will appear most benign with respect to the stagehands because it erases the erasure, is that of training, persuading and seducing the stagehands into *loving* the actors and taking actors' interests and commitments unto themselves as their own. One significant advantage to this solution is that the actors can carry on without the guilt or confusion that might come with annihilating, replacing or falsely forgetting the stagehands. As it turns out, of course, even this is a less than perfect solution. Stagehands, in the thrall of their commitment, can become confused and think of themselves as actors—and then they may disturb the play by trying to enter it as characters, by trying to participate in the creation and maintenance of Reality. But there are various well-known ways to handle these intrusions and this seems to be, generally speaking, the most popular solution to the actor's dilemma.

. . . The king is in his counting house. The king is greedy and will count for himself everything he dares to. But his greed itself imposes limits on what he dares to count.

What the king cannot count is a seer whose perception passes the plane of the foreground Reality and focuses upon the background. A seer whose eye is attracted to the ones working as stagehands—the women. A seer in whose eye the woman has authority, has interests of her own, is not a robot. A seer who has no motive for wanting there to be no women; a seer who is not loyal to Reality. We can take the account of the seer who must be unthinkable if Reality is to be kept afloat as the beginning of an account of what a lesbian is. One might try saying that a lesbian is one who, by virtue of her focus, her attention, her attachment, is disloyal to phallocratic reality. She is not committed to its maintenance and the maintenance of those who maintain it, and worse, her mode of disloyalty threatens its utter dissolution in the mere flick of the eye. This sounds extreme, of course, perhaps even hysterical. But listening carefully to the rhetoric of the fanatic fringe of the phallocratic loyalists, one hears that they do think that feminists, whom they fairly reasonably judge to be lesbians, have the power to bring down civilization, to dissolve the social order as we know it, to cause the demise of the species, by our mere existence.

Even the fanatics do not really believe that a lone maverick lesbian can in a flick of her evil eye atomize civilization, of course. Given the collectivity of conceptual schemes, the way they rest on agreement, a maverick perceiver does not have the power to bring one tumbling down—a point also verified by my own experience as a not-so-powerful maverick. What the loyalists fear, and in this I think they are more-or-less right, is a contagion of the maverick perception to the point where the agreement in perception which keeps Reality afloat begins to disintegrate.

The event of becoming a lesbian is a reorientation of attention in a kind of ontological conversion. It is characterized by a feeling of a world dissolving, and by a feeling of disengagement and re-engagement of one's power as a perceiver. That such conversion happens signals its possibility to others.

Heterosexuality for women is not simply a matter of sexual preference, any more than lesbianism is. It is a matter of orientation of attention, as is lesbianism, in a metaphysical context controlled by neither heterosexual nor lesbian women. Attention is a kind of passion. When one's attention is on something, one is present in a particular way with respect to that thing. This presence is, among other things, an element of erotic presence. The orientation of one's attention is also what fixes and directs the application of one's physical and emotional work.

If the lesbian sees the woman, the woman may see the lesbian seeing her. With this, there is a flowering of possibilities. The woman, feeling herself seen, may learn that she *can be* seen; she may also be able to know that a woman can see, that is, can author perception. With this, there enters for the woman the logical possibility of assuming her authority as a perceiver and of shifting her own attention. With that there is the dawn of choice, and it opens out over the whole world of women. The lesbian's seeing undercuts the mechanism by which the production and constant reproduction of heterosexuality for women was to be rendered *automatic.* The nonexistence of lesbians is a piece in the mechanism which is supposed to cut off the possibility of choice or alternative at the root, namely at the point of conception.

The maintenance of phallocratic reality requires that the attention of women be focused on men and men's projects—the play; and that attention not be focused on women—the stagehands. Woman-loving, as a spontaneous and habitual orientation of attention is then, both directly and indirectly, inimical to the maintenance of that reality. And therein lies the reason for the thoroughness of the ontological closure against lesbians, the power of those closed out, and perhaps the key to the liberation of women from oppression in a male-dominated culture.

My primary goal here has not been to state and prove some rigid thesis, but simply to *say* something clearly enough, intelligibly enough, so that it can be understood and thought about. Lesbians are outside the conceptual scheme, and this is something done, not just the way things are. One can begin to see that lesbians are excluded by the scheme, and that this is *motivated,* when one begins to see what purpose the exclusion might serve in connection with keeping women generally in their metaphysical place. It is also true that lesbians are in a position to see things that cannot be seen from within the system. What lesbians see is what makes them lesbians and their seeing is why they have to be excluded. Lesbians are woman-seers. When one is suspected of seeing women, one is spat summarily out of reality, through the cognitive gap and into the negative semantic space. If you ask what became of such a woman, you may be told she became a lesbian, and if you try to find out what a lesbian is, you will be told there is no such thing.

But there is.

NOTES

1. The analysis that follows is my own rendering of an account developed by Carolyn Shafer. My version of it is informed also by my reading of "Sex and Reference," by Janice Moulton, *Philosophy and Sex,* edited by Robert Baker and Frederick Elliston (Prometheus Books, Buffalo, New York, 1975).
2. This solution is discussed in *The Transexual Empire: The Making of the She-Male,* by Janice G. Raymond (Beacon Press, Boston, 1979).

PERMISSIONS

Dorothy Allison, "A Question of Class" from *Sisters, Sexperts, Queers,* edited by Arlene Stein. Copyright © 1993 by Arlene Stein. Reprinted with the permission of Dutton Signet, a division of Penguin Putnam, Inc.

LaRay M. Barna, "Stumbling Blocks in Intercultural Communication" from *Intercultural Communication, A Reader,* edited by Larry A. Samovar and Richard E. Porter. Copyright © 1994. Reprinted with the permission of the author and Wadsworth, an imprint of the Wadsworth Group, a division of Thomson Learning.

William Bowen and Derek Bok, "The Shape of the River: Long-Term Consequences of Considering Race in College and University Admissions." Excerpts from "Summing Up" from *The Shape of the River: Long-Term Consequences of Considering Race in College and University Admissions.* Copyright © 1998 by Princeton University Press. Reprinted with the permission of the publisher.

F. James Davis, "Who is Black? One Nation's Definition" (originally entitled "The Nation's Rule") from *Who is Black? One Nation's Definition.* Copyright © 1991 by The Pennsylvania State University. Reprinted with the permission of The Pennsylvania State University Press.

Benjamin DeMott, excerpts from "Women-Becoming-Men" from *Killer Woman Blues: Why Americans Can't Think Straight About Gender and Power.* Copyright © 2000 by Benjamin DeMott. Reprinted with the permission of Houghton Mifflin Company. All rights reserved.

Cynthia Fuchs Epstein, excerpts from "Similarity and Difference: The Sociology of Gender Dysfunctions" from *Handbook of the Sociology of Gender,* edited by Janet Saltzman Chafetz. Copyright © 1999 by Kluwer Academic/Plenum Publishers. Reprinted with the permission of the author and publisher.

Yen Le Espiritu, "Asian American Panethnicity" from *Asian-American Panethnicity: Bridging Institutions and Identities.* Copyright © 1992 by Temple University. Reprinted with the permission of Temple University Press.

Anne Fausto-Sterling, "The Five Sexes: Why Male and Female are Not Enough" from *The Sciences* 22, no. 2 (March/April 1993); and

"The Five Sexes, Revisited" from *The Sciences* (July/August 2000). Both reprinted with the permission of *The Sciences.*

Carlos A. Fernández, "La Raza and the Melting Pot: A Comparative Look at Multiethnicity" from *Racially Mixed People in America,* edited by Maria P. P. Root. Copyright © 1992 by Sage Publications, Inc. Reprinted with the permission of the publishers.

Ruth Frankenberg, "Whiteness as an 'Unmarked' Cultural Category" from *White Women, Race Matters.* Copyright © 1993 by the Regents of the University of Minnesota. Reprinted with the permission of the author and the University of Minnesota Press.

Sally French, "'Can You See the Rainbow?' The Roots of Denial" from John Swain, Vic Finkelstein, Sally French, and Mike Oliver (eds.), *Disabling Barriers—Enabling Environments.* Copyright © 1993 by The Open University. Reprinted with the permission of Sage Publications, Ltd.

Marilyn Frye, "Oppression" and "To See and Be Seen" from *The Politics of Reality: Essays in Feminist Theory,* edited by Marilyn Frye. Copyright © 1983 by Marilyn Frye. Reprinted with the permission of The Crossing Press, Freedom, CA.

Rosemarie Garland-Thomson, "Toward a Poetics of the Disabled Body" from *Marginal Groups and Mainstream American Culture,* edited by Yolanda Estes, Arnold Lorenzo Farr, Patricia Smith, and Clelia Smyth. Copyright © 2000 by the University Press of Kansas. Reprinted with the permission of the publishers.

Beth Omansky Gordon and Michael Oliver, "How Long Must We Wait? Unmet Promises of Disability Law and Policy." Previously unpublished article, 2002. Reprinted with the permission of the authors.

Barbara Sherman Heyl, "Homosexuality: A Social Phenomenon" from *Human Sexuality: The Societal and Interpersonal Context,* edited by Kathleen McKinney and Susan Sprecher (Norwood, NJ: Ablex, 1989). Reprinted with the permission of Ablex Publishing Corporation.

David Ingram, excerpt from "Affirmative Action and the Legacy of Racism" from *Group Rights: Reconciling Equality and Difference.* Copyright © 2000 by the University Press of Kansas. Reprinted with the permission of the publishers.

M. Annette Jaimes, "Federal Indian Identification Policy: A Usurpation of Indigenous Sovereignty in North America" (including notes) from M. Annette Jaimes (ed.), *The State of Native America: Genocide, Colonization, and Resistance.* Copyright © 1992 by M. Annette Jaimes. Reprinted with the permission of South End Press, Cambridge, MA.

Jonathan Ned Katz, excerpts from *The Invention of Heterosexuality.* Copyright © 1995 by Jonathan Ned Katz. Reprinted with the permission of Dutton, a division of Penguin Putnam, Inc.

Cheryl Zarlenga Kerchis and Iris Marion Young, excerpts from "Social Movements and the Politics of Difference" from Dean A. Harris (ed.), *Multiculturalism from the Margins: Non-Dominant Voices on Difference and Diversity.* Copyright © 1995 by Bifocal Publications. Reprinted with the permission of Greenwood Publishing Group, Inc., Westport, CT.

Nancy Krieger and Mary Bassett, "The Health of Black Folk: Disease, Class, and Ideology in Science" from *Monthly Review* 38, no. 3 (July–August 1986). Copyright © 1986 by Monthly Review, Inc. Reprinted with the permission of Monthly Review.

John Lamberth, "Driving While Black" from *The Washington Post* (August 16, 1998). Copyright © 1998 by John Lamberth. Reprinted with the permission of the author.

John Larew, "Why Are Droves of Unqualified, Unprepared Kids Getting into Our Colleges? Because Their Dads are Alumni" from *The Washington Monthly* (June 1991). Copyright © 1991 by The Washington Monthly Company. Reprinted with the permission of *The Washington Monthly,* 1611 Connecticut Avenue, N.W., Washington, DC 20009.

Charlie LeDuff, "At a Slaughterhouse, Some Things Never Die" from *The New York Times on the Web* (June 16, 2000). Copyright © 2000 by The New York Times Company. Reprinted with permission.

Robert G. Lee, "The Cold War Origins of the Model Minority" and "The Model Minority as Gook" from *Orientals: Asian Americans in Popular Culture.* Copyright © 1999 by Temple University Press. Reprinted with the permission of the publishers. All rights reserved.

Heidi Levine and Nancy J. Evans, "The Development of Gay, Lesbian, and Bisexual Identities" from *Beyond Tolerance: Gays, Lesbians and Bisexuals on Campus.* Copyright © 1991 by the American College Personnel Association. Reprinted with the permission of the American College Personnel Association.

George Lipsitz, "The Possessive Investment in Whiteness" excerpted from *The Possessive Investment in Whiteness: How White People Profit from Identity Politics.* Copyright © 1998 by Temple University. Reprinted with the permission of Temple University Press. All Rights Reserved.

Jordan Lite, "Please Ask Me Who, Not 'What' I Am" from *Newsweek* (July 16, 2001). Copyright © 2001 by Newsweek, Inc. All rights reserved. Reprinted with permission.

Eric Liu, excerpt from *The Accidental Asian: Notes of a Native Speaker.* Copyright © 1998 by Eric Liu. Reprinted with the permission of Random House, Inc.

Michael Patrick MacDonald, excerpt from *All Souls: A Family Story from Southie.* Copyright © 1999 by Michael Patrick MacDonald. Reprinted with the permission of Beacon Press, Boston.

Arturo Madrid, "Diversity and Its Discontents" from *Academe* 76, no. 6 (November–December 1990). Copyright © 1990 by Arturo Madrid. Reprinted with the permission of the author.

Jerry Mander, excerpts from "What Americans Don't Know About Indians" from *In the Absence of the Sacred: The Failure of Technology and the Survival of the Indian Nations.* Copyright © 1991 by Jerry Mander. Reprinted with the permission of Sierra Club Books.

Daniel P. McMurrer and Isabel V. Sawhill, Chapters 4 and 6 from *Getting Ahead: Economic and Social Mobility in America.* Copyright © 1998 by The Urban Institute. Reprinted with the permission of Urban Institute Press.

Lydia Y. Minatoya, "The Day of Remembrance" from *Talking to High Monks in the Snow: An Asian American Odyssey.* Copyright © 1992 by Lydia Y. Minatoya. Reprinted with the permission of HarperCollins Publishers, Inc.

Nobuko Joanne Miyamoto, "What Are You?" from *Asian Women* (Berkeley: Asian American Studies Program, University of California Berkeley). Reprinted with the permission of the author.

Robert B. Moore, "Racism in the English Language" from *Racism in the English Language* (New York: Council on Interracial Books for Children, 1976). Reprinted with the permission of Lawrence Jordan, Literary Agency, 250 West 57th Street, Suite 1527, New York, NY 10107.

Melissa Nobles, "Race, Censuses, and Citizenship" from *Shades of Citizenship: Race and the Census in Modern Politics.* Copyright © 2000 by the Board of Trustees of the Leland Stanford Junior University. Reprinted with the permission of the Stanford University Press.

Michael Oliver, excerpts from "Disability Definitions: The Politics of Meaning" and "The Cultural Production of Impairment and Disability" from *The Politics of Disablement: A Sociological Approach.* Copyright © 1990 by Michael Oliver. Reprinted with the permission of Palgrave Publishers, Ltd.

Sherry B. Ortner, excerpts from "Reading America: Preliminary Notes on Class and Culture" from *Recapturing Anthropology: Working in the Present,* edited by Richard G. Fox (Santa Fe, New Mexico: School of American Research Press, 1991). Reprinted with the permission of the author.

Barbara F. Reskin and Irene Padavic, "Sex, Race, and Ethnic Inequality in United States Workplaces" from *Handbook of the Sociology of Gender,* edited by Janet Saltzman Chafetz. Copyright © 1999 by Kluwer Academic/Plenum Publishers. Reprinted with the permission of the authors and publisher.

Laurel Richardson, "Gender Stereotyping in the English Language" from *Feminist Frontiers 5,* edited by Laurel Richardson, Verta Taylor, and Nancy Whittier (New York: McGraw-Hill, 2001). Adapted from Laurel Richardson, *The Dynamics of Sex and Gender: A Sociological Perspective* (New York: Harper & Row, 1987). Reprinted with the permission of the author.

Ronald Schmidt, Sr., excerpts from *Language Policy and Identity Politics in the United States.* Copyright © 2000 by Temple University. Reprinted with the permission of Temple University Press. All rights reserved.

Leonard Steinhorn and Barbara Diggs-Brown, excerpt from "A Day in the Life of Two Americas, Part 1" from *By the Color of Our Skin: The Illusion of Integration and the Reality of Race.* Copyright © 1999 by Leonard Steinhorn and Barbara Diggs-Brown. Reprinted with the permission of Dutton, a division of Penguin Putnam, Inc.

Laura Sessions Stepp, "A Lesson in Cruelty: Anti-Gay Slurs Common at School" from *The Washington Post* (June 19, 2001). Copyright © 2001 by The Washington Post Writers Group. Reprinted by permission.

Roberto Suro, excerpts from "Children of the Future" from *Strangers Among Us: How Latino Immigration Is Transforming America.* Copyright © 1998 by Roberto Suro. Reprinted with the permission of Alfred A. Knopf, a division of Random House, Inc.

Deborah Tannen, excerpts from "Both Sides Come Out Fighting: The Argument Culture and the Press" from *The Argument Culture: Stopping America's War of Words.* Copyright © 1998 by Deborah Tannen. Reprinted with the permission of Random House, Inc.

Thandeka, excerpts from "The Cost of Whiteness" from *Tikkun: A Bimonthly Jewish Critique of Politics, Culture and Society* 14, no. 3. Reprinted with the permission of *Tikkun: A Bimonthly Jewish Critique of Politics, Culture and Society.* 26 Fell Street, San Francisco, CA 94102.

The Washington Post, "The Evolution of Identity" from *The Washington Post* (August 13, 2001): A13. Copyright © 1991 by The Washington Post Writers Group. Reprinted by permission.

Patrick Welsh, "Our Classroom Barrios," originally entitled "For Hispanic Students, American Schools Can Be a Nightmare" from *The Washington Post* (September 8, 1991). Copyright © 1991. Reprinted with the permission of the author.

Patricia J. Williams, "Of Race and Risk" from *The Nation* (December 29, 1997). Copyright © 1997 by Patricia J. Williams. Reprinted with the permission of Brandt & Hochman Literary Agents, Inc. All rights reserved.

Walter Williams, "The Berdache Tradition," originally entitled "Of Religions and Dreams: The Spiritual Basis of the Berdache Tradition"

INDEX